Silk Stalkings

More Wom(...)r

Victoria Nichols   Susan Thompson

The Scarecrow Press, Inc.
Lanham, Maryland, and London
2000

SCARECROW PRESS, INC.

Published in the United States of America
by Scarecrow Press, Inc.
4720 Boston Way, Lanham, Maryland 20706
www.scarecrowpress.com

4 Pleydell Gardens, Folkestone
Kent CT20 2DN, England

British Library Cataloguing in Publication Information Available

The hardback edition of this book was previously catalogued by the Library of Congress
as follows:
Library of Congress Cataloging-in-Publication Data
Nichols, Victoria, 1944–
    Silk stalkings : more women write of murder / Victoria Nichols and Susan
Thompson.
       p. cm.
    Includes indexes.
      1. Detective and mystery stories, English—Stories, plots, etc. 2. Detective and
mystery stories, American—Stories, plots, etc. 3. Characters and characteristics in
literature—Bibliography. 4. American fiction—Women authors—Bibliography.
5. English fiction—Women authors—Bibliography. 6. Women and literature—
Bibliography. 7. Crime in literature—Bibliography. 8. Monographic series—
Bibliography. I. Thompson, Susan, 1946– II. Title.
    PR830.D4N53   1997
    823'.0872099287—dc21   97-24372
    ISBN 0-8108-3393-X (cloth : alk. paper)   CIP
    ISBN 1-57886-012-1 (pbk. : alk. paper)

First edition published as *Silk Stalkings: When Women Write of Murder*
(Berkeley, Calif.: Black Lizard Books, 1988).

♾™ The paper used in this publication meets the minimum requirements of
American National Standard for Information Sciences—Permanence of
Paper for Printed Library Materials, ANSI/NISO Z39.48-1992.
Manufactured in the United States of America.

In loving memory of Ellen Nehr
for all of her enthusiastic support, encouragement,
and fruitful lines of inquiry

CONTENTS

PREFACE

Silk Stalkings began over fifteen years ago as the authors' personal shopping list. Shortly after we met, we discovered a mutual love of mystery fiction, particularly those books written by women. After exhausting our own accumulations and the "other titles by the same author" lists on the inside covers of books, we went to the library. There we discovered a wealth of reference books with the exception of just what we were looking for—something that listed only the women authors and the titles of their books.

Each of us has research experience so the logical next step seemed to be to compile such a listing. Slightly daunted by the vast number of women writing in the genre, we limited our list to those women who had created ongoing characters (appearing in two or more titles). As our list grew, so did our book collections. The more we read, the more we realized that others might find the information we gathered of interest.

Silk Stalkings: When Women Write of Murder, published in 1988 by Black Lizard Books, was an instant success and most of the few copies printed are treasured and dog-eared by their owners. As the years went by, the genre grew. We kept discovering new authors, reading their works, and—most important—keeping our list current. At conferences and other mystery gatherings we were constantly reminded how valuable and original a resource the book was and frequently we were asked, "When will the next SS be out?" Early in 1994 we reviewed all of our data and decided that the time had come. *Silk Stalkings: More Women Write of Murder* is the result.

The book consists of eighteen chapters that describe the characters in a variety of series. Those familiar with the original *Silk Stalkings* will find the chapter headings familiar. The characters themselves actually dictated these headings by nicely dividing themselves into categories according to profession, avocation, or the inclination that draws them into the investigation of crime. Some of the characters we have chosen to chronicle are popular—or at least well known; others are a bit more obscure. There have been a few changes, however, which are perhaps a reflection of the times in which we live.

Five new chapters have been added. "After the Fall: Historical Mysteries" features detectives who operate in times gone by. "Another Side to Reality: The Supernatural and the Occult" includes vampires, a witch, a psychic, and a couple of other characters less easy to classify. "The Game's Afoot: Sports and Games" marks the entry of those playing and documenting sports and games into the world of characters created by women mystery authors. Criminals as protagonists are represented for the first time in "The Other Side of the Law," and older and wiser individuals have been given their own chapter, "Senior Sleuths," as their numbers have increased significantly.

The other changes are actually omissions. Much to our dismay, there are few new aristocrats in the world of detection, so the blood no longer runs blue. The one titled soul we found is considered in "Unexpected Detectives." Curators, librarians, and art experts have been put together with visual artists in "Portraits in Crime: Arts and Letters," and there was no room to include those valiant spouses, butlers, housekeepers, secretaries, and assistants who formerly picked up the pieces and held down the fort.

These chapters offer a survey of characters created since 1976—the beginning of the current swell. Despite our interest in and dedication to our subject, more than 1,300 characters and 6,900 titles are an overwhelming prospect, so we have provided samples of detecting styles and detectives' personalities. Individual taste in mystery fiction, as in all things, is a highly subjective matter and few readers will agree with all we have to say. *Vive la différence.*

The second half of this book consists of lists to complement the descriptive chapters that make up the first half of the book. A Master List and three appendixes contain detailed information about authors and their series characters. Please see pages 299–301 for more information on how to use the Master List of authors and the appendixes in conjunction with the descriptive chapters.

We have enjoyed the process of putting this book together. We trust that you will enjoy using it.

ACKNOWLEDGMENTS

Work on *Silk Stalkings* has spanned more than fifteen years during which time we have relied on the assistance of most of our relatives and—at one time or another—all of our friends. We have also come to depend on the kindness of strangers in the nicest of ways. We have encountered countless wonderful individuals whose knowledge has augmented our own and whose enthusiasm has reinforced our sometimes flagging spirits. Thanks to you all.

Our deepest gratitude goes to our respective spouses: Corwin Nichols for the idea in the first place, for our computer, and for the original computerized data base—not to mention the many hours spent performing the requisite "Great Marriage"—and for the use of the resources of his company, MicroTech Conversion Systems; and Geoffrey Thompson for countless airline miles, for tireless promotion, and for the original working title. To both of them, our thanks for keeping us well in spite of our many weeks away from home and for saying they actually enjoyed hastily prepared meals eaten facing the covers of an open book and for providing us with the opportunity and wherewithal to travel and buy ever more books.

Our undying appreciation goes to Bill Deeck for exhaustive fact cross-checking, meticulous text editing, and companionship at some of the finest meat and potato dinners we've had and to Meredith Phillips for her persevering editorial skills, excellent lunches, holidays at the beach, and general all-around support.

Many thanks to Professor B. J. Rahn for more than we can say; Creative Arts Book Company for giving *Silk Stalkings* its first outing; Howard Kurtzman, Steven Cannell, and The Cannell Studios for wanting our title for television—for money—and Stu Segall Productions, Inc., for carrying on with the show—and for more money; Grandma Opal Seith for channeling her negotiating skills; Carole F. Barrett of Severson & Werson for legal advice; John Harpootlian for undertaking the vast task of transporting our data and preparing us for the twenty-first century; The Moms: Betty R. Shumaker for reading and editing and Nell B. Sorenson for financial assistance; Dean E. Wooldridge, Jr., for rest and respite, a glorious view, a bottomless wine bottle, and a comfortable couch; Sue and Derek Debevec for their gracious hospitality every spring (Matt, we miss you); Lora Roberts Smith, one of the mysterious ladies who lunch; Jackie Drew and the membership of the Menlo Park Library Mystery Readers; Janet Rudolph of *Mystery Readers International;* Priscilla Ridgway of Mystery Writers of America and former Los Altos resident; the Sisterhood of Sisters in Crime; Alan J. Hubin, for the whole nine yards; Jim Huang of *The Drood Review;* Bruce Taylor of the San Francisco Mystery Bookstore and his cohort in crime, Steven Stilwell of Once Upon a Crime, Minneapolis; Maxim Jakubowski of Murder One, London, for letting us go on about Dame Beatrice; the resources of the Palo Alto Library System; Jean Schroeter of Future Fantasy; Tom Barry of Printer's, Inc.; Michelle Robinson of Borders; Ann Douglas of Kepler's; Ben Varkentine of Know Knew Books and all the women at Two Sisters for having the books we needed when we needed them and some we didn't even know about; Priscilla Kapel of The Bioenergy Balancing Center; Kim, Karl, and Madisen Brosing; Lori, Jon, Jade, and Tristen Hodges; Chris Kruss; Wendell and Jennifer Encinas Milburn; Sarah Milburn; Jules; Vern; Dolly; Wolfie; Henry and June; and the late Buffer, Bosco, Indiana, and the Fish, key contributors, one and all.

We are each particularly grateful to the partnership of Nichols/Thompson, which has endured not only the years of effort on this book but also the many exigencies of life including but not limited to raising and launching five children; four weddings; one divorce; a couple of funerals; the arrival of four grandchildren; the catering exploits we have executed together; and our travels, those in the air, on the road, and of the mind. Our friendship knows no bounds.

Finally and, in all probability, most important, to all the women who have created the irresistible characters and written the wonderful mysteries upon which our work is based, we sincerely hope that *Silk Stalkings* at least partially discharges our obligation to them.

INTRODUCTION

As observers and chroniclers of women writing crime and mystery fiction, our continuing goal has been to introduce authors to their reading public. Now, however, rather than searching out lost or forgotten authors, characters, and titles, it's all we can do to maintain our pace with the new and developing ones. Fortunately, thanks to the growth of conventions and other gatherings of fans, authors, and booksellers such as Bouchercon, Malice Domestic, and Left Coast Crime, it is possible to meet and speak with a variety of writers covering the full spectrum of style. These authors have not only become more accessible but are extremely generous as well. A number of the series authors we have met kindly replied to a questionnaire we sent. We include some of their observations here.

Carolyn G. Hart, creator of two series, comments, "Mystery sales are increasing at a steady pace. Mystery bookstores have proliferated, which argues a tremendous depth of support among readers. Mysteries are being published in ever increasing numbers. I believe this is happening because the quality of mystery writing is so high, as high as it has ever been since Poe penned the first. Mystery fiction is drawing superbly talented authors who are repelled by modern fiction's continued drift and lack of focus."

There is no sign that the tide is turning. Marilyn Wallace, author of three books featuring the police sergeants Cruz and Goldstein and editor of five *Sisters in Crime* short story collections, thinks that "the field will continue to grow. Every time a new writer comes along with the ability to tell a good story, create complex characters, breathe life into settings and engage my interest from start to finish, I'm pleased and excited because that author is expanding the audience for good mystery fiction."

The number of books is impressive, and the type of writing being done shows important changes as well. Today's series by women include several new types of protagonist: romance writers, art historians, veterinarians, several vampires, a twelfth-century monk, futuristic police officers, and a paid assassin, to name a few. There is a groundswell of cultural diversity in mystery novels today. To the best of our knowledge, Helen Keremos, created by Eve Zaremba, was the first openly lesbian series detective. She has been joined by several more sisters whose sexual preference is just a matter of course in the books in which they are featured. African-Americans, Native Americans, and Armenian-Americans all have representatives in the roster of investigators. These are not characters with a narrow audience—one limited to members of their own group. Rather, their authors are making what have long been felt to be differences a little more familiar for readers.

Female characters themselves are taking new roles within the genre. Although strong and independent women characters have existed in the past, they have been in the distinct minority. There is a new wave of female professional private investigators and law enforcement officers. Marcia Muller's character, San Francisco private eye Sharon McCone—the prototype for a new breed of protagonist—is a true hero. Berkeley, California, police officer Jill Smith created by Susan Dunlap and the New York Police Department's Norah Mulcahaney by Lillian O'Donnell are representatives of women's rise in ranks formerly closed to them. These characters are providing readers of all ages—both men and women—with strong, healthy role models. The authors present their female characters as women creating a new design within the fabric of their lives and not relying on old patterns, long established by men and accepted by society as a whole. These characters have made a major shift from the role of heroine who existed in a story to add romance, an element of danger, and a need to be rescued to the role of hero who may or may not find romance as a part of her investigation, courts danger, and is fully capable of rescuing herself and others.

Ann and Evan Maxwell, a wife-and-husband writing team using the name A. E. Maxwell, have created two characters for their successful series: Fiddler and Fiora, who break with tradition in almost every way. The Maxwells point out, "The role of women in society began changing twenty or thirty years ago, but the genre of crime writing somehow seemed rooted in social/masculine archetypes of the twenties and thirties. What has happened with our series and with others is that we've tried to change the parameters of the genre to conform to the new and evolving reality of America in the late twentieth century. That has occasionally upset some of the traditionalists but it has also generated a strong positive response among readers, both men and women."

This is indeed an exciting and terrifying time in which to be living. Not only is literature taking new directions, but the world itself is changing at a more rapid pace than ever before. Are there parallels between world events and literature? History seems to support that theory. We may, individually, even collectively, hold human life sacred. Nevertheless, we are less surprised by murder as the twentieth century draws to a close and we become no strangers to violence.

Society has not done a thorough job of preparing most women for many of the harsher realities of life; consequently, they are at greater risk in these times of rising, often random, acts of violence. Families are not always bastions of security for women and children; wife-beating and marital rape are not restricted to the lower classes, and child abuse is not uncommon in any community nationwide. Savvy women constantly monitor their dress and behavior and exercise extreme caution when on their own after dark. Even a momentary lapse in personal vigilance can result in, at best, unwanted attention—at worst, battery, rape, or even murder. A simple date can turn into an act of brutal violation because a man just cannot believe that the female object of his desire really means *no*. Paradoxically, at the same time, we're living in an era where most of us, male and female, still take our personal safety for granted.

Even the most supportive and understanding of men has a difficult time relating to the bottom line of fear with which women contend, for themselves and their children, every day. While violence may be directed toward the smaller and weaker members of society, the consequences of any violent action reverberate far beyond the obvious effects on the victims. The media make murder and terrorism an outrageous part of everyday life. In the United States, in 1993, one person was killed by a gunshot wound every twelve minutes. Mass murder and serial killings have risen astronomically since the '60s. Snipers use freeways as shooting galleries, and *carjacking* is a chilling new word in our vocabulary. Children are abducted by strangers and often tortured and murdered by their captors. On an international scale, the drug culture provides a broad range of death and deception from a street killing during a drug transaction to the controlled-substance-big-money death games played by drug lords. Terrorists operating around the globe have hijacked airplanes and cruise ships, taken hostages, and bombed public places.

What does the current popularity of crime and mystery fiction mean in the context of these local and global events? Is there a correlation between the rise of crime in fact and crime in fiction? Does the rising rate of violence in the home and on the street have an effect on what some people choose to write and others to read? If so, why are they choosing this particular literary form for their escape from reality? Writing the series featuring Robert Forsythe under the pseudonym E. X. Giroux, Canadian Doris Shannon feels, "Mystery is very much escape reading and with the world we live in I feel readers are even more willing to escape into a fairly small fantasy world where all questions are answered and many problems solved." Women writers of crime and mystery fiction have a particular perspective—perhaps stemming from vulnerability of their sex—that is worthy of attention. In crafting their novels focused on murder, violence, and deceit, they are, in effect, creating contemporary cautionary tales that, if we are paying attention, can serve as illumination of the new, unsafe world in which we all must live.

Many writers of crime and mystery fiction today are using important social issues as vehicles for their characters and stories. For this reason, we want to look farther than, "Is this a good mystery? Does the author play fair with clues and red herrings? Can I figure out whodunit before the author tells me?" We want to look toward, "Who are these people and why are their problems important? Do I really care what happens in this protagonist's future? Does the story's setting capture my attention? Is this new, valuable information for me?" This focus on current issues is not to dismiss the mystery aspect of a piece of crime and mystery fiction. The detection of murder is, after all, what brings the characters in any of these stories together, and rising sales indicate that writers in this genre are giving dedicated mystery fans what they want. Furthermore, the motivations behind the ultimate act of murder are taking the reader well beyond Colonel Mustard, in the conservatory, with the lead pipe.

Today's writers are provocative, providing readers with new contexts for their own thoughts on social issues and personal safety. For example, *Murder by Deception* by D. R. Meredith deals with the issue of nuclear waste disposal. In *June Mail,* Jean Warmbold provides a possible alternative explanation to the genesis of the syndrome known as AIDS. Subplots to Kathryn Lasky Knight's mystery *Trace Elements* include underground nuclear testing and academic and governmental duplicity. An orthomolecular approach to the treatment of schizophrenia is propounded by Lee Martin in *Too Sane a Murder.* Nancy Pickard addresses the battered wife syndrome in *Marriage Is Murder.* Patricia D. Cornwell's character, pathologist Kay Scarpetta, provides forensic insight into a serial killer who preys on women in *Postmortem,* and Janet LaPierre illustrates women's loss of power when, in *The Cruel Mother,* one of her main characters is kidnapped while on vacation. These writers create scenarios that offer some insight into how people cope with such monumental risks and problems.

Works of crime and mystery fiction are appearing on bestseller lists with increasing frequency. Unfortunately, when this occurs, reviewers are quick to point out that "this book transcends the genre"—implying that something is inherently lacking in this form of fiction and the author must have had something else in mind all along or people would not be reading, much less buying, the thing. Shelley Singer, who writes two series, feels, "This is utter hogwash. The genre itself is an art form, and a really good mystery is fine literature. A good book is a good book, a mediocre one a mediocre one. Ghettos are created by narrow minds."

The original Golden Age in crime and mystery fiction (1928–1946) was golden, in part, because it described prevailing social conventions, mores, and ethics of the times. Relationships between men and women were clearly dictated by propriety, and a certain decorum existed between the sexes. Codes of honor seemed more well defined than they are now. Patriotism in the '20s, '30s, and '40s had a different, positive meaning. War was honorable and service to one's country, in any capacity, was expected. Fewer questions were asked of those in power, and they, in turn, subscribed to a code of ethics that often seems long past. Many authors of this earlier era eloquently captured the essence of their times. Today's authors are faced with more rapidly changing social conventions, mores, and ethics. Their task is to capture something far more multifaceted than that of their foremothers. And they are doing it.

Many questions do arise in the course of a research project, and it is impossible to provide answers to all of them. Even the question of whether we are in the midst of a new Golden Age cannot be fully answered until we have a more historical perspective. However, many women authors agree—some emphatically—that there is one. Susan Kelly, whose character Liz Connors is featured in six books, says, "Golden Age? It's a Golden Explosion!" And Marcia Muller, creator of Sharon McCone and two other series, states, "If it is a New Golden Age, it's a different kind. The emphasis in mystery fiction has shifted from intricate (and often gimmicky) plotting to in-depth characterization and social consciousness. There's a great deal more variety within the genre than there was back then. Writers now have a freedom as to characters, subject matter, type of plot, that the earlier Golden Age authors didn't enjoy." According to Elizabeth Peters, author of four series, "There are so many new (within the past decade) and excellent writers—male and female—many of whom I believe will be considered classics in the future. The mystery itself is evolving, both broadening its scope and becoming richer in characterization and literary merit." Cass Jameson's creator, Carolyn Wheat, agrees: "I think the writers coming along today will be remembered as fondly as the Christies and Queens of yesteryear. Not because of their intellectual puzzles, but because of character development, social satire, insight into abnormal psychology, good writing, and just plain readability. It's not just women who are part of the Golden Age, but it's true that we are a big part of it—a fact that makes me very proud."

One question Nichols/Thompson are sometimes asked is, "Why does your work focus only on women?" The obvious answer is that this is what interests us. As women, we are always curious about what other members of our sex have to say on almost any subject. If and how they manage to apply a feminine point of view to a subject such as crime—especially murder—is of great interest to us. Another answer, only slightly less obvious, is that there are few comprehensive books on women's writing. A growing interest in this subject and a sufficiency of women writing in the genre make it one well worth investigating.

A look at the bookshelves in stores and libraries would seem to indicate that men dominate the field numerically, if in no other way. Our research indicates that this is not precisely the case, though the reason for this apparent imbalance may be that booksellers, librarians, and the reading public are less aware of the work being done by women. This raises the interesting issues of publicity and recognition. If work by women isn't promoted, it cannot gain readers or win awards. In 1987, an international organization known as Sisters in Crime (SinC) was created to redress this imbalance. The membership is open to all who wish to see women and their work accorded respect and recognition. As Linda Grant, 1993–1994 president of this organization and author of a six-book series, articulates, "These books range from the grittiest to the most genteel. Our books do cover the waterfront—and the tea shop. We have something for everyone, and we want the world to know it."

Margaret Maron, 1989–1990 president of SinC and creator of two series, has observed, "I hope one day to look up from my computer and see that the playing field has become absolutely level. In some areas, especially among publishers and buyers, it's already beginning to happen. There are still those who dig in their heels and refuse to concede that romantic suspense is as 'significant' as hard-boiled private eyes, or that 'women's mysteries' sell just as well as 'men's' when equally promoted; but little by little, I do see compliments and contracts, reviews and respect beginning to flow more freely in both directions across the gender gap. This is a new Golden Age, both in the quality of the writing and in the monetary rewards, and it does feel all the richer for the contributions women have made: the tangible books we have written and the intangible perceptions which we are changing and redefining."

Although Nichols/Thompson do hold some strong opinions on style, character type, and story line, and those opinions become apparent in our writing, we do not attempt literary criticism or qualitative evaluations of individual books. We respect, defend, and celebrate every writer's right to whatever perspective she chooses to present. Writing a book is no small accomplishment. Getting a book published these days is nothing short of a miracle, and, if sales and popularity are legitimate indicators, there is a market for every character and story type.

AFTER THE FALL:
Historical Mysteries

One interesting turn that crime and mystery fiction has taken in the recent past is a backward one. Several writers have moved away from the contemporary to take a more historical view of wrongdoing—especially the act of murder. All of the entries in this category hold true both to the times and to the crimes.

The series reflecting these earlier eras have several levels of interest for readers. One level is, of course, the accuracy of the age portrayed. Today's reader is a sophisticated and demanding creature, and woe betide the writer who has not done her homework properly. Another level is the similarity/difference in the investigative processes of these disparate periods. Finally, the most revealing level in these series is the ultimate disclosure that people and motivations remain essentially the same despite the epoch.

England in the twelfth century is the setting for the twenty-one-book series (1977–1994) in which Brother Cadfael, a Benedictine monk, is the protagonist. Cadfael joined the order after an active, worldly life; now in his middle years, he is the monastery's herbalist and is well known for his medical knowledge and healing skills. These abilities allow him to leave the monastery on occasion, often to assist his friend, Sheriff Hugh Beringar, to solve a murder. To the best of our knowledge, this series is the first to take mystery readers to a medieval past made accessible by the engaging portrayals Edith Pargeter, writing as Ellis Peters, drew.

Crimes generally considered modern are at the core of a seventeen-book series (1979–1997) set in the Victorian era. In these books, well-born Charlotte Ellison meets and eventually marries London metropolitan policeman Thomas Pitt. This unlikely union actually works exceedingly well as a device for looking at both sides of the societal issues of the day. Pitt, representing officialdom, is often thwarted in his duties by a repressive and often hypocritical ruling class. Charlotte, a member—by birth—of this order, has access to settings from which Pitt is barred. Their devotion to one another and to the cause of justice in harsh, unsavory social climates

1

make resolution a necessity for them in their respective roles. Author Anne Perry writes with a masterly touch about the time, the place and the people of Victoria's England. Readers soon realize that the era in which we live now is not so vastly different from the life lived then.

In 1975, Barbara Mertz, under the pseudonym Elizabeth Peters, introduced Miss Amelia Peabody, a spinster of the Victorian era. With the untimely combination of an education, a substantial inheritance, and a taste for adventure, Miss Peabody travels to Egypt. There she meets her match—in every sense of the word—in the form of Radcliffe Emerson, a brilliant archaeologist. The pair and their growing entourage are featured in nine books (1975–1997). Most of the action takes place in Egypt and author Peters plies her formidable knowledge of both Egyptology and human nature in each of the books.

History is essentially based on gossip. Who did what to whom? Why did they do it? Is this the truth or is it supposition? If the details seem salacious enough, does it matter? Who cares? Delicious rumors abound and interpretation is all. Those choosing to write in this subgenre have fertile grounds in which to play.

MARCUS DIDIUS FALCO & HELENA JUSTINA
1989–1996   8 books
Lindsey Davis

The series opens in A.D. 70; Nero has fallen and the year of four emperors is over. Vespasian now rules and must consolidate his power and his supporters. Treachery and intrigue are coin of the realm, and there are plots to unseat or overthrow anyone who takes the imperial role—even among the most trusted allies and family members. Enter Marcus Didius Falco, an enterprising young man with a strong personal code and wry sense of humor. He has served in the imperial army, has traveled afar, and has been invalided out of the military at the end of his tenure. Now, at the age of thirty, he works as a private informer gathering information and evidence for whomever will pay his fees. The only living son of a large family, Falco supports not only himself but his mother and the woman and child his late brother left behind. Needless to say, his purse is almost always empty.

In *Silver Pigs*, a young woman asks for Falco's assistance and protection. When she is murdered, her family asks Falco to find her killer. In doing so, he uncovers a quiet drain on the imperial coffers. Titus Caesar, Vespasian's elder son, sends Falco to Britain to get to the heart of the crime and the conspiracy. There he meets Helena

Justina, former wife of Atrius Pertinax and cousin to Sosia Camillina, the murdered woman. Much adventure awaits both Falco and Helena in Britain and, upon their return, in Rome. Ultimately, the drain is plugged and the conspiracy broken, though some unanswered questions remain at the conclusion of the story—not the least being the direction Falco and Helena's relationship will take.

Shadows in Bronze takes up the plot. Falco, operating as Vespasian's imperial informer, and Helena are embroiled in the dregs of the failed scheme. The third book, *Venus in Copper*, finds Falco a private informer once again. He is asked to make a prenuptial investigation of a woman suspected of killing all of her previous husbands for monetary gain. Before the planned marriage can take place, however, the groom dies. *The Iron Hand of Mars* takes Falco to the wilds of Germany. Helena finds her way to this untamed territory as well. Once again, acting for Emperor Vespasian, Falco is commissioned with many tasks: delivering a gift, finding a missing Roman general, co-opting the services of a German tribal leader, and neutralizing the influence of a Druid priestess. With Helena Justina's tenuously loving assistance, it's all in a day's work for Marcus Didius Falco.

Falco is a rogue, albeit a lovable one. His modesty takes the form of self-deprecation and his expressions of affection for others often take the form of calculated insult. A republican at heart, Falco mistrusts things imperial and yet he admires Vespasian the man and so is willing to work for him. Helena Justina is a fair match for Falco. She more than holds her own in their verbal battles, and her bravery and honor equal his. As a senator's daughter, she is several flights of steps above Falco in the social order. Her marriage to Atrius Pertinax was a failure and was terminated by the lady herself. By taking this step, Helena has joined Falco beyond society's pale and, at the same time, has ensured that she is always viewed as her own woman.

Ancillary characters add much to the series. The emperor and his sons wander in and out of the stories and are always in the background. Falco's mother berates him, his five sisters annoy him, and their husbands appall him. His best friend is Petronius Longus, a former tentmate in the army, now patrol captain of the Aventine watch—Falco's neighborhood. Petro is happily married and the father of several little girls. Despite their differences, Petro and Falco rely on one another for comradeship and more.

This is one of the most enjoyable series we've found. Each book is dense with information, and author Lindsey Davis truly makes history come alive through the actions and words of her characters. Most of the historical record is of major figures and epic events. Writers like Davis bring the bit players to the fore and place the major figures and their larger-than-life events into a more manageable perspective for the mortal reader.

SIGISMONDO
1992–1997   6 books
Elizabeth Eyre (Jill Staynes and Margaret Storey)

Once upon a long—unnamed—time ago in Italy when treachery, intrigue, conspiracy, and feuds were the order of the day, soldiers of fortune never lacked for work. Sigismondo is one such man. Tall, shaven of scalp, and always dressed in black, he is often taken for a man of the cloth; however, his broad shoulders and carriage allude to his possible history as a soldier.

As *Death of the Duchess* opens, Sigismondo is Duke Ludovico's man, charged with finding the abducted daughter of one of the duke's allies. A feud between the girl's family and another is thought to be at the heart of the abduction. Tempers run high, and the passions of the moment are only temporarily set aside for the festival honoring the marriage of the duchess's closest friend and mistress of the robes. At the festival, a dancer spills wine down the duchess's dress, forcing her to excuse herself to change clothing. Shortly thereafter, she is found murdered in her bed, which shows obvious signs of amorous transport. The plot thickens in a fashion unique to the Italians, and Sigismondo finds that his tasks require all the arts of statesmanship he can bring to bear. As the story draws to its close, the plots—for now cross-currents have entered the stream—thicken even more. The denouement is as complex as the tale itself, and Sigismondo unravels each knotty aspect of the plot.

The dramatic beheading of a son by his father opens *Curtains for the Cardinal*; Sigismondo and the boy's sister are among the witnesses to this horrific deed. Knowing that madness has fueled this murder, and treachery and jeopardy have replaced all rationality, Sigismondo removes the murdered boy's young sister, Lady Minerva, niece of Duke Ludovico, to insure her safety. Minerva is betrothed to Astorre, son of Duke Grifone of Nemora, and their marriage has been arranged to unite the two families and to strengthen the political alliance between Montenero and Nemora. Cardinal Petrucci is the next victim. This time, immolation is the means of death. Sigismondo is charged with finding the Cardinal's killer. More foul play takes place than could ever be credited to anyone other than the ancient Italians. Once again, Sigismondo provides the wrench for all the machinations. The marriage takes place and order is restored—for the moment.

Benno, a disreputable-looking fellow who is able to appear half-witted at the drop of a drumstick or of a bit of vital information, becomes Sigismondo's servant in the first book. Biondello, a small, one-eared mongrel, joins the pair then too. Angelo, whose countenance reflects his name and belies his true nature, is the dancer who spills wine on the duchess in the first book. Performing as a Tarot reader, he gives aid and a disguise to a refugee in the second. A variety of dwarves—popular in courts of the times—pop up with alarming and regular frequency.

Jill Staynes and Margaret Storey, using the joint pseudonym Elizabeth Eyre, bring as much subtlety to the telling of these novels as exist in the times themselves—whenever they were. Readers fond of the Montague/Capulet debacle will find these stories delectable. The authors' choice of words illustrates rather than narrates, and creates highly effective and evocative mental images for the readers. Staynes and Storey, under another joint pseudonym, Susannah Stacey, also write a series featuring the very British and quite contemporary Supt. Robert Bone discussed in the chapter "Behind the Badge: Provincial Police."

OWEN ARCHER
1993–1997   5 books
Candace (M.) Robb

In 1363, the city of York was the capital of northern England. Situated midway between London and Edinburgh, Scotland, and connected to the North Sea by the tidal River Ouse, it was an important market town and trading center. With its great cathedral and an archbishopric second only to that of Canterbury, York was a force with which to be reckoned. The archbishop of the city at that time was John Thoresby, who also held the title of Lord Chancellor of England under King Edward III. Edward was an ambitious king with aspirations for—among other things—the French throne.

To an archer, the loss of an eye meant the loss of profession. Owen, primary character in this series, is one such. Captain of Archers under the Duke of Lancaster, Owen had been a noted marksman and strong leader. The loss of his eye, not in battle yet in defense of his duke, earned him a place in that nobleman's entourage. At the death of the duke, Owen declines the honor of serving his successor, John of Gaunt, son of Edward III, and is summoned to London by John Thoresby. A suspicious death in the infirmary of St. Mary's Abbey in York has raised questions about an earlier demise, and Thoresby sends Owen to serve as an apprentice to York's apothecary in order to solve the puzzle raised by these two apparently unrelated passings. Owen's appearance, with his eye patch and scar, can be disconcerting; it is effective disguise for the fact that the vision in his remaining eye is sharp and clear.

The mystery in *The Apothecary Rose* is a tangled skein and the process of unraveling it causes pain to both the innocent and the guilty. In the process, however, Owen falls in love. He and Lucie marry off the page and in *The Lady Chapel* are husband and wife. The plot in the first novel is familial. That of the second incorporates a family cabal into the national scheme of things and illustrates the various connections and complicities of power.

These novels vividly capture the everyday life of the fourteenth-century citizens of York, providing glimpses into Britain's royal court and ecclesiastical palaces of that era. Readers may find themselves pleasantly transported to this other time and place by the intriguing characters and their settings. Once there, sense and sensibilities take on new meaning and the strange and foreign become familiar.

ROGER THE CHAPMAN
1991–1996   7 books
Kate Sedley (Brenda Margaret Lilian Honeyman Clarke)

A chapman is an itinerant peddler—a purveyor of pins, needles, thread, ribbons, and buttons. In the late 1400s, many people living outside of towns relied upon these merchants of the road not only for some of life's necessities but also for the news and gossip they carried along with their wares. Cities provided chapmen with opportunities to sell, but even more opportunity to replenish their stock-in-trade, both verbal and material. Roger, the chapman of these tales, is a strong, well-set-up young man. Given to the Glastonbury Benedictines at an early age by his mother, he has been educated and, while he is grateful to the brothers for his skills in reading and writing, he is not quite sure that Christianity provides *all* the answers.

The tales take the form of memoirs written by Roger in his later years. They are addressed to his children, who may or may not be interested in where their sire's inquisitiveness and stubborn streak took him. In *Death and the Chapman*, Roger is fairly new to his most recent calling. His mother's death at her home in Wells the previous Christmas had provided him with a small—a very small—inheritance with which he bought his first stock. Now, in the month of May, he is on his way through the gates of Bristol to see what the city has to offer. The first thing he sees is a procession, that of Queen Margaret of Anjou and her attendants, one of whom is a young woman of fragile appearance. Later events put Roger more closely in the path of this young woman and of the royal house itself, but Roger is reluctant to credit or burden himself with more involvement in royal politics and intrigue than necessary, so the main thrust of the tale is directed toward his solution of the mystery of the alderman's missing son.

The Plymouth Cloak thrusts Roger into the thick of royal doings, like it or no. While in Exeter, Richard of Gloucester—later the infamous Richard III—asks Roger to accompany a messenger to Brittany in the capacity of bodyguard. The messenger is murdered with a cudgel belonging to Roger, who sets forth to clear his name and, in the process, discovers that retribution can be its own reward.

The Weaver's Tale finds Roger back in Bristol and the victim of influenza. The kindness of a widow and her daughter, coupled with his own naturally robust constitution, brings about his rapid recovery. His ever-growing ability to land square in the center of a puzzle in need of solution propels the story through guilds and heresy to its surprising conclusion.

Though Roger may be reluctant to involve himself in royal machinations, readers may enjoy tracing the royal lines of the times and the accuracy with which they are reported by the chapman in the course of his trade. Sedley captures the flavor of the fifteenth and sixteenth centuries in a variety of ways. By choosing a chapman as her protagonist, and, by giving that young man a head start with the Christian brotherhood, she has created a character who is able to operate successfully on a number of different planes. Roger may be invited into the parlor, but he always enters an establishment by the kitchen door. He can pay his way at an inn but most always prefers to sleep outdoors. This protean soul is an ideal one to chronicle both everyday life and the broad-reaching, turbulent events of the era.

THE TONNEMAN FAMILY OF NEW YORK
1992–1998   6 books
Maan Meyers (Annette [Brafman] Meyers and Martin Meyers)

This unusual series begins in New York, then known as New Amsterdam, a city under the rule of Pieter Stuyvesant, director-general of the Dutch West India Company. In 1660, at the urging of the Burgomasters, Stuyvesant had been persuaded to separate the city from the company. As the first story, *The Dutchman*, opens, Pieter Tonneman has been named schout (sheriff) and serves in that capacity. A suspicious hanging—called suicide—a disappearing dead body, the reappearance of the body, several other seemingly unrelated deaths, and a missing man provide the mysteries central to the tale. The city of 1664, under Dutch control, is a very cosmopolitan place. The age of exploration and a Europe grown too small for its dissident political and religious factions have sent forth into the new world new inhabitants that include Dutch, Portuguese, English, and Germans to join several tribes of Native Americans. New Amsterdam is truly a new city in a truly new country. The coming of the English provides the pivotal point for all of the historical events and much of the action of the players in this novel.

The Kingsbridge Plot takes place in 1775. America is in the early stages of revolution and the city of New York is divided between patriots and loyalists. John Peter Tonneman, descendant of Pieter Tonneman and his second wife, Racqel Mendoza, is a physician newly returned from his studies in England. John has inherited his late father's house, medical practice, and title as coroner. On his first day home, the decapitated head of a red-haired woman is delivered to the mayor's office. Soon after, Constable Goldsmith discovers a headless corpse at the construction site of the city's new reservoir. The perpetrator of murder must be discovered and some semblance of common order must prevail.

The times are tumultuous; the English have been in power since the mid-1600s and the populace of the new world is growing weary of heavy taxation by the English monarch and of having little say in their own governance. History swirls around John Tonneman and his companions, compounding and complicating the investigation. At the conclusion of this installment, this Tonneman strengthens his own family ties by his marriage to Mariana Mendoza.

The High Constable takes place some thirty years later. The embargo, declared by President Thomas Jefferson in 1807, is having a strongly negative effect on the city and its inhabitants. "O Grab Me" was a sarcastic anagram that bemoaned the lack of goods and supplies. John Tonneman is still the coroner, but his medical practice has dwindled. His only living son, Peter, has no interest in medicine and seems to be wasting his life away on strong drink taken in dubious company. Peter's employer, James Thaddeus "Tedious" Brown, is murdered, and Peter is suspected of causing his death. Jacob "Old" Hays, the city's high constable, believes in Peter's innocence and puts him to work—as a special constable—on the investigation. The discovery of a skull under Brown's body brings an old crime to light, and John Tonneman and retired Constable Goldsmith join Peter and Old Hays in concluding both the old and the new cases.

Maan Meyers, joint pseudonym of Annette and Martin Meyers, has done a thorough job of research. The historical facts supporting each story are accurate, and it really does take four hundred pages of well-written historical fiction to get to the end of the mystery.

At the conclusion of each book, readers shouldn't be surprised if they want to read more of the fascinating history of New York. Subsequent stories return to the original Tonneman family. Under her own name, Annette Meyers has created the series featuring Xenia Smith and Leslie Wetzon, Wall Street headhunters in modern New York City who appear in the chapter "Killings on the Market: Business and Finance."

JOHN RAWLINGS
1994–1995   2 books
Deryn Lake (Dinah Lampitt)

London, England, during the reign of George II is the setting for this series, which introduces John Rawlings, apothecary, to the art of detecting. One soft and balmy evening in *Death in the Dark Walk*, John and his good friend Samuel Swann take themselves to the famous Vaux Hall Pleasure Gardens to celebrate the end of their seven-year indenture as apprentices in their respective trades. After consuming several bumpers apiece of the infamous Vaux Hall punch, the men become separated and John finds himself near one of the dark walks—where lovers often disport themselves. Hearing a woman's cry, John rushes to her aid but is too late. The beautiful young woman he and Samuel had noted with appreciation earlier in the evening is dead, strangled with her own stocking.

A beak runner arrives on the scene and takes John to the Bow Street home and public office of the principal magistrate of London. Mr. John Fielding—known as the Blind Beak—was the half brother of Henry, noted novelist and founder of the organization first called the Thief Takers. John Fielding succeeded to his brother's office, where, despite the loss of his sight at the age of nineteen, he carried on as Henry had begun. A tall and imposing figure, John Fielding was noted for his acute mind and fairness. Quickly discarding the idea that the apothecary might be responsible for the murder, the Blind Beak enlists John Rawlings's aid in bringing the perpetrator to justice. Using his trade, Rawlings is able to insinuate himself into the homes and confidences of those connected to the case. Finding it necessary to interview several people who have left the city, he travels to the Sussex countryside in order to gather simples—herbs and botanicals necessary for his ointments and potions. After he has gathered his simples and enough information to close the case, the Blind Beak summons all the murder evening's guests back to the pleasure garden for the denouement.

David Garrick and his Drury Lane theatre are parts of the action in *Death at the Beggar's Opera*. At the opening of the famous play, the actor taking the role of Macheath is actually hanged to death in the scene where he is supposed to make his escape. John Rawlings is in the audience and rushes to the stage to see if he can resuscitate the actor. Failing in this, he asks his good friend Sam to run to Bow Street and summon the Blind Beak. Once again, Mr. Fielding asks Rawlings to assist him, and the young man, now with a shop of his own in Shug Lane, agrees to make enquiries for the magistrate on alternate days. His travels take him to the villages of Kensington and Chelsea and place him among the players from London's well-known theatre district. Once again, his perspicacity leads him to the bitter conclusion of another heinous case.

John Rawlings, apothecary, really lived at the time these stories take place. He resided at number two Nassau Street and, some hundred years later, this address was one given for H. D. Rawlings Ltd., Soda Water Manufacturers. Perhaps John, as the original maker of sparkling water, was known for his equally ebullient personality. In any case, historical novelist, Dinah Lampitt, writing as Deryn Lake, has found an interesting soul and created a delightful series surrounding the young apothecary and weaving in other historical figures living then as well.

MADAME VICTOIRE VERNET
1993–1993   2 books
Quinn Fawcett (Chelsea Quinn Yarbro and Bill Fawcett)

The early 1800s and Napoleon Buonaparte's rise to power form the backdrop for this series featuring Madame Victoire Vernet. Married to a major in Napoleon's army, Mme Vernet is every bit a dutiful wife to her husband, Lucien. In *Napoleon Must Die*, Victoire has accompanied Lucien to his post in Egypt. A pharaoh's golden scepter is stolen and a young guard horribly tortured and killed. The generals on the campaign place themselves above the suspicion that then falls on Major Vernet. Napoleon himself takes charge of matters, instigates an investigation, and separates Mme Vernet from the major by dispatching him to Jaffa.

Roustam-Raza, a Mameluke guard, and Mme Vernet become reluctant companions. Together with Gen. Joachim Murat, they undertake a perilous journey across the desert and down the Nile to trace the missing treasure. They recover it only to have it stolen once again. Victoire effects various disguises in the process of recovery and, coincidentally, uncovers a plot to assassinate Napoleon. All ends well. Victoire restores the pharaoh's scepter and her husband's honor. Napoleon shows his gratitude by promoting Lucien to colonel and posting him back to France.

Another plot to kill Napoleon before he is crowned emperor is central to *Death Wears a Crown*. Six British officers from the Royal Horse Artillery—under direct command of their king—join forces with fourteen Frenchmen and form a cabal. Their goal is to end Napoleon's sweep of conquest and restore the monarchy to France. Once again using clever disguises, Mme Vernet uncovers a nefarious plot and, this time willingly assisted by Roustam-Raza and General Murat, brings the miscreants to light. At the end of the book, Lucien Vernet's reward for service to the throne is an annual pension of 20,000 francs. Victoire's more personal reward to him is the news that he is to become a father.

Quinn Fawcett is a joint pseudonym for Chelsea Quinn Yarbro and Bill Fawcett. Under her own name, Yarbro writes a series featuring San Francisco lawyer and Native American medicine man Charles Spotted Moon. While we cannot vouch for the accuracy of the history as presented in the Vernet tales, we can state that all of Yarbro's books are captivating stories; the characters are engaging and the plots entertaining.

JULIAN KESTREL
1993–1997   4 books
Kate (Katherine J.) Ross

England in the 1820s is the setting for these books. Society is clearly stratified, and the aristocracy reigns as much as the monarchy. Young gentlemen-about-town rule the London evenings and move from their comfortable clubs to the theatre and into late-night gaming hells. Not only does Julian Kestrel fit into this noble category, he is the leader of the pack. Appearing on the social scene a year or two earlier—from whence, no one is quite sure—Kestrel sets the standards of fashion as well as the pace. In demand in drawing rooms, at fashionable dinner parties, and, it is implied, in ladies' boudoirs, he moves through life with an uncommon grace. It therefore comes as a surprise to Kestrel's fellow dandies, in *Cut to the Quick*, when he takes up young Hugh Fontclair's invitation to serve as best man at his upcoming nuptials.

The story moves from London to the country home of the Fontclairs, where Hugh's bride-to-be and her father are also guests. It is apparent to Julian from the outset that tension and discomfort run high among those gathered. When a dead woman is discovered in Julian's bed, the story takes an even more ominous turn. Julian's valet, the redoubtable Dipper, is charged with the crime, and even when he is released for lack of evidence, Kestrel feels he must clear his servant's name. With the help of the Fontclairs' physician Dr.

MacGregor and others, Julian concludes the case and restores Dipper's reputation.

A Broken Vessel finds Julian back in his London digs, ably tended by Dipper. Dr. MacGregor also is in town, serving as locum for an ailing colleague. Dipper is reunited with his long-lost sister Sally, a lady of the evening, who has been beaten by one of her customers. The siblings return to Kestrel's rooms, where they encounter the master himself, who summons Dr. MacGregor to treat the young woman's injuries; Sally becomes a temporary member of the household. A mysterious note, a refuge for fallen women, and the death of one of the refuge's inmates catch Julian's attention. A too-hasty inquest into this death impels him to pursue the issue and, with the backing of Samuel Digby, a London magistrate, Julian and his cohorts delve into the mystery.

Point and counterpoint are hallmarks of these stories. Honor is always the crux of the matter at hand and all the disparate elements of Julian's inquiry form the links of the chain by which so many individuals are bound. As revelations are made in the course of investigations, members of the upper crust often come off looking cold, unresponsive, and insensitive to anything but their own position, well-being, and, of course, honor. Kestrel's social position enables him not only to make the revelations but to make sense of them in their particular context. Author Kate Ross gives readers a fine grasp of how life was lived in that time and place. Manners and mores, fashion and gossip, and, as always, the various human strata are well portrayed and make up the harmony of each tale.

WILLIAM MONK
1990–1996   7 books
Anne Perry

Anne Perry, creator of the Victorian series featuring Charlotte Ellison Pitt and her policeman husband, Thomas Pitt, has crafted a second series set in Victorian England. Perry adds another device to that of historical setting in these novels. The protagonist is William Monk, who, as the first book, *The Face of a Stranger*, opens, is in hospital recovering from injuries sustained in a cab crash. When Monk awakens from a three-week coma, all of his memory has been obliterated; he does not even recognize his own reflection. One of his first discoveries is that he is a London police detective. After a period of recovery, he returns to the station, whereupon his superior, Runcorn, sets him to work on a case more than a month old. The story is a study in parallels: while Monk is uncovering the secrets that led to murder, he is beginning to discover just who he has been and who he is.

Sgt. John Evan is assigned to the case along with Monk and proves to be a staunch and admiring ally. Miss Hester Latterly, recently returned from nursing alongside Florence Nightingale in the Crimea, becomes involved in Monk's case through a connection with her own family and her friendship with Lady Callandra Daviot, aunt to the murdered man. When Monk and Miss Latterly meet, each takes an instant dislike to the other and this tension is maintained throughout all of the stories.

A Dangerous Mourning opens with the trial of the perpetrator of the murder in the first book. Barrister Oliver Rathbone is introduced and becomes a part of Monk's coterie. Lady Callandra has helped Hester secure a position as an infirmary nurse; however, Miss Latterly is rightly disobedient to authority and soon finds herself in need of a another situation. Events proceed and, in partial consequence of the investigation central to this story, Monk is charged with insubordination and forced to leave the police. Lady Callandra assists him in setting up as a private investigator and aids Hester in becoming a private-duty nurse as well. In this position, Hester is hired to care for the mother of the young murdered woman. Monk—abetted by Sgt. Evan and Hester—continues his indagation and the case is successfully concluded.

Every inquiry in which Monk becomes involved is complicated and protracted by the repressive society of the time. Ladies and gentlemen, by virtue of their status, are considered exempt from distasteful or dishonorable actions and, by extension, from intrusive questions surrounding criminal acts. The police operate at the behest of society and are thereby often constrained by that body. As an independent agent, Monk has more latitude than the public servant in the guise of the Peeler, while at the same time he lacks the support that even a reluctant superior could provide. Only his emerging nature impels Monk's progress in what appear to be cases impossible to resolve.

Through her characters, their activities, and the nature of the crimes that fuel these novels, Perry awakens all of us to our sensibilities and social conscience.

GLYNIS TRYON
1992–1997   5 books
Miriam Grace Monfredo

The series opens in Seneca Falls, New York, in the year 1848. The Married Woman's Property Act has just been passed by the New

York state senate and, for the first time in United States history, married women are allowed to receive property by gift or inheritance. That they are unable to dispose of said property is thought (by most men) to be irrelevant. However, many of the women instrumental in the passage of the act want more in the way of rights for women and are beginning to quietly agitate.

Glynis Tryon is the Seneca Falls librarian and a graduate of Oberlin College in Ohio—the first four-year college to admit women. Her patron, Friedrich Steicher, had provided Glynis with her tuition and promised her the job when she received her degree. As *Seneca Falls Inheritance* opens, Friedrich and his wife have been killed in a river accident. Glynis has received the contents of his personal library as a bequest to the town and discovers that the family Bible has been sent along by mistake. Glynis also discovers the drowned body of a woman she had met the day before and plunges into the mysteries surrounding the dead woman's presence in town, her need to meet with Elizabeth Cady Stanton, and her connection to the Steicher family.

Most of the series' ancillary characters are introduced in this book. Cullen Stuart is the town's police constable; Jacques Sundown, half French, half Seneca-Iroquois, is Cullen's deputy; Jeremiah Merrycoyf is an attorney and golf companion to Glynis; Quentin Ives is the town physician; Serenity Hathaway is a madam who owns the local tavern; and Abraham Levy runs the dry goods emporium known as Levy's Hardware store. Glynis boards with Harriet Peartree and both are friends with Vanessa and Aurora Usher—wealthy sisters with a flair for things theatrical. Real, historical figures make their appearances in these well-crafted tales. Along with Elizabeth Stanton, Glynis has encounters with Susan B. Anthony, Dr. Elizabeth Blackwell, Charlotte Woodward, and Frederick Douglass.

Each story features at least one suspicious death of which Glynis is instrumental in discovering the perpetrator. Running parallel to the murder mystery are several counterthemes involving events of the time and place. *North Star Conspiracy* documents some of the activity of fugitive slaves and their passage along the Underground Railroad and details the Usher sisters' establishment of a theatre in the town. *Blackwater Spirits* introduces Neva Cardoza, a newly graduated physician from the Female Medical College of Pennsylvania and relative by marriage to Abraham Levy. Her struggles to practice medicine are chronicled as are the tribulations of Serenity Hathaway to comport her business as she sees fit and is legally entitled to. *Through a Gold Eagle* treats counterfeiting and women's fashions as the events leading to the Civil War unfold.

Miriam Grace Monfredo does a masterful job of weaving fiction and history together in compelling, believable tales. Her characters ring true to themselves, their stories, and the times. Readers may learn a great deal about issues pertinent to the lives of historical and contemporary women, including the early women's rights movement, slavery, temperance, and prejudice toward women and other minorities. Though filled with the stuff of which history is made, these books are not dry or weighty but rather vibrant and entertaining reads.

CHEF AUGUSTE DIDIER
1986–1997   10 books
Amy Myers

In 1891, the British Empire is at the height of its glory, Victoria is queen, and England is a bastion of security and moral rectitude. Stately manors are still held by the succeeding generations of the families that built them. (The British National Trust has yet to be invented—much less needed.)

As this series opens in *Murder in Pug's Parlour*, Maitre Chef Auguste Didier, a former apprentice to The Great Escoffier, is in charge of the kitchens of Stockbery Towers, Kent. The twelfth duke of Stockbery and his duchess reign on one side of the green-baize door; Greeves, the steward, holds suzerainty on the servants' side of that portal. Greeves is murdered and aspersions are cast upon the chef and his creations. Under suspicion, Auguste determines to find the miscreant and his investigations carry him to the family side of the dividing line. When a guest of the ducal couple meets her own untimely end, the matter of the sudden, suspicious deaths is taken out of the hands of the Kent constabulary and placed in the purview of Scotland Yard in the person of Insp. Egbert Rose. Ably assisted—not to mention well fed—by Maitre Didier, Rose delivers the culprit to justice, of sorts.

Three years later—1894, in *Murder in the Limelight*—Didier is maitre chef of the Galaxy Restaurant, attached to the theatre of the same name, on the Strand in London. Several showgirls are found dead in various locations around London. All have been bound in a similar fashion. These murders require the attention of Scotland Yard, and Rose is assigned to the cases. Once again, Didier is on the scene and the solution is clarified by his actions.

Murder at Plum's finds Auguste cooking for the gentlemen of an exclusive London club in 1895. At the annual celebration known as Plum's Passing, Colonel Worthington is shot to death in the conservatory. Ladies are present in the club for the first time in history and, for the third time in this series, Rose and Didier must identify the ingredients and recreate the receipt for murder.

Murder at the Masque finds Didier on holiday with his parents at their home in Cannes, France. Insp. Rose, in his official guise, comes to Cannes, hot on the trail of stolen Fabergé eggs—gifts from the Russian Grand Duke Igor to his many mistresses. The denouement takes place at a cricket match at Grand Duke Igor's villa. Although on foreign soil, Rose and Didier triumph, *encore!*

Though his name is French, Maitre Auguste Didier is half-English. His training in the continental style of cooking has been of the highest order, yet his heart remains true to the honest products of the English countryside. Didier is able to lose himself in ecstatic transports over the humble turnip while, at the same time, turning out the most exquisite and complex of sauces. His heart also remains true to the fair Tatiana, a young Russian princess with whom he shares a mutual love that, alas, must remain unrealized due to their respective stations in life.

Amy Myers tantalizes her readers with well-plotted mysteries. The menus created by Auguste are appropriate to each setting and fascinating. Detail is not spared either in the detection or in the preparation of Didier's gastronomical extravaganzas. Readers are invited to devour the lightly humorous series in its entirety.

IRENE ADLER
1990–1994   4 books
Carole Nelson Douglas

American Irene Adler is an international opera star. She is best known, however, as the only woman to ever have outwitted Sherlock Holmes—who henceforth refers to her as *The* Woman. The first book, *Good Night, Mr. Holmes*, is Conan Doyle's story, "A Scandal in Bohemia," expanded and told from Irene's perspective and chronicled by her companion, Penelope Huxleigh. In this novel, the five primary players are Irene, Penelope, Holmes, Watson, and British barrister Godfrey Norton, eventually Irene's husband. As the series progresses, other historical ancillary characters make their appearance, including The Divine Sarah Bernhardt, Lillie Langtry, Oscar Wilde, Louis Comfort Tiffany, Charles Fredrick Worth, and Baron Alphonse Rothschild. The entrances, exits, and involvements of each of these figures are well timed and properly carried out.

At the end of the second book, *Good Morning, Irene*, Irene and Godfrey Norton are involved in a train crash in the Alps and are presumed dead. Like Holmes after his encounter with Moriarty at Reichenbach Falls, they find it convenient to allow the fiction of their demise to continue. The French village Neuilly, just outside Paris, becomes the Nortons' and Miss Huxleigh's home and headquarters for their continuing adventures.

Irene at Large, although third in the series, begins nine years earlier than the second, in Afghanistan, where Dr. Watson and Quentin Stanhope meet during the battle of Maiwand. Spies operating under code names Tiger, Cobra, and Sable all play pivotal roles in this narrative and make appearances in later tales, especially *Irene's Last Waltz*. This third tale finds Irene, Godfrey, Penelope, Holmes, and Watson back in Bohemia, where they are all involved in international politics and intrigue of the highest, most sensitive order.

Carole Nelson Douglas uses a double blind in her attributed authorship of the Adler accounts. The fictional Miss Huxleigh is clearly the original diarist. However, the long-sequestered and fictional diaries were found in a Shropshire bank safe-deposit box, and the fictional Fiona Witherspoon, Ph.D., F.I.A. (Fellow of the Institute of Actuaries), has seen to their contemporary publication. Dr. Witherspoon addresses the issue of the possible suppression of the Huxleigh journals by looking at the accepted view of women of the Victorian era. Adler's behavior—as seen from the male-dominant view of the time—would have been considered highly unsuitable, even immoral and/or promiscuous. Viewed from today's perspective on women, Adler is in the vanguard of the truly liberated woman.

All of the books in this series are lavish with historical and artistic detail. Each runs around four hundred pages in length and, while the information between the covers is dense, the stories are all well paced and hold the reader's interest. Author Carole Nelson Douglas has done her Sherlockian homework and knows the canon intimately. Not only does she deftly and believably weave characters found in Watson's chronicles of the world's first consulting detective into her own narrative, she gives them a new and acceptably credible twist.

Douglas has also created two other series—one featuring psychiatrist Kevin Blake, the other, Midnight Louie, a feline detective.

MARY RUSSELL & SHERLOCK HOLMES
1994–1996   3 books
Laurie R. King

Miss Mary Russell was fifteen when she became *The Beekeeper's Apprentice*. The half-American orphan returned to her English mother's home in Sussex, where she is made the unhappy ward of her maternal aunt, who is a harsh and penurious woman (though lavish on her own behalf). As the book opens, Mary—possessed of a fierce, uncompromising, and tenacious intelligence—is striding across the Downs with her nose buried in a volume of Virgil when she literally stumbles over the beekeeper—none other than the legendary Sherlock Holmes himself. In his mid-fifties, Holmes has retired to a cottage in Sussex, kept for him by the loyal Mrs. Hudson.

Holmes is immediately struck by Mary's intelligence and her habit of keen observation. Mary, starved for companionship and care, soon feels quite at home under Mrs. Hudson's wing and Holmes's tutelage. For the next two years, Mary finds ways to spend most of her time with Holmes, who hones her instincts and feeds her hunger for knowledge while Mrs Hudson feeds her growing body. Mary goes up to her first year at Oxford University and, on her return to Sussex for the long vacation, she and Holmes together solve the case of the "Mistress of the Hounds." Mary, with some aid from Holmes, solves the mystery of the purloined hams in "A Case of My Own." When the daughter of an American senator is kidnapped and held for ransom, Holmes is well aware of the usual outcome of such crimes and reluctant to take the case. He does, however, and, with Mary's able assistance, embarks upon "The Vagrant Gipsy Life." The pair conclude the case in "A Child Gone from Her Bed."

In December of Mary's second year at Oxford, Holmes arrives—in heavy disguise—and informs her that they are in danger and must leave immediately. They set out for the Middle East, where they solve several politically sensitive cases and decide that their only hope of ending the threats to their lives is to return to England and separate. A carefully orchestrated yet personally taxing ruse is put into play and the case is brought to a brilliant conclusion. Throughout the book, the redoubtable Dr. Watson makes occasional appearances as does Mycroft Holmes, Sherlock's elder brother.

A Monstrous Regiment of Women opens just days before Mary's majority, at which time she will inherit her parents' considerable estate. Fed up with a house full of unappealing relatives, Mary escapes first to Holmes's cottage, then, finding him absent, to London. There she encounters her former Oxford classmate, Lady Veronica Beaconsfield, who takes her to a "service" held by the charismatic Margery Childe. Three hundred twenty-six riveting pages later the denouement is achieved. Mary and Holmes shake hands to acknowledge the successful conclusion of the case and to honor the future of their unorthodox partnership.

The material for these cases was purportedly anonymously sent in a large tin trunk to Laurie R. King, self-described editor of all that follows. The contents of the trunk included items of clothing, jewelry, newspaper clippings, and a variety of other oddments along with a great number of handwritten pages. After years of careful scrutiny, copying, and editing, King sent the re-worked manuscript to her editor as her own work. Eventually King confessed the origin of the material to her editor and, with lawyerly advice taken, the first book was published. The second book derived from the same source and, in the editor's note prefacing this work, King describes a postcard sent from Utrecht with the unsigned message, "More to follow." We are as thrilled as King must be that the chronicles of Sherlock Holmes and Miss Mary Russell are to be continued.

King's work begins after Holmes's supposed retirement from active detecting. Clearly established as a legend, what is left for the man to prove—or even to do? In creating Mary, King has devised the antithesis to Holmes's ennui. Given the time and state of the world, only a young person and probably only a female could jolt Holmes from his languor; and jolt him she does. Not only has King crafted a counterpoint to the Master, she has humanized one who has always been viewed as almost purely cerebral. This is a wonderful, vibrant series that brings new life to a well-loved fictional hero and gives birth to a new one.

King also develops another series—a police procedural—featuring Kate Martinelli.

PHRYNE FISHER
1989–1996   8 books
Kerry Greenwood

Australia in the late 1920s is the setting for this series featuring the Honorable Phryne Fisher. Three untimely deaths have brought Phryne's father a title, a vast inheritance, and estates in England. Whisked from Australian poverty to lordly luxury, most of the family have settled into their new life comfortably. Phryne, however, has grown bored with her status as dilettante and is chafing for more adventure than England—or even the Continent—can offer her. In *Death by Misadventure*, Phryne has returned to Melbourne, Australia, at the behest of Colonel and Mrs. Harper, who are worried about their married daughter Lydia, who now also resides there.

Greenwood introduces most of the series' characters early in the first volume. Dr. MacMillan, a friend of Phryne's from England, travels on the same ship as she to take up a post at the Queen Victoria Hospital in Melbourne. The first people the two women meet in Melbourne are Bert and Cec, taxi drivers, who move them—and all of Phryne's luggage—from the dock to their respective residences. A chance encounter outside a glove shop puts Phryne together with the young woman who becomes her new maid/secretary, Dorothy Bryant. Once established in the Windsor Hotel, Phryne sends out cards to all the local notables in order to secure invitations that will place her in the path of her quarry (Lydia), and the plot thickens.

Phryne is the epitome of the "modern" young woman—she smokes cigarettes, drinks cocktails, and is not averse to sharing her bed with a succession of comely young men. She drives a bright-red Hispano-Suiza and flies an airplane. Her methods of investigation are direct, and most of her risks are calculated. Phryne's friends are staunch and devoted, despite the fact that some of her professional requests put them in jeopardy. Her wealth is definitely an asset in providing the necessary entree into society and providing all she needs for her life-style and her detecting.

In *Flying Too High*, Phryne and Dorothy have moved to 221B, The Esplanade, St. Kilda, just outside Melbourne. Phryne has found her metier and is now officially an investigator. The kidnapping of the six-year-old daughter of the Irish Christmas lottery winner is intertwined with the demise of businessman William McNaughton. The challenges thrown up to the intrepid band put them on their mettle.

En route to visit relatives in *Murder on the Ballarat Train*, Phryne's detective skills are called into play when the entire company of the first-class carriage in which she and Dot are traveling is subdued by chloroform and one of the passengers is abducted. The action returns to Melbourne, where Phryne's cronies are all too ready and willing to lend their assistance.

Subthemes run through each of these humorous stories. They provide both an interesting counterpoint to the plot and historical information on Australia during a lively era. Illegal abortion and some of its unsavory practitioners, cocaine traffic and use, and white slavery are among the secondary plots. Despite the gravity of these subjects, Greenwood treats them with a light yet respectful hand. Phryne and her cohorts provide readers with action and an insightful look at a place far away and long ago.

LUCAS HALLAM
1987–1990   3 books
L(ivia) J. Washburn (Reasoner)

Lucas Hallam has been a Texas Ranger, a town marshal, a Pinkerton operative, and a movie cowboy. Now in his fifties, Hallam still occasionally rides on the silver screen but more often hires out as a private investigator. He is a quiet man who does not call attention to himself, and his reputation often precedes him—for good or ill.

Set in the late '20s and early '30s, the stories run true to form for those days. Hollywood is a boom town populated by oil magnates and members of the burgeoning film industry. Prohibition is in effect, speakeasies abound and citizens regularly defy the law to quench their thirst. Though it is rapidly being tamed, the West is still frontier territory. A man of action like Lucas Hallam fits here; there may be fewer gunfights but those that happen are just as lethal as the earlier ones. At times, it is necessary to take the law into one's own hands, and that comes naturally to Hallam.

The movie industry is central to each of the multi-layered stories featuring Hallam. In *Wild Night*, while scouting for possible shooting locations, he meets Lis Fletcher, owner of the ghost town of Chuckwalla, California. No movies ever get made there, though shooting (of the bullet variety) does take place. Hallam is also hired as a bodyguard for Elton Forbes, the charismatic founder of the Holiness Temple of Faith. Two men are shot, and Hallam is led on a merry chase back to Kansas in search of a mystery woman. Added story elements are a lecherous director with an active casting-room couch and the resulting besmirched honor of young ladies led astray by his promises and blandishments. Despite the convolutions of plot, the story is a good one.

Dog Heavies takes place on the Flying L Ranch just outside Ft. Worth, Texas. Hallam and several other cowboys have been hired by studio production head J. Frederick Darby to teach young Eliot Tremaine the tricks of the trade in order to turn him into a star of Western movies. Cattle rustling, bootlegging, and young love are all counterthemes in this story, and Hallam's skills and physical prowess are all put to the test before the tale's end.

The legacy of Mad Ludwig of Bavaria and the aftereffects of World War I enter into *Dead-Stick*, which takes place on the set and in the skies of a movie entitled *Death to the Kaiser!* Accidents have plagued the production, and Hallam is hired to find out what's going on behind the scenes. Spies, thieves, international art treasures, love affairs, and early airplanes are all featured, and once again Lucas Hallam triumphs.

For all the complexities in each of the stories, Washburn gently weaves in a remarkable amount of history. In an era of changing standards of behavior, moral attitudes still exact severe penalties from those who transgress the unwritten code. Huge fortunes are being made; the stock market is rising to astronomical heights and then plunging to the lowest depths, bringing ruin in its wake. Land is available and cheap in the Los Angeles basin; Southern California is just entering its phase of rapid growth. Already Hallam mourns the loss of the quiet agrarian place he remembers. He is rapidly becoming an anachronism himself and in this transitory position is the perfect foil for the settings of these novels.

History is comprised not only of notable characters and large events but also of gossip—information and conversation about other people. Gossip is generally considered in the negative and yet, in reality, all of us engage in it on a regular basis. Through gossip we are better able to understand one another and ourselves; motivations become clearer as we discuss who has said or done what to whom and why. While all mystery writers use the device of gossip to enhance and extend their stories, those using past times as the setting for their works can take things far beyond the realm of the impersonal straight to the intimate heart of matters by using the tattle of their chosen era. History buffs will not be disappointed by these fictional incursions into the past, as all of the writers have well researched their respective centuries. Readers who have disdained the study of the past because of its supposed dry nature are in for a pleasant surprise with any of these works.

SOME OTHER HISTORICAL SLEUTHS

Kate Ardleigh
Sophy Bancroft
Nell Bray
Enrico Caruso
Cassidy & Devlin
Paris Chandler
Clively Close
Iris Cooper & Jack Clancy
Abigail Patience Danforth
Dr. Jeremy Faro
Jack Fleming & Charles Escott

Sister Frevisse
Fremont Jones
Kyra Keaton
Catherine LeVendeur
Lord Meren
The Pennyfoot Hotel
Hollis Powell
Sano
Kathryn Swinbrooke
Miss Harriet Unwin
Insp. Witherspoon & Mrs. Jeffries

ANOTHER SIDE TO REALITY:
The Supernatural and the Occult

Reality is, at best, equivocal. However, most would agree that magic and the supernatural fall outside any conventional boundaries of the word. This chapter introduces characters inhabiting this other area.

At least three earlier characters are a precedent for this addition to our lexicon. The first is Gladys Mitchell's Dame Beatrice Lestrange Bradley, who appears in sixty-eight books (1929–1984). In one persona, she is a highly respected consulting psychiatrist to the British Home Office; her other, less obvious body of knowledge lies in the misty netherworld of folklore and mysticism to which she is, by birth, no stranger.

Charles Spotted Moon also has a dual identity. He is a lawyer in the offices of Ogilvie, Tallant and Moon in San Francisco and a medicine man for his Native American tribe in Canada. While Charles adheres to the letter of the law in his practice, he is not above calling on the spirits to help exonerate an innocent client. Over a seventeen-year period (1976–1992) Chelsea Quinn Yarbro wrote, unfortunately, only four books with Spotted Moon. We want more.

Mrs. Edwina Charles, created by Mignon Warner, appears in seven books (1976–1985). She is a clairvoyant with the Tarot as her medium. The cards give her insights not only into the future but into the human heart and mind. With legitimate claim to all the several names by which she is known, Mrs. Charles is something of an enigma. Few individuals have the vision to see this woman as anything but a fortune-teller. Those who do are invited to share the view from this interesting character's perspective.

The newest offerings in this otherwordly realm make contributions to the recent crossover phenomenon that combines crime and mystery fiction and other genres. Some readers may be familiar with the crossover between romance and mystery. Here fans of fantasy will find themselves quite at home; fans of the traditional mystery are invited to join us on the other side.

J. J. JAMISON
1983–1989 4 books
L(aurie) A(ylma) Taylor

Joseph Jamison is a computer engineer. By his own admission, he is not terribly dedicated to his job but is simply a competent technician. His passion—or perhaps preoccupation—is for an organization called the Committee for Analysis of Tropospheric and Celestial Happenings, or CATCH. J. J. is CATCH's chief of field investigation for Minnesota and the Dakotas and travels around doing follow-up reports on unidentified flying objects (UFOs).

In *Only Half a Hoax*, J. J. is called by his good friend Mack Forrester, an officer with the Minneapolis Police Department, to come and interview two teenagers who have come to report a UFO sighting from a hospital parking lot. In the course of his field work, J. J. discovers the body of a man who had been shot to death and stuffed into a car in the parking lot. In spite of Mack's protests on his behalf, J. J. becomes the prime suspect for the murder. When his wife, Karen goes into labor, J. J. takes her to the hospital and attends the delivery of his son, Joey. Returning home, he discovers that his bedroom has been torched. The plot then begins to really thicken.

In *Deadly Objectives*, "Aunt Yuk" is an experimental pattern recognizer J. J.'s company has been developing for the Department of Defense. The machine disappears in transit, and subsequently the engineer accompanying "Aunt Yuk" is found murdered. Meanwhile, a scam artist is promising elderly UFO enthusiasts passage on an alien spaceship and, in the process, bilking them of their life savings and property. Karen and Joey are kidnapped, and J. J. must divide his time between searching for the machine and for his family.

Shed Light on Death finds J. J. and Karen taking a busman's holiday when J. J. is called to investigate a UFO sighting in a farmer's field. They are witnesses to the death of Cameron Rogers, a self-important Ph.D. who is also dedicated to the study of UFO sightings. Although he was as odious as was humanly possible, death seems a harsh response. J. J. and Karen must stay until released by the police, and they get involved in the murder investigation as well as the one around the UFO report.

Mack Forrester has left the police department in *A Murder Waiting to Happen* and has opened his own detective agency. His first major job is to provide security for a science fiction convention. J. J. has been invited to speak on the subject of UFO investigations, and Mack asks for his assistance. A number of pranks interfere with the planned events. Skinny-dipping in the hotel pool provides some distraction, as does a hot game of "Killer," but when "Killer" becomes murder and another corpse is found as well, the stakes are raised.

Along with Mack and Karen, several other satellite characters appear. Lars Pederson, a.k.a. The Great Dane, is J. J.'s office mate and sometime accomplice in detecting. Mrs. Eskew is Joey's babysitter, their neighbor, and, not incidentally, a crack shot. Prunella Watson never appears but, as the director of CATCH, is featured in almost every story. Although short, each of the four books is dense and a pleasant diversion.

Minneapolis resident and author L. A. Taylor was an award-winning poet and author of several nonseries mysteries in addition to the Jamison series. Unfortunately, the series ends with these four titles, as Taylor died in 1996.

THERESA FORTUNATO
1986–1993   2 books
Kate Green

Theresa Fortunato is a psychic. As a child growing up in Boston, Massachusetts, her odd behavior drove her mother to seek the parish priest's counsel. Because Theresa did her homework and didn't smoke, steal, or go with boys, the priest's advice was to leave her alone. Theresa's grandmother sought other counsel—a Gypsy fortune-teller who recognized fourteen-year-old Theresa's gift and presented her with a deck of Tarot cards. A year of college, marriage at nineteen, a stint in a mental institution, and divorce at twenty-four all create the context in which Theresa's gifts become both useful and accessible.

When *Shattered Moon*, first book in the Fortunato series, opens, Theresa is twenty-nine and living in Venice, California. The sign in her front window reads, "FORTUNATO, PSYCHIC CONSULTANT, READER/ADVISOR." Dr. Frank Brandon, a psychiatrist with whom Theresa has worked, has sent the parents of a missing nineteen-year-old named Bonnie to her. Using Bonnie's ring, Theresa begins to receive images about the girl's fate and her location. Homicide Det. Lt. Oliver Jardine responds to Theresa's phone call reporting Bonnie's death. Neither Theresa nor Jardine has ever worked in quite this fashion before, but the contact between them is strong and each is piqued with curiosity by the other. Two more deaths prove to be related to the first. Theresa and Jardine—each in their own fashion—learn more about the case through the victims and the sites at which they are discovered. The unlikely combination of police and psychic procedure works to filter through the welter of conflicting information and unmask the killer.

In the second book, *Black Dreams*, Theresa is awakened by the voice of a child. The psychic receives the impression that the child has been abducted and phones her friend, Lt. Jardine, who suggests she contact the Simon Foundation for Missing Children. Jardine himself is on the way to the scene of a suspicious death. The two cases overlap, and eventually each forms the basis of the solution of the other.

Since their first meeting nine years earlier, they have occasionally worked together and Theresa is helping Jardine develop his own paranormal gift. Using what Theresa has taught him in his professional capacity is giving Jardine a reputation for being a bit strange. His detractors are forced to admit, however, that for all his strangeness the lieutenant is an excellent detective who often picks up information no one else has noticed.

Kate Green's unusual, well-plotted, and well-written novels are difficult to quantify or qualify. The non-linearity of the stories, while confusing at first, actually provides readers with a glimpse of the workings of the psychic mind. In *Shattered Moon*, Theresa learns that only by putting absolute trust in the information she receives will she be able to sort out what appears to be conflicting data. This advice is good for readers to keep in mind, as numerous, apparently disparate elements woven throughout each tale become relevant to the outcome.

PROF. JAMES ASHER & SIMON YSIDRO
1988–1995   2 books
Barbara Hambly

James Claudius Asher is a professor of philology at New College in Oxford, England, as the nineteenth century turns into the twentieth. One would hardly expect to discover that this brown sort of fellow, as described by his wife, Lydia, had for some sixteen years also served queen and country as a spy. The carnage in South Africa during the Boer War had so soured him for what he calls The Great Game that when *Those Who Hunt the Night* opens, he has been living simply for some years as an Oxford don. Then one night he meets Don Simon Xavier Christian Morado de la Cadena-Ysidro, a three-hundred-year-old vampire of Castilian descent.

Someone is killing vampires and Ysidro, being familiar with Asher's history as a government agent, comes to him for help. One of Ysidro's greatest fears is that another vampire has made an unholy alliance with a mortal and the two are systematically disposing of

London's undead. Using lightly veiled threats against Lydia, Ysidro forces Asher to aid him in his quest. Lydia is herself, however, a force with which to be reckoned. Vastly wealthy, the young Mrs. Asher is also a physician possessed with a boundless curiosity, very little fear, and a deep devotion to her husband. The search for the vampire killer takes Asher and Ysidro to Paris, where they meet not only the master vampire of the city of light and his coterie, but the guilt-ridden, six-hundred-year-old vampire who lives in the depths of the catacombs and calls himself Brother Anthony.

Back in London, Lydia submerges herself in researching property exchanges, wills, and birth and death records at Somerset House to discover possible vampire lairs. When Asher and Ysidro return from Paris, they add her information to what they have ascertained and the culprit is dispatched in a startling fashion. With a perverse sort of gratitude, the London vampire master and several of his followers allow Asher and Lydia to continue their lives, unmolested.

Traveling with the Undead opens on the eve of World War I when Lydia finds it necessary to appeal to Ysidro for his assistance in matters that threaten world security. James recognizes Ignace Karolyi—a Hungarian nobleman, Austrian spy, and sympathizer to the German cause—and is horrified to discover that Korolyi's traveling companion is a vampire. Fearing the consequences of this unholy alliance, Asher follows the pair to Paris, Vienna, and Constantinople. Lydia, Ysidro, and Margaret Potton, a young woman recruited by the vampire to act as Lydia's maid, follow Asher as he crosses the continent and enters Asia Minor. More vampires are encountered along the way and things are brought to a denouement before events even worse than the War to End All Wars happen.

Barbara Hambly, a noted science fiction/fantasy writer, has turned her hand to blending genres. Her writing is engaging and her characters' development always allows for the less-than-sympathetic view James and Lydia feel toward Ysidro and his kind. Hambly's portrayal of vampires and their making, powers, and needs adds considerable depth to what is already a rich historical era. Her mortal protagonists, James and Lydia, provide an ideal focal point that serves to anchor the timeless nature of the vampire to a particular period.

JACK FLEMING & CHARLES ESCOTT
1990–1992   6 books
P(atricia) N(ead) Elrod

Charles Escott is an Englishman, a former actor, and, in the mid-1930s, when the series is set, a private agent working out of Chicago, where gangsters hold sway. Nightclubs provide a glossy backdrop for those who arrive in tuxedos and evening gowns for their night's entertainment in sometimes bulletproof saloon cars and limousines. Al Capone is incarcerated on Alcatraz Island in the San Francisco Bay, Hitler's power is on the rise in Europe, and America is just coming out from under the effects of the 1929 crash of Wall Street and the ensuing Depression.

In the first book of *The Vampire Files* series, *Bloodlist*, Escott meets Jack Fleming, a former journalist from New York and a newly born vampire who cannot remember his last five days of life. The mystery is to find out how and why he died. Together, the two answer the question and find that there is yet a deeper, underlying issue. The next, *Lifeblood*, delves further into unresolved matters: Maureen Dumont, Jack's vampire maker, has been missing for five years; her mortal sister Gaylen contacts Jack—ostensibly to get information about her lost sibling; and two rabid vampire hunters are hot on Jack's trail. Bloody confrontations conclude several story elements.

Book three, *Bloodcircle*, actually finalizes the first book. Charles and Jack travel to New York on their continuing search for Maureen Dumont, Jack's vampire maker, and they meet her vampire maker, who aids them in the resolution of the last question remaining about Jack's past. By the end of this book, Jack and Charles are not only fast friends but business partners and roommates. Jack has moved into part of the three-story brick, once bordello, house that Charles is restoring. Jack's rooms on the second floor are just for show, however, as he spends his days in a small, hidden room in the basement.

Three more books follow and all six stories take place within one year. A few ongoing, but subordinate, characters include Jack's girlfriend, Bobbi Smythe, a nightclub singer, and her accompanist, Marza Chevreaux, who hates Jack—for some reason not related to his being a vampire as she does not know what he is. Marza's boyfriend, Madison Pruitt, a well-to-do dilettante who spouts Communist rhetoric, doesn't have a clue, either. Club owner Gordy is one of the few who knows Jack's secret and keeps it.

This amusing series is a spoof on the pulp fiction popular in the '30s and '40s, with all the features that made the pulps popular reads in their day and classics now. The series has as an added component the problems of a day sleeper. Murder and deception are the core of each story, and Fleming and Escott as private agents detect admirably. Even though these are spoofs, the tales are well told and as full of action as the originals they imitate. Author Elrod has captured the flavor of the times she has chosen to chronicle—in many senses of the term.

VICKI NELSON & HENRY FITZROY
1991–1997   5 books
Tanya Huff

Vicki Nelson, a former police officer in Toronto, is suffering the effects of an incurable disease; retinitis pigmentosa has forced her to resign from the force. As the series opens with *Blood Price*, she has lost all night sight and twenty-five degrees of peripheral vision in each eye. The prognosis is uncertain. She had been a good cop, on the force for eight years, and decorated three times. Known to her colleagues as "Victory" Nelson, she is five foot ten, lithe, and glowing with fair-haired good health. No one would guess that without her thick glasses, the world is a meaningless blur.

Off the force for eight months, Vicki has established herself as a private investigator. Her professional life may be getting itself back in order but her personal life leaves something to be desired. In the series opener, Vicki is on her way home when she hears a scream rising from the subway station. Rushing toward the sound, she discovers a young man's corpse on the platform. His throat has been torn out. After two more similar deaths—in both cases the bodies have been drained of blood—the newspaper headlines scream, "VAMPIRE STALKS CITY," and Vicki is hired by the girlfriend of the first victim to find his killer. In pursuit of her job, Vicki comes upon a fourth corpse, this time with a figure bending over it. Thinking she has caught the perpetrator in the act, Vicki rushes forward to collar him. As sirens draw closer, the figure rises, scoops up Vicki, and carries her off.

When Vicki regains consciousness, she is in the fourteenth-floor apartment of Henry Fitzroy. She asks him what he was doing bending over a corpse; he tells her he was hunting a demon and asks what she was doing there. She tells him she was hunting a vampire. Fitzroy, the twenty-four-year-old romance writer and former duke of Richmond and Somerset, earl of Nottingham, Lord President of the Council of the North, knight of the Garter, and bastard son of King Henry VIII, laughs and tells Vicki the story of *his* making as a vampire 450 years earlier.

The two agree to join forces in the hunt for the demon. Fitzroy explains that there must be a human control—a summoner—for the beast, and Vicki begins her search for that summoner while Henry tracks the demon itself. Mike Celluci, Vicki's former police partner and occasional lover, also enters the fray. Still on the Toronto force,

Celluci represents the rational side of law and order. The case, however, is clearly irrational, and when Celluci is confronted by the demon as it attacks Vicki, he finds his rational mind put on hold while he does what is necessary. Henry, Vicki, and Celluci succeed in vanquishing the demon, his human master, and the demon lord.

Blood Trail takes Vicki, Henry, and—eventually and reluctantly—Mike Celluci to a farm outside London, Ontario, to end the killing that is plaguing a family of werewolves. With the help of a mummy from Egypt's sixteenth dynasty, the trio saves Toronto from the powerful grasp of an Egyptian god in *Blood Lines*. In *Blood Pact*, zombies are loosed from the Life Sciences Department of Queen's University, and the three comrades must bring the immoral experimentation to a halt.

Readers must not be put off by our wry descriptions of these stories, as they are delightful. Even though the series is humorous, fans of H. P. Lovecraft, Edgar Allan Poe, and Anne Rice will feel right at home. Author Tanya Huff turns the tables a bit and makes some of her otherworldly creatures surprisingly sympathetic and others appropriately horrific. We look forward to more in this series—which may never end. . . .

THE ADEPT, SIR ADAM SINCLAIR
1991–1996   5 books
Deborah Turner Harris and Katherine Kurtz

The primary character in this series is Sir Adam Sinclair, a man of learning and power. Sinclair is a Scots nobleman and a practicing psychiatrist who, among other things, acts as a consultant to the police in crimes involving the occult. Sir Adam relies on more than medical expertise in these cases; his true calling is as an adept and master of the Hunt, dedicated to protecting the Light and eradicating the dark forces that threaten it.

Det. Chief Insp. Noel McLeod of the Lothian and Borders Police in Edinburgh is Adam's closest friend and companion in the Hunt; Noel's gift is the ability to act as a medium. In the first book, *The Adept*, Peregrine Lovat, a well-established portrait artist, is troubled by the unseen things he is able to paint. Adam recognizes Peregrine's trouble as the Gift of Sight, helps the young man to accept his talent, and trains him to use and respect it. From Strathmourne House, the Sinclair family seat for generations, the redoubtable butler Humphrey holds forth. Janet Lady Fraser and her husband, Matthew, one of Adam's medical colleagues, have both been friends of Adam since childhood. Each of these characters makes an appearance in all of the stories, although Adam, Noel, and Peregrine are central to each tale.

On ordinary days, Adam makes rounds at the hospital and sees patients in his office, Noel investigates run-of-the-mill crime in and around Edinburgh, and Peregrine paints portraits of well-born and well-known folk. However, not every day is ordinary and these three are occasionally called upon to ply their special talents and guard the Light against dark forces that take many forms. A wizard, the undead, the faerie flag, a magic sword, and the philosopher's gold are trophies sought by an individual seeking vast and evil power in *The Lodge of the Lynx*. This lodge is a coven seeking to increase the strength of ancient Druidical relics and unleash the relics' destructive powers. In *The Templar Treasure*, the Crown, Sceptre, and Seal of Solomon—treasures long under the protection of the ancient order of the Knights Templar—are in jeopardy.

Katherine Kurtz and Deborah Turner Harris are well known for their science fiction/fantasy writing. In their collaboration on the Adept series, they have made a contribution to the crossover between genres.

KAREN HIGHTOWER
1994–1996   3 books
Rosemary Edghill

Karen Hightower is a graphic artist for Houston Graphics in the borough of Manhattan in New York. She lives in a studio apartment within walking distance of her workplace and holds a particular view of her home and city. She is convinced that when all is said and done and yuppification is complete, people will wonder just where the charm of the old neighborhoods has gone and why it is impossible to rent a studio apartment for less than fifteen hundred dollars per month.

Bast is this character's other name and, to her and readers of this series, the most important one. Bast is a practitioner of wicca and can best be described as a witch of the highest order. Her coven is called Changing and her high priestess is Lady Bellflower. The lineage of the Changing Coven is Gardnerian as opposed to the Crowleyites or the Odinists. From Bast's point of view, each of these is just a part of the New York occult community and each holds its rightful space in the One True Polytheism.

In *Speak Daggers to Her*, Bast receives a call from her friend and co-wiccan Lace telling her that their friend Miriam is dead. Rushing to Miriam's apartment, Bast finds herself alone with the corpse, items present and missing, and a dusty altar that speaks volumes. A call for help from Miriam awaits Bast on her answer box along with a message from someone from Baba Yaga, Miriam's Russian wiccan coven, telling Bast that everything is fine and to stay out of things not her business. Needless to say, after Miriam's death, Bast makes many things her business and enables the Goddess to bring justice—in her own time and fashion—to the perpetrator.

Mary, Queen of Scots is a featured character in *Book of Moons*. Another witch asks Bast to help search for her *Book of Shadows*, every witch's personal record of spells, ritual, and diary of magic. At the Ecumenipicnic in celebration of Beltane, Bast overhears several conversations in which a lost or misplaced *Book of Shadows* or notes pertaining to the magic other-life is discussed. She receives a package and is told not to open it. But, after the owner of the package is murdered and Bast is no longer under thrall of her promise, she opens it and finds not only the stolen diaries but also the *Book of Moons*, an apparently four-hundred-year-old tome purported to belong to none other than Mary Stuart. Common sense and, perhaps, a bit of magic come to Bast's aid and the murderer is captured by several of New York's finest and, one presumes, brought to mundane justice.

Although Bast considers herself to be a practicing and fully believing witch, she is a pragmatic one. Whatever one calls the religion of witchcraft, it is an old, long-forgotten polytheic practice. Bast views television as the religion of the masses, so her money is on what she describes as the First Church of Star Trek and she credits the program—in all of its versions and revivals—with having far more impact on people than any other system of belief. Bast strives for a morally ethical life with actions stemming from her better nature. She views evil as the "autism of altruism," and any action she takes must contain no element of evil.

Rosemary Edghill has crafted a distinctive series with an original character who operates from a particular—though uncommon—set of principles. The stories are an axiological blend of the magical and the mundane. Edghill uses the language as both toy and tool and even the most erudite reader may find that it is necessary to resort to *Webster's*.

NICHOLAS SEGALLA
1994–1996   3 books
Ann Dukthas (P[aul] C. Doherty)

Nicholas Segalla is a man cloaked in mystery. Inviting Ann Dukthas to luncheon in an elegant Dublin restaurant, Dr. Segalla tells her he attended her recent lecture at Oxford University and was interested in her subject, the murder—in Scotland in 1567—of Lord Darnley, the husband of Mary, Queen of Scots. Ann asks if he had visited Oxford before her lecture. When Segalla replies that he was last there in the winter of 1561, Miss Dukthas is aghast and rises to leave. Segalla then produces two items as credentials: a gold chancery ring and a bag of ancient coins. When he offers her a drawing of a mermaid sitting on an oar, Miss Dukthas recognizes it as a sixteenth-century original. After their luncheon and meeting ends, she receives through the mail a series of postcards—reproductions of famous paintings that feature the face of the man she recognizes as Segalla—and a manuscript upon which *A Time for the Death of a King* is based.

The pair next meet at a cafe off the Champs Elysees in Paris after Ann has flown from Dublin on a ticket provided by Segalla and spent an expense-paid week following the itinerary he had included with his gift. Her tour had been oriented on the period surrounding the French Revolution—a time Miss Dukthas knows only from the novels of the Baroness Orczy. Once again, Segalla presents Miss Dukthas with a manuscript telling a tale of betrayal, treachery, treason, and murder. The central figure in Segalla's story is the young Dauphin, Louis Charles, son of Queen Marie Antoinette and King Louis XVI, who at the age of ten had been taken from his mother several months before she was guillotined. Segalla had been the Queen's confidante and her last thoughts—mingled with the sorrow of losing her crown, son, and head—may well have been regrets for not heeding the advice of her wise and kind adviser.

In the author's note at the end of the first book, Miss Dukthas details some of her research on the man who never dies. She traces her object as he slips across the events of history—more than nine hundred years to the Battle of Hastings in 1066, to Kirk O'Field in 1567, to an 1860s inquiry directed by Napoleon III, and into the early days of World War II, when a man answering Segalla's description gave information about the use of plutonium long before atomic energy was discovered. These very facts raise further questions in our minds. Is Segalla the man who cannot die or is he but one of a number of dedicated members of a cabal entrusted over the centuries with preserving as much of the world's safety as possible? Is Miss Dukthas herself perhaps an invention conveniently devised to write the stories based on Segalla's manuscripts?

With the popularity of Anne Rice's Vampire series and the movie based on her book *Interview with the Vampire*, of Francis Ford Coppola's cinematic treatment of *Bram Stoker's Dracula*, and of Jack Nicholson's wonderful portrayal of a werewolf in the film *Wolf*, interest in the fantastic is clearly on the rise. The discipline of the murder mystery is appealing and seems to invite writers to blend their own fictional style with crime fiction's traditional form. Although murder is at the core of these novels, readers will not find these mysteries conventional. The characters we've introduced in this chapter do not fit the usual detective mold, yet they get the job done—one way or another. Mystery readers have been suspending their disbelief for generations; it seems a small step to raise the level of suspension just a bit higher to accommodate these new offerings.

SOME OTHER SLEUTHS BEYOND REALITY

Anita Blake
Det. Mitch Greer & Deirdre Griffin
Jo Hughes
Insp. Garret Mikaelian
Diana Tregard

A BLOT IN THE COPYBOOK:
Academia

The hallowed halls and ivory towers of academia are not totally isolated from the follies of their habitues. In fact, these locales are often ideal settings for all manner of mayhem. In addition, the scholarly life often requires its practitioners to abandon the questionable security of halls and towers for other, even less secure venues. No matter where these professorial types are found, they are well advised to adhere to the requirements of their calling—namely, the pursuit and dissemination of knowledge—for when these dictates are applied to detecting crime, the results can be illuminating.

In 1964 Kate Fansler—mirroring Athena's creation—was delivered, fully formed, from the brow of her creator, Amanda Cross. Kate Fansler detects with a curious mixture of logic and intuition held together by literary links she forges. Reed Amhearst, an assistant district attorney who becomes her husband, does not always see the connection Kate has made, yet trusts her intuitive process and is willing to provide whatever resources he can to support her.

Kate Fansler did not achieve her position of respect within the academic community on a feminist platform. Readers actually know very little about Fansler's history and what her achievements may have cost her along the way. We are presented with an adult (probably mid-forties) woman comfortable with herself and her position, who exudes an admirable confidence. Carolyn Heilbrun, writing under the name Amanda Cross, has given us the prototype for a whole and complete woman who serves as a role model throughout the twelve books (1964–1997) in which she appears over the span of thirty years.

Nineteen sixty-four also saw the introduction of another professorial detective only slightly more conventional than Fansler. Author Jane Langton created Homer Kelly, who has been a policeman and has attended a small, nameless city college and obtained a law degree at night school. Through curiosity and hard work, he has elevated himself to some eminence as a scholar of nineteenth-century American literature, authored numerous books, and served as an associate professor at Harvard. In the first novel, Homer meets his future wife, Mary. They marry at the end of *The Transcendental Murder*, and their relationship of amiable intimacy proceeds apace throughout the series.

Most of the twelve books (1964–1996) featuring Homer Kelly take place on the eastern seaboard. The curmudgeonly professor's scholarly interests frequently take him from his home in Concord to other historically relevant locales. All of the books in the thirty-three-year-long series rely on a sense of place, and the events in each story are well defined by location. Like Fansler, Kelly relies on his formidable literary knowledge to connect events and suspects and to arrive at the solution to whatever mystery is at hand.

Predecessors to these exemplary academicians tended to follow a rather more conventional pattern. In the '40s, Professors Penny-feather (author D. B. Olsen) and Mandrake (coauthors John and Emery Bonett) represented traditional aspects of academia. These series were amusing incursions into a profession long thought to be rather isolated from the real world, and both of these gentlemanly representatives fit the norm of the day.

Peter Shandy, created by Charlotte MacLeod, is a professor at the mythical Balaclava Agricultural College, Balaclava Junction, Massachusetts. His exploits are recorded in eleven novels (1978–1996). In terms of values and attention to his duties and responsibilities to the student body, his fellow faculty, and the administration, Shandy is a paragon of convention and tradition. The stories themselves are humorous and feature a cast of recurring characters.

Another humorous note is struck in Elizabeth Peters's series featuring Amelia Peabody (Emerson) and Radcliffe Emerson, who marry after their joint adventures in the first story. The nine books of the series (1975–1997) take place primarily in Egypt during the Victorian era, with Radcliffe working as an unsponsored archaeologist. Amelia is anything but conventional. Intelligent—at a time when that quality was not admired in the fair sex—and independently wealthy—when women were usually at the fiscal mercies of fathers, brothers, and/or husbands, the fiercely outspoken Amelia launches herself out of society and into adventure. Together with Emerson, she produces a "catastrophically precocious" and altogether human offspring known (affectionately?) as Ramses. This unlikely field crew encounters all manner of peril—burning desert heat, a walking mummy, several curses, and a master criminal. Historically accurate and often hilariously funny, these are good adventures with sufficient mysterious twists and turns.

While Oxford University provides office space for the next pair of characters, none of the adventures of Dr. Penelope Spring and

Sir Tobias Glendower actually takes place there. Dr. Spring is an anthropologist and Sir Toby is an archaeologist. She is American; he is English. Their training and field work have prepared them well for investigating crimes—past and present. From the beginning of the twelve-book series (1979–1995), little personal history is given for either of these two scientists, who are well into middle age and highly respected in their fields.

The far-flung locations of the stories are crucial to each plot, and Petronelle Cook, writing as Margot Arnold, gives readers interesting, germane information on each locale. Mythology, superstition, and tradition run rife through the tales that involve these erudite protagonists. The series is good light reading, full of gentle humor and a sense of true friendship and camaraderie.

Scholarship often provides avenues of detection not open to law-enforcement officers. Writers at home in the academic world are wise in using representatives of this intelligent and highly trained community as investigators parallel to those officially charged with the task of preserving the peace. Readers will find much more adventure than dust between the pages featuring any academic sleuth.

ELIZABETH MACPHERSON
1984–1995 8 books

JAY OMEGA
1987–1992 2 books
Sharyn McCrumb

As the Elizabeth MacPherson series opens, MacPherson is a recent college graduate with a B.A. in sociology. As it progresses, she decides on a career in forensic anthropology and acquires a Ph.D. in the subject. Along the way, she also acquires a second title—Mrs., when she marries Cameron Dawson, a Scottish marine biologist, in *The Windsor Knot*, the fifth of the series.

Murder is central to the stories of Elizabeth and her eccentric family. In the first novel, she is pressed into service as a bridesmaid for her cousin Eileen at the family manor in Chandler Grove, Georgia. We meet Captain Grandfather and Aunt Amanda, Uncle Robert, and their offspring, Eileen, Geoffrey, and Charles. Across the street from the family homestead, in a replica of Mad Ludwig of Bavaria's castle, reside Aunt Louisa and cousin Alban. Elizabeth's brother, Bill, a law student, makes a brief appearance at the denouement of the tale. Their parents, Margaret and Doug, having missed the wedding in favor of a sales convention, turn up periodically in other stories.

Forensic anthropology is a convenient hook for the author to use in creating this character. Though professional expertise does come to the fore in several of the books, Elizabeth relies less on her academic background than on her general intelligence, intuition, and firm family connections to reach her conclusions in the bulk of the novels.

Dr. James Owens Mega, the second main character with a series that Sharyn McCrumb created, is an electrical engineering professor. His professorial title and duties are of less interest than his avocation of sci-fi writer and his nom de plume of Jay Omega (a physics term meaning frequency times the square root of negative one). The two books in which he appears have probably the most compelling titles we have ever come across—*Bimbos of the Death Sun* and *Zombies of the Gene Pool*. The stories themselves are light romps through the often fantastic world of science fiction fandom. In *Bimbos*, as the dungeonmaster in a role-playing game, Omega solves the murder of the odious victim. In *Zombies*, the opening of a thirty-year-old time capsule that was buried in the '50s by a group of writers known as the "Lanthanides" threatens both the victim and his killer with unwanted exposure. Omega gently unveils the old secrets and, in the process, heals numerous old wounds.

Probably the most delightful aspect of all of the books penned by Sharyn McCrumb is her mastery of storytelling. In each of the Elizabeth MacPherson (Dawson) books, readers get information on Scots lore, Appalachian history, the Civil War, the British Royal Family, the West Virginia Highland Games, and other equally fascinating subjects. In the Jay Omega series, McCrumb pulls out all the stops and has a roaring good time mixing if not her metaphors at least her genres. Although she may overlabor her points, at the end of all her books the reader feels both entertained and informed.

McCrumb also has created the Sheriff Spencer Arrowood series described in the chapter "Behind the Badge: Provincial Police."

GILLIAN ADAMS & DET. CHIEF INSP. EDWARD GISBORNE
1984–1993   3 books
Nora Kelly

While all three books in this series have a feminist theme, the main character is no strident, radical representative of the order. Gillian Adams, a Ph.D. in history from Cambridge University, England, is a professor at the University of the Pacific Northwest (UPNW) in Vancouver, British Columbia. As a proponent and supporter of women's rights, she is in a position to effect change within her sphere. The first book, *In the Shadow of Kings*, looks at the fact that Cambridge University (in 1984) often rates sex higher than merit. In *My Sister's Keeper*, the university (UPNW) is faced with a stellar scholar who is an ardent feminist and does not fit the conventional model; the idea of true scholarship is addressed, and serious questions about appropriate departmental funding are raised. *Bad Chemistry* treats the issues of women's professional advancement and reproductive rights.

The arguments presented in each of these novels are cogent and timely. Author Kelly cleverly offers both sides of each topic and—though her position is clear—serves as an excellent devil's advocate for the opposition. This is not male bashing, nor is it wholehearted support for women's rights without requisite responsibility. Rather, she looks at some very contemporary issues in a balanced way. The rights of women in the workplace are new enough to still engender debate. Kelly makes a persuasive case for judgment on merit while clearly outlining the responsibilities adherent on women who take up this challenge. And, on the much broader issue of reproductive rights, she puts her characters on the front line of the cause.

Each of her books *is* a murder mystery. The man in Gillian's life, Edward Gisborne, is a Scotland Yard detective. In the first book, Edward attends a lecture Gillian gives at Cambridge and is on the scene when murder is done. While he may head the investigation, information provided by Gillian is vital to his solution. The second book finds Edward as the provider of information that helps Gillian solve a crime an ocean and a continent away from Scotland Yard's resources. Book three involves the couple's friends and requires a combination of their resources.

The pace of these novels is pleasant. Gillian, her friends, and her colleagues offer an interesting collection of viewpoints operating in the present time. Kelly handles geographic location and the more immediate landscape of the workplace with a deft hand and the international quality of the relationship between Gillian and Edward provides much of the vital tension.

PAULA GLENNING
1985–1996   9 books
Anna Clarke

All of the stories in which Professor Paula Glenning appears are best described as English. Were a color to be ascribed to them, it would invariably be grey. The characters, both primary and ancillary, seem only partially defined and, at the same time, are archetypally English. The books offer little or no resolution at their conclusion; oddly enough, despite the foregoing, these complex—often convoluted—tales do engage the reader, make sense in and of themselves, and offer the promise of continuity. Death is not always the focus of the story, and the deaths that do occur may or may not be murder. Far less important than who is guilty is how and why events evolve to constitute the particular mysteries Glenning feels motivated to solve.

We meet the main players of the series in the first book, *Last Judgement*. Famous English novelist G. E. Goff is living in retirement and seclusion as he approaches his ninetieth birthday. He is cared for by his long-suffering yet infinitely patient stepdaughter Mary Morrison. James Goff, grandson to G. E., teaches with Paula at London University and has been persona non grata in G. E.'s household for years due to his grandmother's defection from her marriage. At stake are the "Goff papers," the rights to which would guarantee any scholar's position in the academic world. James's rival in the matter is literary critic Richard Grieve. Paula has been dating James and is also an old friend of Richard. James feels smitten by Mary, and Richard enlists Paula's aid in his cause for obtaining the Goff papers. Without compromising the mystery it must suffice to say that in the second book, *Cabin 3033*, Paula decides not to marry Richard and James is not mentioned.

To date, there are nine books in the series. All are easy reads and oddly compelling. The stories range in locale from London and its environs, over the high Atlantic seas, to the suburban or bucolic English countryside with a literary thread running throughout. Subordinate characters include a literary agent and her husband, who writes mysteries, a reclusive writer of romance novels, students, Paula's mentor, and colleagues of both Paula and James. In all of these venues and with all these individuals, Paula is the constant; she is curious, impetuous, and strong willed. James Goff, who appears in all of the books save the second, grows and develops into a very sympathetic character. He is indulgent and solicitous toward Paula, who remains just who she has always been. Their relationship progresses yet does not really develop. In *The Case of the Ludicrous Letters*, they have purchased a house and are living together. Love may form the core of their relationship—there is obviously mutual respect—yet physical intimacy between them is never even alluded to. There is a lot of repressed emotional energy between the two primary characters but what energy is present is directed toward mystery solving, academia, and general, all-round nosiness.

Anna Clarke has succeeded in creating gothic tales without the requisite brooding moors and moldering mansions. By a careful use of shading, she has managed to present convincing slices of life and an almost microscopic view of individual lives that take place under the gloss of apparent normalcy. This series is memorable. Readers may find themselves—as we do—left with a level of frustration due to a lack of resolution, yet, as in a morality play, there are lessons. Perhaps we are gripped by the author's rendition of reality.

JANE WINFIELD & ANDREW QUENTIN
1987–1991   6 books

CLAIRE CAMDEN
1992–1995   3 books
Audrey Peterson

The first series created by Audrey Peterson features Jane Winfield and Andrew Quentin. In the opening story, Jane is working on her doctorate in music history and Andrew is her adviser; as it progresses, Jane achieves her degree and maintains her friendship and professional connection with Andrew. All of the stories in this set are complicated. Romance is a prime ingredient, as is a plethora of characters. Each book is predictable, and part of the predictability is in the twist at the end of each tale. For readers of romance novels, these stories are the perfect crossover into the realm of the mystery.

While both Winfield and Quentin are American, all of the tales take place abroad—generally in England. In the first, *The Nocturne Murder*, Jane meets James, a solicitor and son of her landlady. Jane, accused of the murder of her lover, turns to James for assistance in her defense. Andrew arrives from southern California on a research project of his own and is in time to offer not only aid and comfort to Jane but also the ultimate solution of the murder.

All of the books follow the same pattern. Jane is pragmatic, and ably, though unknowingly, assists Andrew in gathering information and hard evidence. Andrew's personal history casts him as a rather tragic figure. His sensitivity may make him more susceptible to the emanations of the guilty party, and his actions lead to the climax. Musical scholarship forms the foundation of the series, and Peterson provides readers with interesting—if fictional—insights into the world of the composer, performer, and impresario. Characters involved in the various plots are more or less connected by and with music, and many of the clues to the explanation of the crime are musical. Romance plays a major role in each story, relationships are paramount, and red herrings abound. For readers who care about the development of primary characters and look for satisfactory resolution, these six books offer both.

Peterson's second series revolves around the adventures in the

British Isles of another American academic, Claire Camden. As with the Winfield & Quentin books, teeming relationships are at the crux of the Camden books. Claire's involvement with crime is exacerbated by her relationship with Det. Supt. Neil Padgett. Her other personal relationships—with her former mother-in-law, Bea Camden, her own daughter, Sally, and Sally's father—contribute to the tales.

In *Dartmoor Burial*, Camden is writing a biography of M. L. Talbot, one of Victorian England's most lively and daring female novelists. This subplot strikes close to our hearts. In the author's note at the opening of the book, Peterson draws a parallel between Talbot, her fictional creation, and nineteenth-century novelist M. E. Braddon. (See: "Master List" and "Appendix I: Series Character Chronology.")

MACKENSIE SMITH & ANNABEL REED SMITH
1989–1995   5 books
(Mary) Margaret Truman

Mackensie Smith is a professor of law at Georgetown University and a former criminal lawyer. Annabel Reed, who becomes his wife in the second book in the series, owns a gallery specializing in pre-Columbian art and is also a former lawyer whose expertise was in divorce. Well past the first flush of youth, Mackensie and Annabel have a relationship that is one of mutual respect and warm intimacy. Though both have given up the actual practice of law, they retain their personal integrity and professional acumen. Personal connections engage Mackensie Smith in addressing the legal aspects of the mysteries in which he and Annabel appear. In *Murder at the Kennedy Center*, Smith stumbles over the dead body of an aide to a presidential candidate. A sequence of convoluted family ties and potentially damaging secrets are the hub of this mystery. With the aid of former Washington police detective Anthony Buffolino, Smith and Reed unravel the tangled skein of intrigue.

In *Murder at the National Cathedral*, Mackensie Smith and Annabel Reed are married, and the officiating clergyman is murdered. Smith and his new bride feel obligated to solve the crime. *Murder at the Pentagon* pits Smith against the mighty military machine that is determined to possess the newest ultimate weapon. International arms dealing and homosexuality in the military add to the covert need of this governmental arm to perpetrate lies and disclaimers to an uninformed public. Smith acquits himself and the young woman lieutenant set up to take a heavy part of the fall in this drama. Mackensie Smith's formidable legal background and far-reaching professional associations serve him well in the delicate task of protecting both his clients and the sensitive information often crucial to the matters at hand.

The author's insider knowledge of the environs and inhabitants of the nation's capital (as daughter of a United States president) provides the reader with a real sense of the people charged with governing our country and the inner workings of the branches of government. Margaret Truman has created a believable and sympathetic set of characters whose only goal is to preserve true justice in the name of the union. Since 1980 Truman has written fourteen books; only five titles feature these characters. In our opinion, they are the best part of her Washington, D.C., collection.

WINSTON MARLOWE SHERMAN
1990–1993   5 books
M(argaret) K(eilstrup) Lorens

The relationships in all of the books featuring Winston Marlowe Sherman can best be described as tribal. And there are numerous tribes—some defined by proximity and/or like-mindedness, others forged by a mixture of design and desire. Throughout the five-book series, Sherman—despite a large cast of regulars and an even larger cast of casual characters—remains central to the unity of the stories. Sometimes chief, sometimes shaman, even at times reluctant brave, this large, ponderous, sixty-plus former—though not retired—professor of Shakespeare at DeWitt Clinton College spins and holds the threads connecting whatever disparate crew is playing out the scenes in each novel.

Sarah Bernhardt Cromwell is Sherman's life partner in unwedded bliss. Sherman himself describes their state as one of "tender sin." A concert pianist of some renown, Sarah also teaches piano at her ancestral home and gives classes once or twice a week at Juilliard. The rambling abode inhabited by Winston and Sarah is all that is left of her father, Erskine Cromwell's, once vast estate in Ainsley, New York.

David Garrick Cromwell, Sarah's much younger half brother, raised by Sarah (and Winston) after David's mother's desertion and their father's death, is an actor trained at the Royal Academy of Dramatic Art in London. Married to the gorgeous Alexandra and father of their daughter, Gemma, David has trodden the boards in numerous Shakespearean epics on both sides of the Atlantic and successfully paid his dues on American television as private eye Nick Greyhawk.

Retired professor Eddie Merriman lives in the former servants' quarters of Sarah and Winston's home. After his wife's death, Merriman had rented rooms from widow Blanche Megrim; however, her Tuna Surprise casseroles, Perry Como recordings, and romantic inclinations drove him to seek sanctuary in the Cromwell/Sherman enclave. When not assisting Sherman in detection, Merriman passes his time painting the same Hudson Heights view in watercolor and, in the wee small hours when sleep eludes, playing his clarinet. These characters form the core of Winston's tribe and appear prominently in all the novels. Other individuals, less primary, also make their appearances with regularity.

Henrietta Slocum, Winston Sherman's nom de plume in the world of mystery fiction, and her creation, the redoubtable G. Winchester Hyde, a detective of the gilded age of the nineteenth century, provide some literary grist for Winston's detective mills. David's mastery of disguise and immersion into character inevitably enter the plot. While Winston looks at the surface and investigates what seems to be going on, David delves into the underbelly of matters at hand and provides clues and insight into motive, means, and method.

Other tribes are represented in each of the five novels. In *Sweet Narcissus*, first in the series, the theatre is at the core of deception and death that reaches back over thirty years. In the second book, *Ropedancer's Fall*, charitable foundations, publishers, literary-prize givers, and the homeless are groups that touch and influence the outcome of the crime of defenestration. *Deception Island* takes another retrospective view of Sarah's life and her connection to Frances Woodville, an artist in seclusion on the eponymous site. Spies, David's mother, and long-standing secrets are featured in a story that revolves around the art world and its practitioners—both fair and foul.

From the initial appearance of Winston and his tribe, author M. K. Lorens has created a series that encourages readers to suspend their disbelief and turn the pages to find out what happens next. This series of verve and eloquence can be slowly consumed and relished but always leaves one wanting more.

JACKIE WALSH
1992–1997   9 books
Melissa Cleary

Jackie Walsh is a film instructor at Rodgers University. In the first book, *A Tail of Two Murders*, Jackie and her son, Peter, find a large, injured dog on their back stoop. After being treated for a gunshot wound, Jake (an Alsatian) becomes a member of the Walsh family.

When the dean of the communications school at the university is murdered, Jackie finds the body and meets Det. Mike McGowan. McGowan discovers that Jake is a retired police dog who belonged to Matt Dugan, a police officer dismissed from the force. Dugan himself was murderd. The plot continues to thicken. Jackie's film expertise leads her to the killer of the dean and, assisted by Jake and McGowan, she brings the perpetrator to justice. Dugan's murder remains unsolved. As the series progresses, readers learn more about Jackie, Peter, Jake, and their friends and colleagues.

The world of dog shows and dog owners is featured in book two in the series, *Dog Collar Crime*, and once again Jake is in on the denouement. The mystery surrounding Matt Dugan's death and his dog's involvement in events during and after that crime persists through the third book, *Hounded to Death*, where Jake, Jackie, and McGowan, together with reporter Marcella Jacobs, find Dugan's killer and uncover corruption on a grand scale in the Palmer city government. In *Skull and Dog Bones* a faxed biography, a missed appointment, and a poisoned corpse found floating in a swimming pool provide the intrigue. Jake is maced, and this violation propels Jackie into still another case. An archer with deadly intent, coupled with a wealthy university benefactor, creates a piercing conclusion to the fourth novel.

Romance blossoms for Jackie and McGowan in the first novel and slowly develops throughout the eight books. All of the ancillary characters and their interrelationships grow and we find ourselves looking forward to future installments of Jake and his cohorts in detection.

Detectives in this category cover a wide range of fields and disciplines. The rigors of scholarly training give these academic protagonists an edge on the investigative process relative to crime; they often prove to be admirable adjuncts to officers of law enforcement. Thesis, antithesis, synthesis—Hegelian dialectics—form the foundation of the professorial mode of research. The result is a number of series featuring characters whose curiosity and compulsion to tie up loose ends provide readers with good, well-plotted mysteries as well as subplots that are elucidating far beyond whodunit.

SOME OTHER ACADEMIC SLEUTHS

Lauren Adler & Michael Hunt	Barbara Bettencourt
Beth Austin	Lisa Davis
Andrew Basnett	Sarah Deane
Christine Bennett	Brian Donodio

John Fenchurcht
Glad Gold
Tom Hammer
Roz Howard
Laura Ireland
Joanne Kilbourn

Hannah Land
Loretta Lawson
Amanda Pepper
Molly Rafferty
Lee Squires
Valerie Stevens

BEHIND THE BADGE:
Major Metropolitan Police

An organized and paid police force is a rather recent innovation in the Western world. Before the middle of the nineteenth century, the laws of the land were enforced selectively at the discretion of the governing and judicial bodies of a local/regional jurisdiction. The industrial revolution brought an influx of people from the agrarian districts into the cities; concurrently, the crime rate in those metropolitan areas rose dramatically. Enforcement of law and the maintenance of order grew to be a grave problem, and a hired force dedicated solely to those ends became a necessity.

Webster's tells us that the term "police" comes from the Greek and Latin words referring to citizens engaged in government or administration. The first definition of the word "police" reads, "the internal organization or regulation of a political unit through exercise of governmental powers especially with respect to general comfort, health, morals, safety, or prosperity." The concept of a paid police force is no longer a strange one and the job description remains the same as first mandated.

Although the job description hasn't changed, the scope of crime has broadened over time and those dedicated to keeping the peace and maintaining the well-being of their citizens find their tasks have grown heavy. The representatives of the forces of law and order that follow meet these challenges ably and with dedication. Honest citizens should frequently and reverently wish that the force be with them.

In the city, there are many occasions for violence and certainly a large population from which to draw victims and suspects. Unfortunately, in these days of slashed budgets, the officers charged with public safety are severely handicapped. More crime happens, in part, because there are fewer officials to prevent it and detection of a crime already committed is hampered due to these same constraints. And yet, despite these staggering odds, there are still those willing to take on this Sisyphean task.

Anna Katharine Green celebrated one of these early defenders in

47

her novels featuring New York City police detective Ebenezer Gryce. When the first book in the series, *The Leavenworth Case*, was published, it sold well enough to become known as the first American bestseller, but sadly, of the thirteen books in the series (1878–1917), only the first is still in print. Gryce is a competent detective, yet, like today's police, he operated under severe constraints having less to do with any fiscal crises the city may have been suffering than with social class and his chosen profession. The police were not welcomed at many front doors at the turn of the century. All of the novels by Green—known as the Mother of Detective Fiction—capture the essence of the times and of the man, his strengths and weaknesses.

Today's investigative techniques are highly sophisticated compared to what was available in the early 1900s, but the basics of detection remain the same. Ebenezer Gryce possesses these basics and uses them judiciously in his pursuit of wrongdoers. Clues are gathered and evidence is carefully treated in hopes it will clinch a conviction. One way or another, in questioning those involved in the crime, Gryce brings his ability to read character into play. He sets surface considerations aside to reach the heart of the matter and understands the limits and excesses of emotion. This is a believable character and a fine exemplar for those who follow.

While police involvement is nearly always a feature of crime and mystery fiction, women authors—for the most part—chose detectives other than officers of the law until Elizabeth Linington, writing as Dell Shannon, created Lt. Luis Mendoza, homicide detective of the Los Angeles Police Department. For twenty-seven years (1960–1987) the urbane Latino met and enjoyed the challenges of police work. The stories themselves are procedural and hard-edged in nature. Shannon's depiction of recurring characters in this thirty-eight-book series (one of four series she created) rings true even though almost everyone is rather unconventional, even by the standards of the '60s. These are enjoyable books, fairly accurate in their constabulary detail and colorful in their characterizations.

At the end of the '60s, the writing team of Maj Sjowall and Per Wahloo introduced Chief Insp. Martin Beck of the Stockholm Homicide Squad. Sjowall and Wahloo chose their protagonist and his milieu carefully and used them, in a ten-book series (1967–1976), to exemplify the changes in their country's political system and its new nationalized police force.

The late '60s and '70s opened doors for women in professions traditionally dominated by men. This expanded the potential field for women writers in an exciting way. No longer were they limited to developing their female protagonists as amateur detectives; now they could place them actively on the force and in positions of command. In 1968, Dorothy Uhnak began a series which unfortunately, consists of only three books (1968–1970). It features Christie Opara as a detective for the New York County District Attorney's Special Investigations Squad and addresses, from a woman's perspective, the maintenance of order in an unruly world. Uhnak does a credible job of balancing her character's feminine instincts against her position as a player in a game with rules written by men.

In twenty-two years (1972–1994), author Lillian O'Donnell created a sixteen-book series featuring Norah Mulcahaney of the New York City Police Department. In *The Phone Calls*, the first book, Norah is one year out of the Police Academy and O'Donnell then plausibly traces Norah's career on the force, maintaining throughout the series a fine balance between her personal and professional lives. Unlike female police officers in other series, Norah has a large and complex family who make frequent appearances in each story. Her Irish father is a cop, as is her Italian husband, and their interest in her career can, at times, be less supportive than interfering. In spite—or perhaps because—of this loving interference, Norah knows how to use her intellect, insight, and empathy to diffuse potentially volatile situations with colleagues, victims, and suspects alike. This series possesses both coloration and depth. The crimes Mulcahaney investigates are contemporary and often involve those perpetrated against women and children. O'Donnell's contribution to the genre is of major proportions.

Englishwoman Magdalen Nabb has been a resident of Florence, Italy, for many years and has crafted an unusual eleven-book series (1981–1996) featuring Marshal Guarnaccia of the Italian Carabinieri, a military-like organization that is only one of a vast (to Western readers) complexity of law-enforcement and judicial bodies. Guarnaccia, despite the confusion attendant on the multiplicity of governance and enforcement, serves as Everyman in his approach to human folly and circumstance and demonstrates that law enforcement is the same around the world.

In the annals of crime and mystery fiction, there is a tradition of the elegant gentleman police detective. In 1929, Elizabeth MacKintosh, under the pseudonym Josephine Tey, introduced Alan Grant, a Scotland Yard detective (1929–1952). Although Grant is not an aristocrat, he is a well-educated gentleman with an independent income. The aristocracy is represented by Roderick Alleyn of Scotland Yard, author Ngaio Marsh's creation, who made his first appearance in 1934. Featured in thirty-three books (1934–1989), Alleyn is a paragon of British reserve and rectitude. The upper classes feel almost comfortable under his professional scrutiny; his humanity and compassion, however, provide him with access to the sensibilities of those from the lower classes as well.

The Force has been with us since the beginning of the genre and will continue playing a major role in detective fiction.

JANNA BRILL & MAHLON "MAMA" MAXWELL
1979–1990   3 books
(Karen) Lee Killough

The three books in this crossover series were written over a span of eleven years. All take place in Topeka, Kansas, in what is most probably the twenty-first century. Janna and Mama are police officers attached to the Crimes Against Persons Division of the Shawnee County Police Department and are partnered in the first book, *The Doppelganger Gambit*, after Janna's partner of five years is disabled in the course of a chase. Janna is the more linear thinker and Mama is the intuitive one; Mama is much more flamboyant than the rather staid Janna. In spite of their obvious dissimilarities, they become an effective team in the first book and their union continues into the third.

Aside from the time shift and all its implied differences, these novels are all fairly straightforward police procedurals. In the first book, the killer is known to the reader at the outset. The police soon discover the murderer's identity, and most of the book is concerned with gathering the evidence necessary to convict him. In *Dragon's Teeth*, a pair of ordinary robberies—with a murder and several futuristic twists—have Janna and Mama doing typical investigative legwork. *Spider Play*, second in the series, is the only one that actually involves Janna and Mama in offworld activities. After the theft of a hearse and the body it contains, the pair are sent to the Lanour Space Platform to follow through on the investigation. There they discover just how far people will go to keep bits of technology secret.

The future as written by Lee Killough is reminiscent of the '70s and that time's expectations for the next century. The most important possession for nearly everyone is the Scib Card; it serves as identification, credit card, medical information, and possibly much more. One is registered for the Scib Card at birth, and all of one's actions are recorded and documented throughout one's entire life. There are those who choose—quite legally—to live outside this system; they are collectively known as Slighs and tend to operate on the fringes of the more regimented society.

Though there are major differences between the present and the future in transportation, dress, legal recreational drugs, and sexual standards, all of which are very relaxed, other moral and ethical conventions mirror standards of today. In the first story, shady business practices jeopardize the health, safety, and welfare of a group of colonists on their way to a planet seventy-three light years away. In the third, hostile company takeovers lead to the death of a billionaire businessman. Murder is still the ultimate crime, and the police work necessary to find and convict the perpetrator is persistent. Jargon of the twenty-first century is the device that reminds readers that in spite of all that is familiar and similar, they are, after all, reading about the future.

Lee Killough is best known for her science fiction writing, so it comes as no surprise that she has chosen to set what can be described as a traditional mystery in the future. Clearly she is at home in tomorrowland and creates a reasonably believable place for mystery readers who may be less so.

DET. SIGRID HARALD
1981–1995   8 books
Margaret Maron

When she is introduced in *One Coffee With*, Sigrid Harald is presented as well qualified, able, and well suited to her position as a lieutenant in the Detective Bureau of the New York Police Department. As the story progresses and the private side of this character is revealed, it rapidly becomes apparent to readers that the professional aspect of this woman is far more developed than the personal. Tall, slim, and dark haired, Harald is a cool individual—an admirable attribute for a police officer. Personally, however, she is seen as cold, unfeeling, and insensitive; she is reluctant to let anyone get close. The character evolves along with the series, however, and in all of the books Sigrid is the focus of the story both as a pursuant of the details of a particular case and as an increasingly active participant in personal relationships.

Anne Lattimore Harald, Sigrid's mother, is a successful photojournalist. Petite, dark haired, and a true Southern belle, Anne often wonders just where her daughter came from. Grandmother Lattimore, Anne's sisters, and their daughters all wonder the same thing when Anne and Sigrid visit them in their Southern stronghold. Sigrid Harald feels herself to be a social misfit. Initially, she mistrusts her own feminine nature and, in part because of the profession she has chosen, dismisses it in favor of her intellectual side; she has no doubts about her intelligence and capability.

The principal players in the series are all introduced in the first book even if they do not make a personal appearance there. Leif

Harald, Sigrid's late father, was a police officer, killed in the line of duty when she was a toddler. Sigrid's superior officer, Captain McKinnon, was her father's partner (a fact she doesn't learn until the fourth book, *The Right Jack*). Roman Tramegra, an unusual fellow, gradually insinuates himself into Sigrid's life through an odd chain of events. In *Death in Blue Folders* the two become official roommates in a new home. Oscar Nauman, a noted artist and the chairman of the arts department at Vanderlyn College, is fascinated by this ice maiden and sees qualities Sigrid herself has yet to discover. Their attraction deepens throughout the series until the surprise in the seventh book.

Sigrid's partner, Det. Charles Tildon, is known by his colleagues as "Tillie the toiler." Tillie's specialty is his penchant for detail; no chain of evidence in any of his cases has ever been compromised thanks to his fanatical record keeping. The crimes Sigrid and Tillie investigate are fairly complex in nature, and these two officers are excellent in finding all of the threads that make up the weave, following them, discarding the irrelevant ones, and tracking the central line to its conclusion.

Sigrid's intellectual qualities have made it possible for her to rise within the ranks of a traditionally male profession. The security her position offers her may be giving her the opportunity to invent her own personhood. As Sigrid learns to feel comfortable with aspects of her own femininity, she can incorporate those aspects into her persona and begin moving about the world with a new completeness.

Margaret Maron, using her knowledge of Southern manners and mannerisms, provides readers with an interesting development process for her detective. In an author's note at the beginning of *Fugitive Colors*, Maron explains that although fourteen years have passed for writer and readers, the action of all the novels combined actually spans only one tumultuous year. Each book is written in the "now," which may be a bit confusing as many changes have taken place—in the world, in attitudes, and in the author's perspective. Oddly enough, the series works the way it is presented, though we suggest that it is best enjoyed when read from the beginning.

Maron's newest character, Judge Deborah Knott, appears in her own series and is discussed in the chapter "Legal Eagles: Lawyers."

DET. KATE DELAFIELD
1984–1997   6 books
Katherine V(irginia) Forrest

Under most circumstances, the sexual preference of a given character is not one of the first things we choose to mention in discussing the books in which they appear. However, this series was one of the first to address the issue of homosexuality at its outset, and one of the first in which the primary character's personal preference is vital to her professional responses. All of the books in this excellent series deal with some aspect of gay life and do so in a well-balanced fashion. The life-style is presented as simply a way of being, yet author Katherine V. Forrest adds appropriate measures of righteous political anger at the inequities directed toward those with a same-sex preference.

In *Amateur City*, first novel in this series, the work of Det. Kate Delafield of the Los Angeles Police Department (LAPD) is introduced as solid, meticulous, and well documented. Throughout the ensuing five books, nothing is offered to counter this introduction. Forrest's portrayal of a female police detective rings as one of the truest we've read. Like Det. Chief Insp. (DCI) Jane Tennison of *Prime Suspect*, Delafield must adhere strictly to the letter of the law and does so in a gently admirable style. Delafield is the epitome of the honest, straightforward police officer.

The subjects of these novels are powerful and diverse. *Amateur City* deals with big business, and *Murder at the Nightwood Bar* treats a killing arising from child molestation. In *The Beverly Malibu*, individuals and their relationship to the House Un-American Activities Committee are at the center of the murder of a former Hollywood film director. *Murder by Tradition* addresses gay bashing. Forrest does not pull her punches. Her character has the full force of the law behind her in investigating crimes and, true to the nature of her creation, Forrest places the full force of Kate's integrity behind the treatment of each of these engrossing subjects.

DET. DEB RALSTON
1984–1996   12 books
Lee Martin ([Martha] Anne [Guice] Wingate)

Debra Ralston is an investigator on the Major Case Squad in the city of Fort Worth, Texas. It is early in the morning on New Year's Day when *Too Sane a Murder* opens, and Deb has been called to the scene of a particularly grisly shotgun murder of four people. The alleged perpetrator, a twenty-six-year-old man, is in his house under the watchful eye of a uniformed officer. Olead Baker, the young man in question, is known to have a long history of mental illness. Deb's superior, Captain Millner, knows Olead and his history—has had official dealings with him, in fact. Two of the murder victims are children, half-siblings of Olead, and one child, only fifteen months old, is missing.

Deb is quick to say that she's been a mother longer than she's been a cop, so it comes as no surprise that her first instinct is to protect the children, any children. She will also be the first to admit that much of her detection is based on instinct and that she is almost always correct. She stands about five-foot-two and weighs one hundred twenty pounds. People are always telling her she doesn't look like a cop and she has ceased to be bothered by that fact, which may, in the long run, actually work in her favor. Deb's instinct proves true for the first book.

Readers are slowly introduced to Det. Ralston's family. Harry, her husband, is a helicopter test pilot for Bell Laboratories; they have three children—all adopted and all of mixed parentage. In the first book, Vicky, the eldest, is married and about to become a mother; Becky, the middle child, falls in love with Olead; and Hal, youngest in the family, is a typical fifteen-year-old.

Throughout the series, readers discover that Deb's domestic/maternal nature is at the root of her success as a police officer. These same qualities have made it possible for her to be more easily accepted by her male colleagues. She has no agenda, is not threatening, and simply wants to do the best job she possibly can. In *A Conspiracy of Strangers*, Deb's particular knowledge of the difficulties in adopting give her an edge in investigating the murders of women who have recently delivered babies. The discovery of her own pregnancy is both a surprise and a delight. She hasn't quite worked up the courage to notify Captain Millner of her condition in *Death Warmed Over* and presses through another difficult case involving a kidnapped child. At the end of *Hal's Own Murder Case*, she gives birth to Cameron after exonerating Hal and rescuing his girlfriend, Lorie (Lori in some books).

The Day That Dusty Died is a watershed book for both the character and her author, for it centers on what must be one of the most difficult aspects of police work—the sexual brutalization of children. Deb has been temporarily moved to the Sex Crimes Unit and does not want to be there. Peripherally, the story addresses some of the outmoded thinking about rape and its victims and the long-held notion of a man having the right to the services of any woman under his protection. In this book, readers meet Deb's sister and learn the reasons for the tenuous relationship between the sisters and their mother along with other insidious behaviors related to the cases in which Deb is involved.

In an Author's Note at the end of the book, Martha Wingate, who writes the series as Lee Martin, explains the personal significance of this story. Even though all of the books are based on Wingate's practical knowledge gained as a mother and former police officer, the revelatory nature of this tale is unusual. Deb Ralston is not Superwoman; she is well grounded, has clear-cut priorities, and is flawed, as most of us are. Martin presents a competent woman doing the best she can in all of her areas of responsibility. Over time, Deb has developed into just the character her author needed as the vehicle for personal exploration.

DET. SGT. MARIAN LARCH
1985–1997   7 books
Barbara Paul

Homicide Det. Sgt. Marian Larch of the New York Police Department (NYPD) is introduced in *The Renewable Virgin* when she is assigned to investigate the death, by cyanide poisoning, of a television writer. Rudy Benedict had no enemies and his death seems to serve no purpose, making it appear that he may have been the wrong victim. One of the potential suspects, Kelly Ingram, is the glamorous co-star of the *Lefever* television series, who, after being cleared of suspicion, becomes Marian's friend and ally in the search for Rudy's murderer. After two more deaths, Marian decides that Rudy really was the intended victim and that all of the killings are linked. Kelly accidentally discovers the identity of one of the killers and resourcefully saves herself before Marian and her partner arrive on the scene.

Good King Sauerkraut and *He Huffed and He Puffed* are odd additions to the series as each is told from the perspective of either the killer or the victim and sometimes from that of all of those involved. In each of these books, Marian, her partner, Ivan Malecki, and other officers enter in the last third of the story and serve as the official persons tying up the loose ends. Each story is a wonderful study of the many sides and aspects of human nature. All the individuals under scrutiny are provocative, inciting an unusual series of responses in the reader. Because of the unconventional presentation of the crimes, the motivations behind them, and the characters involved in the commission and detection of wrongful death, these two books almost don't belong in the series. Nonetheless, late on the scene as she is, Marian Larch *is* instrumental in winding up both cases and is credited with the collars.

In *You Have the Right to Remain Silent*, Marian has been transferred (almost demoted) to the Ninth Precinct. Foley, her new partner, is inept, lazy, and dangerous to anyone with whom he is paired. Precinct Captain DiFalco frequently steps into his officers' cases and overrides their authority solely for his own glory. It's a bad situation, yet one Marian must endure for the sake of her career.

Kelly Ingram reenters this story and actually assists Marian and FBI agent Curt Holland in capturing the killer of four men. At the end, both Marian and Holland are considering giving up their respective careers.

The Apostrophe Thief opens the day after the denouement of *You Have the Right....* Kelly asks for Marian's assistance in discovering the identity of a thief whose actions are causing confusion and consternation on the set of the successful Broadway play in which she is starring. Wanting a break from the Ninth Precinct and all its attendant miseries, Marian takes some time away and offers her services to Captain Murtaugh of the Midtown South Precinct. The investigation takes Marian into the heart of the theater world and beyond as she traces the channels of memorabilia trading and collecting. A killing complicates matters and the thefts take on greater and more sinister significance. At the end, after still another successful collar, Captain Murtaugh asks Marian to stay on with Midtown South. After seeing Captain DiFalco hoist with his own petard, she happily agrees to do so and continues her police career.

Barbara Paul provides her readers with fair puzzles and believable, if not sympathetic, characters. Although Marian Larch appears in all six books in the series, she is not, with the exception of *The Apostrophe Thief*, the driving force behind any of them. We meet some of her friends and colleagues—even a lover or two—and still know very little about the woman behind the badge. The tales are told with quiet style and wit. Paul's other series features the famous opera tenor, Enrico Caruso, and further capitalizes on her love of theatre.

DET. J. P. BEAUMONT
1985–1995   13 books
J(udith) A(nn) Jance

J. P. Beaumont is a veteran homicide cop in Seattle as the series opens, yet the stories in this thirteen-book series are far from simple police procedurals. Beau has both a professional and a personal history, and each case provides readers with a window into some part of the life of this complex and compelling character. For example, in the first book Beau is in his mid-forties and has been divorced from his wife, Karen, for five years. She and their children, Scott and Kelly, now live in Cucamonga, California, with Karen's second husband. J. P. Beaumont is a dedicated cop. His dedication, however, may have led to the breakup of his marriage and the alienation he feels from his children. Karen, Kelly, and Scott make several appearances throughout the series and none of these ancillary characters are there for diversion or filler. Each makes a contribution, not only to that particular plot but to the ongoing development of J. P. Beaumont himself.

Professionally, Beaumont does not always play by the book. His instincts are—for the most part—sound and he is inclined to follow them. Beau is the underdog's champion; he almost always believes that the prime suspect in any murder case in which he is involved is innocent, and frequently he takes heroic measures to prove his point. Even in cases that happen off his patch, Beau's involvement generally runs counter to the grain of the investigation. His honor and integrity are always on the line and, at the same time, always provide his fallback position.

Ron Peters is Beau's partner in the first book. The two men are new to one another, and while Beau feels that Peters is probably the best of the bunch, their differences are more apparent than their similarities and they have not settled into an easy working union. Beau's former partner enters the first story and the easy camaraderie between those two is a sharp contrast to the association between Beau and Peters. Peters does prove his mettle, and even though he is injured early on in the series, their relationship continues to grow. Beau relies on Peters, as a friend and a colleague, and depends upon his professional knowledge.

Maxwell Cole, columnist for the *Seattle Post-Intelligencer*, is Beau's antagonist. Cole's sense of rivalry with Beau began in the fraternity they both belonged to in college when Max dated Karen first. Beau not only stole her away from him but married her. Ever since then, Max has dogged Beau's steps and challenged his decisions and actions. Early on in both of their careers, Cole gifted Beau with the epithet "killer cop." Maxwell Cole would say that he is simply doing his job—as Beaumont is doing his. Readers detect a strong note of vengeance in his style of reportage.

J. A. Jance explores a wide range of topics through the perceptions and actions of her protagonist. In the series opener, *Until Proven Guilty*, a murdered child leads to the investigation of a religious cult. Politics and greed are at the center of *Injustice for All* and racial tensions are addressed in *Trial by Fury*. In *Dismissed with Prejudice*, Beau's attorney Ralph Ames tells him that arrangements will be made for Beau's entry into an alcohol-recovery program. The action in *Minor in Possession* takes place at Ironwood Ranch in Arizona, where Beau and his family have gone to address the issue of addiction and its far-reaching effects. The community of Ashland, Oregon, and its attendant world of Shakespearean theatre feature in *Failure to Appear*. Because events in the first book color all of the rest of the novels and we don't want to give away any of the plot, we recommend the series be read from the first title onward.

Seattle and its environs are at the center of this thirteen-book series, and author Jance presents it as a living place. Because the locations are so credibly drawn they possess a vitality that is passed along to the characters. Jance's other character, Sheriff Joanna Brady, appears in the chapter "Behind the Badge: Provincial Police."

SGT. PETER DECKER & RINA LAZARUS DECKER
1986–1996 9 books
Faye Kellerman

With the characters she has chosen as protagonists, Faye Kellerman has created a new sort of police procedural novel. Peter Decker is thirty-eight, divorced, the father of a teenaged daughter, and a sergeant in the Los Angeles Police Department attached to the juvenile and sex-crimes division. Rina Lazarus is an Orthodox Jew, mother of two young boys, and the widow of a Talmudic scholar. The two meet in *Ritual Bath* when a woman is brutally beaten and raped as she is returning to her home from the *mikvah*, the yeshiva's bathhouse for ritual cleansing. Rina, as a witness, is the only member of the community willing to deal with Decker and help him navigate the maze of Jewish religious law that places strict and severe constraints on his official investigation.

While all the murders and their attendant mysteries in each book are well crafted and puzzling, it is the progressive relationship between Peter and Rina that sets the pace and provides the cohesion for the series. Attracted to one another in the first book, Peter and Rina face the formidable barriers between a man raised as the adopted son of Southern Baptists and a religious Orthodox Jewish woman twelve years his junior. These seem insurmountable. However, Rina's appeal for Peter is overwhelming and motivates him to investigate his own heritage as the birth son of Jewish parents. Peter undertakes conversion under the wise and kindly tutelage of Rabbi Schulman and makes important discoveries about himself and his desire to learn and to make sense of the world in which he operates.

Peter and Rina's courtship is—to say the least—fraught with complexities. Rina has been inculcated with the full panoply of Jewish religious tradition. She covers her hair, dresses modestly, wears no makeup, and, until her meeting with Peter, is never alone with a man not of her family. Peter, on the other hand, treads the mean streets and confronts human brutality on a daily basis. Despite all the contradictions between Peter's and Rina's backgrounds, their attraction and their personal integrity are strong enough to suspend, if not surmount, those contradictions long enough for the pair to enter the formal steps of courtship.

The crimes in all nine books are compelling ones, at a level of brutality consistent with the job Decker does. His personal life and chosen significant other offer the antithesis to his profession. Rina has led a sheltered life, protected from most harsh realities by her religious seclusion. Her connection with Peter places her in the direct path of those things she has been raised to avoid. Rina's love for Peter and her growing appreciation for human behavior have broadened her base of compassion and understanding of the human condition. On the other side, Peter has been given a new sense of direction for his career.

Child abuse, kiddie porn, kidnapping, prostitution—both voluntary and coerced—rape, battery, sexual and racial prejudice, and the ultimate crime of murder are all treated in these stories. The solutions are based and grounded upon the two primary characters' divergent points of view. Each learns from the other and the sum is definitely greater than the parts.

Faye Kellerman, her husband, Jonathan—also a novelist—and their four children are practicing Orthodox Jews. Using a traditional storytelling form, she has enhanced and elaborated on the simple fact that the Talmud is concerned with the laws governing human behavior and that religious observance is a form of honoring them. Religion can be pertinent; and together Peter Decker and Rina Lazarus Decker personify the tenuous junction of the spiritual and the secular.

DET. INSP. THOMAS LYNLEY
1988–1997   9 books
(Susan) Elizabeth George

Elizabeth George, an American, is the most recent writer to create an aristocratic policeman operating out of Scotland Yard, Det. Insp. Thomas Lynley, eighth earl of Asherton. The combination of the Yard, murder, and the lives of members of a select social group is almost a guaranteed win for some readers.

The prime players in all of the novels are introduced in *A Great Deliverance*, the first in this series. Called away from the wedding of his closest friends, Simon Allcourt-St. James and Deborah Cotter, Lynley and his sergeant, Barbara Havers, travel to Keldale Valley to pick up the threads of an investigation already some days old. Quite by accident, at dinner one evening, Lynley and Havers encounter the newlyweds. In spite of the delicacy of the situation, St. James, a forensic scientist, is pressed into service. Later, in London, another of Lynley's close friends, Lady Helen Clyde, becomes involved and she too travels to the Keldale Valley to join in at the denouement.

Coincidence is rife in all of these stories and centers on the romance, passion, and honor connecting the primary characters. In *Payment in Blood*, Lady Helen is a guest at a hotel in Scotland where an acquaintance of hers is stabbed to death. In *Well-Schooled in Murder*, while on a photo shoot Deborah St. James stumbles upon the dead body of that story's victim. *A Suitable Vengeance*, the fourth in the series, actually predates the chronological order of the other books. Deborah has just returned to England from school in the United States. She, her father, Joseph Cotter (Simon Allcourt-St. James's valet), Lynley, Lady Helen, and St. James go to the seat of the Asherton estate in Cornwall to officially announce Thomas and Deborah's engagement to Lynley's family. Simon's sister, Sydney, and Peter Lynley, Thomas's younger brother, join the party hosted by Lady Asherton, and all are involved—one way or another—in the cross-connected webs of action that result in two murders and their solutions.

Thomas Lynley is classically handsome and always impeccably turned out. When he arrives at the scene of a crime in his Bentley, "the Yard has arrived" is not anyone's uppermost thought. In spite of his breeding, bearing, and exquisite manners, however, he is portrayed as an insightful and compassionate police officer. While Lynley and murder are central to each of these novels, neither the person, nor the event, nor the relationship of the cop to the crime carries the story along. In fact, more than is usual in a mystery novel the ultimate misdeed is a device for moving the main characters from one scene to another at a directed pace. Also, because readers mainly come to know Lynley through the eyes and thoughts of the other players, he himself is not the driving force of the series. He does tend toward sometimes painful introspection, yet all of the main characters seem to agonize as well. While Lynley's agonies are perhaps more pronounced because he is the pivot point, we cannot say we know him well from any point of view—as a police officer, an earl, or a man.

The qualities of the interconnections and romantic complications of the five principal characters make this an interesting series. Detection is based less on solid police grind work than experience and intuition, and the service of justice seems less important than getting the right people connected to the right partners. Each of the nine books runs to more than 300 pages and the last two hover around 500. Many mystery fans will throw up their hands at all the extraneous entanglements that fill the pages between the commission and the solution of the crime at hand. Others will be pleased that an author is finally exploring her detective's heart and mind with the close scrutiny usually reserved for the criminal investigation itself. George is a gifted storyteller who has successfully made the cross-over from the genre of romance to that of mystery.

CHIEF INSP. MICHAEL OHAYON
1988–1991   3 books
Batya Gur (translated from the Hebrew by Dalya Bilu)

For all we know, there may be a great Hebraic tradition of crime and mystery fiction—and, if one counts the Old Testament, that is surely the case. Few works of Israeli contemporary fiction, however, ever get translated into the English language and reach our faraway shores. Happily, the work of Israeli Batya Gur has made the translation and the journey. With three books in the series available to American and British audiences, her character Chief Insp. Michael Ohayon, deputy head of the Investigations Division of the Jerusalem Subdistrict, brings to light the particular difficulties of crime investigation in this newest Middle Eastern state.

Israel is not only a new state but one whose founders were born elsewhere. Ohayon himself was born in Morocco, arriving in Israel when he was three years old and the nation itself was young. An early, untimely pregnancy forced Michael into a brief, loveless marriage and brought to an end his promising academic career in medieval history. After his mandatory army service, he reluctantly entered the police force in order to support his wife and son.

The cases Ohayon investigates are set in small, tightly knit communities. Each story is complex and complicated by a full cast of multinational, multidimensional characters. *The Saturday Morning Murder* involves Jerusalem's psychiatric community, *Literary Murder* takes place within the academic domain of the Hebrew University, and *Murder on the Kibbutz* involves members of a well-established fifty-year-old commune. Ethics, professional pride, socialist unity, loyalty, and secrecy are at issue in each novel, and Ohayon finds delicacy essential in eliciting information from a victim's colleagues and those suspected of the crime. With a historian's dedication to assembling an entire picture, the inspector probes to reveal truths about the people involved in the case and, in the process, unveils the entire scenario for readers.

Ohayon prefers working independently and gives his subordinates autonomy in their roles in an investigation. He and his team have operated together for many years, and this method works well until his promotion in the third book; then his new superior officer tells him that things are not done that way in his division. Long divorced, Michael is a loner in his personal life as well. In the first book, his mistress is married to another man, and in the second book she returns to her husband. The only person to whom Michael feels close is his son, Yuval. Even here, he hesitates to make a declaration to the boy, fearing disaffection or rejection. Parts of Michael's nature are revealed in each story and some of these revelations serve to explain his aloof quality.

Batya Gur is a professor of literature in Jerusalem. Her novels featuring the rather enigmatic Michael Ohayon have become bestsellers in her native country. Dalya Bilu's translations read well and provide English-speaking readers with the delights of mystery in a truly new land.

DET. SKIP LANGDON
1990–1997   7 books
Julie Smith

New Orleans is the setting for this series. The hot, steamy climate of a city renowned for its decaying beauty and eccentricity provides a wonderful backdrop for what might be a conventional police procedural in any other location. Magic and secrecy thrive unquestioned here, and these elements are carefully woven throughout the six books featuring police officer Skip Langdon.

Skip, born Margaret, is a native daughter. Her father, Don, a local notable, is known as "the society doc." He stopped speaking to Skip when she entered the police academy. Her mother, Elizabeth, is a professional volunteer who speaks to her daughter only in disapproving tones. Her brother, Conrad, is following in their parents' social-climbing footsteps. A Junoesque six-foot-tall, Skip is not the stereotypical Southern belle, despite all the proper upbringing, attendance in the right schools, and exposure to the requisite steps leading to social acceptance.

While living in San Francisco, Skip intervened in a mugging and successfully collared the miscreant. Her personal sense of justice was awakened and she realized that this, coupled with her size and strength, could make her an ideal candidate for law enforcement. There are hints of revenge in Skip's decision to return to New Orleans to pursue her career. Her choice of profession is a fairly positive way in which to cash in on her self-described alienation from her family.

Once back in her home town, Skip begins to create a new family of choice. She rents an apartment in a house in the French Quarter belonging to Jimmy Dee Scoggin, a gay lawyer who not only provides her with a place to live, but also serves as her fashion consultant. Through a mutual friend, Cookie Lamoreaux, she meets Steve Steinman, a filmmaker from Los Angeles. Steve thinks Skip is absolutely gorgeous—a totally new concept for Skip—and they begin a long-distance relationship that lasts through the third book. In the second story, Skip meets Cindy Lou Wootten, a psychologist called in to assist in the investigation of a possible serial killer. Cindy Lou is smart, slim, elegant, and black and has terrible taste in men; she and Skip become fast friends. Lt. Joseph Tarantino is responsible for Skip's transfer to homicide. Sgt. Sylvia Capello, Skip's immediate superior, becomes a close friend and staunch supporter of Skip's stand against misogyny on the force as represented by Frank O'Roarke.

Because New Orleans resembles a village much more than a city, to whom one is related is of paramount importance and where one lives defines the social stratum one occupies. Within this close-knit community, other definite subgroups exist and play major roles in each of the six novels. *New Orleans Mourning* features Mardi Gras krewes and the importance of social position. *The Axeman's Jazz* deals with twelve-step programs and the anonymity they provide. *New Orleans Beat* introduces the relatively new concept of virtual reality through computer networks and women's union through witchcraft. A constant thread uniting these diverse groups is, of course, the community of law enforcement.

This is the third series Julie Smith has devised. The first features San Francisco lawyer Rebecca Schwartz and the second Paul MacDonald, an ex-reporter for the *San Francisco Chronicle* turned mystery writer. Smith draws heavily on her own experience as a reporter in New Orleans and San Francisco for the character and color for which her series are noted. *New Orleans Mourning* won the 1991 Edgar Allan Poe Award given by Mystery Writers of America for Best Novel, making her the first American woman to win the award in that category since 1956.

DET. CHIEF INSP. JANE TENNISON
1991–1994   3 books
Lynda La Plante

Det. Chief Insp. (DCI) Jane Tennison is an excellent officer. Several years at different levels within the London Metropolitan force have given her the training and experience she needs to become the leader of any murder investigation. Yet, eighteen months after her assignment to the special Area Major Incident Team (AMIT) she has still not been assigned a murder case. Her superior, Supt. Mike

Kernan, does not think women belong on the force. He runs a tight ship and has a strong and loyal team of men working for him. Kernan intends to subtly thwart Tennison until she leaves his command of her own accord, but the death of DCI John Shefford at a crucial juncture in a murder case, coupled with the unavailability of anyone else qualified to lead the inquiry, forces him to put Tennison in charge.

Prime Suspect, the first in the series, details not only an intense murder investigation with emphasis on police procedure but also the difficulties a woman of high rank experiences in a predominantly male profession. Despite her impressive record, Tennison finds the ranks firmly closed and bolted against her. Supt. Kernan doesn't want her in the first place; Det. Sgt. Bill Otley, the late Shefford's close friend, resents her intrusion into both the case and his own grief. The locker-room atmosphere among the men of the major-case squad is hostile to Tennison's mere presence and her leadership is anathema to them. Determination and perseverance are two of Tennison's strongest attributes, however. As the case develops, thick skin and healthy self-image serve as her defensive weapons in skirmishes with opponents on both sides of the law.

Although the stories revolve around police work and are filled with tension and action, the three books (to date) in this well-crafted set focus on Jane Tennison as an individual. Author Lynda La Plante gives readers a character who is aggressive, assertive, and ambitious and, at the same time, confounded by desires for some sort of traditional life. In the first book, Jane lives with Peter Rawlins, a divorced father in the building trade. In an interesting juxtaposition, Tennison and Rawlins each play—rather poorly, as it turns out—their traditionally opposite role in the relationship. La Plante deftly and informatively handles the scenes in which this is made apparent. In subsequent books, Jane finds herself in other sorts of relationships, from the casual encounter to the reconnection with one whom she truly loves. Her profession intrudes in all of these unions and continues to define her both professionally and personally.

The original incarnation of each of these novels was an English television series featuring Helen Mirren as DCI Tennison. Readers who have seen the productions (shown on the Public Broadcasting System [PBS] in the United States) are struck by the fact that the books read as the shows look. We recommend these books as some of the most compelling police procedurals by a woman we have read. We also recommend these books as being a highly accurate representation of a dedicated professional woman and the challenges she faces. Beyond that, we recommend these books without qualification.

La Plante has written another series featuring four women that is found in the chapter "The Other Side of the Law."

OFFICER DELTA "STORM" STEVENS
1991–1996   5 books
Linda Kay Silva

River Valley is a fictional community in Southern California. Between the desert and the sprawl of Los Angeles, it covers a large area and requires a substantial number of law-enforcement officers. Delta Stevens is one of these officers. As the series opens, she holds her dying partner Miles in her arms. In a brief flicker of time, a van and a shotgun blast alter Delta's life as a beat cop forever.

Miles's death arises out of a clandestine investigation he has been making into a drug operation he believes originates within the police force. His only link to information connecting other officers to illicit activities was Megan Osbourne, a hooker. Delta almost makes contact with her at Miles's funeral, but not until a misty night some weeks later do Delta and Megan make their first real connection. Delta's fear has been that Miles has been using the services of this lady of the night. Over coffee and doughnuts, Megan tells Delta of her friendship with Miles since high school, of the information she has held, and of her assistance to him in gathering information and evidence against members of the force.

Delta's investigation in *Taken by Storm* moves her outside the conventions of officialdom. Together with Connie Rivera, the computer expert of the River Valley Police Department, Delta tracks the cops responsible for Miles's death and ends their involvement in drug traffic. As all of these events unfold, readers learn that Connie is not only Delta's best friend, she is also a lesbian, partnered with Gina, a psychologist. Delta too is a lesbian, and her recent breakup with her lover, coupled with Miles's death, has precipitated an emotional crisis. When she and Megan meet, their chemical reaction is intense and, at the end of the first book, the two women are investigating commitment to one another.

Delta Stevens becomes a "rogue" cop; not one, as the term might imply, who has gone wrong, but rather one who operates outside the strict boundaries of the law-enforcement code. In *Storm Shelter*, Delta has defied the limits of acceptable police procedure and at the end of the book has been put on suspension. As *Weathering the Storm* opens, she is put back to work as a field training officer. Captain Henry, the new commanding officer, wants to keep Delta on the active force in spite of her disregard for procedure; he assigns her a new partner in training, an eager beaver ready to rush into anything as long as it smells of action.

Author Silva has created a female supercop. Delta "Storm" Stevens is not bound by convention in any of the five books. She is heralded as a hero from the first and is given an enormous amount of latitude to do whatever it takes. Even so, Delta, aided and abetted by Connie, far exceeds her authority. Readers may wonder why Delta has chosen a career in law enforcement when her stand is clearly *not* for law and order. Delta's stance is for *raw justice*. "Make my day" is a phrase that could fall easily from Delta's lips; *The Good, the Bad and the Ugly* would welcome her as a member of the vengeance team. Characters portrayed by Clint Eastwood, Charles Bronson, and Gene Hackman have frequently gone beyond the strictures of the law to achieve their perception of order. For us, this is the first woman police officer portrayed as operating with any degree of acceptability outside the bounds. However, no matter how well portrayed this character may be, she still falls into the male mode of operation.

JOSS O'BANNION & EVAN GLYNDOWER
1991–1992   3 books
Diane Duane and Peter Morwood

High technology and the flavor of the old, lawless West are well blended in this series featuring Solar Patrol Rangers, known as SOPs, Joss O'Bannion and Evan Glyndower. As the first story, *Mindblast,* opens, each has lost his partner: O'Bannion's has transferred to Pluto and Glyndower's (Lon Salonikis) has been killed. The two join and travel to Freedom II, a colony in the far reaches of our solar system, to investigate Salonikis's murder. While neither of these characters could be described as a "dumb cop," Joss O'Bannion is clearly the more intellectual of the two. Standing more than two meters tall, Evan Glyndower radiates physical prowess; in his powered exosuit, his natural strength is enhanced—perhaps even overshadowed—by the suit's intimidation factor.

Freedom II is where most of the pharmaceutical companies have set up zero-gravity manufacturing sites. Coexisting with the legitimate drug trade is the illicit dealing that has recently expanded to include Hyper, a new and very dangerous designer drug. Joss's expertise in chemistry serves to give the pair a bit of clout with the scientists on Freedom II. Evan's suit enables them to penetrate into the perilous underworld of the warehouse complex located in the lowest levels of the underground site. Allied uneasily with the colony's roving gangs, O'Bannion and Glyndower locate the nexus of the smuggling operation and uncover multilevel embezzlement and corruption in the colony's administration and police force.

In *Kill Station*, the disappearance of several miners and their ships sends O'Bannion and Glyndower out to Willans in the asteroid belt, where law is, at best, an iffy proposition. Theoretically, the Solar Patrol maintains order according to the tenets of the United Planets. In reality, because of the vastness of the belt and its relatively low population, every man and woman is for him- or herself. To make the trip, Joss and Evan are given a brand-new ship. Joss has seen to her outfitting and she boasts quite a bit more than the usual Solar Patrol vessel does. The miners—a generally suspicious lot—don't take kindly to the law's interference, and Joss and Evan are challenged and thwarted at every turn. Mell Fontenay, a mechanic, and Cecile from Willans's communication center aid and abet the pair, and intergalactic disaster is averted.

Diane Duane and Peter Morwood have created a fantastically interesting milieu in which their characters operate. There is enough gadgetry to satisfy most ardent techies, and the tang of the Old West is sufficient to ground the more earthbound readers.

Detecting and action are almost evenly matched; the space cops are tough without being excessively macho and smart without geekiness.

DET. DAVID SILVER
1992–1995   4 books
Lynn S. Hightower

This series takes place in the near future—around the mid-'60s of the twenty-first century. Aliens have come to earth in the bizarre form of the Elaki. Over seven feet tall, these highly intelligent creatures have brains in their midsections, mouths under their mantles, and eyes on stalks. Their bodies are scaly and they glide on their bottom fringes. Though they are extremely flexible, sitting is difficult, so the vehicles they drive are modified to accommodate them and are as uncomfortable for humans as human vehicles are for Elaki.

Little is said about their arrival on the earth. In *Alien Blues*, the first book in the series, the Elaki are well established and involved in all aspects of life as it is known. Their expertise is in the social sciences, and they have provided cures for many of the plagues of humankind. The Elaki presence is akin to the British colonials in the far-flung outposts of an earlier time. Elaki are arrogant, superior, slightly racist, and almost always right.

David Silver is a homicide detective for the Saigo City police force; his partner is Mel Burnett. In the first book, they are joined by Elaki adviser String, a member of the elite Elaki law-enforcement organization, Izicho. A serial killer has been operating in Saigo City, and David and his team are charged with apprehending the murderer. Their investigation leads to illegal drug testing and trafficking and involves David's wife, Rose, an animal-rights activist, and also Mel's sister.

The series is a police procedural and, more than that, a study in sociology. There are enough technological advancements to make the futuristic aspects of the story seem believable, and all of the problems the humans and Elaki encounter are familiar. Crime and punishment are almost the same as in our time, and the exceptions only add interest to the characters and their actions. Rose has a particular way of solving some of her cases that hearkens back to the days of the Old West.

While the Elaki have solved some of society's ills, some things have become worse. The sun's rays continue to beat down on the earth through a badly compromised ozone layer and skin cancer is epidemic. One of the proposed solutions to this problem was to create underground communities. This, however, proved to be too expensive to be practical even for the wealthy. Humans have resorted to wearing more clothing and the tunnels built to link the failed underground communities are now inhabited by those who exist on the fringes of society and who provide extra challenges to the forces of law and order.

Lynn Hightower has created a fast-paced action series that fans of the type will enjoy despite its otherworldly qualities. David, Rose, their three daughters, and the people and Elaki with whom they interact are multifaceted characters who are, for the most part, sympathetic. We care about what happens to them, and we recommend the series.

COMM. GUIDO BRUNETTI
1992–1997   6 books
Donna Leon

Commissario of Police Guido Brunetti of Venice, Italy, is introduced in *Death at La Fenice*. A world-famous maestro is found dead after the second interval of *La Traviata*, the opera he was conducting; his death was caused by a dose of cyanide in the coffee he had drunk in his dressing room. Unlike most violent crimes in the city, there is a mystery surrounding this death, and as Brunetti's investigation unfolds, suspects abound. In this story, we meet Brunetti's family. His wife, Paola, teaches English. His daughter, Chiara, is a brilliant student who both likes and does well in the subject of mathematics. Guido's son and heir, Raffaele, possesses, at the tender age of fifteen, a Jesuitical turn of mind in his reasoning against both getting an education and getting a job. Count and Countess Falier, Paola's parents, live in an ancient palazzo on the Grand Canal, which has been inhabited by Falieri for three centuries. Brunetti does not know just how many rooms the palazzo contains—and is embarrassed to ask—but is well aware that it requires an army of workers to keep it from simply dissolving into the waters that define La Serenissima.

Death in a Strange Country provides Brunetti with more intrigue with both local and international implications when the body of a young man is found washed up against the embankment of the canal at San Giovanni e Paolo. When the corpse proves to be that of an American from the military post in Vincenza and his death is determined to have been caused by a careful stab wound rather than drowning, Brunetti's (nominal) superior officer is eager, in the name of tourism, to prove the murder was committed by an outsider—any outsider. As the case continues, Brunetti encounters the less than ethical practices of the Italian government and the force of the Mafia.

Brunetti is devoted to his wife and children as well as to the Italian ideal of family and its traditions. He is also, as a native Venetian, thoroughly imbued with the place and its people. In spite of these strong feelings, Brunetti's relationship with his in-laws is at best equivocal. Count Orazio Falier is said to be "in finance" and possesses not only vast wealth but also vast power and knowledge. Some of Brunetti's reticence toward the count and countess stems from unfamiliarity with the business and social milieus in which they move, but the greatest measure of Guido's discomfort comes from a deep reluctance to become either obligated to or dependent upon the count—for anything.

Venice is a city with a long history of great romance and high drama. The stories featuring Guido Brunetti possess, in a fitting way, these timeless qualities. Today, Venice is a shadow of her former self, a faded courtesan who still tantalizes—in the right light— but whose raddled appearance is all too apparent in the harsh glare of sunlight bouncing off her fetid canals. Brunetti's detecting takes the contradictions of ages and turns them into contemporary classics. Donna Leon is to be congratulated—and encouraged.

DET. JESSIE DRAKE
1993–1994   2 books
Rochelle Majer Krich

Los Angeles is a place where almost anything goes; even murder is an everyday occurence. Murderers in and around greater Los Angeles must work hard to make their killings worth any more than a brief mention on the six o'clock evening news. In her thirteen years on the force, homicide Det. Jessie Drake has seen just about every sort of violence one human can do to another. Yet in *Fair Game* she comes up against a murderer whose bloodless victims speak of a painless death that is more horrific to her than even the grisliest she has seen. When Jessie discovers that the killer is playing an elaborate and deadly game of Monopoly, using the city of Los Angeles as the game board, the cold calculation behind each murder chills her further.

In *Angel of Death*, Jessie has moved to a new precinct. The first case in which she becomes involved is not a suspicious death. In fact there is no death for her to investigate at all, only a series of malicious threats against a man and his family. The man in question is Barry Lewis, a Jewish attorney known for championing controversial causes. Perhaps, in defending the First Amendment rights of a neo-Nazi organization, he has gone too far. When Lewis is killed by a car bomb, it is unclear whether his death was caused by a Jew angered by Lewis's apparent betrayal of Jews or by one of the members of the neo-Nazi group Lewis had been representing.

In only two books, author Rochelle Majer Krich has devised a captivating character—a forthright individual with a healthy curiosity. As events in the first book unfold, readers discover that Drake is not without problems and challenges in her own life. The source of many of these problems has actually given Jessie the ability to balance a paradox, that is, to simultaneously hold two utterly divergent views of a subject. Abuse is the centerpiece of the first book, and Jessie is forced to come to terms with her personal knowledge of that crime in order to understand the mind of the killer she is tracking. Personal choice and personal heritage are at the crux of the second novel, and again Jessie's own challenges aid her in unraveling the twisted strands of racial hatred and murder.

By making her character a female Los Angeles homicide detective and by using almost familiar contemporary crimes as vehicles for investigation, Krich has nearly guaranteed herself an instant readership. She has, however, taken her character much further than mere surface appeal by imbuing Jessie Drake with a peculiar, parallax vision. The stories themselves raise questions on serious issues and present unusually unbiased looks at situations and their underlying causes that often generate polarity. Jessie's view prevails, and as the crimes are solved, Jessie's personal image gains in substance and solidarity.

Even though the foregoing characters are all law enforcement professionals, and crime is much the same universally, the individual officers we have described bring their own personal style of detecting to their cases. This diversity of style keeps these series from being the least formulaic and almost always surprising.

BEHIND THE BADGE:
Provincial Police

Population density is an ever-increasing problem for law-enforce-ment officers in major metropolitan areas. Those charged with keep-ing the peace in the world's smaller communities have different problems. Crimes remain basically the same regardless of location, but the solution of those crimes may differ because of the more personal perspective the rural police officer brings to the job and to those affected by the commission of a crime.

Some of the forerunners of those featured in this section are ex-emplars of these distinctions. Charmian Daniels is one of fiction's earliest female police detectives to be featured in her own series. Popular in England, the books are harder to find in the United States, even though Daniels has been on the job for more than thirty years. Writing under the pseudonym Jennie Melville, Gwendoline Butler has cast Charmian in eighteen books (1962–1996). We recom-mend the series for its author's perspicacity, among other reasons.

Ruth Rendell is best known for her one-offs, yet she has created a series character in the person of Det. Chief Insp. Reg Wexford, whose patch is the English town of Kingsmarkham, Sussex, and its surrounds. The well-plotted mysteries that Wexford and his col-league Mike Burden investigate are offset by the personal lives of the two officers, which offer both interest to the reader and continu-ity for the series of seventeen books (1964–1997).

English author Dorothy Simpson has placed her fictional detec-tive Criminal Investigation Division (CID) Insp. Luke Thanet in her own home territory of Kent. By viewing his methodology alone, a reader might well nickname Insp. Thanet "Insp. Plod." He relies on clear and concisely written reports as his cases progress, but he is by no means deskbound. Thanet and his partner, Sgt. Mike Lineham, diligently work the field in and around the community of Sturren-den and hold countless interviews with those involved in the cases. As with the Wexford series, the private lives of the partners add a vital aspect to their detecting, and throughout the thirteen books (1981–1996) readers watch Thanet and Lineham develop as men faced with a rapidly changing world.

71

As crime and mystery fiction has grown in popularity, writers have begun to use areas outside major cities as settings for their books featuring police detectives. Readers may enjoy these excursions away from any country's meanest streets to the lanes and gravel roads of its countryside; a surprising amount of action, malice, and all the deadly sins are alive and well in the hills, hollows, and small communities of the world, past, present, and future.

DET. SGT. STEVE ARROW
1978–1984   5 books
Laurie Mantell

The only unusual thing about this series of five books is its location. New Zealand—being at the bottom of the world from a United States perspective and the top from its own—seems fairly exotic. There is a large time difference, the seasons are the reverse of ours, and water swirls down the drain in the opposite direction. In contrast, the action in these stories is quietly conventional. The primary character, Det. Sgt. Steven Arrow, a mild-mannered, competent law-enforcement officer of no particular brilliance, is married to the niece of his commanding officer, Det. Chief Insp. Peacock; his father-in-law is an official on the force of a nearby town.

Arrow works out of the police station in the Hutt Valley, which rises gently from Wellington Bay. The pace of life is slower than that found in many parts of the United States or Europe and is rather reminiscent of mysteries set in the English countryside of the '40s and '50s. Violent death is not unknown; New Zealand is, after all, something of a frontier, and death is, more often than not, a straightforward matter. Arrow's job is much more directed toward keeping the peace than detecting, yet when necessary he finds his usual methods stand him in good stead in uncovering covert actions.

The books are competently crafted and lean toward the procedural, puzzle type. Laurie Mantell provides her readers with color-washed line drawings of the people and places she depicts. Good reading on an otherwise do-nothing day.

DET. INSP. LLOYD & DET. JUDY HILL
1983–1997   8 books
Jill McGown

All of the novels by author Jill McGown are marvelous puzzles and exercises in logic. The complexity of the tales is ingenious, and McGown plays fair with her readers by laying out all the clues as the story unfolds. These are low-key police procedurals, and all of the officials portrayed operate by the book. The detection is solid, and although no great intuitive leaps are taken by the investigators, readers will soon realize that Lloyd and Hill have a particular bent for their craft.

The series opens with Lloyd—whose first name remains a deep secret—and Hill working in the Stansfield Criminal Investigation Division. Although Judy Hill has recently been posted to Stansfield, she and Lloyd have known one another for more than fifteen years. At the time of their first meeting, in London, the two were attracted to one another; Lloyd, however, was married. Now he is divorced and Judy has been married—more or less—for ten years. The attraction between Lloyd and Hill is still strong, and in the first book, *A Perfect Match*, the two become lovers.

The course of the relationship between the two protagonists in these novels is at the core of the series and comprises the theme upon which the individual tales build. As Lloyd and Judy work out the various aspects of their union, this effort is mirrored and amplified by the case they are investigating at the moment. The first book is about matches between individuals, for good or ill and for true or false. The second, *Murder at the Old Vicarage*, is about ties that bind—those that secure and those that constrain. *Gone to Her Death* treats the truths that underlie social institutions, and *The Murders of Mrs. Austin and Mrs. Beale* looks at strong and independent women, their place in the contemporary world, and the world's acceptance of them—or lack of it. *Murder Now and Then* deals with the many different permutations and definitions of marriage and the fact that things are seldom as they appear.

McGown plays fair with her readers in laying out all the information needed to reach the conclusion of the murder case. She also plays fair with her two protagonists in putting them in a series of situations—both professional and personal—in which each is forced to draw upon intelligence, honor, and honesty for refuge.

HAMISH MACBETH
1985–1997   13 books
M. C. Beaton (Marion Chesney)

Lochdubh is a small community in the far northwest of the Scottish Highlands. It is on the sea and has an abundance of fresh water running down from the lovely mountains surrounding it. In the summer, the region can be idyllic and draws tourists from all points of the globe. Winters are harsh and demanding. Hibernation is the only way to cope with raging seas, torrential rains, and freezing snows that occasionally obliterate all familiar landmarks, and the inhabitants are content with the requisite state of dormancy. The residents of Lochdubh are, for the most part, quiet and law-abiding. It takes only one constable to maintain the peace, and in these novels he is personified by Hamish Macbeth.

Hamish is not a native of Lochdubh. His parents and six younger siblings live on the family croft in Ross and Cromarty. Tradition requires that the eldest child of the family make a contribution until the next in line becomes self-supporting. Hamish has chosen to be a village constable for the simple reason that it enables him to send most of his pay home. Anything he is able to earn on the side goes home as well. His job makes it possible for this young man to shoulder his responsibilities without compromising his values. On the surface, Hamish's values are not particularly lofty. He seems to be without ambition. As the series progresses, it becomes clear that Hamish does not aspire to the heights of the CID.

Introduced in *Death of a Gossip*, Hamish starts out as he means to go on. Though reasonably new to Lochdubh, he has managed to have a new police station built and has prised a new automobile out of the authorities as well. He arrives at Lochdubh Hotel in time for coffee nearly every morning and turns up for sandwiches at noon. There are hints that he may be a game poacher, and he is known to be lenient toward some transgressors of some laws. When murder occurs in his village, Hamish's first instinct is to let his superiors deal with the unpleasantness. However, when Det. Chief Insp. Blair arrives on the scene with his assistants Anderson and McNab and tells Hamish he thinks he's a bit too inexperienced for this sort of high-class crime, Hamish develops a burning desire to ferret out the details for himself.

It is more or less the same in the succeeding twelve stories; Hamish appears to lack ambition and the object of his desire, Priscilla Halburton-Smythe, wishes him more of it. An inspired aide to Hamish's method of detecting, Priscilla can be cool to the point of coldness to his ardor. Police Supt. Daviot and his wife, Susan, support Priscilla in her quest to raise Hamish above the run-of-the-mill. No one—not Blair, who considers him cloddish and slightly stupid, or Priscilla, who believes she can make a man of him, or the Super, who feels that Hamish should assume the position rightfully his—understands that Hamish is that rare thing, the truly contented man. Much to Blair's ongoing chagrin, Hamish, for all his country ways, does solve each of the murders committed on and around his patch.

M. C. Beaton has created a character who embodies a hefty chunk of reality. Readers soon discover just what Hamish's priorities are and just how valid they are. Another series penned by Beaton features Agatha Raisin, a senior sleuth.

SGT. KARL ALBERG & CASSANDRA MITCHELL
1985–1996   8 books
L(aurali) R. Wright

Karl Alberg is a staff sergeant in the Royal Canadian Mounted Police. As the series opens, his detachment—for the past eighteen months—has been the Sechelt peninsula of British Columbia. The area, known as the Sunshine Coast for its moderate climate, is some eighty miles long and accessible only by ferry. The village of Sechelt is in the middle of the peninsula. Although its population is less than other towns there, its location makes it a convenient center for people who work and live nearby. The tempo of life matches the climate—not much crime beyond traffic violations and petty theft occurs. Murder is highly unusual, yet *The Suspect* opens with one. Alberg is introduced as he questions George Wilcox, the old man who found the body of his neighbor.

Cassandra Mitchell is the librarian in Sechelt. We meet her, in the first book, at the newspaper office in Vancouver where she has gone to pick up responses to a personal ad she has placed. Alberg had responded to her ad, and the two meet for lunch, where they make the usual initial inquiries into one another's life. There is no immediate, intense attraction between the two but no apparent antipathy and they agree to meet again. As Alberg's investigation into the murder continues, he finds himself affected by some of the insight Cassandra brings to the matter.

While there are several satellite characters in the series, the relationship between Karl and Cassandra is central to the stories and progresses through each book. However, there is little momentum toward commitment by either party until the end of the fifth book, *Prized Possessions*. In the one that follows, *A Touch of Panic*, Karl has moved into Cassandra's house and they are looking forward to marriage. Then Cassandra is abducted and Karl is forced to truly acknowledge the depth of his feelings for her.

The stories are unusual in that readers often know who the murderer is at the outset. The interest lies in watching Alberg build his case and, in the process, uncover the passions and secrets that underlie the killer's motivation. In most of the books, there are several parallel plots that coalesce at the denouement—often in an improbable fashion. As Alberg and Cassandra are pragmatic individuals, not given to flights of fancy, the improbability works. Shifts in perspectives catch readers unaware and add to the suspense of each book.

Wright provides her audience with believable portraits of all the characters she crafts. She gifts each of them with typical human foibles and places them in coincidental yet credible proximity to one another.

L. R. Wright won an Edgar Allan Poe Best Novel Award from Mystery Writers of America for the first book in this series. She has lived up to that potential in all that have followed.

SUPT. ROBERT BONE
1987–1995   7 books
Susannah Stacey (Jill Staynes and Margaret Storey)

Supt. Robert Bone is a police officer in Tunbridge Wells in the English county of Kent. Bone is tall and slim, and his countenance can be—though rarely is—transformed by his smile. Part of the reason for his glumness has to do with the death of his wife, Petra, and their infant son in a car crash that injured him and, more seriously, his daughter, Charlotte. In *Goodbye Nanny Gray*, he and his partner, Det. Insp. Steven Locker, are called in on the death, some time past, of Miss Phoebe Gray of Mouse Cottage, Saxhurst. Nanny Gray had cared for many of the children in the surrounding area and was beloved by nearly all. She apparently had her enemies, however, and it is Bone's responsibility to sift through her acquaintances and arrive at the one instrumental in her demise.

Many of the ongoing characters in this series are introduced in the first two novels. Rock star Ken Cryer, his son, Jem, and the necessary entourage live in the manor in the village of Saxhurst. Jem is featured in the first book and his father is central to the third. Grizel Shaw, a biology teacher at Charlotte Bone's school, is introduced in *A Knife at the Opera*; she grows closer to both Charlotte and her father as the series progresses. Mrs. Playfair, a neighbor of the deceased Nanny Gray, is gifted with the "Sight" and numerous cats. She becomes friends with Robert, Charlotte, and Grizel and supplies the two households with cats—respectively, Ziggy and The Bruce. Pathologist Ferdy Foster makes his appearance in all of the books, and other colleagues of Robert and Grizel drop in from time to time.

The seven books in the series are definitely centered on the primary character and those closest to him, but the murders are not simply puff pieces designed to showcase a group of repertory players. The investigation into each crime is invested with countless twists and turns; red herrings abound; and the conclusion is almost always a last-minute and worthwhile surprise. Bone uses his "Nose" and the offices of his colleagues to their best advantage in the process of the devolution of the crime. At the same time, he maintains a close, caring—though not suffocating—relationship with his daughter, "Cha," who in the early books still suffers the aftereffects of the car crash.

Susannah Stacey is in reality Jill Staynes and Margaret Storey. Under another pseudonym, Elizabeth Eyre, the pair also write the series featuring Renaissance soldier of fortune Sigismondo. His exploits are described in the chapter "After the Fall: Historical Mysteries." Readers could hardly ask for more diversity from a writing team and will not be disappointed by either series.

SHERIFF ARLY HANKS
1987–1997   10 books
Joan Hess

Arly Hanks is the sheriff of Maggody, Arkansas (pop. 755). She holds this position because she is the most highly qualified citizen ever to have applied for the job. Arly managed to make an escape from her natal place by going to college and further by marrying an advertising man and moving into the glittery world of Manhattan. Unfortunately, after a few months, the bloom faded from the rose of wedded bliss. After a fast and ugly divorce, Arly removed herself to Maggody to recuperate and be cosseted by her mother Rubella Beatrice, known to all Maggodians as Ruby Bee. Fat chance.

Ruby Bee, owner of the local saloon and the Flamingo Hotel, and her best friend, Estelle Oppers, proprietor of Estelle's Hair Fantasies, truly believe they have Arly's best interests at heart. But when push comes to shove—as it usually does—the masters of obfuscation that they are thwart her every move and compromise evidence, clues, and anything else that falls into their collective paths.

Ruby Bee and Estelle are not the only crosses Arly must bear. The mayor, Jim Bob Buchanon, and his wife, Barbara Anne Buchanon Buchanon (known as Mrs. Jim Bob); Brother Verber of The Voice of the Almighty Lord Assembly; Roy Stiver, Arly's landlord and owner of Roy Stiver's Antiques and Collectibles; Dahlia O'Neill and her ardent suitor Kevin Buchanon; Larry Joe Lambertino, the high school auto shop teacher, and his wife, Joyce; and a wide variety of members of the clan Buchanon including Raz, the local moonshiner, and his hog Marjorie and daughter, Robin, who carries on Daddy's fine distilling traditions and adds prostitution to her list of achievements, all join in what can only be called a conspiracy to prevent law and order from ever settling permanently in their fair burg.

Maggody is usually a quiet little place that isn't even marked on a map. However, when trouble and crime strike they do so with a vengeance usually reserved for cities like Sodom and Gomorrah. Maleficence takes many forms in Maggody. The local inhabitants are more than capable of causing untold damage to friend, neighbor, family, foe, household pet, and self. When outsiders arrive on the scene—as they do for strange and inexplicable reasons—there is a mighty clash of cultures, the reverberations from which echo all the way to Stump City.

Joan Hess has applied her acerbic wit with formidable style in creating these well-drawn characters. For her readers' delectation, she rarely stops at drawing but continues on to quarter her creations as well. Hyperbole abounds in this parody of rural life. No one escapes her scathing pen, and the lines between the good guys and the bad ones often blur, causing the reader to wonder if justice, rough or smooth, is being served by anyone, including Arly.

In spite of the hurdles and challenges she constantly faces, Arly is well suited to her job. She knows the town and its inhabitants and is adept at sifting the meager crop of wheat from the enormous tonnage of chaff each case contains. Hess pulls no punches when writing about her native state and yet will be the first to kick six ways to Sunday any non-Arkansawyer who bad-mouths her home.

Noted drive-in movie critic Joe Bob Briggs, if asked, would rate this series quite highly as it contains, among other elements, aliens and UFOs, one three-hundred-pound lust goddess, countless breasts, highway dawg mashing, a psychic, bovine mutilation, and FBI and IRS-fu.

Hess has also created Claire Malloy, who appears in the chapter, "Killings on the Market: Business and Finance." Also, under the name Joan Hadley, Hess has written a short series featuring retired florist Theo Bloomer.

POL. CHIEF MITCHELL "MITCH" BUSHYHEAD
1989–1996   4 books
Jean Hager

Mitchell Bushyhead, chief of police in the town of Buckskin, Oklahoma, is half Cherokee and half white, though he had never given the Native American side of his heritage much thought until he is faced with the murder of Cherokee artist Joe Pigeon in *The Grandfather Medicine*. One of the officers under Mitch is his closest friend, Virgil Rabbit. Rabbit is a member of a secret Indian society called the Nighthawk Keetoowah. Because one of the society's members is a suspect in the murder, Mitch needs to know more than Virgil feels comfortable telling him. The two go to visit John Irons, known as Crying Wolf, in his role as medicine man for most of the members of the society. At their meeting, Mitch discovers not only a deep respect for the traditions Crying Wolf speaks of but also curiosity about his own origins.

Crying Wolf is a minor, though important, figure in all of the stories. His ceremonial actions and responsibility as medicine man put him in the path of both the victim and the killer in every book. Mitch finds that his position—as law enforcement incarnate—is similar to Crying Wolf's, and while the two don't actually work together, the respect each holds for the other—as men and as representatives of something greater—binds them in their quest for unmasking the wrongdoer and their desire for a whole and healthy community.

Signs and rumors in the second book point to a Cherokee witch, known as a night walker, being loosed because of the violation of a Native American graveyard by a newly developed resort hotel. When the resort manager dies a horrible death on the third night of the screech owl's call, superstition and reality merge. In *Ghostland*, the death of an eight-year-old girl, a student at a Native American boarding school, unleashes a fearsome evil presence. From their own respective positions, Mitch Bushyhead and Crying Wolf apply their expertise and restore harmony—temporarily, at least.

As the series opens, Mitch is a recent widower with an adolescent daughter, Emily. In the first book, Emily has been accepted into the pom-pom squad at her school, and Mitch has to attend a meeting to discuss team business. There he meets Lisa Macpherson, the squad's adviser and Emily's English teacher. In *Nightwalker*, the second in the series, Mitch and Lisa have been dating for three months, but he has been unable to talk with Emily about their growing relationship. In typical adolescent fashion, Emily resents her father's interest in another woman so soon after her mother's death and decides to run away from home, which puts her in the direct path of the killer. Mitch is forced to confront his reluctance to discuss his feelings with both his daughter and Lisa.

Jean Hager crafts this series with a light touch. Her characters are believably human, without being burdened with too much excess baggage. She won the Oklahoma Tepee Award for *The Grandfather Medicine* and was named Oklahoma Writer of the Year in 1982. Hager is the author of two other mystery series, one featuring Molly Bearpaw, an investigator for the Cherokee Nation, and another centered on Tess Darcy and her bed-and-breakfast establishment Iris House.

SHERIFF SPENCER ARROWOOD
1990–1996   4 books
Sharyn McCrumb

Location is crucial to these tales, featuring Sheriff Spencer Arrowood of Hamelin, Tennessee. The Appalachian mountain range that runs the length of the eastern United States forms the dividing line between North Carolina and Tennessee; the history of the area—both geological and human—is determined by the hills and hollows formed by the mighty range. Immigrants from Ireland, Wales, England, and Scotland found the land familiar and knew how best to husband it. Coal mining, sheep raising, and whiskey making were skills the incomers brought and used to temper, though never quite tame, the area. They brought their music, their instruments, and the custom of orally passing history from one generation to the next. The first wave of the industrial revolution passed by this region, and as a result poverty is common. The economic situation forces many to go north for work; however, the immeasurable wealth of beauty and tradition is a strong attraction from which some never escape and to which others hasten to return.

Spencer Arrowood is a native son. One great-grandfather was a Confederate corporal and another was a circuit preacher. The story of *If Ever I Return, Pretty Peggy-O*, the first in the series, begins on Memorial Day with Spencer decorating the grave of his older brother Cal, a victim of the Vietnam war. Deputy Joe LeDonne, a transplant from Gallipolis, Ohio, is another sort of victim of that infamous war, the effects of which run fuguelike through the first three books. Like Spencer, Martha Ayers is native born. In the first two books, she is the dispatcher for the Hamelin Sheriff's Office and in the third, *She Walks These Hills*, she becomes the second deputy and first woman on the force. Martha and Spencer were high school classmates and have a sort of shared history. In the first story, Martha and some of the other women of the class of 1966 are planning the twentieth class reunion. Many of the events of this story are linked to this gathering and to the past it celebrates.

Nora Bonesteel is a relatively minor character in the series, but through her the stories gain much of their color and continuity. From her isolated home on the slope of Ashe Mountain, Nora's view is almost as impressive as her vision. A descendant of Scots ancestors, Nora is gifted with the "Sight," though, as she is prone to point out, she hardly ever gets anything she'd set a store on knowing. She gently keeps the old ways and holds ends of the threads of the past. She weaves, knits, and sews and her handcrafts incorporate fragments of these threads for those who have the eyes to see them.

There are those who are all too ready to dismiss the denizens of this region as poverty-stricken, backward hillbillies. Without sentimentality, Sharyn McCrumb reinstates the dignity of these people by documenting their heritage and validating the struggles that have left many virtually stranded in their homelands. McCrumb is a storyteller of the first water, and the four books in this series are gems of the storyteller's art to be enjoyed by even those not fond of the mystery genre. Fortunately for mystery fans, murder and its requisite detection do occur in each book so they get the full benefits of McCrumb's craftsmanship.

McCrumb's other two series characters, Elizabeth MacPherson and Jay Omega, are described in the chapter "A Blot in the Copybook: Academia."

KATE SHUGAK
1992–1997   7 books
Dana Stabenow

Alaska is incredibly large, beautiful, and dangerous. It is a place populated by a wealth of wildlife, hardy souls, misfits, and adventurers. Most of the two-legged inhabitants have come from somewhere else, though some rightfully claim the title "Native." While incursions into the territory have cut the purity of the Aleut stock, the additions of other racial qualities have infused the basic native gene pool with many positive characteristics. This series is as much about Alaska and its people as it is about Kate Shugak and her investigations into murder.

Kate resides on a homestead in what is referred to as The Park, a vast tract covering some twenty million acres, most of which is virtually inaccessible. Kate's nearest neighbor is five miles away; the closest town, Niniltna, is twelve. She is related to nearly everyone living in the Park as most of them are Aleuts. Those not able to claim true Native status have earned the right to live in this splendid isolation by dint of hard work and the capacity for sheer survival.

Fourteen months before the action in *A Cold Day for Murder*, Kate was the star investigator for the Anchorage district attorney's office. The story behind her leaving that job is woven throughout the series and involves a child molester, a knife, and an injury that radically changes her appearance and life. Jack Morgan is her former boss and the man responsible for putting her in jeopardy. When he and an FBI "suit" arrive at her cabin wanting her to look for a missing park ranger and the investigator Jack had sent to locate him, Kate's first reaction is to answer flatly and emphatically, "No." That the ranger is the son of a United States congressman carries no weight in their argument. What changes Kate's mind is that the missing investigator is her current lover; reluctantly, she agrees to take on the search—for a price.

Shugak is a prickly character. Her retreat from the city to her homestead is not a return to the security of home, for Kate straddles both generational and cultural concerns. Her grandmother Ekaterina Moonin Shugak is the respected matriarch of all the tribes in the area and the person from whom all officials—Native American tribal and United States governmental—must seek counsel. Ekaterina wants to maintain Aleut traditions and to keep her people on the land. Kate realizes that the only survival tactic that can work for the tribe as a whole is for her people to leave an area that, without education and training, can offer merely a subsistence living. In spite of the love and respect between the two women, they are at loggerheads over fundamental issues and neither will back down.

The crimes that Kate is inveigled into investigating all involve murder; the chance that she knows the perpetrator as well as the victim is highly likely. Regulars in the series are Jack Morgan; "Chopper" Jim Chopin, an Alaska state trooper; Bobby Clark, a black wheelchair-bound Vietnam veteran; and Mutt, half Husky and half wolf. They alternately love and hate Kate and she returns their emotions in kind. The stories contain action, danger, and suspense; the pace is good without being fast; and Kate's character is well developed. We recommend reading the books in the order in which they were written to get the full impact of the place and its people as well as for the continuity in Kate's life.

DET. MARTI MACALISTER
1992–1996   5 books
Eleanor Taylor Bland

Marti MacAlister is an African-American single mother of two. She is also a homicide detective and the widow of a Chicago vice officer shot to death while on an undercover operation. After Johnny's death, Marti left Chicago for the smaller community of Lincoln Prairie on the shore of Lake Michigan and moved in with her friend Sharon, a teacher and divorced mother of one daughter, Lisa. Together, the two women share living expenses and responsibilities, though as Marti's hours are unpredictable, Sharon handles most of the practical household matters. Marti's children, Joanna and Theo, like the fact that she is a cop and are as supportive as possible. Their father's death has caused them grief and some uncertainty about their mother's safety but they keep it together for the most part. Joanna has become a bit obsessed with diet and cooks nothing but health food, yet this seems a reasonable response to the risks her mother often must face on the job.

Matthew "Vik" Jessenovik, a twenty-year veteran of the force, is Marti's partner. As the first book, *Dead Time*, opens, they have been together for just over a year. Initially, Vik was far less than comfortable with his new partner, but time and Marti's competence have assuaged any reservations he may have had and the two work as a highly effective team. They share an office with vice officers Slim and Cowboy—macho types with little sensitivity toward women and quite a bit of hostility. Marti gives them as good as she gets and the banter between them becomes rote after a while. All of these officers care passionately about their work. Doing what it takes to keep their community peaceful in the face of the harsh challenges of contemporary society is each individual officer's prime directive, and all of them work together to ensure as much security as possible.

Each story deals with family at some level. In the first, a group of homeless children create the closest thing to family any of them have ever known and are instrumental in bringing a perpetrator to justice. *Slow Burn* deals with sisterhood as embodied by a women's clinic. The murder of a man in *Gone Quiet* raises questions about the man and all the women in his family. As the tale unfolds, it becomes apparent that each woman had strong reasons for wishing him dead. Without Marti and Vik's tenacity in following procedure and presenting solid cases to the DA, the wrong person could easily have been charged with the crime. Johnny MacAlister's death is the focus of *Done Wrong* as Marti determines to exonerate him from the suspicion of suicide tainting her husband's memory. The family of police officers is central here and the code of honor binding them is brought into question. The methods Marti and Vik rely upon not only lead to the resolution of Johnny's death but uncover corruption within the Chicago force itself. Two families are featured in *Keep Still* and two apparently unconnected deaths eventually link them in a story involving pride, deception, honor, and greed.

Throughout all of the novels, Marti struggles to balance her professional life with her personal one. Ben, a paramedic with the Lincoln Prairie Fire Department and a widower with one son, becomes increasingly important in Marti's life. Ben and his son, Mike, go about creating, with Sharon and Lisa, an extended family united by common interests, need, and love rather than by consanguinity; Marti's participation is integral to it but not necessarily constant.

Eleanor Taylor Bland writes driving tales fueled by a strong sense of connectedness. Relationships are paramount in each story, and Marti's sensitivity to the subtext present in most human exchanges leads her and Vik along some twisted paths to what is almost never the obvious solution. Compassion is a strong feature in every story, and Marti seems able to draw that quality out of even those whose hearts seem the most hardened. Black culture is portrayed in an engaging style and is a welcome new venue for crime and mystery fiction. We eagerly await the next installment of Marti MacAlister's professional life and the continuation of her private saga.

DEP. MARTY HOPKINS
1993–1995   2 books
P(atricia) M(cEvoy) Carlson

Nichols County is a mythical place located in southern Indiana, just down the road from Bloomington and Indianapolis. Limestone defines its geography and has contributed to its prosperity; the quarries of Nichols County have provided much of the building material that has shaped the major cities east of the Mississippi. Dep. Sheriff Marty Hopkins's grandfather used to say that he, personally, had dug the entire Empire State Building out of the stone. Although Nichols County is an invention of this series' author, it provides an accurate reflection of the values and mores of the real area.

Martine LaForte Hopkins grew up here and, in high school, played basketball (boys' rules) under Coach Cochran, the Nichols County sheriff. She moved away for a while, went to college—until the money ran out—then fell in love, married, and had her daughter, Chrissie. Marty's husband, Brad, is a dreamer. His goal is to be a well-known radio personality, preferably in New York City. Marty and Chrissie followed Brad in his dream quest until the need to be settled became apparent to Marty for her daughter's sake. Back home, Marty approached Sheriff Cochran for a job. He started her out in the office, answering phones, and let her nag him into letting her out on patrol. Now she is one of his deputies and still expects to play by boys' rules. Unfortunately, Nichols County has clear ideas about the propriety of that.

Here, as in many rural parts of this country, men are considered leaders and protectors of women, who are designed for the role of helpmeet to the man. Sexual equality is slow to reach these quiet backwaters and not always welcome when it does arrive. The stories featuring Dep. Marty Hopkins focus not only on her personal confrontations with the status quo but on the long-term effects of the preservation of that status quo. The cases Marty investigates have their roots in history—some early, some more recent. In *Gravestone*, a well-kept family secret and the illusion of that family's unity hide other crimes and an even darker act of vengeance. *Bloodstream* discloses other illusions and long-kept secrets, as Marty investigates the disappearance of a young boy, his subsequent death, and the death of another child.

P. M. Carlson's choice of location and protagonist brings one major theme to light—the status and treatment of women and children. Marty's position in the sheriff's office is at once timely and tenuous. The law may mandate equality between men and women on the job, but the community relies on and supports old values and the roles that define them. While these issues have gained visibility in recent years, their importance is still in question. The crimes on which the stories are focused relate to the place women and children have held historically. The juxtaposition of today and yesterday brings the respective times into the same frame, yet rather than a pair of superimposed images blurring together, the reader is given an enhanced double image.

Carlson has penned another series featuring Maggie Ryan, which can be found in the chapter "Unexpected Detectives."

SHERIFF JOANNA BRADY
1993–1997   5 books
J(udith) A(nn) Jance

As *Desert Heat* opens, Andrew Brady, the assistant deputy sheriff of Cochise County, Arizona, is late for the tenth-anniversary celebration he has arranged for his wife, Joanna. Joanna's call to the sheriff's office tells her Andy had left early for their date and sends her out into the night to look for him. Not far from their ranch, just off High Lonesome Road, her worst nightmare is realized as she discovers Andy's truck in a culvert and Andy himself lying in front of it, shot in the belly. He is rushed to University Hospital in Tucson by helicopter. Joanna, driven by Sheriff Walter McFadden, follows and begins the long vigil, first outside the surgical suite, then outside the intensive care unit.

As Joanna waits for news of her husband's condition, disturbing rumors reach her. The first assumption is that Andy has been shot by a person or persons unknown. Now, with corroborating information from the surgeon, attempted suicide is suspected; further innuendo suggests that he may have been involved in the illicit drug trade. While Joanna believes firmly in Andy's innocence, she finds she may not have known him as well as she thought. There is formidable evidence speaking to his complicity. For her own peace of mind and that of their daughter, Jennifer, Joanna determines to find the truth—whatever it is.

In this first story, most of the ongoing characters are also introduced. Bisbee, Arizona, is a small place where almost everyone knows everyone else and where Joanna and Andy were buying their ranch from Andy's parents, Jim Bob and Eva Lou Brady. Joanna's mother, Eleanor Lathrop, lives in the town and maintains propriety. Rev. Marianne Maculyea, pastor of the Canyon Methodist Church, is Joanna's close friend, and Clayton Rhodes, an octagenarian and one of the last of the old-time cowboys, is her helpful neighbor. Milo Davis, Joanna's employer since her high school graduation, was also a close friend of her late father. As both the daughter and the wife of law-enforcement officers, Joanna knows most of the members of the local force. Adam York, a district agent for the federal Drug Enforcement Agency, and Angie Kellogg, a former hooker, are also fixtures in the books.

Joanna gathers the evidence to close the case and clear her husband of all suspicion. She has been so determined in her efforts—in the face of the harshest of allegations against Andy—and so successful in her pursuit of the truth that she finds herself proposed as candidate for the office of sheriff. *Tombstone Courage* opens on the day of the election. Joanna wins the three-way race by a landslide and is confronted with a double homicide the following day. Instead of waiting until January to take up her official duties, she is sworn in immediately and takes over as sheriff of Cochise County. This story is fraught with the secrets of a family, a fight over an inheritance, and a pending lawsuit brought against a father by his daughter. With what is becoming her trademark determination, Joanna takes over her new office and concludes her second—though first official—case.

Joanna Brady is one of the more admirable characters developed recently. J. A. Jance's earlier character is Seattle Homicide Detective J. P. Beaumont, described in the "Behind the Badge: Major Metropolitan Police" chapter preceding this one. While Beau is an effective character in his own right, his sex places him in a much more traditional position than that of Sheriff Brady. At the outset of this new series, Jance gifts Joanna with uncommon good sense and a clear presence. Even when beset with uncertainty, her honest and forthright nature clears her path to the unremitting truth. We like the character, the writing, and the promise of a long-lived series.

No matter where it takes place—in the town or the country, *on Earth or off*, detection requires the same general applications. Crime and punishment may take some of their definition from geographical boundaries. Certainly, cultural differences influence the view from each end of the pole, yet it is only within recent years that readers of crime and mystery fiction have been exposed to some of these disparities. As the world—nay, the universe—grows smaller, readers are well advised to prepare to expand their horizons and unlimit their expectations.

The variety of law-enforcement officials in this chapter is much more extensive than in the past. Women are well represented for the first time in the annals of crime and mystery fiction, and some authors are taking their characters into the future and beyond the stars. In some series, readers are treated to accurate detail and correct police procedure; in others, what is written must be taken with a grain of salt, as literary license is fully applied. Most of the officers of law and order wear the white hats, and the fictional presentation of these public servants who are dedicated to keeping the peace honors their place in any society.

As the police are almost always involved in some fashion in this type of fiction, listing other series in which they appear would be an exercise in futility.

CRIME AND THE CORPUS DIVINE:
Clerical Mysteries

Other than the aristocracy, no one can be as well-mannered as members of the clergy. Through their ministrations, they observe those who come to the church for celebration, refuge, confession, spiritual health, and healing. These servants of the church find themselves privy to many secrets and often hear what is unsaid more clearly than what is spoken. They have come to recognize many of the darker motivations of those about them. Because of their vocation, these detectives are sensitive and alert to others' feelings. The cleric's process of detection is usually followed through with thoughtfulness and care.

The six-book series written by Margaret Scherf (1949–1965) featuring the Rev. Martin Buell of Farrington, Montana, is among the earliest evocations of the church by a woman author of a crime series. Her character is an honest and outspoken soul who tends his flock with all care and consideration yet does not hesitate to balk when an issue on which he feels strongly is at stake. A portly, middle-aged man, Buell is an Episcopalian priest whose overall view of humanity is with a jaundiced eye. In 1949, Big Sky Country was still a frontier—underpopulated and lacking big-city sophistication. Buell, at the helm of Christ Church, is well suited to both his congregation and the land. If he sometimes harbors ill will toward a select few of his parishioners, it is probably well justified.

In a series filled with gentle humor, the author pokes as much fun at her protagonist as she does at any of her more outrageous satellite characters and outright scoundrels. Reality is at the core of these books, which combine the truly spiritual with the earthy mundane.

Edith Pargeter, writing under the name Ellis Peters, has created an unusual historical series. Brother Cadfael (1977–1994) solves crimes in the harsh England of the 1100s. In his early life he had fought as a crusader, worked as a tradesman, and known—in all senses, including the biblical—many members of the fair sex. In his middle years, seeking tranquillity and a place to expand his knowledge of healing and herbal remedies, he enters the monastery of

Saint Peter and Saint Paul outside the city of Shrewsbury. The twenty-one-book series is filled with all the richness and machinations of the age. Using Cadfael, his brother monks, and a variety of other denizens, Peters has created a fascinating chronicle of the twelfth century.

Though an older and unfamiliar England is presented here, the motives leading to criminal acts and the acts themselves are no different from those of contemporary times. The series moves slowly. These are not quick reads, though the stories are by no means difficult to follow. Peters provides readers with historical facts and believable scenarios of the era she has chosen to chronicle.

In another series, a Frank Lloyd Wright mansion on Walton Street in Chicago is the home of the last three sisters of the Order of Mary and Martha. Along with seeing to their own particular religious business, these sisters of the cloth hold to their own brand of justice and seek resolution via decidedly odd means.

Sister Mary Teresa Dempsey is barely five-feet-tall and weighs in at close to two hundred pounds. She is the eldest nun of the order of Mary and Martha and holds that her fifty-plus years as a historian give her better qualifications than Chicago's finest in ferreting out truth. Of course, this attitude ensures that the sisters will often run afoul of the minions of law and order. The minion closest to the three inhabitants of this unconventional convent is Sister Kimberly's brother Richard Moriarty. The remaining sister is Joyce, a young, twenty-something nun who holds forth in the kitchen. The results of these clashes are nine (1981–1997) well-written, humorous stories that are good mysteries as well. Monica Quill—in reality, Ralph McInerny—tells a lively and believably improbable tale of life as perceived within a modern cloister.

Sister Carol Anne O'Marie is the author of a series that features seventy-five-year-old Sister Mary Helen. A former history professor, Sister Mary Helen moves in her retirement to Mt. St. Francis College for Women in San Francisco. There, she is involved in her first murder and meets Kate Murphy, a homicide detective for the San Francisco Police Department (SFPD). The action in five of these seven books (1984–1997) takes place in San Francisco and involves members of Sister Mary Helen's order, the SFPD, and the personal side of Kate's life.

Sister Carol Anne has obviously chosen to write what she knows best. Forty years of religious life have probably given her material for many more books. Readers of this series not only get to enjoy well-plotted mysteries but get to see what really goes on within the confines of the convent and what goes on in the minds of (some) nuns.

As murder is the ultimate sin, it should come as no surprise to find members of the clergy doing battle with its perpetrators.

DEACONESS THEODORA BRAITHWAITE
1991–1996   6 books
D(iane) M. Greenwood

At the beginning of this series, the Church of England, in England, did not allow women at the altar. Their talents were not, however, despised, and a titular niche had been found for them in the role of deacon(ess). This gave women the right to marry, baptize, and bury, while withholding from them the responsibilities of consecration of the host and wine at the Eucharist and the absolution from sin.

Deaconess Theodora Braithwaite has been well raised and schooled in the dicta of the church. Her late father was an Anglican priest; her great-uncle Hugh is a canon of the church. As written, Theodora's religious beliefs and practices are fitted to the contemporary church while stemming from a place of profound personal spirituality. She was educated at Cheltenham and Oxford, and her first posting as a representative of the Church was in Nairobi; her second, in a parish in the south of London.

The first book in the (United States) series, *Clerical Errors*, places her in the Cathedral in Medewich where her duties include clerical services as well as pastoral support for Canon Wheeler. At the opening of the book, the decapitated head of a local priest is found in the font of the St. Manicus Chapel of the Cathedral. Father Paul Gray had been a figure of some controversy within the parish. He had substituted high church for low—without a by-your-leave from his parishioners—and was rumored to have had some rather unsavory involvement with a youth group from his former posting. None of these allegations seem enough to have brought him to the horrible end he suffered. The police need to draw a swift conclusion to the case, and pressure from within the Cathedral close to find the killer runs high as well. Theodora gathers like minds around her to discuss the situation. It becomes clear that there is a palpable level of evil abroad and that truth is the only effective weapon against this amorphous force. In the second (U.S.) book, *Unholy Ghosts*, she uses the same discussion methods, with yet a different group, to find the murderer of Father Hereward Marr, pastor of the congregation of Oldfield.

We have put "U.S." in parentheses in the foregoing text as we believe that—based on chronological information within the stories themselves—the second book published in the United States is actually the first in the British series. Chronology notwithstanding, Braithwaite is a superior character. There is not much personal history given, nor is there all that much about the present Theodora in either story, yet her attitudes and actions are quite explicit and well fitted to the cases in which she becomes involved. The deaconess's style of detecting relies more on inference and she brings all of her resources and the resources of those she respects and trusts to that inference. Some may describe the Deaconess Theodora as cold. Perceptive readers, however, will discern that, beneath the cool, objective exterior that she presents to the world at large, Theodora is a woman of uncommon depth and compassion.

CHRISTINE BENNETT
1992–1997   9 books
Lee Harris

Christine Bennett is a former Franciscan nun. Due to family circumstances, Christine was given special dispensation to enter the convent of St. Stephens at the age of fifteen. Now, fifteen years later, she (the erstwhile Sister Edward Francis) has found that she has gotten and given all she needed from the Franciscans and has taken up a secular life. Christine has inherited a house from her Aunt Meg and also the guardianship of her retarded cousin, Gene.

In *The Good Friday Murder*, the council of the city of Oakwood, New York, where Christine now resides, is considering the approval of a group home for the moderately retarded. Gene is one of those residents who would benefit from this arrangement. Sentiment against the proposed home runs high, as one of the residents is alleged to have murdered his mother. Charged with the task by the council, Christine investigates this forty-year-old crime. Inquiries bring her into contact with her new neighbors, twin savants, lawyer Arnold Gold, and Brooklyn homicide detective Jack Brooks. The successful conclusion of Christine's investigations in the first book sets the scenes for those that follow. Oakwood truly becomes her home and replaces the religious community she has left. Much sooner than she expected, Christine becomes romantically involved with Jack and finds herself rapidly adjusting to her new, worldly life.

Christine is a woman of strong convictions and abiding faith. Her need to enter a convent at an early age was matched with desire. Her decision to leave was well thought out and managed with loving support from her friend and spiritual director Sister Joseph. While the Franciscan order met both spiritual and educational needs for the young Sister Edward Francis, the older Christine discovers a need to apply the careful instruction she received within a broader context. Trained as a teacher, Christine found that what she truly loved was the teaching. Trained as a religious, she found that what she truly loved was the ritual. Both are far more accessible to her in the world beyond the convent walls.

Much care and consideration has gone into the creation and development of this character. Each task Christine takes on in her worldly existence is vested with appropriate gravity. She is an optimist and, at the same time, a realist. She trusts in the fact that her God is one of love, justice, and compassion, and she comports herself in support of that belief. Author Lee Harris writes a woman's life as it may well be lived by a contemporary woman, and it is an exemplary life.

SISTER FREVISSE
1992–1997   7 books
Margaret Frazer (Gail Bacon and Mary Monica Pulver [Kuhfield])

Fifteenth-century England is the venue for this series featuring Dame Frevisse, hosteler of the Benedictine priory of St. Frideswide. Her calling and her capacity require her to make arrangements for the accommodation of all who come to the priory. In *The Novice's Tale*, the first in the series, we meet Sister Frevisse's uncle Sir Thomas Chaucer, son of the poet and customs officer Sir Geoffrey. The priory is governed by Domina Edith, an ancient who came into her power at the same time as Henry IV came into his.

The series is full of all manner of morality, mores, and mortality of the era and, as in the series featuring Brother Cadfael, is faithful to the times and their sentiments. Frevisse is a bit more worldly than many of her sisters, as she has lived in her uncle's household and has assisted him in his intellectual pursuits. She is quick of wit, and in all probability the best place for her to ply her talents is within the confines of the convent. St. Frideswide provides Frevisse with protection and prerogative; she uses these judiciously—relying on the sanctity of the cloister or the voice of her office when appropriate—to see that justice is done.

The physical location of the stories is less important than the actions of Sister Frevisse and those who accompany her. The first two novels take place within the gracious, trellised walls of the nunnery. The third in the series, *The Outlaw's Tale*, occurs beyond those walls, yet well within the confines of the calling of Sister Frevisse and her companions, Sister Emma and Master Naylor. In these tales, readers are presented with the concept of a betrothal more binding than a marriage, the salvation of souls threatened by worldly contamination, and the concept of forgiveness by right of rank.

The contrast between the convent of the fifteenth century and the convent of the twentieth is strong and apparent. Whereas the woman of the fifteenth century had few choices, the woman of the twentieth has almost too many. The convent walls offer a secure place for the innocent and for the intellectual. In both the fifteenth and twentieth centuries, other avenues for women have been possible—marriage and motherhood are the obvious first options, the care of one's aging parents, or of the offspring of a deceased sibling, and servitude are others. The cloister provides a place for thought, reflection, peace, and all the time necessary to make a choice in a worldly direction.

CATHERINE LEVENDEUR
1993–1996   4 books
Sharan Newman

The backdrop for this series is twelfth-century France, when the Church held ultimate authority over every aspect of life and prelates were as powerful as the reigning monarch. Questions raised on the prevailing dogma were considered heresy and those who raised those questions, heretics. While death was not an uncommon punishment for those who dared wonder at the validity of all of the Church's declarations, excommunication and social censure were usually sufficient to keep most folk in line. In spite of this, there were those who kept logical thought alive and encouraged others to do so in the face of entrenched beliefs. One such was Peter Abelard, a cleric scholar who taught at the great cathedral school of Notre Dame.

As the series begins with *Death Comes as Epiphany*, many years have passed since the passion of Abelard and Heloise burned and brought grave consequences to the pair. Abelard still teaches in Paris and has established Heloise as abbess of the Paraclete, a new religious house of his making. Catherine LeVendeur is a young novice at the convent. While unsure of her religious commitment, she is devoted to her studies and has found a preceptor in Heloise. Rumor reaches the convent that a psalter, copied and bound at the Paraclete under Catherine's direction and presented to the abbot of the cathedral at Saint-Denis, contains heretical passages. The repercussions of these charges would threaten not only the Paraclete and its head, but also its founder, Peter Abelard. Catherine is charged with ascertaining the truth in the matter and agrees to be suspended from the convent for disobedience. She is escorted by her uncle Roger to her father's house in Paris, where she is met with anger from her father and madness from her mother.

In Saint-Denis, Catherine meets her old friend Garnulf, a stone carver, and his apprentice Edgar. On her way to dinner in the abbot's quarters, Catherine is saved from being struck by a body falling from the transept tower. The body at her feet is that of Garnulf and Edgar saved her. These two form an unlikely union to discover the cause of what can only be the murder of the stone carver. In the process, each uncovers other, even more dangerous, secrets; both Catherine and Edgar's lives become at risk. At the end of the story, the matter of the altered psalter is resolved although Catherine's own future is called into question.

As *The Devil's Door* opens, Catherine is back at the Paraclete, though it is clear that her life has taken a turn away from that of a contemplative. The death of a badly injured woman who had been brought to the convent and questions surrounding the woman's bequest of forest land to the Paraclete take both Catherine and her newlywed husband, Edgar, on a mission to discover the truth. Once again, the two are imperiled as they delve into the mystery and old secrets are disclosed. The story ends happily for some, while justice is served deservedly to others.

One of the things this series did for us was make us review the personal history of Heloise and Abelard. As we read of their lives and love, we realized what a good and thorough job Sharan Newman had done in capturing the flavor of medieval life. While this is not a scholarly work and Newman writes a brief explanation of her work and a disclaimer at the end of *The Devil's Door*, her curiosity has led her on a fascinating search through archival records and contemporary writings. Her books have encouraged us to do the same, and we are grateful.

MOTHER LAVINIA GREY
1995–1997   4 books
Kate Gallison (Dunn)

Lavinia Grey is an Episcopal priest and vicar of St. Bede's Church in Fishersville, New Jersey. As the series opens, Mother Vinnie's flock is small and dwindling. The bishop of the diocese has placed Mother Vinnie at St. Bede's in order to close the church. Fr. Rupert Bingley will take on the parishioners of St. Bede's and has his eye on the fine stained-glass windows, the brass communion rail, and the walnut pulpit for his own church, St. Dinarius. Mother Vinnie is determined to keep St. Bede's alive. Fishersville needs an Episcopal church as well as the social services and counseling Mother Vinnie is able to provide.

In *Bury the Bishop*, Mother Vinnie is a prime suspect in the murder of His Grace Bishop Wealle at the annual Episcopal Convention. Det. Dave Dogg is the investigating officer who finds himself smitten with the petite vicar despite his suspicions that she may have been the agent of two deaths. Ralph Voercker, Mother Vinnie's thirty-year-old acolyte and staunch supporter, becomes involved with Saraleigh Kane, unwed mother of Freddy and an unnamed three-month-old. Rex Perskie, father of Saraleigh's youngest, pursues Saraleigh with murderous intent and succeeds in burning down the apartment building in which they have been living. Mother Vinnie follows an obscure lead, discovers the motive for the bishop's murder, and finds herself face-to-face with the killer. She saves herself in time to be rescued by Det. Dogg, who then proposes. She does not accept.

Weddings, antiques, Satanism, missing cats, Mother Vinnie's plans for a daycare center, and the money necessary to carry those plans through are all elements in the tale of the *Devil's Workshop*. Ralph and Saraleigh are planning to marry but Rex is determined to thwart their dreams. Freddy, together with Danny and Schwartz—Freddy's friends from the halfway house—conspires to get rid of Rex once and for all. Det. Dogg is away in Boston at the funeral of his former mother-in-law, and Mother Vinnie must solve the death of Simon Ratcher almost singlehandedly. Fortunately for the good mother, her parishioners are willing and able detective assistants.

Horace Burkhardt, property owner and Mother Vinnie's friend, has sold the town's baseball field to a greedy developer and has become a pariah in *Unholy Angels*. Too many guns confuse an already complex issue and, as usual, plans are afoot to dispose of Rex Perskie. The developer dies, a park ranger is killed, and Freddy is kidnapped. Mac Barrow, former pro baseball player and musician extraordinaire, offers his services as church organist to Mother Vinnie. Det. Dogg is back together with his former wife, and Saraleigh and Ralph have a new baby. A cross-country chase takes much of Mother Vinnie's congregation away from Fishersville in search of Freddy and, once again, Mother Vinnie confronts a killer and solves the crimes.

Lavinia Grey is in her mid-thirties and was widowed before she was called to the church. Small and cute (an adjective she hates), she seems at first an unlikely pastor. As one gets to know this character, however, one realizes that she possesses all of the qualifications for shepherding her flock and that her apparent naivete is true innocence. She prefers believing the best about people but is savvy enough to realize that not everyone deserves her finest feelings. What everyone does deserve from her and gets, in well-measured doses, is her Christian charity.

Kate Gallison has also created a series featuring investigator Nick Magaracz. Her Mother Grey stories are poignant without being sloppy and funny without being ridiculous. Her characters are all fairly portrayed, and some of those most flawed by life in this harsh world are at once the most endearing and exasperating. We wish her a long tenure at St. Bede's.

Clerical detectives are not a new phenomenon, and their entry into the world of crime and even the mind of the criminal should come as no surprise to readers. The individuals we have chosen to write about bring not only the weight of the church to their investigations but a sense of justice that goes well beyond the sometimes narrow definition given by the forces of secular law and order.

SOME OTHER CLERICAL SLEUTHS

The Rev. Claire Aldington
Father Simon Bede
Sister Cecile
The Rev. Rodney Chelmarsh
The Rev. Fairchild
The Rev. Jabal Jarrett
Sisterr Joan

CRIME ON CUE:
Stage, Screen, and Television

No matter the medium, all of the individuals in this chapter are required—in pursuit of their craft—to put their best face forward for an audience. As actor or television personality, each is required to perform and performance becomes a part of the fabric of their lives. Those intimately familiar with a life lived behind the lights are equally familiar with the added dimension that is necessary to succeed from that position. Once acquired, this added dimension becomes integrated into that individual's persona, and it colors virtually all of their waking (and even some of their sleeping) perceptions.

For Carolyn Wells's character, Kenneth Carlisle, the added dimension actually led him away from Hollywood and the silver screen and into his second career as a New York detective. The three-book series (1929–1931) featuring Carlisle is not noted for tight plotting or for its adherence to the rules of fair play set forth by that venerable British institution, The Detection Club. Nevertheless, they are entertaining stories and Wells did get the actor part right.

Even though they are not as besotted with stars as Americans are, the English do take the theatre even more seriously. Tessa Crichton, created by Felicity Shaw under the pseudonym Anne Morice, is a thespian whose career embraces screen and television drama as well as the London and provincial stages for which she is best known. Tessa's marriage to Scotland Yard detective Robin Price gives her an edge in solving the crimes in which she becomes embroiled. Tessa could be described as a nosy gossip; however, her desire to prove the innocence of the prime suspect in each case is a redeeming feature. The twenty-five-book series (1970–1990) became a bit formulaic over the years, yet still provides predictable enjoyment.

Merlin Capricorn is a trained magician. Scion of the Great Capricornus, Merlin is expected to follow in his late father's footsteps. Even though he has chosen another path—that of the police force—he finds his father still leading the way from time to time.

We chose to put Capricorn in this chapter because of his understanding and use of the world of illusion in his police work. None of the novels could ever pass for a police procedural, but the detection is solid nonetheless. There are only six books (1975–1982) and, while a chronology exists in the tales, it is not reflected in the order in which the books were released. When the books are read as published, the reason for the discrepancy becomes apparent. Pauline Glen Winslow practices sleight of literary hand in her creation, and, like Capricorn's, her magic is subtle and veiled.

In actual life the noted historical biographer Lady Antonia Fraser is a fixture of the London literary scene. Married to playwright Harold Pinter, she and her cohorts were outspoken opponents of Margaret Thatcher during that woman's term as prime minister. Fraser's creation, Jemima Shore, is a television personality appearing in eleven books (1977–1994). Billed as an investigator, she addresses weighty issues such as poverty, birth control, and euthanasia. Her high visibility and professional excellence give her credibility and access to a wide range of people. Conversation is her primary investigative method, whether for her program or her detection. Shore's research talents are impressive and her instincts for both people and issues are formidable. Given Fraser's major focus, we would not be surprised to discover that she created Jemima Shore to provide still another platform for her own social and political viewpoints.

Jane Dentinger began her six-book series (1983–1995) featuring Jocelyn O'Roarke more than ten years ago. Jocelyn O'Roarke is not a starving artist; theatre work and television commercials come her way often enough that she does not need to expend her energies waiting tables or clerking in a department store when she's between plays. Respected in her craft, she teaches acting and so is familiar with both sides of the footlights. Drawn to detection by a killing within the theatrical community, O'Roarke meets Det. Sgt. Phillip Gerrard, who finds her vast knowledge of the denizens of this community of inestimable value.

The stage offers many opportunities for invention. Oddly enough, detection also provides some of the same openings because, particularly in the early stages of an investigation, all things are possible. The actor investigates the role in much the same way the detective investigates the crime scene; however, an ability to extemporize is also valuable. Each plays every plausible scenario to its logical conclusion to eliminate the impossible.

The performers in this chapter bring their powers of study and inventiveness to their roles as detectives. Believability is created out of supposition and nuance, and, when a life hangs in the balance, the play's the thing.

EVANGELINE SINCLAIR & TRIXIE DOLAN
1986–1995   5 books
Marian Babson (Ruth Stenstreem)

Evangeline Sinclair and Trixie Dolan are long-standing members of the Hollywood acting community. Far from being superannuated, however, these two are still hitting their respective marks and, in Trixie's case, kicking up heels. In *Reel Murder*, the two ladies have been invited to London by an old crony, Beauregard Sylvester. Sylvester, a former silent-screen actor himself, is hosting a retrospective highlighting the careers of Evangeline and Trixie. A scalped corpse is found in the garden of the St. John's Wood house where the ladies reside. Det. Supt. Heyhoe and his sergeant Julian Singer come to investigate. They are variously aided and thwarted by Evangeline, Trixie, the rest of the members of their household, and other significant souls.

The second book, *Encore Murder*, takes place in the same setting and with basically the same cast. Another body is found in the garden—not scalped this time, but shot with an arrow. Sgt. Singer, a film buff, is helping Evangeline write her memoirs and becomes a part of the investigation when his superior officer arrives on the scene. Introduced in this tale is Griselda von Kirstenberg, an aging Teutonic temptress and contemporary of Evangeline and Trixie.

Evangeline, Trixie, and Griselda are appearing in a film together— *Shadows in Their Blood*. The village of Whitby is not an appealing place in January but lends just the right ambiance to their remake of *Dracula*. To call the director a miserly and harsh taskmaster is an understatement; everyone on the set is stressed and overworked. This book's victim—a bloodless corpse—is found on the set, and rumors of real vampires abound among the minions essential to the smooth running of things. As in all of the books, Trixie narrates and both she and Evangeline detect, eventually solving the case before the police do. These are light romps carried off by a standing repertory company.

Marian Babson, a well-known, award-winning mystery writer, is versatile and unpredictable. Douglas Perkins, the character in her first series, is a London-based public relations specialist, and the four books in that series also are humorous. The light approach is not the only one Babson takes. Most of her works are one-offs, straight suspense. We are captivated by this author's style of writing; she tells a good story. Even though we don't really care about what happens to the ongoing characters she has created, we enjoy all of her work.

VERITY BIRDWOOD
1989–1995   6 books
Jennifer Rowe

Although Verity "Birdie" Birdwood is the protagonist of these Australian novels and certainly solves the murders around which each book is centered, she herself is a bit of an enigma. Readers must pay close attention for the snippets of information about this character that are scantily scattered throughout the series. The surface Birdie is unprepossessing—small of stature, poorly dressed, and generally careless of her appearance. Although qualified to practice as a solicitor, Birdie supports herself as a researcher for ABC (Australian Broadcast Commission) Television. No one meeting her for the first—or second or even third—time would guess that she is the daughter of a well-known and very well-to-do financier and that she has given away much of her share of the family fortune. Just where and how Birdie gets involved in solving murders is explained only in the first short story in a collection entitled *Death in Store*.

In *Grim Pickings*, the first book in the series, Birdie, goes to the small mountain town of Atherton, Queensland, at the behest of her good friend Kate Delaney, for a weekend of apple picking with the Tender family. A man dies by poison and Det. Sgt. Simon Toby is assigned to the case. Simon has heard of Birdie from his brother Dan, a Sydney homicide detective who has worked with and against the ubiquitous Miss Birdwood on several occasions. Much like his brother, Simon finds Birdie's presence both useful and upsetting. In the end, after an attempted murder and a conflagration that consumes an eighty-year-old farmhouse, Birdie gathers the Tender family and their friends together for the denouement.

The differences in the setting add to the charm of the series. In *Murder by the Book*, Kate Delaney's world of books and publishing takes the spotlight. *The Makeover Murders* take place at Deepdene, an exclusive countryside spa near Windsor, New South Wales, and in *Stranglehold*, Birdie's family and old friends are involved in the death of a young woman.

All of the books in this series contain remarkable similarities, and yet these similarities in no way detract from the well-crafted plots by Jennifer Rowe. Verity Birdwood may be a shadowy character but victims, villains, and innocent bystanders in each story are colorful and well-developed personalities. Almost everyone is a potential suspect, and Birdie is merciless with their secrets as she explains the case and exposes the killer.

As written by author Rowe, Australia comes off as a rather familiar place. The settings are ordinary and there is little—aside from the occasional mention of a kangaroo or koala—in the way of colloquial speech to give the location away. We would like more of the flavor of that Down Under continent as well as more of Miss Birdwood's exploits.

MAGGIE MACGOWEN
1989–1997   6 books
Wendy (Nelson) Hornsby

Maggie MacGowen is an independent investigative filmmaker; her full legal name is Margot Eugenie Duchamps MacGowen. Her mother still calls her Margot and, if she had any living siblings, they would probably still call her Maggot. This is an enormously competent character in all the roles she plays. Though each of the six books in the series uses Maggie's professional duties as the vehicle for the action of the story, it is her personal life and connections that are at the core of each tale set in southern California.

In *Telling Lies*, Maggie's older sister and brother are pivotal figures in the mystery. To solve the crime, it is necessary for Maggie to review events that occurred twenty-two years earlier and to relate those events to actions and reactions of the present. In this first book, Maggie meets Mike Flint, a homicide detective with the Los Angeles Police Department (LAPD). The physical chemistry between the two of them is intense; the differences in their upbringing, politics, and outlook are equally so. The tensions of the burgeoning relationship between Maggie and Mike are made more complex by the addition of the adolescent offspring of each of them and their former spouses, parents, friends, and colleagues. Maggie brings a particular clarity of vision to the entanglements of her personal life and extends that clarity to the focus of her work.

As a filmmaker, she has to know what lens to use in each scene for maximum effect. As a result, Maggie is used to shifting back and forth from the macro view to the micro before she frames her shot. People are important to Maggie—in the abstract as well as in the specific—and she utilizes her frame-shifting technique in her efforts to know her object. In *Midnight Baby*, Maggie and her cameraman Guido meet a young hooker who may be a potential subject for a piece on child-raising experiences. Pisces is about the same age as Maggie's daughter, Casey, and for that reason arouses Maggie's maternal instincts. The child exhibits a canny street sense, and Maggie respects Pisces's survival instincts to the point that Maggie is unwilling to interfere—uninvited. Unfortunately, street smarts are not enough to prevent murder, and Maggie and Mike are thrown together to untangle a twisted skein of events and passions.

Maggie is a savvy professional who is willing to take carefully calculated risks in pursuit of a story. Her work speaks for itself, and her credentials are well earned. She has a sharp business sense too, and markets her products competently. Maggie is also willing to take risks in her personal life. Successful as a single mother, she has raised her daughter to face life with skill and capability. She is even willing to make a leap of faith in her relationship with Mike Flint. We'll say no more and invite readers to discover Maggie's virtues for themselves.

ALICE NESTLETON
1990–1997   14 books
Lydia Adamson (real name unknown)

Almost anyone who has ever had a house pet is familiar with the phenomenon of the phantom cat, dog. . . . Out of the corner of one's eye, this creature is glimpsed sometimes scurrying, at other times just rounding a corner or sitting just beyond the periphery of vision. Most of us are surprised when we appear to encounter this small, harmless beast and, at the same time, chagrined to be caught yet again by this animal shade. In spite of our disquietude, we take this creature's presence for granted.

As an actress, Alice Nestleton is fully conversant with the world of illusion. For her, there is a constant blurring of the boundaries between reality and illusion, and within this gray area the solution to crime arises. Many boundaries are blurred in this series. For example, we never see Alice actually tread the boards. Her acting reputation often precedes her, and many people recognize her even if they can't quite remember the play in which she appeared.

She also knows cats—those present in all of their feline glory as well as those who make only a portion of themselves manifest at odd times. Alice derives her steadiest income from her work as a cat sitter, and we do see her in this role in many of the books in the series. Her own two cats, Bushy and Pancho, are among the recurring cast. Bushy is a Maine Coon cat—large, solid, and earthbound. Pancho is a fey soul perpetually fleeing his unseen enemies—hardly ever at rest. Cats, in one form or another, are central to the plot of each story and are often integral indicators to the resolution of murder. Unfortunately, illusion too easily becomes a form of reality for Alice, and she usually takes her first active detective steps in the wrong direction, thus damaging her credibility with the substantial forces of law and order.

Tony Basillio is Alice's occasional lover and equally occasional partner in detection. In *A Cat in the Manger*, the first book in the series, Tony is the owner of the Mother Courage copier chain with shops scattered around Manhattan and the other boroughs. He is married and the father of several children. After being out of touch for several years, Alice contacts him for help in solving a murder. Eventually, Tony sells the chain of copy shops, leaves his wife and children with most of the proceeds, and returns to his first loves— stage design and Alice. She relies not only on Tony's knowledge but also on his leg work and finely tuned sense of anxiety.

This is an enigmatic series. We have not given much concrete information on character, plot, or progression, because what is there can only be caught out of the corner of one's eye. The author is equally enigmatic. Rumor has it that Lydia Adamson is the pseudonym for a well-known male author but we have never discovered his real name. Obviously, whoever is writing this series wishes to remain pseudonymous.

CHARLOTTE GRAHAM
1990–1997   8 books
Stefanie Matteson

Four-time Oscar winner Charlotte Graham is a famous fixture on both the screen and the stage. As the series opens, the sixty-something actress is still active in her profession and has become noted for her sleuthing talents as well. Her first case happened before this series begins and was documented by journalist Tom Plummer in *Murder at the Morosco*—a book only fictional mystery fans may enjoy. The novel does, however, give Miss Graham some credence in the domain of detection.

Charlotte Graham is gifted with privilege on many levels. Her celebrity is based not only on her still-apparent beauty but also on a solid talent and a life lived above censure. Her privileged status provides entree and acceptance to many diverse situations and gives her cachet with all manner of folk. Each book in which Miss Graham appears takes place in a different locale and all involve murder. In every case, she is asked to aid in an investigation by a person in authority, and it is then that readers must make their greatest suspension of disbelief. And that is just fine for a series of this type; after all, we're not talking about a police procedural here.

If pressed for a descriptive phrase for this series, we'd have to call it an action cozy. No matter the locale, the murder occurs within a relatively small group of people, and suspects are limited to that group. Miss Graham detects primarily through conversational inquiry, though she is not averse to scrambling over wave-washed rocks or hiking to and around a dinosaur-fossil ground. In this regard, Charlotte Graham more closely resembles Mrs. Pollifax than Miss Marple.

Stefanie Matteson informs as well as entertains. In *Murder at Teatime*, herbs and their lore are at the center of the story. Newport, Rhode Island, is featured in *Murder on the Cliff*, along with some Japanese history and the true story behind the characters in Puccini's *Madame Butterfly*. *Murder on the Silk Road* takes readers to a remote region of China that is both an ancient center of Buddhist worship and a fertile ground for paleontologists. New Jersey back roads and the history and accoutrements of American diners are explored in *Murder at the Falls*, and *Murder on High* looks at aspects of Henry David Thoreau and the transcendental movement in America. The books in this series are good, light reading. We look for a long and happy career path for Miss Graham the actress and Charlotte the sleuth.

WILLIAM HECKLEPECK
1992–1993   2 books
Molly McKitterick

This new series uses the nightly news, a form familiar to the entire American television audience. News viewers regularly invite their favorite anchorperson into their homes and rely on that individual to keep them abreast of events of the day. The successful news anchor commands a great deal of loyalty. News anchors are performers, yet their performance goes beyond mere believability. William Hecklepeck is the number-one anchorman in St. Louis, and his viewers love him. Hecklepeck's mobile and expressive face reflects his opinion and feelings on whatever subject he is presenting, which his loyal audience takes as a mark of respect for their sensibilities and intelligence.

Much like any business, television operates on its bottom line; high ratings translate into high revenues for station owners. In news programming, high ratings are directly related to sensational stories. As the series opens, Hecklepeck has been number-one anchor for more than six years, and it does not look as though his title is threatened. He presents the news as it is written, yet with each facial nuance makes his own editorial comment and leads his viewers to their own conclusion on his interpretation of the story. In spite of his highly paid position as figurehead and icon, Hecklepeck is a journalist. He understands what sells news programs to advertisers; unfortunately for his personal values, he respects *hard* news.

In *The Medium Is Murder*, the station's "Cautious Consumer" Laurel Michaels is murdered just before the final installment of her series "Mistresses: Mystique or Misery?" The women Michaels had interviewed for the series are connected to powerful men in St. Louis business, politics, and society. In Hecklepeck's opinion, Laurel is a nuisance and people's sex lives are really no one's business and certainly unrelated to the issue of consumerism. Laurel's murder doesn't change Hecklepeck's view of her, but it makes him wonder just what she uncovered to cause her death; it induces him to find her killer.

In *Murder in a Mayonnaise Jar*, the deaths of several young boys sniffing toluene, known on the street as "tulio," come to the attention of the KYYY news director. The director wants Hecklepeck to investigate the story but the anchorman declines.The assignment is given to rookie reporter Jennifer Burgess, whom "Heck" offers to advise. The story takes several sinister turns, and murder becomes the paramount issue. Hecklepeck is drawn into the investigation.

Even though the stories are written with a light hand and many of the characters—including Heck himself—take their comic turns, the issues addressed are important ones. Readers will have to discover the depth of the issues for themselves because discussing the twists of the plots would give away much of the surprise these tales hold. Author Molly McKitterick has capitalized on the news viewer/ anchor relationship. This engagement is often one of emotion. Those of us who watch the news with a degree of cynicism know full well that while one may relate to a person giving us information, one cannot always trust the information given. William Hecklepeck plays true to that conflict. Readers will enjoy Heck's brand of honesty.

ANNIE MCGROGAN
1992–1994   2 books
Gillian B. Farrell

In each of the two books in this new series, Annie McGrogan makes her first appearance in her guise of actor. In *Alibi for an Actress*, she reads an article about Duke DeNobili, an ex-cop turned private investigator. The description of what the Duke does makes it seem the perfect alternative career for an actor at rest . . . and stony broke. Annie calls to offer her services. Three days later, she's on a job with her new partner, Sonny Gandolfo.

For all but a select few, acting is not the most secure form of employment, and almost everyone who treads the boards in any sense of the term also has a side job. In choosing to work as an investigator, Annie is in a position to put her acting talents to work and to keep them polished while she is resting. At the same time, she discovers that an investigator has access to a world of information and character types few others have. Consciously and unconsciously, she stores this data to draw on for future roles. At fifteen bucks an hour, private investigator Annie McGrogan has become a well-paid actor.

The crimes in each book involve both of Annie's worlds. In the first story, the husband of a well-known daytime soap-opera actress is murdered. Annie and Sonny have been hired to protect this actress and end up providing her with a foolproof alibi. In the second book, *Murder and a Muse*, Annie lands a "significant part" in a "major project" with a "name director." The director is murdered in Annie's hotel room, and she becomes the prime suspect. In each case, all of Annie's skills and talents are called upon and, in the process, a fascinating story unfolds.

Like Annie, author Gillian B. Farrell has experience in both of these spheres. She has created a pragmatic character who understands the value of illusion. Farrell has also gifted Annie with an innate curiosity and a finely tuned sense of responsibility. On the surface, these characteristics may seem contradictory; however, from time to time one encounters a character who can balance a seeming paradox. Farrell has created one.

Mystery writers who choose performers as their sleuths are biting off a large chunk. Almost any author will tell you that at some point her character often begins to direct the plot. When an author has chosen a performer, that author must contend with her own fictional creation's willfulness as well as the willfulness of her fictional creation's fictional creations. We can envision a perpetual tug-of-war between the writers and their creations' creations unto the nth generation. It's a wonder that books featuring this type of character ever get written, and we are glad they do.

SOME OTHER PERFORMING SLEUTHS

Victoria Bowering	Nina McFall
Nell Bray	Emma Shaw
Enrico Caruso	Margo Simon
Molly DeWitt	Cordelia Thorne
Kimmey Kruse	Amy Tupper

CURE IT OR KILL IT:
Medicine and Science

Medicine and science are natural adjuncts to the detection of crime. Physicians and scientists are at home with the time-consuming, tedious routines required by investigation as they are often detectives in their own right, tracing the course of a disease and tracking down a specific causative agent. Law enforcement agencies have, in recent years, come to rely on science and the medical arts for assistance with physical evidence, and the cooperation between these fields enhances the operation of both. These professionals may be called upon to give expert testimony on behalf of both victim and suspected perpetrator and thus, by exposure, become familiar with police and legal procedure.

One of the earliest physicians to aid and abet the forces of law and order made her first appearance in 1929. Dame Beatrice Adela Lestrange Bradley, created by Gladys Mitchell, is featured in sixty-eight books (1929–1984). A well-established practicing psychiatrist as the series opens, Mrs. Bradley is a woman possessed of a fierce intellect and a highly developed—if sometimes unconventional—sense of justice. Many disparate elements combine to make her an engaging character, not the least of which is her having studied medicine and made her mark around the turn of the century, a time when women did not find it easy to pursue any academic course.

One of the earliest fictional representatives of the distaff side to medicine—members of the nursing profession be they male or female—was Mary Roberts Rinehart's Nurse Hilda Adams. Dealing directly with patients, yet seldom receiving the glory given to physicians as a matter of course, nurses are often treated no better than servants—almost invisible even to those most dependent upon their care. Frequently, however, such invisibility works to their advantage, as when they are involved in investigating crime.

The sobriquet "Miss Pinkerton" was bestowed upon Nurse Hilda Adams by the police officer who calls her in to assist him in some of his cases. Rinehart is the founder of the "had-I-but-known" school of writing, and Nurse Adams is not immune to her share of perils as she plies her trade in four books (1932–1950).

Two other psychiatrists joined the ranks of fictional medical experts in the late '30s and early '40s: Dr. Basil Willing (1938–1980) and Dr. Hillis Owen (1942–1948) made their appearances around the time that the study of the mind was becoming acceptable to the general public. Both of these gentlemen use their specialized knowledge to uncover criminal motivations and acts. Officials in charge of the proceedings are surprised by the accuracy of the doctors' insights. Helen McCloy's creation Basil Willing appears in thirteen books and makes a number of forays into the realm of the paranormal. Like Dame Beatrice—and unlike many other psychiatrists—Dr. Willing accepts the inevitable fact that there are some things medical science cannot explain. Anna Mary Wells's Hillis Owen operates along more conventional lines in his three-book series. Both of these characters are well worth reading, for the stories in which they appear speak of real, timeless issues in settings that themselves are clearly dated.

Retirement doesn't sit well with Dr. Grace Severance (1968–1978). Her career as a pathologist has come to an end, but her energy, curiosity, and interest run as high as ever. In fact, the boredom of a life with no fixed schedule and the feeling of being at the mercy of a well-meaning relative may serve to sharpen this lady's keen senses. We do not see her in her laboratory nor are we given much in the way of gruesome forensic detail from her past profession. Rather, this four-book series focuses on an older woman with an unusual history who uses her wits and training toward the solution of crime. Margaret Scherf's Dr. Severance is a well-drawn forerunner to the current crop of female pathologists.

Gordon Christy is a fictional veterinarian invented by Barbara Moore. Sadly, as Dr. Christy and his Doberman Gala are charming characters, there are only two books in this series (1983–1986). Making a diagnosis on patients who cannot describe their symptoms or tell the doctor just what hurts is excellent training for a detective. Christy, reluctantly at first, applies diagnostic methods to the crime of murder and works out plausible solutions to the two crimes in which he becomes involved. We wish for more.

Not only those dedicated to the practice of medicine are intimate with the finer points of illness and disease. Those at the mercy of some form of pathology can be fully conversant with the etiology of their particular malady. Nowadays patients are encouraged by some medical experts to take an active role in managing their own chronic ailments. When such an ailment colors individuals' perceptions and management is critical to their mental well-being they, in effect, become experts in their own field. In this chapter, we have elected to include one such character. Read on. . . .

CHARLIE MEIKLEJOHN & CONSTANCE LEIDL
1985–1995   7 books
Kate (Gertrude) Wilhelm (Knight)

Constance Leidl and Charlie Meiklejohn made their first appearance in print in a short story entitled "The Gorgon Field" in *Isaac Asimov's Science Fiction Magazine*, August 1985. (The story was reprinted in a 1989 collection by Wilhelm, *Children of the Wind*.) Two years later, these two characters were featured in a full-length novel, *The Hamlet Trap*. Currently, there are seven books in the series. Despite the science fiction venue of their debut, Constance and Charlie *are* detectives. We describe this series as a crossover, but not a simple one combining with only one other category. We'll leave it to the reader to discover just which other categories these books may belong to. For now, we'll concentrate on Constance and Charlie and their involvement in solving the crime of murder.

Constance holds a Ph.D. in psychology. Charlie is a former fireman—later arson specialist—and homicide detective. He has retired from the forces, quite literally suffering burnout. Constance has retired from active practice and full-time teaching, yet continues to hold workshops and write articles and books on her subject. They live with cats on what they describe as a miniature farm in upstate New York and enjoy traveling. They only take on cases that seem worth disturbing the pleasant state of inertia they have drifted into and usually get involved through a personal connection.

Constance and Charlie have (to our way of thinking) an enviable union. Both are experts in their particular field, and each can and does operate independently of the other; they are self-defined individuals. Their conjugation, however, creates another definition, and the sum is greater than its parts. Married for more than twenty-five years, this couple is effortlessly sensitive to one another's every nuance. Their nonverbal communication is reliable and articulate, and their trust in one another is unquestioned. Each is capable of setting the other on edge, yet there is enormous latitude—on both sides—for incorporating this edginess into their totality.

Murder is central to each of the novels in which Constance and Charlie appear. Their investigations involve all the usual: procedure, interviews, and consultations. The conclusions they draw are well supported by all the facts given throughout each story. The author plays fair with the readers in providing all the necessary clues to the solution and yet . . . Constance and Charlie and the relationship they share bring an added element to the summation.

Kate Wilhelm is perhaps best known as a science fiction author. Her awards in that genre (to date) include three Nebulas, one Hugo, and a Jupiter. With the Meiklejohn/Leidl series, Wilhelm has crafted stories in which two very likable and believable characters operate within the prescribed realm of crime and mystery fiction. Remaining true to what may be described as her calling, Wilhelm takes these two beyond the prescription and into new, less explored realms. We recommend this series highly and do not want to give away any surprises other readers may encounter and enjoy.

KIERNAN O'SHAUGHNESSEY
1989–1994   3 books
Susan Dunlap

Strictly speaking, this character belongs in the "Private Eye" chapter, as that is her current profession. However, because Dr. Kiernan O'Shaughnessey is a former pathologist and refers to herself as a medical detective, we have put her in this category. As the series opens, we meet a competent, capable woman in her mid-thirties asking questions for a living. She now has what she describes as a decadent life-style in one side of a La Jolla, California, beachfront duplex. Her houseman, Brad Tchernak, a former offensive lineman for the National Football League, lives in the other half. Ezra, a Labrador/Irish Wolfhound, divides his time between them.

Kiernan is a complex character. A personal obsession initially drew her to medical school and the specialized field of pathology. Practice in her field has stripped Kiernan of the illusion that all things can be explained by careful scientific study. As a result of her disillusionment, she accepts dismissal from her job and goes on a journey to learn to identify the right questions to ask. On her return, the foundation of her original obsession is shaken and Kiernan's process of self-discovery edges further toward completion.

O'Shaughnessey is able to pick and choose her cases, and her fee is high. In the first book, *Pious Deception*, her prejudices incline her to turn down a job for the Roman Catholic Church. Kiernan's good friend and mentor, Sam Chase, piques her curiosity and prevails upon her to take it on. With a tight time limit and a cast of highly uncooperative characters, Kiernan sets out to earn her fee. In the heat of the desert near Phoenix she uncovers many dark secrets, both personal and institutional.

Rogue Wave involves Kiernan in the worlds of art, commercial fishing, environmental politics, and death. She begins by confronting a former lover, Dr. Marc Rosten, the acting coroner of the city and county of San Francisco, who denies her access to a body associated with her investigation. Old connections and unevened scores come to light as she delves into the character of the woman she has been hired to find.

As we've said, Kiernan is a complex character. Though she may have overcome her earliest obsessions, she remains an idealist and wants all the loose ends tied up, conclusions drawn, and resolution made. Intimate relationships are not her strong point; everyone is kept at a distance. This is a character with great potential. Author Susan Dunlap has given Kiernan both a full history and a limitless future.

One of Dunlap's other series characters, Jill Smith, is a Berkeley, California, homicide detective. While solid background knowledge is required to make both of these characters and their stories believable, Dunlap takes Jill and Kiernan several steps further by deftly weaving the personal side of these characters' lives into their professional responsibilities. This is what puts life into these series. Another of Dunlap's characters is Vejay Haskell, a Pacific Gas and Electric meter reader for communities along California's Russian River.

EDWINA CRUSOE, R.N.
1990–1995   6 books
Mary Kittredge

In *Fatal Diagnosis*, the first book in the series, Edwina Crusoe is nursing supervisor for the evening shift at Chelsea Memorial Hospital in Hartford, Connecticut. A shocking double murder is committed in one of the laboratories. One of the victims, a seventeen-year-old nursing volunteer, was a friend of Edwina; the other victim was the chief technician in the immunology lab. The reason for the murders is immediately apparent. All the material relative to a controversial custody case is stolen from the lab, the child in question disappears, and the case is stalled. The story is filled with engaging medical information, yet readers do not feel overwhelmed by the detail author Kittredge presents. Homicide detective Martin McIntyre finds Nurse Crusoe as compelling as the information she gives him. They meet in the first book, and their relationship progresses with the series.

Edwina's family background has hardly prepared her for her chosen career. The only daughter of a wealthy industrialist-turned-diplomat and a highly successful romance novelist, Edwina elected to become a nurse because she needed an outlet for her intelligence and wanted to be useful somehow. She is very good at what she does and is highly respected by colleagues, physicians, and staff members at Chelsea Memorial. At the end of the first book, however, Edwina decides to leave the practice of nursing and start her own consulting venture—investigating medical inequity and fraud. In this capacity, her intelligence and curiosity are well exercised, and crimes that might have gone undisclosed or unsolved are brought to resolution.

Edwina's mother figures in most of the stories. Harriet Crusoe is an outspoken soul, and her instincts and insights are direct and illuminating. She may not hand Edwina the solution, but she does suggest alternate views of a situation for her daughter to ponder. Other characters recur throughout the books. Det. Talbot is McIntyre's partner and close friend; Mr. Watkins is Harriet's majordomo; and Maxie is Edwina's spoiled cat. All play their roles well.

Edwina is a likable primary character in a well-written and informative series. Author Mary Kittredge, a respiratory therapist, has done her medical homework for these books. Beyond that, she has crafted stories that are well layered with character, medical lore, and plot. Each tale has twists at the end, and we are always surprised.

DR. KAY SCARPETTA
1990–1997   8 books
Patricia D(aniels) Cornwell

This riveting series features Dr. Kay Scarpetta, the chief medical examiner (CME) operating out of Richmond, Virginia. She is a highly trained forensic pathologist, as well as a lawyer. By law, Scarpetta as CME has full investigative powers with regard to cause and manner of death. About the only thing she can't do is make an arrest. Consequently, her investigation begins at the scene of any suspicious death, is carried on in the autopsy suite and the forensic laboratory, and often ends in the courtroom.

All of the novels featuring this intriguing character are multidimensional and overflowing with detail. She herself is central to each story as is her profession and its myriad requirements. One phone call from Dr. Scarpetta's office is generally enough to crack loose any information or specialist she might need in pursuing facts in a case she is investigating. Her credentials are impeccable, and the demands on her office—and her person—run high. It is fair to say that this character is dedicated to her job, and the conflict between her dedication and her personal needs creates a measure of the tension present in all of the books.

Like Susan Dunlap's character Kiernan O'Shaughnessey, Scarpetta is complex. There are elements of Kay's personal life that remain unaddressed, unexplored, and consequently unresolved. Occasionally, one of these elements arises in the course of a professional investigation and adds to her involvement with the case. Like O'Shaughnessey, Scarpetta maintains a distance between herself and others, although at times she does let people get close enough to surmount her defenses. The difference between these two characters lies in the way in which their obsessions have directed their lives. O'Shaughnessey was compelled by hers to follow a particular path (when the answers didn't come up the way she expected them to, she abandoned her profession and became a somewhat loose cannon). Scarpetta, on the other hand, has continued to be driven by her obsessions and has extended what began as a personal quest to encompass a much larger arena.

Scarpetta is fortunate to have two formidable allies: homicide Det. Lt. Pete Marino and niece Lucy. Marino is a rough diamond, responsible for the police presence in all of the inquiries requiring Scarpetta's expertise. Despite their apparent differences, a strong and abiding trust exists between them and each is willing to go the distance for the other. Lucy is a vital and perhaps only connection between Kay and her family. Lucy's precocity on the computer serves the doctor well in at least two of the novels. Both Pete and Lucy grow and develop along with Kay as the series progresses. Benton Wesley, an FBI agent, sometimes works in close concert with Scarpetta and Marino; at other times, the heavy FBI veil comes down between them, and professional as well as personal issues become clouded. Other characters make appearances in more than one book, but either their position or their usefulness seems to be easily exhausted.

In the span of seven years, Patricia D. Cornwell has reached the lofty heights of fame. With this series she provides readers with not only a compelling set of characters and crimes but also an inundation of state-of-the-art forensic detail. The use of lasers in latent fingerprint identification, the science of fiber analysis, DNA testing and identification, and sophisticated blood testing and typing are all used appropriately by Scarpetta and are well documented by author Cornwell.

Although one of the fascinations of the series is the attention to minutiae Cornwell brings to her writing, we did not find these books easy to read. Part of the difficulty was the graphic detail of death and torture that Cornwell presents, which is never easy for us to endure; however, none of these descriptions is gratuitous. Another part of our fascination had to do with the technical aspects of the detection Scarpetta does; yet, these novels mirror the repetition of procedure, the intersection of investigative technique, and the tedium of the labyrinthine inroad into the heart of crime. We will continue reading. . . .

CLAIRE SHARPLES
1991–1995   3 books
Rebecca Rothenberg

Although this character's patients are never human, her scientific investigations are vital in saving lives and influencing many *Homo sapiens* on a nutritional level. Claire Sharples is a microbiologist specializing in mycology—the study of molds and fungi. In *The Bulrush Murders*, Claire has had it with the academic life at Massachusetts Institute of Technology in Boston. Her boss there, Dr. Mulcahey, is an egotistical tyrant and her former lover, Phil, a cold and calculating golden boy of science. She answers an ad for a position in the San Joaquin Valley in California—the heart of the state's citrus and stone fruit industry—and, when she is offered the job, she moves three thousand miles away from heartbreak and professional stagnation.

Claire's first task is to investigate *Monolinea fructiola*, commonly known as brown smut—a fungus that ruins crops and, by extension, the small farmer. She is on the scene when the son of the family whose crops are infected with the disease is found drowned, and she notices that some of the weed tangled in his motorcycle does not belong to the site of his death. Her curiosity is piqued, and together with Sam Cooper, her coworker at the Citrus Grove Experimental Field Station, she investigates not only Tony Rodriguez's mysterious death but also events leading up to the ruin of the Rodriguez family fortunes. Using sound scientific logic and at the same time making uncharacteristically wild intuitive leaps, Claire discovers the motivation behind the crime and the identity of the murderer. She returns to Boston to face some unresolved feelings including homesickness. However, the attractions of California, her own laboratory, and Sam Cooper draw Claire back to Citrus Grove and her job with the University of California.

Claire finds a body floating in an irrigation canal and hauls it to shore in *The Dandelion Murders*. After she determines that the victim is beyond resuscitation, she calls Police Chief Tom Martelli, who begins an official investigation into the death of a man who turns out to have been a reporter for the *Los Angeles Free Press*. Jonathan Levine is the area's third drowning case in three months and his death raises questions about the two previous ones—both migrant workers. The illegal use of highly toxic pesticides, undocumented workers, a young widow, an unscrupulous labor contractor, and a grower greedy for profits all enter the story. Once again, Claire uses her scientific savvy and her new found intuition to resolve the untimely deaths.

The story that parallels the mystery is that of Claire and Sam's relationship. Each is a competent scientist and both are comfortable in the world of cold, scientific truth. Both of these characters are riddled with insecurities and indecision, and neither is at ease with the often messy aspects of personal interaction; their story is fraught with all manner of complication. Despite this, the two fall in love in the first book and are dazzled by the very act. In the second book, Sam's children come to spend a month with the pair, and Claire is faced with the prospect of stepmotherhood. Linda, an old flame of Sam's, enters the picture and throws both Sam and Claire for a loop. In the end, Claire stays on in California but moves out of Sam's house. As in the beginning, she is living on her own, trying to figure out just what's going on.

To many minds, science is golden and the scientist has become a priest of the highest calling. Claire Sharples is far more down-to-earth than many of those whose skills have been honed against the abrasive wheel of academic policy. Rebecca Rothenberg has created a passionate character whose scientific mind compels her, yet allows circumstances to drive both her personal and professional decisions. Claire Sharples's life may lack balance, but she is out there on the edge using her basic training in inquiry to carry her through both the solution of murder and the solution of things relational.

BARBARA "BO" BRADLEY
1993–1997   5 books
Abigail Padgett

The primary character in this new series is a medical expert in the narrowest sense. Bo Bradley suffers from manic depression, has been institutionalized, and by current medical standards should be on a maintenance dose of lithium for the rest of her life. Instead, Bo has learned to manage her disease by moderating her diet, increasing her exercise, and reducing her stress level. While lithium may slow Bo's speedy manic state, it causes her to gain weight and, worse, dulls her perceptions. Those perceptions—always higher and sharper than those of most "normal" people—are for Bo both the gift and the curse of her disease. Even when she is in control of her equilibrium, her awareness of subtleties in human behavior is acute and contributes to her success as a child abuse investigator for San Diego County's Juvenile Court.

The first two books in which Bo appears are similar in plot and character. In *Child of Silence*, a four-year-old Caucasian boy is found abandoned in a derelict building on an Indian reservation. Bo is given his case file and goes to visit the child in the hospital. Johnny

Doe is classified as retarded, but when Bo meets him she realizes that he is deaf and far from mentally deficient. Annie Garcia, the Paiute woman who found the boy and notified the authorities, also plays a pivotal role in the denouement of the story. Bo's malady serves her and Weppo (as the boy calls himself) well as the story draws to its taut conclusion.

An Iroquois woman, Dr. Eva Blindhawk Broussard, is featured in *Strawgirl*. Bo is charged with finding a child supposedly kidnapped by the alleged murderer of the child's sister. As in the first story, Bo takes enormous personal and professional risks on behalf of her small charges. The bureaucratic process does not always serve the best interests of those it is charged with protecting. Bo's awareness of this fact, her innate compassion, and the perceptions she brings to each case make her a worthy advocate for imperiled children.

Ancillary characters are well drawn. Dr. Andrew LaMarche, Estrella Benedict, Bo's dog, and the late Dr. Lois Bittner are Bo's close friends and allies. Madge Aldenhoven, Bo's supervisor and nemesis, represents most of what is wrong with social service departments. Details crucial to the plots are deftly woven into the narrative at a rate designed to give readers a sample of the way in which this character's mind functions in its most acute state. Bo's sensibilities toward her own condition, her family background, and the plight of far too many of today's children are strong points upon which to build a unique series. We look forward to more.

Abigail Padgett has been a court investigator and is currently an advocate for the mentally ill. She brings her own knowledge and experience to this series and presents it in a fashion that illustrates Bo's unusual perceptive state.

DR. DEIRDRE "DIDI" QUINN NIGHTINGALE
1994–1997   8 books
Lydia Adamson (real name unknown)

Hillsbrook, Duchess County, New York, is the home of veterinarian Dr. Nightingale. Educated at the University of Pennsylvania, Didi spent a postgraduate year in Madras, India, studying elephants under the highly respected expert on pachyderms, Dr. Mohandas Medawar. In Southeast Asia, under the auspices of the Fund for Animals, Didi did field research on elephants still used for work. Upon her return to the United States, she held a number of different positions, from staffing a variety of dog and cat clinics to mending broken-down racehorses. The death of her mother brought Didi home to the house she grew up in and a veterinary practice among the dairy farms of upstate New York.

Other regular characters are introduced in the first book in the series, *Dr. Nightingale Comes Home.* Along with the house, Didi has inherited a staff—of sorts: Mrs. Tunney, cook/housekeeper; Trent Tucker, general handyman; Abigail, a frail, rather enigmatic creature who has a way with pigs; and seventy-something Charlie Gravis, Didi's veterinarian assistant. None of the four receives a salary or has a formal job description. Just how they came to be a part of Didi's mother's household is a long and very complex series of stories and to change things would take much more effort on Didi's part than maintaining the status quo takes. Police officer Allie Voegler has had a crush on Didi ever since they were in high school and he felt she was patronizing and arrogant. Didi, on the other hand, was afraid of him in those early days because he rode a motorcycle and had a reputation as a wild one. As adults, their relationship is still prickly, professional, and, on rare occasions, personal.

Dr. Nightingale is pragmatic, down-to-earth, and competent in her profession. Her love of animals is not romanticized but rather expressed through her intuitive understanding of each beast's nature and her precise treatment of their ailments. While Didi loves animals without restriction, she is drawn to some species with a passionate attraction. In the second book, *Dr. Nightingale Rides the Elephant*, she becomes the on-site vet for a small circus passing through Duchess County simply because it offers her an opportunity to tend to elephants. The exotic setting of the circus doesn't deflect Didi from her responsibility toward the animals, however, and she gets to the bottom of bizarre behavior and solves three murders.

For all the earthy pragmatism of the main character, the stories in the series featuring Dr. Nightingale and her ménage are not straightforward whodunits. A great deal of what occurs in these stories is unwritten and below the surface. Murder is at the center; revealing the identity of the perpetrator is certainly a vital part of the action in each of the books, yet there is much more. Because *it* is unstated, it may be indefinable. *It* is information that depends upon the reader's own perceptions and may be different for each individual. The pseudonymous author Lydia Adamson also writes a series featuring Alice Nestleton, who is described in the chapter "Crime on Cue: Stage, Screen, and Television."

DR. GAIL MCCARTHY
1994–1997   3 books
Laura Crum

California's northern coastal range is the location for this series featuring equine specialist Gail McCarthy. Low yet jagged peaks and golden and rolling hills fringed with monumental redwoods, firs, and scrub oaks, all within view of the Pacific Ocean, provide a marvelous backdrop for this character's activities. Orphaned at the age of eighteen when her parents were killed in a car crash on the treacherous Highway 17, Gail struggled to put herself through college and graduate school at University of California at Davis to become a veterinarian. Santa Cruz is Gail's hometown and she is happy to be back doing what she knows and loves. The practice of veterinary medicine in a rural area is demanding. Animals rarely fall ill during conventional business hours, and it is difficult to bring an ailing horse into a clinic, so for much of Gail's working day she is on the road, between ranches.

In *Cutter*, Gail gets an emergency call from Casey Brooks, a Quarter Horse trainer. Half of his horses are colicky and two are already dead. When she arrives at Indian Gulch Ranch, Gail administers a sedative to one horse and performs a stomach tap to discover murky, greenish fluid—a sign that the animal's intestine has ruptured. There is no cure; only a quick, merciful death, and Gail puts the animal down with a lethal injection. The rest of the horses recover and Casey tells Gail that he is sure all of the animals were poisoned by a rival trainer. Casey is killed while riding. Det. Jeri Ward investigates and is ready to write off his death as an accident, but Gail, knowing the gentle nature of his horse, suspects foul play and tells the detective about the poisoned horses and Casey's accusations.

Gail discovers two murdered bodies in the course of an early morning call and is drawn into the coils of another investigation in *Hoofprints*. The murdered man, Ed Whitney, was the black-sheep scion of a Scotts Valley software entrepreneur; his wife, Cindy, was a beautiful woman with a secret past. Ed's family had written him off; Cindy's fundamentalist Christian parents considered her dead; and, the reason for their actual deaths is a mystery. Gail is lured to a deserted ranch hidden in the mountains by a bogus emergency call and is shot at. However, when she reports the incident to the sheriff's office, the detective who takes her statement appears to doubt her story. Jeri Ward takes Gail more seriously and subtly engages Gail's assistance in unmasking the Whitneys' killer.

Gail McCarthy is a hard-working veterinarian with solid training in her profession and a deep love for the animals she treats. Her close friends are all involved with horses in one way or another and add to the development of the series and the resolution of each story. Bret Boncantini and Gail grew up together. Bret works as a horseshoer and makes rapid progress with women. When he is between relationships, he stays over at Gail's house making minor contributions to the larder and doing the housework. Lonny Peterson, a semi-retired Sierra pack station owner, becomes romantically involved with Gail in the first book and their relationship continues to grow in the second. Kris Griffith has five well-tended acres, the antithesis of Gail's little log cabin in the woods, and she boards Gail's horse, Gunner, here. The doctor and her friends are instrumental in solving the cases, and Gail's knowledge of horses—their individual characters as much as their requirements—puts her in the way of information germane to each solution.

Laura Crum keeps Quarter Horses on her ranch in the Santa Cruz mountains and is a competitor in cutting and team-roping events. She points out that none of the bad guys in her books are derived from personal knowledge as everyone in her horsey world is a paragon. Although Crum takes some geographical liberties, as a fourth-generation Californian, she is very familiar with the territory she portrays and applies her literary license in a plausible fashion.

Death comes in many guises. In the realm of science and medicine, the perpetrator can often be described as a natural cause and may come in the form of a virus, bacteria, or systemic breakdown. Medical practitioners are also confronted with less natural causes of death such as head trauma, gunshot, knife wound, or drowning, to name a few. Some scientific investigators are content to unmask a killer organism. Others are not content until they have brought the human agent of death to light in the wider court of world justice.

SOME OTHER MEDICAL SLEUTHS

Megan Baldwin	Kate Manion
Kevin Blake	Dr. Tina May
Dr. Jack Caleb	Dr. Amy Prescott
Nurse Agnes Carmichael	Imogen Quy
Jason Frank	T. D. Renfro
Samantha Holt	C C Scott
Kate Kinsella	Dr. Maxene Sinclair
Amanda Knight	Dr. Samantha Turner

THE GAME'S AFOOT:
Sports and Games

By tradition, sports and many games have been dominated by men. Only in recent years have women begun—as players and as those assigned to cover games, teams, and prominent sports figures—to make headway against this male bastion. Women and their perspectives are making a powerful impact on the sports world. In the '50s and '60s, Wilma Rudolph made her mark in track and field events and has been admirably succeeded by Jackie Joyner Kersee and Kersee's sister-in-law, Florence Griffith Joyner. In tennis, Billie Jean King put her money where Bobby Riggs's mouth was by soundly trouncing him in a challenge game. Gabrielle Reece is making people pay attention to women's volleyball as much for the game as for the players' bounces. Summer Sanders has captured four Olympic medals in swimming, Bonnie Blair holds Olympic gold and countless records for speed skating, and Katarina Witt is an undisputed champion in women's figure skating. The list goes on and keeps growing.

It has taken a while for mystery fiction to catch up with reality in these endeavors. To the best of our knowledge, Miss Melinda Pink, a character created by Gwen Moffat (1973–1994) is the only early series protagonist who qualifies as a sports participant. Miss Pink is a mountaineer, and all of the sixteen books in which she appears feature climbing as a plot element. So far, only ten characters qualify for this "Sports and Games" chapter, and some of those are not players themselves but rather approach sports journalistically. While these three characters also fit other categories, special knowledge in their fields is necessary for the sports-related job each does.

When murder enters the playing field, the game is almost literally afoot for these characters. It may be simple curiosity, dedication to sport or job, or perhaps hatred of anything that unfairly tips the competitive balance bringing these following characters to detecting. Whatever the reason, these sports-minded sleuths provide their own expertise to crime and strive to level the field, once again, for all the players.

T. T. BALDWIN
1980–1983   3 books
Shannon OCork

Theresa Tracy Baldwin is always known as "T. T." and always has her camera ready for a possible Pulitzer. She got her press pass by mail order from a body-building magazine and won her position at the *New York Graphic* with photos of an illegal cock fight. In *Sports Freak*, T. T.—playing second-string photographer to misogynistic Floyd Beesom and *Graphic* senior sports writer Gilbert Ott, a.k.a. "Gilly Fats"—has been sent to cover the first game between two new National Football League franchises. The game is being played at the High Mountain Climbers' Sports Complex, and T. T. is in the perfect spot to catch the action. When Lovable Lou LaMont is butted in the Adam's apple by Billy "The Badman" O'Leary, T. T. keeps snapping as Lou is carried off the field and follows him, the doctor, and the coach to the locker room, where Lou is soon declared dead. One of the crew of The Scenic View, the team's cheerleading squad, is murdered, Floyd Beesom is poisoned with a hot dog, and T. T. is dragged from underneath a Cadillac. And *then* the plot thickens until finally resolved by T. T.

The opening scene in *End of the Line* takes place on the *Neptune Jones*, a fifty-foot sportfishing boat entered in the Scrimshaw Township's annual shark-fishing contest. T. T. and Floyd have been sent to Scrimshaw—ostensibly to cover the event for the *Graphic*, but actually at the behest of their editor Barkley to investigate a missing jewel merchant and an equally missing antique necklace. T. T. is shooting fast as the first shark is hooked by boat owner Gordie Kittridge. In the tumult of setting the hook, Jeremy Yunker, an insurance agent, falls overboard into the melee of sharks. He is rescued, relatively unscathed, but dies on the deck as the boat heads back to shore. The plot in this story is even thicker than the one in the first book. Once again, T. T., doing her job, unsnarls things in a final scene even more compelling than the opener's.

Hell Bent for Heaven—with a plot even thicker than those of its predecessors—takes place at a rodeo held in Madison Square Garden. The events and the cast of this story are highly colorful, and the motive for the several deaths stretches the readers' imaginations *almost* past the point of belief, yet T. T., operating covertly for Barkley and without Floyd this time, captures the action on film and solves the numerous crimes.

Shannon OCork wrote these three novels between 1980 and 1983, and T. T. Baldwin hasn't been heard from since, which is a shame as both the character and the stories in which she appears are unusual and complex. T. T. herself is a feisty and independent creature in a highly competitive, male-dominated field; hers is a demanding profession that requires not only a good eye but an instinct for being in precisely the right place at exactly the right time. Near misses don't count at all and T. T. rarely misses. The tales themselves are best described as Byzantine yet hold together well enough to be believable. OCork not only tells a ripping good yarn, she pulls it off in around two hundred action-packed pages. We would like more of this character and the odd milieus in which she operates. It is understandable, however, that OCork may need quite a bit of time to recover from the efforts of producing the first three.

KATE HENRY
1989–1995   4 books
Alison Gordon

Baseball is America's national sport and a game full of stars, heroes, winners, and losers. Love of this sport has migrated across seas and borders, and this series, featuring Canadian sportswriter Kate Henry, centers on her home team, the Toronto Titans. Kate loves baseball and sometimes finds it hard to believe that she is actually being paid—by the *Toronto Planet*—to follow the Titans and write about her favorite game. In the five years Kate has been a sportswriter, she has proven herself with accurate and fair reporting and has won respect—some honest, some grudging—from colleagues, players, and her readers.

Sally Parkes and her young son, T. C., live on the first floor of Kate's house. Kate shares the second and third floors with her twenty-pound tomcat, Elwy. It is a nice arrangement; Kate watches T. C. when Sally has to stay late at the photo gallery where she works, and T. C. feeds Elwy when Kate is on the road with the Titans.

As *The Dead Pull Hitter* opens, the Titans are celebrating a winning season and facing their first shot at the World Series. The celebration is dampened when one of the players, Sultan Sanchez, is found in his apartment, killed with his own bat in an apparent robbery attempt. When a second player is killed in the team shower room, the two deaths are linked, and Staff Sgt. Andy Munro of the Toronto Homicide Department is called in to investigate the cases. Kate's relationship with the players enables her to elicit information for which the police would have to dig long and hard. Andy, finding himself attracted to Kate, fears for her safety and, as the story reaches its denouement, is fully justified in that fear.

In *Safe at Home* Kate and Andy have become lovers. They don't live together but each has a key to the other's house and their relationship is growing in closeness. In this story, Andy is tracking a serial killer who has murdered three young boys. When Sally's son, T. C., is threatened by the killer, Kate and player Joe "Preacher" Kelsey come to his rescue. Once again, Andy is piqued by Kate's apparent disregard for her own safety.

In *Night Game*, Kate has traveled with the Titans to their spring training in Sunland, Florida. She and a fellow writer find a beautiful young woman reporter shot dead on the beach. One of the Titan rookies is charged with her death, and Kate is asked by his teammates to prove his innocence. Staff Sgt. Munro realizes that whether he likes it or not, Kate is going to do what she can to unmask the real killer. He also realizes that she is fully capable of doing so, and after some heartfelt discussion, offers his long-distance assistance.

Andy, Sally, and T. C. appear in all of the books as do many of the Titans. Each story is filled with insider information on players, their idiosyncrasies, and their stats. Readers see Kate at work in the press box, on the field, and in the locker room. The game itself is treated with loving respect, and baseball fans will feel as much at home with this series as mystery fans will. Author Alison Gordon writes what she knows; she was the first woman writer on the American League beat when she covered the Toronto Blue Jays for the *Toronto Star*.

LEE OFSTED
1989–1995   2 books
Charlotte Elkins and Aaron Elkins

Professional golf is at the heart of this series featuring young, attractive first-year pro Lee Ofsted. *A Wicked Slice* takes place at the gorgeous Carmel Point course on California's Monterey Peninsula, where the first Pacific-Western Women's Pro-Am tournament is being held. Lee is playing with three women amateurs who have paid hefty sums for the privilege of eighteen holes with a professional. Unfortunately, Lee is literally off her stroke as she slices a surprising number of shots. After the game, she retreats to the practice green, where she continues to slice with her three wood. Giving up for the day, she is wading in the water hazard, retrieving her lost balls, when she steps on the dead body of a fellow pro, Kate O'Brian.

Lt. Graham Sheldon of the Carmel Police Department arrives on the scene. A seven-year veteran of Oakland's finest, Sheldon has removed himself to the sleepy little village suffering the aftermath of severe burnout. Prepared to encounter the rich and spoiled country club set, Sheldon is pleasantly surprised to meet Lee, who lists her home course as the North Portland Municipal Golf Course and whose first exposure to golf came while serving a stint in Germany with the United States Army. After Lee makes another vicious slice, she discovers not only that is she not using her own three wood but that it is the murder weapon. While assuring Sheldon of her innocence, Lee also insists that his inquiries will be severely handicapped by his lack of knowledge of the game and offers her assistance. Reluctantly at first, then with growing enthusiasm as the case progresses, Sheldon includes Lee in his detecting. Her insider's grasp of the players, their rivalry, the game of golf, the scramble for position, and the lucrative area of manufacturers' endorsements are all important elements leading to the conclusion of the case. At the end of play, Lee has won $17,000, holds eleventh place in the tournament, and is in ninety-eighth position on the money list.

Rotten Lies takes place in New Mexico at the Cottonwood Creek golf course, where the American Sports Network is filming events for its *Golf on Tour* series. A $500,000 purse is at stake in the High Desert Classic. Lee is in good position and playing a fantastic game when play is called due to a thunderstorm. On her way back to the clubhouse, Lee comes upon the body of a man apparently struck by lightning. As she applies CPR to him, the bursitis in her elbow flares up. Despite her intervention, the man dies; because of her injury she is forced to drop out of the forthcoming match.

One of the men giving on-site television coverage of the golf match has been injured by lightning. Lee is asked continue his coverage and is given a salary of $400 per day. Sheldon arrives unexpectedly and adds his insight and expertise to questions around the death. Any number of people had reasons for wanting the man dead. Once again, Lee's familiarity with golf, its players, and her new job enables her to assist Sheldon and Det. Ruben Torres to successfully conclude the case. At the end of this book, Sheldon gives up his police force work in favor of private security, taking a job with the Women's Professional Golf League and therefore able to keep Lee company as she makes the rounds of tournaments on her quest.

The stories featuring Lee Ofsted are paced about the same as a round of golf—that is, slowly. In spite of the lack of fast action, Charlotte and Aaron Elkins have crafted sound plots and make Lee a convincing detective as well as a believable rookie pro golfer. Charlotte is a serious amateur golfer and brings her love of the game vividly to the page.

CHICAGO NORDEJOONG
1990–1994   3 books
Victoria McKernan

Eric Nordejoong, a Norwegian seaman, married Tassia, a woman from the island of Trinidad, and together they produced Chicago, a child as unusual as her name. When Chicago was five her mother died; her father took to the sea once again and carried his daughter along. The woman Chicago has become is an interesting amalgam of parentage, ancestry, and upbringing, and these elements have forged a strong, independent person at home on, in, or under the sea. As the series opens with *Osprey Reef*, Chicago lives on board her boat, the *Tassia Far*, built by her father and now berthed in Miami.

Chicago supports herself in part by collecting exotic fish for public aquariums and undersea wildlife parks. On an expedition to Osprey Reef to collect some Lookdowns, possibly a Spotted Eagle ray or two, and to scout for a potentially tractable Moray eel, Chicago and her sixteen-year-old Haitian assistant, Umbi, are menaced by unusually aggressive sharks while diving. They surface to find that their dinghy has been set adrift. The pair are rescued by Alex Sanders and his partner Frank "Wonton" Baxter, out for some early-morning fishing before heading for their jobs with the Miami Police Department. Back in port, Chicago is faced with the loss of a substantial portion of her livelihood and a hospital bill she could have avoided by doing her own suturing; she is not exactly welcoming to Alex when he comes to see how she is.

Alex is drawn to danger like a moth to a flame, so it is hardly a surprise that he is drawn to this tall Viking woman with ice-blue eyes and shining, waist-length black hair. After her initial explosion over her fate, stated in a rousing and impressive stream of expletives, Chicago also admits to a certain attraction to Alex, and a bond is formed. Working together, they clean up a small drug-smuggling endeavor and thwart a larger one as well.

Definitely a character-driven series, the stories are adventures, and the protagonists are more than equal to all the tasks they encounter. Chicago and Alex begin as equals and there is never (much of) a question of either holding the other back for the sake of safety. Alex is drawn to danger; Chicago is drawn to the sea; and, between their individual passions, the spark of personal passion flames. The tensions in each book are both sexual and plot related, and all center on Chicago and Alex.

In *Crooked Island*, the two are hired as divers on an expedition, the outcome of which may change the course of the English succession to the throne. In a clever, diverse blending of the British royal family, a young girl named Annabel Lee, Scottish separatists, North Sea oil interests, the European Economic Community, the British spy cell MI5, and, of course, Chicago and Alex, the story rolls on to an honorable conclusion of three hundred years of history.

Victoria McKernan describes herself as a boat bum who has supported her diving habit in a variety of ways; she is a world traveler and no stranger to adventure herself. Not only are Chicago Nordejoong and Alex Sanders products of this author's imagination, they are derived from her most particular and highly interesting experience.

JAZZ JASPER & INSP. OMONDI
1990–1994   3 books
Karin McQuillan

At one time, not all that long ago, an African safari promised sport of the highest order, with the goal being the getting of game. Today, if someone says they are going to the dark continent on safari, the assumption is that the only shooting that will be done is through a camera lens. This series, featuring Jazz Jasper, is set in Kenya and is full of the beauty and mystery of that place.

Jazz is an American grown tired of cities and academia. Recently divorced, she has moved to Africa and is attempting to fulfill her lifelong dream of running a safari company. In *Deadly Safari*, an old friend arranges a custom trip with Jazz Jasper Safaris for an entourage that is mounting an advertising campaign for Wild and Free Shampoo. Included on the trip are the ad agency's president, his assistant, a photographer, the model, and the clients. Murder happens and Insp. Omondi of Nairobi Homicide is sent to investigate. As the success or failure not only of the trip but of her company rest squarely on Jazz's shoulders, she takes an active role in the detecting and actually discovers the perpetrator.

Both *Elephant's Graveyard* and *The Cheetah Chase* weave the solution of murder with illegal game poaching in a national park and the preservation of endangered wildlife. The locale, with its outstanding scenery and exotic species, adds a glorious dimension to rather ordinary human dilemmas. The herd grazes, the lion sleeps or stalks, and flocks of birds color the skies in flight while the tribesman watches over his flock, tills the soil, or hunts for food. A delicate balance exists, one in which natural and violent death plays an integral part. This balance is under constant threat these days as human greed and the cruelty it engenders are set in opposition to the natural predatory violence of the environs.

A balance of a different sort is struck between Jazz and Omondi. What appear to be almost insurmountable differences between the two actually turn out to be complementary elements that contribute to the whole of a very successful detecting team. Jazz is female, American, white skinned, and impetuous. Her passion is nature and she takes an individualistic approach to her life. Omondi is male, African, black skinned, cautious, and married. He is city bred and, until his meeting with Jazz, has never even visited one of his country's national parks. His approach to life stems from tribal tradition and relies on the social relations within the dominant group. Jazz is direct; Omondi circuitous. Their disparity actually provides them with a multifaceted view of situations and each is able to learn from the other. The sexual tension that exists between them is heightened by their overall dissimilarity and adds another level of interest to the stories.

Jazz's life is complicated. She is a foreigner trying to succeed in a tough, competitive, male-dominated profession. Not only is she attracted to Omondi, she has an intimate relationship with Dan Striker, an activist nature writer. Theirs is a courtship fraught with tension beyond the purely sexual as his personal standards are rapidly being compromised by developments in Kenya, while that same development spells success for Jazz's business. Karin McQuillan has crafted a series with a provocative backdrop and compelling characters. We recommend it.

KIT POWELL
1992–1994 2 books
Julie Robitaille

Television newscasting is, among other things, fickle and unpredictable. News viewers expect instant on-site coverage, and a major part of the reporter's job is to be at the right place, at the right time, with the right equipment. Those who appear before the camera have a double duty to their viewers because much of a station's audience allegiance is based on the connection each member feels for that channel's news anchors and field reporters. Ultimately, the success of a station's news team rests with those who toil behind the scenes checking detail, verifying facts, and doing the necessary research to provide all the pertinent information to those reading the news at six and eleven o'clock.

Station KSDG in San Diego employs Kit Powell. In the first book, her job is newswriter. However, as the story opens, the station's sportscaster arrives for the evening broadcast three sheets to the wind—not an unusual condition for him—and proceeds to pass out in his makeup chair. Casting about for a replacement with some measure of credibility, Doll Garr, the station manager, discovers that Kit is a fount of knowledge on the subject of teams, players, their statistics, and the general trivia that goes into making a dedicated sports follower. Her fill-in broadcast is a success, and over drinks afterward Doll tells Kit that the station owner wants her to continue providing "color" reporting on the air.

The title of the first book, *Jinx*, refers to the black cloud hovering over the Sharks, a major league football team recently moved to San Diego from Galveston. With her reporter's instinct, Kit knows that the team is a good source for ongoing coverage, especially after the accidental death of one of the team owners. When she is approached by the Sharks' public-relations representative and asked to focus on the positive aspects of the team and its players without whitewashing the issues, Kit is willing to provide as much balance to her coverage as possible. Because Kit's original job is investigative reporting, her tendencies are to go for all the facts and depth she can bring to the sports news she reports. In the course of covering the Sharks, she discovers unknown rivalries and multifarious problems.

In *Iced*, Kit is sent to cover the Pro-Am Invitational Figure Skating Championships being held in a new sports complex built by a controversial local entrepreneur. Protesters disrupt the opening ceremonies and continue their picketing throughout the event. Several of the skaters receive threats with racial overtones, and one of the coaches, an East German woman, is killed. Evidence points to the involvement of a white supremacist group called the White Nation. Police Det. Nick Strummer, introduced in the first book and moderately romantically involved with Kit, warns her of the potential dangers of investigating anything that has to do with the organization. Though mindful of Nick's warning, Kit continues her investigations, unravels the tangled skein of clues, and unmasks the killer.

EVA "BUCKET NUT" WYLIE
1993–1997   3 books
Liza Cody

This professional lady wrestler is the most original character to appear in crime and mystery fiction in a long, long time. Eva Wylie is one of the hardest-boiled characters we've ever read about and she operates out of the meanest streets imaginable to anyone. Her father is unknown, her mother is a whore, and her sister has been, according to Eva, stolen by some rich dweebs. Eva is a survivor, self-made in an image to which few women could or would aspire.

Eva not only wrestles (under the moniker of the London Lassassin), she also night guards a junkyard and does the odd job now and then for rather shady characters who pay well and in cash. She has a sense of honesty and code of personal honor that may, at first, seem skewed yet make oddly perfect sense as one delves further into this character's makeup. Her junkyard guarding chores are shared with two dogs, Ramses and Lineker. Eva is clearly alpha dog and continues to do what it takes to maintain her superiority, over Ramses in particular, as he always has his beady little yellow eyes out for her first sign of weakness.

In *Bucket Nut*, one of the shady characters for whom Eva works occasionally decides that she is expendable and sets up a situation in which she is to die and where three others do lose their lives. As Eva has always followed this employer's directions to the letter and he has no professional reason to want her dead, she decides she has been ill done by. The stakes of the game are far beyond Eva's ken, however, and her survival is almost an accident. Almost. At the end of the story, Eva manages to assist in her own salvation the only way she knows how—using her substantial size and sheer brute strength.

Monkey Wrench finds Eva still guarding the junkyard with Ramses and Lineker, still training at George Deeds's gym, and being promoted by Deeds for the occasional wrestling match. She also takes on the job of teaching a group of hookers self-defense after the brutal death of one of their number. Initially, Eva has no respect for the slags nor they for her, but as the story unfolds and the women begin to understand the reasons and motivations behind their choices, some respect is grudgingly exchanged. Once again, Eva's size and power are her saving graces.

Each story gives a bit more of Eva's background and explains her personal development. Her goal is to become a famous baddie in the professional wrestling circuit, and she has chosen the ideal mentor for that task. Harsh, another wrestler from Mr. Deeds's stable, has taught Eva everything important about her training, diet, and mental discipline. He understands the subtle difference between stupidity and ignorance and feels Eva is worthy of whatever education he may be able to provide. Her willingness to learn is all to her credit as Eva is responsible for inventing herself—almost from her beginning—and is reluctant to listen to just anyone's suggestions or advice.

Liza Cody presents this character and the stories in which she appears with a bold and consistent truth that captivates even those readers who don't think they like this type of novel. True, the stories are harsh, brutal, and full of the kind of violence most of us wish didn't exist, but because it does, it is almost refreshing to be given a glimpse of it from the perspective of one who has no agenda other than survival and personal betterment. Eva Wylie is not a crusader for some vague sense of right and order. Her impressions have been formed by what she has seen and experienced and her actions are based upon her knowledge and desire to make sense of the world as she knows it.

As far as the mystery aspect, the stories are as unconventional as the primary character. The forces of law and order are only peripherally involved and have little to do with detection or the outcome. There is no conventional resolution at the conclusion of the tales, and justice is, at best, only roughly served.

Cody's first character, private investigator Anna Lee, makes brief appearances in the Wylie series and serves as counterpoint to a character who makes the hard-boiled Lee look positively ladylike. Eva Wylie as protagonist must be difficult for the writer to sustain. She exists so far out of the boundaries of ordinary, acceptable society that it's almost asking too much of readers to find her sympathetic. Cody has managed it for three novels, and we hope she can handle more.

CASSIE SWANN
1993–1996   4 books
Susan (Elizabeth) Moody

Bridge is a game that offers many possiblities for players at any of several levels. It can be sheer fun and it can be cutthroat. Bridge is often a social exercise yet can be highly profitable for those gifted enough to play for high stakes. It is also possible for a talented player to develop a following and make a respectable living as a teacher. The game is one of strategy and anticipation and can provide an interesting setting for murder.

Cassandra Swann, an Englishwoman, is a bridge expert. In *Death Takes a Hand*, she is teaching at a bridge weekend held at a Cotswold country-house hotel. When she arrives late for a lesson, "Cassie" discovers her three students dead, with an unfinished hand on the table. Det. Insp. Mantripp and Sgt. Walsh arrive to investigate the deaths and discover seething resentments between members of the party, many directed toward the only one of the three victims who was obviously murdered. Unfavorable publicity severely curtails Cassie's teaching career, and she decides that the only way to clear her name and regain her hard-won position in the bridge world is to unmask the killer.

Charlie Quartermain, a former student of Cassie, arrives at Honeysuckle Cottage, her home outside the village of Market

Broughton, bearing champagne and sympathy. Charlie, a rough-hewn stonemason, is clearly smitten with Cassie though the lady herself is not drawn to him in the least and lets him know it in no uncertain terms. Charlie is undaunted. Enormously self-confident, this master craftsman is willing to take whatever crumbs Cassie lets fall while making no secret of his devotion. As the story draws to its end, Charlie's devotion is what saves Cassie from death at the hands of the murderer.

Grand Slam finds Cassie dividing her time between teaching bridge to inmates at a local prison and playing professional high-stakes games with Royston Chilcott as her partner. After a disastrous game and abandonment by her partner, a murder is discovered at Halkam Court, site of the debacle. Once again, Mantripp and Walsh arrive to investigate and Charlie comes several times to Cassie's rescue. Sgt. Walsh extends his investigation into the personal, and he and Cassie enjoy several not-so-brief and very intimate interludes.

Other characters appear in both stories. All—Cassie's Uncle Sam, a vicar; his wife, Polly; and their twin daughters, the diminutive Hyacinth and Primula—serve as constant reminders of Cassie's insalubrious upbringing and Reubenesque stature. Katherine Kurtz, an American, is Cassie's neighbor and good friend. Giles Laughton, a widower who lives with his eccentric mother, Mercy, desperately wants to marry—someone. After numerous unsuccessful proposals to Cassie, Giles turns his attentions toward Katherine, who accepts him.

The game of bridge is liberally laced with clues. Partners send messages to one another through their bids and canny players can outguess an opponent through the bidding process as well. An expert can reconstruct a game by looking at the order of play, tricks taken, and cards held by each player. Keen observation is necessary to a bridge expert; the same talent is required in detecting crime, so Cassie's abilities in that direction are really no surprise. The stories are lightly entertaining and bridge fans will find them fascinating.

JORDAN MYLES
1994–1997   3 books
Martina Navratilova and Liz Nickles

The last two decades have seen the rapid growth of interest in the professional aspects of the sport of tennis. Speed and strength count for a lot, but experience and strategy are of equal importance; youth may shine, yet older players can continue holding their own in fierce competitions. The pro tennis circuit represents big bucks for players, agents, coaches, and equipment manufacturers. All of this brings a great deal of pressure to bear on the individual players, who must keep at the top of their form in order to take advantage of the vast sums the game and its offshoots offer.

Of course, players must stay in peak physical shape to meet the demands of their sport and Jordan Myles, physical therapist for the Desert Springs Sports Science Clinic, plies her trade to that end. She is a former tennis star herself, but her career was cut short by a mountain climbing accident that shattered her leg when she was only twenty-two. Her insider's understanding of the game gives Jordan a significant edge when working with players.

In *The Total Zone*, a sixteen-year-old comes to the clinic to work on her failing game. Ranked fourth on the circuit, the young player is the success behind a $9 million business known as Audrey Armat Enterprises. During an evaluation of Audrey's condition, Jordan discovers that the young woman is severely disturbed and ready to quit. When Audrey disappears from the clinic, detective Noel "the Fish" Fisher is hired by the girl's agency, Global Sport, to find her in time for Wimbledon. As the venerable English tournament begins, Audrey is still missing and a young Japanese opponent of hers is stabbed to death. When Audrey is found, she too is dead, an apparent suicide. Her parents lay the blame for their daughter's death on Jordan's shoulders and threaten to bring suit against her and her clinic. Jordan joins forces with the Fish and together, the pair uncover much more than distress and poor sportsmanship.

Breaking Point begins at the French Open held at the Roland Garros Stadium in Paris. During an exclusive reception hosted by Global Sport in a huge greenhouse, a young woman plunges through the glass roof to her death. The Fish is hired by Catherine Richie's parents to find her killer and once again, he and Jordan team up. After a brutal beating, however, the Fish is sidelined at the American Hospital in Paris under the care of his devoted mother, a woman with a taste for elaborate hats and possessing hidden talents. Back in Palm Springs, Jordan's assistant is killed by a car bomb. Undaunted, Jordan continues to investigate and has a number of close calls of her own. Ultimately, all is disclosed, the Fish recovers, and Jordan and her old nemesis, Kelly Kendall, reach accord.

As a player, one of Jordan's advantages was her ability to change strategies midgame. She brings this talent to her detecting and is able to rise to all the various challenges her cases present her. With the exception of her assistant, Tony, Jordan's colleagues at the clinic appear to be less than supportive; fortunately for everyone, Jordan can count on the Fish. Noel Fisher is a former Green Beret trained in surveillance. In spite of being a large, untidy man, the Fish is easily overlooked. He is also always underestimated. The pair make effective codetectives; however, while solving murder is what they do, the psychology of the tennis players and their game are at the center of these tales.

Martina Navratilova's career achievements make her *the* unsurpassed world tennis champion. Winner of more than 1,400 matches, she holds 168 singles titles and nine Wimbledon singles crowns and has set more records than any other player in the history of the sport. With coauthor Liz Nickles, Navratilova applies her knowledge and insight of the high-stakes game to a new series that gives readers background for the ecstasy of winning and the agony of defeat. Their character provides a look at the life of an athlete engaged though no longer playing in, what has become a very dangerous game.

Americans' love of sports and games of all kinds is legendary. Those who play, those who report on the games and their players, and those who simply observe are linked together in rites as sanctified as organized religion. Watching contests between professional football teams of national rank keeps a sizable segment of the population (male for the most part) glued to couches and recliners most Sunday afternoons and Monday evenings during the season. The Boys of Summer drive young men's minds in a highly predictable direction, and even golfers and bowlers have their television following.

The participation in sports requires a measure of devotion as well as determination, and these characteristics are necessary for those who solve the crime of murder. Death on the field may be honorable, yet at times it is not the clean death of a fair fight but something far more sinister. The characters in this chapter combine their love and knowledge of their respective sports and games to bring justice to those who seek to bring dishonor into play.

SOME OTHER SPORTING SLEUTHS

Adrienne Bishop
Jacob Chaos

KILLINGS ON THE MARKET:
Business and Finance

The area of business and finance has changed in crime and mystery fiction as a whole as well as in our society. Women are making their mark in the marketplace and are showing signs of true entrepreneurship—perhaps because there is little room in the world of business for those who appear to lack conventional skills and perhaps because women prefer the freedom that owning and operating their own business provides.

Some of the ventures undertaken by women include operating bed-and-breakfast establishments and providing catering services. More or less traditional positions are also represented by some of the characters. Secretaries are the backbone of the offices they run and are in the ideal position to know what's really going on. And when it comes to knowing secrets, no one holds more than the domestic worker. In real life small independent bookstores provide more than a few of us with much more than any anonymous chain store ever could, and in the stories featuring booksellers, solutions to murder are a part of what they offer.

Margaret Scherf created five books featuring Emily and Henry Bryce (1948–1963). Placing them in the sophisticated world of interior decorating in Manhattan in the '40s, Scherf tells brisk, witty, and well-plotted tales.

John Putnam Thatcher is an investment banker who appears in twenty-four books (1961–1997). Thatcher is the epitome of the gray-flannel banker, and readers never see him outside his professional venue. The identity of Emma Lathen was a well-kept secret for many years: Martha Henissart and Mary Jane Latsis each had a professional position they feared would be compromised if their penchant for writing mysteries leaked out to their clients.

In 1984, Nancy Pickard created foundation director Jennifer Cain. There are now ten books in the series (1984–1995). Each uses comtemporary social issues as themes with interesting aspects of business, finance, and the law.

All of the following characters are talented, many are creative,

137

and most are risk takers. When murder occurs, as it inevitably does in all these books, the qualities possessed by each series protagonist are well applied to solving the crime at hand.

DORAN FAIRWEATHER CHELMARSH & THE REV. RODNEY CHELMARSH
1986–1997   7 books
Mollie Hardwick

This sentimental series features young, beautiful Doran Fair-weather and the Rev. Rodney Chelmarsh. Star-crossed and uncon-summated lovers in the first book, *Malice Domestic*, the progress of their relationship is at the core of all of the stories. Doran was born and raised in Oxford, where her father was a don. After her father's death, Doran and her mother moved to Eastgate, Kent, to be near the sea for her mother's health. After only one year, Mrs. Fair-weather died, leaving Doran comfortably well off. Using a portion of her inheritance, Doran opened an antique shop in the old harbor area of Eastgate and moved into Bell House in the valley village of Abbotsbourne. Her closest friend is the Rev. Chelmarsh. Both would like the nature of their alliance to deepen, but Rodney's crip-pled daughter, Helena, keeps them apart through spite and tan-trums, because of a seething hatred for Doran. At the end of this book, Rodney and Doran profess their love but their virtue is quite literally saved by the bell.

In *Parson's Pleasure*, the two manage to sneak away together and register at a small bed-and-breakfast establishment near Oxford as Mr. and Mrs. R. H. Barham of Tappington, Everard, Kent. Doran's business partner, Howell Evans, has purchased a clock that Doran recognizes as having come from a house she toured as a schoolgirl. Fearing it is a stolen piece, Doran and Rodney visit the house, meet the rather gaga Lady Timberlake, and discover that valuable an-tiques and jewelry are missing. Doran discovers the perpetrators of the theft as well as murder and is abducted. She saves herself just as Rodney comes to rescue her and at the end of the book the two are married, despite Helena's vocal protests.

Life for the newly blended family does not run smoothly in *Un-easeful Death*. Doran goes away for a weekend antiques roadshow at the lovely, well-run Caxton Manor, where she falls over one body in the car park, becomes snowbound with the rest of the guests, and discovers a second corpse on the conservatory roof. Rodney arrives in a helicopter. In her haste to leave home, Doran has forgotten her birth-control pills and dreads the thought of bringing a new child into the stressful situation at Bell House. However, other events in this story have caused Helena to have a total change of heart.

As *The Bandersnatch* opens, the family welcomes newborn Christopher "Kit" into its bosom. Doran has found for the baby's room a charming carved cherub, which rouses envy in many hearts. Their home is ransacked as they sleep, outrageous offers are made for purchase of the cherub, and Kit is kidnapped and taken to the isle of Jersey. Doran follows close on his heels, and Rodney arrives in a small plane.

The reformed Helena sickens and dies off the page just before *Perish in July*, which opens with her funeral. Rodney's grief is mixed with the effects of both a personal and a professional midlife crisis. Known to his bishop as a dangerous reactionary because he favors the old Anglican prayer book over the new one, Rodney is relieved of most of his parish duties, leaving Doran to provide most of the household's economic support. When both become involved with a Gilbert and Sullivan production and Doran discovers a decapitated body hidden inside a prop, domestic chaos ensues. Tiggy, an old friend of Doran, comes for a visit, and her competence in restoring order to Bell House is almost beyond belief. However, her presence is nearly the undoing of Rodney and Doran's marriage. Howell's mother arrives on the scene and puts things nicely back into perspective. At the end of the book, Rodney's spirits are on the rise.

An unsigned painting in the Pre-Raphaelite style comes to light in *The Dreaming Damozel*, and Doran becomes fascinated with the life of Elizabeth Siddal, mistress of nineteenth-century British painter Dante Gabriel Rossetti. Doran instigates a search for more of that artist's undiscovered works, which, of course, leads to murder. When Doran breaks a solemn promise to Rodney and once again places herself in danger, Rodney arrives in a huff. When she announces that she is expecting their second child, all is forgiven.

Mollie Hardwick is best known for her television writing, which includes *Upstairs, Downstairs* and *The Duchess of Duke Street*, and has won wide acclaim for her historical novels. In this Doran Fairweather (and Rodney Chelmarsh) series Hardwick draws on some of her research to feed Rodney's penchant for quoting almost anyone at the drop of a hat. Despite what some may see as a surfeit of saccharine sensibility, the stories are tightly plotted and the ancillary characters provide enough spice to offer the anodyne.

CLAIRE MALLOY
1986–1996   11 books
Joan Hess

Claire Malloy is a widow. Carlton Malloy's encounter with a chicken truck gave her that status just before she was about to become a divorcee, having lost him to the latest in a long succession of his nubile students. As *Strangled Prose* opens, eight years have passed since Carlton's death. Claire is the proprietor of The Book Depot, a renovated train station that was until the late '40s, when the last train made its final stop there, the focal point of the town of Farberville, Arkansas. The bookstore, while not a huge profitmaker, provides almost enough of a living for Claire and her teenaged daughter, Caron.

Events in the first story bring several previously unknown details of Carlton's affairs to light along with the minor misbehavior of a couple of other Farberville residents. After two murders, Claire becomes involved and meets Lt. Peter Rosen of the Farberville Criminal Investigation Department. When Caron's best friend, Inez, is kidnapped, Claire rushes to the rescue with Rosen hot on her heels. They wind up the case to everyone's relief and almost everyone's satisfaction.

Farberville is a small and thriving community. Farber College is a provincial institution with an emphasis on the liberal arts. Carlton Malloy had been a professor of English there, and several of the characters who appear and reappear in the series are affiliated with the establishment as well. Luanne Bradshaw owns the used-clothing store Second Hand Rose and, in *A Really Cute Corpse*, is in charge of the Miss Thurberfest Beauty Pageant. *Tickled to Death* finds Luanne and the dentist with whom she is enamored at the center of a curious mystery. Miss Emily Parchester and her Basset Hounds Nick and Nora figure in several of Claire's dramas—most notably in *Roll Over and Play Dead*, in which Nick and Nora are dognapped by an unscrupulous underground pet dealer.

As the single parent of an eternally adolescent daughter (Caron ages only two years in the entire course of the series), much of Claire's work is cut out for her. That she takes on amateur detection only highlights her inquisitive qualities plus her desire to gain and keep the upper hand with Lt. Rosen, a thoroughly nice man who wants to marry her and do his own job to the best of his considerable abilities. The Book Depot is almost always in a financial crisis, and Claire's accountant is a frequent, but (at least to readers) invisible, caller to remind her of quarterly tax installments and other unpleasant fiscal realities of life.

Joan Hess's notorious wit is relatively subdued in this series but is present in its acidic glory personified by the well-, if brashly, spoken Claire Malloy. Hess has created two other series. Retired florist Theo Bloomer appeared in only two books, *The Night Blooming Cereus* and *The Deadly Ackee*. Sheriff Arly Hanks, introduced in 1987, can be found in the chapter "Behind the Badge: Provincial Police."

BONNIE INDERMILL
1987–1996   7 books
Carole (Summerlin) Berry

Bonnie Indermill is a not-quite-young woman of thirty-six. A former tap dancer, she lives in Manhattan with her cat, Moses, and is looking for a career and a husband—not necessarily in that order. When she is introduced in *The Letter of the Law*, Bonnie is office manager for a law firm. One of the law partners is found dead in a seedy hotel room; it is assumed that he was there with a prostitute and that his death is a result of robbery. Not so. A spark is ignited between Det. Anthony LaMarca of the NYPD and Bonnie, and, as the story progresses and she becomes more embroiled in the case, he cautions her against putting herself at risk. Of course she does, to the point of solving not only the current murder but also one that had occurred some twenty years earlier. Legal chicanery complicates things and leads to the law firm's dissolution.

Year of the Monkey finds Bonnie working as a trainee for Creative Financial Ventures (CFV), a company offering tax shelters and capital equipment lease-back arrangements. Despite her intelligence and the training program, Bonnie knows next to nothing about the work she is to do. This matters little as there doesn't seem to be much business going on. Several of the ongoing characters in the series are introduced in this story: Bonnie's office mate, compulsive gambler, and all-around shady character "Fast" Eddie Fong and the gorgeous Amanda Paradise, a secretary who can't type. When the chief executive officer of CFV is murdered right after the company Christmas party, Bonnie begins breaking the rule she had established for herself about getting involved with her coworkers. And then Derek Thorensen, a part-time graphic artist, shows an interest in her, and she throws all the other self-imposed rules out too. High-speed car chases, a mysterious scar-faced Chinese man, and an equally mysterious gym bag are added to the chaos of CFV's business. Once again, Bonnie solves more than one crime and is out of another job.

The world of ballet is the next venue for our heroine in *Goodnight, Sweet Prince*. Working with a temporary agency, Bonnie takes a position with the Gotham Ballet Company to assist with their fund-raising drive. When a newly defected Russian dancer falls to his death at his debut, Bonnie is, as always, at the heart of the crime. Both Tony LaMarca and Derek Thorensen are pressing their suits for Bonnie in this story. Then Tony tells her that he's met someone else, and Bonnie moves in with Derek.

In *Island Girl*, Bonnie is back in her own apartment and very little is said about the obvious end of her relationship with Derek. Still working for the temporary agency, she is free to take a friend up on the offer of a position as aerobics instructor at the Flamingo Cove Hotel in the Bahamas. None of the other characters we've met in earlier books are in this one, so Bonnie is on her own when it comes to discovering the identity of her roommate's killer.

The Death of a Difficult Woman finds Bonnie in a place she said she'd never be again—working for a law firm, temping to help the lawyers and staff make a move into new quarters. Tony LaMarca is one of the investigating officers when the odious Kate Hamilton is found bludgeoned to death, wrapped up in curtains, and stuffed in a closet. Sam, one of the Five Finkelstein Boys Moving Company, becomes the object of Bonnie's ardor. After she and Tony solve the crime, Bonnie and Sam move in together.

In *The Death of a Dancing Fool*, Bonnie and Sam are planning their wedding. Fast Eddie Fong reappears along with Tony and Amanda Paradise LaMarca. Eddie has opened a nightclub and wants Bonnie to help him with the office management. There is a matter of forty thousand dollars—last seen in book two—and possible drug and Mafia connections, celebrities, and, of course, murder.

Carole Berry has chosen an interesting collection of vehicles with which to propel her character and the series. Bonnie herself has no particular propensity for solving murders, yet she keeps moving into work situations that provide it. Everyone knows that New York City is a dangerous place and the business world can be cutthroat. Berry combines a compelling location and an interesting variety of occupations for Bonnie to search for support, a spouse, and solutions.

ANNIE LAURANCE DARLING
1987–1995   9 books
Carolyn G(impel) Hart

Broward's Rock is a skillet-shaped island off the South Carolina coast. Not quite as well known as Hilton Head, Broward's Rock is growing in popularity thanks to a high-priced housing development. Annie Laurance had been coming to visit her Uncle Ambrose on Broward's Rock since she was eleven years old. Nine months before the events in *Death on Demand*, Ambrose had fallen off his boat and drowned, leaving Annie heir to his estate, which included the stock and goodwill in his mystery bookstore, Death on Demand.

As the story opens, Annie receives a phone call from Max Darling—a young, handsome, and improbably rich young man with whom she had been involved while both of them were living in Manhattan. Although she feels a strong attraction for Max, Annie is reluctant to get further involved with a man whom she feels takes a far too frivolous attitude toward life. His money notwithstanding, Annie believes that Max should do something meaningful and useful with his life. Max feels one should never let money become one's master, and he sets about diffusing its potential power by spending it as rapidly and as pleasurably as possible. Needless to say, this diametric opposition between the two primary characters sets the tone for much of what follows in the series.

Annie is the prime suspect in the first book not only for the death of an author appearing at her store but for the death of a local veterinarian and her uncle Ambrose as well. Together, she and Max clear suspicion against her and bring the perpetrator to justice. As *Design for Murder* opens, Max has taken Annie's suggestion on useful employment to heart. Though licensed to practice law in the state of New York, Max is unwilling to take the South Carolina bar exam or to get a private investigator's license. Taking a few liberties though breaking no laws, he has opened Confidential Commissions, an advice agency. This proves useful, as Annie continues getting involved with murder, which is, of course, the focus of each book.

Regular characters are introduced throughout the series. Ingrid Jones is Annie's shop assistant. Mrs. Henrietta "Henny" Brawley is one of the store's best customers, even if she does try to cheat on the monthly guessing game that involves renderings, by local artists, of scenes from famous mysteries. The one who correctly guesses both the title of the mystery and its author wins the book of their choice and free coffee for a month. As Annie makes wonderful coffee—served in one of the hundred mugs emblazoned with a title on the side and the author's name on the bottom—the prize is truly worth something. Agatha is a small, sleek black feline who resides in Death on Demand. She is not too fond of people and is usually to be found well hidden under one of the shop's lush ferns. Max's mother, Laurel Darling Roethke, is always in the grip of a new enthusiasm. Max adores her and Annie finds her hard to take. Miss Dora Brevard, a native of Chastain, is introduced in the second book and eventually joins forces with Henny and Laurel to aid and abet Annie and Max in their detection as well as their lives in general.

Award-winning author Carolyn G. Hart's love and knowledge of mystery fiction are well displayed in every book featuring Annie and Max. Through her lively characters, she draws wonderful parallels between the action in her books and that of both well-known and obscure books by other authors in the genre. Among the honors Hart has accrued are two Anthonys, two Agathas, and a Macavity. Her newest series features retired newspaperwoman Henrie O, who may be found in the chapter "Murder between the Pages: Writers and Journalists."

JASON LYNX
1989–1997   6 books
A. J. Orde (Sheri S. Tepper)

Series, by definition, follow some sort of order, and the development of character—most particularly that of the primary one—is vital to the series' continuing success. The books featuring antique dealer Jason Lynx have all the requisite elements, yet the processes of convolution and evolution of plot and character add unusual and rather piquant dimensions to this collection. Disparate elements of Jason's life are introduced in the first book. Left in a foundling home at the age of three with a yellow blanket and healing burn wounds, Jason had the makings of a first-class crook until caught by Jacob Buchnam, who took Jason under his wing, gave him a job, and taught him the antique trade.

As *A Little Neighborhood Murder* opens, a pair of Jason's neighbors are found dead in their home. Their murders are closely linked to the overriding sorrows of Jason's life: the disappearance of his wife and the ongoing care of his institutionalized, brain-dead son. The story progresses, and Jason meets Det. Grace Willis, who prefers the appellation cop to that of policewoman. Together, the two solve the current killings and lay old ghosts to permanent rest.

Jason likes puzzles, and those presented by the human condition provide more fascination than any found on paper. In *Death and the Dogwalker*, Grace is in San Francisco to bail out her ne'er-do-well brother, Ron, and so Jason is on his own to unmask the murderer of his broker's brother-in-law. An earlier murder comes to light as the puzzle comes together, and this too is solved, although the mystery of Jason's identity deepens. Inadvertently, the question of Jason's parentage becomes central to *Death for Old Time's Sake*; in the process of discovering who he is and where and from whom he came, many of Jason's ideals and beliefs are thrown open to reconsideration.

While Jason's background is shrouded in mystery from the outset, it is never really of compelling importance to him. He is content with the person he has become (thanks to Jacob); once the painful reason for his wife's disappearance is disclosed, he seems content to go on with life as he has designed it. After his origins are uncovered in the third book, he feels somewhat cut adrift, and when an old and close friend asks Jason to look into his brother's murder, Jason readily agrees and hastens to Santa Fe, New Mexico, for the action in *Dead on Sunday*. At the end, Jason is in almost more of a quandary about himself and his future than he was at the beginning.

In *A Long Time Dead*, Grace's brother, Ron, is infected with AIDS and comes to Denver to be cared for by his sister. When Ron is killed in an explosion, Grace is guilt ridden and appeals to Jason to help her find Ron's murderer. More family secrets are exposed in this tale, and at least two families are affected by the disclosures. Both Jason and Grace are confronted with the effects their histories have had on their respective personal development and on their growing love for one another.

Other characters appear with regularity. Mark MacMillan is Jason's employee in Jason Lynx Interiors. Mark is intelligent, creative, and very pragmatic about his wealthy family's world view. Eugenia Lowe is the backbone of the business. Wheelchair-bound Nellie Arpels is Jason's back-alley neighbor who keeps a close eye on the neighborhood and is always available to provide Jason with a little advice and counsel. Bela, a Hungarian Kuvasc, is Jason's canine companion, and Schnitz, a twenty-pound Maine Coon cat who is a son of Grace's thirty-pound Critter, is Bela's feline counterpart. The two animals travel with Jason and are involved in the denouements of several of the stories.

A. J. Orde is one of the pseudonyms used by Sheri S. Tepper, a well-known science fiction writer. Under the pseudonym B. J. Oliphant, Tepper has created another mystery series, this one featuring Shirley McClintock, a rancher of a certain age who may be found in the chapter "Senior Sleuths." With the Jason Lynx series, Tepper has used family as an orientation point for clever, compelling mysteries. Murder is only the tip of the iceberg in these complex tales, and readers may find themselves looking among the branches of their family trees for possible deception and the odd skeleton or two.

XENIA SMITH & LESLIE WETZON
1989–1997   7 books
Annette (Brafman) Meyers

In New York City The Street (with a capital "T" and a capital "S") is Wall Street. The work Xenia Smith and Leslie Wetzon do is officially known as professional recruitment. The fact that they deal with the movers and shakers of the financial community makes the pair at home with the sobriquet "headhunter" and, as women in a man's world, they are rather pleased that their names call up visions of the gunsmiths.

Smith came to the profession from the business world, where she had worked in personnel; Wetzon had been a dancer on and off Broadway. She knew that there was a limit to how many years she could meet the arduous demands of that profession, and, when Smith suggested they join forces, she hesitated only one New York minute. Their office is the ground floor of a converted brownstone near the corner of Second Avenue and Forty-ninth Street. Much of their business is done on the phone, but an even more significant part is conducted in up-scale bars and restaurants, the Four Seasons being their favorite.

In *The Big Killing*, Wetzon meets with Barry Stark, a broker on the move, at The Grill Room. Barry is clearly nervous and leaves to make a phone call. When he doesn't return, Wetzon goes to the phone bank, where she discovers Barry's dead body in a phone booth. When the police arrive on the scene, the officer in charge is Sgt. Silvestri of the Seventeenth Precinct. As Wetzon is the person with whom the victim was meeting and she discovered his murdered body, she is high on the suspect list. Layers of duplicity unfold as Wetzon asks questions in an attempt to clear herself, and in the end she provides all of the elements leading to the murderer's identity.

Smith and Wetzon are almost polar opposites. Smith is tall, slender, and dark haired; her clothes and grooming are always impeccable and she wouldn't dream of sweating. She is divorced from a man who worked for the CIA and has a son, Mark, who is devoted to her. Wetzon is five-foot-two, with a dancer's body and fine blond hair always worn in a dancer's topknot. She still works out at the ballet barre in her apartment's dining room and takes an occasional dance class. Her closest friend is Carlos Prince, another former dancer and almost exactly Wetzon's size. After leaving the theater, Carlos started a housecleaning service providing temporary work for other resting actors and dancers. More recently, he has reentered the theatrical world as a choreographer. Smith despises Carlos and much else; she usually refers to stockbrokers as "scum" and "dirtbags" and can find a way to put down anyone and anything. Oddly enough, this mismatch works well. Even though Smith is inclined to be harsh and judgmental toward her, Wetzon is not intimidated by Smith's aggressive nature.

The stories themselves are fascinating. Readers are taken behind the scenes of the dynamic, cutthroat business of finance. Smith and Wetzon are well-drawn characters who play off one another and are the ideal human vehicles for the action of each book. Annette Meyers is the ideal author for this complex—almost Machiavellian—series. Formerly executive assistant of Broadway director-producer Hal Prince, Meyers is senior vice president of an executive search and management consulting firm. Under the joint pseudonym Maan Meyers, she collaborates with her husband Martin on an historical mystery series featuring the Tonneman family of old New York that may be found in the chapter "After the Fall: Historical Mysteries."

DARINA LISLE
1989–1996   8 books
Janet Laurence

Darina Lisle, a chef par excellence, is introduced in *A Deepe Coffyn* when she is invited to prepare a meal using historical recipes and ancient techniques for forty guests of the Society of Historical Gastronomes. The annual event, cofounded by Digby Cary and Professor Nicholas Turvey, provides those attending with the opportunity to sample and critique a vast array of uncommon foodstuffs. Although Digby is Darina's cousin, her position as author and executor of the elaborate menu is based on merit rather than nepotism. Digby's death brings Det. Sgt. William Pigram onto the scene, and, when it is discovered that Darina is Digby's heir, she is immediately moved to the top of the suspect list. In her efforts to exonerate herself, Darina uncovers a host of secrets, unknown personal connections, and, eventually, the killer.

The course of events in the first book sets the tone for those that follow. At the center of each novel is food: those who purvey it, purchase it, prepare it, and partake of it. Darina is an inventive and capable chef with high standards, good business sense, and lofty ambitions. Thanks to the inheritance from her cousin, she is in the enviable position of having the time to carefully explore her career options. And explore she does. In *A Tasty Way to Die*, Darina assists a former classmate in running her catering business; in *Hotel Morgue*, she exercises her longtime dream of going into partnership in a country hotel and restaurant; *Recipe for Death* places Darina in the position of judge in a cookery contest; in *Death and the Epicure*, she has been commissioned to write a cookbook of recipes using products a long-established family firm imports from exotic locales; and *Death at the Table* puts Darina in the spotlight of a television food series.

While food is the central theme of this series, murder runs a close second. Each book features a small group of people bound by ties of blood and/or business. Secrets add a spicy tang, and it falls to

Darina to identify the players and make their often obscure connections. She does so using her knowledge of food, cookery and technique, and an understanding of the fierce rivalry among those striving to succeed in a highly competitive arena. Greed in various guises is often the foundation for the murders Darina solves, and cuisine and killing are carefully blended into a delicious stew.

In the course of the series, Darina and William discover a mutual attraction, and the development of their relationship occupies a substantial place in the proceedings. William is a traditionalist who envisions a wife who holds him and his profession at the center of her life. Darina, on the other hand, is a career-oriented woman who would like a relationship that supports her ambitions as well as those of her mate. Much of the interaction between the pair revolves around this seeming incompatibility, and it takes four books for William to see the light and to understand that Darina is not making unrealistic demands for equality. Love does not conquer all, however, as family complications cause the postponement of their nuptial plans.

Janet Laurence knows her onions and all the other ingredients for a successful culinary series.

GOLDY BEAR
1990–1997   7 books
Diane Mott Davidson

"Goldilocks' Catering, Where Everything Is Just Right!" is located in Goldy Bear's house in Aspen Meadow, Colorado—some forty miles east of Denver. Goldy is the divorced mother of a son, Arch, and supports the two of them by feeding the affluent citizens of her community. Although Goldy's abusive former husband, John Richard Korman—a.k.a. The Jerk—can be numbered among the elite, his child support payments are often late, missing, or in the wrong amount.

In *Catering to Nobody*, Goldy supplies the funeral baked meats for Arch's former teacher, Laura Smiley. At the gathering at Laura's home after the service, John Richard's father, Fritz, becomes ill. The Jerk accuses Goldy of poisoning him and vows retribution. Although Fritz recovers and he and his wife, Vonette, clearly hold no grudge against Goldy, Investigator Tom Schulz of the Furman County Sheriff's Department is forced to close the catering business until further notice. To clear her name and get her business up and running before the busy Christmas holiday season, Goldy must get to the bottom of Fritz's mysterious illness. In the process, she uncovers a murder, unmasks the perpetrator of both crimes, and strikes up a relationship with Schulz.

Some of the ongoing characters are introduced in the first book. Marla Korman, another of The Jerk's ex-wives, is Goldy's best friend. Arch is a quiet and rather precocious child of eleven. Julian Teller doesn't enter the series until the second book, *Dying for Chocolate*, and takes a pivotal role when he does. He meets Goldy and Arch at the home of General Bo and Adele Farquhar, where Goldy is employed as live-in cook while an alarm system is being installed in their home. Goldy's relationship with Tom Schulz is on hold while she rekindles an old flame, Dr. Philip Miller. When the doctor dies right before Goldy's eyes on the twisting road leading to town, she suspects his death is no accident. Following her instincts, Goldy once again solves the crime.

As *The Cereal Murders* opens, Arch has become a full-time student at Elk Park Prep and Julian has moved into the Bear household. After catering a dinner for the senior class and their families, Goldy is loading her Volkswagen van when she falls over the body of the class valedictorian. Another murder takes place and Goldy—to her peril—figures out the who and why, and then is rescued by Tom, whom she agrees to marry. *The Last Suppers* opens at the church where their wedding is to take place. Tom calls and tells Goldy that their officiating minister is dead. Tom disappears and Goldy is brought into the investigation of both the minister's murder and the disappearance of her husband-to-be.

Two months after the pair is finally wed, Goldy is asked, in *Killer Pancake*, to cater an event to launch a new line for a cosmetics company. At the party, Julian's girlfriend is hit by a car and killed in the parking lot. Goldy, Tom, and Julian work in opposition and in harmony and discover danger and deception within an industry dedicated to promoting beauty.

This series is a '90s version of the English Village Murder Mystery. As a caterer, Goldy knows everybody; as a homicide inspector, Tom Schulz knows everything about everybody, and, as a gynecologist, The Jerk has the inside scoop on nearly half the population. Given the antipathy both Goldy and Marla feel for their common former spouse and the growing sympathy between Goldy and Tom, there is an interesting tension that heightens some of the action in the series. Keeping secrets in a small, affluent mountain community proves to be as difficult as it is in St. Mary Mead.

The books abound with recipes from Goldy's arsenal, and we know for a fact that Diane Mott Davidson, Goldy's creator, has tested each and every one. Her cookies are to die for.

FAITH FAIRCHILD
1990–1997   8 books
Katherine Hall Page

"Have Faith" was the name of Faith Sibley's successful New York catering business. A confirmed city dweller, Faith had made a pact with her younger sister, Hope, never to marry a clergyman and never to leave the Big Apple. As her series opens with *The Body in the Belfry*, Faith has broken the pact. She met Tom Fairchild at a wedding she catered and, too late, discovered he had performed the ceremony. After their marriage, Faith moved into the parsonage in Aleford, Massachusetts, and gave birth to their son, Ben.

As the first book opens, Faith climbs, with Ben in his Snugli, up Belfry Hill for an alfresco sandwich. The belfry houses the reconstructed bell that had been used to sound the alarm on the fateful eighteenth of April more than two hundred years earlier. Faith's lunch plans are disrupted by the dead body of a member of Tom Fairchild's parish, the president of the Young People's Club. In the course of the ensuing investigation, Faith learns more than she might want to know about the peccadilloes of the various members of the Aleford community. When her natural curiosity puts her in the path of threats, Police Chief Charley MacIsaac and Det. Lt. John Dunne of the Massachusetts State Police join Tom in sending Faith to safety with her family in the heart of Manhattan. In spite of their best efforts, Faith returns, figures out the killer's identity, and is trapped in a cellar with her son and another young victim.

Pix Miller and her husband, the Fairchilds' next-door neighbors, are featured in several of the stories. One of Faith's adventures, *The Body in the Kelp*, takes place in Maine, on Sanpere Island, where the Miller family has a summer home and where Faith spends an enjoyable if rather mystery-fraught month. In the fifth book, *The Body in the Basement*, the story is presented from Pix's perspective and Faith only makes brief appearances as dogsbody.

Faith Sibley Fairchild is nothing less than a food snob so it comes as no surprise to find in the third book, *The Body in the Bouillon*, that she has opened another "Have Faith" if for no other reason than to provide herself, her family, and close friends with what she considers edible food. *The Body in the Vestibule* takes Faith and Tom to Lyon, France, where Tom plans to finish research for his doctorate and four-months-pregnant Faith plans to indulge in French cuisine and begin writing a cookbook entitled *Have Faith in the Kitchen*. She finds the body of a *clochard* (tramp) in the trash bin of their apartment and becomes embroiled in murderous mystery once again. *The Body in the Cast* puts Faith and her catering crew, which temporarily includes Pix, on location with a film crew making a modern version of Nathaniel Hawthorne's *The Scarlet Letter*. First, Faith's black bean soup is sabotaged with chocolate-covered laxative, then a young production assistant cum star's stand-in dies in her arms, and finally Faith finds the body of one of Aleford's candidates for selectman in the Town Hall basement. Faith is once again immersed in murder.

Bill Deeck introduced us to Katherine Hall Page in 1991 as one of his favorite new authors. We can't help but agree with this knowledgeable gentleman; and the Malice Domestic Convention voted *The Body in the Belfry* the Best First Mystery Novel of 1990.

PETER BARTHOLOMEW
1990–1997   7 books
Sally Gunning

Although Nashtoba, Maine, is really a peninsula, it is considered an island because the only connection between it and Cape Hook, the larger peninsula jutting out from the coastline, is a wooden causeway, built in the year dot. Nashtoba is an odd place inhabited by odd souls. It has the sense and sensibility of a village, yet is big enough so that it is possible not to know everything everyone is doing. Peter Bartholomew is a Nashtoba native. In his sophomore year of high school, needing a summer job, he contemplated "walking the plank" and finding work on Cape Hook. Before he crossed the causeway the word "factotum" and its definition—a person employed to do all kinds of work—sprang into his mind and a business was born.

Twenty years later, Peter still resides on Nashtoba and *is* Factotum. Of course, as with all things, both the island and its inhabitants have experienced changes. Probably the biggest change, and the one certainly central to the entire six-book series, is Peter's marriage and divorce. In *Hot Water*, not only does Peter find a dead body in a bathtub but discovers that his ex-wife, Connie, is back in town. The action of this story is a combination of detection—as Peter and the new chief of police, Will McOwat, track down the killer of Edna Hitchcock—and Peter's avoidance of Connie. Peter is successful in tracking the murderer and bringing the case to a conclusion. He even manages to avoid Connie throughout most of the story, but in the end she proves unavoidable.

The ongoing characters are all introduced in the first story and play parts of varying importance throughout the series. Sarah Abrew, Peter's first customer, still relies on him to read her the morning newspaper. Beston's porch holds a Coke machine that still dispenses old-fashioned bottles of Coca-Cola for a quarter and also supports three local characters. Functioning as Greek chorus, they note and comment on all that goes on in Nashtoba. Rita Peck, Peter's business partner, is the single mother of the challenging teenaged Maxine. Dr. Hardiman Rogers lives hardily with an impressive physique, despite his sixty-something years. He has delivered most of the island's crop of babies over the years and has seen out more patients than he might have chosen to. Peter's sister, Polly, is mentioned in the first book yet does not become a part of the action until the fifth.

Water is in the titles of all of the books, and the adjective used to modify the titular noun has as much to do with the state of Peter and Connie's relationship as it does with the murder mystery. While the killings may be shrouded in secrecy, old and new, the real clouds obscuring each story hang over Peter and Connie. It takes six books covering a span of some three years for these two to admit (to themselves much less to each other) that they may have some talking to do. We are privy to every main character's thoughts and feelings: Peter's thoughts about what he might—yet never does— say to Connie, Connie's anger at Peter's not getting it, Sarah's voiced and unvoiced desires to get the two of them together, and Rita's maunderings on Maxine's whereabouts and Peter's well-being. *Hot, Under, Ice, Troubled, Rough*, and *Still* sum up the couple's progress. In the sixth book, they finally decide to try it again.

JUDITH MCMONIGLE FLYNN
1991–1996   10 books
Mary Daheim

Families and holidays are salient elements of this series featuring Judith Grover McMonigle, proprietor of the Hillside Manor Bed-and-Breakfast. Judith's own family looms large and includes her mother, Gertrude, her cousin Serena "Renie," Judith's son, Mike, and largest of all, her late husband, Dan. While Dan was alive, Judith was the sole support of her husband and son and worked two jobs. During the day, she was a librarian; at night she tended bar at the Meat and Mingle. After she was widowed, Judith discovered an entrepreneurial streak that led her to convert the Grover family home into a B & B.

In *Just Desserts*, Judith is the reluctant hostess for the post-Christmas visit of the contentious Brodie clan, who have sought refuge at the B & B from the effects of exterminators at their own domicile. Graphic designer Renie is pressed into service as Judith's assistant, and the weekend gets off to a sputtering start. When a fortune-teller whom Oriana Brodie has hired for an evening's entertainment dies after eating a cream puff made by Gertrude, homicide investigator Lt. Joe Flynn—erstwhile lover of Judith—arrives to take charge of the case and to throw the McMonigle/Grover ménage into more of a turmoil than murder does.

Judith and Renie are involved in more familial complexities, all of which lead to death. The second book, *Fowl Prey*, takes the pair to an old and famous hotel in British Columbia where they meet a former schoolmate and retired ballet star. Blood, as always, proves thicker than water. The cousins' need to get home for Thanksgiving compels them to assist the strike-hampered Canadian police to sort out the family relationships and solve the murder of a popcorn vendor and his parakeet.

Holy Terrors finds Judith and Renie back in their unnamed city, which closely resembles Seattle. After an Easter egg hunt at Our Lady Star of the Sea (SOT), a woman is found dead in the nursery room. Judith and Renie, both devoted SOTs, delve into this investigation and unearth more secrets and hidden blood ties connected to an inheritance by which someone named Stella Maris benefits.

In the midst of all of these relational killings stand Judith's particular personal relationships. Judith's mother, Gertrude, is an odious woman who has nothing good to say about anyone or anything, especially her daughter. Renie's mother, Deb, may be one of Gertrude's prime nemeses, but Joe Flynn is the recipient of most of her copious venom. The possibility that Joe and Judith might rekindle the spark of their long-lost passion ignites Gertrude's rancor into an impressive pyrotechnic display. When they marry—off the page, between the third and fourth books—Gertrude announces that she will not have Joe Flynn, that "shanty Irishman," living under her roof. Judith, for once, makes it clear that it is *her* roof, and Gertrude finds it necessary to remove herself to her sister-in-law's apartment. That arrangement doesn't last much longer than one book, *Dune to Death*, and *Bantam of the Opera* finds Gertrude abiding in the newly converted toolshed at Hillside Manor.

Although Joe, by virtue of his professional calling, is the official representative of law and order, Judith and Renie are the detectives in every book in this series and are responsible for all the solutions. Their understanding of the convolutions of human nature and the complexities of coupling is astute. While one (or both) may find herself (themselves) in jeopardy as a result of their snooping, their placement in that situation comes about only because the ultimate solution has not become fully apparent.

The bed-and-breakfast appears to have replaced the English country manor home as the site for murder involving small groups of interrelated individuals. Mary Daheim has done a good job of creating the correct ambiance for these nefarious goings-on and compounding the interest by devising an inner circle of individuals closely connected to the protagonist. The series follows a timetable and the development of characters adheres to the time frame, although each book reads well on its own. Fans of the '30s and '40s manor home mysteries will feel right at home with this series.

Emma Lord, Daheim's other series character, may be found in the chapter "Murder between the Pages: Writers and Journalists."

ALISON HOPE & DET. INSP. NICK TREVELLYAN
1991–1996   5 books
Susan B. Kelly

The Hop Valley on the west coast of England is a lovely and imaginary place. Among the towns and villages within the valley are Hopbridge, Little Hopford, and Greater Hopford. Alison Hope's godmother, Lady Molly, lives there with her husband, Sir Anton Armitage, in a house on a cliff overlooking Hop Bay. Tired of London, Alison is ready for some country tranquillity. When she finds a house called Hope Cottage, she knows she has found home and, in *Hope Against Hope*, is in the process of moving not only her residence but her very successful software company there. Det. Insp. Nick Trevellyan of the Hopbridge Criminal Investigation Division (CID) is introduced early in the first story; his initial meeting with Alison is not auspicious.

Aidan Hope arrives in Hopbridge, looking for his cousin Alison. When he finds her, readers learn that he had been her business partner in the early days of Hope Software and had been bought out by Alison after a few unsuccessful years of business. Now that the company is thriving, Aidan wants to reactivate his partnership and, as he had never signed a dissolution agreement, has Alison over the proverbial barrel. When he is found murdered in his room at the Bird in Hand pub, Alison becomes the prime suspect. Nick's sergeant, Bill Deacon, is convinced that Alison is the killer. Nick isn't sure and, while he is unwilling to have his professional integrity compromised by his attraction to her, wants to believe that she is innocent. The proof of Alison's innocence comes at her peril. Nick quite literally saves her and recognizes, in the process, that attraction has turned to love.

In the second book, *Time of Hope*, Nick and Alison are more or less living together and, well aware of their differences, are investigating their similarities. On their return from a well-earned vacation in Venice, Nick's leave is cut short by the murder of the young child of nature, San Francisco "Frisco" Carstairs. When Molly Armitage is attacked and Nick questions Sir Anton on his whereabouts at the relevant time, Alison goes nova over what she perceives as Nick's insensibility yet, when she visits Molly in the hospital, is taken aback by the praise the couple heaps on Nick for his kindness in the very necessary questioning of them both. Although some personal issues between Alison and Nick are resolved in this story, the murderer is brought to justice, and another—seemingly unrelated—spate of crime curtailed, the interesting tension between the two primary characters continues and carries over into the third book.

In a sincere attempt to help a friend and business colleague in *Hope Will Answer*, Alison goes undercover at his London office to track down a computer hacker using the stock market–related products of Orion Software to commit fraud. Nick tries to dissuade her by pointing out that the hacker is not likely to take kindly to possible exposure. Alison ignores his warnings and, of course, finds herself at the mercy of a brutal and unscrupulous criminal. Nick, in the meantime, is involved in tracking a rapist terrorizing the women of Hop Valley. The denouement of each case comes only after fascinating twists and turns of plot and character.

As a native son of the Hop Valley, Nick has long-established connections to the place. Bill Deacon is both his sergeant and his close friend, and that stolid worthy plays an important role in investigating crime and acting as a sounding board for the reticent Nick. Detective constables Carol Halsgrove and Paul Penruan provide backup. Their personal partnership grows along with the series. Reg Grey, Nick's immediate superior, clouds issues and causes consternation among his subordinates, yet he too grows with each book.

Susan B. Kelly's portrayals of place and people are well founded in reality. The author is a computer consultant and clearly knows the ins and outs of that volatile industry. The mythical Hop Valley and its denizens ring true to the English countryside and are reminiscent of Kelly's own home in the Thames Valley.

KATE JASPER
1991–1997   8 books
Jaqueline Girdner

Kate Jasper is the owner of "Jest Gifts," a mail-order gag gift company. She has a warehouse in Oakland where all the shipping and receiving takes place but handles all of the paperwork and phoning from her home in Marin County. On doctor's orders Kate is a vegetarian and seems to have adjusted well to an herbivorous life. Her husband, Craig, is also a vegetarian, which appears to be one of the few things the pair have in common. As *Adjusted to Death* opens, Kate and Craig are separated for the second time and Kate is seriously considering divorce.

In this first story, while waiting to see her chiropractor, Maggie, Kate discovers the dead body of another patient, Scott Younger. Although the police are actively investigating, Maggie asks Kate to find the murderer and save her practice. Wayne Caruso, Scott's bodyguard, is a big, ugly man. In spite of his fearsome appearance and black belt in karate, Wayne is a gentle soul. Kate is strongly attracted to him and the feeling is mutual. As heir to Younger's substantial wealth, Wayne is a prime suspect for his murder. Kate desperately wants to prove him innocent and does.

The series is populated by a strong cast of ancillary characters. Kate's closest friend is Barbara Chu, an electrician and practicing psychic. Barbara's sweetie, Felix Byrne, is a reporter who constantly berates Kate for falling over dead bodies and NOT TELLING him. Craig Jasper is featured in the second book, *The Last Resort*, when his fiancé is murdered and he asks Kate to come to his aid. The "twins" Edna Grimshaw and Arletta Ainsley are ancient, venerable women and close friends who save Kate's bacon in the second book and reappear in the fourth. Wayne's mother, Vesta, enters not only the picture but Kate's house in *Fat-Free and Fatal*, after Kate and Wayne decide to live together. Vesta had been institutionalized and overmedicated for twenty years. When she is taken off the medication and no longer needs custodial care, she is released to her son. Not only is Vesta a generally nasty, spiteful woman, she hates Kate in particular. In *Tea-Totally Dead*, Wayne and Vesta's family take center stage and secrets are spilled along with the blood of two victims.

Marin County is almost a country unto itself. Laughingly known as the hot tub capital of the Western world and affectionately referred to as Mellow Marin, this collection of small, affluent communities is also known for its high number of alternative healers, crystal practitioners, health-food stores, vegetarian restaurants, film and rock stars, gorgeous scenery and weather, and close proximity to The City—San Francisco. Few of the residents of this mystical, magical realm find anything odd about the place, and Jaqueline Girdner treats Marin, its environs, and its denizens with a gentle touch. Kate laughs at herself as often as she laughs at her friends, and the humor in the stories is as warm as it is well deserved.

Kate Jasper exemplifies the new generation of independent women who have created original business ventures to support themselves. Clever, smart, and resourceful, Kate is an ideal amateur detective, which is useful because her friends and associates seem to be murdered with great regularity. She is also a woman with serious questions about the institution of marriage, and Girdner addresses these concerns with all due respect. Gone are the days when the hero rode off on his white charger with the heroine seated behind him, clasping his manly waist. While there is waist clasping to be sure, it is bi-lateral, and Kate Jasper is the hero of these stories.

JULIE BLAKE & VIC PAOLI
1991–1997   4 books
Sally Chapman

California's Silicon Valley was once known as the Valley of Heart's Delight. Land then covered with small farms and orchards is now covered with concrete and asphalt. Meandering creeks falling from the coastal mountain range to the San Francisco Bay have been straightened and lined with Gunite; estuaries are being filled in and built upon. This valley, once considered one of the finest agricultural areas in the continental United States, is no more; the fertile nature of the valley has undergone some radical changes and now technology is the valley's produce.

Julie Blake is typical of the new breed of valley inhabitants—young, highly intelligent, serious-minded, type A workaholic. She is vice president of one of Silicon Valley's highest high-tech companies and, in *Raw Data*, her current project for International Computers, Inc. (ICI), is the development of molecular memory. Arriving at work one morning, Julie is met by one of her programmers babbling about a body in the mainframe of the ICI 9000. Because of the sensitive nature of the work the company has been doing, the local police—embodied by Lt. Dalton—are joined by the FBI and the National Security Agency (NSA) in the investigation of not only the murder but also the sale of the molecular memory design to the Soviets. Vic Paoli is an information systems analyst for NSA. Together, he and Julie plug the leak to the Soviets and solve Ronald's murder but not before two more ICI employees are killed—one of them, Julie's fiancé.

Vic and Julie share a mutual attraction, and, at the conclusion of the first book, Julie leaves ICI and Paoli comes up with the idea of starting an agency specializing in detecting computer fraud. As *Love Bytes* opens, Data 9000 Investigations is a reality. The pair is running out of start-up capital when Lorna Donatello, a bail bondsperson, asks them to find Arnie Lufkin, a client who has skipped his bond. Julie is reluctant to take the case until Lorna explains that they are probably the only people who can find Arnie, a hotshot programmer designing very sophisticated virtual reality software.

Arnie had embezzled nearly half a million dollars from his employer, Anco International, so Julie and Paoli offer their professional services to the president of that company to discover the flaws in Anco's financial software. However, working undercover, the pair begin to track the elusive Arnie. Two women are murdered, Lt. Dalton gets involved, and the stakes of the case are raised. With the help of her best friend Maxine "Max" LaCoste, and Max's fiancé, Wayne Hanson, Julie gets some firsthand experience in the world of virtual reality and unmasks the killer.

The wedding of Max and Wayne is a subplot of *Cyberkiss* in which Julie and Paoli are hired by Bernie Kowolsky, a.k.a. Whip Boy, to find the identity of the sender of some kinky messages and a death threat signed Night Dancer and sent via the Net. Julie and Paoli sign on with Biotech, the company for which Bernie works, and discover that the messages originate within the building. After Bernie and his girlfriend, Gloria, are found murdered, Lt. Dalton enters the scene and asks for Julie's help. The case is brought to an exciting and surprising conclusion right after Max and Wayne's wedding, which takes place in the virtual reality of the planet Saturn.

Sally Chapman is a veteran of nine years with IBM in the heart of Silicon Valley. Using her extensive knowledge of the computer world and its inhabitants, she has created an engaging pair of high-tech detectives and a raft of interesting and credible ancillary characters. Chapman's plots are intricate and fast-paced, and we look forward to more investigations into cyberspace and other electronic realms.

SIMONA GRIFFO
1991–1997   7 books
Trella Crespi, Camilla T. Crespi (Camilla Trinchieri)

In *The Trouble with a Small Raise*, Simona Griffo decides it's time to ask for a salary increase after eighteen months working as art buyer for HH&H Advertising, Inc. When she finds Fred Critelli, her boss and the agency's creative director, dead on the floor of his office, it appears her timing is off. Italian-born Simona is a woman of passion, healthy appetites, and an almost insatiable curiosity. Despite strong warnings from Det. Stan Greenhouse against getting involved in a police investigation, Simona persists with her questions, finds the perfect face for a client's new perfume ads, gets pushed in front of a bus, and unmasks the killer.

On vacation from the agency in *The Trouble with Moonlighting*, Simona is asked by an old friend, film director Sara Varni, to work as dialogue coach on a movie Varni is filming in New York. A series

KILLINGS ON THE MARKET: BUSINESS AND FINANCE • 159

of accidents befalls the beautiful Hollywood star playing the lead in Varni's film *Where Goes the Future?* and she is found, by Simona, garroted in her hotel bedroom. Once again, Greenhouse, now Simona's lover, is on the case and continues to implore her to stay out of police business. She is as incapable of minding her own business as she is of turning down a steaming bowl of "Pasta Crisi." (Recipe found on page 287 of *The Trouble with Too Much Sun*.) At the successful conclusion of the case, Greenhouse tells Simona that he thinks they need a break from one another. As he is almost totally uncommunicative about himself, Simona agrees that perhaps theirs is not a love that is meant to be, and the two part.

The Trouble with Too Much Sun finds Simona and a crew from HH&H at a Club Med working on an ad campaign for a new sun-protection product, Beau Sol, a line produced by a French cosmetics firm hoping to break into the American market. A young mother named Iguana is murdered and Simona finds her body. She and Greenhouse haven't seen one another for four months, and as she gets deeper into the questions surrounding Iguana's death and the possible involvement of some or all of her crew, Simona actually finds herself wishing as much for Stan's protection as for his warm, sexy body. When he flies to Guadeloupe on a fourteen-hour furlough, Simona realizes that he has missed her as well. In *The Trouble with Thin Ice*, the two, joined by Stan's fourteen-year-old son, Willy, go to Connecticut for Christmas week at an inn.

Simona is a *Romana*—a woman of Rome. Her father is a diplomat, and she attended Barnard College when her family was living in Boston. She returned to Rome, where she worked in the film industry and married. After six years, Simona made the discovery that her husband, Carlo Linetti, had been unfaithful to her from the first month of their marriage. She divorced him and moved to New York, where she hoped to heal her heart and find a new life. Five-foot-four, with a generous bosom and a bit of extra padding around her midsection, Simona is an attractive woman. Her genuine interest in people, coupled with her burning curiosity, wins her friends and puts her in jeopardy. Her relationship with Stan Greenhouse is not without complications, but these arise on both sides and stem in part from pain and fear. They continue to learn to be together and the development of their union makes up an interesting part of the series.

Camilla Trinchieri has written this series under two names—Trella Crespi for the first three books, and Camilla T. Crespi for the last four. No matter what name she is using, she writes with a deft hand and uses her own life as the source of many of Simona's traits and adventures.

BLANCHE WHITE
1992–1994 2 books
Barbara Neely

This unique character is introduced in a Farleigh, North Carolina, courtroom where she is being sentenced to thirty days in jail for passing a bad check. Blanche White had thought there was enough money in her account to cover the checks she'd written, and if four of her employers had paid her before they left town on their vacations, she would have had more than enough. The judge—with his mind halfway to the golf course and seeing before him a black woman who had been charged with the same "crime" before—takes no time to consider the fact that she could now cover the checks and pay any fine levied against her. The gavel falls and the sentence is passed. Escorted by a matron to her cell, Blanche asks to go to the bathroom. A commotion in the hallway gives her the opportunity to slip away. Her path of escape takes her directly to a house where a job, arranged through a domestic agency, awaits her. In one ten-page chapter, readers are given the essence of both this character and the story in which she is featured.

Even though the action in *Blanche on the Lam* devolves around a family's secrets and their murderous outcome, the primary character's perspective is highly unusual. Blanche is a well-informed outsider. Her position as domestic help makes her almost invisible and her black skin aids in keeping her quite literally in the shadows. In reality, as anyone who has done domestic work knows, "who cleaneth the rooms, possesseth the secrets" (a Nichols original). Employers are more than likely to regard any knowledge those who serve them may gather, along with the dust bunnies, as unimportant in their view of reality. Feeling that all is not as it appears with her employers, Blanche begins paying close attention to things around the house and taps into her old-girl network for more information on who's who and what's what. Blanche discovers the motive for the three obvious deaths, figures out who caused them, and sends her only ally for help just before the killer comes to ensure that Blanche's suspicions remain unvoiced.

With a substantial gratuity from her ally in the first book, Blanche moves to Boston, where she enrolls her wards—the children of her late sister—in a private school. The parents of a pair of Taifa and Malik's friends invite the children and Blanche to spend some of the summer with them, and, as *Blanche Among the Talented Tenth* opens, she is packing for a trip to Amber Cove, a Black resort on the coast of Maine. An accidental death and a suicide lead Blanche and Mattie Harris, a well-known feminist writer, on a search for the reason behind the suicide of Mattie's godson; in the process they uncover potentially incriminating secrets. In this story, readers learn why Blanche feels as much an outsider in the realm of wealthy, light-skinned blacks as she is in the all-white world. Despite Blanche's mistrust of the "other classes," she is determined to give Taifa and Malik all the advantages a good education will provide even if it means exposing them to the temptation to buy into snobbery and racism.

Barbara Neely provides us with a full-blown character in full color. Blanche White is by no means a second-class citizen even though most of the world tends to treat her as such. She is fully aware of her gifts and the power she commands in the world, while being very realistic about her situation and other people's perception of her. With this character, Neely is definitely blazing new trails in the territory of detective fiction and giving readers a rare glimpse into Black culture and the workings of a black woman's mind. Two books are not enough.

EMILY "EM" HANSEN
1994–1997   3 books
Sarah Andrews (Brown)

The oil patch is a rugged and volatile place to work and for years it has been unquestionably male dominated. At the beginning of the most recent oil boom in the early '70s, American women demanded their fair share of the new jobs for the first time, and the field, quite literally, opened up in a new way. In the first book, *Tensleep*, Em Hansen holds a degree in geology but is working as a mudlogger on the Tensleep field near Meeteetse, Wyoming, where she is the only woman on the crew. The death of Em's mentor, field geologist Bill Kretzmer, rocks her but she has no reason to question the verdict of accident until young pumper Willie Sewell is found dead. Things don't add up to the sheriff's conclusion that Willie was trampled by wild mustangs in the course of a rustling attempt. Em begins to wonder if the two deaths are connected and if perhaps Bill's car wreck wasn't an accident. When drilling is shut down by an act of sabotage, Em travels to Denver to talk with Bill's widow. Elyria Kretzmer, a consulting economist making predictions for petropricing, reacts with a mixture of anger and relief to Em's suggestion that her husband's death may have been murder and agrees to give Em whatever assistance she needs.

Back on the field, Bill's replacement, Alix Chadwick, has been courted then rejected by Chet, the son of the wealthy oil field owner Garth Hawkins. A visit to the Hawkins ranch with Alix gives Em the clue to piece all of the evidence together, and, in an exciting denouement, she is set upon by a cowboy dressed all in black and a seemingly vicious horse. Narrowly escaping death, Em presents the sheriff with motive, means, and method, and the case is brought to a successful conclusion.

As a reward for service rendered in the field, in *A Fall in Denver*, Em is given a position as field geologist for the parent company, the giant corporate entity in Denver, Blackfeet Oil. Her grandmother, an upstanding Boston matron, is delighted with Em's promotion and provides her with the necessary wardrobe and urgings to connect with old school chums now living in Denver. Reluctantly, Em meets three of her former classmates and has as much trouble relating to them as she does to Pete Tutaraitis, a very attractive fellow geologist.

At her meeting with the president to welcome her to the company, Em sees what appears to be a body falling past his twelfth-floor office window. After visiting personnel and meeting her office mate, Maggie McNutt, Em's curiosity gets the best of her and she goes outside to find that her imagination had not been playing tricks. An accountant had fallen to his death from a sixteenth-floor window with a map of Hat Rock oil field in his pocket. Em has been assigned Hat Rock field as her first project but getting information on the project proves difficult and then, after her nominal boss denies her access to company records, impossible. Oddly enough, her grandmother proves to be a staunch, if unwilling, ally as Em unravels the strands of deception and greed that lead unfortunately to another murder before the solution to the killings becomes apparent.

After Em's success in solving Bill Kretzmer's death, Elyria offers to share her home with Em. Together with Sgt. Carlos Ortega, the investigating officer on the case and one of Elyria's neighbors, Maggie McNutt and Archie Arch—mudman, poet, and street citizen of the universe—join forces to discover the killer and the reasons behind the murders. In the process, Em uncovers a major scam that could put Blackfeet Oil out of business.

Sarah Andrews is a geologist who began her career with the United States Geological Survey. In the '80s she joined the oil boom as a field geologist for Amoco. Now she is involved in the environmental services industry, where she works on toxic spills and Superfund sites. Her knowledge of the oil industry and the rigors of the oil patch are clearly apparent in her protagonist. Em Hansen begins as a smart but insecure woman working in a man's world and gains confidence and respect in the stories in which she is featured. By the end of the second book, Em is comfortable with who she is and what she knows. Andrews's series can only get more interesting.

Business and finance are often referred to as cutthroat, and the foregoing series capitalize on that appellation. In an ever-expanding and global marketplace it behooves those in mercantile and fiscal endeavors to keep their eyes not only on the bottom line but on those who are out to make real killings on the market.

SOME OTHER BUSINESS AND FINANCIAL SLEUTHS

Finny Aletter	Viera Kolarova
China Bayles	Jane Lawless
Tess Darcy	Lloyds of London
Catherine Dean	Stoner McTavish
Lark Dodge	Pam Nilsen
Abigail Doyle	Hana Shaner
Fiora	Teal Stewart
Callahan Garrity	Jane Tregar
Pat Goodenough	John Waltz
Anneke Haagen	Liz Wareham
Amanda Hazard	Magdelana Yoder
Guinevere Jones	

LEGAL EAGLES:
Lawyers

At the twilight of the ancient Roman gods, mortals were in a state of turmoil and the earth was awash in the blood of conflict. One by one, the gods abandoned the earth and left the mortals to govern themselves. The last of the immortals to leave was Astraea, goddess of justice, innocence, and purity. Deserted by their deities, mortal Romans were forced to devise a system of laws whereby justice could be fairly meted out. This is the system upon which the courts of law in many parts of the world, including the United Kingdom and the United States, rely today. Images of Astraea may be seen around these courts; this goddess, representing justice, is the blindfolded woman holding aloft the scales on which she weighs opposing claims.

Today's practitioners of the law follow an ancient and honorable tradition, and while there are those who argue that the law has been subverted—if not perverted—others staunchly uphold the law's letter and spirit. English solicitor Arthur G. Crook proclaims, "My clients are *always* innocent!" and in the fifty books in the series that features him (1936–1974), he sets about proving that proclamation far beyond the shadow of a doubt. Under the pseudonym Anthony Gilbert, Lucy Beatrice Malleson created a wonderfully rumpled, loud, and rather boisterous gentleman of the bar whose tactics can easily be admired by today's readers.

Cut from a completely different bolt of cloth is English barrister Antony Maitland. Quiet and reserved to the point of personal repression, Maitland is nevertheless a formidable advocate. Throughout the forty-eight books in this series (1962–1987) this character uses the sheer strength of his professional will and well-honed sense of justice to reach the truth. Sara Hutton Bowen-Judd, writing as Sara Woods, uses the English court of criminal law as the foundation for all the stories, which are wonderful exercises in puzzle solving. If readers can overlook some of Maitland's more annoying mannerisms, they're in for a delightful time.

The antics of five young English lawyers and their former law professor are chronicled in three books (1981–1989) written by Sarah Cockburn under the name Sarah Caudwell. The brilliant professor Hilary Tamar is one of crime and mystery fiction's most enigmatic characters because no one—not even the author herself—is sure of Tamar's sex, giving proof to Coleridge's declaration, "The truth is, a great mind must be androgynous." Crafted in the full flower of the Queen's English, these tales take the scholar's approach to the solution of crime and are worth enduring what may appear to some to be overblown verbosity.

An ocean and a continent away from the British courts of law is Rebecca Schwartz, a young San Francisco lawyer. The city and its denizens feature colorfully in this five-book series (1982–1993) by Bay Area writer Julie Smith. The ongoing cast is Rebecca, her father—a noted lawyer himself—her archetypal Jewish mother, and the rest of her rather wacky family. The tales are fast paced with reality often stretched to the boundaries of our belief.

Cass Jameson is a criminal defense lawyer for the Legal Aid Society in New York, and it is her responsibility to provide the best possible defense for clients often obviously guilty. In the five books in this series (1983–1997) readers observe Cass treading the fine line between an innate idealism and harsh, often dangerous, reality. Carolyn Wheat treats her character and the cases in which Cass becomes involved with proper gravity, and there is a gritty authenticity to each story which Cass's basic humanity saves from being ponderous.

Back across the "pond" Doris Shannon writing as E. X. Giroux has created English barrister Robert Forsythe. Like Sara Woods's Maitland, Forsythe enjoys a mildly repressed nature as the series opens. However, through the ten books (1984–1993), he confronts that which has hindered him and makes as much personal progress as professional. Ably assisted by his legal secretary cum office manager and close friend, Miss Sanderson, Forsythe cerebrates his way through investigations and is not above letting the divine intervene.

This bevy of barristers, selection of solicitors, and legion of lawyers are apt forerunners to those who follow in the fading footsteps of Astraea.

LENNOX KEMP
1984–1996   9 books
M(argaret) R(eid) D(uncan) Meek

In the first book in this series, *Hang the Consequences*, Lennox Kemp is working as a private investigator for a small agency owned by former policeman George McCready and his wife, Grace. Lennox is a fully qualified solicitor; however, he has been struck—quite rightly—from the lists by the Law Society for embezzling trust funds. In the second novel, *The Split Second*, he has been reinstated to the bar and does Grace the favor of looking into her niece's inheritance and well-being. *Remembrance of Rose* finds Lennox the head of Gillorn's Law Office on the outskirts of London. Lennox remains a practicing lawyer for the rest of the series, but his fall from grace and the path he followed from that point have taught him new skills and given him new perspectives on the practice of the law.

Small of stature and rather unprepossessing in appearance, Lennox made a good private operative; his quiet demeanor and his ability to fade into the woodwork served him and his clients well. Despite Lennox's ethical lapse, his sense of honor is impeccable. When the reason for his transgression is explained, his motive is clearly seen as one of probity; his innate integrity got him reinstated to the bar and won him his current position. As a respected member of a respected law firm, he is a bit more noticeable, and, while he is still less than handsome, his looks serve to only disconcert some people.

If this character has any failing, it is a weakness for women. Lennox's admiration for the fair sex is always manifested in a gentlemanly fashion, and sometimes the objects of his attraction may not even be aware of his notice; in some cases, they may not even be aware of just what he has noticed. Unfortunately for Lennox, all of his affections are inappropriate; fortunately for the series, they are all interesting.

M. R. D. Meek has devised an unusual character. Lennox Kemp's fallibility is no secret; he has erred, paid the consequences, and been reinstated. Moreover, he has learned much more about human nature during his exile than he might have had he stayed on the straight and narrow path. Like Hester Prynne, he wears his transgression like a scarlet letter. This openness, combined with a shrewd intelligence, makes Lennox Kemp a character we always enjoy.

WILLA JANSSON
1987–1997 6 books

LAURA DI PALMA
1988–1995 5 books
Lia Matera

Lia Matera has created two series characters. Both Willa Jansson and Laura Di Palma are women, both are lawyers in San Francisco, and there the similarities end.

As the series featuring Willa opens in *Where Lawyers Fear to Tread*, she is in her last year of law school, fifth in her class, and an editor of the *Malhousie Law Review*. Child of radical-leftist parents, Willa plans to use her training and expertise in defending the leftist cause and has accepted a position in the offices of Julian Warneke, an old radical himself and defender of the Left. Murder intrudes on Willa's last weeks in school, and she finds herself both prime suspect and potential victim. After a narrow escape, Willa uncovers the murderer, graduates, and passes the California State Bar Examination.

In *A Radical Departure* Willa has taken her position with Warneke's office. Unfortunately, her employer is murdered by hemlock poisoning, and once again Willa finds herself under suspicion. Not until Willa's mother inherits Warneke's rather large estate does suspicion shift to Mrs. Jansson. Working with San Francisco Homicide Det. Don Surgelato, introduced in the first book, Willa deftly exonerates her mother and nails the true perp.

With the demise of Warneke and his law firm, Willa is out of a job; beyond that, she is tired of being underpaid. In *Hidden Agenda*, she interviews with several firms and ultimately takes a high-salaried position with a firm that has actually solicited her. Wailes, Roth, Fotheringham & Beck is an extremely conservative Wall Street–based firm, and it doesn't take Willa long to wonder just why she was hired. The death of the senior partner in the office gives her a clue. Surgelato's skills help her untangle the knotty problem of murder. At the end of the story, she moves to the firm's Los Angeles office, but *Prior Convictions* finds her back in San Francisco one year later, clerking for federal court judge Michael J. Shanna.

Willa Jansson's development in this series epitomizes the idealist who follows a logical path and is confronted with all the obstacles reality can cast. Raised to believe in the necessity of championing the underdog, Willa has applied herself in a demanding profession with a high regard for excellence and has succeeded admirably. Her experience in the practice of the law has shown her that it is a profession designed to represent both sides of any issue and that fairness and inequity apply equally to each. Willa is an intelligent and honorable individual, and readers are given the opportunity to observe her questioning the early object of her convictions and making a choice from personal integrity.

Laura Di Palma is, as her series opens, the kind of lawyer to whom sharks extend professional courtesy. As a high-profile criminal defense attorney for the firm of White, Sayres & Speck in San Francisco, Laura has recently completed the successful defense of a man charged with the shooting deaths of two Republican senators.

In *The Smart Money*, brilliant and ambitious Laura returns to her hometown, a small unprosperous community on the coast of northern California. She has come back after an absence of eleven years for one compelling reason—to wreak vengeance on her ex-husband, Gary Gleason. Once back in Hillsdale, Laura reconnects with her estranged family, including her cousin Hal. Events in this first story actually lead Laura to believe that vengeance is not all it's cracked up to be. Yet, in the ensuing stories, demons she has thought laid to rest are dragged up by their wings by other, even more vicious spirits.

The locations of the novels alternate between Hillsdale and San Francisco, and Laura's dilemmas are both personal and professional. Her cousin Hal Di Palma plays a large role in the first three (of five) books, and her sometime partner, former lover, and close friend, private investigator Sander "Sandy" Arkelett, is featured in all of them. Anger and stubbornness fuel this intelligent advocate. When these are coupled with a sense of righteousness, Laura Di Palma is a dangerous adversary, one not to be crossed.

Lia Matera is a graduate of Hastings College of Law in San Francisco. While there, she was the editor of the *Constitutional Law Review*. After graduation, she was a teaching fellow at Stanford Law School. She has given up the practice of law to write about it and, in the process, has created two diametrically opposite characters to demonstrate some of the diversity in the legal profession. Both of her characters are well developed, and the scenes in which they appear are believable and engaging. The legal background is solid, and readers will learn about the ethics and the subtleties upon which the profession depends. Matera's background provides a solid foundation for her novels, and we recommend them.

HELEN WEST & DET. SUPT. GEOFFREY BAILEY
1988–1997   6 books

SARAH FORTUNE
1991–1994   2 books
Frances Fyfield (Hegarty)

As a crown prosecutor, Helen West operates on the same side of the law as Det. Supt. Geoffrey Bailey. In *A Question of Guilt*, they meet when Helen is assigned to a case Bailey has brought to trial. The evidence against Stanislaus Jaskowski is clear; he has confessed to killing Sylvia Bernard, the wife of solicitor Michael Bernard. In spite of the apparently straightforward evidence of Jaskowski's guilt, both West and Bailey are certain that there is another agent of death—one who merely used a desperate man to do her bidding and commit murder.

Quietly, the two go about building evidence and play a waiting game to bring the case to a successful close. In this first novel, there is no mystery as to the identity of the murderer; there is not even any mystery as to the true perpetrator or the reasons behind the death of Mrs. Bernard. The mystery is centered on the one missing piece to the puzzle.

As they work to discover that piece, West and Bailey discover one another. Neither of these characters is in the first flush of youth and they fall "into like" long before either will admit to love. Part of this bilateral reticence stems from their respective professions, which expose not only the harsh side of life but the sheer banality of most crime. Another part of the couple's reticence arises from their earlier marital ventures, and in spite of their similar outlook on life, the differences between them are legion.

In *Not That Kind of Place*, West and Bailey move together to a borrowed house in the village of Branston, not far outside of London. Their commitment to one another is growing, and each is reluctant to tell the other just how much they despise the house in which they are living and the pretentiousness of the village and its inhabitants. Added to this tension is the fact that Helen does not believe that the man Bailey has charged with the death of a young woman is guilty. With only a strong instinctive feeling in her favor, Helen goes about finding evidence to support that intuition. Bailey, trusting the person he knows and has come to love, is inclined to heed her judgment. At the denouement, Helen, having been proved right, is put in jeopardy and that event allows the tension between the pair to come to a head. Honesty ultimately prevails and each admits hatred of their current situation to the other.

While the mystery central to each of the novels in this series is well crafted and compelling, much of the ongoing pleasure in reading Fyfield's books has to do with the complexities in the relationship between her primary characters. The passion present in this relationship is not primarily a physical one. Readers follow the courtship of West and Bailey through their conversations with one another and come to realize—as much as the two do themselves—that what is unspoken has as much, if not more, impact as what is spoken. Intelligence, maturity, and the aforementioned reticence of the two protagonists play counterpoint throughout the series. Each is willing to question long-held beliefs in light of the other's sensibilities and both work hard toward mutually desired accord.

Sarah Fortune, on the other hand, is a physical creature from the outset of the series that features her. A solicitor for a prestigious

London Mayfair firm, Sarah often wonders just what she is doing there as she knows full well that she makes it all up as she goes along. In spite of this—or perhaps because of it—Sarah is well regarded in her profession. Privately, however, her activities might raise some eyebrows, for one of the things Sarah does the best is give men the pleasure of her company and her body.

Evil is at the base of the first novel, *Shadows on the Mirror*, and Sarah's response to the personification of that evil both surprises and frightens her. The end of the story is in some ways no surprise, but the ultimate scenes come as a shock to the reader as well as to Sarah Fortune herself. The story continues in *Perfectly Pure and Good* as Sarah goes to the seaside town of Merton to help a family sort out a confusing estate. The evil present in the first novel reasserts itself in the second, yet this time Sarah is more ready to deal with it and whatever unpleasant aspect of herself it reveals.

In all of these novels, there is an overabundance of fact, much of which is irrelevant to the outcome of the official inquiry. At the same time, the stories would suffer from the omission of any single piece, as Fyfield uses the volume of the raw stuff of life to suffuse character and tale with a living quality. The mixture of total honesty and British reticence prevents the books from resembling cozies; they are not police procedural novels either, as there are too many points of view presented. The ending of each novel may not be a happy one, nor as tidy as one might wish it to be. It is believable and very true to life in all its messy reality.

Frances Fyfield is a practicing solicitor in the Crown Prosecution Service in London, specializing in criminal law. The characters she so accurately portrays in both her series are based on her own personal and professional experience. Although Helen West, Geoffrey Bailey, and Sarah Fortune are the primary characters in the books in which they appear, all of the characters crafted by Fyfield are believable and add dimension to the fabric of the stories. Fyfield does not write about her subjects as much as she writes around them. While her use of language appears to circumnavigate her characters and the situations that engage them, her choice of words and structure cuts directly to the center of things. Readers find that they have to do a lot of the work in building the images Fyfield outlines for them in these novels.

JOHN LLOYD BRANSON & LYDIA FAIRCHILD
1988–1993   5 books
D(oris) R. Meredith

Although the town of Canadian is located in the Texas Panhandle, it is not what one would consider typically Texan. Granted, there are cattle ranches that require vast tracts of range land, but the town itself is an oasis of civilization with a river running through it and a substantial number of trees. Amarillo is the nearest major city and is just far enough away to be convenient without interfering with the character of Canadian.

Lawyer John Lloyd Branson is a Canadian native who attended Harvard School of Law, clerked for a Supreme Court justice in Washington, D.C., and made a name for himself in the annals of jurisprudence. However, the sleaze and sneakiness of Washington lawyers and politicos offended John Lloyd's sense of honor. He saw the actions taken as a matter of course as betrayals of almost everything the United States represents. Unwilling to compromise his values by playing an unfair game with bent rules, John Lloyd had removed himself back to his place of origin, where he could be sure of dealing only with the homegrown variety of crook.

Enter Lydia Ann Fairchild: twenty-four years old, a second-year student at Southern Methodist University School of Law with the highest grade-point average in her class. With a recommendation from the dean, she interviews Lawyer Branson for a position as his clerk. Tension between the two is apparent from their initial meeting. At least privately, each admits to an attraction to the other; both are of striking appearance. However, outwardly they are in opposition, as Lydia looks to score against John Lloyd at every opportunity and she is not above using physical force to make her point.

The first case the two work on, in *Murder by Impulse*, puts the pair at swords' point as they are called to defend a bigamist charged with the unsuccessful murder of his first, and only lawful, wife. In *Murder by Deception*, the degree of guilt of their client sets Lydia and John Lloyd at odds. A serial killer and a surprising denouement in *Murder by Masquerade* begin a shift in Lydia's perceptions, and *Murder by Reference* forces her to come to terms with the revelations she has had. By the time *Murder by Sacrilege* opens, Lydia and John Lloyd have acknowledged the facts that each is entitled to hold a point of view divergent from the other's and that there is more than a shared love of the law to keep them together.

John Lloyd Branson is a passionate man, and this passion is expressed in his impeccable approach to the law, to the land and its people, and, above all, to his own sense of honor. Lydia is also passionate, though her passion is that of impulse. Trained to believe true justice is blind, Lydia is inclined to believe in the immutability of the law. John Lloyd's understanding of the blindness of justice is more subtle and incorporates even more understanding of human fallibility than Lydia's impassioned feelings do.

This series is character-driven; the crimes and misdemeanors chronicled pale by comparison to the activities of the two main characters. D. R. Meredith has recreated a lot of what passed between Tracy and Hepburn at their cinematic peak. Almost always "she v. he" makes for an interesting story and, juxtaposed against murder, the relationship takes on an added dimension. When the two actually come to terms with their differences and their similarities and let the sparks fly, the series begins to hold the promise of greater latitude for whatever may be possible.

One of the most outstanding novels in this series has to be *Murder by Deception*. Single-handedly author Meredith takes on the Texas legislature, the Department of Energy, and, in a sense, the United States government. Despite having crafted a work of fiction, Meredith addressed the very real problem of nuclear-waste disposal and its potential threat to a four-state aquifer. She paid a very real price for her fictional treatment of a factual situation. If you ask, she may tell you about it.

Meredith has also penned a series in which Sheriff Charles Matthews is the featured character.

NEIL HAMEL
1988–1996   7 books
Judith Van Gieson

The original Neil Hamel was a colonel of the Tenth Mountain Division who died in an alpine avalanche in December 1945. His namesake is female, his niece, and a lawyer in Albuquerque, New Mexico. Neil shares an office with her partner, Brink Harrison, and their secretary, Anna. Not a particularly prosperous practice, it is enough, more or less, to support the three of them. In the normal course of events, Neil handles real estate transactions and divorce and child-custody cases; she doesn't do wills but she does do murder cases when she can, and in this series she can in all seven books.

Neil does not pursue justice for its own sake or even for her own sense of right versus wrong. For the most part, she doesn't even like her clients. She is not driven by any passion but works as a craftsman who knows that every problem has a solution and, using the tools of her trade, finds it. Neil views most of life as simply inevitable and is rarely surprised by the actions of others or their outcome. Although she is presented with several opportunities, Neil does not take the law into her own hands even when she knows that the prescribed punishment will not come close to suiting the crime. She serves justice nominally and meets the letter, if not the spirit, of the law.

While murder is at the center of each story, the peripheral elements are where most of the interest of the tales lies. Crimes against the land and animals draw Neil's attention and advocacy. She is not a passionate activist for animal rights or environmental causes, yet these are areas where she expends her energies and talents to the fullest. As a product of the late '60s, she feels empathy for the survivors of that era—particularly those who were caught up in the moral questions surrounding the Vietnam war.

The land and its inhabitants play important roles in this series: the sere beauties of New Mexico, the poverty, overpopulation, and emptiness of Old Mexico, the Big Sky beauty of Montana, the native flora and fauna and people at their best and at their worst. Neil is not a New Mexico native; The Kid, her lover, isn't either. Both are transplants from separate parts of the country, the world, cultures, decades. The two have found a geography that suits them and they have found each other. There is an ease in the relationship between the woman and her young man, and, if they are not at ease with the harsh and beautiful high desert they inhabit, they feel acceptance and admiration for its varied qualities.

There is a spare, almost Zen quality to this series. Scenes are laid and overlaid with a chiaroscuro technique. Author Van Gieson's writing is evocative rather than descriptive and gives readers the essence of place and action without buffeting them with detail. Neil Hamel is one of the most completely independent individuals we've encountered and one who operates without rancor or a need for vengeance. Her development isn't dependent on her history, and her sense of self isn't dependent on any other being. She is the ideal character to reflect this economy of style as her life is just that—basic, frugal, unadorned.

JAMES FLEMING
1990–1995   5 books
Ann C. Fallon

This series is set in Ireland, with that lovely country and its people an integral part of every story. The featured character, James Fleming, is a solicitor and owner of a small law firm that specializes in estate management and drawing up wills and trusts. While Fleming's area of expertise is a fairly pedestrian avenue of the practice of law, he does seem to have a flair for solving puzzles related to the detection of murder. Although Fleming's office is in Dublin, his work often takes him out into the countryside, as does his flair, and when murder occurs he is frequently on the spot.

James Fleming is tall, slim, and muscular. Good at both his profession and his avocation of detection, James reserves his deepest passion for locomotives and train travel, and this long-standing love is brought into each story. In fact, in *Potter's Field* a chance meeting on a train in Peru provides the opening to the case. James is a loner. In a country where late marriage for men is not unusual, no one is surprised at his lack of romantic attachment. However, James's mother, Vivienne Fleming, berates him for his bachelor status and tries to arrange matches for him among her friends' eligible daughters, while remaining conspicuously silent on the matter of James's physician brother's lack of wife and family.

James does admire women and has even considered marriage on one or two occasions, but he seems to be missing some vital information about women and what draws them to men. In *Blood Is Thicker* he meets and is immediately attracted to Sarah Gallagher, a young violin virtuoso. The story centers on Sarah and her family, and even though the conclusion is in the family's favor, James is decidedly not. He carries the torch for Sarah in the next three books, but their union is not to be. James meets Dr. Geraldine Keohane in *Where Death Lies* and they seem to be getting to know one another, but she apparently finds James's brother, Donald, more compatible. James's frustration level rises until the end of *Hour of Our Death*, when he finally takes Geraldine into his arms.

This series is very much about James Fleming. The detection in each book arises out of his innate curiosity, and his tenacity keeps him working on the small, seemingly insignificant things that lead to a puzzle's solution. James is introspective and interested in other people's personalities. Perhaps his interest in human psychology is an attempt on his part to understand his lack of success with the fair sex. He does achieve a great understanding of human motivations and, in several cases, unravels fairly tightly knotted family secrets. Oddly enough, James's efforts rarely generate thanks as he often brings facts to light that almost everyone would rather keep dark. His sense of fair play has brought him a certain notoriety, however, and it is reasonable to expect that he will continue unearthing nasty little secrets for many books to come. We hope so.

JUDGE DEBORAH KNOTT
1992–1997   5 books
Margaret Maron

Lee, Stephenson & Knott is the firm for which Deborah Knott practices law as this series opens in *Bootlegger's Daughter*. The first chapter of this novel clearly explains why this lawyer wants a change. The long and short of it is that she decides to run for the elected office of district judge. Once her name is on the slate, Deborah takes stock of the strikes already against her. First of all, she is female in an area that relies heavily upon good old boys and their inevitable network. Secondly, she is the daughter of a former maker of 80-proof white lightnin' who has served prison time for possession with intent to sell untaxed liquor. Colleton County is small and everyone is either related to everyone else or married to someone who is. Who one is and how they fit into the community is fixed from birth. Deborah will always be female and will always be Kezzie Knott's daughter.

The stories are all connected, and to discuss the second and third books in the series would give away vital bits of the first. Suffice it to say that murder and its solution play a major role in each story. However, an even larger role is played by the small and tightly linked communities of which Deborah and her large family are a part.

Margaret Maron is a Southern gentlewoman with a deep understanding of the subtlety and nuance of Southern connections and behavior; she conveys this acuity through her protagonist. She also gifts Deborah with a keen sense of justice that is carefully balanced against the personal knowledge this character holds of all the people with whom she deals. Her justice is tempered with mercy, and she is known to be a fair player, one to whom people turn when they are troubled. Deborah holds a special place in her large and diverse family and through the course of five books comes to find that the place fits her as well as she fits it. Maron crafts the personal and the professional aspects of this character in a tight, close harmony and gives readers a new steel magnolia to admire.

We would love to write reams in praise of this series and all of the inventions of Maron's fertile mind. We cannot, so will simply let readers know that *Bootlegger's Daughter* won the Edgar, Agatha, Anthony, and Macavity awards for 1992—a sweep of the mystery awards for that year.

Sigrid Harald, Maron's other series character, appears in the chapter "Behind the Badge: Major Metropolitan Police."

BARBARA HOLLOWAY
1991–1996   3 books
Kate (Gertrude) Wilhelm (Knight)

Death Qualified refers to the necessary requirement for an attorney practicing criminal law to be eligible to represent a client accused of a crime that could invoke the death sentence. *The Best Defense* is what a defending attorney *must* provide her client regardless of that client's perceived guilt or innocence. In these books, the titles are taken from legal terms and the practice of law is a major story component. Much of the action takes place in the courtroom where Barbara Holloway—assisted by her father, Frank, also an attorney—defends her clients against charges of murder.

Barbara is disillusioned by a profession that relies upon, and excludes her from, good-old-boy connections. These exclusive connections operate behind the scenes in almost every legal transaction, and as Barbara takes a sharp blow to her idealism, she discovers she has a glass jaw. Both novels present Barbara as a reluctant defense counsel.

A woman is charged with the shooting death of her long-absent husband in *Death Qualified*. Nell Kendricks is a friend and neighbor of Frank Holloway, and, when she is arrested for the murder of her husband, Lucas, Frank wants to secure the best possible attorney to serve as her defense. That attorney is his daughter, Barbara. Barbara, however, has left the practice of law for the relative simplicity of running a women's clothing shop in Phoenix. A request for help by Frank comes as somewhat of a surprise to Barbara, and though she knows he has an ulterior motive, she responds to his request for help by returning to Oregon. In *The Best Defense*, Barbara is dispensing simple, low-cost legal advice to citizens of a Eugene neighborhood. A woman comes to Barbara with an impassioned plea. When she takes on the case of the woman accused of murdering her child, Barbara's curiosity as well as her sense of personal responsibility is provoked,

Societal strictures and conventions operate in both cases to give plausibility to the charges brought against the two women. A husband absent for more than six years may well be a threat to the life his abandoned wife has created for herself—enough for her to want him dead. A woman taking her child and running from a husband in fear for her safety is called a child abuser and baby killer when her daughter dies as a result of arson at the shelter where the two have gone. Something about the very plausibility of the charges doesn't ring true for Barbara when faced with the reality of the women she represents and the stories each tells. There is plausibility there as well, and Barbara accepts the challenge of finding the truth in both cases.

The second half of each novel takes place in the courtroom, and it is here that author Kate Wilhelm makes her character shine. In spite of a reluctant beginning in each instance, Barbara Holloway is a gifted defense attorney; through direct examination, cross-examination, and redirect, she is able to manipulate witnesses for both sides to give the testimony she needs on her client's behalf. As she deftly elicits vital information from these witnesses, a story emerges that is vastly different from the one on which the charges depend. Barbara and her father, Frank, go out in the field when necessary, but the vital action is played out before the bar.

Kate Wilhelm is an award-winning science fiction writer with more than twenty books in that genre. She also has another mystery series featuring Charlie Meiklejohn and Constance Leidl and described in the chapter "Cure It or Kill It: Medicine and Science."

NAN ROBINSON
1993–1996   3 books
Taffy Cannon

A Pocketful of Karma introduces Nan Robinson, an attorney-investigator for the California State Bar Association. In this story, Debra LaRoche, a young woman for whom Nan once babysat and, more recently, her former—and highly competent—secretary, has disappeared. Debra's life is an apparent series of contradictions. As Nan looks further into what this young woman has been doing since the tragic death of Debra's infant son, she realizes that there are significant inconsistencies between the Debra she knows and the Debra she discovers. The trail leads Nan from Debra's abusive ex-husband, to the Past Lives Institute located on a hill overlooking the Pacific Ocean in Malibu, to a run-down music club called Papillon in the heart of Los Angeles. After Debra's body is discovered, Nan feels compelled to find her killer and the real reason behind her death. Which she does.

In *Tangled Roots*, Nan's younger sister Julie is pregnant. Her husband, Adam, has been charged with the murder of his close friend Shane, scion of the Pettigrew flower dynasty. Nan goes to the town of Floritas to lend support to her family and gets involved with Adam's legal defense. Feeling that attorney Ramon Garza isn't providing his friend Adam with the best possible defense, Nan becomes involved in the investigation into Shane's death. Julie and Nan's mother arrives from Illinois, and her presence seems to complicate family matters. Once again, Nan pulls all the pieces together and the crime is solved.

This character seems to operate somewhat outside her own life. Raised as a Roman Catholic in the Midwest, Nan left much of her early upbringing behind as she moved west. Divorced and childless, she is kind of looking for a partner, yet in the first story she is attracted to a man with whom she could never become more than physically intimate. Nan's closest relationships are with Shannon Revell, a realtor and former child television star, her sister Julie, and

Moira Callahan, a woman she tutors in reading. There is, however, more convenience to these relationships than true closeness.

While Nan's skills as an investigator are called into play in all three books, none of them show her practicing her profession. This is a shame as we think that a lawyer investigating charges against lawyers offers countless plot possibilities. Instead, Nan goes to her office to do her job, then uses professional contacts and legal knowledge to operate quite outside the purview of the State Bar Association.

With only three books in the series to date, there is potential for this character's development.

Astraea may be long gone but some of the qualities with which this deity is credited remain. Those mortals pledged to uphold justice, flawed though they may be, are doing the best they can with what they have. It behooves them to look at images of Astraea and remember. . . .

SOME OTHER LEGAL SLEUTHS

Nina Fischman
Ellie Gordon
Vicky Holden
Whitney Logan

Annie MacPherson
David Middleton-Brown
Kate Millholland
Dee Street

MURDER BETWEEN THE PAGES:
Writers and Journalists

Though some will argue that printed media are going the way of the dinosaur, there are those of us still firmly wedded to words on paper as opposed to words and/or images on a glowing screen. For us, the pen is still mightier than the sword—and all of the electrons in existence. Many people don't consider their day truly begun until they have read at least the top of the news and possibly the sports and comic pages in their daily newspaper. Others can't imagine a complete day without reading at least one chapter in the book they wish will never end. Fortunately there are still people dedicated to producing these words on paper. Against tight deadlines and monumental odds, they ply their trade to give readers that for which they clamor.

In 1929, Nancy Barr Mavity created the five-book series featuring character James Aloysius Piper (1929–1932). Known as Peter to his colleagues at the *Herald* in San Francisco, this part-time law student is committed to the hot lead and the fast-breaking story. Peter Piper approaches his reportage with a real sense of humanity. He does not simply go for the shock value but delves deeply into the more obscure details. Truth is paramount to this reporter, and he works hard following a story and uncovering everything that will help him attain that lofty goal and solve the murders that are at the heart of those stories.

The *Globe* in New York provides the beat for Barney Gantt in eight books (1936–1976) penned by John Stephen Strange. Introduced as staff photographer for the paper, Barney's career progresses, and in the rest of the books he is billed as the *Globe's* star reporter. These are lively tales with well-plotted crimes. Strange was a highly regarded mystery writer who created two other series characters and many one-offs. The closely held secret—for more than forty years—was that he was in reality Dorothy Stockbridge Tillett.

In 1966 Lilian Jackson Braun introduced Jim Qwilleran (1966–1997) as a journalist new to a small Midwestern newspaper. *The Daily Fluxion* is a far cry from the major metropolitan papers where

Qwill made his name, but after divorce and alcoholism took their toll, he moved down several rungs on the ladder of success. Three books in this series appeared between 1966 and 1968; eighteen years elapsed between the third and fourth books and, since 1986, sixteen more books featuring Qwill and his cats, Koko and Yum Yum, have been written. Qwill has gone through several changes over the years. A substantial inheritance caused his priorities to shift though his values remain the same. Qwill and his cats change residences frequently; with every new location, there is a new mystery to solve and Koko is instrumental in solving every case.

In Lucille Kallen's five-book series (1979–1986), the *Sloan's Ford Reporter* in Sloan's Ford, Connecticut, is literally the home of the primary character. C. B. Greenfield, former NBC news staff writer, has semi-retired and become a small-town news crusader. Chief reporter Maggie Rome narrates the often risky murder investigations into which Greenfield's machinations inevitably lead her. Their relationship, while not warm, is respectful. They bicker and disagree on almost every issue, which creates the tension that holds this light and humorous series together.

Orania Papazoglou created a five-book series (1984–1990) that features Patience C. McKenna. Events in the first book alter the life of "Pay," who likes to think of herself as a serious writer though penning category romance novels has paid her rent. The twelve-room apartment that becomes her home at the end of *Sweet, Savage Death* also becomes the gathering place for her friends and fellow sleuths, which include sister romance writer Phoebe Damereaux, Greek lawyer Nick Carras, and Camille, the black cat. Papazoglou seems to have dropped this series in favor of the one featuring former FBI agent Gregor Demarkian, which she writes under the name Jane Haddam.

Leslie Grant-Adamson wrote of Rain Morgan, an English gossip columnist for the *Post*, a London daily. In the five books in the series (1985–1990) the curiosity that serves Rain so well as a gossip writer propels her to the solution of the murders she encounters in each story. Although she is based in London, most of the action takes place in small villages with limited casts of suspects.

Susan Kelly writes a series that draws directly on her own experience as a Ph.D. in English literature and an instructor at the Cambridge, Massachusetts, Police Academy. Her characters, free-lance writer Liz Connors and Liz's companion, homicide detective Jack Lingemann, search more for the why than the who in the murders they solve in this six-book series (1985–1992).

Despite the erosion by electronic media, the printed word still holds an awesome power. Authors using the purveyors of that power in crafting a mystery tale are making a dual statement. Both they and their characters are presenting ideas and information in a form readers can choose or ignore, can pursue or discard. Writing is a risky business and whether the writing is done for a daily newspaper, a weekly tabloid, a monthly periodical, or a novel, the writer's words stand forth as a statement—quite possibly a testament.

SARAH CALLOWAY
1986–1989　3 books
Jean Warmbold

Although the last book in this series was released in 1989 and the previous two came out in '86 and '88, respectively, these three books are among the most contemporary and the most compelling we've read. They are not standard murder mysteries nor are they strictly espionage. Rather, they are an admixture of styles and are quite believable fictional(?) first-person accounts.

Sarah Calloway, a free-lance journalist, is at the center of each story and narrates them from her perspective. In all three cases, what starts out as one thing rapidly mutates into another and Sarah finds herself immersed, well over her head. Her training and credentials as an investigative reporter give Sarah entree into what becomes the opening level of her investigations. Information she uncovers and events subsequent to her initial queries lead her along obscure side paths into the heart of intrigue and deception on a grand scale.

June Mail looks at a perfectly plausible explanation for the genesis of the AIDS virus. In *The White Hand*, community militia, mercenaries, and white supremacists are featured in a tale reaching beyond United States shores and involving international coups. *The Third Way* addresses the global effects of Middle Eastern terrorism. All of these issues are timely, pertinent, and, unfortunately, have become permanently woven into our national fabric. The AIDS virus and concomitant fears of all sexually transmitted diseases are a looming spectre casting a pall over many human relationships. In the not-too-distant past, with his support for the Iran-contra operation, Oliver North actually declared that, in the name of national security, anything goes, and the 1995 bombing of the Oklahoma City federal building has brought the rise of the militia movement in the United States to broad public attention. The turmoil between the Israelis and the Palestinians over a small slice of real estate has only escalated with the years.

Jean Warmbold has chosen significant topics for her fiction and has done a first-rate job in executing them. We found ourselves taking a fresh look at these disturbing subjects and realized that, as always, there are no real answers and that the best any conscientious individual can do is figure out just what the right questions really are. For readers interested in pursuing some of the issues and questions raised by Warmbold, we suggest the Christic Institute and the recent book by Laurie Garrett, *The Coming Plague*; we also recommend that everyone PAY ATTENTION.

LINDSAY GORDON
1987–1993   4 books
Val McDermid

Lindsay Gordon is a Scotswoman. She grew up in a small community where her father had wrested his family's livelihood from the sea. A socialist by nature, Lindsay attended Oxford University in England, where she took a degree in journalism. As the series opens, she has been working as a reporter for some years for the *Daily Nation*, a Glasgow tabloid, but has been made redundant. An old Oxford friend, Paddy Callaghan, has arranged for Lindsay to write an article on Paddy's school's forthcoming fund raiser for a periodical called *Perspective*. Lindsay, eager to establish herself as a free-lance writer, takes on the task. Cellist Lorna Smith-Cooper, the featured guest performer for the Derbyshire House Girls School gala, is found garroted by a cello string moments before her scheduled performance. Lindsay's friend Paddy is arrested for the murder and Lindsay, together with noted novelist and Derbyshire House "old girl" Cordelia Brown, begins an investigation to clear their friend's name. Needless to say, the two women are successful and Paddy is freed. Lindsay and Cordelia become lovers and, as *Common Murder* opens, the two are trying to reconcile very different life-styles.

Lindsay is sent to Brownlow Common by the *Daily Clarion* to report on the women's peace camp established in protest of the siting of cruise missiles at the American airbase there. Although the women are mounting a nonviolent protest, some of the neighbors, namely, Rupert Crabtree, are in less than peaceful opposition to the camp. The women have been harassed and threatened by unknown assailants and many fear for their safety. When Rupert's murdered body is discovered and the last known person to see him alive is Deborah Patterson, she is arrested and charged with his murder. As the story nears its end and Lindsay proves Deborah's innocence, she uncovers secrets that involve MI6 and aspects of national security. Lindsay's own personal security is placed at risk by her discoveries, and she is forced to flee the country.

Eighteen months later, in *Open and Shut*, Lindsay returns to the

British Isles only to discover that a close friend has been jailed for the murder of another woman. In addition, Lindsay's lover, Cordelia, has formed an new alliance. The surprises uncovered by Lindsay's investigation hold personal significance for her and, at the end of the book, she moves to Northern California with a new lover, Sophie Hartley, a gynecologist.

Union Jack, the fourth in the series, takes place in Sheffield, England, where Lindsay, accompanied by Sophie, has returned for a trades union conference. When Tom "Union" Jack meets death by defenestration from Lindsay's tenth-floor apartment, she is immediately jailed for the crime. She is released when a fellow conferee provides her with an alibi, and, as the mystery unfolds, she traces the murder of Tom Jack to events in 1984 involving another death.

Like her character, Val McDermid is a Scotswoman, a feminist, and a lesbian. She is also a former journalist and a tireless worker for the National Union of Journalists. She brings a wealth of knowledge and experience to this series and her very believable characters reflect the plights and triumphs of contemporary women. Her other character, Kate Brannigan, may be found in the chapter "Private Eyes."

SAMANTHA ADAMS
1988–1997   7 books
Alice Storey, Sarah Shankman

In *First Kill All the Lawyers*, Samantha Adams has returned to Atlanta after what her Aunt Peaches and Uncle Henry refer to as her exile in San Francisco. Almost immediately after her arrival, a distinguished attorney dies. His death has been declared accidental by Sheriff Buford Dodd but Samantha disagrees and proceeds to search for the truth. To get the proof she needs, Sam must wade through a trail of dirty money, adultery, and the good-old-boy mentality.

Samantha left home originally when her boyfriend Beau Talbot ended their summer romance. Stanford University seemed far enough away for her heart to mend, and after graduation she simply stayed on. Life was both hard and good for Sam; she married and divorced and floated along for several years in a state of alcoholic oblivion. She saved herself through Alcoholics Anonymous and enjoyed a successful career. While Samantha pondered an offer she had received from Atlanta's *Journal-Constitution*, her lover, Sean O'Reilly, San Francisco's chief of detectives, was killed by a drunk driver. For various reasons, it was time for Sam to go home again.

Then Hang All the Liars also takes place in Atlanta and, once again, Sam plunges into an investigation of murder. When scammer Randolph Percy dies, Sam finds more than she'd bargained for as a fifty-year-old buried scandal rises up and leads to death.

Samantha goes to New Orleans at Mardi Gras to visit her friend Kitty Lee. While she is there, she meets sexy Harry Zack, an insurance investigator ten years her junior, and begins a new relationship. She also finds a murder to solve and, in doing so, moves about in the rarefied atmospheres of old New Orleans society and contemporary drug dealing. *Now Let's Talk of Graves* is the gem of this series and is the first written under Shankman's real name rather than the Storey pseudonym.

In *She Walks in Beauty*, Samantha is sent to Atlantic City to cover the Miss America pageant, which is a bit of a comedown for Sam, who has been covering the Atlanta crime beat. She determines, however, to make the best of it by looking behind the scenes at one of the country's biggest glitz events. When a judge for the event nearly drowns and then completely disappears, Sam, Harry, and Sam's Shih Tzu Harpo are on the trail again. Matters at the heart of *The King Is Dead* include barbecue, Elvis Presley, and Bikers for Jesus. Samantha is on leave from the *Journal-Constitution*, working on a book tentatively titled *American Weird*, and Tupelo, Mississippi (Elvis's birthplace), is a good place to carry out some research.

In *He Was Her Man*, Samantha has moved to Louisiana on the north shore of Lake Pontchartrain. However, she and Harry have fallen out over a young, skinny, beautiful woman who has captured Harry's attention if not his heart or other vital anatomical bits. When Sam receives an invitation to her friend Jinx's engagement party in Hot Springs, Arkansas, it seems sensible to leave Louisiana before she succumbs to the temptation to blow away her possibly unfaithful lover and his possibly new amour.

The fourth, fifth, and sixth books in this series take flight much like a flock of unruly pigeons and yet they have their charm; we haven't read the seventh. Shankman writes witty and convoluted tales that poke gentle fun at some Southern stereotypes and, at the same time, pay homage to true Southern hospitality, kindness, and generosity.

CAT MARSALA
1990–1997   7 books
Barbara D'Amato

Chicago and its environs are the setting for this series featuring free-lance journalist Catherine "Cat" Marsala. As an independent, she is able to choose the issues she wishes to scrutinize and make public, and the questions her investigations raise are timely and of great public interest. Cat's reputation is solid and publishers will often ask her to take a specific assignment and apply her particular perspective to the matter. Chicago, one of this nation's largest and most diverse cities, provides fertile ground for the type of writing Cat does.

The proposed repeal of Michigan's drug laws, how the rich differ from the rest of us, the Michigan State Lottery, various levels of prostitution, and Chicago's trauma centers are the subjects of some of the books in this series. These themes, coupled with Cat's role as investigative reporter, are ideal arenas for murder and detection.

As the series opens in *Hardball*, Cat is injured when a bomb explodes near her, killing her interview subject, a strong proponent of drug law repeal. Cat's brush with near death and the volatile nature of the topic of drug decriminalization compel her to seek the truth, and her journalistic instincts lead her to some sad conclusions. In *Hard Tack*, an assignment offered by the *Chicago Today* editor strikes Cat as a personal challenge as well as the perfect way to avoid choosing between the two significant men in her life over the fourth of July weekend. Two deaths and an attempt on her own life demonstrate to Cat that while the rich may be slightly different, their motives for murder are quite similar to those of the less privileged.

While escorting her mother to the doctor's office, the body of Cat's next scheduled interview lands at the feet of the two women in *Hard Luck*. That seems more than enough reason for Cat to look into the lottery system and to discover that while it may be simply another business venture, high stakes make it worth killing for.

In *Hard Women*, Cat is on assignment for a Chicago television station and plunges into the seamy world of women in the life of prostitution. The death of a college-bound nineteen-year-old hooker sets Cat on the trail of the killer, and, in the process, she discovers some hard truths about the oldest profession.

Hard Case takes a look into the taut drama of one of the city's trauma centers where death is battled by dedicated individuals. On Cat's first day of observation, the director is murdered, providing a sharp contradiction to the high value of the center's life-saving work.

Although Cat is a competent and dedicated journalist and her territory comprises some of this country's meanest streets, illumination rather than detection is this character's prime goal. That murder happens in Chicago is hardly a surprise to anyone, and that it happens during the course of some journalistic investigations is not even that uncommon. Cat is a good, if amateur, detective, and the skills she brings to her reporting are believably applied to unmasking a killer. Cat's private life and personal connections—her raucous parrot, Long John Silver, the men with whom she is romantically involved, and Captain Harold McCoo of the Chicago Police Department—are well enough drawn to provide character continuity without shifting the focus of the story. Barbara D'Amato has chosen her protagonist well. Clearly this author has done her homework on all the issues she highlights in the series and has created a character who does not get in the way of the gravity of each subject.

HOLLY WINTER
1990–1997   10 books
Susan Conant

Buck and Marissa Winter may have been a little surprised when they produced one two-legged creature shortly after two of their Golden Retriever bitches produced large litters of perfectly acceptable four-legged ones. Holly was raised alongside Golden pups and manifested all the requisite characteristics of a well-bred, -raised, and -trained canine. After Marissa's death, Buck stayed in Maine although he gave up the business of breeding goldens and switched to raising wolf-dog hybrids.

Holly graduated with a degree in journalism and moved to Cambridge, Massachusetts, where she lives in part of a three-story house on the corner of Appleton Street and Concord Avenue. She rents out the other parts of the house to pay her mortgage and derives the rest of her income from a column she writes for *Dog's Life* magazine. Holly's life is centered on dogs: their habits, mannerisms, behaviors, breeding, and, above all, their training. As the series opens, Holly's champion Golden Retriever Vinnie has died and, for the first time in her thirty-something years, Holly is without a canine companion. She still attends the Thursday night training sessions at the Cambridge Armory, however, and when one of the human attendees of the class is found murdered with his own dog's leash, Holly takes the newly orphaned Alaskan Malamute Rowdy home with her and promptly falls in puppy love. Rowdy is obviously a purebred animal; however, his American Kennel Club (AKC) registration papers cannot be found among his owner's other relevant bits. Who killed Dr. Stanton? and Where are those vital AKC papers? are the two questions central to this case. Holly finds the answers and at the end of the story has adopted the beautiful Rowdy.

Throughout the next nine books, more murders occur. Each of the cases involves Holly, Rowdy, a second Malamute, Kimi, and several humans and their canine companions. Rita the therapist with her Dachshund, Groucho, and Scottie, Willie, is Holly's second-floor tenant. Steve Delaney owns India, a German Shepherd, and is Holly's veterinarian and lover. Kevin Dennehy lives next door to Holly with his mother. Kevin is one of the most Irish-looking individuals imaginable and one of Cambridge's finest; he does not have a dog. Leah is Holly's young cousin and resembles Holly's mother in both looks and dog training ability. Although she still lives at home with her parents, Leah is a frequent and welcome visitor at Holly's home.

In detecting, Holly uses her knowledge of canine behavior and successful training methods to solve murders, and each of the stories features some aspect of the world of registered dogs. For example, *A New Leash on Death* deals with pedigree, registration, and conformation to standard. In *Dead and Doggone*, readers learn about the variety of grooming styles acceptable for working dogs, pets, and show dogs. *Bloodlines* addresses puppy mills, forged AKC papers, and mistreated animals. *Ruffly Speaking* features Ruffly, a mixed breed trained as a hearing-ear dog.

According to Holly, life would be just fine if everyone had a dog and spent time training the dog and themselves to be the best each could possibly be. All of the books are informative and Holly's quirk of relating all life to canine standards actually makes sense.

MELISSA CRAIG
1990–1996   6 books
Betty Rowlands

A cottage just outside the village of Upper Benbury in the English Cotswolds is the new home of mystery writer Melissa Craig. As the series opens in *A Little Gentle Sleuthing*, Melissa is ready to move in but finds that the work she had contracted has not been completed and her furniture and boxes arrive from London into chaos. Iris Ash, Melissa's nearest neighbor, is a well-known artist whose fabric designs rival those of Laura Ashley. She arrives to introduce herself and suggests Melissa enlist the aid of her housecleaner, Gloria Parkin, to deal with the cleanup. Gloria arrives and not only sets Melissa's cottage to rights but fills Melissa in on all the local gossip, of which there is much.

A series of mysterious anonymous phone calls come in on Melissa's new telephone. Iris uncovers a murdered body whilst digging mulch for Melissa's future garden. Melissa and her friend newspaperman Bruce Ingram pursue the mysterious phone caller and, in the process, uncover a hotbed of salacious activity centering around a stripper's bar called The Usual Place. Det. Chief Insp. (DCI) Kenneth Harris, head of the local Criminal Investigation Division, arrives to put official closure to the case, and Melissa settles into what she trusts will be a quiet and productive life in the country.

Alas, it is not to be so, for in *Finishing Touch*, Melissa begins teaching a writing class at the Mid-Cotswold College of Arts and Technology in Stowbridge and murder occurs. Her knowledge of both the victim and the prime suspect places Melissa in the middle of the investigation and, in the end, she is the one who finds the solution.

Over the Edge takes place at Centre Cevenol d'Études, a school in France where Iris has gone to teach an art class for her friend the director, Monsieur Philippe Bonard. Melissa has accompanied Iris in order to do some research for a book she is planning to write using some of the locale's geographical features for her plot. A body is found at the foot of a high cliff—an apparent accident. After the death of M. Bonard's assistant in the same manner, the question of murder arises. Melissa's investigation into the two deaths uncovers old rancors that ultimately explain the reasons for both murders.

A haunted manor house turned luxury hotel is the scene of murder in *Exhaustive Enquiries*. Melissa has written a "pantocrime" for the birthday celebration of Mitch, a wealthy businessman whose origins as a London barrow boy and reputation for straight and honest dealing inspire deep loyalty in his friends and associates. This loyalty leads to the death of Will Foley. Once again, Melissa is called to look into what at first appears to be an accidental death. As usual, she discovers a nefarious subplot involving some of Mitch's less loyal employees.

Over the course of the series, Iris and Melissa become close friends. Even though the two women are in their middle years, their amorous interests are still active. Each is capable of making wrong choices in companions and these choices add to the story lines as much as they do to the development of the characters. DCI Ken Harris appears in all but one of the books and in the fourth has been divorced and is becoming a romantic contender for Melissa's affections. We find ourselves comfortable with these characters and curious about what will be happening to them. The stories are written with a light touch and are definitely in the mold of the English Village mystery.

KATE MULCAY
1991–1995   4 books
Celestine Sibley

Kate Mulcay is an Atlanta newspaperwoman. She makes her home in a small, three-room log cabin she and her late husband, Benjamin "Benjy" Franklin Mulcay, had built in the countryside, some distance from the metropolis. While moving to the city might make more sense for Kate, memories and friendships have kept her in her familiar surroundings. Although she is apparently a well-respected professional, we do not see her at work as a reporter for the *Atlanta Searchlight*. All of the books center around her private life and the connections between Kate and people she and her husband have known together over the years.

In *Ah, Sweet Mystery*, Kate's neighbor Miss Willie Wilcox has been summarily moved into a nursing home by her beloved yet nonetheless greedy stepson Garney. Garney has been developing his share of the family homestead into luxurious homes. When he is found murdered, few mourn his loss. When Miss Willie confesses to the crime, Kate knows she must get involved to protect her dear friend. With the aid of the young Gandy sisters, Sheena and Kim Sue, the real killer is found. Miss Willie is restored to her home and all ends well.

Straight as an Arrow takes place on Ila Island off the Florida Gulf Coast, where Kate and Benjy had maintained a summer home. A desperate phone call from Nora Noble, year-round resident on Ila, prompts Kate to make her first visit to the island since Benjy's death. When she arrives, she finds that Nora's husband, Philip, has been hospitalized with a heart attack. Nora tells Kate that this is only one part of the trouble that has been visited on the island in recent months, and she relates the sad tales of several mysterious deaths. When Philip suffers a second, fatal heart attack and Nora is convinced its cause is deliberate, she persuades Kate to look into the matter, and ultimately Kate finds resolution.

The death of a Native American legislator just before his scheduled meeting with Kate involves her in the mystery central to *Dire Happenings at Scratch Ankle*. Return Pickett had represented one side of a historical land dispute between his tribe and the descendants of the early white settlers. Kate determines to find Pickett's killer and when a local woman also dies, the ante is upped. A gathering of spelunkers and a crazy fat woman enter the story as do the Gandy sisters. Kate prevails, the land dispute is resolved, and order is restored.

Celestine Sibley has crafted a sweet series. Some readers may find it a bit cloying; however, the stories fit well into the cozy mystery tradition and are a welcome contribution for those who relish the gentle side of murder.

BRITT MONTERO
1992–1997   5 books
Edna Buchanan

Britt Montero is a thirty-something Miami native. Her father had been a Cuban Freedom Fighter against Castro and was executed for his efforts. Her mother had never forgiven him for his disaffection and death nor Britt for her resemblance to him, so had farmed her out to a variety of relatives from both sides of the family. As a result, Britt grew up confused and unsure of her identity. She escaped to Chicago, where she attended journalism school at Northwestern University. The harsh Midwestern weathers proved too much for her and her final two years of university were spent back in Miami. After graduation, she was hired by one of Miami's best newspapers and, as the series opens, is covering the police beat on the *Miami Daily News*.

As *Contents Under Pressure* opens, Britt has responded to a call coming into police headquarters reporting a hostage situation at a local elementary school. Knowing the officer in charge of the scene and that she's onto a hot story, Britt follows Officer Ted Ferrell as he chases after the suspect. Her instincts prove as sound as Officer Ferrell's reputation, and the perpetrator is collared with no shots exchanged. Lottie Dane, the staff photographer for the paper, arrives on the scene to document Britt's story.

No sooner has Britt filed her story than she receives a call from one of her sources. Rico, an intensive care nurse, tells her that D. Wayne Hudson, a former Los Angeles Raiders and Miami Hurricanes football star who turned coach to disadvantaged youngsters, is in the hospital technically dead and being maintained on life support until his organs can be harvested. Hudson had died from a beating administered by officers after his apparent attempt to flee from the police.

As Britt continues to cover the story, she discovers strong racial tension lying not too far below an apparently calm surface. She also uncovers a cell of corruption within the police department. When the officers charged with Hudson's death are acquitted of his murder, the black populace is outraged and a riot breaks out. Britt, her close friend Officer Francie Alexander, and Francie's toy poodle, Bitsy, are caught in a surge of uncontrolled violence and Officer Alexander is killed.

In *Miami, It's Murder*, the focus is a rapist operating unseen in women's restrooms in downtown Miami. Britt becomes the rapist's specific target when her coverage of his crimes provokes his anger. Britt's old recently retired friend, Det. Daniel Flood, cautions her against pursuing or further provoking the rapist and Britt, mindful of her friend's longtime connection with the force, pays some heed to his words. However, things Dan has left unspoken turn out to be of interest in clearing up several unsolved homicides and his cautions to Britt still leave her unprepared for her eventual confrontation with the rapist.

Suitable for Framing places Britt in a new sort of jeopardy as both her professionalism and her competence are called into question. Trish Tierney has taken a position in the newspaper's library when Britt first meets her. Trish confesses her aspirations to the newsroom and Britt becomes her mentor. After losing several hot stories to Trish, who always seems to be in just the right place at just the right time, Britt begins to question the wisdom of her sponsorship. The death of a young witness and information given by an accused killer and a security guard raise serious questions. Britt must find the answers in order to maintain her professional reputation and keep her job.

Edna Buchanan, a Pulitzer Prize–winning writer in Miami, has created a riveting series. Her character may be based on the author's own experience as a reporter covering one of the nation's most challenging urban police beats. The character is a good foil for the stories, and the pacing of each tale is exquisite.

EMMA LORD
1992–1997   8 books
Mary Daheim

Alpine, Washington, is a small isolated community nestled in the western foothills of the Cascade mountains. Most of the denizens of Alpine have long histories connecting them and their forebears to the place. A journalist for her entire working career, Emma Lord always had the fantasy of publishing her own paper. With a windfall inheritance, Emma purchased the *Alpine Advocate* from its former owner and finds herself swept into the lives and concerns of Alpine's populace.

In *The Alpine Advocate*, Emma's son, Adam, a student at the University of Hawaii, informs his mother that she is to have a houseguest. Adam's roommate, Chris Ramirez, has family in Alpine but, as his mother had been disinherited by her father, Neeny Doukas, Chris is uncertain of both his welcome and his own filial feelings. When Mark Doukas is found murdered, Chris is suspected of killing his cousin. With the more than able assistance of Vida Runkel, the *Advocate* House and Home editor, and the official hand of Sheriff Milo Dodge, Emma investigates and uncovers old secrets and hidden passions. While delving into the mystery of Mark's death, Emma has some history of her own to contend with in the form of Tom Cavanaugh—Adam's father—to whom Emma had never been married.

In *The Alpine Betrayal*, a film company arrives in Alpine for some location shooting and a former Alpine resident has the starring role.

Once again, Emma, Vida, and Milo uncover old secrets and solve several murders. As the story draws to its conclusion, Adam telephones his father, Tom, and introduces himself for the first time.

In *The Alpine Christmas*, Emma's brother Ben is on vacation from the Arizona parish where he is priest to a Navajo congregation. Father Fitz, Alpine's longtime Roman Catholic clergyman, suffers a series of small strokes, and Ben is asked to remain until Father Fitz recovers or a replacement can be found. While out fishing, Sheriff Milo Dodge reels in something unexpected—a human leg. Ben and Emma, while on an expedition to get a Christmas tree, come across the frozen body of a young woman. Questions abound around the Nyquist family. The Whistling Marmot, Alpine's movie theatre, features in the story that once again involves things of historical significance.

Fourth in the series, *The Alpine Decoy* pits Emma and her staff against bigotry as well as murder. A beautiful African-American woman, Marilynn Lewis, has come to Alpine and taken a job as a nurse in the local clinic. When a young black man is found shot through the head, Marilynn is immediately suspected. The end of the story is a surprise even for Emma and Vida.

Emma takes a vacation in *The Alpine Escape*. When her car breaks down, Emma calls Jackie Melcher, daughter of an Alpine resident, to see if she can stay until her car is fixed. Jackie eagerly agrees since she and her husband have discovered a skeleton in the basement of their house. The secrets in this tale span over a hundred years and extend far beyond the small community of Alpine. The answer is, however, there and in a very surprising form.

Emma Lord is a woman we would like to meet. There is a healthy balance between her strength and her vulnerability and, although she is a newcomer to the community, she is accepted and respected because of her equanimity. Besides Vida Runkel, Emma's staff includes Ed Bronsky, the lugubrious advertising salesman who can't understand why businesses want to spend their good money on newspaper ads. Carla Steinmetz is the solitary reporter and photographer for the *Advocate*. Her inability to spell or to center photos are only small drawbacks. Ginny Burmeister is the secretary and office manager and picks up everyone's pieces. Emma's son, Adam, and his father make appearances throughout the series and the relationship between the three grows and develops. We look forward to more issues of news from Alpine.

HENRIE O
1993–1997   3 books
Carolyn G(impel) Hart

Henrietta O'Dwyer Collins is retired from a career spanning fifty years as a newspaper reporter; her wits have not dimmed with the passage of time. The prologue to the first Henrie O novel is actually a short story complete with a beginning, a middle, and an end that gives readers a clear picture of just who this woman is and just how and—perhaps more important—why she works. And work she does. Even though she is officially retired, Henrie O has maintained her contacts and does not hesitate to use them to answer questions and fill in gaps in her formidable personal data base.

As the main story of *Dead Man's Island* opens, Henrie O receives a call from media czar Chase Prescott, a man from whom she had parted more than four decades earlier. Loyalty is a strong and compelling force and when Chase says, "Henrie O, I need you," her response is almost completely automatic. The following day, she arrives at the shore of South Carolina, where she is met by a taciturn boatman and conveyed to Prescott Island, the palatial retreat of Chase Prescott, a man living under the threat of murder. The help he wants from Henrie O is nothing less than for her to discover who, among the assembled guests on the island, wants him dead. Reluctantly, she agrees to the task but not until after Chase's death, another murder, several injured persons, and a hurricane that obliterates the island, does Henrie O completely unravel all of the mysteries leading to the tumultuous ending.

In *Scandal in Fair Haven*, a relaxing stay in a friend's mountain cabin turns into another murder investigation when Craig Matthews, the nephew of Henrie O's friend Margaret, is accused of killing his wife. Patty Kay Prentiss Pierce Matthews had been a warm, vibrant, wealthy, and powerful woman. Evidence strongly points to Craig as a man likely to do away with his wife and yet Henrie O's instincts tell her that he is innocent. For her friend Margaret's sake, Henrie O assumes the disguise of Craig's aunt and begins to dig for the truth. When all is uncovered, a dark and sinister picture of greed, deception, and misplaced protection emerge. The citizens of Fair Haven will never be quite the same.

Carolyn G. Hart's first series, featuring Max and Annie Laurance Darling, is light, romantic humor and may be found in the chapter "Killings on the Market: Business and Finance." The Henrie O novels—while far from chronicling the mean streets—treat far darker themes. The sixty-odd years of Henrie O's life have been full of experience and no small amount of danger. She is clear in her mind as to just what is important and how vital the preservation of the important truly is. She is an admirable character who some have declared is the Miss Jane Marple of the '90s. We agree that there are some parallels between Jane and Henrie O, but there is little comparison between the stories themselves. Like Agatha Christie's work, Hart's newest series is well and tightly plotted; however, Hart's characters are multi-dimensional and finely drawn. We wish

Henrie O a long and healthy life as we are eager to read more of this compelling woman's adventures.

IRENE KELLY
1993–1997   5 books
Jan Burke

This series opens with *Goodnight, Irene*, and Irene Kelly's best friend O'Connor has been murdered by a package bomb left on his doorstep. O'Connor had been Irene's mentor at the newspaper where they had both worked until Irene had quit in a fit of pique with the owner and gone into public relations. After the death of her friend, she is induced to return to *Las Piernas News Express*. The owner is a stupid man and Irene easily allows him to think that his wishes are what have brought her back to the paper. She takes O'Connor's desk and resumes the stories he was working on when he died. One of them, a thirty-year-old unsolved murder, is of particular interest for O'Connor's devotion to the "Jane Doe" known as Handless Hannah and his annual tribute to her in his column.

The investigating officer on the O'Connor murder is Det. Frank Harriman. He and Irene have known one another for some years but their paths have not crossed recently. Immediately, there is tension between the cop and the reinstated reporter. Only part of this tension is due to their respective professions; the rest is pure sex. Harriman is protective of Irene, who resents what she sees as interference with her job. Eventually, the two of them do solve not only O'Connor's murder but the death of Handless Hannah as well. In the process they also uncover political corruption and bribery, and at the end the two have resolved some of their differences.

Politics and Satanism are featured in *Sweet Dreams, Irene* when the opponent of a candidate for the office of Las Piernas district attorney threatens to expose the candidate's son with photos of him at an alleged Satanic cult meeting. Once again, Irene and Frank—from their almost opposing professional positions—are drawn into the investigation, which reaches far beyond the political and philosophical rings and the denouement of the story places Irene in extreme jeopardy.

As *Dear Irene* opens, Irene is recovering from injuries and the fear incurred at the hands of her captors. As a well-known reporter, she receives a great deal of mail, some from fans and some from undoubted nut cases. The letter signed "Thanatos" seems to fall into the latter category until the discovery of the first body. Mythological references abound in Thanatos's letters to Irene and all are clues to his next victim. Irene's neighbor Jack Fremont—introduced in the second book—has been raised on a steady diet of Greek and Roman mythology. He becomes Irene's primary source of information on the subtleties of the missives, but Irene herself discovers the reasons for Thanatos's rampage and is once again the object of violence.

In five books, Jan Burke has created a cast of believable and sympathetic characters. We care about what happens to Irene, her friends, and her colleagues. In spite of the obvious conflict between the press and the police, Irene and Frank are determined to maintain their romantic connection along with their professional integrity. Their superiors are pressured to create a working arrangement between the two, and the result is a sum greater than its parts. Ancillary characters only add to the stories. Irene's best friend, Lydia Ames, is always there for comfort and hard advice. Frank's partner, Pete Baird, keeps his eye out for Irene even if Frank hasn't asked him to. Irene's news editor, John Walters, trusts her instincts and judgment and goes to bat for her against the bureaucratic machinery that drives Frank's profession. Wild Bill Cody, the cat, and two large, unnamed dogs round out the cast of this series.

Whether an author writes fact or fiction there is an unspoken obligation to the reader. The factual writer owes her readers the most complete and concise rendering possible for that reader's edification. The fiction writer, depending on her reader's suspension of disbelief, must craft her tale to create the context for that suspension from the outset. Those writing sensationalized accounts of facts must do a bit of both as they must enlist the reader's complicity in making more of the story than pure fact may support. Some writers compel their readers to face some awful truths yet present their facts or fictions in a light that enables those readers to come to terms with reality. Others take a light approach to those same truths and use humor to soften the horrors that life may hold. The written word holds the power to balance the paradox between immediacy and reflection. We respect, honor, and celebrate the words and their creators.

SOME OTHER WRITING SLEUTHS

Angelina Amalfi	Morgana Dalton
Bernard	Egan & Kingston
Pete Brady	Daisy Field
Hollis Carpenter	Sophie Greenway
Molly Cates	Judith Hayes
Paris Chandler	Katherine Henry

Nikki Holden
Kate Ivory
Jessica "Jessie" James
Tyler Jones
Charlotte Kent
Libby Kincaid
Chris Martin
Georgia Lee Maxwell
Paul McDonald
Tori Miracle

Jay Omega
Ben & Carrie Porter
Georgina Powers
E. J. Pugh
Rick & Rosie Ramsay
Amanda Roberts
Charlotte Sams
Winston Marlow Sherman
Mitch Stevens

THE OTHER SIDE OF THE LAW

Most crime and mystery fiction is dedicated to the tenet that justice will be served. The protagonist in most mystery novels is one of the good guys, even if he or she operates outside the strict bounds of the law. There are exceptions to this rule of thumb, and a significant number of exceptions have made their appearance in recent years.

Predecessors to this new crop of criminal-as-protagonist set an interesting standard. At the turn of the century, authors Elizabeth Thomasina Meade and Robert Eustace, under the pseudonym L. T. Meade, created two characters with decidedly criminal bents. Each appeared in only one short story collection (Madame Koluchy in *The Brotherhood of the Seven Kings* [1899] and Madame Sara in *The Sorceress of the Strand* [1903]). In 1905, Baroness Orczy began a series of stories featuring the original armchair sleuth Bill Owen, the Old Man in the Corner. Not until the end of the eight-book series (1905–1925) do readers learn of this character's crimes, and so they read his brilliant solutions of other crimes with an untainted view.

In 1955, Patricia Highsmith introduced Tom Ripley, a truly amoral individual. Fifteen years passed before the second book in the series came out, and since then three more novels have been published. These five works (1955–1991) are probably the most repellently compelling books we have ever read. Ripley starts out in *The Talented Mr. Ripley* as a rather innocuous young man in his mid-twenties. An orphan, Tom was raised by an aunt who may have done her duty by the boy but never gave him love or even affection. His activities as the book opens are definitely criminal; however, one gets the feeling that this may be a passing phase for a person of obvious intelligence who is just down on his luck for the moment. His first murder is committed almost as a whim; the second, to cover the first, is more of a necessity. As time goes by, Tom learns just how gullible most people—including the police—can be and just how believable he can appear.

On the surface, all the enterprises in which Tom is involved are credible. He is part-owner of the Buckmaster Gallery London, the Derwatt School of Art, and Derwatt Ltd., an art supply shop, all in London. All of these operations are covers for fraudulent art, and

Tom is much more than a sleeping partner. He appears to be an ordinary fellow who lives in France with a lovely wife in a nice house. Below the surface, however, Tom will brook no interference and will not be thwarted; killing comes easily to him if it is expedient and essential. There is little malice aforethought in any of the killings (at least eight) that Mr. Ripley commits, and it is doubtful that he even considers them to be acts of murder.

Probably the most striking feature of the series is just how mundane Tom's life is. Highsmith writes of travel, destinations, and domestic detail with eloquent simplicity. The reader is lured into a sense of comfort and then, with the same elegant style, Highsmith inserts an appalling death scene. Readers used to a positive relationship with the protagonist in a mystery novel find themselves in sympathy with Tom Ripley, even after they know he has killed. We want him to get away with whatever he has done. "There will be some mitigating circumstance or some redeeming feature to explain things," we might say to ourselves as we continue to turn the pages. Often, it is not until the end of the book that we realize that none of our hopes and wishes for this character have come to pass. We are left with a sense of our own gullibility at the hands of the malevolent Mr. Ripley.

Patricia Highsmith has set a certain standard with Tom Ripley. Happily, there are only a few female authors who aspire to that lofty(?) height. Readers may judge the following characters by their own standards.

ANNA PETERS
1976–1997   9 books
Janice Law (Trecker)

Anna Peters is the primary character in nine books and she is fascinating. In the first book, *The Big Payoff*, we find that she has gotten all of her earlier jobs through the dubious art of blackmail. Money is important to Anna but power—in the form of psychological mastery—holds much more appeal. Job security in the New World Oil megacompany has allowed her to put a glove on her Black Hand although, as the series progresses, she once again finds her talent for extortion useful to consolidate her power within New World Oil. Anna's tasks for the company take her from murder in the oil fields in the North Sea, through liberating trade secrets from behind the Iron Curtain, to uncovering spoils from the Central American jungle. Espionage, smuggling, and international intrigue are all features of the stories in which this character appears. In the fourth book of the series, *The Shadow of the Palms*, Anna moves out on her own as an investigator. Her new company, Executive Security, Inc., provides among other things background searches on individuals being considered for high positions within large companies.

The fascination this character holds is, in part, her operation outside ethical boundaries. One of the earliest independent female private investigators, Anna sets an unusual standard. Her morality is unconventional and springs from her own sense of self-interest and a code of personal honor. She can admit to a degree of corruption—not necessarily a handicap in the world of corporate maneuvering—and lets one recipient of this admission know that she holds a line between justice in a legal sense and justice in a larger, moral one.

NURSE AGNES CARMICHAEL
1982–1995   13 books
Anthea Cohen (Doris Simpson)

WARNING! PLOT REVEALED!

Just mentioning this character's name in this chapter violates one of our prime directives, namely, not to give away the end of any mystery we write about. With full apologies to author Anthea Cohen and with all due respect to the reader, in order to properly introduce this character we must break our own rule.

It is not until the last two pages of the first book, *Angel Without Mercy* (dedicated "to Patricia Highsmith, in admiration"), that readers find out that Nurse Agnes Carmichael is the murderer of the odious Sister Marion Hughes. Throughout the story, Hughes, an effective and efficient supervisor, has manipulated, used, abused, and insulted everyone from the senior surgeon to the cook in the hospital canteen. Hughes's death in a car crash, while she was driving under the lethal influence of Nembutal, comes as a relief to the victims of her machinations.

The story is set out as a standard whodunit. There are numerous suspects for the killing, which is ruled simply death by misadventure, and Cohen builds a plausible case against each of them. Nurse Carmichael is an unattractive, insecure, and easily intimidated soul. Her intelligence is sufficient to propel her up the career ladder in her profession, yet she is sorely lacking in confidence—in short, the perfect prey for the vitriolic Sister Hughes. Readers used to the protagonist as hero are ready to believe that Carmichael solves the crime, yet are not surprised to find that she has actually committed it and gets away with it.

At the end of the first book, we see a new, more confident Nurse

Carmichael ready to rise to all the challenges her profession has to offer. In *Angel of Vengeance*, she has become a sister of the outpatient department at a new hospital and has begun to enjoy the power of her position. Unfortunately, the role model she emulates is the late, despised Sister Marion Hughes. Agnes Carmichael is still the same unattractive, insecure individual she has always been. Agnes is an orphan who was raised in institutions and has never experienced love or affection in any form. She possesses no social skills and is uncomfortable with people in any situation. Her first murder did not win the nurse much more than the bit of confidence she needed to rise in the ranks. While the nurse's next victims are no great loss to society, her motivation for causing their deaths is not profound and no one gains through her acts.

In *Angel of Death*, Agnes falls in love, and in this book the full extent of her wounded nature becomes apparent. The object of her desire is a professor of medieval history. Though Harry Maitland is blind and suffers from diabetes, he leads a full life and lives in a beautiful home with his wife, Emily. Befriended by the Maitlands, Agnes is appalled by what she perceives as Emily's cavalier treatment of her husband. When she learns that Harry's wife is unfaithful to him, Agnes decides to end what she sees as a painful relationship and kills Emily in order to supplant her. In this story we clearly see how a lack of understanding of human nature can cripple individuals and distort their perceptions.

Agnes Carmichael is a lonely, alienated creature. Her perceptions may be valid, but she does not know how to read or interpret them, much less put them to practical use. She is constantly confronted with her own ineptitude, and her wounds fester with each faux pas and rejection. This is not a conventionally sympathetic character, although she does evoke pity. Each death diminishes Nurse Carmichael and we feel slightly diminished as well, for many of us have known people much like Agnes and few of us summon the compassion to help them alter the course of their lives.

Agnes is not one of our favorites and we have not followed her career. Eight more novels have been added to this series since we described the character and her actions and we will leave it to the reader to discover whether she, who appears to us to be a poor and misguided soul, finds her redemption.

THE WIDOWS
1983–1985   2 books
Lynda La Plante

There are only two books in this series, written after the successful British production of a television serial called *Widows*. Author

Lynda La Plante wrote both the teleplay and the books. Neither *Widows* nor *Widows 2* is a conventional mystery novel; each is a crime/adventure story.

Three women are widowed when the heist in which their husbands are involved goes awry. The men were successful career criminals, and the leader, Harry Rawlins, kept faithful records of all the operations he ever headed. The police and Harry's crime rivals want the ledgers, but Harry's widow, Dolly, cops the pot. She enlists the other two widows, Linda Pirelli and Shirley Miller, and together they decide to complete the aborted heist. The widows are joined by a fourth woman, Bella O'Reilly, and set to work on the elaborate preparations necessary to carry the event off successfully.

The relationships of the four women are among the most unusual and the most interesting we've ever read. Because they are constantly watched by the police and Harry's rivals, the only time they are together is when they are working on their preparations. They do not bond in the more traditional female fashion. None of the women has ever done anything like this before. Dolly, using her husband's careful records and plans, takes on the role of leader. Each of the women has assigned tasks: Shirley has to purchase vehicles and equipment in an untraceable fashion; Linda must learn auto mechanics and steal just the right van; Bella needs to practice cutting into the side of a truck with a chainsaw. All of them pitch in to disguise the vehicles, and they learn to handle shotguns with ease. Timing is critical. There is only one location at which the heist can be carried out with any degree of promise for their escape. With only four minutes to do the deed and sacks of heavy bank notes to carry, the women must scout, time, and practice the arduous run. As the story progresses, tension and discord run high among the four women. Shirley and Linda are suspicious of Dolly's intentions and fear that she may just be using them for her own unspoken ends. Bella is far more pragmatic and often serves as peacemaker. Dolly's careful plans and the hours spent in preparation pay off. The team, despite all the dissension, functions like clockwork; however, a surprise twist near the end of the book throws the outcome into doubt.

The second book effectively ends the series and loudly proclaims the following messages: crime does not pay and there is no honor among (some) thieves. The odd relationships between the four women continue, yet the women never betray one another. Dolly is still the leader and the other women depend on her knowledge, resourcefulness, and grace under pressure. Harry Rawlins is alive and his existence poses a constant threat to the women and their ill-gotten gains.

No one comes out of the final installment of the series looking good. Despite the honorable way in which Dolly comports herself in relation to her partners, none of the women wins anything in the end. Harry and his cohorts receive justice though not necessarily from the forces of law and order. The police do not even make a good showing. When they are finally involved, it is almost an accident and one based on a tip-off.

La Plante has created an entire cast of unusual yet highly believable characters and depicts the evolution of each character in a manner that enhances the story's cohesiveness. The four inexperienced women in an enterprise of uncommon magnitude, Harry Rawlins's villainous rivals, and the overburdened and frustrated London Metropolitan Police are well drawn and run true to form throughout the tightly plotted novels. These are not books to suit everyone's tastes, yet for exceptional characterization and an intense read, we recommend them.

This author is perhaps best known for her creation of the *Prime Suspect* series, featuring Det. Chief Insp. Jane Tennison, also originally produced for British television and aired on American Public Broadcasting Service (PBS). Det. Chief Insp. Jane Tennison of the London Metropolitan Police may be found in the chapter "Behind the Badge: Major Metropolitan Police."

MISS SUSAN MELVILLE
1986–1993   5 books
Evelyn E. Smith

Manhattan and its upper-class denizens form the backdrop for this series. Born into wealth and social position, Susan Melville is living in reduced circumstances in the first book, *Miss Melville Regrets*. Inflation has eroded her small trust fund, the only thing left after her father's defection with his own family's millions as well as the millions of several other families. The school where she has been employed as an art teacher is closing, and none of her paintings has ever sold. To add insult to injury, the rent-controlled apartment in which she lives is going co-op. Miss Melville decides that death is preferable to penury and plans to kill herself at a benefit dinner for the homeless where her unscrupulous landlord is to be the guest speaker. Fortunately for her and for her many fans, the speaker's words galvanize her into action in another direction. Rather than shoot herself as planned, she shoots her (now) erstwhile landlord. Amazingly, no one has seen her commit this act; in fact, no one has even noticed this attractive, modestly dressed, middle-aged woman with the notable exception of Alex Tabor.

Miss Melville's meeting with Alex is timely in every sense. He helps her make a clean escape from the scene of her first crime, disposes of the gun, and serves as the only true sounding board she has ever had. He also tells her that his boss may be interested in employing her. This proves to be so and Susan Melville embarks upon a new career—as a well-paid assassin. Her targets are public figures who for one reason or another have eluded justice for a variety of heinous crimes. Payment for plying her new trade is legitimized—to satisfy the IRS, an old enemy of the Melville family—by the exchange of one of her paintings for a check drawn on a corporation formed solely for this purpose.

In the second novel, *Miss Melville Returns*, Susan has become an artist of note. Her paintings form the centerpiece of a collection hanging in a wing of the Museum of American Art in New York and command astronomical prices in the marketplace. The death of her employer has ended her career as a gun for hire, but she remains close to Alex, who has married Tinsley, the daughter of one of Susan's close friends. While Susan may no longer get paid for killing, she manages to keep her hand in. *Miss Melville's Revenge* finds her doing away with foreign diplomats who are quite literally, thanks to diplomatic immunity, above the law for crimes committed on United States soil.

The stories are convoluted, weighty with detail, and populated with an abundance of ancillary characters. Dr. Peter Franklin, a professor at Columbia University, is Susan's longtime companion. He makes a few brief appearances in the stories, but he is usually off in some exotic locale doing field research. Mimi Fitzhorn LaFleur Livingston DelVecchio Tibbs Carruthers Hunyadi von Schwabe is Susan's oft-married best friend from boarding school days. Amy Patterson, mother of Tinsley, is another of Susan's old friends. Dodo Pangborn, when not in prison or recovering from yet another scam she has failed to pull off, drops into Susan's life to add the odd bit of (off) color. The contingent of party crashers including Freddy, Shirley, Dana, Hilary, Shalimar, and Rhonda aid and abet Susan in the first book and appear in the second. These diverse elements are well blended, however, and the pace of the books is moderate enough to accommodate the various connections and relationships. Each book stands alone, and read from beginning to present the series holds together in a grander scheme.

Using a criminal as the protagonist of a series may not be a new convention in the annals of crime and mystery fiction though, to our minds, it is a chilling one. Despite the Robin Hood qualities of one of the characters, all of them are dealing with death and/or deception—reprehensible crimes, whatever way one looks at it. In this genre, it is customary for killers to be brought to justice and readers have come to expect a moral outcome. The authors who have created the foregoing series provide their audience with the unique opportunity to scrutinize their own values.

PORTRAITS IN CRIME:
Arts and Letters

Arts and letters are a powerful force within any society. Painting, sculpture, photography—all the visual arts—can speak directly to the mind and soul of viewers. Words are potent tools with which to reinforce, sway, or change a reader's point of view. Artists and writers must possess a vision; they also need the talent, skill, and dedication to bring their vision to life for others' response. Specialized talents are necessary for the preservation, protection, and cataloguing of these artistic creations and renderings; individuals who pursue this artistic avenue are responsible for their own vision as well as that of the original artist or writer. When the visionary and protective talents of creators and preservationists are brought to bear on the realm of detection, the results can be illuminating.

In 1938, author Ngaio Marsh introduced painter Agatha Troy to her successful fictional detective Roderick Alleyn. Troy, as she is known, is an early example of the strong, independent woman. Her career is of vital importance to her. If love and marriage are to happen, they must fit in with her prime directive of utilizing her talent to its fullest. Fortunately for the reader, both love and marriage do happen and form one of the most positive marital unions in this genre. Troy makes her first appearance in the sixth book of the series and appears in most of the succeeding twenty-eight (1938–1982) novels.

In a sixteen-book series (1940–1951) Elizabeth Daly created Henry Gamadge, known primarily as an expert in rare and unusual books and manuscripts. His avocation, however, is detection and he brings the same level of dedication to each of his tasks. The stories in which he appears are enigmatic, provocative, and, because they are written and set in New York of the '40s, of historical value.

Dorothy Dunnett's seven-book series featuring portrait painter Johnson Johnson (1968–1991) is almost a spoof on the spies so popular in the '50s and '60s. The rumpled, bifocaled Johnson, master of *Dolly*—a quietly and expensively fitted, gaff-rigged auxiliary ketch—is a spy's spy. Johnson's artistry and his elegant craft carry him and his current "bird" wherever his peculiar talents are required in the service of Her Majesty. His portrait subjects include royalty and a pope or two.

Martha Kay Renfroe, using the pen name of M. K. Wren, created Conan Flagg, known primarily as a bookstore owner, but also a licensed, though unadvertised, private investigator. Wealthy from his share in his family's Ten Mile Ranch, Conan does not need to work at anything. The Holliday Beach Book Shop is his passion and investigation is his compulsion. Conan's tall, dark good looks reflect his Nez Percé ancestry. His Native American heritage is manifested in his love of the land and a sense of justice that extends beyond man-made law. There was a nine-year gap between the sixth and seventh book in this eight-book series (1973–1994). We hope the most recent addition to the list is an indication that more adventures are in the works for this quietly captivating character.

Barbara Ninde Byfield's character Helen Bullock is featured in a four-book series (1975–1979). She is a respected photojournalist whose work has appeared in many periodicals of note and in a book or two her own creation. Together with Father Simon Bede, an Anglican priest and aide to the archbishop of Canterbury, she solves a series of crimes. Struck from the mold of Dorothea Lange and Margaret Bourke White, Bullock is an early example of fictional women to come.

In writing her five-book series (1977–1988) author Clarissa Watson merges art, murder, and espionage in a light, faintly romantic serial. The self-described starving artist Persis Willum is actually a well-known and respected painter. Watson treats art fraud and personal and professional misrepresentation and features a wealth of recurring characters.

To say that Charlotte MacLeod is a prolific author is a vast understatement. She has created a total of four series with twelve books in the Kelling one (1979–1995). The set opens upon the trials and tribulations of newly widowed Sarah Kelling, a Boston Brahmin. At the end of the first book, she has acquired a boarder, Max Bittersohn, who later becomes her husband. Max's job is restoring lost or stolen objets d'art, paintings, or jewelry to their rightful owners or to the company that insured them. All of the murders in which he becomes involved center on Sarah's eccentric family but that does not diminish Max in anyone's eyes. His worldly knowledge and particular expertise serve Max and the Kelling family more than well.

All the above are worthy predecessors to the following characters. Before the '80s, the world must have seemed a larger place where fraud, chicanery, and murder were as rare as the true masterpiece.

Today's artistic sleuths may be surprised at their initial encounters with murder, but in a world where stakes are high and human life can seem less valuable than something with a high price tag, their gentler sensibilities are soon set aside for the practical necessity of uncovering whodunit.

ANDREA PERKINS
1984–1993   5 books
Carolyn Coker

Andrea Perkins is red-haired, an art expert, and in her thirties. As the series opens in *The Other David*, she is in Florence, Italy, on leave from her teaching position at the Harvard School of Fine Arts. In Florence, she has taken an apprenticeship as assistant curator at the Galleria dell'Accademia; she also undertakes commissions to restore some of the country's finest art treasures. Returning from Perugia, where she has worked on frescoes at a villa built by Lorenzo de'Medici, she meets an old priest who gives her a painting he says has been in his family for generations. The painting is nothing less than a portrait of David that Michelangelo is said to have painted as a gift to his patron Lorenzo Il Magnifico. Andrea goes to the Florence Police Department to request additional security while the painting is being validated. At the police station, she meets Captain of Detectives Aldo Balzani.

Andrea's specialty is art of the Italian Renaissance, and this series focuses mainly on places and pieces from that era. In *The Vines of Ferraro*, the summer villa built for Lucrezia Borgia and a deck of Tarot cards said to have belonged to that lady are at the crux of the tale. Central to *The Hand of the Lion* are the Basilica of St. Mark's in Venice and a bronze death mask. The action in the fourth book in the series, *The Balmoral Nude*, moves to London, where Andrea is working on a project at the Victoria and Albert Museum, and *Appearance of Evil* takes place in Southern California, where she has gone to work on the restoration of Gainsborough's *Blue Boy*.

Aldo Balzani is a native of Florence who, after the death of his mother when he was ten, moved to New Orleans. He won an athletic scholarship to Tulane University, where he starred on the football field, performed with the Opera Club, and earned a master's degree in political science. Five years before the series opens, Aldo had taken a trip to Italy to visit his father's family and stayed on. He and Andrea meet in the first book, and their relationship deepens throughout the series. Aside from a few intense meetings, however, theirs is not a smooth courtship. One of the pair is generally bemoaning the absence of the other, though ultimately they do aid each other in solving whatever crime is at hand and achieve their reunion.

The art and the history woven into this series by Carolyn Coker are interesting and well founded. The romance of the location will appeal to many readers, and the romance between Andrea and Aldo will appeal to others.

JOANNA STARK
1986–1989   3 books
Marcia Muller

Marcia Muller is best known for her series featuring San Francisco private investigator Sharon McCone. But the series that features Joanna Stark is unusual for several reasons, not the least being that it is complete in three books, a beginning, a middle, and an end. Other interesting aspects of the stories are their settings and the perspective on the art world by the primary character.

Joanna Stark is an art security expert whose company, Security Systems International (SSI), specializes in providing protection for museums, art galleries, and auction houses. As the series opens in *The Cavalier in White*, Joanna, a widow, has been spending her time renovating the Victorian farmhouse in Sonoma, California, left her by her late husband. Joanna's partner in SSI is trying to lure her back as an active participant in the company. A Dutch painting has been stolen from the M. H. de Young Museum in San Francisco. Not only is Joanna familiar with the museum's security system, she knows most of the people involved in the situation, including, as it turns out, the thief.

All three of the books in this series center on Joanna, her nemesis, Antony Parducci, and the tangled web of their relationship. Most of the ongoing characters in the stories are connected to Joanna or Parducci in one way or another, and the complexities of the interplay among the characters add to the overall tension of each mystery. The circle of characters is small, but their range encompasses both time and space. *There Hangs the Knife* takes place in London and on the English coast of Cornwall as Joanna, driven by an obsession, finds that what she has set in motion is rapidly running out of her control. *Dark Star* brings the story back to Sonoma and San Francisco, where the years of fear and uncertainty are brought to a dramatic finale.

While each of the books can be read as a single, complete story, the cumulative events of the three bring years of dishonesty and obsession to resolution. For readers fond of Sharon McCone, the Joanna Stark books will provide an interesting contrast. We recommend these, not only for purposes of comparison, but for good mystery reading.

HARRIET JEFFRIES & INSP. JOHN SANDERS
1986–1994   6 books
(Caroline) Medora Sale (Roe)

Even though the character we've chosen to highlight here does not appear until the second book in this series, once she arrives on the scene, she begins to steal it. In all fairness to Toronto homicide detective John Sanders, in *Murder on the Run*, the first book, his actions establish him as much more than a mere placeholder. This story is basically a police procedural involving the pursuit of a serial killer. John Sanders, the detective in charge of the case, is romantically paired with a real estate agent named Eleanor. Suffice it to say that the case is successfully concluded. In the second book, Eleanor is history and Harriet Jeffries, an independent architectural photographer, enters in chapter three. She immediately captures John's attention, his heart, and the series, more or less in that order.

Readers finding themselves bored with predictable characters involved in run-of-the-mill murder mysteries will enjoy the variety this series has to offer. Not only is there a shift in protagonist between the first two books but the series as a whole is almost impossible to classify. *Murder in Focus*, the first featuring Harriet, involves international intrigue and espionage. *Murder in a Good Cause* is a straight murder mystery. *Sleep of the Innocent* is another straight whodunit, but John and Harriet are on vacation in Martha's Vineyard, Massachusetts, and don't get involved until the end. In *Pursued by Shadows*, Harriet's past rises up and quite literally smites her. John is there to pick her up and help her arrange the pieces of a suspenseful tale. *Short Cut to Santa Fe* takes Harriet away from Toronto on an assignment. After winding up his most recent case, John flies to Santa Fe to meet her and enjoy some vacation time in the desert. Although the pair is central in this book, the actual police work is done by others.

In her first appearance, Harriet is literally run down by Sanders. His attempts to help only exacerbate the situation, and Harriet, trying to catch the five o'clock sun on a particular building, has no time for niceties or for her assailant. However, as she misses the sun, she takes Sanders up on his offer of a drink and finds herself inadvertently involved in a complex situation centered on international security and corruption within the Canadian forces of law and order. John is, of course, a part of the cause of Harriet's entanglement and has a hand in her eventual salvation. As the case devolves, Harriet's independent nature becomes not only apparent but also crucial to the plot. She is the match for the six-foot-three homicide detective that Eleanor could never have been.

While Harriet's professional activities and personal connections get the pair involved in most of the stories, it is the relationship between the cop and the photographer that carries the series by author Medora Sale. Both Harriet and John are strong and resourceful characters; each has a stubborn streak, and the attraction the two enjoy is fraught with tension and danger. We've enjoyed this series and look forward to their continuing adventures.

CALISTA JACOBS
1986–1994   4 books
Kathryn Lasky Knight

While Calista Jacobs holds the title of artist in this series, all of the characters, operating fully and competently within their respective disciplines, can be described in this fashion as well, and they add the weight of their artistry to all of the books. Kathryn Lasky Knight treats astrophysics, computer technology, archaeology, and paleontology as fields of study that benefit from an artistic approach and application. Her series brings out many of the lyrical qualities that each of these scientific realms possesses and often are neglected or overlooked in the misguided belief that the purity of these activities lies solely in their logic.

Calista is a well-known illustrator of children's books who has received countless awards of merit and is extremely well paid. In *Trace Elements*, Calista's husband, Tom, a renowned astrophysicist, is killed at an archaeological site where he has been using a device he has invented—the Time Slicer. The agent of his death is *Crotalus horridus horridus*, the rattlesnake. As their grief recedes to a bearable level, Calista and her eight-year-old son, Charley, begin to resume their lives. At the same site, the death of an archaeologist by rattlesnake leads Calista to believe that her husband may have been murdered and that the information his Time Slicer provided was of more than simple scholarly interest.

Mortal Words, the second in the set, looks at the difference between the validation of a theory by rigorous scientific investigation and selective experimentation. Deception, another art, is brought into play in this story. Calista unveils her skill as a mythmaker, and Charley discovers the beauty and elegance of computer linguistics. Archie Baldwin, an archaeologist with the Smithsonian, introduced in the first book, falls in love with Calista, who reciprocates in spades.

Calista, Charley, and Archie form the investigative triad in all of the books. Each is an independent operator with skills, talents, and resources that prove, in combination, to be an inimical force against their foes. Though Calista illustrates fairy tales and fantasies, she does so with a pragmatism that incorporates all of the weakness and strength of humanity. For her, there is a fine line between good and evil, innocence and worldliness, right and wrong. Archie deals in a much more objective world where empirical proof represents the Holy Grail. Charley is being raised in an atmosphere where all things may be possible. His specialties are curiosity, dedication, and youthful enthusiasm.

Knight's choice of subjects provides her characters with a variety of arenas in which to ply their respective talents. Asides, throwaway comments, Freudian slips, and adolescent misutterances give ballast to both story and characterizations. The mysteries themselves are well crafted and hold a measure of intrigue. It is not difficult to care what happens to any of these three or to those they choose as friend, colleague, or confidante. We highly recommend all of these books.

CLAIRE BRESLINSKY
1990–1995   3 books
Mary Anne Kelly

Queens, New York, is the setting for this three-book series featuring photographer Claire Breslinsky. The middle one of three daughters of Polish Stan and Irish Mary, Claire has just returned after ten years away from home. Her sisters—the eldest, beautiful, dark-haired fashion columnist Carmela, and the youngest, fair-haired policewoman Zinnie—and Zinnie's four-year-old son, Michaelaen, are all back in the family homestead on Park Lane South as well. Besides the human contingent, house space is also shared with the Mayor, a black, mostly English Bulldog who gained his title because he takes care of all things around the neighborhood. Claire had left all those years ago because she could not bear the grief of losing her twin brother, Michael, a rookie policeman, to a knife wielded by a tear-streaked thirteen-year-old. Her travels had taken her around the world. Feeling jaded by her jet-setting lifestyle around Europe, Claire traveled east to the Himalayas, where she found a measure of the tranquillity she had been seeking. Her last months away were spent in an ashram in Rishikesh, India, assisting Swamiji.

In *Park Lane South, Queens*, Claire—thirty years old and home again—is trying to figure out what life holds for her and what she is to do about it all. The body of a small boy is found in a circular clearing in the nearby woods, and the investigation decides Claire's course of action for the immediate future. At the kosher butcher shop where the Mayor has just helped himself to a fresh chicken, Claire meets the large, rough-hewn police detective Johnny Benedetto. Another child dies in the same manner as the first, and the Breslinsky family, friends, pets, and hangers-on are drawn into the drama of the deaths. At the end of the story, Claire and Johnny are hopelessly and passionately in love and the Mayor is involved in a heroic and successful rescue.

Foxglove takes place four years later. Claire and Johnny are married and have a three-year-old son, Anthony. After their wedding, Claire moved into Johnny's old apartment overlooking Aqueduct Racetrack. Needless to say, she longs for a house—preferably in her old neighborhood. The one she finds is right across the street from her childhood friend Tree. Shortly after moving into her dream house, Claire learns of Tree's sudden, swift death. At the wake, she sees Tree's husband, looking bewildered though not particularly bereaved. At his side is a beautiful woman, Portia McTavish. On the steps outside Mahegganey's Roman Catholic Funeral Parlour, Claire encounters Tree's daughter, Dharma, and sweeps her gently into the bosom of the family. The whole family, natural and extended, now use Claire and Johnny's house as headquarters. From this center, a new mystery and an old one are finally laid to rest.

Like viewing an impressionist painting, the closer one gets to the words of these stories, the vaguer they become. Even from the proper distance, the edges are blurry and yet, at that distance, the picture is full and complete. Mary Anne Kelly writes her characters from their insides out so, while one may not know what papa Stan's face looks like, one could describe the way his legs look in shorts and what he smells like. We find these to be alluring tales. We like the characters and we care about what happens to them. Not all of the endings are happy, yet this seems to be just the way things are supposed to happen—*almost* like real life.

LIBBY KINCAID
1991–1994   4 books
Kerry Tucker

Although photojournalist Libby Kincaid lives and works in Manhattan she is still a small-town girl in many ways. *Still Waters* takes her back to her hometown of Darby, Ohio, where she attends the funeral of her brother Avery, an apparent suicide. Charged with executing Avery's estate, Libby makes some discoveries which pique her curiosity. Avery's good friend, Dan Sikora, and his former fiancée, Pam Bates, the local veterinarian, provide information that only adds to Libby's confusion and grief. In the end, Libby proves that her brother did not kill himself but was, in fact, murdered. She returns to her life and loft in Manhattan thinking that Ohio is a closed chapter in her life story.

In *Cold Feet*, Libby almost achieves the separation she desires. On leave from *Americans*, the magazine for which she works, she has sought her own form of therapy—photography—and she has found her subject in a jazz tap dance group known as the Nonpareils. She also finds that her father, the elusive Max, has won the $1.2 million West Virginia Lottery. After Libby discovers the dead body of the leader of the tap troupe, she and Silver Gaines, another member of the troupe, are accused of the murder. Libby begins her own investigation to clear her name and prove Silver's innocence as well. Max's current marital convolutions serve as a minor distraction for Libby, and in the end father and daughter are no closer than they have ever been.

Death Echo takes Libby back to Echo, Ohio. After a camping trip with her long-distance lover, Dan Sikora, Libby returns to Darby, where she encounters veterinarian Pam Bates, who reluctantly asks a favor. Libby herself is reluctant to respond to Pam's request, but Pam provides the perfect bribe in the form of an interview—with pictures—of the reclusive author of the best-selling *The Tree of Life*, who happens to be the sister of Pam's foster mother. Libby goes to Echo, where she unravels an old, sad, and sordid tale of greed and mendacity.

Kerry Tucker writes evocative tales. The ongoing characters— Libby, Max, Dan, Pam, roommate Claire, and boss Octavia—are all slightly flawed. Their flaws and their desires to rise above them are what make this an accessibly human sort of series. We want Libby and her friends to learn from their mistakes, be freed from their self-imposed restrictions, and be the very best they can be. One of us is an Ohio native, and Tucker's descriptions of that state's places and people ring nostalgically true. Even the scenes that take place in Manhattan resonate with the Midwestern connection to the land and flair for storytelling.

AURORA TEAGARDEN
1990–1996   5 books
Charlaine Harris

Lawrenceton, Georgia, is a small, quiet community, not far from Atlanta. As the series opens in *Real Murders*, Aurora "Roe" Teagarden, the town librarian, is scheduled to make a presentation to the members of Real Murder, a literary club to which she belongs. Her subject is the Wallace case, a murder that occurred in England in 1931. Arriving a bit early, Aurora discovers the body of another club member in the kitchen of the Veterans of Foreign Wars (VFW) hall where the Real Murder meetings are held. Roe notices that the body is arranged in precisely the same fashion as the body in the Wallace case had been. Several more deaths occur, with each of the murders set up to resemble one of historical note. Together with her ex-husband, police officer Arthur Smith, and mystery writer Robin Crusoe, Roe figures out whodunit.

Aurora is four foot eleven and almost thirty. Her mother, Aida, is a real estate agent who also owns several rental properties, including the townhouse complex that Roe manages. Aida Brattle Teagarden resembles Lauren Bacall and is the quintessential Southern gentlewoman. In *A Bone to Pick*, Aida marries John Queensland, the former president of Real Murders. The ceremony is performed by the Reverend Aubrey Scott, Lawrenceton's new Episcopal priest. The Reverend Scott next officiates at the funeral of Roe's friend Jane Engle, former secretary of Real Murders, who has died of cancer. After the funeral, Jane's lawyer informs Roe that she is Jane's heir. Roe's inheritance is not without a catch, however, nor without other, unwanted complications. Roe's neighbor Lynn Liggett Smith—now married to officer Arthur Smith and *very* pregnant— assists Roe in capturing this story's miscreant.

Roe's inheritance allows her to leave the library. In *Three Bedrooms, One Corpse*, she is considering a new career in real estate, but when the first house she shows has the dead body of a realtor in the master bedroom, she wonders at the wisdom of her choice. She does meet Martin Bartell in the process, and her love life picks up in intensity. More killings take place and Martin becomes a prime suspect. At the denouement, Roe corners the killer and is rescued at the last possible moment.

Charlaine Harris has written a light-hearted series. Aside from finding dead bodies, Roe leads a fairly typical life. The small community of Lawrenceton becomes familiar, as do many of the characters who appear in the stories.

MISS HELMA ZUKAS
1994–1996   4 books
Jo Dereske

The Bellehaven, Washington, Public Library boasts a book collection four times as large as the population of the city, and its per capita circulation is the envy of every librarian in the state. To say that this library is a model of organization and sound management is a gross understatement. Miss Helma Zukas has been working at this institution for fourteen years and, as the archetype of all librarians, is no doubt responsible for much of the library's success. In her mid-thirties, Miss Zukas has worn the same hairstyle for the past twenty years. Her clothing is fastidiously cared for and always color coordinated. She drives the Buick given to her upon her high school graduation and has lived in apartment 3F of the Bayside Arms since her arrival in Bellehaven.

As *Miss Zukas and the Library Murders* opens, Miss Zukas's routine is shattered by the dead body found by the janitor in the library's fiction section. She quickly regains her customary equilibrium and sets about restoring order to her world and inadvertently gathering clues to the identity of the murderer. Police Chief Wayne Gallant recognizes Miss Zukas as an observant person and has several conversations with her regarding things she has seen and her interpretations of the pattern they form. He soon realizes that she is a very attractive woman whose shyness and naivete only add to her appeal. In personal peril, Miss Zukas discovers the miscreant and nicely rescues herself just before Chief Gallant arrives to do those honors.

Miss Zukas and the Island Murders finds her keeping a twenty-year promise to arrange a reunion of her Scoop River, Michigan, high school classmates. True to her nature, Miss Zukas has carefully husbanded the money entrusted to her as class treasurer and has made enough on her investments to bring the entire class to Washington. The weekend event is to be held at the Victorian Gull Rock Inn on Saturday Island in the San Juans. Anonymous letters, thinly veiled accusations, and minor sabotage threaten Miss Zukas's carefully laid plans. Undaunted, she perseveres and lays to rest both an old mystery and several new killings. Once again, Chief Gallant arrives just after Miss Zukas has saved the day and herself.

Author Jo Dereske has rendered the quintessential librarian every reader recognizes. At an early age, the order of the Dewey Decimal System provided an irresistible draw for Miss Zukas and has provided a natural extension of her personal image. Ruth Winthrop, her best friend since they were ten years old, is nearly the polar opposite of Miss Z. A six-foot-tall artist, Ruth is loud, flamboyant, excessive, and disorganized to the hilt. Her lusty approach to life is the perfect counter to Miss Zukas's rather repressed one; together, they make one complete, healthy individual. It is safe to say, however, that Ruth is the one to keep the relationship afloat by always being unconditionally there for Helma. Chief Gallant is, in fact, a gallant man. While he finds himself attracted to Helma, he is cautious in pressing his suit as he is aware that any precipitous action on his part will hinder the blossoming process of this retiring flower.

The stories are light and humorous. Miss Zukas is an engaging character, one whom readers will cheer on to her next liberation. All of the ongoing characters add substance to the stories, and the murders that draw them closer are both straightforward and well drawn.

ALBENIA "BENNI" HARPER
1994–1997   4 books
Earlene Fowler

This series seems to epitomize the tension between feisty female and macho man. The female half of the equation is Albenia "Benni" Harper, widow, folk-art expert, former cowgirl, and currently curator of the Folk Art Museum in San Celina, California. The male half is Gabe Ortiz, acting police chief of the town and Ph.D. aspirant. The initial meeting between these two puts them at instant loggerheads. In *Fool's Puzzle*, Benni is a suspect in the murder of a potter, and Ortiz, a veteran of the worst that east Los Angeles has to offer an officer of the law, will broach no interference in *his* investigation. It doesn't matter to him that another—missing—suspect is Benni's cousin Rita, and that Benni just might have some legitimate familial reason for concern over Rita's whereabouts. As far as Chief Ortiz is concerned, police business is just that—police business with no civilians allowed, much less invited.

Of course, Benni cannot refrain from getting involved. Her father and her grandmother Dove live together on the Ramsey Ranch. Benni with her late husband, Jack Harper, and his brother Wade worked the Harper family's ranch together. Both families have long and strong connections to the land and its adjacent community. Little wonder that Benni, her father, and her grandmother have a vested interest in Rita's well-being. Even less wonder that ranchers, living in relative isolation, take care of their own and help out their neighbors in ways city folk cannot understand.

A sure collision course between Gabe and Benni is set in the first book and holds true in the second, *Irish Chain*, after two friends of Benni—residents of San Celina's retirement home—are murdered during an event given by Benni in celebration of Mardi Gras. The first two books in the series deal with old secrets and pit the newcomer, Gabe Ortiz, in his official capacity against Benni Harper and her long-standing connections to her home town. Oddly enough, any collision between these two is caused as much by mutual attraction as it is by mutual animosity.

We have to describe this series as one of those crossovers between romance and mystery. Benni is an admirable modern-day heroine who resists rescue by the strong, protective man in her life until the last possible second. Gabe is just about as manly as one can get yet has a touch of the sensitive new-age guy (SNAG) about him. Apparently, this touch is enough for Benni. We know some readers will really enjoy these stories.

The foregoing characters represent a variety of approaches to art and the printed word. These characters run the gamut from the flamboyant artist to the repressed librarian and touch all points between. Each brings a well-honed power of observation to all her tasks, and though their detecting methods may vary according to personality, when it comes to murder these sleuths are meticulous in applying the results of their observations, ferreting out the criminal, and rendering a finished work.

SOME OTHER ARTISTS, ART EXPERTS, AND BIBLIOPHILE SLEUTHS

Katherine Craig
Sophie Greenway
Mis Susan Melville
Cassandra Mitchell
Elena Oliverez
Annabel Reed Smith
Glynis Tryon

PRIVATE EYES

The professional private investigator (PI) is one of crime and mystery fiction's most popular characters. The job of investigating beyond the parameters of officialdom is harsh and demanding, and writers have used those demands and challenges to create some of the most lasting and memorable fictional individuals. In 1909, Fleming Stone, known as The Great Man, was introduced by author Carolyn Wells. Though he appeared in sixty-one novels (1909–1942), Stone's methods are not dwelt upon; he makes his appearance to provide the solution for the baffled participants in the case. Wells knew a good thing when she saw it, and if she didn't create a memorable person in her character, she certainly created a long-lived one.

Lee Thayer gave readers Peter Clancy (1919–1966), who appeared in sixty books and during the long span aged very little. Justice was the cause Clancy served, with personal integrity of prime importance in all of his cases. Thayer was ninety-two when she wrote the last book in the series and must be considered the doyenne of this subgenre.

Agatha Christie's contribution to the field of private investigation is the possessor of the little grey cells—none other than the celebrated Hercule Poirot. He appeared in forty-seven books (1920–1984), and must have been about two hundred ten in his last adventure, which winds the series up in a tidy, if surprising, fashion. Another Englishwoman, Dora Turnbull, using the pen name Patricia Wentworth, created the redoubtable Miss Maud Silver, a discreet private enquiry agent. She appeared in thirty-two books (1928–1961) and presented the same demeanor of the calm schoolmistress in all of them.

One of the delights of the late '30s is the short series (1938–1942) featuring Mary Carner, who starts out as a department store detective, then marries the head of the store's security, and the couple adopt a child. Mary is so successful at solving murders, however, that she is asked to investigate things outside the confines of the store. Zelda Popkin wrote only five books starring this character. All are hard to find and treasures if one does.

In 1947 another female private investigator—Gale Gallagher,

head of the Acme Investigating Bureau—came on the scene and appeared in two well-crafted books (1947–1949) by the writing team of Margaret Scott and Will Oursler under the joint pseudonym Gale Gallagher.

P. D. James made a contribution to the private side of crime detection with Cordelia Gray (1972–1982). In spite of appearing in only two books, James's creation is an appropriate one. Being the daughter of a minor revolutionary provides Cordelia with the raw material for making her a good, intuitive investigator. Her mentor and employer recognized her talents and the rest, as they say, is history. Cordelia meets Supt. Adam Dalgliesh during one of her cases and for several years readers hoped for a reunion between the two. Unfortunately, James seems to have forgone her female PI in favor of her more official detective.

Sharon McCone's creator, Marcia Muller, is considered the godmother of the current spate of female private eyes. McCone has appeared in nineteen books to date (1977–1997). Coming into her profession through the route of security guard, Sharon was employed as the staff investigator for the All Souls Legal Cooperative. Her skills and talents include the ability to gently elicit information from people and to synthesize that data into a solution. A loner who discovers her otherness as the series progresses, Sharon is a full and compelling character who continues to grow and develop.

An English entry to the affray is Liza Cody's character Anna Lee (1980–1994). She appears alone as an investigator for Brierly Security in London in the first six books and as a minor character in the last three Cody books featuring the unusual Eva Wylie, a.k.a. Bucket Nut, who appears in the chapter "The Game's Afoot: Sports and Games." Dexterous and mechanically inclined from the outset, Anna Lee has progressed and honed her detecting abilities to a keen edge. This likable loner possesses a wry sense of humor and conducts her investigations with a clear tenacity and intelligence.

A banner year for the female detective was 1982, with the debuts of both V. I. Warshawski and Kinsey Millhone. Warshawski operates in Chicago and is one of the hardest of the hard-boiled investigators. Sara Paretsky has featured this tough, independent, and tenacious woman in nine books (1982–1995). She may leave much to be desired as a role model, but the stories in which she is featured are fast-paced, hard-hitting, and brilliantly executed.

Kinsey Millhone works in and around a fictional California coastal town very like Santa Barbara. Her author, Sue Grafton, says that she devised this character as a means of exorcising the desire to murder her own ex-husband and to date has carried Kinsey almost halfway through the alphabet in thirteen books (1982–1996). Kinsey is a former police officer who found the job too restricting and opted for the less well-defined horizon of the private operative. A competent detective at the outset, Kinsey has polished her skills throughout the series and in the process has become a more fully rounded character.

One of the most notable features of the contributions by women authors to this category of private detective is the introduction of a great number of women in a field considered by many for years as only appropriate for men. It should come as no surprise that women excel in this profession, as one of the necessary and important attributes of a good investigator is the ability to present a calm demeanor and inspire confidence. Most women have a strong disinclination for violent or confrontational behavior that may have to do with their generally smaller size and sometimes lesser strength. Nevertheless, the women who follow are as well prepared to handle the physical challenges of the job as they are to cope with the mental ones.

HELEN KEREMOS
1978–1997   6 books
Eve Zaremba

One of the earliest—and, to our minds, most riveting—female private investigators is Canadian Helen Keremos. Details of Helen's appearance and early life are sparsely sprinkled throughout the five books in the series, yet readers get a clear sense of just who this individual is and how she operates through the action of the stories and her investigative style.

Three of the books are fairly straightforward detective novels, but the third and fifth books break out of that mold. *Beyond Hope* carries Helen and her skills into the Canadian interior, where, while tracing a missing woman, she gets involved with multinational terrorism, world arms trade, and fanatical survivalists. *The Butterfly Effect* takes Helen on an ostensibly routine assignment to Tokyo, where she becomes involved with a missing person, an international art-smuggling ring, and the Yakuza, Japanese equivalent to the Mafia.

No matter where she is or what manner of case she works on, Helen Keremos is equal to the tasks at hand. She is not young— forty in the second book, *Work for a Million*—yet is fully capable of taking care of herself in a physical confrontation. Licensed to carry a gun, and qualified to use it, Helen rarely relies on a weapon even in the tightest of corners. She counts far more on her brains than her brawn or hardware and also depends on a wide network of friends and acquaintances to get the answers to the puzzles she faces.

One of the small hints about Helen's past is that she served in the United States Naval Security Division in the late '50s. The training she received in that phase of her career serves as a solid foundation for her expertise and competence as an investigator.

Basically, Helen is a loner; her resources are wide and varied, making her choice of profession a natural one. Comfortable in her camper living in the Canadian wilderness and capable of dealing with the practical aspects of life in the rough, she also fits well in a cityscape and has a circle of friends to aid and abet her wherever she goes.

Several of these friends and lovers appear throughout the series. Alex Edwards, a free-lance researcher and production assistant for the Canadian Broadcasting Commission, provides Helen with a bed and information in the first two stories, *A Reason to Kill* and *Work for a Million*. Nate Ottoline, a man who walks a fine line between legitimate and criminal activity, is a player in those two plus the fourth, *Uneasy Lies*. Alice Caplan, who serves as liaison between Helen and legal matters in the third, *Beyond Hope*, becomes Helen's lover at the end of that story, and the two are still together in the one that follows. Wayne Tillion is introduced in the fourth book and plays a major role in the fifth. Helen's relationships with these ancillary characters are pivotal to each story, and the nature of these connections goes a long way toward explaining Helen's character.

Eve Zaremba is a longtime feminist activist. She has created just the sort of protagonist we would hire in an instant and would love to have for a friend. We strongly recommend all of the books in the series and further, that they be read in order so that the full force of the character and her actions can be savored.

FIDDLER & FIORA
1985–1993   8 books
A. E. Maxwell (Ann [Elizabeth Lowell] Maxwell and Evan Maxwell)

Fiddler is just Fiddler. If he has other names, readers never learn them, nor do others who come into contact with him in the course of his investigations. Fiora Flynn was, at one time, Fiddler's wife. Even though she—feminist and professional woman that she is— probably never took his last name, it is likely that she knows it. Fiddler describes himself as a social critic. As the series opens, he is a licensed private investigator with a piece of paper that allows him to carry a concealed weapon; he is also, thanks to Fiora's fiscal expertise, independently wealthy. Consequently, Fiddler criticizes society freely and not only in ways that support his life-style. His *nom de guerre* harks back to a time when Fiddler played the violin. He was good but not good enough to meet his own high standard and perfect pitch. Consequently, he pitched his violin under the wheels of a southbound Corvette, brushed the dust from his hands, and never looked back.

The original source of Fiddler's wealth was a steamer trunk full of unmarked, nonsequential ten-, twenty-, and fifty-dollar bills, a legacy from his Uncle Jake, Fiddler's mother's much younger brother, who made his pile importing Mexican agricultural products. Jake's drug of choice was adrenaline; Fiddler shares this family trait. Fiora was a small-town girl with a notable talent. Pomona College, Harvard Business School, the London School of Economics, and the University of Tokyo—all attended on scholarship—placed Fiora at the crux of high-stakes financial sorcery. For her, turning Uncle Jake's questionably gotten gains into a respectable fortune was mere child's play.

Fiddler and sometimes Fiora live in Uncle Jake's house in Crystal Cove, California. Fiddler's next-door neighbor owns Kwame N'Krumah, a Rhodesian Ridgeback who has annexed Fiddler's territory and guards it with all appropriate ferocity. Lord Tornaga is the undisputed ruler of the Koi pond in the back yard. A tacky glass and plastic feeder attracts small, savage aerial fighters to battle for the nectar it contains. When Fiddler is in residence, so is the Shelby Cobra. When Fiora is there, the Cobra is joined by whatever BMW is current.

New Zealander Benny Speidel, a.k.a. The Ice Cream King of Saigon, was made a paraplegic by "friendly fire" in Vietnam. Now he resides in a beachfront duplex where he plies his trade—electronic wizardry. Through the magic of computer technology, Benny is able to gather any information Fiddler needs. Through his multifarious connections, he is also able to lay his hands on all manner of esoteric hardware and gadgetry. Although Benny and Fiddler are friends, Benny is devoted to Fiora and would protect her from any threat—even Fiddler.

Although each book involves murder and detection, none of the stories in this action-packed series remotely resembles the classic whodunit. The two protagonists, their relationship, and their shared philosophical style are the focus of the tales as are the connections the pair have to other characters appearing throughout the series. Uncle Jake is made manifest as a threnody until his murder is finally solved in the eighth book, *Murder Hurts*. In *Just Another Day in Paradise*, the first book, United States Customs agent and Jake's opponent Aaron Sharp becomes Fiddler's ally and features posthumously in the fourth, *Just Enough Light to Kill*. Volker, Fiddler's mirror image, also appears in these two books and wreaks vexation on Fiddler and Fiora's unity. The characters' synergy and cohesiveness add a vital element to each separate plot. Though each book may be read on its own, we encourage readers to get full value from this well-constructed series by starting with the first and following Fiddler and Fiora wherever they may go.

A. E. Maxwell is the joint pseudonym of Ann and Evan Maxwell. They have found that their coauthorship is most rewarding by an amalgamation of both points of view—a you and a me become an us.

QUIN ST. JAMES & MIKE MCCLEARY
1987–1995   10 books
T(rish) J(aneshutz) MacGregor

To say that these stories are complex, convoluted, and often confusing is a huge understatement. There are plots and subplots, themes and counterthemes, as well as conflict and resolution. As the series opens in *Dark Fields*, one of the primary characters, Mike McCleary, is a homicide detective with Metro-Dade in Miami. He meets Quin St. James when her lover is killed and he is called in to investigate the murder. At the end of the story, McCleary has resigned from the force, and when *Kill Flash* opens, he and Quin are married and partners in a private investigation firm.

The stories range through straightforward investigations, including threats made against an old friend of McCleary and a serial killer who alters Quin and McCleary's marriage. A plot to permanently remove McCleary from the investigative scene segues into the realm of paranormal psychology. While Quin is no stranger to risk and is willing to put herself into threatening situations to bring a case to a successful close, it is McCleary whose life is most frequently on the line. He is injured in every story and in *On Ice* suffers from amnesia. In *Death Flats*, he is shot and clinically dead for more than a minute, and in *Blue Pearl* another gunshot wound causes aphasia. The stories follow a definite path, and it is strongly recommended that readers begin with *Dark Fields* (if it can be found) and continue in order of publication.

Mistress of the Bones, the tenth in the series, takes place in Tango Key, where resides Aline Scott, another of T. J. MacGregor's characters (created under MacGregor's pseudonym Alison Drake). Scott doesn't appear in the story, but we wonder if the two series will be linked after the surprise ending of this compelling tale.

The connecting thread through all ten of these novels is the relationship between Quin and McCleary. In some respects, theirs appears to be a match made in heaven; the physical attraction between them is strong and their sexual relationship is active and well documented. There is a dark side to their pairing, however, that manifests itself through McCleary and his inability to completely connect with and commit to Quin. Pivotal events in the first book affect their relationship from the outset, and in *Death Sweet* he reconnects with Sylvia Callahan, a former lover who still fires his lust. Quin is aware of their attraction and challenges him with it. McCleary is forced to admit that he is unsure of his feelings for Sylvia, and, when she is murdered, those feelings remain unresolved. The lack of resolution between McCleary and Sylvia colors the personal connection between Quin and McCleary and in some ways defines both their personal and professional partnerships.

Miami is a port city, a tropical, multiethnic, tourist mecca. The "native" population is diverse in terms of economic status, racial background, and interests. Expatriates from a variety of Caribbean islands have added their religions and politics to the conservative, Southern, good-old-boy establishment. Old money is well established in well-known watering spots, and the new money of international drug dealing overrides almost everything. McCleary and St. James are at home in this milieu and possess the savvy and the connections that enable them to figure out just what's going down in any of the cases they are called upon to investigate. When Quin becomes pregnant, the two decide that Miami is no place to raise a family and relocate north to West Palm Beach. The arrival of Michelle Maia McCleary further alters both Quin and McCleary's world view.

For mystery fans of the hard-boiled persuasion, this series will meet, if not exceed, their highest expectations. However, the characters, primary and ancillary, and their interrelationships are so well developed and evolve so thoroughly throughout the series that they appeal to those less fond of action-packed, hard-boiled novels. MacGregor's experience as a teacher, a journalist, and a prison librarian pays off in this exciting and fast-paced series. We like the characters, the stories, and the writer's style and look forward to more.

CARLOTTA CARLYLE
1987–1997   7 books
Linda (Appelblatt) Barnes

Carlotta Carlyle is six-foot-one, wears a size-eleven shoe, and has wild red hair. Her father is a Scots-Irish ex-cop; her mother is a Russian-Jewish radical socialist who is full of Yiddish quotes from her late mother. Carlotta lives in a house left to her by her Aunt

Bea. She shares it with Thomas C. Carlyle, a cat of uncertain origins, in whose name the telephone is listed and to whom magazines are addressed; a parakeet who answers to none of her given names—Fluffy, Red Emma, or Esmerelda; and Roz, a punk artist who changes her hair color and style with alarming regularity and who gets reduced rent in exchange for doing the housework and sometimes assisting Carlotta in private investigations. Roz is a karate student whose instructor, known as Lemon, provides a variety of exercises on the mats that cover the floor of Roz's room as well as extra assistance for Carlotta. Volleyball and blues guitar are Carlotta's recreations. She is good at both.

In *A Trouble of Fools*, Carlotta and all of the people who are featured throughout the series are introduced. Gloria is the co-owner and sexy-voiced dispatcher for Green & White Cabs. She is black, wheelchair-bound, weighs in at somewhere around three hundred pounds, and is a junk-food junkie. The other owner of G&W Cabs is Sam Gianelli, fourth son of mob boss Anthony Gianelli, Sr. Sam and Carlotta have an intense on-again, off-again relationship. Carlotta's ex-husband, Cal Therieux, is Cajun, a musician, and a cokehead. Lt. Mooney of the Boston Police Department is Carlotta's former boss and would like to have a different—more intimate—relationship with the feisty PI. Paolina and Carlotta met through the Big and Little Sisters organization. Paolina lives with her brothers and their mother in one of the infamous housing projects of Cambridge, Massachusetts. Carlotta spends whatever time she can with Paolina.

All of the stories in this series involve Carlotta, her friends, and some aspect of their interconnected lives. The first book deals with a missing man, his old cab driver buddies, and their revival of the Gaelic Brotherhood Association raising money for the Irish Republican Army. In *The Snake Tattoo*, Mooney asks Carlotta to find a missing woman who witnessed the barroom confrontation that caused his suspension. At the same time, she is hired to find a fourteen-year-old runaway. *Coyote* involves Carlotta in the world of illegal aliens, the Immigration and Naturalization Service, and a serial killer whose victims are the disenfranchised workers in Boston's sweatshops. *Steel Guitar* brings Carlotta's earlier musical life to the fore when an old friend and Cal bring murder—past and present—to Carlotta's attention. In *Snapshot*, a child dies of an easily controlled disease in one of the city's hospitals and her distraught mother asks Carlotta to investigate. Paolina's real father emerges in this story, and his political and drug connections confuse Paolina, Carlotta, and the case. Sam Gianelli's family and their Mafia connections are at the center of *Hardware*.

Carlotta Carlyle, her friends, and her associates are great multidimensional characters, and the stories in which they are featured are well plotted, exciting, and believable. Carlotta herself is an apt representative of the new breed of PI. She is an independent and stubborn loner who, without losing the edge or danger inherent in this type of tale, brings intuition, intelligence, and compassion to a hard-boiled profession. Linda Barnes has done a wonderful job in this series, not only with the characters she has created but with the cab driver's view of Boston that she provides her readers. Her other series features Michael Spraggue, sometime actor, occasional vintner, and formerly licensed PI.

CATHERINE SAYLER
1988–1998   6 books
Linda Grant (Linda V. Williams)

Detecting white-collar crime in the city of San Francisco and up and down its peninsula is Catherine Sayler's specialty. Her office, in an unreconstructed Victorian on Divisadero, is shared with her secretary, Amy, and her assistants Chris and Jesse. In *Love Nor Money*, Jesse's computer skills, determination, and intelligence move him up to full partner. Catherine and Jesse have saved substantial sums of money for more than one company and have prevented numerous business disasters. Catherine finds herself more comfortable dealing with dishonesty and greed than with cruelty and violence. Her lover and fellow private investigator Peter Harman, an unreconstructed hippie, has his own area of expertise in the darker arenas of crime.

Fortunately for readers, Catherine's personal connections and loyalties lead her into cases that involve all of the seven deadly sins. When Peter is arrested for murder in *Random Access Murder*, Catherine doesn't hesitate to get involved in the investigation to clear him. Her background in high-tech chicanery serves her well as the case centers on espionage within the computer industry. In *Blind Trust*, Catherine is hired to find a missing banker before money changes hands in a major acquisition. Peter assists her and, in the process, is shot.

In *Love Nor Money*, at a friend's request, Catherine takes an excursion away from her usual cases to prove that a highly respected judge is in fact a pedophile. Her skills in business matters bring her the satisfaction of sweet revenge against a client who has betrayed her as he is linked—albeit innocently—to the judge's unsavory practices. In *A Woman's Place*, sexual harassment in the corporate world is the focus when Catherine is hired to discover the identities of practical jokers, malicious misogynists, and eventually a murderer.

Unlike many of today's female private investigators, Catherine Sayler is not a loner. She works with a staff, has a lover, and, as the series progresses and her niece Molly moves in with her and Peter, she has a family. She is also a dedicated student of aikido, a martial art that provides its adherents the means only of defense—never of offense. Her workouts and teaching at the dojo are integral parts of her persona. Her study of this martial art is a serious discipline and an active form of meditation that has taught Catherine the importance of getting out of her own way and using any opponent's energy to her benefit. She uses the principles of aikido in confrontations—both physical and mental—in each of her stories, yet is not hesitant to rely on more conventional forms of backup when necessary or available.

Linda Grant is a Stanford University graduate who began the study of aikido while attending that institution. Her character is a smart, savvy woman comfortable in the world of haute technology and contemporary business practice. While Catherine Sayler may prefer unmasking embezzlers and is a dab hand at corporate wrangling, she is equally talented at disclosing killers and handling physical confrontation. Grant has created a well-rounded individual as a role model and, perhaps, an inspiration.

KAT COLORADO
1989–1997   8 books
Karen Kijewski

Kat Colorado's mother died the night of Kat's high school graduation by falling down the stairs in a drunken stupor and breaking her neck. Kat never knew her father, and her mother didn't care enough for her to give Kat her own last name. She started out as Kate—named for the Shakespearean heroine of *The Taming of the Shrew*. Her last name is for the place her mother thought her father may have come from. Alma Flaherty entered Kat's life soon after her mother's death and became Kat's adoptive grandmother. Alma is a pistol—eighty-something with a hollow leg and a productive kitchen. Her capacity for love seems boundless, and she reserves judgment on the major stuff of life while keeping a running commentary on most everyone's failings and her favorite soap operas.

Kat is a private investigator with an office in downtown Sacramento in a Victorian building just on the edge of the gentrified area. Her downstairs neighbor, Mr. Addison, repairs adding machines, quotes statistics, and keeps an eye on Kat, whom he calls "Doll

Face." Charity Collins, Kat's closest friend, is an advice writer whose syndicated column, "Consult Charity," appears in newspapers around the country. The two met when Kat worked as an investigative reporter for the *Sacramento Bee*. In *Katwalk*, Charity asks Kat to find out what has really happened to $200,000 her soon-to-be ex-husband squirreled away. Kat reluctantly agrees, and the case takes her to Las Vegas, where she meets homicide Det. Hank Parker. The plot thickens when she discovers Charity's husband Sam's involvement in a company called New Capital Ventures. Sam is killed, Kat's arm gets broken by a hit-and-run driver, and she is threatened by an old friend. With Hank's help, she brings the case to its conclusion.

Katapult opens with a five A.M. call from Alma telling Kat that a copper is in her house saying that another of her adopted grandchildren has been murdered. Alma asks Kat to find out who killed Johnny and why and also to find his long-missing sister. As Kat ponders these large questions of her extended family, she is approached by a young hooker who asks Kat to investigate the street killing of her close friend. Lindy is an in-your-face fourteen-year-old who alternately touches and exasperates Kat. The two cases run in parallel, and Kat makes some unpleasant discoveries about families and the kind of closeness they share.

Several themes run through this character-driven series. Kat is central to all of the stories and her perspective on people, for the most part, is clear and true. On occasion, her judgment is clouded, yet what she learns from her wrong calls aids her in pursuing her chosen profession. Family unity and disharmony feature heavily in several books, and the plight of the abandoned child is a frequent scenario as well. Perhaps the strongest recurring motif is that of a woman's ability to redeem herself in spite of staggering odds against her. All of the female characters who appear in this series are strong, and their strength is not limited to heroism or altruism; there are also some of the best women villains we've ever encountered. The males in these stories fare less well, as most of them have serious character flaws.

Karen Kijewski plays fair with her readers in terms of laying out clues and steadily building the story to an exciting and plausible climax. Despite her warm and loving adoptive family and close friends, Kat Colorado is a loner. Though she is capable of defending herself and anyone else she cares for, Kat is not an innately violent individual. When in the course of events she finds it necessary to take a human life, Kat's remorse and regret weigh heavily on her. Kijewski has crafted a likable and effective role model and has won several awards for her sterling efforts, namely, the Shamus from Private Eye Writers of America and the Anthony from the Bouchercon convention.

JERI HOWARD
1990–1997   7 books
Janet Dawson

Oakland, California, and the environs of the eastern shore of the San Francisco Bay make up Jerusha "Jeri" Howard's home territory. Daughter of Dr. Timothy Howard and Marie Doyle Howard, Jeri was born in Berkeley as her father achieved his graduate degree in history. The family moved to Alameda when the professor took a position at Cal State, Hayward. Though her parents divorced after Jeri and her brother, Brian, were grown, Jeri has yet to forgive her mother.

Jeri started her career path as a legal secretary, then moved into position as a paralegal. Errol Seville plucked her from that mundane world and trained her as an investigator. She worked with him for five years and, when a heart attack compelled his retirement, took over his business and renamed it J. Howard Investigations. Most of the work she does is for insurance companies and law offices, with the occasional skip trace. In *Kindred Crimes*, Jeri's ex-husband, Sgt. Sid Vernon of the homicide section of the Oakland Police Department, recommends Jeri to a husband looking for his missing wife. Following the woman's trail, Jeri crosses the path of an old, somewhat familiar, murder and finds a new dead body. The solution to both crimes is lodged in the past.

Till the Old Men Die provides readers with an instructive look at the recent history of the Philippines and the struggles of its people during World War II. A colleague of Jeri's father is murdered, and a woman claiming to be his widow comes to the college to collect his belongings—five months after his death. Jeri is hired to find out if the woman does in fact have a claim to Lito Manibusan's papers and in the process discovers why he was killed and by whom.

In *Take a Number*, a woman involved in the first story recommends Jeri to her daughter Ruth Raynor, who is seeking a divorce and needs to find some well-hidden assets. When her abusive husband is shot to death in her apartment, Ruth is charged with his murder and Jeri undertakes to prove her innocence.

Don't Turn Your Back on the Ocean is sound advice and the title of the fourth novel. Jeri travels to the Monterey Peninsula to visit her mother and her extensive Irish-Italian family. Jeri's cousin is being held under suspicion in the disappearance of his girlfriend and is charged with her murder when her dead body washes to shore.

Jeri offers to look into the matter for the family, finds the killer, solves another old mystery, and uncovers the perpetrator of sabotage against her mother's restaurant.

Jeri Howard is a loner. From the outset of the series, she is a self-described daddy's girl with strong antipathy toward her mother. Dr. Howard comes into all of the stories, but it is not until the fourth that we meet Marie Doyle Howard and get a look at the other side of the family portrait. Jeri seems better at resolving conflict with and for other families than her own, and all of the stories involve strife and dysfunction among related persons.

Janet Dawson's own background as an East Bay resident, as an enlisted journalist in the navy, and as a legal secretary provides her character with the necessary qualifications for the job she has taken on. Dawson's extensive knowledge of the greater San Francisco Bay area forms a part of the framework of the books, and the United States military, its personnel, and its installations are featured elements. Janet Dawson won the Private Eye Writers of America Best First Private Eye Novel Contest for the first book in this series.

BARRETT LAKE
1993–1996   5 books
Shelley Singer

In *Following Jane*, Barrett Lake is a forty-year-old history teacher in Berkeley at Technical High School and at the edge of a midlife crisis. She has recently purchased a red Mazda RX7 sports car that has helped improve her outlook on life, yet something still seems to be missing. After the murder of a fellow teacher and the disappearance of a student in one of Barrett's senior history classes, Barrett is approached by Francis Broz, a private investigator. Broz, known as "Tito," has been hired by the student's natural father to discover the whereabouts of his missing daughter, and Tito is asking questions of everyone who had come in contact with her. Barrett likes Tito and finds herself fascinated with his job. She cares about what may have happened to the student and offers Tito her services—at no pay.

Barrett Lake was adopted by a couple who emigrated from the Soviet Union. The Lakes owned a small grocery store in the low end of the old North Side of Minneapolis and were staunch upholders of the work ethic. By birth, Barrett is a mixture of Chippewa, French, and Swedish—not strange for someone born in Minnesota—and Jewish by adoption. As a child, she fantasized herself as a hero cut in the mold of Robin Hood or Ivanhoe. As she grew older, she allowed herself to be convinced by her parents that nice girls didn't do such things, so she attended college, got a master's degree in medieval history and made a career of teaching in the hope that she could at least influence young lives. Teaching did not even begin to meet the needs of some of the lost and disenfranchised children who passed through Barrett's classes, and she began to feel almost totally ineffectual.

After successfully finding the student and solving a murder in the first book, Barrett asks Tito to hire her permanently. Although he is reluctant to let her give up the security her teaching position provides for the hit-or-miss profession of investigator, Tito agrees to let her continue moonlighting for him. As *Picture of David* opens, Barrett is getting ready for the start of the school year. She has arranged to job share in order to maintain her financial security while allowing herself more time to do the job she much prefers. When Barrett's oldest and closest friend and fellow Minneapolis expatriate asks her to help an immigrant family whose son has been kidnapped, she readily agrees. The long arm of revenge is at the center of this story, and Barrett must pry old secrets from the frightened parents in order to find the missing boy.

Searching for Sara takes Barrett to the Tenderloin district of San Francisco looking for a fifteen-year-old runaway. Although Barrett finds Sara, there are two murders at the Loughlin Street Youth Center and the director hires her to find the killer. *Interview with Mattie* opens with the murder of a thirteen-year-old boy soon after an interview with him appeared on the front page of *The Berkeley Word*. The publisher is being held responsible for the child's death and has received threatening letters. He hires Barrett to investigate the threats and the killing. In the process, she discovers neglected children, a kiddie-porn ring, and the effects of professional greed.

Though she may be too tall to wear the suit of armor she has named Ivanhoe that stands in her hallway, Barrett's idealism well serves her and the young victims she assists. Her choice of friends and companions is a fitting adjunct to her new part-time profession. Aside from Tito, Barrett is occasionally assisted by her sixty-five-year-old landlady and best friend, Gilda, an animal-rights activist and proud Gray Panther.

Shelley Singer has created a modern-day hero who is well placed to make a difference in the lives of those least able to help themselves. In doing so, she paints a vivid picture of kids at risk and the dangers that face them. Singer's first series features Berkeley jack-of-all-trades Jake Samson and his lesbian carpenter sidekick Rosie Vicente. No titles have been added to that series since 1988, and we hope for more.

LAUREN LAURANO
1991–1996   4 books
Sandra Scoppettone

Lauren Laurano is five-foot-two with brown hair going grace-fully gray. She's a third-generation Italian-American who grew up in New Jersey. Her father is an attorney, her mother an alcoholic housewife. As the series opens, Lauren is forty-two and has been in a relationship with Kip Adams for eleven years. The two women own a brownstone in Greenwich Village where Kip has an office for her therapy practice. They rent apartments to William and Rick and another couple known only as the PITAS (pains in the ass). Lauren and Kip have a wide circle of friends—some gay, others straight—and in *Everything You Have Is Mine*, Jill, one of the J's who own Three Lives Bookstore, tells Lauren about a friend who needs Lauren's help.

Lauren is a private investigator, so Jill's request could be related to that profession. But Lauren's personal experience as a rape victim is even more to the point for Lake Huron, a beautiful young woman raped by a man on their second date. When Lake is found hanged in her own bathroom, suicide is everyone's first supposition, includ-ing that of Lauren's friend and police connection Lt. Peter Cecchi. Money, motherhood, and memories are all elements of this labyrin-thine case. In the course of tracing Lake's rapist, Lauren evolves from computerphobe to computerphile.

The theme for this series is established in the first book; each case Lauren becomes involved with consists of perplexing connections between seemingly unrelated persons. Links are made, affinities un-raveled, and disunities revealed in every story, and Lauren seems to have an uncanny ability to gather all the stray threads into a coher-ent strand that leads to the killer. Each story has several plot lines running concurrently, as well as those that carry over from one book to the others. In the second book in the series, *I'll Be Leaving You Always*, the description of the guest list for Lauren and Kip's twelfth-anniversary dinner party is a prime example of theme and countertheme. A surprise in *My Sweet Untraceable You* would make Bill Deeck's favorite author, James Corbett, feel right at fictional home.

Whether describing Manhattan life, street people, or friends of Lauren and Kip, Sandra Scoppettone hits notes that resonate with appropriate harmony or dissonance. While murder is taken seri-ously by both author and character, there is an overall sense of humor that enlivens these well-written tales; some of the dialogue between Lauren and others could be done as stand-up comedy. The

Big Apple is noted for its multifarious life-styles and the comedy, tragedy, pathos, and Eros endemic to this place are vital elements of the books featuring this intriguing character. Though Scoppettone also writes young-adult fiction and has penned three hard-boiled mysteries under the pseudonym of Jack Early, we are glad she has added Lauren Laurano to the growing list of believable and readable female PIs.

HANNAH WOLFE
1991–1995   3 books
Sarah Dunant

Englishwoman Hannah Wolfe works for the firm of Comfort and Security, whose owner, Frank Comfort, is an ex-cop. Their office is located between London's two biggest railway stations, and the building that houses it has seen better days. Some of Comfort and Security's clients have seen better days as well, especially those who turn up dead. Much of Hannah's work involves personal security as companion and bodyguard for wealthy women. Hannah's politics are what prevented her from joining the police force, a fact she considers fortunate as she probably never would have met Frank, who had left the force before she might have joined it.

As *Birth Marks* opens Hannah has returned from escorting a rich matron on a shopping spree in Hong Kong. She is confronted with a water-damaged apartment and a stack of unpaid bills. In spite of her disdain for the sort of jobs Frank has to offer her, Hannah calls him, and Frank sends her to Miss Augusta Patrick, who has not heard from a young protégée in over a month and wants to know what has happened to her. When Carolyn Hamilton's eight-months-pregnant body is hauled out of the Thames, an apparent suicide, the case seems to have come to a logical conclusion. However, as far as Hannah is concerned, some ends remain loose and some burning questions remain unanswered. When Hannah is told by a solicitor that his client wishes her to continue the investigation, she does. The case takes her to a chateau in France where she finds as many questions as she does answers. Eventually, all is made known, yet the outcome is such that both Hannah and the reader are left with only partial resolution.

In *Fatlands*, a simple escort job for a recalcitrant teenage girl comes to an abrupt end when the young woman is killed in a car explosion almost before Hannah's eyes. The apparent culprits are a group of animal-rights activists protesting the involvement of the girl's father in the genetic alteration of animals for profit. Once again, Hannah is dissatisfied with the pat answers and pursues matters to a violent conclusion.

Sabotage at Castle Dean Health Farm brings Hannah to the scene of crimes in *Under My Skin*. Deception is more than skin deep in this story and Hannah finds herself looking at the societal imperative for women to maintain a youthful appearance at all costs. As in the first two novels, the case seems closed to everyone except Hannah, and she passionately follows her own lines to an inevitable end.

Hannah Wolfe is a modern-day Paladin, the outstanding protagonist of a cause. While those in power may be satisfied with a particular outcome, Hannah's personal sense of ethics will not let her rest until the causal issue—greater even than that of death—is addressed. Hannah's actions may serve only to alter a given situation rather than to resolve matters in their entirety, but in reality, what more can one individual do?

Sarah Dunant writes with wit, style, and a wonky-yet-relevant view of contemporary life. Her character is, like most private investigators, a loner whose self-defined isolation allows her to aggressively extract confidential information from those she questions. Few individuals would have the intestinal fortitude to carry an investigation to its farthest, if not most logical, conclusion as Hannah Wolfe does, and Dunant does not write easy, happy endings. We predict that readers will clamor for more.

RONNIE VENTANA
1991–1997   4 books
Gloria White

Veronica Ventana is the daughter of the late Francisco and Olivia Ventana—high-society jewel thieves. A point of pride with Ronnie is that her parents were never convicted. They died in a car crash before their case came to trial; Ronnie was fifteen. The senior Ventanas are held in reverence by the segment of the population their heists benefited; those representing law and order hold the diametrically opposite view; this legacy from her parents is a mixed blessing for Ronnie. Her standards are high and her career reflects them. For a while she worked as a parole officer, but the cumbersome bureaucracy eventually got to her. Now she is a private investigator specializing in security with an office in her studio apartment over the Quarter Moon Saloon in downtown San Francisco.

Ronnie's mentor and teacher is Blackhand "Blackie" Coogan, an ex-boxer and sometime PI. Blackie is around sixty-five and cuts a dashing, if rather seedy, figure; and women adore him. He lives in squalor in a tiny house in the Bernal Heights section of the city, where he spends his time drinking and watching boxing matches on television. When Ronnie needs backup, muscle, or the odd safe cracked, Blackie is her man.

All of the stories show Ronnie investigating murder, yet in none of them is she the hired detective. In *Murder on the Run*, she is the eyewitness to a fight between two men that ends when one throws the other into the San Francisco Bay at just about the same spot where Jimmy Stewart rescued Kim Novak in the film *Vertigo*. In *Money to Burn*, David "Bink" Hanover seeks Ronnie's protection from a woman and her goons who are out to kill him. As *Charged with Guilt* opens, Ronnie is checking security in a supposedly empty house. The police arrive, discover the murdered body of Senator Payton Murphy, and charge Ronnie with the crime. In spite of her lack of charter, Ronnie is determined to get the answers to an ever-growing set of questions in each case. Lt. Harold "Philly" Post of the San Francisco Homicide Department reluctantly helps her and accepts her assistance in all four books.

Other individuals woven throughout the stories are well drawn. Ronnie's cousin Myra runs Tuxedo Messages and has less than great taste in men. Ronnie's ex-husband, Mitchell, pops in and out of her life and her cases and is always trying to get her to take a straight job and make some money. Aldo Stivick, an officer in police administration, has had a major crush on Ronnie since high school and feeds her information and lunch whenever possible. Members of the city's Hispanic community provide her with assistance, information, and comfort out of respect for her parents.

The city of San Francisco and its surrounding communities are wonderful features in these tales. Without dwelling on minute detail, Gloria White evokes the ambiance of the various city neighborhoods and districts and has created a main character who operates comfortably and knowledgeably in her environs. All of these stories are well and intricately plotted, and Ronnie herself is a substantial creation.

FREDDIE O'NEAL
1992–1997   7 books
Catherine Dain (Judith Garwood)

Reno is the setting for this series featuring private investigator Freddie O'Neal. A personality profile test administered as a part of career counseling showed Freddie that she had a strong sense of right and wrong, liked puzzles, needed meaningful work, and didn't like to take orders. Of the several job possibilities presented, the one with the most appeal was that of private investigator. She operates out of the living room of the house she shares with two long-haired cats, Butch and Sundance, and has a reasonable success rate doing skip traces, divorce work, and the more mundane investigative chores.

In *Lay It on the Line*, Freddie is hired to find a stolen car. When she does, she also finds a large bag of white powder in the trunk. Freddie turns the car and its contents over to the police and assumes her case is closed. The murder of her employer's sister brings Freddie back into the picture, and when her employer is also killed, the ante is upped. Of course, there are no simple answers around the murders of the two women. As the tale unfolds, Reno's history, its founding fathers and mothers, and its present politicos figure into a much larger picture. After Freddie survives a forced landing in her sabotaged airplane, she is abducted by those with heavy secrets to keep. Deacon "Deke" Adams, her sometime employee, assists in her rescue and in bringing the bad guys to justice.

Freddie is a native daughter of Reno and has a strong affinity for the schizophrenic city. Those who succeed in this harsh and unforgiving place are made of uncommon stuff, and Freddie is no exception to that rule. She is practical, realistic, and resourceful. Her love and admiration of the scenic splendors of the area are tempered with a healthy respect for the unpredictability of the elements. Freddie knows Nevada's history and has watched changes affect her hometown within her lifetime. While she may not welcome all of those changes, she knows that, in a mutable place, what goes around usually comes around and the city of Reno and the state of Nevada will probably withstand and outlast almost everything.

As the series progresses, readers learn more about Freddie's life and her family. In the second book, *Sing a Song of Death*, her mother, Ramona, and Ramona's second husband, Al, are introduced. They live on the north shore of Lake Tahoe—just far enough away to make visits infrequent. Freddie's father, James Joseph Daniel "Danny" O'Neal the Fourth, is the centerpiece of *Walk a Crooked Mile*, and the crosscurrents and conflicts that plague Freddie's life unfold in these two books. Her independence is demonstrated as much by her choice of vehicles as her profession. Her favorite mode of transportation—and by far the most sensible in this large and empty place—is a Piper Cherokee airplane. Her track record with men is dismal, and her relationship with Deke Adams, a former Air Force survival trainer currently providing night security for the Mother Lode Casino, is testy and solid.

In all of the stories, Catherine Dain's creation comports herself intelligently. Her risks are calculated; she is not a loose cannon. When she finds herself on her own and in jeopardy, she is strong and savvy enough to cope with the situation. Freddie is an exemplary product of her environment who learned the basics of the art of survival at her mother's knee. She still has some rough edges and, as a success in an exacting profession, we hope she keeps them.

KATE BRANNIGAN
1992–1996   5 books
Val McDermid

Kate Brannigan was a first-year law student when she met Bill Mortensen, who was romantically involved with her lodger. Bill, with a first-class degree in computer science from an English university, had discovered that the crooked side of computing was vastly more interesting than any programming task could be. He set up shop investigating computer fraud and expanded to include surveillance and security. Kate started doing small legal tasks for him during her vacations and, after completing her second year in law school, went to work for him full time. As the series opens, Kate is a partner in Mortensen and Brannigan.

Kate and her boyfriend, rock journalist Richard Barclay, have what—to most women we know—is the ideal living situation. They live next door to one another and their respective residences are joined at the back by a beautiful conservatory with a door between the two units that locks. Richard believes that only Chinese food and McDonalds sustain life, and he is a slob. Kate cooks and is careful to throw food out once its sell-by date has passed. She is tidy without being obsessive about it. Kate is naturally disciplined and compounds that quality through her work and the practice of Thai kick boxing. Richard smokes pot and maintains an impressive collection of beer from around the world.

Most of the work the Manchester-based Mortensen and Brannigan does is the investigation of white-collar crime. In *Dead Beat*, Kate is tracing goods in the "schneid" trade. *Kick Back* finds her looking into, among other things, a real estate scam. *Crack Down* opens with Kate and Richard posing as a married couple purchasing a car to uncover fraud in the motor trade, and *Clean Break* features paintings and objets d'art stolen from premises Kate has secured. Each of the books has at least two cases running in parallel, and at least one of them involves murder. The constant thread of Kate's personal life winds through the stories and often overlaps her professional responsibilities, adding to the complexity of the job Kate must do. And she is equal to all tasks.

Kate Brannigan is a woman of many talents—she knows her way around most computers and can access information with the best of them, is a capable photographer with a darkroom at the office, and has learned to kick box and pick locks from her good friend Dennis O'Brien, a burglar by trade. Kate also has a close cadre of friends and acquaintances with whom she exchanges information or skills. Alexis Lee, crime reporter for the Manchester *Evening Chronicle*, is her closest friend. Another friend, Josh, is a financial broker who trades credit record information with Kate for a bang-up dinner out every few months.

Val McDermid read English and received a degree from Oxford. She has been an award-winning journalist and spent three years as northern bureau chief of an English national Sunday tabloid. She writes another series featuring reporter Lindsay Gordon, who may be found in the chapter "Murder between the Pages: Writers and Journalists." McDermid's talent and experience—her journalistic flair for facts and background—show up in her fiction writing. Tantalizing bits of English history and lore crop up in the stories along with well-researched data on current popular scams. Northern British slang is dexterously woven throughout the novels as well as tidbits of gossip about the rock scene and the variety of Chinese food available in the Greater Manchester area.

McDermid has made a stellar contribution to the domain of female PIs. Read the Brannigan series from start to finish and enjoy the humor, tightly woven plotting, local color, and lively detecting.

PHOEBE SIEGEL
1993–1996   3 books
Sandra West Prowell

This series gets off to an explosive start as Billings, Montana, PI Phoebe Siegel goes ballistic over the investigation of her brother Ben's apparent suicide—an event that took place in March, three years before the opening of *By Evil Means*. As a result of Ben's death and that of her beloved Aunt Zelda in the same month, Phoebe doesn't do March any more. She rips it off the calendar and, if her behavior in the first book is an example, throws all caution and good sense to the wind for those thirty-one days.

All of the initial pain of Ben's death reasserts itself when a woman comes to Phoebe and asks her to find out what is happening to her daughter, a patient at the Whispering Pines rehab center. Politics, corruption, ownership of vast tracts of Montana land, betrayal, and abuse (physical, sexual, and mental) are all elements of the story, and Ben's death is intimately linked to several of these elements. Phoebe does solve an old crime but several more people die in the process and the denouement takes place at a shoot-out in which three more people are shot and killed.

When *The Killing of Monday Brown* opens, Phoebe has set many of her ghosts to rest. When Kyle Old Wolf and his family arrive at her newly purchased house to elicit her aid in proving Matthew Wolf's innocence in the death of Monday Brown, she agrees to take on the job and proceeds to discover not only the real killer but the facts behind the thefts of valuable Native American artifacts. *When Wallflowers Die* puts Phoebe on the trail of a killer whose crime occurred some twenty-seven years earlier. Approached by the dead woman's husband, Phoebe finds herself interested in the case but unwilling to work for Robert Maitland, a man with his eye on the governor's mansion. Another man offers to hire Phoebe but he is shot to death just before his first meeting with her. The shades of Ellen Maitland and Frank Chillman compel Phoebe to keep on the case and she uncovers secrets based on levels of immorality hard to imagine.

Phoebe Siegel is a Montana native. Her late father was Jewish and a police officer. Her mother is very much alive and very Irish Catholic. Ben Siegel followed in his father's footsteps and was a cop. Their brother Michael became a priest and their oldest brother Aaron moved east and became a rabbi. Another brother, Sam, was killed in Vietnam and Kehly, the baby of the family, is a recovering alcoholic. Life in the Siegel family is not without its ups and downs. After the events in the first book, Phoebe's relationship with her family takes a turn for the better, and she develops some rapport with her mother, her younger sister, and their former sister-in-law. Michael, the priest, rubs Phoebe the wrong way and she continually lets him know just how much she resents what she sees as his holier-than-thou attitude. She's involved with a man named Roger in the first book and the early part of the second, but eventually she and Kyle Old Wolf develop a mutual attraction that has possibilities for the future.

Recruited by the FBI straight out of college, Phoebe was in training at Quantico when she received word of her brother's death; she never returned to her training. Aunt Zelda had been a free spirit and, upon her death, left Phoebe $1.5 million in an unnumbered Puerto Rican bank account. The only way Phoebe could claim her inheritance was to promise never to reveal its existence and to always live her life free from inhibition; Phoebe does so in spades.

Sandra West Prowell, a fourth-generation Montanan, has developed a gutsy character. She's as tough as V. I. Warshawski but, once Prowell lays the demons driving Phoebe to rest, she allows her protagonist to develop a bit more finesse. Prowell's plotting is elaborate, her characters are believable, and the stories evoke the big sky sensibilities of her home state.

CALEY BURKE
1993–1995   3 books
Bridget McKenna

Cascade, California, is a small fictional community at the northern end of the state's great Central Valley that has been home to Caley Burke for more than fourteen years. Caley's life has taken unexpected twists and turns. As the series opens in *Murder Beach*, she is a newly licensed private investigator. In this story, Caley has returned to El Morado, a small costal community between Los Angeles and San Diego, where she spent the last two years of high school, graduating in 1977. Her best friend, Valerie Hayden, has implored Caley to come to their class reunion and to help her with a serious problem.

The problem, of course, involves murder, and Valerie's grandfather Tony Garza is the prime suspect. As the story unfolds, Caley is faced with more than the task of clearing Tony's name; an old love, Rob Cameron, declares his renewed affection for her, but their reunion is complicated by the fact that he is the investigating police officer and is convinced of Tony's guilt. Other faces from the past arise to complicate Caley's life and the case itself. At the end, Caley is left with as many—if not more—questions as those with which she arrived.

Dead Ahead also takes Caley away from Cascade. In this book, she has been asked by the daughter of Caley's mother's good friend Cass Lowry to investigate Cass's death. Arriving just in time for the funeral and the gathering afterward, Caley meets all of the players in what turns out to be a deadly serious game involving white supremacists led by a man no one has ever seen. The connections for Caley are far less personal than in the first book, but the tension-filled end of the tale, coming only one month after her first official case, takes its toll on her psyche.

When *Caught Dead* begins, Caley is suffering from the effects of the two deaths she has caused in conjunction with her investigations. Her boss, Jake Baronian, tells her to go on leave until she gets some counseling. Reluctantly, Caley agrees to see therapist Maggie Peck for help with her serious loss of appetite, inability to sleep, and increased reliance on alcohol. In spite of the fact that she is officially not working, Caley gets involved in a local murder and brings it to a successful conclusion.

Although all three stories are separated by geography, there are links to Caley, her insecurities, and that which drives her. In the first book, when asked to help a friend, Caley is forced to confront her past and come to terms with who she has become in the present. In the second book, another plea from a family friend puts Caley's personal and political beliefs on the line, and once again she is thrown back on her own resources. In both stories, Caley shoots someone to save her own and another's life. In the third book, she must look long and hard at what she has done to put herself in the way of such violence.

Bridget McKenna's character is a typical private investigator—a loner, somewhat insecure and uncomfortable with people. Jake, her mentor and boss, believes in her and has given her tools and confidence to support herself in a difficult, often boring, and sometimes dangerous job. The cases Caley becomes involved in are intricate, interesting, and well devised.

PATRICIA DELANEY
1994–1995   3 books
Sharon Gwyn Short

Cincinnati, Ohio, is the setting for these stories featuring investigative consultant Patricia Delaney. A stint as a newspaper reporter and editor made Patricia notice that her forte was research rather than writing. After serving a three-year apprenticeship with Adams Security and Investigations, Patricia got her investigator's license and set up her own office. Her expertise lies in background searches on individuals for companies, educational institutions, organizations, or those considering more personal partnerships. The primary tool of her trade is the computer—her little gray box. Patricia is a virtuosa on the system and is able to access almost any information held in the public domain, and some available only to licensed investigators. She uses bulletin boards extensively and has on-line relationships with a variety of experts across the country.

Patricia, the youngest of six children, grew up in Cleveland. At an early age, she showed a marked talent for music and, after graduating from high school, attended the University of Cincinnati's College-Conservatory of Music, where she studied violin. It didn't take her too long to realize that she was living out a dream of her father's rather than her own. She dropped out of school and went to work, first as a stripper, then as a bouncer for a nightclub in a sleazy section of Cincinnati, and she has the tattoo of a parrot on her bottom as a reminder of those bad old days. Patricia still maintains a musical connection by playing drums with the Queen River Band every Tuesday night at Dean's Tavern.

As the series opens in *Angel's Bidding*, Patricia and Dean O'Reilly, owner of the tavern, are friends. He wants more out of the relationship; she is wary. An added complication enters Patricia's life in the form of her moderately rebellious niece Lucy, who comes to stay for several weeks. At the conclusion of a labyrinthian case in which her life hangs in the balance, Patricia acknowledges the fact that her desire for companionship—even love—is nearly as great as her need for solitude.

Past Pretense brings Patricia face-to-face with her bad old days when a woman she knew while working at Poppy's Parrot reenters her life. Readers learn much more about Patricia as she is forced to confront the effects that events from that time have wrought. As the case proceeds to include murder, she consults her attorney, Jay Bell, the Queen River Band's leader. She asks Dean to sit in on the conference as what she must tell Jay about her past are things Dean must know as well.

More personal clarification comes about in *The Death We Share* when Patricia is asked to investigate matters for the family of Carlotta Moses, a retired opera superstar. Patricia's father enters this story and, as Carlotta's biggest fan, is more than happy to assist his daughter in clearing the singer's name. The case takes several Byzantine twists, and at the end the Delaney family has drawn closer and Patricia and Dean are exploring commitment.

With the invention of the CD-ROM and the proliferation of data available on the Internet, almost every public record has become available to those with a personal computer. As computers continue to revolutionize all aspects of life, individuals who make their living accessing information are well advised to make use of these tools to aid them in their searches. Patricia Delaney has capitalized on her talents as a researcher and her appreciation and application of a modern device to join the growing ranks of female investigators.

TAMARA HAYLE
1994–1997 4 books
Valerie Wilson Wesley

One of the more interesting turns taken in this new era of female private investigators is this series featuring Tamara Hayle, a black former cop in Newark, New Jersey. Tamara is street wise, savvy, and knows her community and its members from years of experience. Her former boss, chief of the Belvington Heights Police Department, knew he was losing one of his best officers when Tamara resigned, yet he understood that the undisguised racism and pressures brought to bear on her were more than she could be expected to handle in the line of duty. From her office on Main Street above Jan's Beauty Biscuit, her friend Wyvetta Green's beauty parlor, Tamara handles straightforward investigative work—surveillance, missing persons, divorce, and insurance fraud.

In *When Death Comes Stealing*, Tamara's former husband, DeWayne Curtis, father of her son, Jamal, comes to her office and asks her to find who has murdered his oldest son. This is not the first of DeWayne's sons to be killed. Five years earlier to the day, another of his boys had been shot, and DeWayne is convinced someone has it in for him and plans to kill all of his sons. Tamara knew DeWayne had been married before she became his wife and knew he had fathered three sons, but the existence of a fourth—DeWayne, Jr.— comes as news to her. For Jamal's sake, Tamara agrees to take on the case. Two more Curtis boys die only five days apart, and Tamara knows she has only four days to find the killer and keep Jamal safe. The story unwinds in a surprising fashion, and Tamara finds herself following clues laid long before.

In *Devil's Gonna Get Him*, Tamara moves into the world of high-powered black society when she is hired by wealthy and successful Lincoln E. Storey. Storey's stepdaughter Alexa is keeping company with a man Storey feels is unsuitable, and he wants Tamara to gather "every bit of shit about that motherfucking cocksucker." When she hears the name of her quarry, Brandon Pike, Tamara agrees with the less than complimentary words Storey has used and, despite what may well be a conflict of interest, agrees to tail Pike. Once again, the seeds of the crimes committed in this book are ones sown years earlier. It is only at the last minute, when her life hangs in the balance, that Tamara puts everything together and saves at least two more lives in the process.

Valerie Wilson Wesley has created a stellar character. Tamara knows her way around and relies on her intelligence and connections much more than any physical skills she may possess. She and her friends fit into the milieu where Wesley has placed them in a way that makes the stories compellingly readable. We couldn't put the books down and are looking forward to more action from this exciting new member of the ranks of women private eyes.

LYDIA CHIN & BILL SMITH
1994–1998   5 books
S(hira) J(udith) Rozan

As this new series opens, Lydia Chin (Chin Ling Wan-ju) has been a licensed investigator for six years. Her sometime partner Bill Smith has been in the trade longer. Lydia and Bill maintain private practices but each will hire the other when a case warrants assistance or backup. Professionally, their relationship is egalitarian. Personally—well, let's just say that things get a little more complicated. Lydia, in her late twenties, is the youngest of five children of a very Chinese family. Her four older brothers hold the male prerogative firmly in their hands and they are backed to the hilt by their mother, a tiny tyrant, who speaks only Cantonese and holds male supremacy as her particular law of the land. In spite of this family solidarity against her and in spite of the fact that she still lives with her mother in the New York City Chinatown apartment in which she and her brothers were raised, Lydia carefully balances her traditional role against her independent nature.

Bill Smith is older and more experienced, yet even he would question whether he is the wiser of the two. As an impulsive and tempestuous youth, he was saved from the consequences of most of his follies by his uncle, Police Captain Dave Maguire. Bill's transgressions finally exceeded even Uncle Dave's tolerance and, at the tender age of seventeen, Bill joined the navy. After that, he attended college and was married for a brief, stormy time. From there . . . who knows. Suffice it to say that since turning twenty-five, he has lived in the same loft, over Shorty's Bar in lower Manhattan. Now he is nearing forty.

S. J. Rozan has employed an interesting device in telling her protagonists' stories. As each is a free-lance operator who calls on the other when necessary, whoever gets the case is the boss. Consequently, the novels are written in different voices. *China Trade* is told from Lydia's perspective. The action takes place within her Chinese community and involves Lydia's lawyer brother Tim. In *Concourse*, Bill narrates what follows his being asked by an old friend to investigate the death of one of his security officer employees. The fashion industry and another of Lydia's brothers, Andrew, get her involved in the investigation detailed in *Mandarin Plaid*, and Lydia tells the tale. Bill is outspokenly enamored of Lydia. The reverse is more than likely true although natural reticence prevents Lydia from being quite so blatant about her own feelings and desires. The tension—sexual and otherwise—provides a counterpoint that compounds the interest and adds texture.

New York City and its boroughs are well portrayed and serve as the foundation for the tales involving Lydia and Bill. Communities, cultures, and political agendas all play integral parts in the novels. A combination of instinct, knowledge, and street savvy combine to allow Lydia and Bill to function effectively in this diverse, provocative milieu. And the pair need every edge they can get as their opponents include rival *Dai los* (leaders) from a couple of Chinese Tongs, the mysterious purveyor of old world herbal medicine, art experts, real estate barons, the kingpin of a Black street gang, western medical practitioners, and Lydia's ever protective family.

Rozan is neither male nor Chinese yet she has created two brilliantly executed characters who are one—or the other. Both of her protagonists are believable; in either guise she speaks with an authentic voice. Beyond that, her plots are intricate and, at the same time, credible. As we are both fascinated by Lydia and just a little infatuated with Bill, we want more.

MAX BRAMBLE & WYLIE NOLAN
1994–1996   2 books
Shelly Reuben

Max Bramble is a lawyer and in the first story, *Origin and Cause*, represents the Courtland Motor Company in a $52 million damage suit brought against them by the family of Stanfield Standish, who died in the fire of his 1930 Duesenberg sedan. The family-owned company manufactures high-quality luxury sedans and top-of-the-line recreational vehicles. One of the company's sidelines is Courtland Classic Cars; this branch lovingly restores fine old cars using the highest-quality materials and replacement parts, and this division had done the restoration of the Duesenberg. Courtland's reputation is impeccable, and Max, believing that the fire and subsequent death cannot be laid at Courtland's doorstep, calls his friend Wylie Nolan in to investigate matters.

Wylie Nolan is a former New York City fire marshal with an encyclopedic knowledge of things combustible. Retired from public office, Wylie has set himself up as an independent arson investigator. His office is on the seventh floor of the Lispenard Building in Chinatown, but the kit he carries around with him and the work he does in the field are of far more importance than his address. Wylie's methods are intense and he doesn't rely on high-tech equipment— his hydrocarbon detector is his nose. When he arrives on the scene, he spends the first while just looking; then he asks questions of everyone about everything. When he presents his conclusions, his careful documentation leaves nothing out and his level of certainty is indisputable.

Subplots abound, and readers learn many incidental snippets about other characters and their stories as well as fascinating bits about the science of fire. In the course of determining the actual cause of the fire that destroyed Standish and his Duesenberg—the latter apparently valued higher than the former by many—Wylie discovers that the victim was dead before the fire broke out, and the case becomes one of murder.

An exhibition of Pre-Raphaelite paintings is scheduled to be held at the Zigfield Museum in midtown Manhattan in *Spent Matches*. The day the guest curator Dr. Georgiana Weeks is to arrive, the current exhibit is destroyed by fire in an unusual fashion. Enter the museum's attorney, Max, and Wylie, called in for obvious reasons. As all of the doors to the museum had been locked and none of the alarms—either smoke, heat, or motion—have been triggered, Wylie is faced with a real locked-room mystery. In addition to the destruction of paintings insured for $5 million, Camden Kimcannon, Dr. Weeks's assistant, is charged with the arson death of his mother. As in the first book, subplots are rife on the ground, adding to a lively tale.

Shelly Reuben and her husband are partners in an arson investigation firm in New York. She has written many professional articles on the subject of arson, and her technical expertise is well used in this series. Reuben may wax pedantic at times, but the facts readers may find too detailed at first are always the ones they are glad to have as the story unfolds. Her primary characters are what make these tales come to life as they are knowledgeable, intelligent, and humorous. Each has a definite taste for life and a love of the work they do. Ancillary characters are multidimensional and add to the depth and coloration of each tale. Reuben has given readers an insight into yet another level of professional investigation and we are glad of it.

The individual who investigates matters privately is a character who has taken on new dimensions in real life. Persons looking for lost or missing family members cannot rely on an overworked police force and often must turn to the private operative. Insurance companies use private detectives to investigate possible fraud, and corporations hire PIs to look into the background of prospective employees, solve matters of industrial espionage, and aid them in protecting their corporate selves from hostile takeovers. Changes in society at large have created new demands for those willing to carry secrets and pain for others and, not incidentally, have provided much grist for the crime and mystery fiction writer's mill.

The growing number of women entering this field is a revelation. Not only does it speak to changes in attitudes in the work place but it validates the entrepreneurial tendencies of the "fair" sex. Compassion, empathy, and the ability to listen are strengths long credited to females, and in impressively increasing numbers they are now taking those characteristics out into the streets.

The modern-day Paladins have a personal code of honor that admits them to avenues not open to officials. While it is unfortunate that the world requires more and more of these loose cannons, fiction readers have much to be thankful for.

SOME OTHER PRIVATE INVESTIGATORS

Lilly Bennett
Helen Black
Haskell Blevins
Moz Brant
Sydney Bryant
Roman Cantrell
Maggie Elliott
The Flowers Detectives
Laura Flynn
Nell Fury
Appollonia "Lonia" Guiu
Maggie Hill & Claire Conrad
Kate Kinsella
Meg Lacey
Devon MacDonald
Quint McCauley
Wanda Mallory
Daisy Marlow

Angela Matelli
Layne Montana
Laura Principal
Neal Rafferty
Gwen Ramadge
Caitlin Reece
Cassandra Reilly
Regan Reilly
Lil Ritchie
Sydney Sloane
Sarah Spooner
Blaine Stewart
Alex Tanner
Nyla Wade
Alex Winter
Will Woodfield
Jerry Zalman

STRANGE BEDFELLOWS IN BRASS BEDS:
Military and Government Service

Ask any six people to explain their government or their military forces and you will get answers as diverse as those given by the six blind men asked to describe an elephant. There are as many ways for one to serve one's government as well. In the United States, the two world wars and the interval between them provided fertile ground for crime and mystery fiction featuring military personnel and individuals involved in espionage. The cold war years provided readers with many more spies.

Col. John Primrose is a retired officer from the Army Corps of Engineers but still maintains his ties to the force he served, and he works closely with the police in any city in which he finds crime. Coupled in the second book in the series with Mrs. Grace Latham, a widow, he appeared in a total of sixteen novels (1934–1953). Zenith Jones Brown, writing under the pseudonym Leslie Ford, crafted a series that captures the style and sensibilities of the time in which the books were written.

In 1940, two authors, Adelaide Manning and Cyril Henry Coles, writing as Manning Coles wrote *Drink to Yesterday*, which opens with an inquest into the death of the hero. What follows is a retrospective of the actions of Tommy Hambledon leading to his death. The book was so successful that Manning and Coles were forced to resuscitate Tommy (who had supposedly drowned). He appeared in twenty-six novels (1940–1963) and, though he led a long and active life after his first near miss, the later books don't quite measure up to the earlier ones.

Nineteen sixty-six was a banner year for spies as the diametrically opposed Edmund Brown and Mrs. Emily Pollifax were both introduced. Edmund Brown, penned by Joyce Porter, is a bumbling fool who became a spy only because he was fluent in the Russian language. Egomaniacal, untidy, and incautious, Brown confuses his own side more often than he confounds his opposition. Edmund appeared in four books (1966–1971) but each is memorable for its sarcastic and cynical humor. Mrs. Pollifax, on the other hand, enters the service of the CIA with a sincere desire to serve her country. In her sixties as the series opens, this dauntless character values the skills she has acquired in her lifetime and uses those skills admirably. She likes people and has a very positive outlook on life; she gives and receives respect where due yet is worldly enough to know that not everyone is to be trusted. Unlike Edmund, Mrs. P. is competent and reliable. She has appeared in thirteen books (1966–1997) and we trust that her creator, Dorothy Gilman, will keep her going strong for another decade.

Congressman Ben Safford (Democrat, Ohio) is one of the few main characters that we have discovered who is a politician. Writing as R. B. Dominic, Martha Henissart and Mary Jane Latsis have drawn a character ideal to engage in investigations into areas as diverse as institutions, government and military agencies, and legislative bodies. Murder occurs in each book, and Safford uses his understanding of both the uses and abuses of power to sort out the clues leading to the murderer's identity. The seven-book series (1968–1983) seems to be the authors' exercise in viewing the issue of power. Under another pseudonym, Emma Lathen, the two women created a much longer series that features investment banker John Putnam Thatcher.

Times have definitely changed. The cold war is over and the wars the United States has been involved in since the end of World War II have not generated the popular support that that major conflict and the one that preceded it did. The ways of serving one's country seem to have changed as the characters who follow demonstrate.

TAMARA HOYLAND
1981–1991   6 books
Jessica Mann

Tamara Hoyland is an archaeologist employed by the Royal Commission on the Historical Monuments of England. Ian Barnes, Tamara's lover, is ostensibly a civil servant but in reality is in the employ of MI6. In *Funeral Sites*, the knowledge that Aidan Britton, the man considered England's brightest political hope and potential prime minister, is a cold-blooded killer drives a woman into hiding. Ian is put in charge of maintaining Aidan's safety. Tamara and her friend and former professor Thea Crawford share an active dislike for the prospective PM and a deep distrust of his political motivations. When Rosamond Sholto, sister of Aidan Britton's dead wife, disappears, Ian perceives her as a potential threat to Aidan. Tamara's convictions are convincing, however and, in the nick of time, Ian sees Aidan for just what he is, switches his allegiance, and the situation is saved.

As *No Man's Island* opens, Ian has been killed and Tamara has been recruited by his boss, the enigmatic Mr. Black. Added to her credits as an archaeologist are her abilities to quickly learn the necessary trade craft, a surprising physical strength and agility, and a cold and deadly need for vengeance. Sent to the island of Forway where Ian had grown up and where his widowed mother still lives, Tamara's job is to scout an archaeological site in advance of the British government's takeover of the island as a residence for oil workers. Rather than give up their home, Forway's inhabitants have mounted a move for independence, and Tamara's more hidden agenda is to discover if there is any hostile foreign power behind this impetuous and idealistic movement. After several suspicious accidental deaths occur, Tamara discovers that pure detecting will provide more answers than spying will.

In *Grave Goods*, an East German art exhibit, a forged treasure, a proud woman, and the descendant of the German Joachim Prince of Horn are among the featured elements. A series of seemingly unrelated coincidences bring Tamara, under Mr. Black's guidance, into the picture. The treasure is the regalia from one of the coronations of Charlemagne and the proud possession and symbol of the house of Horn. Margot Ellice, the proud woman, has been working on the story of Artemis Bessemer, a young Englishwoman united in a morganatic marriage with the prince in the middle years of Victoria's reign in England. When Margot is killed, coincidence turns out to be a careful plot both personal and political.

Still under the guise of an archaeologist in *Death beyond the Nile*, Tamara is employed by the British Secret Service when Janet Macmillan, a woman who has discovered a potential cure for epilepsy, resigns her post and leaves the country. It is feared that she intends to sell her secrets to the highest bidder, and Tamara is put aboard a barge cruising the Nile to watch her. Lecturing on Egyptology, Tamara soon discovers that Janet is merely taking a much needed vacation but other sinister forces are at work and it isn't long before there are two deaths. While national security is not in danger of being compromised, a killer must be identified and Tamara does the honors, admirably.

Jessica Mann studied archaeology and Anglo-Saxon at Cambridge University and law at Leicester University. She is the author of numerous mysteries and a study of female characters in crime fiction, entitled *Deadlier Than the Male*. Her first series features Professor Thea Crawford and the stories focus more on the academic side of archaeology. With Tamara Hoyland, Mann has given herself a much larger arena that she has populated with both contemporary and historical figures. The tales are complex and compact. In one line of description or dialogue, Mann manages to convey more than most writers can in three paragraphs. Characters are compelling and believable and one cares what happens to Tamara and even what is left of the mighty British Empire.

ROBERT AMISS
1981–1996   7 books
Ruth Dudley Edwards

This seven-book series gets off to a good start and gets better with each installment. In *Corridors of Death*, we are introduced to Robert Amiss in his capacity of private secretary to Sir Nicholas Clark, permanent secretary of the Department of Conservation. Clark is at the top of the civil servant's heap that supplies information and support to the politicians whom they serve. Early in the story—after Sir Nicholas is murdered with a blunt instrument in a lavatory stall—Amiss meets with Det. Supt. James Milton of Scotland Yard, who asks Amiss for some inside information on the operation of the civil service and the potential suspects. What follows is a quietly hilarious parody of the whole British system of governance. Amiss puts himself out on a limb to give Milton the help he needs and, over much gin and many horrible curries at The Star of India, the two become friends. Amiss, with his knowledge of both the system and the people, solves the crime just in time to save the career of a very nice man who is very ineffectual in his political position. Milton is grateful that he has not been responsible for ruining a man's reputation needlessly and even more so for not causing a tottery government to come even closer to falling to its own level of incompetence.

In each book that follows, Ruth Dudley Edwards takes pokes at aspects of English heritage, culture, and tradition by placing Robert in a succession of truly odd jobs. Disgusted, exasperated, and enraged by the thoughtlessness and inefficiency of the civil service, Robert walks out on his career at the end of *The Saint Valentine's Day Murders*. *The English School of Murder* finds Robert—at the behest of Det. Sgt. Ellis Pooley—teaching English as a second language, initially to waiters and harlots, and later, in the same institution, to those to whom his boss refers as the BPs (beautiful people). Again, at the request of Sgt. Pooley, Amiss takes an undercover job as a waiter at a gentlemen's club run by and for debauched geriatrics. In *Matricide at St. Martha's*, Robert is asked by his old friend and former civil service colleague to take a position as a fellow at St.

Martha's College, Cambridge. Descending into a hotbed of feminist politics and financial intrigue, Amiss is once again on the spot when murder occurs.

James Milton serves as the official police presence in all of the novels. Det. Sgt. Romford, a narrow-visioned, Bible-thumping fundamentalist, is introduced in the first book and appears in those capacities in all but one. After thirty years on the force, Romford seems to exist only to plague his colleagues, obfuscate anything useful in an investigation, and get up the respective noses of almost everyone he encounters. Ellis Pooley is introduced in the second book and soon becomes Milton's sergeant. His initial claim to fame is as a mystery buff with an understanding of—and belief in—the Holmesian dictate that states (more or less) that when one has eliminated the impossible, whatever remains, no matter how improbable, must be the truth. Amiss discovers Pooley's origins as a member of the aristocracy who has been educated at Eton and Cambridge. Pooley eventually overcomes his hesitancy to become friends with his superior and he, Milton, and Amiss form a formidable triumvirate. Milton's wife, Ann, sometimes plays go-between for her husband and Amiss and becomes friends with Robert as well. When Robert decides that Rachel is the woman for him, despite the long-distance aspects of their relationship due to her job with the Foreign Service, Ann and Jim Milton include her in their warm regards too. Plutarch the cat enters Robert's life in the third book and, despite her unlovely countenance and worse habits, continues to share Robert's life and quarters as the series progresses.

Ruth Dudley Edwards writes from experience. She has been variously a civil servant, a teacher, and a writer for *The Economist*. She pens this series with wit, style, grace, and a cutting accuracy about the institutions she skewers. We wish Robert Amiss and his cohorts long, successful, and humorously happy careers.

MARY MINOR "HARRY" HARISTEEN
1990–1996   5 books
Rita Mae Brown and Sneaky Pie Brown

Mary Minor "Harry" Haristeen is the young postmistress of the small town of Crozet nestled at the base of the Blue Ridge Mountains in Albemarle County, Virginia. Born and raised in Crozet, Harry left for a while to attend Smith College and returned to marry her high school sweetheart, Pharamond "Fair" Haristeen, D.V.M. As *Wish You Were Here* opens, Harry and Fair are in the process of divorcing. Harry lives on the farm left her by her late parents and shares the quarters with Mrs. Murphy, a lovely gray tiger cat; Tee Tucker, a Welsh Corgi; and Tomahawk and Gin Fizz, two horses. As postmistress in a small town, Harry knows almost everything about everyone before they know it themselves; she in turn is known by all and sundry.

Susan Tucker is Harry's best friend, who gave her Tee Tucker, so named as she was given to Harry on the fifth tee of the local golf club. Susan's husband, Ned, is Harry's lawyer. Mrs. George (Miranda) Hogendobber is the Bible-quoting widow of Crozet's former postmaster and another of Harry's close friends. Big Marilyn "Mim" Sanburne is the wealthy, snobbish wife of Jim, Crozet's mayor, and mother of Little Marilyn. "Boom Boom" Craycroft is married to Kelly, a local paving contractor. Boom Boom garnered her nickname in high school and we'll let readers find out why for themselves. Peter "Market" Shiflett is the owner of the general store next door to the post office and of Pewter, a fat and nosy gray cat. The sheriff in Crozet is Rick Shaw, and he is assisted by Police Officer Cynthia Cooper. Walk-on characters include Rob Collier, mail carrier; Paddy, Mrs. Murphy's ex-husband; and Simon, a shy possum who lives in Harry's barn.

Each story is purportedly written by Mrs. Murphy and much of the action is told from the animals' point of view. Murder occurs in all of the books and can be grisly. In the first, Kelly Craycroft is dispatched in one of his own cement mixers and the second victim is cut into thirds when she is run over by a train. And, in *Rest In Pieces*, a dismembered corpse with all potentially identifying features obliterated is found in various locations around Crozet. The deaths in *Murder at Monticello* are ordinary—even tidy—by comparison. Needless to say, none of the animals in the series is impressed with their humans' senses or abilities, and quite a lot of time is spent leading the humans toward what is obvious to the four-legged creatures' superior senses.

Rita Mae Brown tells a good story. We only wish she allowed herself full credit for the tales rather than using the cute trick of having her feline companion Sneaky Pie Brown serve as coauthor. Much of what the animals observe cannot be argued. There are, however, other, perhaps more effective, ways of pointing out humans' sensory failings than anthropomorphizing otherwise innocent creatures.

GREGOR DEMARKIAN
1990–1996   14 books
Jane Haddam (Orania Papazoglou)

As this series opens, Gregor Demarkian is fifty-five years old and retired from two decades of service with the FBI, where, in his last years, he headed the Bureau's Behavioral Sciences Department. Now a widower, he has moved from his empty, anonymous apartment just off the Washington beltway to Cavanaugh Street in Philadelphia, where he had been born and raised in the Armenian-American community. Gregor's move back to his former home was almost a whim; he hadn't expected to find things remotely the same as he remembered them. Therefore, it came as a great surprise to Gregor to find that little had changed on Cavanaugh Street and that he was warmly welcomed by the other residents, most of whom he had known from childhood.

The community is well populated with these figures from Gregor's past. Father Tibor Kasparian is the priest of The Holy Trinity Church, where Gregor had spent his early Sundays in the second pew from the front on the right. Tibor is an immigrant whose life has forced him to live and think in Russian, French, Hebrew, English, and even, at times, Armenian. He is a scholar, a gently persuasive leader of his congregation, and a force with which to be reckoned. Lida Kazanjian Arkmanian, the most beautiful of all the girls in the Armenian community in Gregor's youth, is now a wealthy grandmother living in a palatial townhouse where she spends most of her time cooking. Lida's neighbor and best friend since high school is Hannah Oumoudian Krekorian. George Tekemanian lives in the ground-floor apartment of Gregor's building and Donna Moradanyan lives on the floor above. Donna has a penchant for decorating everything in sight at the slightest provocation. In these books, she has ample opportunity as each of them takes place around some holiday or celebration. Ohanian's Middle Eastern Food Store is a frequent meeting place for the ever-shifting cast of regulars. All of these individuals play roles in the stories. Some are active in Gregor's investigations while at other times the group combines to form an Armenian Greek chorus.

Not a Creature Was Stirring marks what Gregor comes to think of as his maiden incursion into extracurricular murder. In this story, he meets Robert Hannaford and his contentious clan; all are wealthy, WASP (white Anglo-Saxon Protestant), and connected to all the famous old-money names lining the Philadelphia Main Line. Bennis, one of Robert's seven children, is a highly successful and well-paid author of a series of sword-and-sorcery novels, and just as well, as she has long been disinherited by her malevolent father. As the series progresses, she moves to Gregor's building on Cavanaugh Street and often joins forces with him, usually to his dismay, to solve murders. There is an attraction between these two characters but the twenty years between them and their highly disparate personalities are enough to keep them romantically unattached. Each knows the other too well and they enjoy simply being friends.

Each of Gregor's involvements in murder and mystery gains him more notoriety and frequently lands him on the pages of *People* magazine, where he is billed as the Armenian-American Hercule Poirot, an honorific he detests. Gregor's background in studying the minds and patterns of some of the country's most infamous serial killers has given him professional credibility and, as the cases often involve highly placed individuals and sensitive situations, his discretion and tact during an investigation are as valuable as the skill he brings to detecting.

Jane Haddam is the pseudonym for Orania Papazoglou, whose earlier series featured romance writer Patience McKenna. However, since Gregor Demarkian's introduction, his well-crafted exploits seem to have taken all his talented author's time and attention.

MEREDITH MITCHELL & CHIEF INSP. ALAN MARKBY
1991–1997   10 books
Ann Granger (Hulme)

Although each of these stories centers on murder and each at the outset involves the police, embodied by Chief Insp. Alan Markby and his formidable Sgt. Pearce of the Bamford Force, British Foreign Service Officer Meredith Mitchell is the character on which the stories focus. In *Say It with Poison*, the first in the series, film star Eve Owens implores her cousin Meredith to come to England for the wedding of Eve's daughter Sara. Meredith agrees and, once installed in her cousin's house, meets Insp. Markby, who has been asked to give the bride away. Philip Lorimer, a local potter, is killed by poison. Meredith finds the young man in his death throes and, of course, is drawn into the investigation. She solves the crime and uncovers another murder in the process. Markby is attracted to Meredith, feels somewhat protective of her, and is annoyed with her involvement.

These feelings of attraction and annoyance plague the couple throughout the following nine books and set the tone for both their relationship and the course of all of their detection. Markby is a native of Bamford and has strong ties to the land. Meredith is a career diplomat with the Foreign Service who is extremely good at what she does. She too feels an attraction for Markby and for Bamford. In *A Season for Murder*, she is posted to London and takes a house in Pook's Common, just outside of the town. In *Cold in the Earth*, she has found the commute too long and frustrating and has moved into an absent colleague's flat in Islington. She returns to

Bamford to take care of the house of Markby's sister Laura while Laura and her family are away on Easter holiday. In *Murder Among Us*, Toby, the absent colleague, returns unexpectedly and the two try sharing his flat. This awkward situation continues in *Where Old Bones Lie*, until Meredith decides that the two of them can never achieve compatibility and begins house hunting . . . in Bamford, where else? As the series progresses, it becomes ever clearer that, while she and Alan have romantic inclinations toward one another, each is set enough in their ways to make a permanent liaison almost impossible.

Bamford is an ancient market town in the Cotswolds, not too far from Oxford. It is described as a village, yet its environs seem to go on forever and incorporate any number of historical sites, stately homes, and farms long held by the same families. The bucolic serenity of the place is threatened not only by murder but by progress in the form of housing developments and the invasion of foreigners from at home as well as abroad. In spite of the changes the place is experiencing, Meredith likes the rural qualities of Bamford and its surrounds enough to keep returning to the scene of many crimes.

As an outsider and as a diplomat, Meredith can see the forest for the trees; she uses her professional skills to elicit information and shed light on dark doings. The crimes themselves are fairly straightforward but convoluted enough to cause the local constabulary due consternation. Alan Markby is a good and conscientious officer of the law and, given enough time, would probably reach the same conclusions Meredith does. That she gets there first and is often in peril in the process causes him no end of angst and complicates their relationship, which is tenuous at best. Though Meredith is often in danger, she never puts herself there through stupidity or carelessness. Alan rescues her moments after she has saved herself and this probably adds to his discomfort. Meredith relies on her diplomacy with Markby and their union struggles on.

Read one at a time, with long intervals between each; these are essentially good books in the cozy tradition. Ann Hulme, writing as Ann Granger, has worked in British embassies around the world. She and her husband, also a career diplomat, are now permanently posted to Bicester, near Oxford. She clearly writes what she knows.

MOLLY BEARPAW
1992–1997   4 books
Jean Hager

Molly Bearpaw is a Cherokee and the sole employee for the northeast Oklahoma office of the Native American Advocacy

League, a national organization charged with upholding the civil rights of registered members of the Cherokee Nation. In *Raven-mocker*, Woodrow Mouse, son of a man who has died in a nursing home, makes a strange request; he asks Molly to attend his father's autopsy to make sure the old man's heart is still in his body. If it isn't, it is a sure sign that he has been killed by a Ravenmocker, one of the most feared Cherokee witches. Molly agrees, not because she fears a Ravenmocker but because there may be cause for legal action against the nursing home for negligence. The agent of death turns out to be *Clostridium botulinum*, and, even though the Health Department gives the nursing home kitchen a clean bill of health, another death by botulism occurs.

Sheriff's Dep. D. J. Kennedy is called to the scene after the first death and agrees to work with Molly on the case when it becomes a matter of murder. The two had dated several times shortly after Molly's return to Tahlequah, but she had broken it off as she was still feeling shaky after a failed romance. Thrown together on the case, the pair begin a hesitant courtship. Molly's reluctance to get too involved with D. J. stems not only from her romantic disappointment but from earlier betrayals by her abandoning father and her mother's alcoholism and subsequent suicide. D. J. is gentle and persistent and, after Molly unmasks the killer in the first book, continues to press his suit in the second.

The Redbird's Cry opens with an exhibit of native crafts at the Cherokee National Museum. A lawyer for the Cherokee Nation involved in actions brought against the Nation by the True Echota Band—a group wanting more political involvement in the tribe's governance—is killed. Molly is asked by the grandmother of the young man who ostensibly caused the death to clear him of the charge. Priceless ancient wampum belts are stolen from the exhibit, and many of the tribe members fear that dark powers have been unleashed by the careless handling of these relics. Once again, working with D. J., Molly uncovers the true perpetrator and the reason behind Tom Battle's death. She also aids in the recovery of the stolen wampum belts and, in the process, allays the tribe's fears.

After her father's desertion, Molly's upbringing was taken over by her grandmother Eva Adair. When her mother killed herself, Molly moved in with Eva and lived with her until leaving for college. After graduation, Molly worked for an insurance company in Tulsa but was dissatisfied with the work and city life. She applied for and got her present position in Tahlequah and, for the past two years, has lived in a garage apartment belonging to retired history professor Conrad Swope. Eva and Conrad appear in these stories and

Homer, an abandoned dog, is adopted—initially by Molly, but later he becomes a member of Conrad's household as well.

Jean Hager, an award-winning Oklahoma author, has another series featuring half-Cherokee Mitch Bushyhead, a police chief operating out of Buckskin, Oklahoma. These stories may be found in the chapter "Behind the Badge: Provincial Police." Hager has also created a third series—this one about Tess Darcy, the owner of Iris House, a bed-and-breakfast in Victoria Springs, Missouri.

ANNA PIGEON
1993–1997   5 books
Nevada Barr

Anna Pigeon as a ranger in the National Park Service is a federally commissioned law enforcement officer. Charged with maintaining order and protecting the multitudes of visitors in the nation's parks and wilderness preserves from wild animals, the elements, and each other, she is trained in search and rescue operations; she carries a gun and knows how to use it.

Track of the Cat takes place in the Guadalupe Mountains National Park in West Texas. On a back-country reconnaissance, Anna discovers the dead body of a fellow ranger. Wounds on the body and tracks leading from it point to a cougar as the likely perpetrator. After an amateur herpetologist is dispatched by a tangle of poisonous snakes, Anna realizes that the small park is a hotbed of secrecy and deception. Then, after Anna herself is injured on another back-country foray, everyone else becomes aware that murder is afoot. Anna solves the crime, loses a lover, and gains a friend.

In *A Superior Death*, Anna has been transferred to the remote Isle Royale National Park in Michigan's Upper Peninsula. This venue is nearly the diametric opposite of the hot, dry wilderness of the Southwest. Even at mid-summer, temperatures rarely rise above the seventies and the lake is *always* cold. The park has several dive sites, and the unique preservation qualities of this large body of cold freshwater becomes a part of the story when a sixth corpse joins the five already long resident in the watery grave of a sunken ship. Once again, at no small amount of personal risk, Anna solves the crime and apprehends the perpetrator.

Ill Wind finds Anna back in the Southwest at the Anasazi ruins of Mesa Verde National Park in Colorado. An unusually high number of medical rescues and the unexplained death of a fellow ranger upset a work force already perturbed by the construction of a new water system for park residents. Anna is assigned to assist FBI Special Agent Frederick Stanton (introduced in the second story) and together, they make lists, ask questions, and draw conclusions. One of the conclusions nearly gets Anna killed, but the inadvertent murderer is caught and dies horribly.

Strong, quiet, and private, Anna Pigeon is ideally suited to the wild areas to which she is assigned. Although she prefers the solitude such places offer, she is at ease in dealing with the people who come to visit, enjoy, and sometimes invade her territory. Her husband's death drove her from the bright lights and bustle of Manhattan and now her only link with that place is the telephone connection she maintains with her sister, Molly, a psychiatrist. Christina Walters and her four-year-old daughter, Alison, become Anna's close friends in the first book, are on the scene several times in the second, but do not appear in the third. Agent Stanton is introduced as an iritant in the second and becomes a valuable ally in the third. Other than those few and very satellite characters, Anna is a loner.

Nevada Barr's creation is highly credible. In addition to being an author, Barr is a ranger at the Natchez Trace Parkway in Mississippi.

LEAH HUNTER
1992–1995   4 books
Sarah Lacey (Kay Mitchell)

Curiosity is a prerequisite for an inspector for Her Majesty's Inland Revenue Service. Poking around in people's closely held financial affairs isn't always easy and is almost guaranteed to put a damper on one's popularity. Leah Hunter is twenty-five, single by choice, and still lives in the town where she was born and raised. Bramfield is an English town that thinks itself slightly better than its Yorkshire neighbors and is the center for all of the action that takes place in these books. In *File Under: Deceased*, a man Leah has just met as they wandered through an art exhibit dies with his head in her lap. When the shock wears off, Leah's curiosity is piqued and she is driven to do more than wonder why a young, apparently healthy man should suddenly drop dead. Det. Sgt. Dave Nicholls of the Regional Force considers Leah a suspect at first, then a possibly unwitting accomplice, then an active participant in something very nasty. Leah is in turn baffled then angry as she tries to figure out just how she has become involved and in just what she is involved.

Leah doesn't initiate the troubles in which she finds herself but once trouble finds her, she is not shy in tracking its source. She knows how to go about getting information and how to synthesize it once it is in hand. Back at her desk after the young man's death, Leah is given his tax information as a matter of course. She finds no cause for suspicion but wonders at his transient work history. The disappearance of a probation officer and his client list, heavily weighted toward addicts, triggers another level of her curiosity. When she is struck by a hit-and-run motorcyclist and hospitalized with minor but painful injuries, she knows she is on the trail of something hot even though she hasn't a clue as to what it is.

To Dave Nicholls, Leah is a puzzle. As he gets to know her better, she becomes an irritating challenge. The attraction between them is electric though the two are careful and cagey with one another. Leah's neighbor Dora provides garage space for Leah's car. Dora is cleverly disguised as a retired, spinster schoolteacher in her seventies. In truth, she has the heart of a lioness and a wide adventuresome streak. After her garage, containing Leah's car, is torched and after she bashes a potential mugger with a milk bottle, Dora signs up for self-defense lessons with Jack, Leah's karate instructor. Jack is one of Leah's valued sources for information as he knows most everything of whatever goes on around Bramfield. Charlie, the auto repair man, is another source for Leah. After her car is destroyed, Charlie provides her with what she refers to as The Hybrid, a Morris Mini with a BMW engine. He also introduces her to Sid, an elegant if shady character, who teaches Leah to pick locks and provides her with a nice little feminine set of picks disguised as a manicure set. Marcie and her toddler son live one floor below Leah's attic apartment. The two women are on casual rather than close terms until events in the second book, *File Under: Missing*.

Once again, Leah finds herself drawn toward trouble when Dora asks her to help a friend whose son has been missing for three months. The police have given Grace little assistance in searching for Andy and, as she is officially on holiday, Leah agrees to do a little research on just what might have happened to him. Inevitably, things become much more complex than anyone could predict. Dave Nicholls is annoyed with Leah's involvement, especially as she seems to be raising the hackles of quite a few people. Jack, Charlie, and Sid all play their respective parts in this episode, and Leah learns a bit more about Sid's livelihood when the women who work for him disguise and assist Leah in a bit of breaking and entering.

Readers don't often see Leah at work as a tax inspector though we do meet her boss when Leah inveigles him into letting her do a little extracurricular searching. Her professional qualifications are enough to give her credibility as she pursues her courses. Leah Hunter is the archetypal new woman—young, independent, resourceful, strong, and physically well trained. She is well drawn by her author, Sarah Lacey, and we look forward to more of Leah's exploits.

The foregoing characters represent a commendable diversity. The agencies they represent (with the possible exception of the United States Postal Service) are ones which fascinate readers and which offer ample scope for the writers' respective talents. It would be difficult to read any one of these series (with the possible exception of the one which features a postal clerk) and not learn something new about the workings of the agency highlighted.

One notable absence for us in this chapter, however, is a series character based on a woman politician. Such a woman would be ideally placed to encounter countless crimes based upon countless social issues. Any takers?

SOME OTHER GOVERNMENTAL SLEUTHS

Patrick & Ingrid Gillard
Davina Graham
David Haham
Madison McGuire

Nick Magaracz
Richard Owen
Robert Renwick

SENIOR SLEUTHS

The senior detective is not a new fictional convention. In 1905, Baroness Orczy placed the Old Man, Bill Owen, in the corner of a tea shop where he expounded upon his cogitations on crime to young reporter Polly Burton. In a series of eight books (1905–1925), Bill Owen discourses on his favorite subject while his hands are busy creating, then unraveling, fantastic knots in a piece of string. His musings are based solely on intelligent reasoning, and he feels no compunction to present his solutions to the proper authorities.

Evan Pinkerton, a small gray Welshman, was created in 1930 by American writer Zenith Jones Brown, writing as David Frome. The shy, retiring Mr. Pinkerton is befriended by J. Humphrey Bull of Scotland Yard and, in the fourteen books (1930–1950) in which he appears, he is instrumental in solving murders in conjunction with Bull's official investigations.

One of the most famous senior detectives in history is Agatha Christie's Miss Jane Marple of the English country village Saint Mary Mead. From her introduction in *The Murder at the Vicarage* through the following nineteen books (1930–1985), Miss Marple uses her experience of life in a small village to unmask the most devious killers. Scotland Yard reluctantly comes to rely on her perspicacity as she keeps turning up at or near the scenes of crime. Despite a highly developed sensibility for evil, she remains thoroughly optimistic about human nature.

Twenty-four books (1931–1951) feature the Down Easter Asey Mayo, often referred to as the Codfish Sherlock. A bit of a jack-of-all-trades, Asey is capable of understanding almost any mechanical object and has an uncanny ability to apply the same innate skill to unmasking murderers. Phoebe Atwood Taylor devised this clever—if laconic—Maine sleuth. Occasionally moved to action, Asey's primary method of detection is contemplative.

Delores Hitchens, writing as D. B. Olsen, crafted a thirteen-book series (1939–1956). All titles include the mention of cats and feature the spinster Murdock sisters. Rachel, younger than Jennifer by two years, is bold and adventuresome in contrast to her sister's prim and proper manner. Yet the pair manage to get themselves mixed up in murder and must rely on their joint abilities to solve the crime. Lt. Mayhew is the official who makes use of the sisters' talents. He retires to a chicken ranch in Ventura, quite possibly to recover from the excesses of ladies of a certain age.

The enigmatic Edwina Charles is the protagonist of a seven-book series (1976–1984) written by Mignon Warner. Edwina and her eccentric brother Cyril Forbes inhabit a cottage on the fringe of the English village of Little Giddings. Suspected of murder in the first book, Mrs. Charles uses the Tarot and her clairvoyant talents to clear her name and point to the real culprit. A retired police inspector comes to rely on this mysterious female and her arcane knowledge in ways that confound him.

Murder occurs shortly after Mrs. Eugenia Potter arrives on the scene, and, in four books (1982–1992) she unmasks the killer— much to her surprise. An excellent cook and great good friend to many people scattered around the country, Mrs. Potter discourses on the best way to do anything at the drop of a white glove. Virginia Rich liberally laced the tales featuring this senior sleuth with recipes and household hints. She died shortly after the third book was published. However, her baton has passed on to Nancy Pickard, who has written the fourth book in the series and plans several more.

For our purposes, the term "senior" is not limited to those advanced in age. We—in our fifties—are not inclined to think of ourselves as elderly. We do believe, however, that we have achieved a certain level of wisdom, just as have several of the amateur detectives that follow. More by experience than by an accumulation of years, these individuals are aptly entitled seniors.

GEORGE & MOLLY PALMER-JONES
1986–1996   8 books
Ann Cleeves

Birdwatchers in the British Isles take the business of spotting the objects of their interest quite seriously. George Palmer-Jones is one of the more obsessed of his nation's birders, and the stories that feature him and his wife, Molly, are centered on his passion and pastime. Now retired, George had, as a civil servant, provided liaison between the police and the bureaucrats of the Home Office. Molly, also retired, had spent forty years as a social worker with the criminal element—youthful offenders and addicts. Both Palmer-Joneses looked forward to their retirement, yet after a year each is surprised to miss the action their respective jobs provided. Even George's compulsive hobby of twitching isn't enough to keep boredom at bay.

When in the first book, *A Bird in the Hand*, George is asked to look into the death of a young twitcher, he doesn't hesitate to become involved in the investigation. In this story, readers learn a great deal about the year, life, and world lists kept by all serious birders. The difference between twitchers, ringers, and stringers is explained, and George Palmer-Jones's expertise is clearly established. The term "twitcher" is derived from a Wessex phrase, "twitching like a long dog," and is used at least once by Thomas Hardy in his brooding, dismally wonderful novels. The Palmer-Jones books have more than one phrase in common with Hardy's writing as they too are steeped in a somber gloom. Even the successful conclusion of an investigation does little to dispel the bleak atmosphere as George carries the failure of the human condition squarely on his rounded shoulders.

A distinct contrast to the tenebrous George, Molly likes people and, despite her years of working with lawbreakers, ultimately believes in the triumph of the human spirit. She conveys warmth, empathy, patience, and genuine interest and is George's most valuable asset in his inquiries. Molly is the background player in all of the books, and not until well into the series does she become a full partner in the business of detecting. Even then she is disregarded by most of the individuals involved in the Palmer-Jones cases. She appears to be incapable of boredom, which is a clear advantage when set against her husband's single-minded dedication to feathered creatures.

While a continuing theme of birding runs through all of the stories, there is a common pattern to them as well. A small group of persons is brought together by relationship or interest. Murder occurs and there are several plausible suspects. Each suspect's motive is complex and almost—yet not quite—sufficient to explain or justify the killing. George and Molly are tuned to the psychological subtleties of each situation and, by dint of perseverance, unravel the sticky knots that have led to murder.

Ann Cleeves discovered birdwatching when working as an assistant cook for a season at the Bird Observatory on Fair Isle. Her interest and knowledge are integral components of her books.

SHEILA TRAVIS & AUNT MARY
1988–1995   7 books
Patricia Houck Sprinkle

Sheila Beaufort Travis was born in Shikoku, Japan, to missionary parents. When she was ready for high school, her father put her on a plane for Atlanta and into the care and keeping of his spinster sister, the wealthy Mary Beaufort. After college, Sheila married Tyler Travis, a career diplomat in the United States embassy in Japan. When he was killed in a mountaineering accident, Sheila took charge of things for the first time in her life. After winding up her duties with the embassy, she moved back to the States and took her first job with the Markham Institute of International Studies in Chicago. There, in *Murder at Markham*, she solves her first mystery.

Murder in the Charleston Manner takes place in South Carolina and involves an old, distinguished family of friends of Aunt Mary when a series of accidents leads up to murder. On vacation with her aunt in Atlanta, Sheila is pushed into her second investigation by the tiny tyrant. In *Murder on Peachtree Street*, Sheila takes a new position as Director of International Relations for Hokosawa International, a Japanese company based in Atlanta. When an executive in one of Hokosawa's subsidiary companies is murdered, Sheila is asked to serve as liaison between her company and the other; her job is to find out what she can. She does and, in the process, solves the murder.

In *Somebody's Dead in Snellville*, a fire in the apartment below Sheila's renders her place uninhabitable, and a neighbor comes to her rescue by taking Sheila to dinner. When the neighbor's mother is murdered, Sheila is once again—with Aunt Mary's urging—up to her ears in detecting.

In *Death of a Dunwoody Matron*, Sheila meets Crispin Montgomery, a horticulturist and brother of the murder victim. This story involves friends and relatives of the Beaufort family and takes place in a prosperous Atlanta suburb. *A Mystery Bred in Buckhead* is almost a continuation of its predecessor and involves many of the same people. An old woman, wanting to clear her conscience before she dies, attempts to return some papers she stole from a former employer some fifty years earlier. That the employer in question was none other than *Gone with the Wind* author Margaret Mitchell adds interest and drama to the tale. Sheila, Aunt Mary, and Crispin track down old secrets and solve murders old and new. In *Deadly Secrets on the St. Johns*, as the relationship between Sheila and Crispin deepens, the pair travel to Jacksonville to meet his family. There, aided and thwarted by various members of his clan, Sheila is once again drawn into discovering who is responsible for violent death.

Patricia Houck Sprinkle's character is a competent and likable woman just coming into her own. Aunt Mary is an imperious, demanding soul—a true steel magnolia. Trouble follows this maidenly lady around like iron filings follow a magnet. Mildred, Mary's housekeeper, is devoted and unquestionably loyal. Jason, Mary's driver and factotum, is equally devoted, though one suspects it may be because Mary holds his less than honest past over his head. Mary is the only person permitted to call her financial adviser, Charles Davidson, "Charlie," and even if she sometimes calls upon him to gather less than ethical information, he is always quick to respond. Mary's force is no less with Sheila, who may resist but always complies. For readers fond of Southern gentility, vast and complicated clans, and historical information, this series will fill the bill.

CLARA GAMADGE
1989–1996   5 books
Eleanor Boylan

Clara Gamadge is the relict of Henry Gamadge, one of mystery fiction's most interesting and enigmatic series characters. The sixteen books featuring Mr. Gamadge appeared in the '40s and were wonderful exercises in puzzlement. In 1989, Clara makes her debut in *Working Murder* and takes up where her beloved husband left off when she is asked by her Aunt May to help get cousin Lloyd buried. The plot thickens when May herself dies and an old family mystery—the disappearance of May's only daughter, Ellen—surfaces and begs to be solved.

Clara, widowed only one year in the first book, has gone to Florida for the winter as the guest of her cousin Charles Saddlier—always known as "Sadd." The two are close friends who, despite widely divergent tastes, get on well together. In fact, as the series progresses the two become practically inseparable and jointly solve every mystery and murder with which they are confronted. When not in residence in Florida, Clara still lives in the old brownstone house she shared with Henry in Manhattan.

Henry Junior and his wife, Tina, are attorneys at the same law firm. They and their son, Hen, live in Brooklyn Heights. The senior Gamadges' beautiful daughter, Paula, lives in Boston with her husband, Andy, and their daughter, Andrea. The family is very close knit and, in spite of job obligations and geographical distance, manages to get together frequently. Of course, when Clara is confronted with a mystery, the entire clan rallies and aids her in finding the answer.

In the four books that follow, love interests and a complexity of cousins abound. One salient feature of every story is the Scoundrel—an individual whose actions are so horrific they make everyone connected to the tale and to Clara sick to their stomachs. In all cases, proof of the Scoundrel's misdeeds must be provided so that just deserts may be dealt. Clara and Sadd are masters at pulling this off in a classically orchestrated denouement.

Author Eleanor Boylan is the niece of Elizabeth Daly, author of the original Gamadge series. Just as Clara has taken up her husband's avocation and carries on in her own fashion, Boylan picks up where her Aunt Elizabeth left off and adds some charming—almost old-fashioned stories—to the Gamadge canon. Readers fond of the mysteries from the '20s, '30s, and '40s will be delighted with Boylan's additions. In less than two hundred pages, a complex problem is laid out; a plethora of characters is introduced; improbable yet believable coincidences occur; and the end is reached in an exciting, if tidy, manner. Relationships are of paramount importance in these little gems, and even the offspring of characters who appeared in the Henry Gamadge books arrive on one scene or another. We recommend this series and, of course, the original Gamadge books.

TISH MCWHINNY
1986–1995   4 books
B(arbara) Comfort

Lofton, Vermont, is the home of this series' protagonist; Tish McWhinny's house is right across the street from the post office where Charlie the Postmaster holds sway. The village store is a mixture of that New York epicurean delight Dean & DeLuca and a hardware store; it is a newsstand and information central for the residents of Lofton and its surrounds. Tish's closest friend, Hilary Oats, is a retired printer who moved to Lofton after his wife's death. Tish became a widow about the same time and while she and Hilary are not romantically inclined—in the beginning—their friendship is deep and abiding. Hilary cooks, Tish paints, and both possess insatiable curiosity.

In *Phoebe's Knee*, after eight quiet years of residence, all hell breaks loose when a quasi-religious group called The Ring of Right moves into an old mansion at the edge of the village. An archaeological find hinting at an early Druidical presence and the suspicion of illegal drug use by the cult members arouse Tish's interest and ire. When the charismatic cult leader is murdered as he is sitting to his portrait by Mrs. McWhinny, she becomes the prime suspect. Tish and Hilary must find not only the real killer, but a missing reporter and also must uncover the true secret of the Ringers.

In *Grave Consequences*, Tish meets her young stepniece Sophie Beaumont when the two make an unsuccessful attempt to catch a fleeing van filled with some valuable items stolen from the Farron Mansur Museum, where Tish is a volunteer. A health spa proposed by a Vermont gubernatorial candidate's wife is connected to the death of Tish's friend, a museum guide. After an unsuccessful attempt is made on Tish's life, she and Hilary, joined by Sophie, track down the killer.

Life, for the most part, continues at a mellow pace for a few years. As *The Cashmere Kid* opens, Sophie has purchased a goat farm and is in the process of breeding and raising Cashmeres. After William the Conqueror, one of Sophie's prize goats, is stolen and one of her neighbors is found with his face beaten to obliteration by a golf club, the three unlikely sleuths are on the trail once again.

Slate quarries, explosives, and rattlesnakes loom large in *Elusive Quarry*. Sophie's house is blown up, one of her suitors is brutally murdered, the village store managers leave town in the dead of night, Hilary wrecks his new car, and Tish sits on a rattler hidden in Hilary's sofa. Everyone is suspect in this tale. Sophie's taste for unsuitable men is compounded when she brings two prospective candidates for her charms into the lives of her extended family. At grave peril—as usual—Tish solves the mystery and unmasks the killer.

Tish McWhinny, Hilary Oats, Sophie Beaumont, and the rest of the recurring cast are likable characters. Lofton is a lovely place to live, even when dastardly deeds occur. The stories penned by B. Comfort are interesting, light reads. Any violence is far from gratuitous and the good guys always win. We like these gentle village mysteries in all of their improbability.

SHEILA MALORY
1989–1996   7 books
Hazel Holt

Sheila Prior Malory is a middle-aged widow living in the seaside town of Taviscombe in England's West Country. Sheila and her husband, Peter, were both Oxford graduates. He was fond of saying to Sheila—a fan of Dorothy L. Sayers—that the only reason she'd married him was that his name was Peter and he was down from Balliol. Peter, also a native Taviscombian, had been a well-regarded solicitor in the small community. Michael, their son, is up at Oxford reading history as the series opens. Two years after Peter's death, Sheila continues to live in the house left her by her mother. She mourns her loss yet, after tending Peter through his long illness, is resigned.

Friends, recognizing her bereft state, have involved her in all manner of good works, and Sheila has taken to committee work like the proverbial duck to water. Her dearest friend, the long-suffering Rosemary, is the mother of Jill, an enlightened young woman living—without benefit of clergy—with Roger Eliot, an inspector with the Taunton Criminal Investigation Division. Rosemary's mother, Mrs. Dudley, is a cross Rosemary and Jill must bear. Sheila, as the daughter of a clergyman and later wife of a respected solicitor, has been deemed by Mrs. Dudley the only one almost good enough to be Rosemary's friend.

Sheila does have her own work, writing the occasional volume of literary criticism, mostly about the more obscure Victorian novelists. She is published by one of the university presses and enjoys sharing theory and countertheory with other scriveners in the field. She is considered rather literary by her fellow Taviscombians and is a bit of a celebrity on the committees on which she serves. One would think that this woman had a nice, fulfilling life. However . . .

Sheila Malory has a penchant for uncovering secrets. Death is always the event that starts her investigative ball rolling, but as often as not it is a death that officials have deemed accidental or consider solved. Mrs. Malory is far less than willing to let sleeping dogs lie and manages to uncover not only the secret leading to the identity of the murderer but several other, unrelated secrets as well. In the process of all this nosing about, she manages to disrupt the lives of countless individuals whose innocence is put on the line by her probing and incessant questions. After roiling the pot, bringing forth several red herrings, and insulting some of her oldest friends with her suspicions of their possible guilt in the matter at hand, Mrs. Malory usually ends up letting the killer off the hook. Some of these guilty parties have the decency to do the right thing by committing suicide—we wonder about the others?

We can only believe that Hazel Holt has taken the murder mystery to its most logical conclusion by showing just how much damage the amateur detective can do. Sheila is always diminished by the discoveries that many of her oldest and dearest friends have not only feet of clay but in several cases hearts of stone. Nevertheless, the stories themselves are little gems of all that make a mystery novel intriguing. The plots are sound, the suspects all potentially guilty, and the culprit is the logical choice in the end. We like these little incursions into morality, and only hope that Ms. Holt is recognized for her true talents.

EMMA CHIZZIT
1989–1993   4 books
Mary Bowen Hall

Emma Chizzit calls herself a picker and is wise in the ways of recycling, restoring, and reselling formerly owned items. Hired to clear out homes and business sites, she is paid for cleaning and hauling and gets to keep anything that turns up in the process. Emma lives in the chauffeur's quarters over the garage of Frannie Edmundson's house in Sacramento, California. Emma and the wealthy Frannie have been friends since high school and, though their lifestyles differ diametrically, are still bosom buddies. Vince Valenti, an almost-retired cop, is introduced in the first book and offers Emma invaluable advice on the murders with which she gets involved. Vince would like to take care of Emma in a much more personal way, although Emma has other ideas. Widowed by her first husband and divorced from her second, Emma is the mother of two grown children who never appear in the stories. Disillusioned by wedlock after her divorce, Emma abandoned her maiden and two married names, chose the surname Chizzit, and is happily independent.

This feisty woman gets herself involved in multilayered, convoluted situations that involve murder and at least three other levels of dishonest dealings. In *Emma Chizzit and the Queen Anne Killer*, she discovers, in the process of clearing out the crawl space of a Victorian house awaiting renovation, the mummified body of a strangled infant. The plot includes an unclaimed inheritance, a property developer's greed, and Native American land rights. *Emma Chizzit and the Sacramento Stalker* pits Emma against a rapist, right-wing political scam artists, and a male chauvinist harassing a women's activist group.

Emma and Frannie go to Buckeye City in California's Gold Country in *Emma Chizzit and the Mother Lode Marauder*. There they encounter Trooper Hadley, a woman whose expensive travel adventures and environmental activism finally get her killed when she bumps up against members of the corrupt Buckeye City Council. As in the two previous novels, Emma, Frannie, and Vince combine their efforts to solve a very mysterious event.

Emma Chizzit in her sixties is a woman who does not let mere chronology provide her only definition. Her job as a salvager requires strength, stamina, and specialized knowledge; her investigations draw on all of her physical and mental fortitude for their solutions. Emma is a good friend to have, though her independence tends to keep even those closest to her at some distance. Lack of financial security does not daunt Emma in her pursuit of a full and active life. She is determined to grow old with as much grace and dignity as she can muster.

Mary Bowen Hall died of cancer in 1994. Her final days were documented in a book that was profiled in *People* magazine. Right to the end, Hall served as an exemplar of a woman unafraid of age or even death. Her character Emma Chizzit shares many of Hall's personal convictions about the environment and the casual disregard of history and heritage. Hall was an enthusiastic amateur historian. Her research took her to Folsom Prison, and in her last years she took pride in the time she spent behind bars. If her life and her Emma Chizzit books tell readers anything, it is: "Don't be afraid of growing old, look for a lifetime of interesting things ahead of you, and *always* stand up for what you believe in."

SHIRLEY MCCLINTOCK
1990–1995   6 books
B. J. Oliphant (Sheri S. Tepper)

Fifty-something and six-foot-three, Shirley McClintock is a rancher on a spread established by her great-grandparents near Denver. She grew up on the ranch but left for college and a career with an unnamed Washington, D.C., bureau. Shirley and her first husband, Martin, had two children; Sal, their youngest, was killed by a drunk driver when she was twelve, and their son, Marty, disappeared in the Amazon while on an expedition. After Marty's death, Martin declined and soon died. Shirley remarried, but her second husband, Bill, died five years later. After his death and that of her father, Shirley returned to Colorado. An old college friend, John Quentin—always known as "J. Q."—came to work on the ranch. The two have a close and loving relationship, and the level of intimacy they share is never fully disclosed.

In *Dead in the Scrub*, eleven-year-old Allison Maxwell enters Shirley and J. Q.'s lives after both of her parents are murdered in separate incidents. Allison's aunt and uncle are ever so gently persuaded to allow her to continue living on the McClintock ranch and do not reappear until *Death Served Up Cold*, fifth in the series. Shirley's close friend and headmistress of Crepmier School, Xanthippe Minging, is introduced in the first story and makes brief appearances in all the following books. In *Death and the Delinquent*, Shirley and J. Q. are acting as chaperones on a school trip to New Mexico. In this story, Miss Minging and Shirley both make career decisions that influence the direction of the next two books.

The arrangement between Shirley, J. Q., and Allison is unconventional, yet a fine example of a fully functional family unit. In order to make the ranch run successfully, everyone must be able and willing to do every job. On the McClintock place, there is no distinction between men's work and that of women. Shirley can mend a fence with the best of them; J. Q.'s menudo is the tastiest soup in the world. Allison comes into this ordered and challenging life and begins making her own contributions. Shirley has never quite gotten over the loss of her children and J. Q.'s own kids are far away. Both take to fostering Allison with relish and enthusiasm. Their shared responsibility for the child and her loving response to their care are strong features of all of the stories.

In every book, there are several stories running in parallel. The tales all converge at the end, and what appear to be disparate events prove to be connected. Shirley holds strong opinions and does not hesitate to deliver what can only be called rants on a variety of subjects ranging from women's rights to the environment and all points between; the harangues she delivers are presented cogently. Further, by establishing Shirley's position on a variety of issues, the author allows the character to define herself to readers. Even though the setting is in the foothills of the Rocky Mountains where ranches cover hundreds, even thousands, of acres, the people living on the land are, if not close knit, at least respectful of one another, helpful, and neighborly. Shirley has many friends of long standing among her fellow ranchers, and their stories contribute to the plotting of each novel.

B. J. Oliphant is one of the pen names used by Sheri S. Tepper, a well-known science fiction writer. Under the pseudonym A. J. Orde, she has written another mystery series featuring antique dealer Jason Lynx whose adventures are chronicled in the chapter "Killings on the Market: Business and Finance." Oliphant was nominated for an Edgar and an Anthony for her first Shirley McClintock book. She lives in Santa Fe, New Mexico, and writes what she knows with style, verve, and well-placed and eloquent rants.

HUBBERT & LIL
1991–1996   4 books
Gallagher Gray (Katy Munger)

Theodore S. Hubbert is a newly—and early—retired personnel manager for the investment bank Sterling & Sterling. Lillian Hubbert, his aunt, is a former assistant fashion designer who, at the tender age of eighty-four, is still called to action during peak season. "T. S." is conservative; his apartment reflects his character, taste, and inclination in its meticulous and fastidious decor and organization. Auntie "Lil," on the other hand, lives in the midst of colorful chaos. Her worldwide travels are lavishly represented by paintings and objets d'art and her talents as a fashion designer are made manifest by countless bolts of cloth designated toward one end or another. Painting supplies and true-crime magazines fill in any gaps. Lil's passions are displayed for all the world to see. T. S.'s are hidden and, if disclosed, would cause severe embarrassment. Each is all the other has in the way of family. While their relationship to one another may at times be equivocal, it is one of devotion.

The quiet, somewhat enigmatic Herbert Wong is the unifying factor between these disparate characters. Originally a messenger for Sterling & Sterling, he becomes T. S.'s close friend and Auntie Lil's champion. A native of Singapore, Herbert is a compact and sartorially savvy soul. Well versed in martial and terpsichorean arts, Herbert keeps himself fit through moderation in all things.

In *Hubbert & Lil: Partners in Crime*, a murder takes place at Sterling & Sterling the day after T. S.'s retirement party, and he is called back to find the killer. Ably assisted by Auntie Lil and the redoubtable Herbert Wong, T. S. solves the crime and, in the process, falls under the sway of newly widowed Lilah Cheswick. In *A Cast of Killers*, while working at a Hell's Kitchen soup kitchen, Auntie Lil summons T. S. to help cook and serve. In the middle of lunch, an old former actress dies and T. S., Lil, Herbert, and Lilah find themselves thrown into the worlds of the disenfranchised and sleazy off-Broadway producers.

Death of a Dream Maker brings some of Lil's past forward and embroils her in the murder of an old flame. T. S. learns a great deal about his auntie in this story and Lil learns a few things about herself as she faces off with a Mafia don, the FBI, her old nemesis, Lt. Abromowitz, and the family of the deceased Max Rosenbloom. At the center of *A Motive for Murder* are the problems of a ballet company and the plight of child film stars. Auntie Lil, as a member of the board of the Metro Ballet Company, is called upon to discover the killer of the father and manager of young Mikey Morgan.

The stories featuring T. S. Hubbert, his octagenarian aunt, and their cohorts are about different sorts of familial relationships. Consanguinity is a major factor only in the third novel but is of some importance in all the others. The respective affiliations of bankers, the homeless, and performing artists are sufficient to create a form of kinship that bears all the complexity and conflict the nuclear family offers. Unfortunately, murder is the outcome of these various arrangements and, fortunately for readers, provides challenges for the protagonists.

Gallagher Gray is really Katy Munger, a native North Carolinian, currently a resident of New York's Hell's Kitchen. She has worked in the personnel division of a private bank on Wall Street and has obviously paid close attention to both her employers and their clients. Her characters—Hubbert, Lil, and Herbert Wong—are lively and, if not totally believable, at least engrossing enough to cause readers to willingly suspend their disbelief for the duration of each story.

MISS EMILY SEETON
1991–1997   13 books
Hamilton Crane (Sarah J[ill] Mason)

Miss Emily Dorothea Seeton is a bit of an institution. The series in which she is featured was begun in 1968 by a man named Heron Carvic, who wrote five books. After his death, the series continued for three more books, all published in 1990 under the pseudonym Hampton Charles, who was in reality Roy Peter Martin. In 1991, Sarah J. Mason, writing as Hamilton Crane, assumed the series and has produced prolifically.

Sweetbriars, Old Mrs. Bannet's cottage at the south end of The Street in the picturesque village of Plummergen, is the home of Miss Seeton—second cousin, goddaughter, and heir to Old Mrs. Bannet. Miss Seeton is a retired art teacher and artist in her own right. Most of her artistic renderings show a marked if ordinary talent; however, some are unique, inspired, even prescient. These efforts, produced from someplace in Miss Seeton's unconscious, have led to the downfall of many an unsuspecting miscreant through the offices of Chief Supt. Delphick (known to all and sundry as The Oracle) of Scotland Yard and his trusty sergeant Bob Ranger.

Plummergen, Miss Seeton's village, is a small place in which the main (and only) thoroughfare is formally known as The Street. There are three shops, all selling groceries in addition to their regular stock. The post office, located in the largest of the three shops, is the central gathering and gossip dissemination point for most of the occupants of the village.

Directly opposite this vital spot is the cottage known as Lilikot, home of Miss Erica Nuttel and Mrs. Bunny Blaine, collectively referred to as "The Nuts." Lilikot, unlike all of the other village cottages, boasts a large plate-glass window overlooking The Street and all its activities. The strictly vegetarian Nuts observe, comment upon, and speculate about any and all who heave into their view. When facts are scarce on the ground, the Nuts—along with any other resident engaged in commerce or conversation within the confines of the post office—are not loath to embroider what little fact exists in the name of local color.

Miss Seeton's habits, activities, and visitors have not gone unnoticed, and she provides the villagers with many happy hours of conjecture on or against her behalf. Although Bob Ranger considers Miss Seeton his unofficial Auntie, his visits do not pass unremarked. When he is accompanied by any of his more senior officers, the first assumption made by the Nuts, and soon taken up by the others, is that the "Battling Brolly" has finally met her comeuppance. The

Brolly in question—though Miss Seeton is the proud possessor of several umbrellas—is a gift from a grateful beneficiary of Miss Seeton's unique skills. The handle of this utilitarian object is gold, albeit hollow—not solid—perhaps for consideration of weight. Needless to say this object raises eyebrows and questions among the villagers and adds much to Miss Seeton's notoriety.

Miss Seeton is paid a consultant's retainer by Scotland Yard. In return, she is required to provide Chief Supt. Delphick with her artistic impressions of scenes, events, and individuals. That Miss Seeton has never been near the location of the scenery in question, is uninformed about the events in question, and has not set eyes on the individuals under police scrutiny matters not. Her subconscious, through her artful hand, pen, and sketch block, reveals all to those who but trust in her powers.

The English village mystery is alive and well in this series. Those fond of slightly eccentric elderly spinsters, in possession of abilities that directly or inadvertently aid the forces of law and order, will welcome these books. Sarah J. Mason has truly taken the bit and run with it, spinning the improbable yet delightful tales of Miss Seeton, The Nuts, The Oracle, and the rest of the cast out to the very edges of probability. Carry on, Heron Carvic, Hamilton Crane . . . whoever.

CAT CALIBAN
1993–1997   6 books
D. B. Borton (Lynnette Carpenter)

Catherine "Cat" Caliban's role models include, and are not limited to, Nancy Drew, Miss Jane Marple, Maud Silver, Mrs. Pollifax, V. I. Warshawski, and Kinsey Millhone. After Cat's husband dies, she decides to make some changes in her life. She sells the family's Cincinnati home and buys a pink brick apartment house from her good friend, realtor Louella Simmons. One Kevin O'Neill, bartender by trade and great amateur cook, is Cat's sitting tenant. Sadie, Sophie, and Sidney, Cat's feline fur people, think Kevin is a deity as his apartment is air conditioned and his cooking divine. Obviously, private investigation holds great appeal for her, so Cat embarks on a training period designed to culminate in Caliban Investigations.

In *One for the Money*, prospective tenants Melanie Carter and Alice Rosenberg, a lesbian couple, come to view an apartment and discover a dead woman in the middle of the living room. Undaunted, the two women take another of Cat's vacancies, and Cat has her first investigation. The body belongs to a woman in her eighties, reduced to living on the streets and known as "Betty Bags." Cat discovers that Betty was formerly a famous silent screen star, who rather than being penniless may have been hoarding a fortune to leave the daughter she had given up for adoption. Retired black police officer Moses Fogg and his Beagle move into the apartment where Betty's body was discovered, and Cat's crew is almost complete; Leon Jakes, a moderately retarded black kid, rounds out the set and this disparate group goes on to solve four more mysteries.

Each story centers on a theme. The first, in *One for the Money*, is the fate of the homeless. *Two Points for Murder* features the murder of a rising high school basketball player and looks at the pressures brought to bear on promising athletes. In *Three Is a Crowd*, Cat and her friends must look back into events begun during the Vietnam era. The specter of the tragedy at Kent State University is invoked, and former protesters and veterans alike are involved in unraveling the murder of a man demonstrating against the United States government's involvement with the Nicaraguan contras. In *Four Elements of Murder*, Cat and part of her crew go to Tennessee when Louella asks for help in proving that her Uncle Red's death was in fact murder. The rest of the Catatonia Arms tenants remain at home providing backup and computer hacking skills to aid the travelers, who uncover a toxic waste dumping scheme. The fifth novel, *Five Alarm Fire*, looks at the racial issue known as passing.

Cat Caliban may be a grandmother approaching sixty but these facts don't stand in her way. This feisty, foul-mouthed female knows how to go about an investigation, and even though she hasn't gotten her PI license by the fifth book, she pursues her inquiries undaunted. She is a good friend and has good friends who are willing and able to assist in her informal involvement in murder cases. Cat's creator, Lynette Carpenter, writing as D. B. Borton, has researched all of the stories with an admirable thoroughness and placed Cat and her cohorts in excitingly plausible situations.

Not all senior detectives are little old ladies or those retired from their work. Some seniors are still defined professionally and appear in other chapters. Many of these fictional detectives have a substantial number of birthdays behind them, yet remain fully employed and continue to make major contributions to society. Retirement no longer means the end of active life, however, and the elders in our society are beginning to be taken more seriously than in the past. As the Baby Boomers reach their golden years, more credence will be given to the musings of those whose physical capacity may have diminished but whose minds remain sharp and clear.

SOME OTHER SENIOR SLEUTHS

Benbow & Wingate
Theo Bloomer
Poppy Dillworth
The Hometown Heroes

Dewey James
G. D. H. Pringle
Fanny Zindel

UNEXPECTED DETECTIVES

This chapter celebrates those characters who defy classification. Their livelihood does not depend on their appearance at an office or other place of business. Some have independent incomes, others—housewives for example—are supported by another in exchange for familial and domestic arranging. Still others may hold jobs but their work hardly ever puts them in a position to detect.

Miss Amelia Butterworth is a lady of independent means. A member of the higher planes of society, she is, nevertheless, fascinated with crime and makes herself available to provide information to Ebenezer Gryce of the New York City Police. Anna Katharine Green created Miss Butterworth in 1897, and she appeared in six books (1897–1917). Green is known as the mother of the detective novel, and Amelia sets a high standard for others in her position who follow in her unexpected detecting footsteps.

When it comes to getting to the heart of murder, no one can doubt the prowess of Lord Peter Wimsey. Second son of a ducal family, his noblesse oblige runs strong and he uses both his affluence and his title to aid him in bringing miscreants to justice—one way or another. Dorothy L. Sayers wrote only eleven novels and several short stories (1923–1982) featuring this exemplary amateur, yet Lord Peter, the ever-present Bunter, and Harriet Vane have gone down in the annals as classics.

Another aristocratic amateur sleuth made his appearance in twenty-one novels and several short story collections (1929–1989). Little is known about Albert Campion's family, although it is reputed to be close to the English throne, and his real name is only hinted at. Together with his tremendous man-of-all-work, Lugg, Campion cuts capers and plays the madcap in bringing wrongdoers their just deserts. Margery Allingham's creation has brought pleasure to several generations of readers and, without a doubt, will continue to do so for several more.

Young widow Abbie Harris is featured in eight books (1944–1954). She lives with her sister Margaret in their family house in upstate New York and falls into detecting out of boredom. Her creator, Amber Dean, weaves bits of lore and history into sweet tales of less than two hundred pages. World War II affects many of the people in these mysteries and contributes to several of the plots. Abbie Harris is one of the few memorable characters to arise out of the "dark ages" of crime and mystery fiction that began in the late '40s and extended well into the '50s.

Julie Hayes, a creation of Dorothy Salisbury Davis, is featured in only four books (1976–1987), yet in her brief life in print Julie meets a wide range of people in an even broader variety of settings. Just twenty-four in the first story, Julie grows up in the series and, in the process, grows in confidence. Davis is a master of her craft, and these lesser-known works of hers are well worth finding and reading.

Charlotte MacLeod created another young widow, Sarah Kelling Kelling. She, her zany family, and their connections are chronicled in twelve books (1979–1995). Like Julie Hayes, Sarah grows up in these stories. Marriage and motherhood are aspects of her life woven into the humorous plots in which the crimes are almost as improbable as the names of some of the characters.

Jack-of-all-trades Jake Samson is partnered with carpenter Rosie Vicente in five books (1983–1988) by Shelley Singer. Child of the '60s, Jake is an ex-cop and an ex-husband. The cover he uses for his detecting is that of a free-lance writer, and one supposes he can do a fair job of stringing words together. Both Jake and his tenant, Rosie, believe in freedom and keeping their options open. They do a great job of solving murders, and we hope Singer brings them back in more adventures.

Although quite a few of the characters in previous chapters could be classed as unexpected, there is usually something about their vocation that puts them in the direct path of crime and/or its solution. Unexpected detectives pop up all over the landscape. Their very unpredictability adds to their charm and makes them good, if unconventional, investigators.

PENNY WANAWAKE
1984–1991   7 books
Susan (Elizabeth) Moody

Six-foot-tall, drop-dead gorgeous, and very black, Penny Wanawake is the twenty-five-year-old daughter of the permanent ambassador to the United Nations for the tiny African Republic of Senangaland. Ancestors (male we presume) on her mother, Lady Helena Hurley's, side have held seats in the British House of Lords for more than six hundred years. Though Penny calls England home, her education has taken her from the English countryside to finishing school in Switzerland, the Sorbonne in Paris, and Stanford University in California. No stranger to wealth and privilege, Penny's life changed during a trip to Africa made at her father's suggestion. When confronted with the deprivation, disaster, and despair of her motherland and faced with the deceptions practiced by organizations ostensibly dedicated to dispensing charitable contributions toward the relief of some of the suffering, Penny took matters into her own capable hands.

Penny met Barnaby Midas in Paris while he was rifling her apartment in search of her jewel case. She distracted him with some of her other charms, and in the process of becoming lovers, Penny enlisted him in her cause. Barnaby's career took a slight turn, and he switched from being a second-rate cat burglar to a Robin Hood–like character who steals only from those who can afford it to aid those in need. Together, they created R. H. Enterprises. With profits licit and il-, Penny and Barnaby send much-needed funds and supplies to beleaguered parts of Africa knowing that 100 percent of their donations reach their intended goal.

The Ivory Domestic Agency, run by one of Penny's sitting tenants, Miss Antonia Ivory, is a clever and innocent front for Penny and Barnaby's brainchild. Miss Ivory's careful placement of well-educated young ladies as nannies and mother's helpers in the homes of the wealthy requires impeccable research into both prospective employer and prospective employee. This research provides Barnaby with a never-ending list of burglary potential. Miss Ivory, daughter of a trainer of noble horseflesh, possesses yet another talent—that of choosing the winner of any sort of horse race or meet. Barnaby considers any betting wins through the offices of Miss Ivory to be simple fund maximizers.

All seven books in the series feature murder, and Penny inevitably becomes involved through friends or family. In *Penny Black*, Marfa Lund doesn't show up for a meeting she has arranged with Penny at the Wanawakes' Big Sur, California, beach house. When she is found dead, Penny is called to identify her body and, of course, is compelled to find out why she has been killed and who has killed her. *Penny Dreadful* takes place in Canterbury, England, when a novelist who is also an instructor at an exclusive public school is found dead in his rooms. *Penny Post* also takes place in England when Penny's friend asks her to find out who is trying to kill him. She does, but not until after the evil deed is done. Italy is the setting for *Penny Royal*, and Penny is thrown into the fascinating and highly competitive world of archaeology while looking for another friend who has allegedly absconded with a pair of priceless gold figurines.

In *Penny Pinching*, Penny's look-alike is found bludgeoned to death on the deck of the Wanawake Big Sur beach house and Penny's father disappears. Senangalinese politics and the illegal export of that country's art treasures are at the center of this mystery that Penny and Barnaby work together to solve. In *Penny Wise*, Lady Helena asks her daughter to go to Greece to visit some old family friends and check out a speculative business venture Lady Helena is considering. The death of one of the partners puts Penny on the trail of yet another murderer. *Penny Saving*, published in England in 1991, is not available in the United States at the time of this writing.

Penny Wanawake resembles female heroes of an earlier time. She almost seems a parody of Honey West or Emma Peel except for the fact that her instincts are sound, she doesn't take too many outrageous chances, and she keeps most of her clothes on most of the time. She is in charge of herself, her person, and her sexuality and carries off these responsibilities in a likably independent fashion. She would be a good friend to have in almost any situation.

Susan Moody's other series features English bridge instructor Cassie Swann, found in the chapter "The Game's Afoot: Sports and Games"—a far cry from the globe-trotting Miss W.

MAGGIE RYAN
1985–1991   8 books
P(atricia) M(cEvoy) Carlson

Although this series first appeared in 1985 with *Audition for Murder*, the story itself takes place in the late '60s. The setting for the first novel is the campus of Hargate College in upstate New York where actors Nick O'Connor and his wife, Lisette, have gone to appear in a production of *Hamlet*. Maggie Ryan makes an entrance early in the story as she swings down from the flies above the stage. While murder is certainly central to this and all of these stories, the characters and their conditions are the most telling and salient features of each book. Nick's relationship with his wife and the reasons behind their difficulties are vital aspects of the story, and Maggie's understanding of their situation is crucial to both the outcome of the tale and the ongoing series itself.

The issues that compound and propel the narrative are presented from separate, often very different, angles of perception and never simply as social abstractions. Aging, rape, the consequences of the violence of wars, and the conflicts of personal needs are personified in the various characters appearing throughout the series. Through it all, the energetic, tenacious, and fierce Maggie Ryan provides not only the solution to the murder but her own analysis of these situations. In conversations with victim, murderer, and those touched by the effects of the crime, she applies a depth of compassionate comprehension of the human condition that goes well beyond the sleuth following clues to a logical conclusion. Maggie works toward resolution, and her support of justice is tempered with a firm belief in the possibility of human redemption.

As a statistician, Maggie is no stranger to analytical reasoning. Starting in the first book as a student, Maggie perseveres until she holds a Ph.D. in statistics. The series sees her through college, marriage, and into motherhood, and each story uses whatever circumstances her life holds as the focal point for her detecting. Maggie is the star, yet her brilliance does not shine alone; she relies on a variety of partners, and her associates codetect with her willingly. With a strong academic background as a foundation, Maggie uses logic and method to arrive at some of her conclusions. Her instinctual paths are, however, equally well trodden as the context of the crime and its human complications do not always lend themselves to a logical approach.

Nick O'Connor, who becomes Maggie's husband before the 1972 events in *Murder Unrenovated*, is a working actor who will take any good job offered. Big, tall, and shaggy, Nick rarely plays the romantic lead. His competence and craftsmanship hold him in good stead and readers seldom find him resting. Their courtship is rocky and their marriage more than ordinary. Of the pair, Maggie has the more conventional job, yet Nick's unpredictable schedule often works to their benefit, especially after their daughter is born. *Rehearsal for Murder* takes place in 1973 and opens with Nick waiting for Maggie to bring five-month-old Sarah to him at the theatre. Much of the story finds one or the other of the couple wearing the baby in a Snugli. Nick's world of theatre is featured in two books and woven throughout all eight. Maggie's profession gets her into a few of her detecting situations, but what she does professionally remains, for the most part, unremarked.

Patricia Carlson holds a Ph.D. in psychology. She has taught psycholinguistics, statistics, and research methodology at Cornell University and has authored numerous academic books and articles. She chose the mystery genre for her fiction series as it offered the largest range of scenarios and subjects while allowing her primary characters to develop completely. Along with the evolution of her protagonists, Carlson plays devil's advocate by using the respective voices of her antagonists and through them presents chillingly plausible motivations for those characters' illegal—often immoral—actions. In short, she gives readers more than a little to contemplate.

Carlson's other series takes place in Southern Indiana and features Deputy Sheriff Marty Hopkins, described in the chapter "Behind the Badge: Provincial Police."

EMMA VICTOR
1987–1997   4 books
Mary Wings

Jill-of-some-trades Emma Victor arrived on the mystery fiction scene in 1987 in *She Came Too Late*. In this story, Emma is on the staff of a women's crisis center in Boston. She is on phone duty on the center's hotline when a call comes in directed specifically to her. When Emma goes to meet the woman who called her, she finds the woman's murdered body. Recognizing Julie Arbeder as an acquaintance, Emma feels compelled to discover the identity of her killer and is launched into her first investigation. As the case progresses, Emma meets Dr. Frances Cohen and the pair fall in lust—followed by love.

In one hundred ninety-seven pages, Emma encounters, among others, union organizers, lesbian and gay activists, a drug addict, yuppies, and new agers. This complex, convoluted tale features money, friendship, artificial insemination, gay rights, and political shenanigans. In the end, Emma discovers the killer and the motive behind not only Julie's death but that of two others.

As *She Came in a Flash* opens, Emma is disenchanted with her relationship with Frances and has moved to the San Francisco Bay Area. She has a job as publicist for a concert benefiting various women's organizations. A call from her best friend, Jonell, sets Emma to finding Jonell's missing sister, who has quit her job as a physicist and joined a cult. A bounced check, a temperamental former punk rock star making a comeback, and the mysterious Vishnu are but a few of the characters Emma meets as she investigates the death of her friend's sister. Lawyer Willie Rossini offers Emma money to clear her corporate client Nevada Storm—the former punk rocker—from any wrongdoing. Neither incarceration nor a bullet in her leg deters Emma from solving the crime and, in the end, Willie pays Emma $1,500 for her services.

Time passes. In *She Came by the Book*, Frances has moved to California and she and Emma live together. In this story, Emma seems to be working as a legal investigator for Willie Rosini (the spelling changes somewhere between stories), who asks her to meet with David Stimson, "professional widow" of the murdered Senator Howard Blooming. This case takes Emma back into her own history as, twenty years earlier, she had been Blooming's publicist. David wants Emma to personally deliver Howard's journals to the

Howard Blooming Lesbian and Gay Memorial Archive and to attend the gala in celebration of the work done by the archive. At the dinner, one of the organizers falls dead at Emma's feet. Drawing on her knowledge of past and present players, Emma discovers the killer, though not before two more people die.

Mary Wings operates within a very fluid timeline and, in fact, creates reality as it goes along. Emma is a whole being at her inception and the stories in which she stars are complete in and of themselves. There is some ancillary character carry-over between the books and, though all of the tales are exercises in involution, not much about who Emma really is or was is divulged. We like these disconnected puzzles, admire the style with which they are written, and want more.

LADY MARGARET PRIAM
1988–1996   8 books
Joyce Christmas

Breeding, background, and an English title are prized in the high social circles of New York. Lady Margaret Priam, sister of the twenty-second earl of Brayfield, has them all; what she does not have is money. Nevertheless, she travels lightly among the old-mon-eyed crowd and is in demand for all the most important social events Gotham can offer.

All of the characters who dot the series appear in the first book, *Suddenly in Her Sorbet*, which opens on Poppy Dill, society columnist nonpareil, writing up an event that has not yet taken place. This is her habit as the same cast will do the same things and the outcome is predictable. Much to Poppy's and everyone else's surprise, the hostess of the event is murdered. Lady Margaret is among the guests—courtesy of a ticket given her by Bedros Kasparian, for whom she works—as is Margaret's close friend Prince Paul Castrocani. Sam De Vere, a homicide detective with the New York City Police Department, investigates officially, but Margaret solves the crime. Prince Paul's mother, Carolyn Sue Dennis Castrocani Hoopes, and her current husband, Benton, also make their appearance.

The elite, the climbers, and the hoi polloi are all well represented, and Margaret moves up and down the social ladder with grace, dignity, and respect, when due. Her title gives her entree to society's top level, and her unfailing good manners win her friends among the lesser orders. She tolerates—nay, even understands—some of the desires compelling the social "wannabes," and, while never suffering fools gladly, she is kind in keeping them well outside the so-important venues to which they desire admission.

Most of the action of the stories takes place in and around the isle of Manhattan, where Margaret goes about her social rounds and occasionally turns up to assist Bedros at his Oriental antiquities shop. She falls into detecting accidentally, and her insights are grudgingly accepted by De Vere, who would prefer that she stay far away from death and danger. New York is not the only place Margaret falls over bodies, however. In *A Stunning Way to Die*, fourth in the series, she accompanies the ashes of a supposed close friend to their final resting place in Los Angeles and unravels an old mystery involving deceit and blackmail as well as the murder of her bare acquaintance.

In *Friend or Faux?* Margaret, feeling oddly distanced from De Vere, almost eagerly travels to England when her brother David calls for her help at the family seat, Priam's Priory. David is besieged by a Hollywood film crew, an old family friend, the friend's two wives, and their entire entourage. The deaths of the Maharani and the Priams' black sheep cousin Nigel add to the earl's dilemma and make it even more essential for Margaret to get to the heart of matters.

In *A Perfect Day for Dying*, Prince Paul is hired to manage the social schedule for Lord Farfaine at the latter's winter home on the Caribbean island of Boucan. Margaret gets herself invited to the festivities to help Paul out and ends up solving two murders and laying the islanders' fears of voodoo to rest. Paul meets his soul mate and young love blooms.

This series is light and entertaining, the characters quirky and interesting, and the class delineations well managed. Joyce Christmas uses society's solipsism as a grand starting point for some very human tales. Christmas's newest series features retired office manager Betty Trenka and takes place in East Moulton, Connecticut.

SUSAN HENSHAW
1988–1996   10 books
Valerie Wolzien

Susan Henshaw is a housewife living in the affluent bastion of Hancock, Connecticut. Her husband, Jed, is an executive in a New York advertising agency and commutes to town by train or car. As the series opens in *Murder at the PTA Luncheon*, the couple's two children, Chad and Chrissy, are nine and twelve, respectively. Susan is involved in murder when two of her fellow PTA members are killed in separate incidents. Because she knows all of the parents and teachers involved in the association, she is asked by Connecticut

State Police Officer Brett Fortesque for her assistance in understanding what might have happened. Brett's official partner in the case is the beautiful widow Kathleen Somerville. Kathleen and Susan become friends in the course of the investigation, and the unlikely pair go on to detect in nine more books.

As *The Fortieth Birthday Body* opens, Kathleen has married Jed's business partner Jerry Gordon and has taken up residence in Hancock. She has left the state police and is running a private security business. This has the potential to be highly lucrative as Hancock is one of the more exclusive and wealthy communities in the whole United States. Mercedes, Jaguars, and Maseratis abound. Imported Italian kitchen cabinets are not unusual, furs and jewels are de rigueur, and no one would dream of being inappropriately attired for any occasion. When a dead body falls out of the new Volvo that Jed is giving Susan for her birthday, she and Kathleen are once again called into action and solve the crime.

What to give one's spouse for Christmas is a major problem for Hancock residents in *We Wish You a Merry Murder*. Despite that hefty challenge, murder takes precedence. After solving the crime with her cohort Susan, Kathleen announces that she is pregnant and thereby provides her husband with a gift that is unrivaled. When said child, Alexander Brandon Colin Gordon, a.k.a. Bananas, is six months old, his parents join the Henshaws on a winter trip to Yellowstone. There, in *An Old Faithful Murder*, the two women encounter several murders and solve them despite being far away from home territory.

With all of their family members otherwise occupied, Susan and Kathleen take themselves Down East for the Fourth of July celebrations where *A Star-Spangled Murder* takes place at Susan's family summer home on an island off the coast of Maine. The corpse of her newest neighbor is discovered in Susan's living room. After the two women solve that killing, they return to Hancock, and in *A Good Year for a Corpse* a body is found in the wine cellar of the Hancock Inn, everyone's favorite restaurant. Brett Fortesque, now Hancock's Chief of Police, is out of town. He arrives on the scene just in time to put the cuffs on the miscreant as identified by the intrepid pair.

The nouveaux riches are well represented in this series. Who's who in the pecking order has much more to do with who has what than any sort of character quality, and the bottom of the ladder is littered with the bodies of those who have fallen—or were pushed—in the clamor for the top rung. In the face of all of this wealth and infighting, Susan and Kathleen manage to hold their own and maintain a more reasonable set of personal standards. They tolerate, perhaps even understand, the foibles of their friends and neighbors while keeping cool heads and catching criminals.

Valerie Wolzien's characters are likable. They may not be everyone's cup of tea, however; we can relate to the exigencies of raising families and are not unfamiliar with the facade of affluent communities. The murders are well plotted and the element of mystery is present throughout. Wolzien's newest character, contractor Josie Pigeon, is introduced in the Henshaw series.

LIZ SULLIVAN, BRIDGET MONTROSE & DET. PAUL DRAKE
1988–1998   6 books
Lora Roberts (Smith)

This series takes place in our hometown of Palo Alto, California, and all of the places mentioned are familiar to us. The series begins with *Revolting Development*, yet the primary character, Liz Sullivan, doesn't appear until the second book. Other major characters include homicide Det. Paul Drake, who investigates the murder of a real estate developer in the first story and appears in the rest of the books, both in his professional capacity and in a more personal one. Bridget Montrose, a housewife and prime suspect in the first book, gets pregnant with her fourth child at the end of that story, has her first daughter by the second book, and continues as Liz's close friend along with Claudia Kaplan and several others. Our fair city can even be considered a vital feature of this series as the action takes place in locales that really exist just as described.

Liz Sullivan is introduced in *Murder in a Nice Neighborhood*. She lives in her 1969 VW microbus on various and sundry streets in Palo Alto and is a free-lance writer whose articles have appeared in diverse publications ranging from *The Smithsonian* to *True Confessions*. Liz teaches creative writing at the city's Senior Center, gardens at the community plots behind the main library, and swims and showers at Rinconada Park's public pool. Her life may be considered marginal by most people's standards—even Liz describes herself as a vagabond—yet she has created a rich, fulfilling milieu of friends and activities and is far from destitute or homeless. Circumstances dictate her reason for not having a fixed abode, and this is explained in the first story in which she appears.

As *Murder in the Marketplace* opens, Liz has become a home owner, with Paul Drake as her neighbor. Coming home from her temporary part-time job, Liz finds Paul talking with a young woman whose personal style is colorful, to say the least. She introduces herself as Liz's niece Amy Sullivan and announces that she has run away from home and plans to stay with Liz for a while. With the door to her past opened a little further, readers learn more about the Sullivan clan and Liz's decision to remove herself from her family's bosom. In *Murder Mile High*, Liz returns to Denver, where her parents, brother, and sister all live and becomes re-enmeshed in internecine conflict. Liz holds out for resolution and discovers hidden reserves of strength and independence.

In each of the books, Liz is suspected of murder. Even though she is exonerated early on in every story, enough of a cloud hangs over her to make it essential that the real killer be identified. First acting in her own best interest, then to assist Paul Drake, and finally to defend her family, Liz becomes an active participant in detection and does it well.

The first book appears under the name Lora R. Smith, and subsequent books are penned as Lora Roberts. We can attest to the fact that these two are one and the same person. Like Liz, Lora lives in Palo Alto, drives a VW microbus, and has a dog. We've met Lora's mother, who doesn't resemble Liz's in the least, and we've heard that her sister is really nice. Whether writing as Smith or Roberts, this author has a fine grasp on the art of storytelling and plies her craft in a captivating fashion.

JANE JEFFRY
1989–1996   8 books
Jill Churchill (Janice Young Brooks)

An unnamed suburb of Chicago is the home of Jane Jeffry and her three children, Mike, Katie, and Todd. Jane's husband, Steve, died in a car crash seven months earlier, and she is still coming to terms with her new status as widow as the series opens with *Grime and Punishment*. Shelley Nowack, Jane's next-door neighbor and best friend, is expecting the first visit from the new housekeeper that she and Jane are going to share. A replacement arrives instead. When Shelley returns from meeting her mother at O'Hare Airport, she finds the housekeeper dead in the guest room. Homicide detective Mel VanDyne arrives to investigate the strangulation and finds Jane and Shelley fonts of information on all of the potential suspects and things of a domestic nature. In spite of VanDyne's protests, Jane, of course, investigates and solves the crime.

Jane is a State Department brat who traveled extensively with her parents and lived all over Europe and the Far East. Her marriage to Steve had been nominally happy until the night of his death, when he told her he was leaving her for another woman. Jane always felt shy and, during her marriage, was dependent upon her husband. As a widow, however, she is discovering untapped strengths and is pleased to find that she is eminently capable of running her home and managing the demands of family. Jane has solid values and relies upon them in raising her children. She holds her own in every situation she encounters, and readers will find themselves cheering Jane on as she and her children evolve. Not only do her good nature, optimism, and basic unflappability benefit her family, they are essential ingredients for the detecting Jane almost inadvertently does.

Jane's relationship with Mel VanDyne undergoes a change from antagonism to romance. Yet, in the sixth book, *From Here to Paternity*, she finds that she likes running her own show and that the prospect of marriage—even to someone she has grown to love and respect—holds little appeal for her. Many women will recognize Jane's equivocal feelings toward Mel.

Each of the eight books in the series adheres closely to a formula; to say too much about it would be to give away some of the charms of the stories. What we can say is that all but one book take place in the unnamed Chicago suburb, every one involves a small, closed group of people, and every title is a takeoff on a well-known book or film title.

Janice Brooks is the author of several historical novels. As Jill Churchill, she has been nominated for an Anthony and has won an Agatha and a Macavity for Best First Novel. Her protagonist is well chosen and well drawn. Neither of us would mind living next door to Jane even if she isn't human first thing in the morning.

JANE DA SILVA
1992–1995   4 books
K. K. Beck (Kathrine Marris)

Jane da Silva is a thirty-seven-year-old expatriate as this series opens. In *A Hopeless Case*, she is singing in a restaurant housed in a building constructed in the mid–seventeenth century in Amsterdam. After finishing a set, Jane is approached by a good-looking man who introduces himself as the cultural attaché from the United States embassy. Jane's uncle Harold Mortensen has died, leaving Jane beneficiary of a large trust. There is a catch, however, and thereby hangs the tale.

Jane had left home for Europe in search of adventure and romance during her junior year in college. She had found both, but the romance had come to an abrupt end when her handsome husband, a Formula One race car driver, died in a fiery crash. His manager had been systematically milking the profits and that, coupled with the precipitous fall of the Brazilian currency, left Jane virtually penniless. She has spent the succeeding ten years at a variety of uninspiring jobs.

Upon returning to Seattle Jane meets with her uncle's attorney to learn what she must do to qualify for the trust. Uncle Harold's aim in life was to deal with what could be considered hopeless cases through the Foundation for Righting Wrongs. He courted no publicity and made no charges to those he benefited. His foundation is now being overseen by a board of directors made up of Uncle Harold's friends, a group of powerful old men. They have the ultimate say on the qualifications of any case Jane takes on, and she is dependent upon their perspicacity and goodwill. Initially, she is given an allowance, the right to live in Uncle Harold's house, and three months to come up with her first hopeless case.

Through attorney and sometime private investigator Calvin Mason, Jane meets her first client, a talented young musician with aspirations for the Juilliard School. With Calvin's assistance and some help from a six-foot-eight, three-hundred-pound Samoan named Bob Manalatu, Jane recovers a lost inheritance and solves a murder. These results are not quite good enough for the board of directors, but Jane's allowance is extended and she is given another chance.

Her second case is more successful, and Jane receives six months of trust income in *Amateur Night*. In this story, one of Calvin's clients may have been wrongfully imprisoned on a murder charge, and Jane sets out to prove his innocence and secure his release. Her investigations take Jane north to British Columbia and into the world of professional strippers.

Feeling a sense of accomplishment, Jane sets out on her third case in *Electric City*. Two people ask Jane to help them find out what has happened to one of their co-workers at a news-clipping service. The path Jane follows in this investigation takes her all over Washington state—to a rodeo, the light show at Grand Coulee Dam, and an impressive number of bars. Jane's path crosses those of a country-western singer, a blackmailer, and a disgraced church deacon, among others. At the successful conclusion, the board doesn't approve, and once again Jane is put on short rations.

In *Cold Smoked*, Jane has returned to her former role as chanteuse and is singing at the International Seafood Show in a downtown Seattle hotel. A young woman is murdered, and Jane takes up the matter of finding her killer for the girl's parents. Almost everything connected to this case is fishy, and Jane travels far afield in search of answers. One trip takes her to the farthest reaches of the Lofoten Islands off the north coast of Norway and only a little south to the Shetland Islands off Scotland. The denouement to this episode takes place in England, and Jane is paid a reasonable sum by a foreign intelligence agency for her efforts.

Readers are left in a state of suspense about Jane's relationship with the foundation board of directors. Can she continue to live in Uncle Harold's Capitol Hill, craftsman-style house? Will she receive another payment of trust moneys? Can she find and solve another hopeless case? The fifth book in the series may hold the answers, yet we won't be surprised if Kathrine Marris, writing as K. K. Beck, provides even more questions in her next installment.

Chance and/or proximity seem to create the unexpected detective, and more often than not these same elements seem to keep them at the task of investigating. Some of these amateurs find the practice of unmasking killers thrilling and find ways to put themselves in the path of murder. The rest continue to be unwillingly drawn to the task. In all cases, readers are rewarded with inventive characters and situations and whole new realms of detection to contemplate.

SOME OTHER UNEXPECTED DETECTIVES

Kate Baier
Ginger Barnes
Peaches Dann
Joe Grey
Ellie Simons Haskell
Vejay Haskell

Midnight Louie
Chris Martin
Lexie Jane Pelazoni
Snooky
Jeet & Robin Vaughn

EPILOGUE

While it is tempting to draw conclusions at the end of one's work, the very mutability of the crime and mystery fiction genre precludes this. However, during the fifteen years of our research and reading on this project we have noticed directions, drifts, and fashions that are of interest to us and may be to our readers.

The red-haired woman is a definite presence, as is she who stands over five-foot-ten inches tall. There are more children actively assisting their parental units in investigations and the niece who comes to visit—and stays to aid and confound the detective—is a notable addition. Housewives, with or without children, have become more involved in pursuing murderers, and domestic animals not only help their owners bring criminals to justice but have begun narrating the exploits of their humans.

In earlier years, the major metropolitan settings for mystery novels were limited to cities such as New York, Chicago, San Francisco, Los Angeles, and London. Today, writers are expanding the action to include New Orleans, Miami, Atlanta, Denver, Santa Fe, Portland, Seattle, Vancouver, Jerusalem, Venice, and Manchester and their suburbs. Rural areas form the backdrop for an increasing number of successful sleuths; the vast desert of the American Southwest, the forested mountains of the Pacific Northwest, and the vales, moors, and downs of the British Isles are also featured locales.

The space/time continuum offers grist for the contemporary writers' mill and detecting is taking place in both the past and the future. Historical epochs offer exciting venues for well-researched novels, and realms once open only to the science fiction writer provide new arenas for murder. Mystery readers have always found it necessary to suspend their disbelief and authors having their characters travel through, bend, or defy time provide new directions for this challenge.

The entrepreneur in mystery novels is taking risks beyond those offered by the business world as she or he tracks down killers and brings them to justice. Women in particular are embarking on ventures that allow them freedom to define the way in which they support themselves and, if they have them, their families. The English manor house has been almost completely replaced by the bed-and-breakfast establishment run, more often than not, by an enterprising woman. The catering trade offers the possibility of fiscal security for its providers and, at the hands of the mystery writer, ample opportunity for physical danger. Booksellers, secretaries, computer experts, art gallery owners, executive headhunters, ranchers, and, of course, private investigators put their livelihoods and often their lives on the line while plying their respective trades.

There is more ethnic, religious, and sexual diversity in this genre than ever before. Members of races seldom represented as the protagonist in a work of mystery fiction before are now taking their place as those committed to bringing miscreants to justice. Religious practice and observance are showing their influence on methods of detection and the detectives themselves. The gay and lesbian contingent is an undeniable presence as those whose sexual preference is no secret take an active, sometimes outspoken role in the annals of mystery fiction.

The tradition of the storyteller is long. Many of the women creating series characters today are true masters of the craft. Using the vast linguistic riches available, they provide information, entertainment, and an element of caution. And they are applying this wealth eloquently, to spin their mystery yarns.

One disturbing trend we have noted is the proliferation of collectors snatching the books we want to read, locking them away in temperature-controlled vaults, and driving the price of a single volume far beyond the meager resources of most readers. It used to be possible to attend library and estate sales and fill some of the gaps on one's library shelves. Now, dealers get there early and gather the precious few for resale—most often at the inflated prices collectors dictate. The saddest effect of this collecting mania is that many of the books remain not only unavailable but unread. Perhaps it is time for some of these treasures to be reprinted. Publishers, take note!

It would be difficult to write a book focused on women authors and their characters without making some observation on the phenomenon of feminism and its attendant consequences over the time span we cover. Given that the chronological age of most of the women currently creating series falls between forty and sixty, it is hard to imagine that they—and by extension, their writing—have not been influenced by this pressing issue, one way or another. Feminist sensibilities were reawakened in the early '70s; interestingly, few series by women were developed in this period.

In the mid-'70s, when numbers of series began to increase, women started to create new character types, yet many of the old models still seemed to be in operation. It wasn't until the '80s that women started to make their female characters respond consistently to situations from a woman's perspective rather than reacting in the time-honored male fashion. Yet, women writing series in this genre seldom resort to strident feminist rhetoric in making the point that our half of the human race holds a valid point of view and that our ways of working in the world are effective.

We have enjoyed the entire process of creating our book and take full responsibility for all of this original research. Bookstore and library shelves, listings of current releases from publishing houses and select periodicals, the highly valuable Sisters in Crime *Books in Print* publication, and the authors themselves are the sources we've used in compiling our list. The foregoing character sketches are based solely on our reading, and all of the observations made are entirely those of Nichols/Thompson.

Silk Stalkings: When Women Write of Murder was nominated for the Edgar Allan Poe Award, Mystery Writers of America's highest honor, and won several other major accolades. The most satisfying reward we have received is to have our work used as source material, cited or not, by other scholars and authors.

Despite being immersed, extensively and exclusively, for the better part of the last three years (or four?), in the bounty of works by women writing series, this still remains one of our favorite forms of recreational reading. We have made some delightful discoveries along the way and have broadened our personal horizons considerably. We invite readers to join us in suspending judgment along with disbelief.

One of the aims of our work is to continue providing other researchers with solid data upon which to base their own investigations. Our passion, however, is to be able to present to an eager and receptive audience the full panoply of the series books that women have been producing in the crime and mystery genre for more than one hundred years.

MASTER LIST

For the past fifteen years, we have been gathering data on women authors who have created characters who appear in two or more titles. The MASTER LIST is the result. It is the most comprehensive and most accurate listing of series characters created by women authors in crime and mystery fiction extant, and is truly the foundation of this work.

While our focus is on women writers, there are a few noteworthy exceptions to this primacy. Male authors using a female pseudonym are a rarity. The decision to write under a woman's guise might have been one based on marketing or may have been dictated by the author's choice of protagonist. Whatever the reason, we include these men for their audacity. In the early part of the twentieth century, it wasn't unusual for a woman to team up with a man to craft a series. More often than not, these mixed writing teams were married couples though some are linked by neither blood nor banns. One result of this joint authorship is the incorporation of the female point of view into the end product.

The MASTER LIST is organized in a hierarchical style with autonym taking first rank. The Autonyms (A:) are arranged alphabetically and all information relating to that individual, e.g., Pseudonym (P:), Series Character (SC:) name, and all Titles in which a given character appears, is listed under that designation. The titles are listed chronologically according to copyright date—when this information is available. Unfortunately, as some books are long out of print, in some cases we have had to resort to the earliest publication date. If a title is a collection of short stories, the designation SS precedes the year. When a book is published under another title, it is listed under the first title as Also Published As (APA).

The MASTER LIST is cross-referenced to both Pseudonym (P:) and Joint Name (JN:). These designations appear in their proper alphabetical sequence and refer back to the Autonym (A:).

P: Harris, Colver
    Please see: Colver, Anne
JN: Hearnden, Beryl
    Please see: Balfour, Eva w/ Beryl Hearnden

When a writing team consists of a woman and a man, the Autonym (A:) entry appears alphabetically by the woman's last name. In the case of two women writing together, the Autonym (A:) entry is given in alphabetical order. Pseudonyms (P:) used by writing teams are treated the same way as names of single authors.

The MASTER LIST also serves as an index to characters presented in the foregoing chapters. Page references are made next to the character's name in the listing.

As there are numerous sources for publication information on the titles listed and a wealth of biographical information on the authors appearing in the MASTER LIST, none is given here.

KEY TO MASTER LIST

A: = Autonym
P: = Pseudonym
J: = Joint Name
SC: = Series Character
SS = Short Story
Year = Year of Copyright
APA = Also Published As

APPENDIX I

SERIES CHARACTER CHRONOLOGY

This chronological listing is designed to assist readers in several ways. With this information, a series can be fixed in time. A favorite character can then be placed with her/his fictional counterparts. Often, writing style and vernacular reflect the era in which a book was written. Trends and character types also vary with different periods.

The first date of each entry marks the series character's first appearance in print. The second date shows when the last book in the series was published. The number of books in which each series character appears is next, followed by the series character's name in bold print. The Autonym appears under the series character's name.

APPENDIX II

PSEUDONYM TO AUTONYM

There are any number of reasons for an author to use a nom de plume. A new name often gives an undeveloped aspect of an author's personality a chance to flourish. Several authors in our MAS-TER LIST have created a new pseudonym for each new series character. An author whose books are well known in another field may want to separate this work from her crime and mystery writing. Some team writers, in the true sense of collaboration, choose a single name under which their works appear.

A man may write under a female pseudonym thinking that readers may be more sympathetic toward a certain character developed by a woman rather than a man. In the not-so-distant past, many women chose to send their work to a publisher under a male pseudonym to improve chances of publication or publishers decreed that a woman adopt a male pseudonym or publish under her first initials. It was felt the market was more receptive to works by men.

Many earlier authors' real names were kept closely guarded secrets—sometimes for decades. Today, some authors still desire anonymity for personal or professional reasons. Our policy is to reveal only those real names that have appeared in print elsewhere. We respect those who wish to remain pseudonymous.

This section makes it possible for readers familiar with only a pseudonym to discover the author's real name and any other pseudonyms she may have chosen to use. Readers may find that a favorite author's name is in fact a pseudonym. This list is compiled alphabetically by pseudonym (last name first). The autonym appears on the same line.

APPENDIX III

SERIES CHARACTER TO WRITER

This appendix links the series character—arranged alphabetically by *first* name—to the writer. In this case, the term writer applies to both Pseudonym and Autonym—whichever name appears on the book jacket.

Because of the sheer number of law enforcement and military personnel represented, no rank or title is given to their name in this list. However, each individual's honorific is shown in the MASTER LIST. Physicians and members of the clergy are listed alphabetically by their honorific.

Readers may be familiar with a certain series character's name. By referring to this list, they can find the writer, then use the MASTER LIST to find all the titles of the books in which that character appears, as well as any other series characters created by the same author (Autonym).

A

A: **Abrahams, Doris Caroline w/ Simon Jasha Skidelsky**
P: **Brahms, Caryl & S. J. Simon**
    SC: Insp. Adam Quill
            1937 A Bullet in the Ballet
            1938 Casino for Sale
                  APA: Murder à la Stroganoff
            1940 Envoy on Excursion
    SC: Ballet Stroganoff
            1937 A Bullet in the Ballet
            1938 Casino for Sale
                  APA: Murder à la Stroganoff

A: **Adams, Deborah**
    SC: Jesus Creek, TN
            1992 All the Crazy Winters
            1992 All the Crazy Pretenders
            1993 All the Dark Disguises
            1994 All the Hungry Mothers
            1995 All the Deadly Beloved
            1997 All the Blood Relations

A: **Adams, Jane**
    SC: Det. Michael Croft
            1995 The Greenway
            1996 Cast the First Stone

A: **Adamson, Lydia**
    SC: Alice Nestleton (see p. 104)
            1990 A Cat in the Manger
            1991 A Cat in Wolf's Clothing
            1991 A Cat of a Different Color
            1992 A Cat by Any Other Name
            1992 A Cat in the Wings
            1993 A Cat with a Fiddle
            1993 A Cat in a Glass House
            1994 A Cat with No Regrets
            1994 A Cat on the Cutting Edge
            1995 A Cat on a Winning Streak
            1995 A Cat in Fine Style
            1996 A Cat in a Chorus Line
            1996 A Cat Under the Mistletoe
            1997 A Cat on a Beach Blanket
    SC: Dr. Deirdre "Didi" Quinn Nightingale (see p. 118)
            1994 Dr. Nightingale Comes Home
            1994 Dr. Nightingale Rides the Elephant

       1995 Dr. Nightingale Goes the Distance
       1995 Dr. Nightingale Goes to the Dogs
       1996 Dr. Nightingale Enters the Bear Cave
       1996 Dr. Nightingale Chases Three Little Pigs
       1997 Dr. Nightingale Rides to the Hounds
       1997 Dr. Nightingale Meets Puss in Boots
  SC: Lucy Wayles
       1996 Beware the Tufted Duck
       1997 Beware the Butcher Bird

A: **Adamson, M(ary) J(o)**
  SC: Balthazar Marten
       1987 A February Face
       1987 Not till a Hot January
       1987 Remember March
       1989 April When They Woo
       1989 May's Newfangled Mirth

P: **Aird, Catherine**
  please see: **McIntosh, Kinn Hamilton**

A: **Albert, Susan Wittig**
  SC: China Bayles
       1992 Thyme of Death
       1993 Witches' Bane
       1994 Hangman's Root
       1995 Rosemary Remembered
       1996 Rueful Death
       1997 Love Lies Bleeding
       1998 Chile Death

A: **Albert, Susan Wittig w/ William J. Albert**
  P: **Paige, Robin**
  SC: Kate Ardleigh & Sir Charles Sheridan
       1994 Death at Bishop's Keep
       1995 Death at Gallows Green
       1997 Death at Daisy's Folly
       1998 Death at Devil's Bridge

J: **Albert, William J.**
  please see: **Albert, Susan Wittig w/ William J. Albert**

P: **Allan, Joan**
  please see: **Grove, Martin**

P: **Allen, Irene**
  please see: **Peters, Elsa Kirsten**

A: **Allen, Kate**
  SC: Alison Kaine
       1993 Tell Me What You Like
       1995 Give My Secrets Back
       1996 Takes One to Know One

P: **Allen, Mary Ann**
please see: **Pardoe, Rosemary**
A: **Allingham (Carter), Margery (Louise)**
SC: Albert Campion (see p. 281)
1929 The Crime at Black Dudley
APA: The Black Dudley Murder
1930 Mystery Mile
1931 Look to the Lady
APA: The Gyrth Chalice Mystery
1931 Police at the Funeral
1933 Sweet Danger
APA: Kingdom of Death
APA: The Fear Sign
1934 Death of a Ghost
1936 Flowers for the Judge
APA: Legacy in Blood
1937 Dancers in Mourning
APA: Who Killed Chloe?
SS 1937 Mr. Campion: Criminologist
1937 The Case of the Late Pig
1938 The Fashion in Shrouds
SS 1939 Mr. Campion and Others
1941 Traitor's Purse
APA: The Sabotage Murder Mystery
1945 Coroner's Pidgin
APA: Pearls Before Swine
SS 1947 The Case Book of Mr. Campion
1948 More Work for the Undertaker
1952 The Tiger in the Smoke
1955 The Beckoning Lady
APA: The Estate of the Beckoning Lady
1958 Hide My Eyes
APA: Tether's End
APA: Ten Were Missing
1962 The China Governess
1963 The Mysterious Mr. Campion
1965 Mr. Campion's Lady
1965 The Mind Readers
1968 Cargo of Eagles
SS 1969 The Allingham Case-Book
SS 1973 The Allingham Minibus
APA: Mr. Campion's Lucky Day and Other Stories
SS 1989 The Return of Mr. Campion

A: **Ames, Sarah Rachel Stainer**
  P: **Gainham, Sarah**
    SC: Julia Homberg
          1967 Night Falls on the City
          1969 A Place in the Country
          1971 Private Worlds

A: **Amey, Linda**
    SC: Blair Emerson
          1992 Bury Her Sweetly
          1995 At Dead of Night

A: **Andreae, Christine**
    SC: Lee Squires
          1992 Trail of Murder
          1994 Grizzly
          1996 A Small Target

A: **Andrews (Brown), Sarah**
    SC: Emily "Em" Hansen (see p. 161)
          1994 Tensleep
          1995 A Fall in Denver
          1997 Mother Nature

A: **Andrews, Val**
    SC: Sherlock Holmes
          1991 Sherlock Holmes and the Brighton Pavilion
               Mystery
          1991 Sherlock Holmes and the Eminent Thespian
          1995 Sherlock Holmes and the Egyptian Hall Adventure
          1995 Sherlock Holmes and the Houdini Birthright
          1997 Sherlock Holmes and the Greyfriars School
               Mystery
          1997 Sherlock Holmes and the Man Who Lost Himself

P: **Anthony, Elizabeth**
    please see: **Traynor, Page w/ Anthony Traynor**

P: **Anthony, Evelyn**
    please see: **Ward-Thomas, Evelyn Bridget Patricia Stephens**

P: **Antill, Elizabeth**
    please see: **Middleton, Elizabeth**

P: **Aresbys, The**
    please see: **Bamberger, Helen w/ Raymond Bamberger**

P: **Arliss, Joen**
    please see: **Martin, Ian**

A: **Armitage, Audrey w/ Muriel Watkins**
  P: **McCall, K. T.**
    SC: Johnny Buchanan
          1957 Dance with Me Deadly

1957 Deadly But Delectable
1957 Fatally Female
1957 Killer Orchid
1957 Killers in Chorus
1957 The Lady's a Decoy
1957 A Redhead for Free
1957 Shroud for Her Shame
1957 Sweet But Deadly
1957 Sweet But Sinful
1957 Velvet Vixen
1957 Tornado in Town
1957 M'amselle It's Murder
1958 Angel Hold Fire!
1958 Babe up in Arms
1958 Black Lace Blackmail
1958 Caviar to Kill
1958 Dame on the Make
1958 Million Dollar Mayhem
1958 Playgirl for Keeps
1958 Stripper Strikes Out
1958 M-MM-Minx

A: **Armstrong, Charlotte**
SC: MacDougal Duff
1942 Lay On, MacDuff!
1943 The Case of the Weird Sisters
1945 The Innocent Flower
APA: Death Filled the Glass

P: **Arnold, Margot**
please see: **Cook, Petronelle Marguerite Mary**

A: **Ashbrook, H(arriette) C(ora)**
SC: Philip "Spike" Tracy
1930 The Murder of Cecily Thane
1931 The Murder of Steven Kester
1933 The Murder of Sigurd Sharon
1935 A Most Immoral Murder
1937 Murder Makes Murder
1940 Murder Comes Back
1941 The Purple Onion Mystery
APA: Murder on Friday

P: **Shane, Susannah**
SC: Christopher Saxe
1942 Lady in Danger
1943 Lady in a Million

1944 The Baby in the Ash Can
1946 Diamonds in the Dumplings
P: **Ashe, Mary Ann**
please see: **Brand (Lewis), (Mary) Christianna (Milne)**
A: **Ashton, Winifred w/ Helen (DeGuerry) Simpson**
P: **Dane, Clemence & Helen Simpson**
SC: Sir John Saumarez
1928 Enter Sir John
1930 Printer's Devil
APA: Author Unknown
1932 Re-Enter Sir John
A: **Atherton, Nancy**
SC: Lori Shepherd
1992 Aunt Dimity's Death
1994 Aunt Dimity and the Duke
1996 Aunt Dimity's Good Deed
A: **Atkins, Meg (Margaret Elizabeth)**
SC: Insp. Henry Beaumont
1975 By the North Door
1976 Samain
1981 Palimpsest
1988 Tangle
A: **Auspitz, Kate**
P: **Belfort, Sophie**
SC: Nick Hannibal & Molly Rafferty
1991 The Marvell College Murders
1992 Eyewitness to Murder
A: **Austin, Anne**
SC: James F. "Bonnie" Dundee
1930 Murder Backstairs
1930 The Avenging Parrot
1931 Murder at Bridge
1932 One Drop of Blood
1939 Murdered But Not Dead
A: **Ayres, Noreen**
SC: Smokey Brandon
1992 A World the Color of Salt
1994 Carcass Trade
1996 The Long Slow Whistle of the Moon
A: **Azolakov, Antoinette**
SC: T. D. Renfro
1989 The Contractees Die Young
1992 Blood Lavender

B

A: **Babbin, Jacqueline**
    SC: Clovis Kelly
            1972 Prime Time Corpse
                    APA: Bloody Special
            1989 Bloody Soaps
P: **Babson, Marian**
    please see: **Stenstreem, Ruth**
A: **Backhouse, (Enid) Elizabeth**
    SC: Insp. Christopher Marsden
            1957 Death Came Uninvited
            1961 The Night Has Eyes
    SC: Insp. Prentis
            1960 The Web of Shadows
            1963 Death Climbs a Hill
A: **Backus, Jean Louise**
    P: **Montross, David**
    SC: Remsen
            1962 Traitor's Wife
            1963 Troika
                    APA: Who Is Elissa Sheldon?
            1965 Fellow-Traveler
A: **Bacon, Gail w/ Mary Monica Pulver (Kuhfeld)**
    P: **Frazer, Margaret**
    SC: Sister Frevisse (see p. 93)
            1992 The Novice's Tale
            1993 The Servant's Tale
            1994 The Outlaw's Tale
            1994 The Bishop's Tale
            1995 The Boy's Tale
            1996 The Murderer's Tale
            1997 The Prioress' Tale
P: **Bailey, Hilea**
    please see: **Marting, Ruth Lenore**
A: **Bailey, Jo**
    SC: Jan Gallagher
            1991 Bagged
            1993 Recycled
            1996 Erased
A: **Bailey, Michele**
    SC: Matilda Haycastle
            1994 Dreadful Lies
            1995 The Cuckoo Case

J: **Bain, Donald**
please see: **Fletcher, Jessica & Donald Bain**
A: **Baker, Marc(eil Genee Kolstad)**
P: **Blair, Marcia**
SC: Tory Baxter
1978 The Final Lie
1978 The Final Pose
1978 The Final Ring
1979 The Final Appointment
1979 The Final Fair
1979 The Final Guest
1979 The Final Target
1980 Finale
A: **Baker, Nikki**
SC: Virginia Kelly
1991 In the Game
1992 The Lavender House Murder
1993 Long Goodbyes
1996 The Ultimate Exit Strategy
A: **Balfour, Eva w/ Beryl Hearnden**
P: **Balfour, Hearnden**
SC: Insp. Jack Strickland
1927 The Paper Chase
APA: A Gentleman from Texas
1928 The Enterprising Burglar
1931 Anything Might Happen
APA: Murder and the Red-Haired Girl
P: **Balfour, Hearnden**
please see: **Balfour, Eva w/ Beryl Hearnden**
A: **Ball, Doris Bell (Collier)**
P: **Bell, Josephine**
SC: Amy Tupper
1979 Wolf! Wolf!
1980 A Question of Inheritance
SC: Claude Warrington-Reeve
1959 Easy Prey
1960 A Well-Known Face
1963 A Flat Tyre in Fulham
APA: Fiasco in Fulham
APA: Room for a Body
SC: Dr. David Wintringham
1937 Death on the Borough Council
1937 Murder in Hospital
1938 Fall over Cliff

1939 Death at Half-Term
      APA: Curtain Call for a Corpse
1939 From Natural Causes
1940 All Is Vanity
1944 Death at the Medical Board
1949 Death in Clairvoyance
1950 The Summer School Mystery
1953 Bones in the Barrow
1954 Fires at Fairlawn
1956 The China Roundabout
      APA: Murder on the Merry-Go-Round
1958 The Seeing Eye

SC: Dr. Henry Frost
1964 The Upfold Witch
1966 Death on the Reserve

SC: Insp. Steven Mitchell
1937 Death on the Borough Council
1937 Murder in Hospital
1938 Fall over Cliff
1938 The Port of London Murders
1939 Death at Half-Term
      APA: Curtain Call for a Corpse
1949 Death in Clairvoyance
1950 The Summer School Mystery
1953 Bones in the Barrow
1956 The China Roundabout
      APA: Murder on the Merry-Go-Round
1958 The Seeing Eye
1959 Easy Prey
1960 A Well-Known Face
1963 A Flat Tyre in Fulham
      APA: Fiasco in Fulham
      APA: Room for a Body
1964 The Upfold Witch

A: **Ball, (Nanoni) Patricia (Maude Hamilton)**
P: **Hamilton, Nan**
    SC: Isamu "Sam Irish" Ohara
        1984 Killer's Rights
        1986 The Shape of Fear

A: **Bamberger, Helen w/ Raymond Bamberger**
P: **Aresbys, The**
    SC: Parrish Darby
        1927 Who Killed Coralie?
        1929 The Mark of the Dead

J: **Bamberger, Raymond**
    please see: **Bamberger, Helen w/ Raymond Bamberger**
A: **Bamburg, Lilian**
    SC: Septimus March
        1926 Beads of Silence
        1927 Rays of Darkness
A: **Banks, Carolyn**
    SC: Jeet & Robin Vaughan
        1993 Death by Dressage
        1995 Groomed for Death
        1995 Murder Well-Bred
        1996 Death on the Diagonal
        1996 A Horse to Die For
A: **Bannister, Jo**
    SC: Dr. Clio Rees Marsh & Harry Marsh
        1984 Striving with Gods
        1989 Gilgamesh
        1990 The Going Down of the Sun
    SC: Insp. Liz Graham, Sgt. Cal Donovan & Supt. Frank Shapiro
        1993 A Bleeding of Innocents
        1994 Charisma
            APA: Sins of the Heart
        1995 A Taste for Burning
            APA: Burning Desires
        1996 No Birds Sing
A: **Barber, Willetta Ann w/ R(udolph) F(rederick) Schabelitz**
    SC: Christopher Storm
        1940 Murder Draws a Line
        1941 Pencil Points to Murder
        1942 Drawn Conclusion
        1942 Murder Enters the Picture
        1945 The Noose Is Drawn
        1947 Drawback to Murder
        1949 The Deed Is Drawn
P: **Barbette, Jay**
    please see: **Spicer, Betty Coe w/ Bart Spicer**
J: **Barclay, Armiger**
    please see: **Barclay, Marguerite w/ Armiger Barclay**
A: **Barclay, Marguerite w/ Armiger Barclay**
    SC: Lavie Jutt
        SS 1911 The Activities of Lavie Jutt
A: **Barker, Elsa**
    SC: Dexter Drake
        1928 The Cobra Candlestick

SS   1929 The C.I.D. of Dexter Drake
      1930 The Redman Cave Murder
P: **Barling, Charles**
    please see: **Barling, Muriel Vere M.**
A: **Barling, Muriel Vere M.**
    P: **Barling, Charles**
        SC: Insp. Henderson
                1968 Accessory to Murder
                1968 Death of a Shrew
    P: **Barrington, Pamela**
        SC: Insp. George Marshall
                1951 The Rest Is Silence
                1953 Account Rendered
                1959 Night of Violence
                1960 By Some Person Unknown
                1963 Afternoon of Violence
                1963 Motive for Murder
                1964 Appointment with Death
                1965 Time to Kill
                1966 Cage Without Bars
                1967 A Game of Murder
                1967 Confession of Murder
                1967 Slow Poison
        SC: Insp. George Travers
                1952 The Mortimer Story
                1953 Among Those Present
                1961 The Gentle Killer
A: **Barnes, Linda (Appelblatt)**
    SC: Carlotta Carlyle (see p. 227)
                1987 A Trouble of Fools
                1989 The Snake Tattoo
                1990 Coyote
                1991 Steel Guitar
                1993 Snapshot
                1995 Hardware
                1997 Cold Case
    SC: Michael Spraggue
                1982 Blood Will Have Blood
                1983 Bitter Finish
                1984 Dead Heat
                1986 Cities of the Dead
A: **Barnett, Glyn**
    SC: Insp. Gramport
                1935 The Call-Box Murder

```
              1936  Murder on Monday
              1937  I Know Mrs. Lang
              1946  Find the Lady
A:  Barr, Nevada
       SC:  Anna Pigeon (see p. 261)
              1993  Track of the Cat
              1994  A Superior Death
              1995  Ill Wind
              1996  Firestorm
              1997  Endangered Species
P:  Barrington, Pamela
       please see:  Barling, Muriel Vere M.
P:  Barron, Stephanie
       please see:  Mathews, Francine
A:  Baskerville, Beatrice w/ Elliot Monk
       SC:  Briconi
              1922  By Whose Hand?
              1931  The St. Cloud Affair
A:  Bayne, Isabella
       SC:  Benedict Breeze
              1952  Death and Benedict
              1956  Cruel as the Grave
P:  Beaton, M. C.
       please see:  Chesney, Marion
P:  Beck, K. K.
       please see:  Marris, Kathrine
A:  Bedford, Jean
       SC:  Anna Southwood
              1990  To Make a Killing
              1992  Worse Than Death
              1993  Signs of Murder
P:  Beecham, Rose
       please see:  Fulton, Jennifer
P:  Belfort, Sophie
       please see:  Auspitz, Kate
P:  Bell, Josephine
       please see:  Ball, Doris Bell (Collier)
A:  Bell, Nancy
       SC:  Biggie Weatherford
              1996  Biggie and the Poisoned Politician
              1997  Biggie and the Mangled Mortician
              1998  Biggie and the Fricasseed Fat Man
A:  Benke, Patricia D.
       SC:  Judith Thornton
              1995  Guilty by Choice
```

1945 The Birthday Murder
1952 The Passionate Victims

A: **Beynon-Harris, Vivian**
    SC: Richard Hanard
        1948 Confusion at Campden Trig
        1948 Trouble at Hanard

A: **Bidwell, Margaret**
    SC: Mr. Hodson
        1939 Death on the Agenda
        1940 Death and His Brother

A: **Birmingham, Maisie**
    SC: Kate Weatherley
        1974 You Can't Help Me
        1976 The Heat of the Sun

P: **Bishop, Claudia**
    please see: **Stanton, Mary**

A: **Black, E(lizabeth) Best**
    SC: Peter Strangely
        1933 The Ravenelle Riddle
        1934 The Crime of the Chromium Bowl

P: **Black, Veronica**
    please see: **Peters, Maureen**

A: **Blackmon, Anita**
    SC: Adelaide Adams
        1937 Murder à la Richelieu
           APA: The Hotel Richelieu Murders
        1938 There Is No Return
           APA: The Riddle of the Dead Cats

P: **Blackmur, L. L.**
    please see: **Long, Lydia**

A: **Blair, Dorothy w/ Evelyn Page**
    P: **Scarlett, Roger**
    SC: Insp. Kane
        1930 The Back Bay Murders
        1930 The Beacon Hill Murders
        1931 Cat's Paw
        1932 Murder Among the Angells
        1933 In the First Degree

P: **Blair, Marcia**
    please see: **Baker, Marc(eil Genee Kolstad)**

P: **Blake, Christina**
    please see: **Halpin, Mary D.**

A: **Blanc, Suzanne**
    SC: Insp. Menendez
        1961 The Green Stone

        1964 The Yellow Villa
        1967 The Rose Window

A: **Bland, Eleanor Taylor**
    SC: Det. Marti MacAlister (see p. 82)
        1992 Dead Time
        1993 Slow Burn
        1994 Gone Quiet
        1995 Done Wrong
        1996 Keep Still

P: **Bliss, Adam**
    please see: **Burkhardt, Eve w/ Robert Ferdinand Burkhardt**

A: **Blizard, Marie**
    SC: Eve MacWilliams
        1946 The Late Lamented Lady
        1947 The Men in Her Death

A: **Block, Barbara**
    SC: Robin Light
        1994 Chutes and Adders
        1995 Twister
        1996 In Plain Sight
        1997 The Scent of Murder

A: **Bodington, Nancy Hermione Courlander**
  P: **Smith, Shelley**
    SC: Jacob Chaos
        1942 Background for Murder
        1947 He Died of Murder!

A: **Boehnhardt, Patricia**
  P: **Hart, Ellen**
    SC: Jane Lawless & Cordelia Thorn
        1989 Hallowed Murder
        1991 Vital Lies
        1993 A Killing Cure
        1993 Stage Fright
        1994 A Small Sacrifice
        1995 Faint Praise
        1996 Robber's Wine
    SC: Sophie Greenway
        1994 This Little Piggy Went to Murder
        1995 For Every Evil
        1997 The Oldest Sin

A: **Bolitho, Janie**
    SC: Det. Chf. Insp. Ian Roper
        1993 Kindness Can Kill

         1994 Ripe for Revenge
         1997 An Absence of Angels

P: **Bond, Evelyn**
     please see: **Hershman, Morris**

P: **Bonett, John & Emery**
     please see: **Coulson, Felicity Winifred Carter w/ John H. A.**
         Coulson

A: **Boniface, Marjorie**
     SC: Sheriff Hiram Odom
         1940 Murder as an Ornament
         1942 Venom in Eden
         1946 Wings of Death

P: **Bonnamy, Francis**
     please see: **Walz, Audrey Boyers**

A: **Bonner, Geraldine**
     SC: Molly Morgenthau
         1915 The Girl at Central
         1916 The Black Eagle Mystery
         1919 Miss Maitland, Private Secretary

A: **Borthwick (Creighton), J(ean) S(cott)**
     SC: Sarah Deane & Dr. Alex McKenzie
         1982 The Case of the Hook-Billed Kites
         1985 The Down East Murders
         1986 The Student Body
         1990 Bodies of Water
         1991 Dude on Arrival
         1994 The Bridled Groom
         1995 Dolly Is Dead
         1997 The Garden Plot

P: **Borton, D. B.**
     please see: **Carpenter, Lynnette**

A: **Bowden, Jean**
     P: **Curry, Avon**
        SC: Jerome Aylwin
           1960 Derry Down Death
           1961 Dying High

A: **Bowen, Gail**
     SC: Joanne Kilbourn
         1990 Deadly Appearances
         1991 Murder at the Mendel
              APA: Love and Murder
         1992 The Wandering Soul Murders
         1994 A Colder Kind of Death
         1997 A Killing Spring

P: **Bowen, Marjorie**
   please see: **Long, Gabrielle Margaret Vere Campbell**
A: **Bowen-Judd, Sara Hutton**
  P: **Burton, Anne**
    SC: Richard Trenton
          1980 The Dear Departed
          1980 Where There's a Will
          1981 Worse Than a Crime
  P: **Challis, Mary**
    SC: Jeremy Locke
          1980 Burden of Proof
          1980 Crimes Past
          1981 A Very Good Hater
          1981 The Ghost of an Idea
  P: **Leek, Margaret**
    SC: Stephen Marryat
          1980 The Healthy Grave
          1980 We Must Have a Trial
          1981 Voice of the Past
  P: **Woods, Sara**
    SC: Antony Maitland (see p. 165)
          1962 Bloody Instructions
          1962 Malice Domestic
          1963 Error of the Moon
          1963 The Taste of Fears
              APA: The Third Encounter
          1964 This Little Measure
          1964 Trusted Like the Fox
          1965 The Windy Side of the Law
          1965 Though I Know She Lies
          1966 Enter Certain Murderers
          1966 Let's Choose Executors
          1967 And Shame the Devil
          1967 The Case Is Altered
          1968 Knives Have Edges
          1968 Past Praying For
          1969 Tarry and Be Hanged
          1970 An Improbable Fiction
          1971 Serpent's Tooth
          1971 The Knavish Crows
          1972 They Love Not Poison
          1973 Enter the Corpse
          1973 Yet She Must Die
          1974 Done to Death

1975 A Show of Violence
1976 My Life Is Done
1977 A Thief or Two
1977 The Law's Delay
1978 Exit Murderer
1979 Proceed to Judgement
1979 This Fatal Writ
1980 They Stay for Death
1980 Weep for Her
1981 Cry Guilty
1981 Dearest Enemy
1982 Enter a Gentlewoman
1982 Most Grievous Murder
1982 Villains by Necessity
1983 Call Back Yesterday
1983 The Lie Direct
1983 Where Should He Die?
1984 Defy the Devil
1984 Murder's Out of Tune
1984 The Bloody Book of Law
1985 An Obscure Grave
1985 Away with Them to Prison
1985 Put Out the Light
1986 Most Deadly Hate
1986 Nor Live So Long
1987 Naked Villainy

A: **Bowers, Dorothy (Violet)**
    SC: Insp. Dan Pardoe
        1938 Postscript to Poison
        1939 Shadows Before
        1940 A Deed Without a Name
        1941 Fear for Miss Betony
             APA: Fear and Miss Betony

A: **Bowers, Elisabeth**
    SC: Meg Lacey
        1988 Ladies' Night
        1991 No Forwarding Address

A: **Boyd, Eunice Mays**
    SC: F. Millard Smyth
        1943 Murder Breaks Trail
        1944 Doom in the Midnight Sun
        1945 Murder Wears Mukluks

A: **Boylan, Eleanor**
    SC: Clara Gamadge (see p. 269)
        1989 Working Murder

```
                    1990  Murder Observed
                    1992  Murder Machree
                    1993  Pushing Murder
                    1996  Murder Crossed
A:  Braddon, M(ary) E(lizabeth)
      SC:  John Faunce
                    1898  Rough Justice
                    1899  His Darling Sin
      SC:  Valentine Hawkehurst
                    1867  Birds of Prey
                    1868  Charlotte's Inheritance
P:  Brahms, Caryl & S. J. Simon
      please see: Abrahams, Doris Caroline w/ Simon Jasha Skidelsky
A:  Bramhall, Marion
      SC:  Kit Marsden Acton
                    1944  Button, Button
                    1944  Murder Solves a Problem
                    1945  Tragedy in Blue
                    1948  Murder Is an Evil Business
                    1949  Murder Is Contagious
A:  Branch, Pamela (Jean)
      SC:  Clifford Flush
                    1951  The Wooden Overcoat
                    1954  Murder Every Monday
A:  Brand (Lewis), (Mary) Christianna (Milne)
      SC:  Insp. Charlesworth
                    1941  Death in High Heels
                    1948  Death of Jezebel
                    1952  London Particular
                          APA:  Fog of Doubt
                    1979  The Rose in Darkness
      SC:  Insp. Cockrill
                    1941  Heads You Lose
                    1944  Green for Danger
                    1946  The Crooked Wreath
                          APA:  Suddenly at His Residence
                    1948  Death of Jezebel
                    1952  London Particular
                          APA:  Fog of Doubt
                    1955  Tour de Force
                    1957  The Three-Cornered Halo
               SS   1968  What Dread Hand?
               SS   1983  Buffet for Unwelcome Guests
```

P: **Ashe, Mary Ann**
  SC: Insp. Chucky
      1950 Cat and Mouse
      1977 A Ring of Roses
A: **Brandes, Rhoda**
  P: **Ramsay, Diana**
    SC: Lt. Meredith
       1972 A Little Murder Music
       1973 Deadly Discretion
       1974 No Cause to Kill
A: **Brandon, Ruth**
  SC: Andrew Taggart
      1991 Mind Out
      1992 The Gorgon's Smile
J: **Brandt, Nat**
  please see: **Brandt, Yanna w/ Nat Brandt**
A: **Brandt, Yanna w/ Nat Brandt**
  SC: Mitch & Valerie Stevens
      1991 Land Kills
      1993 A Death in Bulloch Parrish
A: **Braun, Lilian Jackson**
  SC: Jim Qwilleran (see p. 181)
      1966 The Cat Who Could Read Backwards
      1967 The Cat Who Ate Danish Modern
      1968 The Cat Who Turned On and Off
      1986 The Cat Who Saw Red
      1987 The Cat Who Played Brahms
      1987 The Cat Who Played Post Office
    SS 1988 The Cat Who Had Fourteen Tales
      1988 The Cat Who Knew Shakespeare
      1988 The Cat Who Sniffed Glue
      1989 The Cat Who Went Underground
      1990 The Cat Who Lived High
      1990 The Cat Who Talked to Ghosts
      1991 The Cat Who Knew a Cardinal
      1992 The Cat Who Moved a Mountain
      1992 The Cat Who Wasn't There
      1993 The Cat Who Went into the Closet
      1994 The Cat Who Came to Breakfast
      1995 The Cat Who Blew the Whistle
      1996 The Cat Who Said Cheese
      1997 The Cat Who Tailed a Thief

A: **Brawner, Helen w/ Francis Van Wyck Mason**
P: **Coffin, Geoffrey**
    SC: Insp. Scott Stuart
            1935 Murder in the Senate
            1936 The Forgotten Fleet Mystery
A: **Bream, Freda**
    SC: Rev. Jabal Jarrett
            1982 Island of Fear
            1983 The Vicar Done It
            1983 The Vicar Investigates
            1984 Sealed and Despatched
            1985 The Corpse on the Cruise
            1985 With Murder in Mind
A: **Brennan, Carol**
    SC: Emily Silver
            1994 In the Dark
            1995 Chill of Summer
    SC: Liz Wareham
            1991 Headhunt
            1993 Full Commission
P: **Bridge, Ann**
    please see: **O'Malley, Lady Mary Dolling Saunders**
A: **Brightwell, Emily**
    SC: Insp. Witherspoon & Mrs. Jeffries
            1993 Mrs. Jeffries Dusts for Clues
            1993 The Ghost and Mrs. Jeffries
            1993 The Inspector and Mrs. Jeffries
            1994 Mrs. Jeffries Takes Stock
            1994 Mrs. Jeffries on the Ball
            1995 Mrs. Jeffries on the Trail
            1995 Mrs. Jeffries Plays the Cook
            1996 Mrs. Jeffries and the Missing Alibi
            1996 Mrs. Jeffries Stands Corrected
            1997 Mrs. Jeffries Takes the Stage
A: **Brill, Toni**
    SC: Midge Cohen
            1991 Date with a Dead Doctor
            1993 Date with a Plummeting Publisher
A: **Bristow, Gwen w/ Bruce Manning**
    SC: Wade
            1931 The Gutenberg Murders
            1932 The Mardi Gras Murders
A: **Brochet, Jean Alexandre**
P: **Bruce, Jean**
    SC: Hubert Bonisseur de la Bath
            1963 Deep Freeze

    1964 Double Take
    1964 Short Wave
    1965 Flash Point
    1965 Live Wire
         APA: The Last Quarter Hour
    1965 Photo Finish
    1965 Pole Reaction
    1965 Shock Tactics
    1965 Soft Sell
    1967 Cold Spell
    1967 Dead Silence
    1967 High Treason
    1967 Hot Line
         APA: Trouble in Tokyo
    1967 Top Secret
    1968 Strip Tease

A: **Brod, D(eborah) C(obban)**
  SC: Quint McCauley
    1989 Murder in Store
    1990 Error in Judgment
    1991 Masquerade in Blue
         APA: Framed in Blue
    1993 Brothers in Blood

A: **Brooks, Janice Young**
  P: **Churchill, Jill**
  SC: Jane Jeffry (see p. 291)
    1989 Grime and Punishment
    1990 A Farewell to Yarns
    1993 A Quiche Before Dying
    1994 The Class Menagerie
    1994 A Knife to Remember
    1995 From Here to Paternity
    1996 Silence of the Hams
    1996 War and Peas

A: **Brooks, Vivian Collin**
  P: **Mills, Osmington**
  SC: Insp. Baker
    1955 Unlucky Break
    1956 The Case of the Flying Fifteen
    1957 No Match for the Law
    1958 The Misguided Missile
    1959 Stairway to Murder
    1961 Trail by Ordeal
    1964 Traitor Betrayed

1965 At One Fell Swoop

1966 Enemies of the Bride

SC: Pol. Const. Patrick Shirley & Insp. Rupert "Rip" Irving

1965 Dusty Death

1966 Enemies of the Bride

1967 Death Enters the Lists

1969 Many a Slip

A: **Brown, Morna Doris (MacTaggart)**

P: **Ferrars, E. X.**

SC: Andrew Basnett

1983 Something Wicked

1984 Root of All Evil

1985 The Crime and the Crystal

1987 The Other Devil's Name

1989 A Murder Too Many

1991 Smoke Without Fire

1994 A Hobby of Murder

1995 A Choice of Evils

SC: Supt. Ditteridge

1971 A Stranger and Afraid

1972 Foot in the Grave

1973 Alive and Dead

1976 Blood Flies Upward

SC: Pol. Chf. Rapaso

1969 Skeleton Staff

1972 Birth of Suspicion

1979 Witness Before the Fact

1984 Root of All Evil

SC: Toby Dyke

1940 Give a Corpse a Bad Name

1940 Remove the Bodies

APA: Rehearsals for Murder

1941 Death in Botanist's Bay

APA: Murder of a Suicide

1942 Don't Monkey with Murder

APA: The Shape of a Stain

1942 Your Neck in a Noose

APA: Neck in a Noose

SC: Virginia Freer

1978 Last Will and Testament

1980 Frog in the Throat

1981 Thinner Than Water

1983 Death of a Minor Character

1986 I Met Murder

1990 Woman Slaughter
1991 Sleep of the Unjust
1993 Beware of the Dog

A: **Brown, Rita Mae w/ Sneaky Pie Brown**
  SC: Mary Minor "Harry" Haristeen (see p. 255)
    1990 Wish You Were Here
    1992 Rest in Pieces
    1994 Murder at Monticello
    1995 Pay Dirt
    1996 Murder, She Meowed

J: **Brown, Sneaky Pie**
  please see: **Brown, Rita Mae w/ Sneaky Pie Brown**

A: **Brown, Susan w/ Anne Stephenson**
  SC: Amber Mitchell & Liz Elliott
    1987 The Mad Hacker
    1992 Something's Fishy at Ash Lake

A: **Brown, Zenith Jones**
  P: **Ford, Leslie**
  SC: Grace Latham & Col. John Primrose (see p. 251)
    1937 Ill Met by Moonlight
    1937 The Simple Way of Poison
    1938 Three Bright Pebbles
    1939 False to Any Man
        APA: Snow-White Murder
    1939 Reno Rendezvous
        APA: Mr. Cromwell Is Dead
    1940 Old Lover's Ghost
        APA: A Capital Crime
    1941 The Murder of a Fifth Columnist
    1942 Murder in the O.P.M.
        APA: The Priority Murder
    1943 Siren in the Night
    1944 All for the Love of a Lady
        APA: Crack of Dawn
    1945 The Philadelphia Murder Story
    1946 Honolulu Story
        APA: Honolulu Murder Story
        APA: Honolulu Murders
    1947 The Woman in Black
    1948 The Devil's Stronghold
    1953 Washington Whispers Murder
        APA: The Lying Jade
  SC: Col. John Primrose (see p. 251)
    1934 The Strangled Witness

SC: Lt. Joseph Kelly
        1932 Murder in Maryland
        1933 The Clue of the Judas Tree

P: **Frome, David**
SC: Evan Pinkerton (see p. 265)
        1930 The Hammersmith Murders
        1931 Two Against Scotland Yard
             APA: The By-Pass Murder
        1932 The Man from Scotland Yard
             APA: Mr. Simpson Finds a Body
        1933 The Eel Pie Murders
             APA: The Eel Pie Mystery
        1934 Mr. Pinkerton Finds a Body
             APA: The Body in the Turl
        1934 Mr. Pinkerton Goes to Scotland Yard
             APA: Arsenic in Richmond
        1935 Mr. Pinkerton Grows a Beard
             APA: The Body in Bedford Square
        1936 Mr. Pinkerton Has the Clue
SS   1936 Mr. Pinkerton Is Present
        1937 The Black Envelope: Mr. Pinkerton Again
             APA: The Guilt Is Plain
        1939 Mr. Pinkerton at the Old Angel
             APA: Mr. Pinkerton and the Old Angel
        1939 Mr. Pinkerton: Passage for One
SS   1940 Mr. Pinkerton Lends a Hand
        1950 Homicide House: Mr. Pinkerton Returns
             APA: Murder on the Square
SC: Major Gregory Lewis
        1929 The Murder of an Old Man
        1931 The Strange Death of Martin Green
             APA: The Murder on the Sixth Hole

P: **Browne, Lizbie**
please see: **Marriott, Mary**

P: **Bruce, Jean**
please see: **Brochet, Jean Alexandre**

A: **Bruyer, Kris**
SC: Ashley & Emily
        1995 Whispers
        1996 Out of the Night

A: **Bryce, Mrs. Charles**
SC: Mr. Gimblet
        1914 Mrs. Vanderstein's Jewels
        1915 The Ashiel Mystery

A: **Buchanan, Betty Joan**
   P: **Shepherd, Joan**
      SC: Insp. Jolivet
            1953 The Girl on the Left Bank
            1956 Tender Is the Knife

A: **Buchanan, Edna**
      SC: Britt Montero (see p. 191)
            1992 Contents Under Pressure
            1994 Miami, It's Murder
            1995 Suitable for Framing
            1996 Act of Betrayal
            1997 Margin of Error

A: **Buchanan, Eileen-Marie Duell**
   P: **Curzon, Clare**
      SC: Supt. Mike Yeadings & Sgt. Angus Mott
            1983 I Give You Five Days
            1984 Masks and Faces
            1985 The Trojan Hearse
            1986 The Quest for K
            1988 Three-Core Lead
            1990 The Blue-Eyed Boy
            1992 Cat's Cradle
            1993 First Wife, Twice Removed
            1993 Nice People
            1994 Death Prone
            1996 Past Mischief
            1997 Close Quarters

   P: **Petrie, Rhona**
      SC: Dr. Nassim Pride
            1967 Foreign Bodies
            1969 Despatch of a Dove
      SC: Insp. Marcus MacLurg
            1963 Death in Deakins Wood
            1964 Murder by Precedent
            1965 Running Deep
            1966 Dead Loss
            1968 MacLurg Goes West

A: **Buckholtz, Eileen w/ Ruth Glick**
   P: **York, Rebecca**
      SC: Peregrine Connection
            1986 Flight of the Raven
            1986 In Search of the Dove
            1986 Talons of the Falcon

A: **Buckstaff, Kathryn**
SC: Morgana Dalton
1993 Branson and Beyond
1994 No One Dies in Branson

A: **Budlong, Ware Torrey**
P: **Crosby, Lee**
SC: Eric Hazard
1938 Terror by Night
1941 Too Many Doors
APA: Doors to Death

A: **Burbridge, Edith Joan**
P: **Cockin, Joan**
SC: Insp. Cam
1947 Curiosity Killed the Cat
1949 Villainy at Vespers
1952 Deadly Ernest

A: **Burden, Pat**
SC: ex–Det. Chf. Supt. Henry Bassett
1989 Screaming Bones
1990 Wreath of Honesty
1992 Bury Him Kindly
1993 Father, Forgive Me

A: **Burger, Rosaylmer**
P: **Wallace, C. H.**
SC: Steve Ramsay
1965 Crashlanding in the Congo
1966 Highflight to Hell
1966 Tailwind to Danger
1967 E.T.A. for Death

A: **Burger, Rosaylmer w/ Julia Perceval**
P: **Paull, Jessyca**
SC: Tracy Larrimore & Mike Thompson
1968 Destination: Terror
1968 Passport to Danger
1969 Rendezvous with Death

A: **Burgess, Ellen**
SC: Letitia Hawkins
SS 1933 Miss Hawkins: The Ocean Boarder

A: **Burke, Jan**
SC: Irene Kelly (see p. 196)
1993 Goodnight, Irene
1994 Sweet Dreams, Irene
1995 Dear Irene,

1996 Remember Me, Irene
1997 Hocus
A: **Burkhardt, Eve w/ Robert Ferdinand Burkhardt**
   P: **Bliss, Adam**
      SC: Alice Penny
1931 The Campden Ruby Murder
1935 Murder Upstairs
J: **Burkhardt, Robert Ferdinand**
   please see: **Burkhardt, Eve w/ Robert Ferdinand Burkhardt**
P: **Burnes, Caroline**
   please see: **Haines, Carolyn**
A: **Burnham, Helen**
   SC: One Week Wimble
1931 The Murder of Lalla Lee
1932 The Telltale Telegram
A: **Burrows, Julie**
   SC: Supt. Bowman
1970 No Need for Violence
1973 Like an Evening Gone
P: **Burton, Anne**
   please see: **Bowen-Judd, Sara Hutton**
A: **Burton, Sarah w/ Judith Holland**
   P: **Wakefield, Hannah**
      SC: Dee Street
1987 The Price You Pay
1990 A February Mourning
        APA: A Woman's Own Mystery
A: **Bushell, Agnes**
   SC: Wilson & Wilder
1989 Shadowdance
1993 Death by Crystal
A: **Butler, Gwendoline**
   SC: Insp. John Coffin
1956 Receipt for Murder
1957 Dead in a Row
1958 The Dull Dead
1958 The Murdering Kind
1960 Death Lives Next Door
        APA: Dine and Be Dead
1961 Make Me a Murderer
1962 Coffin in Oxford
1963 Coffin for Baby
1963 Coffin Waiting
1964 Coffin in Malta

1966 A Nameless Coffin
1968 Coffin Following
1969 Coffin's Dark Number
1970 A Coffin from the Past
1973 A Coffin for Pandora
      APA: Sarsen Place
1974 A Coffin for the Canary
      APA: Olivia
1986 Coffin on the Water
1987 Coffin in Fashion
1988 Coffin Underground
1989 Coffin in the Black Museum
      APA: Coffin in the Museum of Crime
1990 Coffin and the Paper Man
1992 Coffin on Murder Street
1993 Cracking Open a Coffin
1994 A Coffin for Charley
1995 The Coffin Tree
1995 A Dark Coffin

SC: Insp. William Winter
1956 Receipt for Murder
1957 Dead in a Row
1958 The Dull Dead
1958 The Murdering Kind

P: **Melville, Jennie**
SC: Charmian Daniels (see p. 71)
1962 Come Home and Be Killed
1963 Burning Is a Substitute for Loving
1964 Murderers' Houses
1965 There Lies Your Love
1966 Nell Alone
1967 A Different Kind of Summer
1970 A New Kind of Killer, an Old Kind of Death
      APA: A New Kind of Killer
1981 Murder Has a Pretty Face
1987 Death in the Garden
      APA: Murder in the Garden
1988 Windsor Red
1989 A Cure for Dying
1990 Footsteps in the Blood
      APA: Making Good Blood
1990 Witching Murder
1992 Dead Set
1993 Whoever Has the Heart

    1995 Death in the Family
          APA: Baby Drop
    1995 The Morbid Kitchen
    1996 The Woman Who Was Not There
A: **Butler, Leslie**
    SC: Horton & Jordan
          1964 Night and the Judgment
          1965 Recover or Kill
          1966 The Man Who Crawled Away
A: **Butterworth, Michael**
    P: **Kemp, Sarah**
        SC: Dr. Tina May
              1984 No Escape
              1986 The Lure of Sweet Death
              1987 What Dread Hand
A: **Byfield, Barbara Ninde**
    SC: Father Simon Bede & Helen Bullock (see p. 208)
          1976 Forever Wilt Thou Die
          1977 A Harder Thing Than Triumph
          1979 A Parcel of Their Fortunes
A: **Byfield, Barbara Ninde w/ Frank L. Tedeschi**
    SC: Father Simon Bede & Helen Bullock (see p. 208)
          1975 Solemn High Murder

C

A: **Cail, Carol**
    SC: Maxey Burnell
          1993 Private Lies
          1995 Unsafe Keeping
          1997 If Two of Them are Dead
A: **Callahan, Sheila MacGill**
    SC: Brian Donodio
          1993 Death in a Far Country
          1994 Forty Whacks
A: **Calloway, Kate**
    SC: Cassidy James
          1996 1st Impressions
          1997 2nd Fiddle
A: **Cameron, Evelyn**
    SC: Sheriff Jack Thompson
          1939 Dead Man's Shoes
          1940 Malice Domestic

A: **Campbell, Alice (Ormond)**
    SC: Insp. Headcorn
          1937 Death Framed in Silver
          1940 They Hunted a Fox
          1941 No Murder of Mine
              APA: The Borrowed Cottage
          1946 The Cockroach Sings
              APA: With Bated Breath
          1948 The Bloodstained Toy
    SC: Tommy Rostetter
          1931 The Click of the Gate
          1934 Desire to Kill
          1938 Flying Blind
          1948 The Bloodstained Toy

A: **Campbell, Harriette (Russell)**
    SC: Simon Brade
          1936 The String Glove Mystery
          1937 The Porcelain Fish Mystery
              APA: The Porcelain Fish
          1938 The Moor Fires Mystery
          1940 Three Names for Murder
          1941 Murder Set to Music
          1943 Magic Makes Murder
          1946 Crime in Crystal

P: **Candy, Edward**
    please see: **Neville, Barbara Alison Boodson**

P: **Cannan, Joanna**
    please see: **Pullein-Thompson, Joanna M. C.**

A: **Cannell, Dorothy**
    SC: Ellie Simons Haskell
          1984 The Thin Woman
          1988 The Widows Club
          1990 Mum's the Word
          1992 Femmes Fatal
          1994 How to Murder Your Mother-in-Law
          1995 How to Murder the Man of Your Dreams
    SC: Flowers Detectives
          1985 Down the Garden Path
          1988 The Widows Club
          1997 God Save the Queen

A: **Cannon, Taffy**
    SC: Nan Robinson (see p. 178)
          1993 A Pocketful of Karma

        1995 Tangled Roots
        1996 Class Reunions Are Murder

A: **Carlon, Patricia (Bernadette)**
    SC: Jefferson Shields
           1970 Death by Demonstration
           1970 The Souvenir

A: **Carlson, P(atricia) M(cEvoy)**
    SC: Maggie Ryan (see p. 284)
           1985 Audition for Murder
           1985 Murder Is Academic
           1986 Murder Is Pathological
           1988 Murder Unrenovated
           1988 Rehearsal for Murder
           1990 Murder in the Dog Days
           1990 Murder Misread
           1991 Bad Blood
    SC: Dep. Marty Hopkins (see p. 84)
           1993 Gravestone
           1995 Bloodstream

A: **Carlton, Bea**
    SC: Carole Loring
           1985 Terror in the Night
           1987 The Secret of Windthorn
    SC: Clay & Linn Randolph
           1984 In the House of the Enemy
           1986 Moonshell

P: **Carnac, Carol**
    please see: **Rivett, Edith Caroline**

A: **Carpenter, Lynnette**
    P: **Borton, D. B.**
    SC: Cat Caliband (see p. 278)
           1993 One for the Money
           1993 Two Points for Murder
           1994 Three Is a Crowd
           1995 Four Elements of Murder
           1996 Five Alarm Fire
           1997 Six Feet Under

A: **Case, Peg w/ John Migliori**
    SC: Felix Guzman
           1987 Total Recall
           1988 Death Blade

P: **Castle, Jayne**
    please see: **Krentz, Jayne Ann**

P: **Caudwell, Sarah**
    please see: **Cockburn, Sarah**
A: **Caverly, Carol**
    SC: Thea Barlow
                1994 All the Old Lions
                1996 Frogskin and Muttonfat
P: **Challis, Mary**
    please see: **Bowen-Judd, Sara Hutton**
A: **Chanslor, (Marjorie) Torrey (Hood)**
    SC: Lutie & Amanda Beagle
                1940 Our First Murder
                1941 Our Second Murder
A: **Chapman, Sally**
    SC: Julie Blake & Vic Paoli (see p. 157)
                1991 Raw Data
                1994 Love Bytes
                1996 Cyberkiss
                1997 Hardwired
A: **Chappell, Helen**
    SC: Hollis Ball
                1996 Slow Dancing with the Angel of Death
                1997 Dead Duck
P: **Charles, Kate**
    please see: **Chase, Carol**
A: **Chase, Carol**
    P: **Charles, Kate**
    SC: David Middleton-Brown
                1992 A Drink of Deadly Wine
                1992 The Snares of Death
                1993 Appointed to Die
                1994 A Dead Man out of Mind
                1996 Evil Angels Among Them
A: **Chase, Elaine Raco**
    SC: Nikki Holden & Roman Cantrell
                1987 Dangerous Places
                1988 Dark Corners
                1989 Rough Edges
A: **Chesney, Marion**
    P: **Beaton, M. C.**
    SC: Agatha Raisin
                1992 Agatha Raisin and the Quiche of Death
                1993 Agatha Raisin and the Vicious Vet
                1994 Agatha Raisin and the Potted Gardener

        1995 Agatha Raisin and the Walkers of Dembley
        1996 Agatha Raisin and the Murderous Marriage

SC: Const. Hamish Macbeth (see p. 73)
        1985 Death of a Gossip
        1987 Death of a Cad
        1988 Death of an Outsider
        1988 Death of a Perfect Wife
        1990 Death of a Hussy
        1991 Death of a Snob
        1992 Death of a Prankster
        1993 Death of a Glutton
        1993 Death of a Travelling Man
        1994 Death of a Charming Man
        1995 Death of a Nag
        1996 Death of a Macho Man
        1997 Death of a Dentist

A: **Chetwynd, Bridget**
    SC: Petunia Best & Max Frend
        1951 Death Has Ten Thousand Doors
        1952 Rubies, Emeralds and Diamonds

A: **Child, Nellise**
    SC: Det. Lt. Jeremiah Irish
        1933 Murder Comes Home
        1934 The Diamond Ransom Murders

P: **Chipperfield, Robert O.**
    please see: **Ostrander, Isabel (Egenton)**

P: **Chisholm, P. F.**
    please see: **Finney, Pauline**

A: **Chittenden, Margaret**
    SC: Charlie Plato & Zack Hunter
        1996 Dying to Sing
        1997 Dead Men Don't Dance
        1998 Dead Beat and Deadly

A: **Christie, Agatha**
    SC: Supt. Battle
        1925 The Secret of Chimneys
        1929 The Seven Dials Mystery
        1936 Cards on the Table
        1939 Murder Is Easy
              APA: Easy to Kill
        1944 Towards Zero
    SC: Harley Quin
        SS 1930 The Mysterious Mr. Quin

SS   1950   Three Blind Mice
               APA: The Mousetrap

SC: Hercule Poirot (see p. 221)

         1920   The Mysterious Affair at Styles
         1923   Murder on the Links
SS   1924   Poirot Investigates
         1926   The Murder of Roger Ackroyd
         1927   The Big Four
         1928   The Mystery of the Blue Train
         1932   Peril at End House
         1933   Lord Edgware Dies
               APA: Thirteen at Dinner
         1934   Murder in Three Acts
               APA: Three-Act Tragedy
         1934   Murder on the Orient Express
               APA: Murder in the Calais Coach
         1935   Death in the Air
               APA: Death in the Clouds
         1936   Cards on the Table
         1936   Murder in Mesopotamia
         1936   The ABC Murders
         1937   Death on the Nile
         1937   Dumb Witness
               APA: Poirot Loses a Client
SS   1937   Murder in the Mews
               APA: Dead Man's Mirror and Other Stories
         1938   Appointment with Death
         1938   Hercule Poirot's Christmas
               APA: Murder for Christmas
         1940   One, Two, Buckle My Shoe
               APA: An Overdose of Death
         1940   Sad Cypress
         1941   Evil Under the Sun
         1942   Murder in Retrospect
               APA: Five Little Pigs
SS   1943   Poirot and the Regatta Mystery
SS   1943   Poirot on Holiday
SS   1943   Problem at Pollensa Bay and Christmas Adventure
SS   1944   The Veiled Lady and the Mystery of the Baghdad Chest
SS   1946   Poirot Knows the Murderer
SS   1946   Poirot Lends a Hand
         1946   The Hollow
               APA: Murder After Hours

SS   1947 The Labours of Hercules
      1948 Taken at the Flood
            APA: There Is a Tide
SS   1950 Three Blind Mice
            APA: The Mousetrap
      1952 Mrs. McGinty's Dead
            APA: Blood Will Tell
      1953 After the Funeral
            APA: Murder at the Gallop
      1955 Hickory Dickory Death
            APA: Hickory Dickory Dock
      1956 Dead Man's Folly
      1959 Cat among the Pigeons
SS   1960 The Adventure of the Christmas Pudding
SS   1961 Double Sin and Other Stories
      1963 The Clocks
      1966 Third Girl
      1969 Hallowe'en Party
      1972 Elephants Can Remember
SS   1974 Poirot's Early Cases
            APA: Hercule Poirot's Early Cases
      1975 Curtain
SS   1984 Hercule Poirot's Casebook
SC: Miss Jane Marple (see p. 265)
      1930 The Murder at the Vicarage
SS   1932 The Thirteen Problems
            APA: The Tuesday Club Murders
SS   1940 The Mystery of the Blue Geranium and Other Tuesday Club Murders
      1942 The Body in the Library
      1942 The Moving Finger
      1950 A Murder Is Announced
SS   1950 Three Blind Mice
            APA: The Mousetrap
      1952 They Do It with Mirrors
            APA: Murder with Mirrors
      1953 A Pocket Full of Rye
      1957 4.50 from Paddington
            APA: Murder, She Said
SS   1960 The Adventure of the Christmas Pudding
SS   1961 Double Sin and Other Stories
      1962 The Mirror Crack'd from Side to Side
            APA: The Mirror Crack'd

          1964 A Caribbean Mystery
          1965 At Bertram's Hotel
   SS 1966 Thirteen Clues for Miss Marple
          1971 Nemesis
          1976 Sleeping Murder
   SS 1979 Miss Marple's Final Cases and Two Other Stories
   SS 1985 Miss Marple: The Complete Short Stories

SC: Parker Pyne
   SS 1934 Parker Pyne Investigates
                 APA: Mr. Parker Pyne: Detective

SC: Col. Race
          1924 The Man in the Brown Suit
          1936 Cards on the Table
          1937 Death on the Nile
          1945 Remembered Death
                 APA: Sparkling Cyanide

SC: Tommy & Tuppence Beresford
          1922 The Secret Adversary
   SS 1929 Partners in Crime
                 APA: The Sunningdale Mystery
          1941 N or M?
          1968 By the Pricking of My Thumbs
          1973 Postern of Fate

A: **Christmas, Joyce**
  SC: Betty Trenka
          1993 This Business Is Murder
          1995 Death at Face Value
  SC: Lady Margaret Priam (see p. 287)
          1988 Suddenly in Her Sorbet
          1989 Simply to Die For
          1990 A Fete Worse Than Death
          1991 A Stunning Way to Die
          1991 Friend or Faux?
          1992 It's Her Funeral
          1994 A Perfect Day for Dying
          1996 Mourning Gloria

A: **Christopher, Laura Kim**
  SC: Insp. Bosco of the Yard
          1974 Insp. Bosco and the Cat Burglar
          1976 Insp. Bosco Spots the Crime
          1977 Insp. Bosco and Lady Indiana
          1988 Insp. Bosco and the End of the Tale
  SC: Lady Indiana
          1989 Lady Indiana on Her Own
          1990 Lady Indiana Meets Her Maker

P: **Churchill, Jill**
   please see: **Brooks, Janice Young**
A: **Chute, M(ary) G(race)**
   SC: Sheriff John Charles Olson
       SS   1942 Sheriff Olson
P: **Clandon, Henrietta**
   please see: **Vahey, John G. H.**
A: **Clark, Carol Higgins**
   SC: Regan Reilly
       1992 Decked
       1993 Snagged
       1994 Iced
       1997 Twanged
A: **Clark, Mary Higgins**
   SC: Henry & Sunday Parker Britland IV
       SS   1996 My Gal Sunday
A: **Clarke, Anna**
   SC: Paula Glenning (see p. 39)
       1985 Last Judgment
       1986 Cabin 3033
       1986 The Mystery Lady
       1987 Last Seen in London
       1988 Murder in Writing
       1989 The Whitelands Affair
       1991 The Case of the Paranoid Patient
       1994 The Case of the Ludicrous Letters
       1996 The Case of the Anxious Aunt
A: **Clarke, Brenda Margaret Lilian Honeyman**
   P: **Sedley, Kate**
   SC: Roger the Chapman (see p. 6)
       1991 Death and the Chapman
       1992 The Plymouth Cloak
       1993 The Hanged Man
       1994 The Weaver's Tale
       1994 The Holy Innocents
       1996 The Eve of St. Hyacinth
       1996 The Wicked Winter
A: **Cleary, Melissa**
   SC: Jackie Walsh (see p. 44)
       1992 A Tail of Two Murders
       1993 Hounded to Death
       1993 Dog Collar Crime
       1994 Skull and Dog Bones
       1994 First Pedigree Murder

     1994 Dead and Buried
     1995 The Maltese Puppy
     1996 Murder Most Beastly
     1997 Old Dogs

A: **Cleeves, Ann**
  SC: George & Molly Palmer-Jones (see p. 266)
     1986 A Bird in the Hand
     1987 Come Death and High Water
     1988 Murder in Paradise
     1989 A Prey to Murder
     1991 Sea Fever
     1993 Another Man's Poison
     1994 The Mill on the Shore
     1996 High Island Blues
  SC: Det. Stephen Ramsay
     1990 A Lesson in Dying
     1991 Murder in My Backyard
     1992 A Day in the Death of Dorothea Cassidy
     1995 Killjoy
     1995 The Healers

J: **Clements, Colin**
  please see: **Ryerson, Florence w/ Colin Clements**

A: **Clements, E(ileen) H(elen)**
  SC: Alister Woodhead
     1939 Let Him Die
     1943 Cherry Harvest
     1945 Berry Green
     1949 Weathercock
     1955 Chair-Lift
     1955 Discord in the Air
     1956 The Other Island
     1957 Back in Daylight
     1958 Uncommon Cold
     1959 High Tension
     1960 Honey for the Marshal
     1961 A Note of Enchantment
     1963 Let or Hindrance

A: **Cockburn, Sarah**
  P: **Caudwell, Sarah**
   SC: Hilary Tamar (see p. 166)
     1981 Thus Was Adonis Murdered
     1984 The Shortest Way to Hades
     1989 The Sirens Sang of Murder

P: **Cockin, Joan**
    please see: **Burbridge, Edith Joan**
A: **Cody, Liza**
    SC: Anna Lee (see p. 222)
              1980 Dupe
              1982 Bad Company
              1984 Stalker
              1985 Head Case
              1986 Under Contract
              1991 Backhand
              1993 Bucket Nut
              1994 Monkey Wrench
    SC: Eva "Bucket Nut" Wylie (see p. 131)
              1993 Bucket Nut
              1994 Monkey Wrench
              1997 Musclebound
A: **Coel, Margaret**
    SC: Father John O'Malley & Vicky Holden
              1995 The Eagle Catcher
              1996 The Ghost Walker
              1997 The Dream Stalker
P: **Coffin, Geoffrey**
    please see: **Brawner, Helen w/ Francis Van Wyck Mason**
A: **Coggin, Joan**
    SC: Lady Lupin Hastings, Clergyman's Wife
              1944 Who Killed the Curate?
              1947 The Mystery of Orchard House
              1947 Why Did She Die?
              1949 Dancing with Death
P: **Cohen, Anthea**
    please see: **Simpson, Doris**
A: **Cohen, Susan Handler**
    P: **St. Clair, Elizabeth**
    SC: Marilyn Ambers
              1978 Murder in the Act
              1979 The Sandcastle Murders
              1980 Trek or Treat
A: **Coker, Carolyn**
    SC: Andrea Perkins (see p. 209)
              1984 The Other David
              1986 The Vines of Ferrara
              1987 The Hand of the Lion
              1990 The Balmoral Nude
              1993 Appearance of Evil

P: **Colburn, Laura**
    please see: **McMahan, Ian**
J: **Cole, G(eorge) D(ouglas) H(oward)**
    please see: **Cole, Margaret (Isabel Postgate) w/ G(eorge)**
             D(ouglas) H(oward) Cole
A: **Cole, Margaret (Isabel Postgate) w/ G(eorge) D(ouglas)**
H(oward) Cole
    SC: Dr. Benjamin Tancred
             1935 Dr. Tancred Begins
             1936 Last Will and Testament
    SC: Everard Blatchington
             1926 The Blatchington Tangle
             1930 Burglars in Bucks
                  APA: The Berkshire Mystery
             1934 Death in the Quarry
             1935 Scandal at School
                  APA: The Sleeping Death
             1941 Knife in the Dark
    SC: Supt. Henry Wilson
             1923 The Brooklyn Murders
             1925 Death of a Millionaire
             1926 The Blatchington Tangle
      SS   1928 Superintendent Wilson's Holiday
             1928 The Man from the River
             1929 Poison in the Garden Suburb -
                  APA: Poison in a Garden Suburb
             1930 Burglars in Bucks
                  APA: The Berkshire Mystery
             1930 Corpse in Canonicals
                  APA: The Corpse in the Constable's Garden
             1931 Dead Man's Watch
             1931 The Great Southern Mystery
                  APA: The Walking Corpse
             1933 End of an Ancient Mariner
             1934 Death in the Quarry
             1935 Big Business Murder
             1935 Dr. Tancred Begins
             1936 Last Will and Testament
             1936 The Brothers Sackville
             1937 The Missing Aunt
             1938 Off with Her Head!
             1939 Double Blackmail
             1939 Greek Tragedy

1940 Counterpoint Murder
1940 The Murder at the Munition Works
SS 1940 Wilson and Some Others
1942 Toper's End
SC: Mrs. Elizabeth Warrender
SS 1938 Mrs. Warrender's Profession
1941 Knife in the Dark
J: **Coles, Cyril Henry**
please see: **Manning, Adelaide Frances Oke w/ Cyril Henry Coles**
P: **Coles, Manning**
please see: **Manning, Adelaide Frances Oke w/ Cyril Henry Coles**
A: **Collins, Anna Ashwood**
SC: Abigail Doyle & Roz Benson
1989 Deadly Resolutions
1991 Red Roses for a Dead Trucker
A: **Collins, Michael**
P: **Collins, Michelle**
SC: Megan Marshall
1979 Murder at Willow Run
1980 Premiere at Willow Run
P: **Collins, Michelle**
please see: **Collins, Michael**
A: **Colter, Eli(zabeth)**
SC: Pat Campbell
1946 The Gull Cove Murders
1947 Cheer for the Dead
1953 Rehearsal for the Funeral
A: **Colver, Anne**
P: **Harris, Colver**
SC: Timothy Fowler
1933 Hide and Go Seek
1936 Going to St. Ives
1938 Murder in Amber
APA: Murder by Proxy
A: **Comfort, B(arbara)**
SC: Tish McWhinny (see p. 270)
1986 Phoebe's Knee
1989 Grave Consequences
1993 The Cashmere Kid
1995 Elusive Quarry
A: **Conant, Susan**
SC: Holly Winter (see p. 188)
1990 A New Leash on Death
1990 Dead and Doggone

1987 A Civil Death

1990 The White Zone

A: **Coulson, Felicity Winifred Carter w/ John H. A. Coulson**

   P: **Bonett, John & Emery**

      SC: Prof. Mandrake (see p. 36)

1949 Dead Lion

1951 A Banner for Pegasus

         APA: Not in the Script

1959 No Grave for a Lady

      SC: Insp. Salvador Borges

1964 Better Dead

         APA: Better Off Dead

1966 The Private Face of Murder

1967 This Side Murder

         APA: Murder on the Costa Brava

1970 The Sound of Murder

1972 No Time to Kill

J: **Coulson, John H. A.**

   please see: **Coulson, Felicity Winifred Carter w/ John H. A. Coulson**

A: **Cowdroy, Joan**

      SC: Chf. Insp. Gorham

1936 Framed Evidence

1944 Murder out of Court

      SC: Li Moh

1931 Watch Mr. Moh

         APA: The Flying Dagger Murder

1933 Murder of Lydia

1934 Disappearance

1936 Murder Unsuspected

1938 Death Has No Tongue

1940 Merry-Go-Round

P: **Craig, Alisa**

   please see: **MacLeod, Charlotte (Matilda Hughes)**

A: **Craig, Georgiana Ann Randolph**

   P: **Lee, Gypsy Rose**

      SC: Gypsy Rose Lee

1941 The G-String Murders

         APA: The Strip-Tease Murders

         APA: Lady of Burlesque

1942 Mother Finds a Body

   P: **Rice, Craig**

      SC: Bingo Riggs & Handsome Kusak

1942 The Sunday Pigeon Murders

                1943 The Thursday Turkey Murders
                1958 The April Robin Murders
SC: John J. Malone & The Justuses
                1939 8 Faces at 3
                        APA: Death at Three
                1940 The Corpse Steps Out
                1940 The Wrong Murder
                1941 The Right Murder
                1941 Trial by Fury
                1942 The Big Midget Murders
                1943 Having a Wonderful Crime
                1945 The Lucky Stiff
                1948 The Fourth Postman
                1957 Knocked for a Loop
                        APA: The Double Frame
                1957 My Kingdom for a Hearse
        SS   1958 The Name Is Malone
        SS   1963 People vs. Withers and Malone
                1967 But the Doctor Died
P: **Venning, Michael**
    SC: Melville Fairr
                1942 The Man Who Slept All Day
                1943 Murder Through the Looking Glass
                1944 Jethro Hammer
A: **Crane, Frances**
    SC: Pat & Jean Abbott
                1941 The Turquoise Shop
                1942 The Golden Box
                1942 The Yellow Violet
                1943 The Applegreen Cat
                1943 The Pink Umbrella
                        APA: The Pink Umbrella Murder
                1944 The Amethyst Spectacles
                1945 The Indigo Necklace
                        APA: The Indigo Necklace Murders
                1946 The Cinnamon Murder
                1946 The Shocking Pink Hat
                1947 Murder on the Purple Water
                1948 Black Cypress
                1949 The Flying Red Horse
                1950 The Daffodil Blonde
                1951 Murder in Blue Street
                        APA: Death in the Blue Hour
                1951 The Polkadot Murder

1953   13 White Tulips
1953   Murder in Bright Red
1954   The Coral Princess Murders
1955   Death in Lilac Time
1956   Horror on the Ruby X
1956   The Ultraviolet Widow
1958   The Buttercup Case
1958   The Man in Gray
    APA: The Gray Stranger
1960   Death-Wish Green
1962   The Amber Eyes
1965   The Body Beneath a Mandarin Tree

P: **Crane, Hamilton**
    please see: **Mason, Sarah J(ill)**
A: **Cranston, Claudia**
    SC: Clarice Claremont
        1934   The Murder on Fifth Avenue
        1935   Murder Maritime
P: **Crespi, Camilla T.**
    please see: **Trinchieri, Camilla**
P: **Crespi, Trella**
    please see: **Trinchieri, Camilla**
A: **Crombie, Deborah**
    SC: Supt. Duncan Kincaid & Sgt. Gemma James
        1993   A Share in Death
        1994   All Shall Be Well
        1995   Leave the Grave Green
        1996   Mourn Not Your Dead
        1997   Dreaming of the Bones
P: **Crosby, Lee**
    please see: **Budlong, Ware Torrey**
P: **Cross, Amanda**
    please see: **Heilbrun, Carolyn G(old)**
A: **Crossley, Maude**
    SC: Guy Bannister
        1931   Crookery Inn
A: **Crossley, Maude w/ Charles Thomas King**
    SC: Guy Bannister
        1925   The Forbidden Hour
P: **Crowleigh, Ann**
    please see: **Cummings, Barbara w/ Jo-Ann Power**
A: **Crum, Laura**
    SC: Dr. Gail McCarthy (see p. 119)
        1994   Cutter

D

1993 The Alpine Betrayal
1993 The Alpine Christmas
1994 The Alpine Decoy
1995 The Alpine Escape
1995 The Alpine Fury
1996 The Alpine Gamble
1997 The Alpine Hero
SC: Judith McMonigle Flynn (see p. 152)
1991 Fowl Prey
1991 Just Desserts
1992 Holy Terrors
1993 Bantam of the Opera
1993 Dune to Death
1994 A Fit of Tempera
1995 Major Vices
1995 Murder, My Suite
1996 Auntie Mayhem
1996 Nutty as a Fruitcake
1997 September Mourn
A: **Daiger, K(atherine) S.**
SC: Insp. Everett Anderson
1931 Fourth Degree
1934 Murder on Ghost Tree Island
P: **Dain, Catherine**
please see: **Garwood, Judith**
A: **Daly, Elizabeth (Theresa)**
SC: Henry Gamadge (see pp. 207, 269)
1940 Deadly Nightshade
1940 Unexpected Night
1941 Murders in Volume 2
1942 The House Without the Door
1943 Evidence of Things Seen
1943 Nothing Can Rescue Me
1944 Arrow Pointing Nowhere
       APA: *Murder Listens In*
1944 The Book of the Dead
1945 Any Shape or Form
1946 Somewhere in the House
1946 The Wrong Way Down
       APA: *Shroud for a Lady*
1947 Night Walk
1948 The Book of the Lion
1949 And Dangerous to Know

        1950 Death and Letters
        1951 The Book of the Crime

A: **Dams, Jeanne M.**
      SC: Dorothy Martin
        1995 The Body in the Transept
        1996 Trouble in Town Hall
        1997 Holy Terror in the Hebrides

P: **Dane, Clemence & Helen Simpson**
      please see: **Ashton, Winifred w/ Helen (DeGuerry) Simpson**

A: **Dank, Gloria**
      SC: Bernard & Snooky
        1989 Friends til the End
        1990 As the Sparks Fly Upward
        1990 Going Out in Style
        1993 The Misfortunes of Others

A: **Danks, Denise**
      SC: Georgina Powers
        1989 User Deadly
        1993 Frame Grabber
        1994 Wink a Hopeful Eye

A: **Darby, Ruth**
      SC: Peter & Janet Barron
        1939 Death Boards the Lazy Lady
        1940 Death Conducts a Tour
        1941 Beauty Sleep
        1941 If This Be Murder
        1943 Murder with Orange Blossoms

P: **Davey, Jocelyn**
      please see: **Raphael, Chaim**

A: **Davidson, Diane**
      SC: Lt. Toni Underwood
        1994 Deadly Rendezvous
        1996 Deadly Gamble

A: **Davidson, Diane Mott**
      SC: Goldy Bear (see p. 148)
        1990 Catering to Nobody
        1992 Dying for Chocolate
        1993 The Cereal Murders
        1994 The Last Suppers
        1995 Killer Pancake
        1996 The Main Corpse
        1997 The Grilling Season

J: **Davis, Burton**
      please see: **Davis, Clare w/ Burton Davis**

A: **Davis, Clare w/ Burton Davis**
   P: **Saunders, Lawrence**
      SC: Wylie King & Nels Lundberg
                1931 The Columnist Murder
                1933 The Devil's Den
A: **Davis, Dorothy Salisbury**
      SC: Jasper Tully
                1957 Death of an Old Sinner
                1958 A Gentleman Called
      SC: Julie Hayes (see p. 282)
                1976 A Death in the Life
                1980 Scarlet Night
                1984 Lullaby of Murder
                1987 The Habit of Fear
      SC: Mrs. Norris
                1957 Death of an Old Sinner
                1958 A Gentleman Called
                1959 Old Sinners Never Die
           SS 1984 Tales for a Stormy Night
A: **Davis, Julia**
   P: **Draco, F.**
      SC: Lord & Lady Tintagel
                1951 The Devil's Church
                1952 Cruise with Death
A: **Davis, Lavinia R(iker)**
      SC: Nora Hughes & Larry Blaine
                1945 Evidence Unseen
                1947 Taste of Vengeance
A: **Davis, Lindsey**
      SC: Marcus Didius Falco & Helena Justina (see p. 2)
                1989 Silver Pigs
                1990 Shadows in Bronze
                1991 Venus in Copper
                1992 The Iron Hand of Mars
                1992 Poseidon's Gold
                1994 Last Act in Palmyra
                1995 Time to Depart
                1996 A Dying Light in Corduba
A: **Dawkins, Cecil**
      SC: Ginevra Prettifield
                1993 Santa Fe Rembrandt
                1994 Clay Dancers
                1995 Rare Earth

A: **Dawson, Janet**
    SC: Jeri Howard (see p. 232)
               1990 Kindred Crimes
               1993 Take a Number
               1993 Till the Old Men Die
               1994 Don't Turn Your Back on the Ocean
               1995 Nobody's Child
               1996 A Credible Threat
               1997 Witness to Evil

A: **Day, Dianne**
    SC: Fremont Jones
               1995 The Strange Files of Fremont Jones
               1996 Fire and Fog
               1997 The Bohemian Murders

A: **Day (Lederer), Lillian w/ Norbert (Lewis) Lederer**
    SC: Frederick Hunt
               1935 Murder in Time
               1937 Death Comes on Friday

A: **Day, Marele**
    SC: Claudia Valentine
               1988 The Life and Crimes of Harry Lavender
               1989 The Case of the Chinese Boxes
               1992 The Last Tango of Dolores Delgado
               1994 The Disappearances of Madalena Grimaldi

A: **de la Torre (Bueno) (McCue), Lillian**
    SC: Dr. Sam: Johnson
          SS 1944 Dr. Sam: Johnson, Detector
          SS 1960 The Detections of Dr. Sam: Johnson
          SS 1984 The Return of Dr. Sam: Johnson, Detector
          SS 1987 The Exploits of Dr. Sam: Johnson, Detector

A: **Dean (Getz), Amber**
    SC: Abbie Harris (see p. 282)
               1944 Dead Man's Float
               1945 Chanticleer's Muffled Crow
               1946 Call Me Pandora
                    APA: The Blonde Is Dead
               1946 Wrap It Up
               1948 No Traveller Returns
               1949 Snipe Hunt
               1951 August Incident
               1954 The Devil Threw Dice

A: **Dean, Elizabeth**
    SC: Emma Marsh & Hank Fairbanks
               1939 Murder Is a Collector's Item

          1940 Murder Is a Serious Business
          1944 Murder a Mile High
A: **DeLoach, Nora L.**
     SC: Mama (Candi) & Simone
          1992 Mama Solves a Murder
          1995 Mama Traps a Killer
          1997 Mama Stalks the Past
A: **Dengler, Sandy**
     SC: Jack Prester & Maxx
          1993 Death Valley
          1993 A Model Murder
          1994 Murder on the Mount
          1995 The Quick and the Dead
     SC: Sgt. Joe Rodriguez
          1993 Cat Killer
          1993 Mouse Trapped
          1994 Gila Monster
          1994 The Last Dinosaur
          1995 Fatal Fishes
A: **Dennison, Dulcie Winifred Catherine Bailey**
     P: **Gray, Dulcie**
     SC: Insp. Cardiff
          1960 Epitaph for a Dead Actor
          1968 Died in the Red
A: **Denniston, Elinore**
     P: **Foley, Rae**
     SC: Hiram Potter
          1955 Death and Mr. Potter
                APA: The Peacock Is a Bird of Prey
          1956 The Last Gamble
          1957 Run for Your Life
          1958 Where Is Nancy Bostwick?
                APA: Where Is Mary Bostwick?
                APA: Escape to Fear
          1959 Dangerous to Me
          1961 It's Murder, Mr. Potter
                APA: Curtain Call
          1962 Repent at Leisure
                APA: The Deadly Noose
          1963 Back Door to Death
                APA: Nightmare Honeymoon
          1964 Fatal Lady

     1965 Call It Accident
     1970 A Calculated Risk
  SC: John Harland
     1949 The Girl from Nowhere
     1950 The Hundredth Door
     1951 An Ape in Velvet

A: **Dentinger, Jane**
  SC: Jocelyn O'Roarke (see p. 100)
     1983 Murder on Cue
     1984 First Hit of the Season
     1988 Death Mask
     1992 Dead Pan
     1994 The Queen Is Dead
     1995 Who Dropped Peter Pan?

A: **Dereske, Jo**
  SC: Miss Helma Zukas (see p. 216)
     1994 Miss Zukas and the Library Murders
     1995 Miss Zukas and the Island Murders
     1995 Miss Zukas and the Stroke of Death
     1996 Miss Zukas and the Raven's Dance
  SC: Ruby Crane
     1996 Savage Cut
     1997 Cut and Dry

A: **Dewhurst, Eileen (Mary)**
  SC: Helen Johnson
     1982 Whoever I Am
     1985 Playing Safe
  SC: Insp. Neil Carter
     1977 Curtain Fall
     1980 Drink This
     1981 Trio in Three Flats
     1984 There Was a Little Girl
     1987 A Nice Little Business

A: **Dick (Erikson), (Sibyl Cicely) Alexandra**
  SC: Alastair MacAlastair
     1944 And Only Man
     1944 An Old-Fashioned Christmas
     1945 The Curate's Crime
     1947 MacAlastair Looks On
     1950 Cross Purposes

A: **Dietz, Denise**
  SC: Ellie Bernstein
     1992 Throw Darts at a Cheesecake
     1994 Beat Up a Cookie

A: **Disney, Doris Miles**
    SC: David Madden
          1956 Unappointed Rounds
               APA: The Post Office Case
          1958 Black Mail
          1961 Mrs. Meeker's Money
    SC: Jeff DiMarco
          1946 Dark Road
               APA: Dead Stop
          1947 Family Skeleton
          1951 Straw Man
               APA: The Case of the Straw Man
          1955 Trick or Treat
               APA: The Halloween Murder
          1957 Method in Madness
               APA: Quiet Violence
               APA: Too Innocent to Kill
          1959 Did She Fall or Was She Pushed?
          1962 Find the Woman
          1971 The Chandler Policy
    SC: Jim O'Neill
          1943 A Compound for Death
          1945 Murder on a Tangent
          1947 Appointment at Nine
          1950 Fire at Will
          1954 The Last Straw
               APA: Driven to Kill

A: **Doherty, P(aul) C.**
    P: **Dukthas, Ann**
    SC: Nicholas Segalla (see p. 32)
          1994 A Time For the Death of a King
          1995 The Prince Lost to Time
          1996 The Time of Murder at Mayerling

A: **Dolson, Hildegarde**
    SC: Lucy Ramsdale
          1971 To Spite Her Face
          1973 A Dying Fall
          1975 Please Omit Funeral
          1977 Beauty Sleep

P: **Dominic, R. B.**
    please see: **Henissart, Martha w/ Mary Jane Latsis**
A: **Donald, Anabel**
    SC: Alex Tanner
          1992 An Uncommon Murder

1993 In at the Deep End
1994 The Glass Ceiling
A: **Donovan, J(ean) B(ernadine)**
SC: Bill Speed
     SS 1961 Meet Bill Speed
          1962 Bill Speed on Hot Ice
          1963 Bill Speed—Special Squad
A: **Douglas, Carole Nelson**
SC: Irene Adler (see p. 16)
          1990 Good Night, Mr. Holmes
          1991 Good Morning, Irene
          1992 Irene at Large
          1994 Irene's Last Waltz
SC: Kevin Blake
          1985 Probe
          1988 Counterprobe
SC: Midnight Louie
          1992 Catnap
          1993 Pussyfoot
          1994 Cat on a Blue Monday
          1995 Cat in a Crimson Haze
          1996 Cat in a Diamond Dazzle
          1996 Cat with an Emerald Eye
          1997 Cat in a Flamingo Fedora
          1997 Cat in a Golden Garland
A: **Douglas, Lauren Wright**
SC: Allison O'Neil
          1996 Death at Lavender Bay
          1997 Swimming Cat Cove
SC: Caitlin Reece
          1987 The Always Anonymous Beast
          1990 Ninth Life
          1991 The Daughters of Artemis
          1992 A Tiger's Heart
          1993 Goblin Market
          1994 A Rage of Maidens
          1995 Cat Dancing
P: **Draco, F.**
please see: **Davis, Julia**
P: **Drake, Alison**
please see: **MacGregor, T(rish) J(aneshutz)**
A: **Dreher, Sarah**
SC: Stoner McTavish
          1985 Stoner McTavish

1986 Something Shady
1987 Gray Magic
1990 A Captive in Time
1993 Other World
1995 Bad Company
1997 Solitaire and Brahms

A: **Dreyer, Eileen**
SC: Nurse Molly Burke
1995 Bad Medicine
1998 Head Games

A: **Drury, Joan M.**
SC: Tyler Jones
1993 The Other Side of Silence
1996 Silent Words

A: **Duane, Diane w/ Peter Morwood**
SC: Joss O'Bannion & Evan Glyndower (see p. 66)
1991 Mindblast
1992 High Moon
1992 Kill Station

A: **DuBois, Theodora M.**
SC: Anne & Jeffrey McNeill
1936 Armed with a New Terror
1938 Death Wears a White Coat
1939 Death Dines Out
1939 Death Tears a Comic Strip
1940 Death Comes to Tea
1941 Death Is Late to Lunch
1941 The McNeills Chase a Ghost
1942 The Body Goes Round and Round
1943 The Wild Duck Murders
1944 The Case of the Perfumed Mouse
1945 Death Sails in a High Wind
1946 Murder Strikes an Atomic Unit
1947 The Footsteps
1948 The Devil and Destiny
1948 The Face of Hate
1949 It's Raining Violence
APA: Money, Murder and the McNeills
1951 Fowl Play
1952 The Cavalier's Corpse
1954 Seeing Red

A: **Duffy, Margaret**
SC: Joanna McKenzie & Chf. Insp. James Carrick
1994 Dressed to Kill
1995 Prospect of Death

SC: Patrick & Ingrid Gillard
    1987 A Murder of Crows
    1988 Brass Eagle
    1988 Death of a Raven
    1990 Who Killed Cock Robin?
    1991 Rook-Shoot
    1993 Gallows Bird

A: **Duffy, Stella**
SC: Saz Martin
    1994 Calendar Girl
    1996 Wavewalker

A: **Duke, Madelaine (Elizabeth)**
SC: Dr. Norah North
    1975 Death of a Holy Murderer
    1976 Death at the Wedding
    1978 Death of a Dandie Dinmont

P: **Dukthas, Ann**
please see: **Doherty, P(aul) C.**

A: **Dunant, Sarah**
SC: Hannah Wolfe (see p. 236)
    1991 Birth Marks
    1993 Fatlands
    1995 Under My Skin

A: **Dunbar, Sophie**
SC: Claire Jennerette Claiborne
    1993 Behind Eclaire's Doors
    1995 Redneck Riviera
    1996 A Bad Hair Day

A: **Dunlap, Susan**
SC: Jill Smith
    1984 As a Favor
    1984 Karma
    1985 Not Exactly a Brahmin
    1987 A Dinner to Die For
    1987 Too Close to the Edge
    1990 Diamond in the Buff
    1992 Death and Taxes
    1993 Time Expired
    1996 Sudden Exposure
    1997 Cop Out
SC: Kiernan O'Shaughnessey (see p. 112)
    1989 Pious Deception
    1991 Rogue Wave
    1994 High Fall

SC: Vejay Haskell
  1984 An Equal Opportunity Death
  1985 The Bohemian Connection
  1986 The Last Annual Slugfest

A: **Dunn, Carola**
 SC: Hon. Daisy Dalrymple & Det. Chf. Insp. Alec Fletcher
  1994 Death at Wentwater Court
  1995 The Winter Garden Mystery
  1996 Requiem for a Mezzo
  1997 Murder on the Flying Scotsman

A: **Dunnett, Dorothy (Halliday)**
 SC: Johnson Johnson (see p. 207)
  1968 Dolly and the Singing Bird
    APA: The Photogenic Soprano
    APA: Rum Affair
  1970 Dolly and the Cookie Bird
    APA: Murder in the Round
  1971 Dolly and the Doctor Bird
    APA: Match for a Murderer
    APA: Operation Nassau
  1973 Dolly and the Starry Bird
  1976 Dolly and the Nanny Bird
    APA: Split Code
  1984 Dolly and the Bird of Paradise
    APA: Tropical Issue
  1991 Morrocan Traffic
    APA: Send a Fax to the Casbah

A: **Durham, Mary**
 SC: Insp. Christopher Marsh
  1951 Forked Lightning
  1952 The Devil Was Sick
 SC: Insp. Randolph York
  1945 Hate Is My Livery
  1945 Why Pick on Pickles?
  1946 Keeps Death His Court
  1947 Crime Insoluble
  1948 Murder by Multiplication

A: **Dymmoch, Michael Allen**
 SC: Dr. Jack Caleb & John Thinnes
  1993 The Man Who Understood Cats
  1995 The Death of Blue Mountain Cat

E

A: **Eades, M(aude) L.**
    SC: Winston Barrows
        1925 The Crown Swindle
        1932 The Torrington Square Mystery
A: **Eberhart, Mignon (Good)**
    SC: Sarah Keate
        1942 Wolf in Man's Clothing
        1954 Man Missing
    SC: Sarah Keate & Lance O'Leary
        1929 The Patient in Room 18
        1930 The Mystery of Hunting's End
        1930 While the Patient Slept
        1931 From This Dark Stairway
        1932 Murder by an Aristocrat
          APA: Murder of My Patient
    SC: Susan Dare
        SS 1934 The Cases of Susan Dare
A: **Eccles, Marjorie**
    SC: Det. Chf. Insp. Gil Mayo
        1988 Cast a Cold Eye
        1989 Death of a Good Woman
        1990 Requiem for a Dove
        1991 More Deaths Than One
        1992 Late of This Parish
        1993 The Company She Kept
        1994 An Accidental Shroud
        1995 A Death of Distinction
        1996 A Species of Revenge
A: **Edghill, Rosemary**
    SC: Karen Hightower (see p. 31)
        1994 Speak Daggers to Her
        1995 Book of Moons
        1996 The Bowl of Night
A: **Edginton (Bailey), May (Helen Marion)**
    SC: Napoleon Prince
        SS 1912 The Adventures of Napoleon Prince
J: **Edington, Arlo Channing**
    please see: **Edington, Carmen Ballen w/ Arlo Channing Edington**
A: **Edington, Carmen Ballen w/ Arlo Channing Edington**
    P: **Edingtons, The**
        SC: Capt. Smith
            1929 The Studio Murder Mystery

1930 The House of the Vanishing Goblets
APA: Murder to Music
1931 The Monk's Hood Murders

P: **Edingtons, The**
please see: **Edington, Carmen Ballen w/ Arlo Channing Edington**

A: **Edmiston, Helen Jean Mary**
P: **Robertson, Helen**
SC: Insp. Lathom Dynes
1956 Venice of the Black Sea
1957 The Crystal-Gazers
1960 The Chinese Goose
APA: Swan Song

A: **Edmonds, Janet**
SC: Linus Lintoul
1988 Dog's Body
1989 Dead Spit
1990 Judge and Be Damned

A: **Edwards, Ruth Dudley**
SC: Robert Amiss (see p. 254)
1981 Corridors of Death
1984 The St. Valentine's Day Murders
1990 The English School of Murder
APA: The School of English Murder
1992 Clubbed to Death
1994 Matricide at St. Martha's
1996 Ten Lords A-Leaping
1996 Murder in a Cathedral

P: **Egan, Lesley**
please see: **Linington, (Barbara) Elizabeth**

A: **Eichler, Selma**
SC: Desiree Shapiro
1994 Murder Can Kill Your Social Life
1995 Murder Can Ruin Your Looks
1996 Murder Can Stunt Your Growth
1996 Murder Can Wreck Your Reunion

A: **Eiker, Mathilde**
P: **Evermay, March**
SC: Insp. Glover
1938 They Talked of Poison
1940 This Death Was Murder

J: **Elkins, Aaron**
please see: **Elkins, Charlotte w/ Aaron Elkins**

A: **Elkins, Charlotte w/ Aaron Elkins**
    SC: Lee Ofsted (see p. 126)
               1989 A Wicked Slice
               1995 Rotten Lies

P: **Ellery, Jan**
    please see: **Ewing, Jan**

A: **Elrod, P(atricia) N(ead)**
    SC: Jack Fleming & Charles Escott (see p. 27)
               1990 Bloodcircle
               1990 Bloodlist
               1990 Lifeblood
               1991 Art in the Blood
               1991 Fire in the Blood
               1992 Blood on the Water

A: **Emerson, Kathy Lynn**
    SC: Susanna, Lady Appleton
               1997 Face Down in a Marrow-Bone Pie
               1998 Face Down Upon an Herbal

A: **Ennis, Catherine**
    SC: Dr. Bernadette Hebert
               1991 Clearwater
               1993 Chatauqua

A: **Epstein, Carole**
    SC: Barbara Simons
               1996 Perilous Friends
               1997 Perilous Relations

A: **Erskine, Laurie York**
    SC: Douglas Renfrew
               1922 Renfrew of the Royal Mounted
               1927 Renfrew Rides Again
               1928 Renfrew Rides the Sky
               1931 Renfrew Rides North
               1933 Renfrew's Long Trail
               1935 Renfrew Rides the Range
               1936 Renfrew in the Valley of the Vanished Men
               1939 One Man Came Back
               1941 Renfrew Flies Again

P: **Erskine, Margaret**
    please see: **Williams, Margaret Wetherby**

J: **Eustace, Robert**
    please see: **Meade (Smith), Elizabeth Thomasina w/ Robert Eustace (Barton)**

A: **Evanovitch, Janet**
    SC: Stephanie Plum
               1994 One for the Money

1996 Two for the Dough
1997 Three to Get Deadly
A: **Evans, Constance May**
   P: **O'Nair, Mairi**
      SC: Pamela Wayne
         SS 1935 The Girl with the X-Ray Eyes
A: **Evans, Geraldine**
      SC: Insp. Rafferty & Sgt. Llewellyn
         1993 Dead Before Morning
         1994 Down Among the Dead Men
A: **Evans, Julie Rendel**
   P: **Hobson, Polly**
      SC: Insp. Basil
         1964 Murder Won't Out
         1968 Titty's Dead
            APA: *A Terrible Thing Has Happened to Miss*
               Dupont
         1970 The Three Graces
A: **Evans, Marguerite Helen Jervis**
   P: **Sandys, Oliver**
      SC: Lady Weybridge
         SS 1912 Chicane
P: **Evermay, March**
   please see: **Eiker, Mathilde**
A: **Ewing, Jan**
   P: **Ellery, Jan**
      SC: Adrienne Bishop
         1979 The Last Set
         1980 High Strung
A: **Eyles, (Margaret) Leonora (Pitcairn)**
      SC: Dr. Joan Marvin
         1936 Death of a Dog
         1936 They Wanted Him Dead!
P: **Eyre, Elizabeth**
   please see: **Staynes, Jill w/ Margaret Storey**

F

A: **Fahrenkopf, Anne w/ Ruth Fox (Hume)**
   P: **Irving, Alexander**
      SC: Dr. Anthony Post
         1946 Bitter Ending
         1948 Symphony in Two Time

A: **Fairstein, Linda**
   SC: Alexandra Cooper
         1996 Final Jeopardy
         1997 Likely to Die
A: **Fallon, Ann C.**
   SC: James Fleming (see p. 174)
         1990 Blood is Thicker
         1991 Where Death Lies
         1992 Dead Ends
         1993 Potter's Field
         1995 Hour of Our Death
A: **Farrell, Gillian B.**
   SC: Annie McGrogan (see p. 107)
         1992 Alibi for an Actress
         1994 Murder and a Muse
A: **Farrelly, Gail E.**
   SC: Lisa King
         1995 Beaned in Boston
         1998 Duped by Derivatives
A: **Farrer, Katharine**
   SC: Insp. Richard Ringwood
         1952 The Missing Link
         1954 The Cretan Counterfeit
         1957 Gownsman's Gallows
J: **Fawcett, Bill**
   please see: **Yarbro, Chelsea Quinn w/ Bill Fawcett**
P: **Fawcett, Quinn**
   please see: **Yarbro, Chelsea Quinn w/ Bill Fawcett**
A: **Feagles, Anita Macrae**
   P: **Macrae, Travis**
      SC: Jim & Kate Harris
            1960 Death in View
            1961 Twenty Per Cent
                  APA: Multiple Murder
A: **Fearon, Diana**
   SC: Arabella Frant
         1959 Death Before Breakfast
         1960 Murder-on-Thames
A: **Feddersen, Connie**
   SC: Amanda Hazard & Nick Thorn
         1993 Dead in the Water
         1994 Dead in the Cellar
         1995 Dead in the Melon Patch
         1996 Dead in the Dirt

1997 Dead in the Mud
1998 Dead in the Chevy

A: **Fell, Doris Elaine w/ Carole Gift Page**
SC: David Ballard & Michelle Merrill Ballard
1985 Mist over Morro Bay
1986 Secret of the East Wind
1986 Storm Clouds over Paradise
1987 Beyond the Windswept Sea

A: **Femling, Jean**
SC: Martha "Moz" Brant
1989 Hush, Money
1991 Getting Mine

A: **Fenisong, Ruth**
SC: Capt. Gridley Nelson
1942 Murder Needs a Face
1942 Murder Needs a Name
1943 Murder Runs a Fever
1943 The Butler Died in Brooklyn
1950 Grim Rehearsal
1951 Dead Yesterday
1952 Deadlock
1953 The Wench Is Dead
1954 Miscast for Murder
        APA: *Too Lovely to Live*
1956 Bite the Hand
        APA: *The Blackmailer*
1958 Death of the Party
1960 But Not Forgotten
        APA: *Sinister Assignment*
1962 Dead Weight

J: **Fenn, Caroline K.**
please see: **McGrew, Julia w/ Caroline K. Fenn**

A: **Fennelly, Tony**
SC: Margo Fortier
1994 The Hippie in the Wall
1996 1 (900) D-E-A-D
SC: Matthew Sinclair
1985 The Glory Hole Murders
1987 The Closet Hanging
1989 Kiss Yourself Goodbye

P: **Ferrars, E. X.**
please see: **Brown, Morna Doris (MacTaggart)**

A: **Fetta, Emma Lou**
SC: Lyle Curtis & Susan Yates
1939 Murder in Style

 1940 Murder on the Face of It
 1941 Dressed to Kill

J: **Fickling, Forrest**
    please see: **Fickling, Gloria w/ Forrest Fickling**
P: **Fickling, G. G.**
    please see: **Fickling, Gloria w/ Forrest Fickling**
A: **Fickling, Gloria w/ Forrest Fickling**
    P: **Fickling, G. G.**
        SC: Erik March
             1957 This Girl for Hire
             1962 Naughty but Dead
             1963 The Case of the Radioactive Redhead
             1964 The Crazy Mixed-up Nude
             1972 Stiff as a Broad
        SC: Honey West
             1957 This Girl for Hire
             1958 A Gun for Honey
             1958 Girl on the Loose
             1959 Girl on the Prowl
             1959 Honey in the Flesh
             1960 Dig a Dead Doll
             1960 Kiss for a Killer
             1961 Blood and Honey
             1964 Bombshell
             1971 Honey on Her Tail
             1972 Stiff as a Broad

A: **Field, Katherine**
    SC: Det. Insp. Ross Paterson
         1941 Disappearance of a Niece
         1942 The Two-Five to Mardon
         1944 Murder to Follow

A: **Field, Moira**
    SC: Det. Insp. Flower
         1950 Foreign Body
         1951 Gunpowder Treason and Plot

P: **Fielding, A.**
    please see: **Fielding, Dorothy**

A: **Fielding, Dorothy**
    P: **Fielding, A.**
        SC: Insp. Pointer
             1924 The Eames-Erskine Case
             1925 The Charteris Mystery
             1926 The Footsteps That Stopped
             1927 The Clifford Affair
                   APA: The Clifford Mystery

1928 The Cluny Problem
1928 The Net Around Joan Ingilby
1929 Murder at the Nook
1929 The Mysterious Partner
1930 The Craig Poisoning Mystery
1930 The Wedding-Chest Mystery
1931 The Upfold Farm Mystery
1932 Death of John Tait
1932 The Westwood Mystery
1933 The Tall House Mystery
1934 The Cautley Conundrum
    APA: The Cautley Mystery
1934 The Paper-Chase
    APA: The Paper-Chase Mystery
1935 The Case of the Missing Diary
1935 Tragedy at Beechcroft
1936 Mystery at the Rectory
1936 The Case of the Two Pearl Necklaces
1937 Black Cats Are Lucky
1937 Scarecrow
1944 Pointer to a Crime

A: **Fielding, Joy**
  SC: Jess Koster
        1991 See Jane Run
        1993 Tell Me No Secrets

A: **Filgate, C. Macartney**
  SC: Charlotte Eliot
        1979 Bravo Charlie
            APA: Runway to Death
        1979 Delta November

A: **Finney, Pauline**
  P: **Chisholm, P. F.**
  SC: Sir Robert Carey
        1995 A Famine of Horses
        1996 A Season of Knives
        1997 A Surfeit of Guns

A: **Firth, Violet Mary**
  P: **Fortune, Dion**
  SC: Dr. Taverner
    SS 1926 The Secrets of Dr. Taverner
  P: **Steele, V. M.**
  SC: Chf. Insp. Saunders
        1935 The Scarred Wrists
        1936 Hunters of Humans

A: **Fiske, Dorsey**
    SC: John Fenchurch & Insp. Bunce
          1980 Academic Murder
          1987 Bound to Murder
P: **Fitt, Mary**
    please see: **Freeman, Kathleen**
A: **Fleming, Joan (Margaret)**
    SC: Nuri Iskirlak
          1962 When I Grow Rich
          1965 Nothing Is the Number When You Die
A: **Fletcher, Jessica & Donald Bain**
    SC: Jessica Fletcher
          1989 Gin and Daggers
          1994 Manhattans and Murder
          1995 Rum and Razors
          1995 Brandy and Bullets
          1995 Martinis and Mayhem
          1996 A Deadly Judgment
          1996 A Palette for Murder
          1997 The Highland Fling Murders
A: **Flora, Kate (Clark)**
    SC: Thea Kozak
          1994 Chosen for Death
          1995 Death in a Funhouse Mirror
          1996 Death at the Wheel
          1997 An Educated Death
A: **Flower, Pat(ricia Mary Bryson)**
    SC: Insp. Swinton
          1958 Wax Flowers for Gloria
          1959 Goodbye, Sweet William
          1960 A Wreath of Water-Lilies
          1961 One Rose Less
          1962 Hell for Heather
          1963 Term of Terror
          1966 Fiends of the Family
P: **Foley, Rae**
    please see: **Denniston, Elinore**
A: **Foote-Smith, Elizabeth**
    SC: Will Woodfield
          1976 A Gentle Albatross
          1977 Never Say Die
A: **Forbes, DeLoris Florine Stanton**
  P: **Wells, Tobias**
    SC: Knute Severson
          1966 A Matter of Love and Death

1967 Dead by the Light of the Moon
1967 What Should You Know of Dying?
1968 Murder Most Fouled Up
1969 Die Quickly, Dear Mother
1969 The Young Can Die Protesting
1970 Dinky Died
1971 The Foo Dog
    APA: The Lotus Affair
1971 What to Do Until the Undertaker Comes
1972 A Die in the Country
1972 How to Kill a Man
1973 Brenda's Murder
1974 Have Mercy upon Us
1975 Hark, Hark, the Watchdogs Bark
1977 A Creature Was Stirring
1988 Of Graves, Worms and Epitaphs

P: **Ford, Leslie**
   please see: **Brown, Zenith Jones**
A: **Forrest, Katherine V(irginia)**
   SC: Det. Kate Delafield (see p. 52)
       1984 Amateur City
       1987 Murder at the Nightwood Bar
       1989 The Beverly Malibu
       1991 Murder by Tradition
       1996 Liberty Square
       1997 Apparition Alley

P: **Fortune, Dion**
   please see: **Firth, Violet Mary**
A: **Fowler, Earlene**
   SC: Albenia "Benni" Harper (see p. 218)
       1994 Fool's Puzzle
       1995 Irish Chain
       1996 Kansas Troubles
       1997 Goose in the Pond

P: **Fox, David**
   please see: **Ostrander, Isabel (Egenton)**
J: **Fox (Hume), Ruth**
   please see: **Fahrenkopf, Anne w/ Ruth Fox (Hume)**
A: **Frankel, Valerie**
   SC: Wanda Mallory
       1991 A Deadline for Murder
       1992 Murder on Wheels
       1994 Prime Time for Murder
       1995 A Body to Die For

A: **Fraser, Anthea**
    SC: Chf. Insp. David Webb & Det. Sgt. Ken Jackson
        1984 A Shroud for Delilah
        1985 A Necessary End
        1986 Pretty Maids All in a Row
        1987 The Nine Bright Shiners
        1987 Death Speaks Softly
        1988 Six Proud Walkers
        1989 The April Rainers
        1990 Symbols at Your Door
        1991 The Lilly-White Boys
            APA: *I'll Sing You Two-O*
        1992 Three, Three, the Rivals
        1994 The Gospel Makers
        1996 The Seven Stars

A: **Fraser, Antonia (Pakenham)**
    SC: Jemima Shore (see p. 100)
        1977 Quiet as a Nun
        1978 The Wild Island
        1981 A Splash of Red
        1982 Cool Repentance
    SS 1983 Jemima Shore Investigates
        1985 Oxford Blood
    SS 1986 Jemima Shore's First Case and Other Stories
        1988 Your Royal Hostage
    SS 1991 Jemima Shore at the Sunny Grave
        1991 The Cavalier Case
        1994 Political Death

P: **Frazer, Margaret**
    please see: **Bacon, Gail w/ Mary Monica Pulver (Kuhfeld)**

A: **Freeman, Kathleen**
  P: **Fitt, Mary**
    SC: Supt. Insp. Mallett
        1938 Expected Death
        1938 Sky-Rocket
        1939 Death at Dancing Stones
        1940 Death Starts a Rumor
        1941 Death and Mary Dazill
            APA: *Aftermath of Murder*
        1941 Death on Heron's Mere
            APA: *Death Finds a Target*
        1942 Requiem for Robert
        1944 Clues to Christabel
        1946 Death and the Pleasant Voices

1947 A Fine and Private Place
1948 Death and the Bright Day
1949 The Banquet Ceases
1951 An Ill Wind
1952 Death and the Shortest Day
1954 Love from Elizabeth
SS 1954 The Man Who Shot Birds and Other Tales
1956 Sweet Poison
1959 Mizmaze

A: **Freeman, Lucy**
SC: Dr. William Ames
1971 The Dream
1973 The Psychiatrist Says Murder
1975 The Case on Cloud Nine

A: **French, Linda**
P: **Mariz, Linda**
SC: Laura Ireland
1992 Body English
1992 Snake Dance

A: **Friedman, (Michaele) Mickey (Thompson)**
SC: Georgia Lee Maxwell
1988 Magic Mirror
APA: Deadly Reflections
1989 A Temporary Ghost

P: **Frome, David**
please see: **Brown, Zenith Jones**

A: **Fromer, Margot J.**
SC: Amanda Knight
1991 Scalpel's Edge
1992 The Gift of Death
1993 Night Shift

A: **Frommer, Sara Hoskinson**
SC: Joan Spencer
1986 Murder in C Major
1994 Buried in Quilts
1997 Murder & Sullivan

A: **Frost (Shively), Barbara**
SC: Marka de Lancey
1949 The Corpse Said No
1951 The Corpse Died Twice
1955 Innocent Bystander

A: **Fulton, Eileen**
SC: Nina McFall & Det. Lt. Dino Rossi
1988 A Setting for Murder

1988 Death of a Golden Girl
1988 Dying for Stardom
1988 Lights, Camera, Death
1988 Take One for Murder
1989 Fatal Flashback

A: **Fulton, Jennifer**
P: **Beecham, Rose**
SC: Amanda Valentine
1992 Introducing Amanda Valentine
1994 Second Guess
1995 Fair Play

A: **Furie, Ruthe**
SC: Frances "Fran" Tremaine Kirk
1995 If Looks Could Kill
1996 A Natural Death
1996 A Deadly Pate

A: **Fyfield (Hegarty), Frances**
SC: Helen West & Det. Supt. Geoffrey Bailey (see p. 169)
1988 A Question of Guilt
1990 Not That Kind of Place
APA: Trial by Fire
1992 Deep Sleep
1993 Shadow Play
1995 A Clear Conscience
1997 Without Consent
SC: Sarah Fortune (see p. 169)
1991 Shadows on the Mirror
1994 Perfectly Pure and Good

G

A: **Gaines (Schultz), Audrey**
SC: Chauncey O'Day
1939 The Old Must Die
1940 While the Wind Howled
1942 The Voodoo Goat
SC: Jeff Strange
1946 Omit Flowers, Please
1952 No Crime Like the Present

P: **Gainham, Sarah**
please see: **Ames, Sarah Rachel Stainer**
P: **Gaite, Francis**
please see: **Manning, Adelaide Frances Oke w/ Cyril Henry Coles**

P: **Gallagher, Gale**
      please see: **Scott, Margaret w/ Will(iam Charles) Oursler**
A: **Gallison (Dunn), Kate**
      SC: Mother Lavinia Grey (see p. 95)
                  1995 Bury the Bishop
                  1996 Devil's Workshop
                  1996 Unholy Angels
                  1997 Hasty Retreat
      SC: Nick Magaracz
                  1986 Unbalanced Accounts
                  1987 The Death Tape
                  1992 Jersey Monkey
A: **Garcia-Aguilera, Carolina**
      SC: Lupe Solano
                  1996 Bloody Waters
                  1997 Bloody Shame
A: **Gardiner, Dorothy**
      SC: Sheriff Moss Magill
                  1956 What Crime Is It?
                          APA: The Case of the Hula Clock
                  1958 The Seventh Mourner
                  1963 Lion in Wait
                          APA: Lion? or Murder?
      SC: Mr. Watson
                  1933 The Transatlantic Ghost
                  1934 A Drink for Mr. Cherry
                          APA: Mr. Watson Intervenes
A: **Garwood, Judith**
   P: **Dain, Catherine**
      SC: Freddie O'Neal (see p. 238)
                  1992 Lay It on the Line
                  1993 Sing a Song of Death
                  1994 Walk a Crooked Mile
                  1994 Lament for a Dead Cowboy
                  1995 Bet Against the House
                  1996 The Luck of the Draw
                  1997 Dead Man's Hand
A: **Gavin, Catherine (Irvine)**
      SC: Jacques Brunel
                  1976 Traitor's Gate
                  1978 None Dare Call It Treason
P: **Gayle, Newton**
      please see: **Marin, Muna Lee w/ Maurice C. Guiness**

A: **Geason, Susan**
    SC: Syd Fish
        SS   1990 Shaved Fish
              1991 Dog Fish
              1993 Shark Bait

A: **George, Anne**
    SC: Patricia Anne & Mary Alice
              1996 Murder on a Girls Night Out
              1996 Murder on a Bad Hair Day
              1997 Murder Makes Waves
              1997 Murder Runs in the Family

A: **George, (Susan) Elizabeth**
    SC: Det. Insp. Thomas Lynley (see p. 59)
              1988 A Great Deliverance
              1989 Payment in Blood
              1990 Well-Schooled in Murder
              1991 A Suitable Vengeance
              1992 For the Sake of Elena
              1993 Missing Joseph
              1994 Playing for the Ashes
              1996 In the Presence of the Enemy
              1997 Deception on His Mind

A: **Gibson, Maggie**
    SC: Grace de Rossa
              1995 Grace, the Hooker, the Hard Man and the Kid
              1996 The Longest Fraud
              1997 Deadly Serious

P: **Gilbert, Anthony**
    please see: **Malleson, Lucy Beatrice**

A: **Gill (Trimble), B(arbara) M(argaret)**
    SC: Insp. Tom Maybridge
              1980 Victims
                   APA: Suspect
              1985 Seminar for Murder
              1991 The Fifth Rapunzel

A: **Gill, Elizabeth**
    SC: Benvenuto Brown
              1931 Strange Holiday
                   APA: The Crime Coast
              1932 What Dread Hand?
              1933 Crime de Luxe

A: **Gilligan, Sharon**
    SC: Alix Nicholson
              1993 Danger in High Places

                1994 Danger! Cross Currents
                1996 Danger on the Levee
A: **Gilman (Butters), Dorothy**
        SC: Mrs. Emily Pollifax (see p. 252)
                1966 The Unexpected Mrs. Pollifax
                        APA: Mrs. Pollifax, Spy
                1970 The Amazing Mrs. Pollifax
                1971 The Elusive Mrs. Pollifax
                1973 A Palm for Mrs. Pollifax
                1977 Mrs. Pollifax on Safari
                1983 Mrs. Pollifax on the China Station
                1985 Mrs. Pollifax and the Hong Kong Buddha
                1988 Mrs. Pollifax and the Golden Triangle
                1990 Mrs. Pollifax and the Whirling Dervish
                1993 Mrs. Pollifax and the Second Thief
                1995 Mrs. Pollifax Pursued
                1996 Mrs. Pollifax and the Lion Killer
                1997 Mrs. Pollifax, Innocent Tourist
A: **Gilpatrick, Noreen**
        SC: Pol. Det. Kate MacLean
                1993 Final Design
                1995 Shadow of Death
A: **Gilruth, Susan**
        SC: Insp. Hugh Gordon & Liane Crawford
                1951 Sweet Revenge
                1952 Death in Ambush
                1954 Postscript to Penelope
                1956 A Corpse for Charybdis
                1957 To This Favour
                1961 Drown Her Remembrance
                1963 The Snake Is Living Yet
A: **Girdner, Jaqueline**
        SC: Kate Jasper (see p. 155)
                1991 Adjusted to Death
                1991 The Last Resort
                1992 Murder Most Mellow
                1993 Fat-Free and Fatal
                1994 Tea-Totally Dead
                1995 A Stiff Critique
                1996 Most Likely to Die
                1997 A Cry for Self-Help
P: **Giroux, E. X.**
        please see: **Shannon, Doris**

A: **Glass, Leslie**
    SC: Pol. Chf. April Woo & Jason Frank
          1993 Burning Time
          1994 Hanging Time
          1996 Loving Time

P: **Glen, Alison**
    please see: **Lowry, Cheryl Meredith w/ Louise Vetter**

J: **Glick, Ruth**
    please see: **Buckholtz, Eileen w/ Ruth Glick**

A: **Glidden, M(inna) W(esselhoft)**
    SC: Carey Brent
          1937 Death Strikes Home
              APA: Come Dwell with Death
          1937 The Long Island Murders

A: **Godfrey, Ellen**
    SC: Jane Tregar
          1988 Murder Behind Locked Doors
          1992 Georgia Disappeared
    SC: Rebeccah Rosenthal
          1976 The Case of the Cold Murderer
          1978 Murder Among the Well-To-Do

A: **Gordon, Alison**
    SC: Kate Henry (see p. 125)
          1989 The Dead Pull Hitter
          1990 Safe at Home
          1992 Night Game
          1995 Striking Out

J: **Gordon, Gordon**
    please see: **Gordon, Mildred w/ Gordon Gordon**

A: **Gordon, Mildred w/ Gordon Gordon**
    P: **Gordons, The**
    SC: D. C. Randall (a cat)
          1963 Undercover Cat
              APA: That Darn Cat
          1966 Undercover Cat Prowls Again
          1974 Catnapped: The Further Adventures of
              Undercover Cat
    SC: Gail & Mitch Mitchell
          1969 Night Before the Wedding
          1979 Night After the Wedding
    SC: John Ripley
          1950 FBI Story
          1953 Case File: FBI
          1957 Captive

1961 Operation Terror
APA: Experiment in Terror
1973 The Informant

P: **Gordons, The**
please see: **Gordon, Mildred w/ Gordon Gordon**

A: **Gosling, Paula**
SC: Lt. Jack Stryker
1985 Monkey Puzzle
1989 Backlash
1992 The Body in Blackwater Bay
1994 A Few Dying Words
1996 The Dead of Winter

SC: Det. Chf. Supt. Luke Abbott
1986 The Wychford Murder
1991 Death Penalties

SC: Sheriff Matt Gabriel
1992 The Body in Blackwater Bay
1994 A Few Dying Words
1996 The Dead of Winter

A: **Goulart, Ronald Joseph**
P: **Kains, Josephine**
SC: Terry Spring
1978 The Curse of the Golden Skull
1978 The Devil Mask Mystery
1979 The Green Lama Mystery
1979 The Whispering Cat Mystery
1979 The Witch's Tower Mystery
1980 The Laughing Dragon Mystery

A: **Goyder, Margot w/ Anne N(eville) G(oyder) Joske**
P: **Neville, Margot**
SC: Insp. Grogan
1943 Murder in Rockwater
APA: Lena Hates Men
1946 Murder and Gardenias
1948 Murder in a Blue Moon
1949 Murder of a Nymph
1951 Murder Before Marriage
1952 The Seagull Said Murder
1953 Murder of the Well-Beloved
1954 Murder and Poor Jenny
1956 Murder of Olympia
1957 Murder to Welcome Her
1958 The Flame of Murder
1959 Sweet Night for Murder

<pre>
        1960 Confession of Murder
        1961 Murder Beyond the Pale
        1962 Drop Dead
        1963 Come See Me Die
        1964 My Bad Boy
        1965 Ladies in the Dark
        1966 Head on the Sill
</pre>

A: **Grafton, Sue**
    SC: Kinsey Millhone (see p. 222)
<pre>
        1982 "A" Is for Alibi
        1985 "B" Is for Burglar
        1986 "C" Is for Corpse
        1987 "D" Is for Deadbeat
        1988 "E" Is for Evidence
        1989 "F" Is for Fugitive
        1990 "G" Is for Gumshoe
        1991 "H" Is for Homicide
        1992 "I" Is for Innocent
        1993 "J" Is for Judgement
        1994 "K" Is for Killer
        1995 "L" Is for Lawless
        1996 "M" Is for Malice
</pre>

A: **Graham, Caroline**
    SC: Insp. Barnaby
<pre>
        1987 The Killings at Badger's Drift
        1989 Death of a Hollow Man
        1993 Death in Disguise
        1995 Written in Blood
</pre>

A: **Graham, (Matilda) Winifred (Muriel)**
    SC: Miss Woolfe
<pre>
        1930 A Wolf of the Evenings
        1930 The Last Laugh
        1931 Wolf-Net
</pre>

A: **Granbeck, Marilyn**
    P: **Henderson, M. R.**
    SC: Jeanne Donovan
<pre>
        1985 By Reason Of
        1989 The Killing Game
</pre>

A: **Granbeck, Marilyn w/ Arthur Moore**
    P: **Hamilton, Adam**
    SC: Barrington Hewes-Bradford
<pre>
        1974 The Xandar Pursuit
        1974 The Yashar Pursuit
</pre>

1974 The Zaharan Pursuit
1975 The Wyss Pursuit

A: **Granger (Hulme), Ann**
    SC: Fran Varady
        1997 Asking for Trouble
        1997 Keeping Bad Company
    SC: Meredith Mitchell & Chf. Insp. Markby (see p. 258)
        1991 A Season for Murder
        1991 Say It with Poison
        1992 Cold in the Earth
        1992 Murder Among Us
        1993 Where Old Bones Lie
        1994 Flowers for His Funeral
        1995 A Fine Place for Death
        1995 A Candle for a Corpse
        1996 A Touch of Mortality
        1997 Word After Dying

P: **Grant, Linda**
    please see: **Williams, Linda V.**

A: **Grant-Adamson, Leslie**
    SC: Rain Morgan (see p. 182)
        1985 Death on Widow's Walk
            APA: Patterns in the Dust
        1985 The Face of Death
        1987 Wild Justice
        1988 Guilty Knowledge
        1990 Curse the Darkness

P: **Gray, Dulcie**
    please see: **Dennison, Dulcie Winifred Catherine Bailey**

P: **Gray, Gallagher**
    please see: **Munger, Katy**

A: **Grayland, (Valerie) Merle (Spanner)**
    SC: Hoani Mata
        1962 The Dead Men of Eden
        1963 Night of the Reaper
        1964 The Grave-Digger's Apprentice
        1965 Jest of Darkness

A: **Greber, Judith**
    P: **Roberts, Gillian**
        SC: Amanda Pepper
            1987 Caught Dead in Philadelphia
            1989 Philly Stakes
            1992 I'd Rather Be in Philadelphia
            1993 With Friends Like These

1994 How I Spent My Summer Vacation
1995 In the Dead of Summer
1996 The Mummers' Curse

A: **Green, Anna Katharine**
SC: Amelia Butterworth & Ebenezer Gryce (see p. 281)
1897 That Affair Next Door
1898 Lost Man's Lane: A Second Episode in the Life of Amelia Butterworth
1900 The Circular Study
1901 One of My Sons
1911 Initials Only
1917 The Mystery of the Hasty Arrow
SC: Caleb Sweetwater
1899 Agatha Webb
1900 The Circular Study
1906 The Woman in the Alcove
1910 The House of the Whispering Pines
1911 Initials Only
1917 The Mystery of the Hasty Arrow
SC: Ebenezer Gryce (see pp. 48, 281)
1878 The Leavenworth Case: A Lawyer's Story
1880 A Strange Disappearance
1883 Hand and Ring
1888 Behind Closed Doors
1890 A Matter of Millions
SS 1895 The Doctor, His Wife and the Clock
1897 That Affair Next Door
1898 Lost Man's Lane: A Second Episode in the Life of Amelia Butterworth
1900 The Circular Study
SS 1900 A Difficult Problem and Other Stories
1901 One of My Sons
1911 Initials Only
1917 The Mystery of the Hasty Arrow
SC: Violet Strange
SS 1915 The Golden Slipper and Other Problems for Violet Strange

A: **Green, Christine**
SC: Chf. Insp. Connor O'Neill & Det. Sgt. Fran Wilson
1993 Death in the Country
1995 Die in My Dreams
1996 Fatal Cut
SC: Kate Kinsella
1992 Deadly Errand

1993 Deadly Admirer
1995 Deadly Practice
1996 Deadly Partners

A: **Green, Edith Pinero**
SC: Dearborn V. Pinch
1977 Rotten Apples
1979 Sneaks
1982 Perfect Fools

P: **Green, Glint**
please see: **Peterson, Margaret Ann**

A: **Green, Kate**
SC: Theresa Fortunato (see p. 25)
1986 Shattered Moon
1993 Black Dreams

A: **Greenwood, D(iane) M.**
SC: Deaconess Theodora Braithwaite (see p. 91)
1991 Clerical Errors
1992 Unholy Ghost
1993 Idol Bones
1994 Holy Terrors
1995 Every Deadly Sin
1996 Mortal Spoils

A: **Greenwood, Kerry**
SC: Phryne Fisher (see p. 19)
1989 Cocaine Blues
APA: Death by Misadventure
1990 Flying Too High
1992 Death at Victoria Dock
1993 Murder on the Ballarat Train
1993 The Green Hill Murder
1994 Blood and Circuses
1995 Ruddy Gore
1996 Urn Burial

A: **Greenwood, L(illian) B(ethel)**
SC: Sherlock Holmes
1986 Sherlock Holmes and the Case of the Raleigh Legacy
1988 Sherlock Holmes and the Case of Sabina Hall
1989 Sherlock Holmes and the Thistle of Scotland

A: **Gregory, Sarah**
SC: Sharon Hays
1995 In Self Defense
1997 Public Trust

A: **Gregory, Susanna**
    SC: Matthew Bartholomew
           1996 A Plague on Both Your Houses
           1996 An Unholy Alliance
           1997 Bone of Contention

A: **Gresham, Elizabeth**
    SC: Jenny Gilette & Hunter Lewis
           1972 Puzzle in Paisley
           1973 Puzzle in Parchment
           1973 Puzzle in Parquet
           1973 Puzzle in Patchwork

 P: **Grey, Robin**
    SC: Jenny Gilette & Hunter Lewis
           1945 Puzzle in Porcelain
           1947 Puzzle in Pewter

A: **Greth, (Le) Roma (Eshbach)**
    SC: Hana Shaner
           1988 . . . Now You Don't
           1989 Plain Murder

P: **Grey, Robin**
    please see: **Gresham, Elizabeth**

A: **Griffiths, Ella**
    SC: Sgt. Rudolf Nilsen
           1982 Murder on Page Three
           1986 The Water Widow

A: **Grimes, Martha**
    SC: Det. Chf. Insp. Richard Jury
           1981 The Man with a Load of Mischief
           1982 The Old Fox Deceiv'd
           1983 The Anodyne Necklace
           1984 The Dirty Duck
           1984 The Jerusalem Inn
           1985 Help the Poor Struggler
           1985 The Deer Leap
           1986 I Am the Only Running Footman
           1987 The Five Bells and Bladebone
           1989 The Old Silent
           1991 The Old Contemptibles
           1993 The Horse You Came in On
           1995 Rainbow's End

A: **Grimes, Terris McMahan**
    SC: Theresa Galloway
           1996 Somebody Else's Child
           1997 Blood Will Tell

A: **Grimshaw, Beatrice (Ethel)**
    SC: Cristina Raye
        SS   1917 Kris-Girl
A: **Grindle, Lucretia**
    SC: Chf. Insp. Ross
           1993 The Killing of Ellis Martin
           1994 So Little to Die For
A: **Groner, Augusta**
    SC: Joe Miller
           1911 The Man with the Black Cord
           1912 Mene Tekel: A Tale of Strange Happenings
           1922 The Lady in Blue
P: **Grove, Marjorie**
    please see: **Grove, Martin**
A: **Grove, Martin**
    P: **Grove, Marjorie**
    SC: Maxine Reynolds
           1978 You'll Die Laughing
           1978 You'll Die Tomorrow
           1978 You'll Die When You Hear This
           1979 You'll Die, Darling
           1979 You'll Die Today
           1979 You'll Die Tonight
           1979 You'll Die Yesterday
A: **Grove, Martin**
    P: **Allan, Joan**
    SC: Valerie Lambert
           1979 Who Killed Me?
           1979 Who's Next?
           1979 Who's on First?
J: **Guiness, Maurice C.**
    please see: **Marin, Muna Lee w/ Maurice C. Guiness**
A: **Gunning, Sally**
    SC: Peter Bartholomew (see p. 151)
           1990 Hot Water
           1992 Ice Water
           1992 Under Water
           1993 Troubled Water
           1995 Rough Water
           1995 Still Water
           1997 Deep Water
A: **Gur, Batya**
    SC: Chf. Insp Michael Ohayon (see p. 61)
           1988 The Saturday Morning Murder: A Psychoanalytic Case

1991   Literary Murder: A Critical Case
1991   Murder on a Kibbutz: A Communal Case

H

A: **Haddad, C(arolyn) (A.)**
    SC: David Haham
          1976   Bloody September
          1978   Operation Apricot
P: **Haddam, Jane**
    please see: **Papazoglou, Orania**
A: **Haddock, Lisa**
    SC: Carmen Ramirez
          1994   Edited Out
          1995   Final Cut
P: **Hadley, Joan**
    please see: **Hess, Joan**
A: **Haffner, Margaret**
    SC: Catherine Edison
          1992   A Murder of Crows
          1994   A Killing Frost
A: **Hagen, Miriam-Ann**
    SC: Hortense Clinton
          1947   Plant Me Now
          1949   Dig Me Later
          1951   Murder—But Natch
A: **Hager, Jean**
    SC: Pol. Chf. Mitchell "Mitch" Bushyhead (see p. 78)
          1989   The Grandfather Medicine
          1990   Nightwalker
          1992   Ghostland
          1996   The Fire Carrier
    SC: Molly Bearpaw (see p. 259)
          1992   Ravenmocker
          1994   The Redbird's Cry
          1995   Seven Black Stones
          1997   The Spirit Caller
    SC: Tess Darcy
          1994   Blooming Murder
          1995   Dead and Buried
          1996   Death on the Drunkard's Path
          1997   The Last Noel

A: Haines, Carolyn
  P: **Burnes, Caroline**
    SC: Ann Tate
        1988 A Deadly Breed
        1988 A Measure of Deceit
    SC: Dawn Markey
        1988 A Deadly Breed
        1988 A Measure of Deceit
        1989 Phantom Filly

P: **Hale, Christopher**
  please see: **Stevens, Frances M(oyer) R(oss)**

A: Haley, Wendy
  SC: Alex Danilov
      1994 This Dark Paradise
      1995 These Fallen Angels

A: **Hall, Mary Bowen**
  SC: Emma Chizzit (see p. 272)
      1989 Emma Chizzit and the Queen Anne Killer
      1991 Emma Chizzit and the Sacramento Stalker
      1992 Emma Chizzit and the Napa Nemesis
      1993 Emma Chizzit and the Mother Lode Marauder

P: **Hall, Patricia**
  please see: **O'Connor, Maureen**

A: **Halpin, Mary D.**
  P: **Blake, Christina**
    SC: Insp. Ronald Dobbs
        1980 A Fragrant Death
        1981 Deadly Legacy

P: **Hambledon, Phyllis**
  please see: **MacVean, Phyllis**

A: **Hambly, Barbara**
  SC: Prof. James Asher & Simon Ysidro (see p. 26)
      1988 Those Who Hunt the Night
      1995 Traveling with the Dead

P: **Hamilton, Adam**
  please see: **Granbeck, Marilyn w/ Arthur Moore**

A: **Hamilton, Elaine**
  SC: Insp. Reynolds
      1930 Some Unknown Hand
          APA: The Westminster Mystery
      1931 Murder in the Fog
      1932 The Chelsea Mystery
      1932 The Green Death
      1934 Peril at Midnight

1935 Tragedy in the Dark
1936 The Casino Mystery
1937 Murder Before Tuesday
A: **Hamilton, Henrietta**
SC: Sally & Johnny Heldar
1956 The Two Hundred Ghost
1957 Death at One Below
1959 Answer in the Negative
1959 At Night to Die
A: **Hamilton, Laurell K.**
SC: Anita Blake
1993 Guilty Pleasures
1994 The Laughing Corpse
1995 Circus of the Damned
1996 The Lunatic Cafe
1996 Bloody Bones
1997 The Killing Dance
P: **Hamilton, Nan**
please see: **Ball, (Nanoni) Patricia (Maude Hamilton)**
A: **Hanshew, Hazel Phillips**
SC: Hamilton Cleek
1931 The Riddle of the Winged Death
1932 Murder in the Hotel
P: **Hanshew, Mary & Thomas Hanshew**
SC: Hamilton Cleek
1920 The Frozen Flame
APA: The Riddle of the Frozen Flame
1921 The Riddle of the Mysterious Light
1922 The House of Discord
APA: The Riddle of the Spinning Wheel
1924 The Amber Junk
APA: The Riddle of the Amber Ship
1925 The House of the Seven Keys
A: **Hanshew, Hazel Phillips w/ Mary Hanshew**
P: **Hanshew, Thomas**
SC: Hamilton Cleek
1915 The Riddle of the Night
1918 The Riddle of the Purple Emperor
J: **Hanshew, Mary**
please see: **Hanshew, Hazel Phillips w/ Mary Hanshew**
P: **Hanshew, Mary & Thomas Hanshew**
please see: **Hanshew, Hazel Phillips**
P: **Hanshew, Thomas**
please see: **Hanshew, Hazel Phillips w/ Mary Hanshew**

A: **Hanson, Virginia**
  SC: Adam Drew & Katherine Cornish
      1938 Death Walks the Post
      1939 Casual Slaughters
      1942 Mystery for Mary

A: **Harcourt, Palma w/ Jack H. Trotman**
  P: **Penn, John**
  SC: Insp. Dick Tansey
      1988 Outrageous Exposures
      1989 A Feast of Death
      1990 A Killing to Hide
      1991 A Knife Ill-Used
      1991 Death's Long Shadow
  SC: Insp. George Thorne
      1983 A Will to Kill
      1984 Mortal Term
      1985 A Deadly Sickness
      1986 Unto the Grave
      1986 Barren Revenge
      1987 Accident Prone

A: **Hardwick, Mollie**
  SC: Doran Fairweather Chelmarsh & Rev. Rodney Chelmarsh (see p. 138)
      1986 Malice Domestic
      1987 Parson's Pleasure
      1988 Uneaseful Death
      1989 Perish in July
      1989 The Bandersnatch
      1990 The Dreaming Damozel
      1997 Come Away, Death
  SC: Insp. Jean Darblay
    SS 1980 Juliet Bravo 1
    SS 1980 Juliet Bravo 2
      1981 Calling Juliet Bravo

A: **Harris, Charlaine**
  SC: Aurora Teagarden (see p. 215)
      1990 Real Murders
      1992 A Bone to Pick
      1994 Three Bedrooms, One Corpse
      1995 The Julius House
      1996 Dead over Heels
  SC: Lily Bard
      1996 Shakespeare's Landlord
      1997 Shakespeare's Champion

P: **Harris, Colver**
    please see: **Colver, Anne**
A: **Harris, Deborah Turner w/ Katherine Kurtz**
    SC: The Adept, Sir Adam Sinclair (see p. 30)
             1991 The Adept
             1992 The Adept, Book Two: The Lodge of the Lynx
             1993 The Adept, Book Three: The Templar Treasure
             1995 Dagger Magic
             1996 Death of an Adept
A: **Harris, Evelyn**
    SC: Largely Lee
             1985 Largely Luck
             1986 Largely Trouble
A: **Harris, Lee**
    SC: Christine Bennett (see p. 92)
             1992 The Good Friday Murder
             1992 The Yom Kippur Murder
             1993 The Christening Day Murder
             1994 The Saint Patrick's Day Murder
             1994 The Christmas Night Murder
             1995 The Thanksgiving Day Murder
             1996 The Passover Murder
             1997 The Valentine's Day Murder
             1997 The New Year's Eve Murder
A: **Harrison, Jamie**
    SC: Jules Clement
             1995 The Edge of the Crazies
             1996 Going Local
A: **Harrod-Eagles, Cynthia**
    SC: Insp. Bill Slider
             1991 Orchestrated Death
             1993 Death Watch
             1994 Death to Go
                  APA: Necrochip
             1995 Grave Music
                  APA: Dead End
             1996 Blood Lines
             1997 Killing Time
A: **Hart, Carolyn G(impel)**
    SC: Annie Laurance Darling (see p. 142)
             1987 Death on Demand
             1987 Design for Murder
             1988 Honeymoon with Murder
             1988 Something Wicked

1989 A Little Class on Murder
1990 Deadly Valentine
1991 The Christie Caper
1992 Southern Ghost
1995 Mint Julep Murder
SC: Henrie O (see p. 194)
1993 Dead Man's Island
1994 Scandal in Fair Haven
1997 Death in Lovers' Lane

P: **Hart, Ellen**
please see: **Boehnhardt, Patricia**

A: **Hart (Shrager), Jeanne**
SC: Det. Sgt. Carl Pedersen
1987 Fetish
  APA: A Personal Possession
1990 Some Die Young
1991 Threnody for Two
  APA: Lament for the Ladies

A: **Hartzmark, Gini**
SC: Kate Millholland
1992 Principal Defense
1994 Final Option
1995 Bitter Business

A: **Haymon, S(ylvia) T(heresa)**
SC: Det. Insp. Benjamin Jurnet
1980 Death and the Pregnant Virgin
  APA: Death of a Pregnant Virgin
1982 Ritual Murder
1984 Stately Homicide
1987 Death of a God
1989 A Very Particular Murder
1992 Death of a Warrior Queen
1993 A Beautiful Death
1996 Death of a Hero

A: **Haynes, Annie**
SC: Insp. Furnival
1923 The Abbey Court Murder
1926 The House in Charlton Crescent
1927 The Crow's Inn Tragedy
SC: Insp. Stoddart
1929 The Crime at Tattenham Corner
1929 Who Killed Charmian Karslake?
1930 The Crystal Beads Murder

A: **Hayter, Sparkle**
    SC: Robin Hudson
            1994 What's a Girl Gotta Do?
            1996 Nice Girls Finish Last
            1997 Revenge of the Cootie Girls
A: **Head, (Joanne) Lee**
    SC: Lexey Jane Pelazoni
            1976 The Terrarium
            1977 The Crystal Clear Case
A: **Healey, Evelyn**
    SC: Det. Supt. Horace Plummet
            1961 Let X Equal Murder
            1963 The Braydon Mystery
J: **Hearnden, Beryl**
    please see: **Balfour, Eva w/ Beryl Hearnden**
A: **Heberden, M(ary) V(iolet)**
    SC: Desmond Shannon
            1939 Death on the Door Mat
            1940 Fugitive from Murder
            1940 Subscription to Murder
            1941 Aces, Eights and Murder
            1941 The Lobster Pick Murder
            1942 Murder Follows Desmond Shannon
            1942 Murder Makes a Racket
            1943 Murder Goes Astray
            1944 Murder of a Stuffed Shirt
            1945 Vicious Pattern
            1947 Drinks on the Victim
            1947 They Can't All Be Guilty
            1948 The Case of the Eight Brothers
            1950 Exit This Way
                    APA: *You'll Fry Tomorrow*
            1950 That's the Spirit
                    APA: *Ghosts Can't Kill*
            1952 Tragic Target
            1953 Murder Unlimited
    SC: Rick Vanner
            1946 Murder Cancels All Debts
            1949 Engaged to Murder
            1951 The Sleeping Witness
P: **Leonard, Charles L.**
    SC: Paul Kilgerrin
            1942 Deadline for Destruction
            1942 The Stolen Squadron

1943 The Fanatic of Fez
   APA: Assignment to Death
1944 The Secret of the Spa
1945 Expert in Murder
1946 Pursuit in Peru
1947 Search for a Scientist
1948 The Fourth Funeral
1949 Sinister Shelter
1950 Secrets for Sale
1951 Treachery in Trieste

A: **Heilbrun, Carolyn G(old)**
   P: **Cross, Amanda**
      SC: Kate Fansler (see p. 35)
         1964 In the Last Analysis
         1967 The James Joyce Murder
         1970 Poetic Justice
         1971 The Theban Mysteries
         1976 The Question of Max
         1981 Death in a Tenured Position
            APA: Death in the Faculty
         1984 Sweet Death, Kind Death
         1986 No Word from Winifred
         1989 A Trap for Fools
         1990 The Players Come Again
         1995 An Imperfect Spy
      SS 1997 The Collected Stories

A: **Hely (Younger), Elizabeth**
      SC: Antoine Cirret
         1959 Dominant Third
            APA: I'll Be Judge, I'll Be Jury
         1960 A Mark of Displeasure

A: **Henderson, Lauren**
      SC: Sam Jones
         1995 Dead White Female
         1997 The Black Rubber Dress

P: **Henderson, M. R.**
      please see: **Granbeck, Marilyn**

A: **Hendricksen, Louise**
      SC: Dr. Amy Prescott
         1993 With Deadly Intent
         1994 Grave Secrets
         1995 Lethal Legacy

A: **Henissart, Martha w/ Mary Jane Latsis**
   P: **Dominic, R. B.**
      SC: Ben Safford (see p. 253)
         1968 Murder, Sunny Side Up

1969 Murder in High Place
1971 There Is No Justice
      APA: Murder out of Court
1974 Epitaph for a Lobbyist
1976 Murder Out of Commission
1980 The Attending Physician
1983 A Flaw in the System
      APA: Unexpected Developments

P: **Lathen, Emma**
    SC: John Putnam Thatcher (see p. 137)
1961 Banking on Death
1963 A Place for Murder
1964 Accounting for Murder
1966 Death Shall Overcome
1966 Murder Makes the Wheels Go Round
1967 Murder Against the Grain
1968 A Stitch in Time
1968 Come to Dust
1969 Murder to Go
1969 When in Greece
1970 Pick up Sticks
1971 Ashes to Ashes
1971 The Longer the Thread
1972 Murder Without Icing
1974 Sweet and Low
1975 By Hook or by Crook
1978 Double, Double, Oil and Trouble
1981 Going for the Gold
1982 Green Grow the Dollars
1988 Something in the Air
1991 East Is East
1993 Right on the Money
1996 Brewing Up a Storm
1997 A Shark out of Water

A: **Henry, Sue**
    SC: Sgt. Alex Jensen
1991 Murder on the Iditarod Trail
1995 Termination Dust
1996 Sleeping Lady
1997 Death Takes Passage

J: **Herald, Beverly Taylor**
    please see: **McCafferty, Barbara Taylor w/ Beverly Taylor Herald**

A: **Herndon, Nancy**
    SC: Elena Jarvis
1995 Acid Bath

        1995 Widows' Watch
        1996 Lethal Statues
        1996 Hunting Game
        1997 Time Bombs

A: **Hershman, Morris**
   P: **Bond, Evelyn**
      SC: Ira Yedder
        1971 Doomway
        1972 Dark Sonata
        1972 The Devil's Footprints
        1972 The Girl from Nowhere

   P: **Hervey, Evelyn**
      please see: **Keating, H(enry) R(eymond) F(itzwalter)**

A: **Hesky, Olga**
      SC: Insp. Tami Shimoni
        1966 The Serpent's Smile
        1967 Time for Treason
        1969 The Sequin Syndicate
        1970 The Different Night

A: **Hess, Joan**
      SC: Sheriff Arly Hanks (see p. 77)
        1987 Malice in Maggody
        1988 Mischief in Maggody
        1989 Much Ado in Maggody
        1990 Madness in Maggody
        1991 Mortal Remains in Maggody
        1992 Maggody in Manhattan
        1993 O Little Town of Maggody
        1994 Martians in Maggody
        1995 Miracles in Maggody
        1997 The Maggody Militia
      SC: Claire Malloy (see p. 139)
        1986 Murder at the Murder at the Mimosa Inn
        1986 Strangled Prose
        1987 Dear Miss Demeanor
        1988 A Really Cute Corpse
        1989 A Diet to Die For
        1991 Roll Over and Play Dead
        1992 Death by the Light of the Moon
        1993 Poisoned Pins
        1994 Tickled to Death
        1995 Busy Bodies
        1996 Closely Akin to Murder

P: **Hadley, Joan**
    SC: Theo Bloomer
          1986 The Night-Blooming Cereus
          1988 The Deadly Ackee

A: **Heyer, Georgette**
    SC: Supt. Hannasyde & Sgt. Hemingway
          1935 Death in the Stocks
               APA: Merely Murder
          1936 Behold, Here's Poison!
          1937 They Found Him Dead
          1938 A Blunt Instrument
          1939 No Wind of Blame
          1941 Envious Casca
          1951 Duplicate Death
          1953 Detection Unlimited

A: **Highsmith, (Mary) Patricia (Maugham)**
    SC: Tom Ripley (see p. 199)
          1955 The Talented Mr. Ripley
          1970 Ripley Under Ground
          1974 Ripley's Game
          1980 The Boy Who Followed Ripley
          1991 Ripley Under Water

A: **Hightower, Lynn S.**
    SC: Det. David Silver (see p. 67)
          1992 Alien Blues
          1993 Alien Eyes
          1994 Alien Heat
          1995 Alien Rites
    SC: Sonora Blair
          1995 Flashpoint
          1996 Eyeshot

A: **Hill, Katharine**
    SC: Lorna Donahue
          1944 Dear Dead Mother-in-Law
          1945 Case for Equity
               APA: The Case of the Absent Corpse

J: **Hitchens, (Hu)Bert**
    please see: **Hitchens, (Julia Clara Catherine) Dolores (Birk) w/ Hu(Bert) Hitchens**

P: **Hitchens, Bert & Dolores**
    please see: **Hitchens, (Julia Clara Catherine) Dolores (Birk) w/ Hu(Bert) Hitchens**

A: **Hitchens, (Julia Clara Catherine) Dolores (Birk)**
    SC: Jim Sader

1955 Sleep with Strangers
1960 Sleep with Slander

P: **Olsen, D. B.**

SC: Prof. A. Pennyfeather (see p. 36)

1945 Bring the Bride a Shroud
      APA: A Shroud for the Bride
1947 Gallows for the Groom
1948 Devious Design
1950 Something About Midnight
1951 Love Me in Death
1952 Enrollment Cancelled
      APA: Dead Babes in the Wood

SC: Rachel & Jennifer Murdock (see p. 265)

1939 The Cat Saw Murder
1942 The Alarm of the Black Cat
1943 Cat's Claw
1943 Catspaw for Murder
1944 The Cat Wears a Noose
1945 Cats Don't Smile
1946 Cats Don't Need Coffins
1948 Cats Have Tall Shadows
1949 The Cat Wears a Mask
1950 Death Wears Cat's Eyes
1951 The Cat and Capricorn
1953 The Cat Walk
1956 Death Walks on Cat Feet

SC: Lt. Stephen Mayhew

1938 The Clue in the Clay
1939 The Cat Saw Murder
1940 The Ticking Heart
1943 Cat's Claw
1943 Catspaw for Murder
1944 The Cat Wears a Noose
1946 Cats Don't Need Coffins

A: **Hitchens, (Julia Clara Catherine) Dolores (Birk) w/ Hu(Bert) Hitchens**

P: **Hitchens, Bert & Dolores**

SC: Collins & McKechnie

1955 F.O.B. Murder
1959 The Man Who Followed Women

SC: John Farrel

1957 End of the Line
1963 The Grudge

A: **Hoag, Tami**
    SC: Ellen North
              1996 Night Sins
              1996 Guilty as Sin
P: **Hobson, Polly**
    please see: **Evans, Julie Rendel**
A: **Hocker, Karla**
    SC: Sophy Bancroft
              1991 The Impertinent Miss Bancroft
              1992 The Incorrigible Sophia
A: **Hocking (Messer), (Mona Naomi) Anne**
    SC: Insp. William Austen
              1939 Old Mrs. Fitzgerald
                    APA: Deadly Is the Evil Tongue
              1940 The Wicked Flee
              1941 Miss Milverton
                    APA: Poison Is a Bitter Brew
              1942 One Shall Be Taken
              1943 Death Loves a Shining Mark
                    APA: Nile Green
              1943 Six Green Bottles
               1945 The Vultures Gather
              1946 Death at the Wedding
              1947 Prussian Blue
                    APA: The Finishing Touch
              1949 At "The Cedars"
              1950 Death Disturbs Mr. Jefferson
              1950 The Best Laid Plans
              1951 Mediterranean Murder
                    APA: Killing Kin
              1953 Death Among the Tulips
              1953 The Evil That Men Do
              1954 And No One Wept
              1955 A Reason for Murder
              1955 Poison in Paradise
              1956 Murder at Mid-Day
              1957 Relative Murder
              1957 The Simple Way of Poison
              1958 Epitaph for a Nurse
                    APA: A Victim Must Be Found
              1959 Poisoned Chalice
              1959 To Cease Upon the Midnight
              1960 The Thin-Spun Thread
              1961 Candidates for Murder

1962 He Had to Die
1968 Murder Cries Out

A: **Hodges, Doris Marjorie**
P: **Hunt, Charlotte**
SC: Dr. Paul Holton
1967 The Gilded Sarcophagus
1968 The Cup of Thanatos
1970 The Lotus Vellum
1972 The Thirteenth Treasure
1974 A Touch of Myrrh
1975 Chambered Tomb

A: **Holbrook, Teri**
SC: Gale Grayson & Katie Pru
1995 A Far and Deadly Cry
1996 The Grass Widow

P: **Holden, Genevieve**
please see: **Pou, Genevieve Long**

A: **Holding, Elisabeth Sanxay**
SC: Lt. Levy
1940 Who's Afraid?
APA: Trial by Murder
1946 The Innocent Mrs. Duff
1947 The Blank Wall
1951 Too Many Bottles
APA: The Party Was the Pay-Off
1953 Widow's Mite

A: **Holland, Isabelle**
SC: Rev. Claire Aldington
1984 A Death at St. Anselm's
1985 Flight of the Archangel
1986 A Lover Scorned
1989 A Fatal Advent
1990 The Long Search

J: **Holland, Judith**
please see: **Burton, Sarah w/ Judith Holland**

A: **Holley, Helen**
SC: Tessie Venable
1946 Blood on the Beach
1947 Dead Run

A: **Holt, Hazel**
SC: Sheila Malory (see p. 271)
1989 Gone Away
APA: Mrs. Malory Investigates
1991 The Cruellest Month

      1993 Mrs. Malory and the Festival Murder
            APA: Uncertain Death
      1994 The Shortest Journey
            APA: Mrs. Malory's Shortest Journey
      1994 Mrs. Malory: Detective in Residence
            APA: Murder on Campus
      1995 Mrs. Malory Wonders Why
            APA: Superfluous Death
      1996 Mrs. Malory: Death of a Dean

A: **Holtzer, Susan**
    SC: Anneke Haagen & Lt. Karl Genesko
      1994 Something to Kill For
      1995 Curly Smoke
      1996 Bleeding Maize and Blue
      1997 Black Diamond

A: **Hood, Margaret Page**
    SC: Gil Donan
      1954 The Silent Women
      1956 The Scarlet Thread
      1957 In the Dark Night
            APA: The Murders on Fox Island
      1959 The Bell on Lonely
      1961 Drown the Wind

A: **Hooper, Kay**
    SC: Hagen
      1987 In Serena's Web
      1987 Raven on the Wing
      1987 Rafferty's Wife
      1987 Zach's Law
      1988 Captain's Paradise
      1988 Outlaw Derek
      1988 Shades of Gray
      1988 The Fall of Lucas Kendrick
      1988 Unmasking Kelsey
      1989 Aces High
      1989 It Takes a Thief
    SC: Lane Montana
      1991 Crime of Passion
      1991 House of Cards

A: **Horansky, Ruby**
    SC: Nikki Trakos
      1990 Dead Ahead
      1994 Dead Center

A: **Hornsby, Wendy (Nelson)**
    SC: Maggie MacGowen (see p. 103)
              1989 Telling Lies
              1993 Midnight Baby
              1994 Bad Intent
              1995 77th Street Requiem
              1996 Swimming with Jonah
              1997 Hard Light
    SC: Roger Tejeda & Kate Byrd Teague
              1987 No Harm
              1990 Half a Mind

A: **Horowitz, Renee**
    SC: Ruthie Kantor Morris
              1996 Rx for Murder
              1997 Deadly Rx
              1998 Rx Alibi

A: **Hosken, Alice Cecil Seymour w/ Ernest Charles Heath Hosken**
P: **Stanton, Coralie**
    SC: Miriam Lemaire
        SS 1906 Miriam Lemaire, Money Lender
           APA: The Adventuress

J: **Hosken, Ernest Charles Heath**
    please see: **Hosken, Alice Cecil Seymour w/ Ernest Charles**
               Heath Hosken

A: **Howe, Melodie Johnson**
    SC: Maggie Hill & Claire Conrad
              1989 The Mother Shadow
              1990 Beauty Dies

A: **Huff, Tanya**
    SC: Vicki Nelson & Henry Fitzroy (see p. 29)
              1991 Blood Price
              1992 Blood Trail
              1993 Blood Lines
              1993 Blood Pact
              1997 Blood Debt

A: **Hughes, Dorothy B(elle)**
    SC: Insp. Tobin
              1940 The Cross-Eyed Bear
            APA: The Cross-Eyed Bear Murders
              1940 The So Blue Marble
              1942 The Fallen Sparrow

A: **Hultman, Helen Joan**
    SC: Tim Asher
              1929 Find the Woman
              1931 Death at Windward Hill

P: **Hunt, Charlotte**
    please see: **Hodges, Doris Marjorie**
A: **Hurt, Freda (Mary E.)**
    SC: Insp. Herbert Broom
           1960 Death by Bequest
           1961 Sweet Death
           1962 Acquainted with Murder
           1963 Death and the Bridegroom
           1964 Cold and Unhonoured
           1966 A Cause for Malice
A: **Huxley, Elspeth (Jocelyn Grant)**
    SC: Supt. Paul Vachell
           1937 Murder at Government House
           1938 Murder on Safari
           1939 Death of an Aryan
                APA: The African Poison Murders
A: **Hyde, Eleanor**
    SC: Lydia Miller
           1995 In Murder We Trust
           1996 Animal Instincts

I

A: **Infante, Anne**
    SC: Micky Douglas
           1989 Death on a Hot Summer Night
           1990 Death Among the Dunes
A: **Ingate, Mary**
    SC: Ann Hales
           1974 The Sound of the Weir
                APA: Remembrance of Miranda
           1977 This Water Laps Gently
P: **Ironside, John**
    please see: **Tait, Euphemia Margaret**
P: **Irving, Alexander**
    please see: **Fahrenkopf, Anne w/ Ruth Fox (Hume)**
A: **Irwin, Inez H(aynes)**
    SC: Patrick O'Brien
           1935 Murder Masquerade
                APA: Murder in Fancy Dress
           1936 The Poison Cross Mystery
           1938 A Body Rolled Downstairs
           1941 Many Murders
           1946 The Woman Swore Revenge

J

P: **Jackson, Marian J. A.**
please see: **Rogers, Marian**
A: **Jacobs, Jonnie**
SC: Kali O'Brien
1995 Shadow of Doubt
1997 Evidence of Guilt
SC: Kate Austen
1994 Murder Among Neighbors
1995 Murder Among Friends
1998 Murder Among Us
A: **Jacobs, Nancy Baker**
SC: Devon MacDonald
1991 The Turquoise Tattoo
1992 A Slash of Scarlet
1993 The Silver Scalpel
A: **Jaffe, Jody**
SC: Natalie Gold
1995 Horse of a Different Color
1996 Chestnut Mare, Beware
A: **James (White), P(hyllis) D(orothy) [Baroness James of Holland Park]**
SC: Supt. Adam Dalgliesh (see p. 222)
1962 Cover Her Face
1963 A Mind to Murder
1967 Unnatural Causes
1971 Shroud for a Nightingale
1972 An Unsuitable Job for a Woman
1975 The Black Tower
1977 Death of an Expert Witness
1986 A Taste for Death
1990 Devices and Desires
1994 Original Sin
1997 A Certain Justice
SC: Cordelia Gray (see p. 222)
1972 An Unsuitable Job for a Woman
1982 The Skull Beneath the Skin
A: **Jance, J(udith) A(nn)**
SC: Det. J. P. Beaumont (see p. 56)
1985 Until Proven Guilty
1986 Injustice for All
1986 Trial by Fury
1987 Taking the Fifth

1988 A More Perfect Union
1988 Improbable Cause
1989 Dismissed with Prejudice
1990 Minor in Possession
1991 Payment in Kind
1992 Without Due Process
1993 Failure to Appear
1994 Lying in Wait
1995 Name Witheld

SC: Sheriff Joanna Brady (see p. 85)
1993 Desert Heat
1994 Tombstone Courage
1995 Shoot, Don't Shoot
1996 Dead to Rights
1997 Skeleton Canyon

A: **Jerina, Carol**
SC: Jackson Fury
1988 Sweet Jeopardy
1988 The Tall Dark Alibi

A: **Jerrold, Ianthe (Bridgman)**
SC: John Christmas
1929 The Studio Crime
1930 Dead Man's Quarry

A: **John, Katherine**
SC: Sgt. Trevor Joseph
1995 Without Trace
1996 Six Foot Under
1997 Murder of a Dead Man

A: **Johns, Veronica P(arker)**
SC: Agatha Welch
1940 Hush, Gabriel!
1941 Shady Doings
SC: Webster Flagg
1953 Murder by the Day
1958 Servant's Problem

A: **Johnson, Dolores**
SC: Mandy Dyer
1997 Taken to the Cleaners
1998 Hung Up to Die

A: **Johnson, Enid w/ Margaret Lane**
P: **Jones, Jennifer**
SC: Daisy Jane Mott
1937 Murder-on-Hudson
1939 Dirge for a Dog
1939 Murder al Fresco

A: **Johnson, Pamela Hansford w/ Neil Stewart**
P: **Lombard, Nap**
    SC: Lord Winterstone
            1940 Tidy Death
            1943 Murder's a Swine
               APA: The Grinning Pig

A: **Johnston, Jane**
    SC: Louisa Evans
            1985 Pray for Ricky Foster
            1987 Paint Her Face Dead

A: **Johnston, Madeleine**
    SC: Noah Bradshaw
            1938 Comets Have Long Tails
            1938 Death Casts a Lure

A: **Jon, Lori**
    SC: Tristen Jade
            1993 Diamonds in April
            1996 Emeralds in May

A: **Jones, Hazel Wynn**
    SC: Emma Shaw
            1988 Death and the Trumpets of Tuscany
            1990 Shot on Location

P: **Jones, Jennifer**
    please see: **Johnson, Enid w/ Margaret Lane**

A: **Jordan, Jennifer**
    SC: Barry & Dee Vaughan
            1987 A Good Weekend for Murder
            1988 Murder Under the Mistletoe
            1993 Book Early for Murder
    SC: Kristin Ashe
            1992 A Safe Place to Sleep
            1993 Existing Solutions

A: **Jorgensen, Christine T.**
    SC: Stella the Stargazer, a.k.a. Jane Austen Smith
            1994 A Love to Die For
            1995 You Bet Your Life
            1997 Curl Up and Die
            1997 Death of a Dustbunny

A: **Joseph, Alison**
    SC: Sister Agnes Bourdillon
            1996 Sacred Hearts
            1997 The Hour of Our Death

J: **Joske, Anne N(eville) G(oyder)**
    please see: **Goyder, Margot w/ Anne N(eville) G(oyder) Joske**

K

A: **Kaewort, Julie**
    SC: Alex Plumtree
        1994 Unsolicited
        1997 Unbound
        1998 Unprintable
P: **Kains, Josephine**
    please see: **Goulart, Ronald Joseph**
A: **Kallen, Lucille**
    SC: C. B. Greenfield & Maggie Rome (see p. 182)
        1979 Introducing C. B. Greenfield
        1980 C. B. Greenfield: The Tanglewood Murder
        1982 C. B. Greenfield: No Lady in the House
        1984 C. B. Greenfield: The Piano Bird
        1986 C. B. Greenfield: A Little Madness
A: **Karl, Kimberly**
    SC: Jules Vern
        1990 20,000 Leagues Before Breakfast
        1991 Jules Vern in the Fur Country
        1992 Lunch with the Traveling Circus
        1994 Jules Vern, Lady Dolly and the Blue Collar Cat
    SC: Roxy & Madisen
        1995 Appointment in Avalon
        1996 The Redwood Ruse
P: **Karl, M. S.**
    please see: **Shuman, M. K.**
J: **Karni, Michaela**
    please see: **Bernell, Sue w/ Michaela Karni**
A: **Keate, E(dith) M(urray)**
    SC: Sgt. Margetson
        1930 A Wild-Cat Scheme
        1931 The Jackanapes Jacket
        1936 Demon of the Air
        1937 Demon Again
A: **Keating, H(enry) R(eymond) F(itzwalter)**
    P: **Hervey, Evelyn**
    SC: Miss Harriet Unwin
        1983 The Governess
        1985 The Man of Gold
        1986 Into the Valley of Death
A: **Kellerman, Faye**
    SC: Sgt. Peter Decker & Rina Lazarus Decker (see p. 58)
        1986 The Ritual Bath

1987 Sacred and Profane
1990 Milk and Honey
1991 Day of Atonement
1992 False Prophet
1993 Grievous Sin
1994 Sanctuary
1995 Justice
1996 Prayers for the Dead

A: **Kellogg, Marne Davis**
SC: Lilly Bennett
1995 Bad Manners
1996 Curtsey
1997 Tramp

A: **Kelly, Mary**
SC: Insp. Brett Nightingale
1956 A Cold Coming
1957 Dead Man's Riddle
1958 The Christmas Egg
SC: Det. Hedley Nicholson
1961 The Spoilt Kill
1962 Due to a Death
APA: The Dead of Summer

A: **Kelly, Mary Anne**
SC: Claire Breslinsky (see p. 213)
1990 Park Lane South, Queens
1992 Foxglove
1995 Keeper of the Mill

A: **Kelly, Nora**
SC: Gillian Adams & Det. Chf. Insp. Edward Gisborne (see p. 38)
1984 In the Shadow of King's
1992 My Sister's Keeper
1993 Bad Chemistry

A: **Kelly, Susan**
SC: Liz Connors & Det. Jack Lingemann (see p. 182)
1985 The Gemini Man
1986 The Summertime Soldiers
1988 Trail of the Dragon
1990 Until Proven Innocent
1991 And Soon I'll Come to Kill You
1992 Out of the Darkness

A: **Kelly, Susan B.**
SC: Alison Hope & Det. Insp. Nick Trevellyan (see p. 154)
1990 Time of Hope
1990 Hope Against Hope

```
              1992  Hope Will Answer
              1994  Kid's Stuff
              1996  Death Is Sweet
```

A: **Kelman, Judith**
    SC: Sarah Spooner
```
              1987  Where Shadows Fall
              1989  Hush Little Darlings
              1991  Someone's Watching
```

A: **Kelner, Toni L. P.**
    SC: Laura Fleming
```
              1993  Down Home Murder
              1994  Dead Ringer
              1995  Trouble Looking for a Place to Happen
              1996  Country Comes to Town
              1998  Tight as a Tick
```

A: **Kelsey, Vera**
    SC: Lt. Diego
```
              1941  The Owl Sang Three Times
              1943  Satan Has Six Fingers
```

P: **Kemp, Sarah**
    please see: **Butterworth, Michael**

A: **Kendall, Carol (Seeger)**
    SC: Roderick "Drawers" Random
```
              1946  The Black Seven
              1952  The Baby-Snatcher
```

A: **Kenealy, Arabella**
    SC: Lord Syfret
```
          SS  1897  Belinda's Beaux and Other Stories
```

A: **Kennett, Shirley**
    SC: Dr. Penelope Jessica "PJ" Gray
```
              1996  Gray Matter
              1997  Firecracker
```

A: **Kenney, Susan (McIlvaine)**
    SC: Roz Howard
```
              1983  Garden of Malice
              1985  Graves in Academe
              1990  One Fell Sloop
```

A: **Kijewski, Karen**
    SC: Kat Colorado (see p. 230)
```
              1989  Katwalk
              1990  Katapult
              1991  Kat's Cradle
              1992  Copy Kat
              1994  Wild Kat
```

    1995 Alley Kat Blues
    1996 Honky Tonk Kat
    1997 Kat Scratch Fever
A: **Killough, (Karen) Lee**
  SC: Insp. Garret Mikaelian
    1987 Blood Hunt
    1988 Bloodlinks
  SC: Janna Brill & Mahlon "Mama" Maxwell (see p. 50)
    1979 The Doppelganger Gambit
    1986 Spider Play
    1990 Dragon's Teeth
A: **Kilpatrick, Florence**
  SC: Elizabeth
    SS 1946 Elizabeth the Sleuth
      1949 Elizabeth Finds the Body
J: **King, Charles Thomas**
  please see: **Crossley, Maude w/ Charles Thomas King**
A: **King, Laurie R.**
  SC: Det. Kate Martinelli & Al Hawken
    1993 A Grave Talent
    1995 To Play the Fool
    1996 With Child
  SC: Mary Russell & Sherlock Holmes (see p. 17)
    1994 The Beekeeper's Apprentice
    1995 A Monstrous Regiment of Women
    1996 A Letter of Mary
P: **Kingsbury, Kate**
  please see: **Roberts, Doreen**
A: **Kittredge, Mary**
  SC: Charlotte Kent
    1987 Murder in Mendocino
    1989 Dead and Gone
    1990 Poison Pen
  SC: Edwina Crusoe, R.N. (see p. 113)
    1990 Fatal Diagnosis
    1991 Rigor Mortis
    1992 Cadaver
    1992 Walking Dead Man
    1993 Desperate Remedy
    1995 Kill or Cure
A: **Knight, Alanna**
  SC: Insp. Jeremy Faro
    1989 Bloodline
    1989 Deadly Beloved

1989 Enter Second Murderer
1991 A Quiet Death
1992 Killing Cousins
1992 To Kill a Queen
) 1993 The Evil That Men Do
1994 The Missing Duchess
1995 The Bull Slayers
1997 Murder by Appointment

A: **Knight, Kathleen Moore**
SC: Elisha Macomber
1935 Death Blew Out the Match
1936 The Clue of the Poor Man's Shilling
APA: The Poor Man's Shilling
1936 The Wheel That Turned
APA: Murder Greets Jean Holton
1937 Seven Were Veiled
APA: Death Wears a Bridal Veil
APA: Seven Were Suspect
APA: Death Wears a Veil
1938 Acts of Black Night
1938 The Tainted Token
APA: The Case of the Tainted Token
1940 Death Came Dancing
1946 The Trouble at Turkey Hill
1947 Footbridge to Death
1948 Bait for Murder
1949 The Bass Derby Murder
1952 Death Goes to a Reunion
1952 Valse Macabre
1953 Akin to Murder
1953 Three of Diamonds
1959 Beauty Is a Beast
SC: Margot Blair
1940 Rendezvous with the Past
1941 Exit a Star
1942 Terror by Twilight
1944 Design in Diamonds

A: **Knight, Kathryn Lasky**
SC: Calista Jacobs (see p. 212)
1986 Trace Elements
1990 Mortal Words
1991 Mumbo-Jumbo
1994 Dark Swan

A: **Knight, Phyllis**
    SC: Lil Ritchie
            1993 Switching the Odds
            1994 Shattered Rhythms
            1996 Lost to Sight
A: **Koehler, Margaret Hudson**
    P: **Mead, Russell**
    SC: Dr. Peter Casey
            1980 The Moses Bottle
            1981 The Nightingale Trivet
            1981 The Third One
A: **Kraft, Gabrielle**
    SC: Jerry Zalman
            1987 Bullshot
            1988 Screwdriver
            1989 Let's Rob Roy
            1990 Bloody Mary
A: **Krentz, Jayne Ann**
    P: **Castle, Jayne**
    SC: Guinevere Jones
            1986 The Chilling Deception
            1986 The Desperate Games
            1986 The Sinister Touch
            1986 The Fatal Fortune
A: **Krich, Rochelle Majer**
    SC: Det. Jessie Drake (see p. 69)
            1993 Fair Game
            1994 Angel of Death
    SC: Det. Sam Ryker
            1990 Where's Mommy Now?
            1991 Till Death Do Us Part
A: **Kruger, Mary**
    SC: Brooke Cassidy & Matt Devlin
            1994 Death on the Cliff Walk
            1995 No Honeymoon for Death
            1996 Masterpiece of Murder
P: **Kruger, Paul**
    please see: **Sebenthal, Roberta Elizabeth**
A: **Kunz, Kathleen**
    SC: Terry Girard
            1993 Murder Once Removed
            1996 Death in a Private Place
J: **Kurtz, Katherine**
    please see: **Harris, Deborah Turner w/ Katherine Kurtz**

L

A: **La Plante, Lynda**
    SC: Det. Chf. Insp. Jane Tennison (see p. 63)
            1991 Prime Suspect
            1993 Prime Suspect 2
            1994 Prime Suspect 3
    SC: Lt. Lorraine Page
            1996 Cold Shoulder
            1997 Cold Blood
    SC: The Widows (see p. 202)
            1983 The Widows
            1985 The Widows 2
A: **Labus, Marta Haake**
  P: **McCormick, Claire**
    SC: John Waltz
            1982 Resume for Murder
            1983 The Club Paradis Murders
            1985 Murder in Cowboy Bronze
P: **Lacey, Sarah**
    please see: **Mitchell, Kay**
A: **Lachnit, Carroll**
    SC: Hannah Barlow
            1995 Murder in Brief
            1996 A Blessed Death
A: **Lackey, Mercedes**
    SC: Diana Tregarde
            1989 Burning Water
            1990 Children of the Night
            1991 Jinx High
P: **Laing, Patrick**
    please see: **Long, Amelia Reynolds**
P: **Lake, Deryn**
    please see: **Lampitt, Dinah**
A: **Lamb, J. Dayne**
    SC: Teal Stewart
            1993 Questionable Behavior
            1994 A Question of Preference
            1995 Unquestioned Loyalty
J: **Lambert, Dudley**
    please see: **Lambert, Rosa w/ Dudley Lambert**
P: **Lambert, Mercedes**
    please see: **Munson, Douglas Anne**

A: **Lambert, Rosa w/ Dudley Lambert**
    SC: Glyn Morgan
           1928 Monsieur Faux-Pas
                 APA: Death Goes to Brussels
           1930 The Mediterranean Murder
           1935 The Mystery of the Golden Wings
           1938 Crime in Quarantine
A: **Lampitt, Dinah**
    P: **Lake, Deryn**
    SC: John Rawlings (see p. 9)
           1994 Death in the Dark Walk
           1995 Death at the Beggar's Opera
A: **Landreth, Marsha**
    SC: Dr. Samantha Turner
           1992 The Holiday Murders
           1993 A Clinic for Murder
           1994 Vial Murders
A: **Lane, (Margaret) Gret**
    SC: Insp. Hook
           1937 Three Died That Night
           1938 The Red Mirror Mystery
    SC: John Barrin
           1930 The Curlew Coombe Mystery
           1932 The Hotel Cremona Mystery
           1933 The Unknown Enemy
           1939 Death Visits the Summer-House
           1940 Death in Mermaid Lane
           1942 Death Prowls the Cove
           1943 The Guest with the Scythe
    SC: Kate Marsh
           1930 The Curlew Coombe Mystery
           1931 The Lantern House Affair
           1932 The Hotel Cremona Mystery
           1933 The Unknown Enemy
           1939 Death Visits the Summer-House
           1940 Death in Mermaid Lane
           1942 Death Prowls the Cove
           1943 The Guest with the Scythe
J: **Lane, Margaret**
    please see: **Johnson, Enid w/ Margaret Lane**
P: **Lang, Maria**
    please see: **Lange, Dagmar Maria**
A: **Lange, Dagmar Maria**
    P: **Lang, Maria**
    SC: Christer Wick
           1966 A Wreath for the Bride

1990 A Tasty Way to Die
1991 Hotel Morgue
1992 Recipe for Death
1993 Death and the Epicure
1994 Death at the Table
1995 Death at La Provencale
1996 Diet for Death

A: **Law (Trecker), Janice**
SC: Anna Peters (see p. 200)
1976 The Big Payoff
1977 Gemini Trip
1978 Under Orion
1980 The Shadow of the Palms
1981 Death Under Par
1992 Time Lapse
1993 A Safe Place to Die
1994 Backfire
1997 Cross-Check

A: **Lawrence, Hilda (Hildegarde Kronemiller)**
SC: Mark East
1944 Blood upon the Snow
1945 A Time to Die
1947 Death of a Doll

P: **Lawrence, Margaret**
please see: **Lorens, M(argaret) K(eilstrup)**

A: **Lawrence, Margery (H.)**
SC: Miles Pennoyer
SS 1945 Number Seven Queer Street
SS 1959 Master of Shadows

A: **Lawrence, Martha C.**
SC: Dr. Elizabeth Chase
1995 Murder in Scorpio
1997 The Cold Heart of Capricorn

J: **Lederer, Norman (Lewis)**
please see: **Day (Lederer), Lillian w/ Norbert (Lewis) Lederer**

P: **Lee, Babs**
please see: **Van der Veer Lee, Marion**

A: **Lee, Barbara**
SC: Eve Elliott
1995 Death in Still Waters
1997 Final Closing

P: **Lee, Gypsy Rose**
please see: **Craig, Georgiana Ann Randolph**

A: **Lee, Jennette (Barbour Perry)**
    SC: Millicent Newberry
            1909 Simeon Tetlow's Shadow
            1917 The Green Jacket
            1922 The Mysterious Office
            1925 Dead Right

A: **Lee, Marie**
    SC: Marguerite Smith
            1995 The Curious Cape Cod Skull
            1996 The Fatal Cape Cod Funeral
            1997 The Mysterious Cape Cod Manuscript

A: **Lee, Norma**
    SC: Norma "Nicky" Lee
            1953 Lover—Say It with Mink!
            1953 The Beautiful Gunner
            1954 Another Woman's Man
            1954 The Broadway Jungle

P: **Lee, W. W.**
    please see: **Lee, Wendi**

A: **Lee, Wendi**
    SC: Angela Matelli
            1994 The Good Daughter
            1996 Missing Eden

  P: **Lee, W. W.**
    SC: Jefferson Birch
            1989 Rogue's Gold
            1990 Rustler's Venom
            1991 Rancher's Blood
            1992 Robber's Trail
            1993 Outlaw's Fortune
            1995 Cannon's Revenge

P: **Leek, Margaret**
    please see: **Bowen-Judd, Sara Hutton**

A: **Lemarchand, Elizabeth (Wharton)**
    SC: Insp. Tom Pollard
            1967 Death of an Old Girl
            1968 The Affacombe Affair
            1969 Alibi for a Corpse
            1971 Death on Doomsday
            1972 Cyanide with Compliments
            1973 Let or Hindrance
                APA: No Vacation from Murder
            1974 Buried in the Past
            1976 Step in the Dark

1977 Unhappy Returns
1978 Suddenly While Gardening
1980 Change for the Worse
1981 Nothing to Do with the Case
1982 Troubled Waters
1984 Light Through Glass
1984 The Wheel Turns
1987 Who Goes Home?
1988 The Glade Manor Murder

A: **Lentolainen, Leena**
SC: Maria Kallio
1993 Ensimmainen Murhani (My First Murder)
1994 Harmin Paikka (Armi of Troubles)
1995 Kuparisydan (Heart of Copper)

A: **Leon, Donna**
SC: Comm. Guido Brunetti (see p. 68)
1992 Death at La Fenice
1993 Death in a Strange Country
1994 Dressed for Death
APA: The Anonymous Venetian
1995 Death and Judgment
APA: A Venetian Reckoning
1996 Acqua Alta
APA: Death in High Water
1997 The Death of Faith

P: **Leonard, Charles L.**
please see: **Heberden, M(ary) V(iolet)**

A: **Leslie, Jean**
SC: Peter Ponsonby
1945 One Cried Murder
1946 Two Faced Murder
1947 Three-Cornered Murder

P: **Lewis, Lange**
please see: **Beynon, Jane**

A: **Lewis (Brown), Sherry**
SC: Fred Vickery
1995 No Place for Secrets
1996 No Place Like Home
1996 No Place for Death
1997 No Place for Tears
1997 No Place for Sin

A: **Ley, Alice Chetwynd**
SC: Anthea & Justin Rutherford
1984 A Reputation Dies

1987　A Fatal Assignation
1989　Masquerade of Vengeance
A:　**Liddon, E(loise)**
　　SC:　Peggy Fairfield
　　　　　1934　The Riddle of the Russian Princess
　　　　　1935　The Riddle of the Florentine Folio
A:　**Lilly, Jean**
　　SC:　Bruce Perkins
　　　　　1929　False Face
　　　　　1934　Death in B-Minor
　　　　　1940　Death Thumbs a Ride
A:　**Lin-Chandler, Irene**
　　SC:　Holly-Jean Ho
　　　　　1995　The Healing of Holly-Jean
　　　　　1996　Grievous Angel
A:　**Lincoln, Natalie S(umner)**
　　SC:　Det. Ferguson
　　　　　1920　The Red Seal
　　　　　1921　The Unseen Ear
　　SC:　Insp. Mitchell
　　　　　1916　I Spy
　　　　　1917　The Nameless Man
　　　　　1918　The Moving Finger
　　　　　1918　The Three Strings
　　　　　1922　The Cat's Paw
　　　　　1923　The Meredith Mystery
　　　　　1925　The Missing Initial
　　　　　1926　The Blue Car Mystery
　　　　　1927　P.P.C.
　　　　　1927　The Dancing Silhouette
A:　**Lindop, Audrey Erskine**
　　SC:　Father Keogh
　　　　　1953　The Singer Not the Song
　　　　　1956　The Judas Figures
A:　**Linington, (Barbara) Elizabeth**
　　SC:　Sgt. Ivor Maddox
　　　　　1964　Greenmask!
　　　　　1964　No Evil Angel
　　　　　1966　Date with Death
　　　　　1967　Something Wrong
　　　　　1968　Policeman's Lot
　　　　　1971　Practice to Deceive
　　　　　1973　Crime by Chance
　　　　　1977　Perchance of Death

1979 No Villain Need Be
1980 Consequence of Crime
1982 Skeletons in the Closet
1984 Felony Report
1986 Strange Felony

P: **Egan, Lesley**
SC: Jesse Falkenstein
1962 A Case for Appeal
1962 Against the Evidence
1964 My Name Is Death
1966 Some Avenger, Rise!
1968 A Serious Investigation
1970 In the Death of a Man
1972 Paper Chase
1977 The Blind Search
1978 Look Back on Death
1980 Motive in Shadow
1981 The Miser
1983 Little Boy Lost
1985 The Wine of Life

SC: Vic Varallo
1961 The Borrowed Alibi
1962 A Case for Appeal
1963 Run to Evil
1965 Detective's Due
1967 The Nameless Ones
1969 The Wine of Violence
1971 Malicious Mischief
1976 Scenes of Crime
1978 A Dream Apart
1979 The Hunters and the Hunted
1980 A Choice of Crimes
1982 Random Death
1984 Crime for Christmas

P: **Shannon, Dell**
SC: Lt. Luis Mendoza (see p. 48)
1960 Case Pending
1961 The Ace of Spades
1962 Extra Kill
1962 Knave of Hearts
1963 Death of a Busybody
1963 Double Bluff
1964 Mark of Murder
1964 Root of All Evil

1965 Death by Inches
1965 The Death-Bringers
1966 Coffin Corner
1966 With a Vengeance
1967 Chance to Kill
1967 Rain with Violence
1968 Kill with Kindness
1969 Crime on Their Hands
1969 Schooled to Kill
1970 Unexpected Death
1971 The Ringer
1971 Whim to Kill
1972 Murder with Love
1972 With Intent to Kill
1973 No Holiday for Crime
1973 Spring of Violence
1974 Crime File
1975 Deuces Wild
1976 Streets of Death
1977 Appearances of Death
1978 Cold Trail
1979 Felony at Random
1980 Felony File
1981 Murder Most Strange
1982 The Motive on Record
1983 Exploit of Death
1984 Destiny of Death
1985 Chaos of Crime
1986 Blood Count
SS 1987 Murder by the Tale

A: **Linscott, Gillian**
SC: Birdie Linnett
1984 A Healthy Body
1985 Murder Makes Tracks
1986 Knightfall
1987 A Whiff of Sulfur
SC: Nell Bray
1991 Sister Beneath the Sheet
1992 Hanging on the Wire
1993 Stage Fright
1995 An Easy Day for a Lady
      APA: *Widow's Peak*
1995 Crown Witness
1996 Dead Man's Sweetheart

A: **Livingston, Nancy**
    SC: G. D. H. Pringle
        1985 The Trouble at Aquitaine
        1986 Fatality at Bath and Wells
        1987 Incident at Parga
        1988 Death in a Distant Land
        1989 Death in Close-Up
        1990 Mayhem at Parva
        1992 Unwillingly to Vegas
        1993 Quiet Murder

A: **Locke, G(ladys) E(dson)**
    SC: Insp. Burton
        1922 The Red Cavalier
        1923 The Scarlet Macaw
        1924 The Purple Mist
        1925 The House on the Downs
    SC: Mercedes Quero
        1914 That Affair at Portstead Manor
        1922 The Red Cavalier

A: **Lockridge, Frances (Louise Davis) w/ Richard (Orson) Lockridge**
    SC: Bernard Simmons
        1962 And Left for Dead
        1964 The Devious One
           APA: Four Hours to Fear
    SC: Insp. Merton Heimrich
        1946 Death of a Tall Man
        1947 Think of Death
        1948 I Want to Go Home
        1949 Spin Your Web, Lady!
        1950 Foggy, Foggy Death
        1951 A Client Is Cancelled
        1952 Death by Association
           APA: Trail by Terror
        1953 Stand Up and Die
        1954 Death and the Gentle Bull
           APA: Killer in the Straw
        1955 Burnt Offering
        1956 Let Dead Enough Alone
        1957 Practice to Deceive
        1958 Accent on Murder
        1960 Show Red for Danger
        1961 With One Stone
           APA: No Dignity in Death

1962 First Come, First Kill
1963 The Distant Clue
SC: Nathan Shapiro
    1956 The Faceless Adversary
        APA: Case of the Murdered Redhead
    1957 The Tangled Cord
    1959 Murder and Blueberry Pie
        APA: Call It Coincidence
    1961 The Drill Is Death
SC: Pam & Jerry North
    1940 The Norths Meet Murder
        APA: Mr. & Mrs. North Meet Murder
    1941 A Pinch of Poison
    1941 Murder out of Turn
    1942 Death on the Aisle
    1942 Hanged for a Sheep
    1943 Death Takes a Bow
    1944 Killing the Goose
    1945 Payoff for the Banker
    1946 Death of a Tall Man
    1946 Murder Within Murder
    1947 Untidy Murder
    1948 Murder Is Served
    1949 The Dishonest Murderer
    1950 Murder in a Hurry
    1951 Murder Comes First
    1952 Dead as a Dinosaur
    1953 Curtain for a Jester
    1953 Death Has a Small Voice
    1954 A Key to Death
    1955 Death of an Angel
        APA: Mr. & Mrs. North and the Poisoned Playboy
    1956 Voyage into Violence
    1958 The Long Skeleton
    1959 Murder Is Suggested
    1960 The Judge Is Reversed
    1961 Murder Has Its Points
    1963 Murder by the Book
SC: Paul Lane
    1962 Night of Shadows
    1964 Quest for the Bogeyman
J: **Lockridge, Richard (Orson)**
    please see: **Lockridge, Frances (Louise Davis) w/ Richard (Orson) Lockridge**

A: **Logan, Margaret**
    SC: Olivia Chapman
        1994 The End of an Altruist
        1995 Never Let a Stranger in Your House
P: **Lombard, Nap**
    please see: **Johnson, Pamela Hansford w/ Neil Stewart**
A: **Long, Amelia Reynolds**
    SC: Edward Trelawney
        1939 The Shakespeare Murders
        1940 Invitation to Death
            APA: The Carter Kidnapping Case
        1940 Murder Times Three
        1941 Four Feet in the Grave
        1943 The Triple Cross Murders
        1944 Death Looks Down
        1944 Symphony in Murder
    SC: Katherine "Peter" Piper
        1940 The Corpse at the Quill Club
        1941 Four Feet in the Grave
        1942 Murder by Scripture
        1942 Murder Goes South
        1944 Death Looks Down
        1948 It's Death, My Darling!
        1951 The Lady Saw Red
    SC: Steve Carter
        1943 Death Wears a Scarab
        1943 Murder to Type
        1944 Death Has a Will
        1944 Murder by Treason
        1945 Once Acquitted
        1947 Murder by Magic
        1950 The House with Green Shutters
            APA: The House with Green Shudders
P: **Laing, Patrick**
    SC: Patrick Laing
        1945 If I Should Murder
        1945 Stone Dead
        1946 Murder from the Mind
        1949 A Brief Case of Murder
        1951 The Lady Is Dead
        1957 The Shadow of Murder
P: **Reynolds, Adrian**
    SC: Prof. Dennis Barrie
        1947 Formula for Murder

1950 The Leprechaun Murders
1952 The Round Table Murders

A: **Long, Gabrielle Margaret Vere Campbell**
P: **Bowen, Marjorie**
    SC: Brother Felipe Bruno
        SS 1934 The Triumphant Beast

A: **Long, Lydia**
P: **Blackmur, L. L.**
    SC: Galen Shaw & Julian Baugh
        1988 Love Lies Bleeding
        1989 Love Lies Slain

P: **Lorac, E. C. R.**
    please see: **Rivett, Edith Caroline**

A: **Lordon, Randye**
    SC: Sydney Sloane
        1993 Brotherly Love
        1994 Sister's Keeper
        1997 Father Forgive Me

A: **Lorens, M(argaret) K(eilstrup)**
    SC: Winston Marlowe Sherman (see p. 43)
        1990 Deception Island
        1990 Ropedancer's Fall
        1990 Sweet Narcissus
        1991 Dreamland
        1993 Sorrowheart
P: **Lawrence, Margaret**
    SC: Hannah Trevor
        1996 Hearts and Bones
        1997 Blood Red Roses

A: **Lottman, Eileen (Shurb)**
    SC: Jaime Sommers
        1976 Extracurricular Activities
        1977 Welcome Home

A: **Lovett, Sarah**
    SC: Dr. Sylvia Strange
        1995 Dangerous Attachments
        1996 Acquired Motives

A: **Lowry, Cheryl Meredith w/ Louise Vetter**
P: **Glen, Alison**
    SC: Charlotte Sams
        1992 Showcase
        1995 Trunk Show

P: **Lynch, Lawrence**
    please see: **Van Deventer, Emma M.**

P: **Lynch, Miriam**
    please see: **Wallace, Mary**
A: **Lyon, (Mabel) Dana**
    SC: Hilda Trenton
            1950 The Tentacles
            1963 Spin the Web Tight
J: **Lyons, Ivan**
    please see: **Lyons, Nan w/ Ivan Lyons**
A: **Lyons, Nan w/ Ivan Lyons**
    SC: Natasha O'Brien & Max Ogden
            1976 Someone Is Killing the Great Chefs of Europe
            1993 Someone Is Killing the Great Chefs of America

M

P: **Mace, Merlda**
    please see: **McCoy, Madeleine**
A: **MacGowan, Alice w/ Perry Newberry**
    SC: Jerry Boyne
            1922 The Million Dollar Suitcase
            1924 The Mystery Woman
            1925 Shaken Down
            1926 The Seventh Passenger
            1927 Who Is This Man?
A: **MacGregor, T(rish) J(aneshutz)**
    SC: Quin St. James & Mike McCleary (see p. 226)
            1987 Dark Fields
            1987 Kill Flash
            1988 Death Sweet
            1989 On Ice
            1990 Kin Dread
            1991 Death Flats
            1992 Spree
            1993 Storm Surge
            1994 Blue Pearl
            1995 Mistress of the Bones
   P: **Drake, Alison**
      SC: Aline Scott
            1988 Fevered
            1988 Tango Key
            1989 Black Moon
            1990 Lagoon
            1992 High Strangeness

A: **MacInnes, Helen (Clark)**
    SC: Robert Renwick
            1980 The Hidden Target
            1982 Cloak of Darkness
P: **Mack, Evalina**
    please see: **McNamara, Lena Brooke**
A: **MacKay (Smith), Amanda**
    SC: Hannah Land
            1976 Death Is Academic
            1981 Death on the Eno
                    APA: Death on the River
A: **MacKintosh, Elizabeth**
P: **Tey, Josephine**
    SC: Insp. Alan Grant (see p. 49)
            1929 The Man in the Queue
                    APA: Killer in the Crowd
            1936 A Shilling for Candles
            1948 The Franchise Affair
            1950 To Love and Be Wise
            1951 The Daughter of Time
            1952 The Singing Sands
A: **MacKintosh, May**
    SC: Laurie Grant & Stewart Noble
            1972 Appointment in Andalusia
            1973 A King and Two Queens
                    APA: Assignment in Andorra
            1974 The Sicilian Affair
                    APA: Dark Paradise
A: **MacLeod, Charlotte (Matilda Hughes)**
    SC: Prof. Peter Shandy (see p. 36)
            1978 Rest You Merry
            1979 The Luck Runs Out
            1982 Wrack and Rune
            1983 Something the Cat Dragged In
            1985 The Curse of the Giant Hogweed
            1987 The Corpse in Oozack's Pond
      SS 1987 Grab Bag
            1989 Vane Pursuit
            1991 An Owl Too Many
            1994 Something in the Water
            1996 Exit the Milkman
    SC: Sarah Kelling Bittersohn & Max Bittersohn (see pp. 208, 282)
            1979 The Family Vault
            1980 The Withdrawing Room

           1981 The Palace Guard
           1983 The Bilbao Looking Glass
           1983 The Convivial Codfish
           1985 The Plain Old Man
SS   1987 Grab Bag
           1988 The Recycled Citizen
           1988 The Silver Ghost
           1990 The Gladstone Bag
           1992 The Resurrection Man
           1995 The Odd Job

P: **Craig, Alisa**
    SC: Insp. Madoc Rhys
           1980 A Pint of Murder
           1981 Murder Goes Mumming
           1986 A Dismal Thing to Do
           1989 Trouble in the Brasses
           1992 The Wrong Rite
    SC: The Grub-and-Stakers
           1981 The Grub-and-Stakers Move a Mountain
           1985 The Grub-and-Stakers Quilt a Bee
           1988 The Grub-and-Stakers Pinch a Poke
           1990 The Grub-and-Stakers Spin a Yarn
           1993 The Grub-and-Stakers House a Haunt

P: **Macrae, Travis**
    please see: **Feagles, Anita Macrae**

A: **MacVean, Phyllis**
  P: **Hambledon, Phyllis**
    SC: Insp. "Tubby" Hall
           1958 Keys for the Criminal
           1959 Murder and Miss Ming

P: **MacVeigh, Sue**
    please see: **Nearing, Elizabeth C.**

A: **Maiman, Jaye**
    SC: Robin Miller
           1991 I Left My Heart
           1992 Crazy for Loving
           1993 Under My Skin
           1994 Someone to Watch
           1996 Baby, It's Cold
           1997 Old Black Magic

A: **Malim, Barbara**
    SC: Simon Chard
           1937 Murder on Holiday
           1939 Seven Looked On

A: **Malleson, Lucy Beatrice**
P: **Gilbert, Anthony**
   SC: Arthur G. Crook (see p. 165)
      1936 Murder by Experts
      1937 Murder Has No Tongue
      1937 The Man Who Wasn't There
      1938 Treason in My Breast
      1939 The Bell of Death
      1939 The Clock in the Hatbox
      1940 Dear Dead Woman
                APA: Death Takes a Redhead
      1941 The Vanishing Corpse
                APA: She Vanished in the Dawn
      1941 The Woman in Red
                APA: The Mystery of the Woman in Red
      1942 Something Nasty in the Woodshed
                APA: Mystery in the Woodshed
      1942 The Case of the Tea-Cosy's Aunt
                APA: Death in the Blackout
      1943 The Mouse Who Wouldn't Play Ball
                APA: 30 Days to Live
      1944 A Spy for Mr. Crook
      1944 The Scarlet Button
                APA: Murder Is Cheap
      1944 He Came by Night
                APA: Death at the Door
      1945 Don't Open the Door
                APA: Death Lifts the Latch
      1945 Lift Up the Lid
                APA: The Innocent Bottle
      1945 The Black Stage
                APA: Murder Cheats the Bride
      1946 The Spinster's Secret
                APA: By Hook or by Crook
      1947 Death in the Wrong Room
      1947 Die in the Dark
                APA: The Missing Widow
      1949 Death Knocks Three Times
      1950 A Nice Cup of Tea
                APA: The Wrong Body
      1950 Murder Comes Home
      1951 Lady Killer
      1952 Miss Pinnegar Disappears
                APA: A Case for Mr. Crook

1953 Footsteps Behind Me
      APA: Black Death
      APA: Dark Death
1954 Snake in the Grass
      APA: Death Won't Wait
1955 A Question of Murder
      APA: Is She Dead Too?
1956 And Death Came Too
1956 Riddle of a Lady
1957 Give Death a Name
1958 Death Against the Clock
1959 Death Takes a Wife
      APA: Death Casts a Long Shadow
1959 Third Crime Lucky
      APA: Prelude to Murder
1960 Out for the Kill
1961 She Shall Die
      APA: After the Verdict
1961 Uncertain Death
1962 No Dust in the Attic
1963 Ring for a Noose
1964 Knock, Knock, Who's There?
      APA: The Voice
1964 The Fingerprint
1965 Passenger to Nowhere
1966 The Looking Glass Murder
1967 The Visitor
1968 Night Encounter
      APA: Murder Anonymous
1969 Missing from Her Home
1970 Death Wears a Mask
      APA: Mr. Crook Lifts the Mask
1971 Tenant for the Tomb
1972 Murder's a Waiting Game
1974 A Nice Little Killing
SC: M. Dupuy
1934 The Man in the Button Boots
1936 Courtier to Death
      APA: The Dover Train Mystery
SC: Scott Egerton
1927 The Tragedy at Freyne
1928 The Murder of Mrs. Davenport
1929 Death at Four Corners
1929 The Mystery of the Open Window

        1930 The Night of the Fog
        1932 The Body on the Beam
        1932 The Long Shadow
        1933 The Musical Comedy Crime
        1934 An Old Lady Dies
        1935 The Man Who Was Too Clever
A: **Malmont, Valerie S.**
    SC: Tori Miracle
        1994 Death Pays the Rose Rent
        1997 Death, Lies, and Apple Pies
A: **Maney, Mabel**
    SC: Nancy Clue
        1993 The Case of the Not-So-Nice Nurse
        1994 The Case of the Good-for-Nothing Girlfriend
        1995 A Ghost in the Closet
A: **Mann, Jessica**
    SC: Tamara Hoyland (see p. 252)
        1981 Funeral Sites
        1983 No Man's Island
        1984 Grave Goods
        1986 A Kind of Healthy Grave
        1988 Death Beyond the Nile
        1991 Faith, Hope and Homicide
    SC: Thea Crawford
        1973 The Only Security
              APA: *Troublecross*
        1975 Captive Audience
        1981 Funeral Sites
        1983 No Man's Island
        1984 Grave Goods
A: **Manning, Adelaide Frances Oke w/ Cyril Henry Coles**
    P: **Coles, Manning**
    SC: Tommy Hambledon (see p. 252)
        1940 Drink to Yesterday
        1940 Pray Silence
              APA: *A Toast to Tomorrow*
        1941 They Tell No Tales
        1943 Without Lawful Authority
        1945 Green Hazard
        1946 The Fifth Man
        1947 A Brother for Hugh
              APA: *With Intent to Deceive*
        1947 Let the Tiger Die
        1948 Among Those Absent

1949 Diamonds to Amsterdam
1949 Not Negotiable
1950 Dangerous by Nature
1951 Now or Never
1952 Alias Uncle Hugo
    APA: Operation Manhunt
1952 Night Train to Paris
1953 A Knife for the Juggler
    APA: The Vengeance Man
1954 Not for Export
    APA: The Mystery of the Stolen Plans
    APA: All That Glitters
1955 The Man in the Green Hat
1956 Birdwatcher's Quarry
    APA: The Three Beans
1956 The Basle Express
1957 Death of an Ambassador
1958 No Entry
1960 Crime in Concrete
    APA: Concrete Crime
1960 Nothing to Declare
1961 Search for a Sultan
1963 The House at Pluck's Gutter

P: **Gaite, Francis**
SC: Charles & James Latimer
1954 Brief Candles
1955 Happy Returns
    APA: A Family Matter
1958 Come and Go

J: **Manning, Bruce**
please see: **Bristow, Gwen w/ Bruce Manning**

P: **Mannon, M. M.**
please see: **Mannon, Martha w/ Mary Ellen Mannon**

A: **Mannon, Martha w/ Mary Ellen Mannon**
P: **Mannon, M. M.**
SC: Sheriff George White
1942 Here Lies Blood
1944 Murder on the Program

J: **Mannon, Mary Ellen**
please see: **Mannon, Martha w/ Mary Ellen Mannon**

A: **Mantell, Laurie**
SC: Det. Sgt. Steve Arrow (see p. 72)
1978 Murder in Fancy Dress

1980 A Murder or Three
1980 Murder and Chips
1983 Murder to Burn
1984 Murder in Vain

A: **Manthorne, Jackie**
   SC: Harriet Hubley
       1994 Ghost Motel
       1995 Deadly Reunion
       1995 Last Resort
       1996 Final Take
       1997 Sudden Death

A: **Marin, Muna Lee w/ Maurice C. Guiness**
   P: **Gayle, Newton**
   SC: James Greer
       1935 Death Follows a Formula
       1935 The Sentry-Box Murder
            APA: Murder in the Haunted Sentry-Box
       1936 Murder at 28:10
       1937 Death in the Glass
       1938 Sinister Crag

P: **Mariz, Linda**
   please see: **French, Linda**

A: **Marlett, Melba (Balmat)**
   SC: Sarah O'Brien
       1941 Death Has a Thousand Doors
       1943 Another Day Toward Death
            APA: Witness in Peril

A: **Maron, Margaret**
   SC: Judge Deborah Knott (see p. 175)
       1992 Bootlegger's Daughter
       1993 Southern Discomfort
       1994 Shooting at Loons
       1996 Up Jumps the Devil
       1997 Killer Market
   SC: Det. Sigrid Harald (see p. 51)
       1981 One Coffee With
       1984 Death of a Butterfly
       1985 Death in Blue Folders
       1987 The Right Jack
       1988 Baby Doll Games
       1989 Corpus Christmas
       1991 Past Imperfect
       1995 Fugitive Colors

A: **Marriott, Mary**
   P: **Browne, Lizbie**
      SC: Elizabeth Blair
          1992 Broken Star
          1995 Turkey Tracks
A: **Marris, Kathrine**
   P: **Beck, K. K.**
      SC: Iris Cooper & Jack Clancy
          1984 Death in a Deck Chair
          1986 Murder in a Mummy Case
          1989 Peril Under the Palms
      SC: Jane da Silva (see p. 292)
          1992 A Hopeless Case
          1993 Amateur Night
          1994 Electric City
          1995 Cold Smoked
      SC: The Body in the . . . series
          1987 The Body in the Volvo
          1992 The Body in the Cornflakes
A: **Marsh, (Edith) Ngaio**
      SC: Insp. Roderick Alleyn (see p. 49)
          1934 A Man Lay Dead
          1935 Enter a Murderer
          1935 The Nursing Home Murder
          1936 Death in Ecstasy
          1937 Vintage Murder
      SC: Insp. Roderick Alleyn & Agatha Troy Alleyn (see p. 207)
          1938 Artists in Crime
          1938 Death in a White Tie
          1939 Overture to Death
          1940 Death at the Bar
          1940 Death of a Peer
              APA: *Surfeit of Lampreys*
          1941 Death and the Dancing Footman
          1943 Colour Scheme
          1945 Died in the Wool
          1947 Final Curtain
          1949 Swing, Brother, Swing
              APA: *A Wreath for Rivera*
          1951 Opening Night
              APA: *Night at the Vulcan*
          1953 Spinsters in Jeopardy
              APA: *The Bride of Death*
          1955 Scales of Justice

        1956 Death of a Fool
              APA: Off with His Head
        1958 Singing in the Shrouds
        1959 False Scent
        1962 Hand in Glove
        1963 Dead Water
        1966 Killer Dolphin
              APA: Death at the Dolphin
        1968 Clutch of Constables
        1970 When in Rome
        1972 Tied Up in Tinsel
        1974 Black as He's Painted
        1977 Last Ditch
        1978 Grave Mistake
        1980 Photo Finish
        1982 Light Thickens
    SS 1989 The Collected Short Fiction of Ngaio Marsh

A: **Martin, Allana**
    SC: Texana Jones
         1996 Death of Healing Woman
         1997 Death of a Saint Maker
A: **Martin, Ian**
    P: **Arliss, Joen**
        SC: Kate Graham
             1979 The Shark Bait Affair
             1980 The Lady Killer Affair
P: **Martin, Lee**
    please see: **Wingate, (Martha) Anne (Guice)**
A: **Marting, Ruth Lenore**
    P: **Bailey, Hilea**
        SC: Hilea Bailey & Hilary D. Bailey III
             1939 What Night Will Bring
             1940 Give Thanks to Death
             1941 The Smiling Corpse
             1946 Breathe No More, My Lady
J: **Mason, Francis Van Wyck**
    please see: **Brawner, Helen w/ Francis Van Wyck Mason**
A: **Mason, Sara Elizabeth**
    SC: Sheriff Bill Davies
         1943 Murder Rents a Room
         1945 The Crimson Feather
A: **Mason, Sarah J(ill)**
    SC: Det. Supt. Trewley & Det. Sgt. Stone
         1993 Frozen Stiff

        1993 Murder in the Maze
        1993 Corpse in the Kitchen
        1994 Dying Breath
        1996 Sew Easy to Kill
        1997 Seeing Is Deceiving

P: **Crane, Hamilton**

    SC: Miss Emily Seeton (see p. 277)

        1991 Miss Seeton Cracks the Case
        1991 Miss Seeton Paints the Town
        1992 Hands Up, Miss Seeton
        1992 Miss Seeton by Moonlight
        1992 Miss Seeton Rocks the Cradle
        1993 Miss Seeton Goes to Bat
        1993 Miss Seeton Plants Suspicion
        1994 Miss Seeton Undercover
        1994 Miss Seeton Rules
        1994 Starring Miss Seeton
        1995 Sold to Miss Seeton
        1996 Sweet Miss Seeton
        1997 Bonjour Miss Seeton

A: **Matera, Lia**

    SC: Laura Di Palma (see p. 167)

        1988 The Smart Money
        1990 The Good Fight
        1992 A Hard Bargain
        1994 Face Value
        1995 Designer Crimes

    SC: Willa Jansson (see p. 167)

        1987 Where Lawyers Fear to Tread
        1988 A Radical Departure
        1988 Hidden Agenda
        1991 Prior Convictions
        1996 Last Chants
        1997 Star Witness

A: **Mather, Linda**

    SC: Jo Hughes

        1994 Blood of an Aries
        1994 Beware Taurus
        1995 Gemini Doublecross

A: **Mathews, Francine**

    SC: Det. Meredith Folger

        1994 Death in the Off-Season
        1995 Death in Rough Water
        1997 Death in a Mood Indigo

P: **Barron, Stephanie**
   SC: Jane Austen
         1996 Jane and the Unpleasantness at Scargrave Manor
         1996 Jane and the Man of the Cloth
A: **Matschat, Cecile Hulse**
   SC: Andrea Reid Ramsay & David Ramsay
         1941 Murder in Okefenokee
         1943 Murder at the Black Crook
A: **Matteson, Stefanie**
   SC: Charlotte Graham (see p. 105)
         1990 Murder at the Spa
         1991 Murder at Teatime
         1991 Murder on the Cliff
         1992 Murder on the Silk Road
         1993 Murder at the Falls
         1994 Murder on High
         1996 Murder Among the Angels
         1997 Murder Under the Palms
A: **Matthews, Alex**
   SC: Cassidy McCabe
         1996 Secret's Shadow
         1997 Satan's Silence
A: **Mavity, Nancy Barr**
   SC: Peter Piper (see p. 181)
         1929 The Body on the Floor
         1929 The Tule Marsh Murder
         1930 The Case of the Missing Sandals
         1930 The Other Bullet
         1932 The Man Who Didn't Mind Hanging
               APA: He Didn't Mind Hanging
P: **Maxwell, A. E.**
   please see: **Maxwell, Ann Elizabeth Lowell w/ Evan Maxwell**
A: **Maxwell, Ann Elizabeth Lowell w/ Evan Maxwell**
   P: **Maxwell, A. E.**
   SC: Fiddler & Fiora (see p. 224)
         1985 Just Another Day in Paradise
         1986 The Frog and the Scorpion
         1987 Gatsby's Vineyard
         1988 Just Enough Light to Kill
         1989 The Art of Survival
         1991 Money Burns
         1992 The King of Nothing
         1993 Murder Hurts

J: **Maxwell, Evan**
     please see: **Maxwell, Ann Elizabeth Lowell w/ Evan Maxwell**
A: **McAllester, Melanie**
     SC: Ashley Johnson & Elizabeth "Tenacity" Mendoza
             1994 The Lessons
             1996 The Search
A: **McCafferty, Barbara Taylor w/ Beverly Taylor Herald**
     SC: Bert & Nan Tatum
             1996 Double Murder
             1997 Double Exposure
A: **McCafferty, Jeanne**
     SC: Mackenzie Griffin
             1994 Star Gazer
             1995 Artist Unknown
             1996 Finales and Overtures
             1998 Exquisite Shades of Grey
A: **McCafferty, (Barbara) Taylor**
     SC: Haskell Blevins
             1990 Pet Peeves
             1992 Ruffled Feathers
             1993 Bed Bugs
             1994 Thin Skins
             1995 Hanky Panky
   P: **McClellan, Tierney**
     SC: Schuyler Ridgway
             1994 Heir Condition
             1995 Closing Statement
             1996 A Killing in Real Estate
             1997 Two-Story Frame
P: **McCall, K. T.**
     please see: **Armitage, Audrey w/ Muriel Watkins**
A: **McChesney, Mary F.**
   P: **Rayter, Joe**
     SC: Johnny Powers
             1954 The Victim Was Important
             1955 Asking for Trouble
P: **McClellan, Tierney**
     please see: **McCafferty, (Barbara) Taylor**
A: **McClendon, Lise**
     SC: Alix Thorssen
             1994 The Bluejay Shaman
             1996 Painted Truth
A: **McCloy, Helen (Worrell Clarkson)**
     SC: Dr. Basil Willing (see p. 110)
             1938 Dance of Death
                     APA: Design for Dying

1940 The Man in the Moonlight
1941 The Deadly Truth
1942 Cue for Murder
1942 Who's Calling?
1943 The Goblin Market
1945 The One That Got Away
1950 Through a Glass, Darkly
1951 Alias Basil Willing
1955 The Long Body
1956 Two-Thirds of a Ghost
1968 Mr. Splitfoot
1980 Burn This

SC: Miguel Urizar
1943 The Goblin Market
1948 She Walks Alone
   APA: Wish You Were Dead

A: **McConnell, Vicki**
SC: Nyla Wade
1982 Mrs. Porter's Letter
1984 The Burnton Widows
1988 Double Daughter

P: **McCormick, Claire**
please see: **Labus, Marta Haake**

A: **McCoy, Madeleine**
P: **Mace, Merlda**
SC: Christine Andersen
1943 Headlong for Murder
1945 Blondes Don't Cry

A: **McCrumb, Sharyn**
SC: Elizabeth MacPherson (see p. 37)
1984 Sick of Shadows
1985 Lovely in Her Bones
1986 Highland Laddie Gone
1988 Paying the Piper
1990 The Windsor Knot
1991 Missing Susan
1992 MacPherson's Lament
1995 If I'd Killed Him When I Met Him . . .

SC: Jay Omega (see p. 37)
1987 Bimbos of the Death Sun
1992 Zombies of the Gene Pool

SC: Sheriff Spencer Arrowood (see p. 79)
1990 If Ever I Return, Pretty Peggy-O
1992 The Hangman's Beautiful Daughter

1994 She Walks These Hills
1996 The Rosewood Casket

A: **McCully, (Ethel) Walbridge**
SC: D. A. Carey Galbreath
1942 Death Rides Tandem
1943 Doctors Beware!

A: **McDermid, Val**
SC: Kate Brannigan (see p. 239)
1992 Dead Beat
1993 Kickback
1994 Crack Down
1995 Clean Break
1996 Blue Genes
SC: Lindsay Gordon (see p. 184)
1987 Report for Murder
1989 Common Murder
1991 Final Edition
APA: Deadline for Murder
1993 Union Jack

A: **McGerr, Patricia**
SC: Selena Mead
1964 Is There a Traitor in the House?
1970 Legacy of Danger

A: **McGiffen, Janet**
SC: Dr. Maxene St. Clair
1991 Emergency Murder
1993 Prescription for Death
1995 Elective Murder

A: **McGown, Jill**
SC: Det. Insp. Lloyd & Det. Judy Hill (see p. 72)
1983 A Perfect Match
1988 Redemption
APA: Murder at the Old Vicarage
1989 Gone to Her Death
APA: Death of a Dancer
1991 The Murders of Mrs. Austin and Mrs. Beale
1992 The Other Woman
1993 Murder . . . Now and Then
1995 A Shred of Evidence
1997 Verdict Unsafe

P: **McGrew, Fenn**
please see: **McGrew, Julia w/ Caroline K. Fenn**
A: **McGrew, Julia w/ Caroline K. Fenn**
P: **McGrew, Fenn**

SC: Lt. Charles Hillary
    1953 Taste of Death
    1954 Made for Murder
A: **McGuire, Christine**
    SC: Kathryn Mackay
        1993 Until Proven Guilty
        1994 Until Justice Is Done
        1997 Until Death Do Us Part
A: **McInerny, Ralph**
  P: **Quill, Monica**
    SC: Sister Mary Teresa Dempsey (see p. 90)
        1981 Not a Blessed Thing!
        1982 Let Us Prey
        1984 And Then There Was Nun
        1985 Nun of the Above
        1986 Sine Qua Nun
        1988 The Veil of Ignorance
        1991 Sister Hood
        1993 Nun Plussed
        1997 Half Past Nun
A: **McIntosh, Kinn Hamilton**
  P: **Aird, Catherine**
    SC: Insp. C. D. Sloan
        1966 The Religious Body
        1968 Henrietta Who?
        1969 The Complete Steel
              APA: The Stately Home Murder
        1970 A Late Phoenix
        1973 His Burial Too
        1975 Slight Mourning
        1977 Parting Breath
        1979 Some Die Eloquent
        1980 Passing Strange
        1982 Last Respects
        1984 Harm's Way
        1986 A Dead Liberty
        1990 The Body Politic
        1994 A Going Concern
      SS 1995 Injury Time
        1996 After Effects
A: **McKenna, Bridget**
    SC: Caley Burke (see p. 242)
        1993 Murder Beach

           1994 Dead Ahead
           1995 Caught Dead
A: **McKenna, Marthe**
     SC: Clive Granville
           1937 Lancer Spy
           1941 The Spy in Khaki
A: **McKernan, Victoria**
     SC: Chicago Nordejoong (see p. 128)
           1990 Osprey Reef
           1992 Point Deception
           1994 Crooked Island
A: **McKevett, G. A.**
     SC: Savannah Reid
           1995 Just Desserts
           1996 Bitter Sweets
           1997 Killer Calories
A: **McKitterick, Molly**
     SC: William Hecklepeck (see p. 106)
           1992 The Medium is Murder
           1993 Murder in a Mayonnaise Jar
A: **McMahan, Ian**
P: **Colburn, Laura**
     SC: Carol Gates
           1979 Death in a Small World
           1979 Death of a Prima Donna
           1979 Death Through the Mill
A: **McNab, Claire**
     SC: Det. Insp. Carole Ashton
           1988 Lessons in Murder
           1989 Fatal Reunion
           1990 Death Down Under
           1991 Cop Out
           1992 Dead Certain
                 APA: Off Key
           1995 Body Guard
           1995 Double Bluff
           1996 Inner Circle
           1997 Chain Letter
A: **McNamara, Lena Brooke**
P: **Mack, Evalina**
     SC: Ann McIntosh
           1952 Death of a Portrait
           1955 Corpse in the Cove
           1957 Death Among the Sands

A: **McQuillan, Karin**
    SC: Jazz Jasper & Insp. Omondi (see p. 129)
          1990 Deadly Safari
          1993 Elephant's Graveyard
          1994 The Cheetah Chase
A: **McShea, Susanna H(ofmann)**
    SC: Hometown Heroes
          1990 Hometown Heroes
          1992 The Pumpkin-Shell Wife
          1994 Ladybug, Ladybug
P: **Mead, Russell**
    please see: **Koehler, Margaret Hudson**
A: **Meade (Smith), Elizabeth Thomasina**
    P: **Meade, L(illie) T(homas)**
    SC: Dr. Clifford Halifax
        SS 1894 Stories from the Diary of a Doctor
        SS 1896 Stories from the Diary of a Doctor: Second Series
            1896 Dr. Rumsey's Patient
        SS 1900 Where the Shoe Pinches
        SS 1901 A Race with the Sun
    SC: Gilchrist
        SS 1901 A Race With the Sun
    SC: Madame Sara (see p. 199)
        SS 1903 The Sorceress of the Strand
    SC: Micah Faraday
        SS 1910 Micah Faraday, Adventurer
A: **Meade (Smith), Elizabeth Thomasina w/ Robert Eustace (Barton)**
    P: **Meade, L. T.**
    SC: Dr. Chetwynd & Dr. Paul Cato
        SS 1900 The Sanctuary Club
    SC: George Conway
        SS 1899 The Gold Star Line
    SC: John Bell
        SS 1898 A Master of Mysteries
    SC: Norman Head
        SS 1899 The Brotherhood of the Seven Kings
    SC: The Oracle of Maddox Street
        SS 1904 The Oracle of Maddox Street
P: **Meade, L(illie) T(homas)**
    please see: **Meade (Smith), Elizabeth Thomasina**
P: **Meade, L. T.**
    please see: **Meade (Smith), Elizabeth Thomasina w/ Robert Eustace (Barton)**

A: **Means, Mary w/ Theodore Saunders**
P: **Scott, Denis**
  SC: Mike James
        1944 Murder Makes a Villain
        1946 The Beckoning Shadow
A: **Meek, M(argaret) R(eid) D(uncan)**
  SC: Lennox Kemp (see p. 166)
        1984 Hang the Consequences
        1985 The Split Second
        1986 In Remembrance of Rose
        1987 A Worm of Doubt
        1989 A Loose Connection
        1989 A Mouthful of Sand
        1990 This Blessed Plot
        1993 Touch and Go
        1996 Postscript to Murder
A: **Meier, Leslie**
  SC: Lucy Stone
        1991 Mail-Order Murder
        1994 Tippy-Toe Murder
        1996 Trick or Treat Murder
        1997 Back to School Murder
P: **Melville, Jennie**
  please see: **Butler, Gwendoline**
A: **Meredith, D(oris) R.**
  SC: Sheriff Charles Matthews
        1984 The Sheriff and the Panhandle Murders
        1985 The Sheriff and the Branding Iron Murders
        1987 The Sheriff and the Folsom Man Murders
        1992 The Sheriff and the Pheasant Hunt Murders
        1995 The Homefront Murders
  SC: John Lloyd Branson & Lydia Fairchild (see p. 171)
        1988 Murder by Impulse
        1989 Murder by Deception
        1990 Murder by Masquerade
        1991 Murder by Reference
        1993 Murder by Sacrilege
A: **Merrick, Mollie**
  SC: Red Hanlon
        1936 Upper Case
        1938 Mysterious Mr. Frame
A: **Mertz, Barbara L(ouise) G(ross)**
P: **Michaels, Barbara**
  SC: Karen & Cheryl Nevitt
        1968 Ammie, Come Home

J: **Meyers, Martin**
    please see: **Meyers, Annette (Brafman) w/ Martin Meyers**
P: **Michaels, Barbara**
    please see: **Mertz, Barbara L(ouise) G(ross)**
A: **Mickelbury, Penny**
    SC: Lt. Gianna Maglione & Mimi Patterson
         1994 Keeping Secrets
         1995 Night Songs
A: **Middleton, Elizabeth**
    P: **Antill, Elizabeth**
    SC: Insp. Simon Ashton
              1950 Murder in Mid-Atlantic
              1952 Death on the Barrier Reef
J: **Migliori, John**
    please see: **Case, Peg w/ John Migliori**
A: **Millar, Florence N.**
    SC: Chf. Insp. Douglas Grant
              1946 Fishing Is Dangerous
              1956 Grant's Overture
A: **Millar, Margaret (Ellis Sturm)**
    SC: Dr. Paul Prye
              1941 The Invisible Worm
              1942 The Devil Loves Me
              1942 The Weak-Eyed Bat
    SC: Insp. Sands
              1942 The Devil Loves Me
              1943 Wall of Eyes
              1945 The Iron Gates
                    APA: Taste of Fears
    SC: Tom Aragon
              1976 Ask for Me Tomorrow
              1979 The Murder of Miranda
              1982 Mermaid
A: **Miller, J(anice) M. T(ubbs)**
    SC: Artie Weatherby
              1987 Weatherby
              1989 On a Dead Man's Chest
A: **Millhiser, Marlys**
    SC: "Charlie" Greene
              1992 Murder at Moot Point
              1993 Death of the Office Witch
              1995 Murder in a Hot Flash
              1996 It's Murder Going Home

A: **Mills, D(eanie) F(rancis)**
    SC: Nathan Kendall
             1991 Spellbound
             1992 Free Fall
P: **Mills, Osmington**
    please see: **Brooks, Vivian Collin**
A: **Milne, Shirley**
    SC: Det. Sgt. Steytler
             1962 Stiff Silk
             1963 The Hammer of Justice
             1964 False Witness
A: **Mitchell, Gladys (Maude Winifred)**
    SC: Dame Beatrice Adela Lestrange Bradley (see pp. 23, 109)
             1929 Speedy Death
             1929 The Mystery of a Butcher's Shop
             1930 The Longer Bodies
             1932 The Saltmarsh Murders
             1933 Ask a Policeman
             1934 Death at the Opera
                    APA: Death in the Wet
             1935 The Devil at Saxon Wall
             1936 Dead Man's Morris
             1937 Come Away, Death
             1938 St. Peter's Finger
             1939 Printer's Error
             1940 Brazen Tongues
             1941 Hangman's Curfew
             1941 When Last I Died
             1942 Laurels Are Poison
             1943 Sunset over Soho
             1943 The Worsted Viper
             1944 My Father Sleeps
             1945 The Rising of the Moon
             1946 Here Comes a Chopper
             1947 Death and the Maiden
             1948 The Dancing Druids
             1949 Tom Brown's Body
             1950 Groaning Spinney
             1951 The Devil's Elbow
             1952 The Echoing Strangers
             1953 Merlin's Furlong
             1954 Faintley Speaking
             1955 Watson's Choice
             1956 Twelve Horses and the Hangman's Noose

1957 The Twenty-Third Man
1958 Spotted Hemlock
1959 The Man Who Grew Tomatoes
1960 Say It with Flowers
1961 The Nodding Canaries
1962 My Bones Will Keep
1963 Adders on the Heath
1964 Death of a Delft Blue
1965 Pageant of Murder
1966 The Croaking Raven
1967 Skeleton Island
1968 Three Quick and Five Dead
1969 Dance to Your Daddy
1970 Gory Dew
1971 Lament for Leto
1972 A Hearse on May-Day
1973 The Murder of Busy Lizzie
1974 A Javelin for Jonah
1974 Winking at the Brim
1975 Convent on Styx
1976 Late, Late in the Evening
1977 Fault in the Structure
1977 Noonday and Night
1978 Mingled with Venom
1978 Wraiths and Changelings
1979 Nest of Vipers
1979 The Mudflats of the Dead
1980 The Whispering Knights
1980 Uncoffin'd Clay
1981 The Death Cap Dancers
1982 Death of a Burrowing Mole
1982 Here Lies Gloria Mundy
1982 Lovers Make Moan
1983 Cold, Lone and Still
1983 The Greenstone Griffins
1984 Crime on the Coast and No Flowers by Request
1984 No Winding Sheet
1984 The Crozier Pharoahs

P: **Torrie, Malcolm**
SC: Timothy Herring

1966 Heavy as Lead
1967 Late and Cold
1968 Your Secret Friend
1969 Churchyard Salad

1970 Shades of Darkness
1971 Bismarck Herrings
A: **Mitchell, Kay**
SC: Det. Chf. Insp. John Morrissey
1990 A Lively Form of Death
1992 In Stony Places
1993 Roots of Evil
APA: A Strange Desire
1995 A Portion for Foxes
1996 A Rage of Innocence
P: **Lacey, Sarah**
SC: Leah Hunter (see p. 262)
1992 File Under: Deceased
1993 File Under: Missing
1994 File Under: Arson
1995 File Under: Jeopardy
A: **Moffat, Gwen**
SC: Jack Pharaoh
1991 Pit Bull
1993 The Outside Edge
SC: Melinda Pink (see p. 123)
1973 Lady With a Cool Eye
1975 Miss Pink at the Edge of the World
1976 A Short Time to Live
1976 Over the Sea to Death
1978 Persons Unknown
1982 Die Like a Dog
1982 Miss Pink's Mistake
1982 The Buckskin Girl
1983 Last Chance Country
1984 Grizzly Trail
1987 Snare
1989 The Stone Hawk
1990 Rage
1990 The Raptor Zone
1992 Veronica's Sisters
1994 Cue the Battered Wife
A: **Monfredo, Miriam Grace**
SC: Glynis Tryon (see p. 13)
1992 Seneca Falls Inheritance
1993 North Star Conspiracy
1995 Blackwater Spirits
1996 Through a Gold Eagle
1997 Ladies, Hoydens, and the President's Wife

J: **Monk, Elliot**
    please see: **Baskerville, Beatrice w/ Elliot Monk**
A: **Montgomery, Ione**
    SC: Christopher Gibson
                1940 The Golden Dress
                1941 Death Won a Prize
A: **Montgomery (Ewegen), Yvonne**
    SC: Finny Aletter
                1987 Scavengers
                1990 Obstacle Course
P: **Montross, David**
    please see: **Backus, Jean Louise**
A: **Moody, Skye Kathleen**
    SC: Venus Diamond
                1996 Rain Dance
                1997 Blue Poppy
A: **Moody, Susan (Elizabeth)**
    SC: Cassie Swann (see p. 133)
                1993 Death Takes a Hand
                       APA: Takeout Double
                1994 Grand Slam
                1995 King of Hearts
                1996 Doubled in Spades
    SC: Penny Wanawake (see p. 282)
                1984 Penny Black
                1984 Penny Dreadful
                1985 Penny Post
                1986 Penny Royal
                1988 Penny Wise
                1989 Penny Pinching
                1991 Penny Saving
J: **Moore, Arthur**
    please see: **Granbeck, Marilyn w/ Arthur Moore**
A: **Moore (Lee), Barbara**
    SC: Dr. Gordon Christy (see p. 110)
                1983 The Doberman Wore Black
                1986 The Wolf Whispered Death
A: **Moore, Margaret**
    SC: Det. Chf. Insp. Richard Baxter
                1987 Forests of the Night
                1988 Dangerous Conceits
                1990 Murder in Good Measure
                1991 Fringe Ending

A: **Moore, Rayanne w/ Serita Stevens**
   SC: Fanny Zindel
          1991 Red Sea, Dead Sea
          1993 Bagels for Tea
A: **Morell, Mary**
   SC: Pol. Det. Lucia Ramos
          1991 Final Session
          1993 Final Rest
A: **Morgan, D Miller**
   SC: Daisy Marlow
          1987 Money Leads to Murder
          1988 A Lovely Night to Kill
A: **Morgan, Kate**
   SC: Dewey James
          1990 A Slay at the Races
          1991 Home Sweet Homicide
          1991 Murder Most Fowl
          1992 Days of Crime and Roses
          1992 Mystery Loves Company
          1994 Wanted: Dude or Alive
          1996 The Old School Dies
P: **Morice, Anne**
   please see: **Shaw, Felicity**
A: **Morison, B(etty) J(ane)**
   SC: Elizabeth Lamb Worthington
          1983 Champagne and a Gardener
          1984 Port and a Star Boarder
          1985 Beer and Skittles
          1987 Voyage of the Chianti
          1992 The Martini Effect
A: **Morris, Jean**
   P: **O'Hara, Kenneth**
      SC: Dr. Alun Barry
             1958 A View to a Death
             1960 Sleeping Dogs Lying
J: **Morwood, Peter**
   please see: **Duane, Diane w/ Peter Morwood**
A: **Moyes, Patricia**
   SC: Insp. Henry Tibbett & Emily Tibbett
          1959 Dead Men Don't Ski
          1961 The Sunken Sailor
                 APA: Down Among the Dead Men
          1962 Death on the Agenda
          1963 Murder a la Mode

1964 Falling Star
1965 Johnny Under Ground
1967 Murder Fantastical
1968 Death and the Dutch Uncle
1970 Who Saw Her Die?
       APA: Many Deadly Returns
1971 Season of Snows and Sins
1973 The Curious Affair of the Third Dog
1975 Black Widower
1977 To Kill a Coconut
       APA: The Coconut Killings
1978 Who Is Simon Warwick?
1980 Angel Death
1983 A Six Letter Word for Death
1985 Night Ferry to Death
1989 Black Girl, White Girl
1993 Twice in a Blue Moon

A: **Muir, D(orothy) Erskine**
    SC: Insp. Woods
            1933 In Muffled Night
            1934 Five to Five

A: **Muller, Marcia**
    SC: Elena Oliverez
            1983 The Tree of Death
            1985 The Legend of the Slain Soldiers
    SC: Joanna Stark (see p. 210)
            1986 The Cavalier in White
            1988 There Hangs the Knife
            1989 Dark Star
    SC: Sharon McCone (see p. 222)
            1977 Edwin of the Iron Shoes
            1982 Ask the Cards a Question
            1983 The Cheshire Cat's Eye
            1984 Games to Keep the Dark Away
            1984 Leave a Message for Willie
            1985 There's Nothing to Be Afraid Of
            1988 Eye of the Storm
            1989 The Shape of Dread
            1989 There's Something in a Sunday
            1990 Trophies and Dead Things
            1991 Where Echoes Live
            1992 Pennies on a Dead Woman's Eyes
            1993 Wolf in the Shadows

        1994 Till the Butchers Cut Him Down
        1995 A Wild and Lonely Place
  SS   1995 The McCone Files
        1996 The Broken Promise Land
        1997 Both Ends of the Night

A: **Muller, Marcia w/ Bill Pronzini**
     SC: Elena Oliverez
          1986 Beyond the Grave
     SC: Sharon McCone (see p. 222)
          1984 Double

A: **Munger, Katy**
   P: **Gray, Gallagher**
     SC: Casey Jones
          1997 Legwork
          1998 Countdown
     SC: Hubbert & Lil (see p. 275)
          1991 Hubbert and Lil: Partners in Crime
          1992 A Cast of Killers
          1995 Death of a Dream Maker
          1996 A Motive for Murder

A: **Munson, Douglas Anne**
   P: **Lambert, Mercedes**
     SC: Whitney Logan
          1991 Dogtown
          1996 Soultown

A: **Murphy, Shirley Rousseau**
     SC: Joe Grey, PI
          1996 Cat on the Edge
          1996 Cat Under Fire
          1997 Cat Raise the Dead

A: **Murray, Donna Huston**
     SC: Ginger Barnes
          1995 The Main Line Is Murder
          1996 Final Arrangements
          1996 The School of Hard Knocks
          1997 Dominance Down

A: **Museo, Laura w/ Stephen Schermerhorn**
   P: **Tanner, Jake**
     SC: B. F. Hopper
          1991 Old Black Magic
          1992 St. Louie Blues

A: **Myers, Amy**
     SC: Chef August Didier (see p. 15)
          1986 Murder in Pug's Parlor

        1987 Murder in the Limelight
        1989 Murder at Plum's
        1991 Murder at the Masque
        1992 Murder Makes an Entree
        1992 Murder Under the Kissing Bough
        1994 Murder in the Smokehouse
        1995 Murder at the Music Hall
        1996 Murder in the Motor Stable
        1997 Murder with Majesty

A: **Myers, Isabel Briggs**
    SC: Peter Jerningham
        1930 Murder Yet to Come
        1934 Give Me Death

A: **Myers, Tamar**
    SC: Abigail Timberlake
        1996 Larceny and Old Lace
        1996 Gilt by Association
    SC: Magdalena Yoder
        1994 Too Many Crooks Spoil the Broth
        1995 Parsley, Sage, Rosemary and Crime
        1996 No Use Dying over Spilled Milk
        1997 Just Plain Pickled to Death

N

A: **Nabb, Magdalen**
    SC: Marshal Guarnaccia (see p. 49)
        1981 Death of an Englishman
        1982 Death of a Dutchman
        1983 Death in Springtime
        1985 Death in Autumn
        1987 The Marshal and the Murderer
        1988 The Marshal and the Madwoman
        1990 The Marshal's Own Case
        1991 The Marshal Makes His Report
        1994 The Marshal at the Villa Torrini
        1995 The Marshal and the Forgery
        1996 The Monster of Florence

A: **Nash, Anne**
    SC: Mark Tudor
        1943 Said with Flowers
        1944 Death by Design
    SC: Nell Winter & Doris "DoDo" Trent
        1943 Said with Flowers

        1944 Death by Design
        1945 Cabbages and Crime
A: **Navratilova, Martina w/ Liz Nickles**
    SC: Jordan Myles (see p. 134)
        1994 The Total Zone
        1996 Breaking Point
        1997 Killer Instinct
A: **Nearing, Elizabeth C.**
    P: **MacVeigh, Sue**
        SC: Capt. Andy & Sue MacVeigh
            1939 Grand Central Murder
            1939 Murder Under Construction
            1940 Streamlined Murder
            1941 The Corpse and the Three Ex-Husbands
A: **Neel (Cohen), Janet**
    SC: Det. John McLeish & Francesca Wilson
        1988 Death's Bright Angel
        1989 Death on Site
        1991 Death of a Partner
        1993 Death Among the Dons
        1997 A Timely Death
A: **Neely, Barbara**
    SC: Blanche White (see p. 160)
        1992 Blanche on the Lam
        1994 Blanche Among the Talented Tenth
A: **Neville, Barbara Alison Boodson**
    P: **Candy, Edward**
        SC: Insp. Burnivel
            1953 Which Doctor?
            1954 Bones of Contention
            1971 Words for Murder Perhaps
P: **Neville, Margot**
    please see: **Goyder, Margot w/ Anne N(eville) G(oyder) Joske**
J: **Newberry, Perry**
    please see: **MacGowan, Alice w/ Perry Newberry**
A: **Newell, Audrey**
    SC: Patrick Michael Doyle
        1930 Who Killed Cavalotti?
        1940 Murder Is Not Mute
A: **Newman, Sharan**
    SC: Catherine LeVendeur (see p. 94)
        1993 Death Comes as Epiphany
        1994 The Devil's Door
        1995 The Wandering Arm
        1996 Strong as Death

A: **Nicholson, Margaret Beda Larminie**
P: **Yorke, Margaret**
  SC: Patrick Grant
      1970 Dead in the Morning
      1972 Silent Witness
      1973 Grave Matters
      1974 Mortal Remains
      1976 Cast for Death
J: **Nickles, Liz**
  please see: **Navratilova, Martina w/ Liz Nickles**
A: **Nielsen, Helen**
  SC: Simon Drake
      1951 Gold Coast Nocturne
         APA: Dead on the Level
         APA: Murder by Proxy
      1966 After Midnight
      1967 A Killer in the Street
      1969 The Darkest Hour
      1973 The Severed Key
      1976 The Brink of Murder
A: **Nisot, (Mavis) Elizabeth (Hocking)**
  SC: Commissaire Payran
      1935 Twelve to Dine
      1936 Hazardous Holiday
      1938 False Witness
      1939 Unnatural Deeds
A: **Nolan, Jeannette Covert**
  SC: Lace White
      1943 Final Appearance
      1945 "I Can't Die Here"
      1955 Sudden Squall
      1956 A Fearful Way to Die
A: **North, Suzanne**
  SC: Phoebe Fairfax
      1994 Healthy, Wealthy and Dead
      1996 Seeing Is Deceiving

O

A: **O'Brien, Meg**
  SC: Jessica "Jesse" James
      1990 Salmon in the Soup
      1990 The Daphne Decisions

1991 Hare Today, Gone Tomorrow
1992 Eagles Die Too
A: **O'Callaghan, Maxine**
SC: Delilah West
1980 Death Is Forever
1981 Run from Nightmare
1989 Hit and Run
1991 Set-Up
1994 Trade-Off
SC: Dr. Anne Menlo
1996 Shadow of the Child
1997 Only in the Ashes
A: **O'Connell, Carol**
SC: Kathleen Mallory
1994 Mallory's Oracle
1995 The Man Who Cast Two Shadows
1996 Killing Critics
1997 Stone Angel
A: **O'Connor, Maureen**
P: **Hall, Patricia**
SC: Laura Ackroyd & Chf. Insp. Michael Thackeray
1993 Death by Election
1994 Dying Fall
1995 In the Bleak Midwinter
1997 The Dead of Winter
A: **O'Donnell, Lillian (Udvardy)**
SC: Gwenn Ramadge
1990 A Wreath for the Bride
1993 Used to Kill
1995 The Raggedy Man
1997 The Goddess Affair
SC: Mici Anhalt
1977 Aftershock
1979 Falling Star
1980 Wicked Designs
SC: Sgt. Norah Mulcahaney (see p. 49)
1972 The Phone Calls
1973 Don't Wear Your Wedding Ring
1974 Dial 577 R-A-P-E
1975 The Baby Merchants
1976 Leisure Dying
1978 No Business Being a Cop
1981 The Children's Zoo
1983 Cop Without a Shield

1984 Ladykiller
1985 Casual Affairs
1986 Shadow in Red
1987 The Other Side of the Door
1989 A Good Night to Kill
1991 A Private Crime
1992 Pushover
1994 Lockout

P: **O'Hara, Kenneth**
please see: **Morris, Jean**

A: **O'Kane, Leslie**
SC: Molly Masters
1996 Just the Fax, Ma'am
1996 Death and Faxes
1998 Cold Hard Fax

A: **O'Malley, Lady Mary Dolling Saunders**
P: **Bridge, Ann**
SC: Julia Probyn
1956 The Lighthearted Quest
1958 The Portuguese Escape
1960 The Numbered Account
1962 The Tightening String
1963 The Dangerous Islands
1965 Emergency in the Pyrenees
1966 The Episode at Toledo
1969 The Malady in Madeira

A: **O'Marie, Sister Carol Anne**
SC: Sister Mary Helen
1984 A Novena for Murder
1986 Advent of Dying
1988 The Missing Madonna
1991 Murder in Ordinary Time
1993 Murder Makes a Pilgrimage
1995 Death Goes on Retreat
1997 Death of an Angel

P: **O'Nair, Mairi**
please see: **Evans, Constance May**

A: **O'Shaughnessy, Perri**
SC: Nina Reilly
1995 Motion to Suppress
1996 Invasion of Privacy
1997 Obstruction of Justice

A: **OCork, Shannon**
SC: T. T. Baldwin (see p. 124)
1980 Sports Freak

1981 End of the Line
1983 Hell Bent for Heaven
A: **Oellrichs, Inez H(ildegarde)**
SC: Matt Winters
1939 The Kettel Mill Mystery
1939 The Man Who Didn't Answer
1940 Murder Comes at Night
1945 And Die She Did
1947 Murder Helps
1949 Death of a White Witch
1964 Death in a Chilly Corner
A: **Offord, Lenore Glen**
SC: Bill & Coco Hastings
1938 Murder on Russian Hill
APA: Murder Before Breakfast
1942 Clues to Burn
SC: Todd McKinnon
1943 Skeleton Key
1944 The Glass Mask
1949 The Smiling Tiger
1959 Walking Shadow
A: **Oleksiw, Susan (Prince)**
SC: Pol. Chf. Joe Silva
1993 Murder in Mellingham
1994 Double Take
1995 Family Album
P: **Oliphant, B. J.**
please see: **Tepper, Sheri S.**
A: **Oliver, Maria-Antonia**
SC: Appollonia "Lonia" Guiu
1987 Study in Lilac
1989 Antipodes
P: **Olsen, D. B.**
please see: **Hitchens, (Julia Clara Catherine) Dolores (Birk)**
A: **Orczy, Baroness (Emma Magdalena Rosalia Maria Josifa Barbara, Baroness Orczy)**
SC: Bill Owen, The Old Man in the Corner (see pp. 199, 265)
SS 1905 The Case of Miss Elliott
SS 1909 The Old Man in the Corner
APA: The Man in the Corner
SS 1923 The Old Man in the Corner Unravels the Mystery of the Khaki Tunic
SS 1924 The Old Man in the Corner Unravels the Mystery of the Pearl Necklace

SS   1924   The Old Man in the Corner Unravels the Mystery of the Russian Prince, and of Dog's Tooth Cliff

SS   1925   The Old Man in the Corner Unravels the Mystery of the Fulton Gardens, and the Moorland Tragedy

SS   1925   The Old Man in the Corner Unravels the Mystery of the White Carnation and the Montmartre Hat

SS   1925   Unraveled Knots

SC: Lady Molly

SS   1910   Lady Molly of Scotland Yard

SC: M. Fernand

SS   1918   The Man in Gray

SC: M. Hector Ratichon

SS   1921   Castles in the Air

SC: Patrick Mulligan

SS   1928   Skin o' My Tooth

SC: The Scarlet Pimpernel

1905   The Scarlet Pimpernel

1906   I Will Repay

1908   The Elusive Pimpernel

1913   Eldorado

1917   Lord Tony's Wife

SS   1919   The League of the Scarlet Pimpernel

1920   The First Sir Percy

1922   The Triumph of the Scarlet Pimpernel

1924   Pimpernel and Rosemary

1927   Sir Percy Hits Back

SS   1929   Adventures of the Scarlet Pimpernel

1933   The Way of the Scarlet Pimpernel

1936   Sir Percy Leads the Band

1940   Mam'zelle Guillotine

P: **Orde, A. J.**

please see: **Tepper, Sheri S.**

A: **Osborne, Denise**

SC: Queenie Davilov

1994   Murder Offscreen

1995   Cut to: Murder

1996   Deadly Treatment

1997   Focus on Murder

A: **Ostrander, Isabel (Egenton)**

SC: Timothy McCarty

1917   The Clue in the Air

1919   The Twenty-Six Clues

1920   How Many Cards?

        1922 McCarty, Incog.
        1923 Annihilation
P: **Chipperfield, Robert O.**
    SC: Barry O'Dell
        1920 Unseen Hands
        1921 The Man in the Jury Box
P: **Fox, David**
    SC: The Shadowers, Inc.
        1920 The Man Who Convicted Himself
        1922 Ethel Opens the Door
        1923 The Doom Dealer
        1924 The Handwriting on the Wall
J: **Oursler, Will(iam Charles)**
    please see: **Scott, Margaret w/ Will(iam Charles) Oursler**
A: **Owens, Virginia Stem**
    SC: Beth Marie Cartwright
        1992 At Point Blank
        1992 Congregation
        1993 A Multitude of Sins

P

A: **Padgett, Abigail**
    SC: Barbara "Bo" Bradley (see p. 117)
        1993 Child of Silence
        1994 Strawgirl
        1995 Turtle Baby
        1996 Moonbird Boy
        1997 The Dollmaker's Daughters
J: **Page, Carole Gift**
    please see: **Fell, Doris Elaine w/ Carole Gift Page**
P: **Page, Emma**
    please see: **Tirbutt, Honoria**
J: **Page, Evelyn**
    please see: **Blair, Dorothy w/ Evelyn Page**
A: **Page, Katherine Hall**
    SC: Faith Fairchild (see p. 150)
        1990 The Body in the Belfry
        1991 The Body in the Bouillon
        1991 The Body in the Kelp
        1992 The Body in the Vestibule
        1993 The Body in the Cast
        1994 The Body in the Basement

            1996 The Body in the Bog
            1997 The Body in the Fjord

P: **Paige, Robin**
      please see: **Albert, Susan Wittig w/ William J. Albert**

A: **Palliser, Iris**
    P: **Wray, I.**
      SC: Insp. Digby
           1930 The Vye Murder
           1931 Murder—And Ariadne

A: **Palmer, Madelyn**
    P: **Peters, Geoffrey**
      SC: Insp. Trevor Nicholls
           1964 The Claw of a Cat
           1964 The Eye of a Serpent
           1965 The Whirl of a Bird
           1966 The Twist of a Stick
           1967 The Flick of a Fin
           1967 The Mark of a Buoy
           1968 The Chill of a Corpse

A: **Papazoglou, Orania**
      SC: Patience C. McKenna (see p. 182)
           1984 Sweet, Savage Death
           1985 Wicked, Loving Murder
           1986 Death's Savage Passion
           1988 Rich, Radiant Slaughter
           1990 Once and Always Murder

    P: **Haddam, Jane**
      SC: Gregor Demarkian (see p. 256)
           1990 Not a Creature Was Stirring
           1991 Act of Darkness
           1991 Precious Blood
           1991 Quoth the Raven
           1992 A Feast of Murder
           1992 A Great Day for the Deadly
           1992 A Stillness in Bethlehem
           1993 Murder Superior
           1994 Bleeding Hearts
           1994 Dear Old Dead
           1994 Festival of Deaths
           1995 Fountain of Death
           1996 And One to Die On
           1996 Baptism in Blood

A: **Pardoe, Rosemary**
    P: **Allen, Mary Ann**
      SC: Jane Bradshawe
        SS 1986 The Angry Dead

A: **Paretsky, Sara**
    SC: V. I. Warshawski (see p. 222)
              1982 Indemnity Only
              1984 Deadlock
              1985 Killing Orders
              1987 Bitter Medicine
              1988 Blood Shot
                    APA: Toxic Shock
              1990 Burn Marks
              1992 Guardian Angel
              1994 Tunnel Vision
      SS   1995 Windy City Blues
A: **Pargeter, Edith Mary**
  P: **Peters, Ellis**
    SC: Brother Cadfael (see pp. 1, 89)
              1977 A Morbid Taste for Bones: A Medieval Whodunit
              1979 One Corpse Too Many
              1980 Monk's-Hood
              1981 Saint Peter's Fair
              1981 The Leper of St. Giles
              1982 The Virgin in the Ice
              1983 The Devil's Novice
              1983 The Sanctuary Sparrow
              1984 Dead Man's Ransom
              1984 The Pilgrim of Hate
              1985 An Excellent Mystery
              1986 The Raven in the Foregate
              1986 The Rose Rent
              1987 The Hermit of Eyton Forest
      SS   1988 A Rare Benedictine
              1988 The Confession of Brother Haluin
              1989 The Heretic's Apprentice
              1989 The Potter's Field
              1991 The Summer of the Danes
              1992 The Holy Thief
              1994 Brother Cadfael's Penance
    SC: Insp. George Felse & Family
              1951 Fallen into the Pit
              1960 The Will and the Deed
                    APA: Where There's a Will
              1961 Death and the Joyful Woman
              1964 Flight of a Witch
              1965 A Nice Derangement of Epitaphs
                    APA: Who Lies Here?

1966 The Piper on the Mountain
1967 Black Is the Colour of My True Love's Heart
1968 The Grass-Widow's Tale
1969 Mourning Raga
1969 The House of Green Turf
1970 The Knocker on Death's Door
1972 Death to the Landlords!
1973 City of Gold and Shadows
1974 The Horn of Roland
1976 Never Pick Up Hitch-Hikers!
1979 Rainbow's End

A: **Parker, Barbara**
    SC: Gail Connor
        1994 Suspicion of Innocence
        1995 Suspicion of Guilt

A: **Parker, Maude**
    SC: Jim Little
        1951 Which Mrs. Torr?
        1952 The Intriguer
            APA: Blood Will Tell
        1955 Murder in Jackson Hole
            APA: Final Crossroads

A: **Patterson, (Isabella) Innis**
    SC: Sebald Craft
        1930 The Eppworth Case
        1931 The Standish Gaunt Case

A: **Paul, Barbara**
    SC: Enrico Caruso
        1984 A Cadenza for Caruso
        1985 Prima Donna at Large
        1987 A Chorus of Detectives
    SC: Det. Sgt. Marian Larch (see p. 55)
        1984 The Renewable Virgin
        1989 Good King Sauerkraut
        1989 He Huffed and He Puffed
        1992 The Apostrophe Thief
        1992 You Have the Right to Remain Silent
        1995 Fare Play
        1997 Full Frontal Murder

P: **Paull, Jessyca**
    please see: **Burger, Rosaylmer w/ Julia Perceval**

A: **Payes, Rachel**
    SC: Forsythia Brown
        1960 Forsythia Finds Murder
        1964 Memoirs of Murder

A: **Pearson, Ann**
   SC: Maggie Courtney
          1979 A Stitch in Time
          1979 Murder by Degrees
          1980 Cat Got Your Tongue?
A: **Pearson, Ryne Douglas**
   SC: Frankie Aguirre & Art Jefferson
          1995 Capitol Punishment
          1996 Simple Simon
A: **Pence, Joanne**
   SC: Angelina Amalfi & Det. Paavo Smith
          1993 Something's Cooking
          1994 Too Many Cooks
          1995 Cooking Up Trouble
          1996 Cooking Most Deadly
          1997 Cook's Night Out
P: **Penn, John**
   please see: **Harcourt, Palma w/ Jack H. Trotman**
A: **Penny, Mrs. Frank**
   SC: Jim Burns
        SS   1900 A Forest Officer
J: **Perceval, Julia**
   please see: **Burger, Rosaylmer w/ Julia Perceval**
A: **Perdue, Virginia**
   SC: Eleanora Burke
          1941 The Case of the Grieving Monkey
          1942 The Case of the Foster Father
A: **Perry, Anne**
   SC: Insp. Thomas Pitt & Charlotte Ellison Pitt (see p. 1)
          1979 The Cater Street Hangman
          1980 Callander Square
          1981 Paragon Walk
          1981 Resurrection Row
          1983 Rutland Place
          1984 Bluegate Fields
          1985 Death in the Devil's Acre
          1987 Cardington Crescent
          1988 Silence in Hanover Close
          1990 Bethlehem Road
          1991 Highgate Rise
          1992 Belgrave Square
          1993 Farriers' Lane
          1994 The Hyde Park Headsman
          1995 Traitors Gate

1996 Pentecost Alley
1997 Ashworth Hall
SC: William Monk (see p. 12)
    1990 The Face of a Stranger
    1991 A Dangerous Mourning
    1992 Defend and Betray
    1993 A Sudden, Fearful Death
    1994 The Sins of the Wolf
    1995 Cain His Brother
    1996 Weighed in the Balance

P: **Peters, Elizabeth**
    please see: **Mertz, Barbara L(ouise) G(ross)**
P: **Peters, Ellis**
    please see: **Pargeter, Edith Mary**
A: **Peters, Elsa Kirsten**
  P: **Allen, Irene**
    SC: Elizabeth Elliot
        1992 Quaker Silence
        1993 Quaker Witness
        1996 Quaker Testimony
P: **Peters, Geoffrey**
    please see: **Palmer, Madelyn**
A: **Peters, Maureen**
  P: **Black, Veronica**
    SC: Sister Joan
        1990 A Vow of Silence
        1992 A Vow of Chastity
        1993 A Vow of Sanctity
        1993 A Vow of Obedience
        1994 A Vow of Penance
        1994 A Vow of Devotion
        1995 A Vow of Poverty
        1996 A Vow of Fidelity
A: **Peterson, Audrey**
    SC: Claire Camden (see p. 41)
        1992 Dartmoor Burial
        1994 Death Too Soon
        1995 Shroud for a Scholar
    SC: Jane Winfield & Andrew Quentin (see p. 41)
        1987 The Nocturne Murder
        1989 Death in Wessex
        1989 Murder in Burgundy
        1990 Deadly Rehearsal

1990 Elegy in a Country Graveyard
1991 Lament for Christobel

A: **Peterson, Margaret Ann**
  P: **Green, Glint**
    SC: Insp. Wield
        1931 Strands of Red . . . Hair!
        1932 Devil Spider
        1933 Beauty—A Snare
        1933 Poison Death

P: **Petrie, Rhona**
  please see: **Buchanan, Eileen-Marie Duell**

A: **Phillips, Stella**
    SC: Insp. Matthew Furnival
        1967 Down to Death
        1968 The Hidden Wrath
        1969 Death in Arcady
        1970 Death Makes the Scene
        1971 Death in Sheep's Clothing

A: **Pickard, Nancy**
    SC: Jennifer Cain (see p. 137)
        1984 Generous Death
        1985 Say No to Murder
        1986 No Body
        1987 Marriage Is Murder
        1988 Dead Crazy
        1990 Bum Steer
            APA: Crossbones
        1991 I. O. U.
        1993 But I Wouldn't Want to Die There
        1994 Confession
        1995 Twilight
    SC: Mrs. Eugenia Potter (see p. 266)
        1993 The 27-Ingredient Chili Con Carne Murders
            [original series by Virginia Rich]

A: **Piesman, Marissa**
    SC: Nina Fischman
        1989 Unorthodox Practices
        1991 Personal Effects
        1993 Heading Uptown
        1994 Close Quarters
        1995 Alternate Sides
        1997 Survival Instincts

A: **Piggin, Julia Remine**
    SC: Sara Hull
      SS 1973 Mini-Mysteries

A: **Pincus, Elizabeth**
  SC: Nell Fury
              1992 The Two-Bit Tango
              1993 The Solitary Twist
              1995 The Hangdog Hustle
A: **Pirkis, C(atharine) L(ouisa)**
  SC: Loveday Brooke, Lady Detective
        SS 1894 The Experiences of Loveday Brooke, Lady
                    Detective
A: **Plain, Josephine**
  SC: Colin Anstruther
              1934 The Secret of the Sandbanks
              1935 The Secret of the Snows
              1936 The Pazenger Problem
A: **Plante, Pele**
  SC: CC Scott & Barbara Bettencourt
              1991 Getting Away with Murder
              1992 Dirty Money
A: **Plum, Mary**
  SC: John Smith
              1930 The Killing of Judge McFarlane
              1931 Dead Man's Secret
              1932 Murder at the Hunting Club
              1933 Murder at the World's Fair
                    APA: The Broken Vase Mystery
A: **Poore, Dawn Aldridge**
  SC: Roxanne Sydney
              1993 The Brighton Burglar
              1993 The Secret Scroll
              1994 The Cairo Cats
              1995 The Mummy's Mirror
              1997 Saint's Haven
A: **Popkin, Zelda**
  SC: Mary Carner (see p. 221)
              1938 Death Wears a White Gardenia
              1940 Murder in the Mist
              1940 Time off for Murder
              1941 Dead Man's Gift
              1942 No Crime for a Lady
A: **Porter, Anna**
  SC: Judith Hayes
              1985 Hidden Agenda
              1987 Mortal Sins

A: **Porter, Joyce**
    SC: Edmund Brown (see p. 252)
            1966 Sour Cream with Everything
            1967 The Chinks in the Curtain
            1969 Neither a Candle nor a Pitchfork
            1971 Only with a Bargepole
    SC: The Honorable Constance Morrison-Burke
            1970 Rather a Common Sort of Crime
            1972 A Meddler and Her Murderer
            1975 The Package Included Murder
            1977 Who the Heck Is Sylvia?
            1979 The Cart Before the Crime
    SC: Insp. Wilfred Dover
            1964 Dover One
            1965 Dover Two
            1965 Dover Three
            1967 Dover and the Unkindest Cut of All
      SS 1968 Dover and the Sense of Justice
            1968 Dover Goes to Pott
      SS 1969 Dover Pulls a Rabbit
      SS 1970 Dover Fails to Make His Mark
            1970 Dover Strikes Again
      SS 1971 A Terrible Drag for Dover
      SS 1972 Dover and the Dark Lady
            1973 It's Murder with Dover
      SS 1975 Dover Tangles with High Finance
            1976 Dover and the Claret Tappers
      SS 1977 Dover Does Some Spadework
      SS 1977 When Dover Got Knotted
            1978 Dead Easy for Dover
      SS 1978 Dover Doesn't Dilly-Dally
      SS 1978 Dover Goes to School
      SS 1978 Dover Without Perks
            1980 Dover Beats the Band
      SS 1995 Dover: The Collected Short Stories
A: **Pou, Genevieve Long**
  P: **Holden, Genevieve**
    SC: Lt. Al White
            1953 Killer Loose!
            1954 Sound an Alarm
            1956 The Velvet Target
            1958 Something's Happened to Kate
A: **Powell, Deborah**
    SC: Hollis Carpenter
            1991 Bayou City Secrets
            1992 Houston Town

J: **Power, Jo-Ann**
    please see: **Cummings, Barbara w/ Jo-Ann Power**
A: **Powers, Alexis**
    SC: Leah Gordon
            1995 Kiss My Tattoo
            1996 Kiss Daddy Goodbye
            1996 Kiss Your Inheritance Goodbye
A: **Powers, Elizabeth**
    SC: Viera Kolarova
            1981 All That Glitters
            1984 On Account of Murder
A: **Press, Margaret**
    SC: Det. Gabriel Dunn & Det. Jake Myles
            1992 Requiem for a Postman
            1994 Elegy for a Thief
P: **Prichard, K. & Hesketh**
    please see: **Prichard, Katherine O'Brien w/ Vernon Hesketh
            Prichard**
A: **Prichard, Katherine O'Brien w/ Vernon Hesketh Prichard**
P: **Prichard, K. & Hesketh**
    SC: Don Q
            SS   1904 The Chronicles of Don Q
            SS   1906 The New Chronicles of Don Q
                        APA: Don Q in the Sierras
                  1909 Don Q's Love Story
    SC: Flaxman Low
            SS   1899 Ghosts
                        APA: Ghost Stories
J: **Prichard, Vernon Hesketh**
    please see: **Prichard, Katherine O'Brien w/ Vernon Hesketh
            Prichard**
J: **Pronzini, Bill**
    please see: **Muller, Marcia w/ Bill Pronzini**
A: **Prowell, Sandra West**
    SC: Phoebe Siegel (see p. 241)
            1993 By Evil Means
            1994 The Killing of Monday Brown
            1996 When Wallflowers Die
A: **Pugh, Dianne G.**
    SC: Iris Thorne
            1993 Cold Call
            1994 Slow Squeeze
            1997 Fast Friends
A: **Pullein-Thompson, Joanna M. C.**

P: **Cannan, Joanna**
   SC: Insp. Guy Northeast
       1939 They Rang Up the Police
       1940 Death at the Dog
   SC: Insp. Ronald Price
       1950 Murder Included
          APA: Poisonous Relations
          APA: The Taste of Murder
       1952 Body in the Beck
       1955 Long Shadows
       1958 And Be a Villain
       1962 All Is Discovered

A: **Pullein-Thompson, Josephine (Mary Wedderburn)**
   SC: Insp. James Flecker
       1959 Gin and Murder
       1960 They Died in the Spring
       1963 Murder Strikes Pink

J: **Pulver (Kuhfeld), Mary Monica**
   please see: **Bacon, Gail w/ Mary Monica Pulver (Kuhfeld)**

A: **Pulver (Kuhfeld), Mary Monica**
   SC: Det. Sgt. Peter Brichter & Kori Brichter
       1987 Murder at the War
          APA: Knight Fall
       1988 Ashes to Ashes
       1988 The Unforgiving Minutes
       1991 Original Sin
       1992 Show Stopper

J: **Punnett, Ivor**
   please see: **Punnett, Margaret w/ Ivor Punnett**

A: **Punnett, Margaret w/ Ivor Punnett**
  P: **Simons, Roger**
   SC: Insp. Fadiman Wace
       1959 The Houseboat Killings
       1960 A Frame for Murder
       1960 Murder Joins the Chorus
       1961 Arrangement for Murder
       1961 Gamble with Death
       1962 The Killing Chase
       1964 Bullet for a Beast
       1965 Dead Reckoning
       1966 The Veil of Death
       1967 Taxed to Death
       1968 Death on Display
       1969 Murder First Class

1970 Reel of Death
1973 Picture of Death
1973 Silver and Death
1974 Murder by Design

Q

P: **Quest, Erica**
please see: **Sawyer, Nancy Buckingham w/ John Sawyer**
A: **Quick, Dorothy**
SC: Lt. Peter Donnegan
1947 The Fifth Dagger
1959 The Doctor Looks at Murder
P: **Quill, Monica**
please see: **McInerny, Ralph**
A: **Quinn, E(leanor) Baker**
SC: James Strange
1936 One Man's Muddle
1940 Death Is a Restless Sleeper
A: **Quinn (Barnard), Elizabeth**
SC: Lauren Maxwell
1993 Murder Most Grizzly
1995 A Wolf in Death's Clothing
1996 Lamb to the Slaughter
1997 Killer Whale
A: **Quinton, Ann**
SC: James Roland
1989 To Mourn a Mischief
1990 Death of a Dear Old Friend

R

P: **Radford, E. & M. A.**
please see: **Radford, Mona Augusta Mangan w/ Edwin Isaac Radford**
J: **Radford, Edwin Isaac**
please see: **Radford, Mona Augusta Mangan w/ Edwin Isaac Radford**
A: **Radford, Mona Augusta Mangan w/ Edwin Isaac Radford**
P: **Radford, E. & M. A.**
SC: Dr. Manson
1944 Inspector Manson's Success

1944 Murder Jigsaw
1945 Crime Pays No Dividends
1946 Murder Isn't Cricket
1947 It's Murder to Live
1947 Who Killed Dick Whittington?
1949 John Kyleing Died
1950 The Heel of Achilles
1956 Look in at Murder
1957 Death on the Broads
1959 Death of a Frightened Editor
1960 Death at the Chateau Noir
1960 Murder on My Conscience
1961 Death's Inheritance
1962 Death Takes the Wheel
1962 From Information Received
1963 A Cosy Little Murder
1963 Murder of Three Ghosts
1964 The Hungry Killer
1965 Mask of Murder
1965 Murder Magnified
1966 Death of a "Gentleman"
1967 Jones's Little Murders
1967 No Reason for Murder
1967 The Middlefold Murders
1968 The Safety First Murders
1968 Trunk Call to Murder
1969 Death of a Peculiar Rabbit
1969 Death of an Ancient Saxon
1969 Two Ways to Murder
1970 Murder Is Ruby Red
1970 Murder Speaks
1971 Dead Water
1971 The Greedy Killers
1972 Death Has Two Faces
SC: Prof. Marcus Stubbs
     SS 1961 Death and the Professor
P: **Radley, Sheila**
    please see: **Robinson, Sheila Mary**
P: **Ramsay, Diana**
    please see: **Brandes, Rhoda**
A: **Raphael, Chaim**
    P: **Davey, Jocelyn**
        SC: Ambrose Usher
             1956 The Undoubted Deed
                   APA: A Capitol Offense

                  1958 The Naked Villainy
                  1960 A Touch of Stagefright
                  1965 A Killing in Hats
                  1976 A Treasury Alarm
                  1982 Murder in Paradise
                  1988 A Dangerous Liaison

A: **Raskin, Ellen**
      SC: Garson
           SS   1975 The Tattooed Potato and Other Clues

A: **Rath, Virginia (Anne)**
      SC: Michael Dundas
                1938 The Dark Cavalier
                1939 Murder with a Theme Song
                1940 Death of a Lucky Lady
                1941 Death Breaks the Ring
                1942 Epitaph for Lydia
                1942 Posted for Murder
                1947 A Dirge for Her
                1947 A Shroud for Rowena
      SC: Sheriff Rocky Allan
                1935 Death at Dayton's Folly
                1936 Ferryman, Carry Him Across!
                1936 Murder on the Day of Judgment
                1937 An Excellent Night for a Murder
                1937 The Anger of the Bells
                1939 Murder with a Theme Song

P: **Rayter, Joe**
      please see: **McChesney, Mary F.**

A: **Rea, M(argaret) P(aine)**
      SC: Lt. Powledge
                1941 A Curtain for Crime
                1941 Compare These Dead!
                1943 Death of an Angel

A: **Redmann, J. M.**
      SC: Michelle "Micky" Knight
                1990 Death by the Riverside
                1993 Deaths of Jocasta
                1995 The Intersection of Law and Desire

A: **Reilly, Helen**
      SC: Insp. Christopher McKee
                1930 The Diamond Feather
                1931 Murder in the Mews
                1934 McKee of Centre Street
                1934 The Line-Up

1936 Dead Man Control
1936 Mr. Smith's Hat
1939 All Concerned Notified
1939 Dead for a Ducat
1940 Death Demands an Audience
1940 Murder in Shinbone Alley
1940 The Dead Can Tell
1941 Mourned on Sunday
1941 Three Women in Black
1942 Name Your Poison
1944 The Opening Door
1945 Murder on Angler's Island
1946 The Silver Leopard
1947 The Farmhouse
1949 Staircase 4
1950 Murder at Arroways
1951 Lament for the Bride
1952 The Double Man
1953 The Velvet Hand
1954 Tell Her It's Murder
1955 Compartment K
      APA: Murder Rides the Express
1956 The Canvas Dagger
1958 Ding Dong Bell
1959 Not Me, Inspector
1960 Follow Me
1961 Certain Sleep
1962 The Day She Died

A: **Rendell, Ruth**
    SC: Det. Chf. Insp. Reg Wexford (see p. 71)
1964 From Doon with Death
1967 A New Lease of Death
      APA: Sins of the Fathers
1967 Wolf to the Slaughter
1969 The Best Man to Die
1970 A Guilty Thing Surprised
1971 No More Dying Then
1972 Murder Being Once Done
1973 Some Lie and Some Die
1975 Shake Hands Forever
1978 A Sleeping Life
1981 Death Notes
      APA: Put on by Cunning
1983 The Speaker of Mandarin

        1985 An Unkindness of Ravens
        1988 The Veiled One
        1992 Kissing the Gunner's Daughter
        1995 Simisola
        1997 Road Rage

A: **Renfroe, Martha Kay**
   P: **Wren, M. K.**
      SC: Conan Flagg (see p. 208)
              1973 Curiosity Didn't Kill the Cat
              1975 A Multitude of Sins
              1976 Oh, Bury Me Not
              1978 Nothing's Certain But Death
              1981 Seasons of Death
              1984 Wake Up, Darlin' Corey
              1993 Dead Matter
              1994 King of the Mountain

A: **Rennert, Maggie**
      SC: Guy Silvestri
              1974 Circle of Death
              1975 Operation Alcestis
              1976 Operation Calpurnia

A: **Reuben, Shelly**
      SC: Max Bramble & Wylie Nolan (see p. 248)
              1994 Origin and Cause
              1996 Spent Matches

A: **Reubens, Aida**
      SC: Cliveden Prince
         SS 1945 Your Verdict Is?

P: **Revell, Louisa**
   please see: **Smith, Ellen Hart**

P: **Reynolds, Adrian**
   please see: **Long, Amelia Reynolds**

A: **Reynolds, Kay w/ Mike Reynolds**
      SC: Fortune's Friends
              1986 Fortune's Friends: Hell Week
              1987 Lucky Lacey

J: **Reynolds, Mike**
   please see: **Reynolds, Kay w/ Mike Reynolds**

P: **Rice, Craig**
   please see: **Craig, Georgiana Ann Randolph**

A: **Rich, Virginia**
      SC: Mrs. Eugenia Potter (see p. 266)
              1982 The Cooking School Murders
              1983 The Baked Bean Supper Murders

1985 The Nantucket Diet Murders
1992 The 27-Ingredient Chili Con Carne Murders
[written by Nancy Pickard]

A: **Rinehart, Mary Roberts**
SC: Leticia "Tish" Carberry
1911 The Amazing Adventures of Leticia Carberry
SS 1916 Tish
1921 More Tish
SS 1926 The Book of Tish
SS 1926 Tish Plays the Game
SS 1937 Tish Marches On
SC: Nurse Hilda Adams (Miss Pinkerton) (see p. 109)
1932 Miss Pinkerton
APA: The Double Alibi
1933 Mary Roberts Rinehart's Crime Book
1942 Haunted Lady
1950 Episode of the Wandering Knife
APA: The Wandering Knife

A: **Ripley, Ann**
SC: Louise Eldridge
1994 Mulch
1996 Death of a Garden Pest

A: **Rippon, Marion (Edith)**
SC: Insp. Maurice Ygrec & Sgt. Paul Michelin
1969 The Hand of Solange
1970 Behold, the Druid Weeps
1974 The Ninth Tentacle
1979 Lucien's Tomb

A: **Rivett, Edith Caroline**
P: **Carnac, Carol**
SC: Insp. Julian Rivers
1945 A Double for Detection
1946 The Striped Suitcase
1947 Clue Sinister
1948 Over the Garden Wall
1950 Copy for Crime
1950 Upstairs, Downstairs
APA: Upstairs and Downstairs
1951 It's Her Own Funeral
1952 Crossed Skis
1953 A Policeman at the Door
1953 Murder as a Fine Art
1954 Impact of Evidence
1955 Murder Among Members

1955 Rigging the Evidence
1956 The Double Turn
     APA: *The Late Miss Trimming*
1958 Long Shadows
     APA: *Affair at Helen's Court*
SC: Insp. Ryvet
1936 Triple Death
1937 Murder at Mornington
1937 The Missing Rope
1939 The Case of the First-Class Carriage
1939 When the Devil Was Sick
1940 Death in the Diving Pool
P: **Lorac, E. C. R.**
SC: Insp. Robert Macdonald
1931 The Murder on the Burrows
1932 The Affair on Thor's Head
1932 The Greenwell Mystery
1933 Death on the Oxford Road
1933 The Case of Colonel Marchand
1934 Murder in Chelsea
1934 Murder in St. John's Wood
1935 The Organ Speaks
1936 A Pall for a Painter
1936 Crime Counter Crime
1936 Post After Post-Mortem
1937 Bats in the Belfry
1937 These Names Make Clues
1938 Slippery Staircase
1938 The Devil and the C.I.D.
1939 Black Beadle
1939 John Brown's Body
1940 Death at Dyke's Corner
1940 Tryst for a Tragedy
1941 Case in the Clinic
1942 Rope's End—Rogue's End
1942 The Sixteenth Stair
1943 Death Came Softly
1944 Checkmate to Murder
1944 Fell Murder
1945 Murder by Matchlight
1946 Fire in the Thatch
1946 The Theft of the Iron Dogs
     APA: *Murderer's Mistake*
1947 Relative to Poison

1948 Death Before Dinner
 APA: A Screen for Murder
1948 Part for a Poisoner
 APA: Place for a Poisoner
1949 Policeman in the Precinct
 APA: And Then Put Out the Light
1949 Still Waters
1950 Accident by Design
1951 Murder of a Martinet
 APA: I Could Murder Her
1952 Murder in the Mill-Race
 APA: Speak Justly of the Dead
1952 The Dog It Was That Died
1953 Crook o' Lune
 APA: Shepherd's Crook
1954 Let Well Alone
1954 Shroud of Darkness
1955 Ask a Policeman
1956 Murder in Vienna
1957 Dangerous Domicile
1957 Picture of Death
1958 Death in Triplicate
 APA: People Will Talk
1958 Murder on a Monument
1959 Dishonour Among Thieves
 APA: The Last Escape

A: **Robb, Candace (M.)**
 SC: Owen Archer (see p. 5)
   1993 The Apothecary Rose
   1994 The Lady Chapel
   1995 The Nun's Tale
   1996 The King's Bishop
   1997 The Riddle of St. Leonards

P: **Robb, J. D.**
 please see: **Roberts, Nora**

A: **Roberts, Carey**
 SC: Det. Annie FitzHugh
   1989 Touch a Cold Door
   1993 Pray God to Die

A: **Roberts, Doreen**
 P: **Kingsbury, Kate**
  SC: A Pennyfoot Hotel Mystery
   1993 Room with a Clue

1994 Do Not Disturb
1994 Service for Two
1994 Eat, Drink and Be Buried
1995 Checkout Time
1995 Grounds for Murder
1996 Pay the Piper
1996 Chivalry Is Dead
1997 Ring for Tomb Service

P: **Roberts, Gillian**
please see: **Greber, Judith**

A: **Roberts, Lillian M.**
SC: Andi Pauling
1996 Riding for a Fall
1997 The Hand that Feeds You

A: **Roberts (Smith), Lora**
SC: Liz Sullivan, Bridget Montrose & Det. Paul Drake (see p. 290)
1988 Revolting Development
1994 Murder in a Nice Neighborhood
1995 Murder in the Marketplace
1996 Murder Mile High
1997 Murder Bone by Bone
1998 Murder Crops Up

A: **Roberts, Nora**
P: **Robb, J. D.**
SC: Ed Jackson
1987 Sacred Sins
1988 Brazen Virtue
SC: Lt. Eve Dallas
1995 Naked in Death
1995 Glory in Death
1996 Immortal in Death
1996 Rapture in Death
1997 Ceremony in Death
1997 Vengeance in Death

P: **Robertson, Helen**
please see: **Edmiston, Helen Jean Mary**

A: **Robinson, Lynda S(uzanne)**
SC: Lord Meren
1994 Murder in the Place of Anubis
1995 Murder at the God's Gate
1996 Murder at the Feast of Rejoicing
1997 Eater of Souls

A: **Robinson, Sheila Mary**
   P: **Radley, Sheila**
     SC: Insp. Douglas Quantrill
            1978 Death and the Maiden
                   APA: Death in the Morning
            1980 The Chief Inspector's Daughter
            1982 A Talent for Destruction
            1983 Blood on the Happy Highway
                   APA: The Quiet Road to Death
            1986 Fate Worse Than Death
            1987 Who Saw Him Die?
            1989 This Way Out
            1992 Cross My Heart and Hope to Die
            1995 Fair Game
A: **Robitaille, Julie**
     SC: Kit Powell (see p. 130)
            1992 Jinx
            1994 Iced
P: **Roffman, Jan**
     please see: **Summerton, Margaret**
A: **Rogers, Marian**
   P: **Jackson, Marian J. A.**
     SC: Abigail Patience Danforth
            1990 The Arabian Pearl
            1990 The Punjat's Ruby
            1991 The Cat's Eye
            1992 Diamond Head
            1994 The Sunken Treasure
A: **Romberg, Nina**
     SC: Miriam Winchester, Medicine Woman
            1989 The Spirit Stalker
            1993 The Shadow Walkers
A: **Roome, Annette**
     SC: Chris Martin
            1989 A Real Shot in the Arm
            1990 A Second Shot in the Dark
A: **Roos, Audrey Kelley w/ William Roos**
   P: **Roos, Kelley**
     SC: Haila & Jeff Troy
            1940 Made Up to Kill
                   APA: Made Up for Murder
            1941 If the Shroud Fits
                   APA: Dangerous Blondes

      1942 The Frightened Stiff
      1944 Sailor, Take Warning!
      1945 There Was a Crooked Man
      1947 Ghost of a Chance
      1948 Murder in Any Language
      1949 Triple Threat
      1966 One False Move

P: **Roos, Kelley**
    please see: **Roos, Audrey Kelley w/ William Roos**
J: **Roos, William**
    please see: **Roos, Audrey Kelley w/ William Roos**
A: **Rooth, Anne Reed**
    SC: Hank Sullivan
        1988 Fatal Stranger
        1990 Eye of the Beholder

A: **Ross, Kate (Katherine J.)**
    SC: Julian Kestrel (see p. 11)
        1993 Cut to the Quick
        1994 A Broken Vessel
        1995 Whom the Gods Love
        1997 The Devil in Music

A: **Ross, Z(ola) H(elen Girdey)**
    SC: Beau Smith & Pogy Rogers
        1946 Three Down Vulnerable
        1948 One Corpse Missing

A: **Roth, Holly**
    SC: Lt. Kelly
        1954 The Content Assignment
          APA: The Shocking Secret
        1966 Button, Button
    SC: Insp. Medford
        1957 Shadow of a Lady
        1962 Operation Doctors
          APA: Too Many Doctors

A: **Rothenberg, Rebecca**
    SC: Claire Sharples (see p. 116)
        1991 The Bulrush Murders: A Botanical Mystery
        1994 The Dandelion Murders
        1995 The Shy Tulip Murders

A: **Rowe, Anne (Von Meibom)**
    SC: Insp. Barry
        1944 Too Much Poison
          APA: Cobra Venom
        1945 Up to the Hilt
        1946 Deadly Intent

A: SC: Insp. Pettengill
          1942 The Little Dog Barked
          1945 The Painted Monster

A: **Rowe, Jennifer**
   SC: Verity Birdwood (see p. 102)
         1989 Murder by the Book
         1991 Grim Pickings
     SS 1993 Death in Store
         1993 The Makeover Murders
         1995 Lamb to the Slaughter
         1995 Stranglehold

A: **Rowland, Laura Joh**
   SC: Sano Ichiro
         1994 Shinju
         1996 Bundori
         1997 The Way of the Traitor

A: **Rowlands, Betty**
   SC: Melissa Craig (see p. 189)
         1990 A Little Gentle Sleuthing
         1991 Finishing Touch
         1993 Over the Edge
         1994 Exhaustive Enquiries
         1996 Malice Poetic
         1996 Smiling at Death

A: **Rozan, S(hira) J(udith)**
   SC: Lydia Chin & Bill Smith (see p. 246)
         1994 China Trade
         1995 Concourse
         1996 Mandarin Plaid
         1997 No Colder Place
         1998 Eating Bitter

A: **Rubino, Jane**
   SC: Cat Austen
         1997 Death of a DJ
         1997 Fruitcake

A: **Ruryk, Jean**
   SC: Cat Wilde
         1994 Chicken Little Was Right
         1996 Whatever Happened to Jennifer Steele?

A: **Rushford, Patricia H.**
   SC: Helen Bradley
         1997 Now I Lay Me Down to Sleep
         1997 Red Sky in Mourning

A: **Russell, Charlotte M(urray)**
   SC: Homer Fitzgerald
         1947 Lament for William

        1949 The Careless Mrs. Christian
        1950 Between Us and Evil
        1952 June, Moon and Murder

SC: Jane Amanda Edwards
        1935 Murder at the Old Stone House
        1936 Death of an Eloquent Man
        1937 The Tiny Diamond
        1938 Night on the Pathway
                 APA: Night on the Devil's Pathway
        1939 The Clue of the Naked Eye
        1940 I Heard the Death Bell
        1942 The Message of the Mute Dog
        1945 No Time for Crime
        1946 The Bad Neighbor Murder
        1948 Ill Met in Mexico
        1949 Hand Me a Crime
        1951 Cook Up a Crime

A: **Russell, E(nid)**
    SC: Ben Louis
        1968 She Should Have Cried on Monday
        1971 Nice Enough to Murder

A: **Rutland, Harriet**
    SC: Mr. Winkley
        1938 Knock, Murderer, Knock!
        1940 Bleeding Hooks
                 APA: The Poison Fly Murder

A: **Ryan, Jessica (Cadwalader)**
    SC: Gregory Pavlov & O'Shaunnessey
        1945 The Man Who Asked Why
                 APA: Clue of the Frightening Coin
        1947 Exit Harlequin

A: **Ryerson, Florence w/ Colin Clements**
    SC: Jimmy Lane
        1930 Seven Suspects
        1931 Fear of Fear
        1933 Blind Man's Buff
                 APA: Sleep No More
        1934 Shadows

S

A: **Sale (Roe), (Caroline) Medora**
    SC: Harriet Jeffries & Insp. John Sanders (see p. 211)
        1986 Murder on the Run

1989 Murder in Focus
1990 Murder in a Good Cause
1991 Sleep of the Innocent
1992 Pursued by Shadows
1994 Short Cut to Santa Fe

A: **Salmonson, Jessica Amanda**
SC: Penelope Pettiweather
SS 1990 Harmless Ghosts

A: **Salter, Elizabeth (Fulton)**
SC: Insp. Michael Hornsley
1957 Death in a Mist
1958 Will to Survive
1960 There Was a Witness
1962 The Voice of the Peacock
1965 Once upon a Tombstone

A: **Sanborn, Ruth Burr**
SC: Angeline Tredennick
1932 Murder by Jury
1935 Murder on the Aphrodite

A: **Sandstrom, Eve K.**
SC: Sheriff Sam Titus & Nicki Titus
1990 Death Down Home
1991 The Devil Down Home
1993 The Down Home Heifer Heist

P: **Sandys, Oliver**
please see: **Evans, Marguerite Helen Jervis**

A: **Santini, Rosemarie**
SC: Rick & Rosie Ramsey
1986 A Swell Style of Murder
1987 The Disenchanted Diva

A: **Sarsfield, Maureen**
SC: Insp. Lane Parry
1945 Green December Fills the Graveyard
1948 Dinner for None
APA: A Party for Lawty

A: **Saum, Karen**
SC: Brigid Donovan
1990 Murder Is Relative
1991 Murder Is Germane
1994 Murder Is Material

A: **Saunders, Claire Castler w/ Marion Van der Veer Lee**
SC: Argus Steele
1944 Measured for Murder

P: **Saunders, Lawrence**
    please see: **Davis, Clare w/ Burton Davis**
J: **Saunders, Theodore**
    please see: **Means, Mary w/ Theodore Saunders**
A: **Sawyer, Corrine Holt**
    SC: Benbow & Wingate
        1988 The J. Alfred Prufrock Murders
        1989 Murder in Gray and White
        1992 Murder by Owl Light
        1993 The Peanut Butter Murders
        1994 Murder Has No Calories
        1995 Ho-Ho Homicide
        1996 The Geezer Factory Murders
        1997 Murder Ole
        1998 Bed, Breakfast, and Bodies
J: **Sawyer, John**
    please see: **Sawyer, Nancy Buckingham w/ John Sawyer**
A: **Sawyer, Nancy Buckingham w/ John Sawyer**
    P: **Quest, Erica**
        SC: Det. Chf. Insp. Kate Maddox
            1988 Death Walk
            1990 Cold Coffin
            1991 Model Murder
A: **Sayers, Dorothy L(eigh)**
    SC: Lord Peter Wimsey (see p. 281)
            1923 Whose Body?
            1926 Clouds of Witness
            1927 Unnatural Death
                 APA: *The Dawson Pedigree*
      SS 1928 Lord Peter Views the Body
            1928 The Unpleasantness at the Bellona Club
            1930 Strong Poison
            1931 The Five Red Herrings
                 APA: *Suspicious Characters*
            1932 Have His Carcase
      SS 1933 Hangman's Holiday
            1933 Murder Must Advertise
            1934 The Nine Tailors
            1935 Gaudy Night
            1937 Busman's Honeymoon
      SS 1939 In the Teeth of the Evidence and Other Stories
      SS 1958 A Treasury of Sayers's Stories
      SS 1972 Lord Peter: A Collection of All the Lord Peter Stories

SS   1972 Striding Folly
SS   1982 The Abominable History of the Man with Copper Fingers
SC: Montague Egg
SS   1933 Hangman's Holiday
SS   1939 In the Teeth of the Evidence and Other Stories
P: **Scarlett, Roger**
please see: **Blair, Dorothy w/ Evelyn Page**
J: **Schabelitz, R(udolph) F(rederick)**
please see: **Barber, Willetta Ann w/ R(udolph) F(rederick) Schabelitz**
A: **Schenkel, S(hirley) E.**
SC: Ray & Kate Frederick
1994 In Blacker Moments
1995 Death Days
A: **Scherf, Margaret (Louise)**
SC: Dr. Grace Severance (see p. 110)
1968 The Banker's Bones
1971 The Beautiful Birthday Cake
1972 To Cache a Millionaire
1978 The Beaded Banana
SC: Emily & Henry Bryce (see p. 137)
1948 Always Murder a Friend
1949 The Gun in Daniel Webster's Bust
1951 The Green Plaid Pants
APA: The Corpse with One Shoe
1954 Glass on the Stairs
1963 The Diplomat and the Gold Piano
APA: Death and the Diplomat
SC: Rev. Martin Buell (see p. 89)
1949 Gilbert's Last Toothache
APA: For the Love of Murder
1950 The Curious Custard Pie
APA: Divine and Deadly
1952 The Elk and the Evidence
1956 The Cautious Overshoes
1959 Never Turn Your Back
1965 The Corpse in the Flannel Nightgown
SC: Lt. Ryan
1945 The Owl in the Cellar
1948 Murder Makes Me Nervous
J: **Schermerhorn, Stephen**
please see: **Museo, Laura w/ Stephen Schermerhorn**

A: **Schier, Norma**
    SC: Kay Barth
        1978 Death on the Slopes
        1979 Death Goes Skiing
        1979 Murder by the Book
        1980 Demon of the Opera

A: **Schmidt, Carol**
    SC: Laney Samms
        1993 Silverlake Heat
        1994 Sweet Cherry Wine
        1994 Cabin Fever

A: **Scoppettone, Sandra**
    SC: Lauren Laurano (see p. 234)
        1991 Everything You Have Is Mine
        1992 I'll be Leaving You Always
        1994 My Sweet Untraceable You
        1996 Let's Face the Music and Die

P: **Scott, Denis**
    please see: **Means, Mary w/ Theodore Saunders**

A: **Scott, Margaret w/ Will(iam Charles) Oursler**
    P: **Gallagher, Gale**
    SC: Gale Gallagher (see p. 221)
        1947 I Found Him Dead
        1949 Chord in Crimson

A: **Scott, Marian Gallagher**
    P: **Wolffe, Katherine**
    SC: Capt. Courtney Brade
        1942 The Attic Room
        1946 Death's Long Shadow

A: **Sebenthal, Roberta Elizabeth**
    P: **Kruger, Paul**
    SC: Phil Kramer
        1966 Weep for Willow Green
        1967 Weave a Wicked Web
        1969 If the Shroud Fits
        1972 The Bronze Claws
        1972 The Cold Ones

P: **Sedley, Kate**
    please see: **Clarke, Brenda Margaret Lilian Honeyman**

A: **Seifert, Adele**
    SC: Gregory Trent
        1939 Deeds Ill Done
           APA: Kill Your Own Snakes

1939 Shadows Tonight
1942 3 Blind Mice
A: **Shaffer, Louise**
    SC: Angie DaVito
        1994 All My Suspects
        1995 Talked to Death
A: **Shah, Diane K.**
    SC: Paris Chandler
        1990 As Crime Goes By
        1992 Dying Cheek to Cheek
A: **Shakespeare, L. M(arguerita)**
    SC: Lloyd's of London
        1987 Utmost Good Faith
        1989 The Gentleman's Mafia
           APA: A Question of Risk
P: **Shane, Susannah**
    please see: **Ashbrook, H(arriette) C(ora)**
A: **Shankman, Sarah**
    SC: Samantha Adams (see p. 185)
        1990 Now Let's Talk of Graves
        1991 She Walks in Beauty
        1992 The King Is Dead
        1993 He Was Her Man
        1997 Digging Up Momma
  P: **Storey, Alice**
    SC: Samantha Adams (see p. 185)
        1988 First Kill All the Lawyers
        1989 Then Hang All the Liars
P: **Shannon, Dell**
    please see: **Linington, (Barbara) Elizabeth**
A: **Shannon, Doris**
  P: **Giroux, E. X.**
    SC: Robert Forsythe (see p. 166)
        1984 A Death for Adonis
        1985 A Death for a Dancer
        1985 A Death for a Darling
        1986 A Death for a Doctor
        1987 A Death for a Dilettante
        1988 A Death for a Dietician
        1989 A Death for a Dreamer
        1990 A Death for a Double
        1991 A Death for a Dancing Doll
        1993 A Death for a Dodo

A: **Sharp, Marilyn (Augburn)**
 SC: Richard Owen, Agent
   1979 Sunflower
   1984 Falseface
A: **Shaw, Felicity**
 P: **Morice, Anne**
  SC: Tessa Crichton (see p. 99)
     1970 Death in the Grand Manor
     1971 Death of a Gay Dog
     1971 Murder in Married Life
     1972 Murder on French Leave
     1973 Death and the Dutiful Daughter
     1974 Death of a Heavenly Twin
     1974 Killing with Kindness
     1975 Nursery Tea and Poison
     1976 Death of a Wedding Guest
     1977 Murder in Mimicry
     1977 Scared to Death
     1978 Murder by Proxy
     1979 Murder in Outline
     1980 Death in the Round
     1981 The Men in Her Death
     1982 Hollow Vengeance
     1982 Sleep of Death
     1983 Murder Post-Dated
     1984 Getting Away with Murder?
     1985 Dead on Cue
     1986 Publish and Be Killed
     1987 Treble Exposure
     1988 Design for Dying
     1988 Fatal Charm
     1990 Planning for Murder
A: **Shelton, Connie L.**
 SC: Charlie Parker
   1995 Deadly Gamble
   1995 Vacations Can Be Murder
   1997 Partnerships Can Kill
   1998 Small Towns Can Be Murder
P: **Shepherd, Joan**
 please see: **Buchanan, Betty Joan**
A: **Shepherd, Stella**
 SC: Insp. Richard Montgomery
   1988 Black Justice
   1989 Murderous Remedy

```
        1991  Thinner Than Blood
        1993  A Lethal Fixation
        1995  Something in the Cellar
        1997  Embers of Death
A:  Sheridan, Juanita
      SC:  Lilly Wu & Janice Cameron
        1949  The Chinese Chop
        1951  The Kahuna Killer
        1952  The Mamo Murders
              APA:  While the Coffin Waited
        1953  The Waikiki Widow
A:  Shone, Anna
      SC:  Ulysses Finnegan Donaghue
        1995  Mr. Donaghue Investigates
        1996  Secrets in Stones
A:  Shore, Viola Brothers
      SC:  Colin Keats & Gwynn Leith
        1930  The Beauty-Mask Murder
              APA:  The Beauty-Mask Mystery
        1932  Murder on the Glass Floor
A:  Short, Sharon Gwyn
      SC:  Patricia Delaney (see p. 244)
        1994  Angel's Bidding
        1994  Past Pretense
        1995  The Death We Share
A:  Shriber, Ione Sandburg
      SC:  Lt. Bill Grady
        1940  Head over Heels in Murder
        1940  The Dark Arbor
        1941  Family Affair
        1941  Murder Well Done
        1942  A Body for Bill
        1943  Invitation to Murder
        1944  Pattern for Murder
        1946  The Last Straw
A:  Shuman, M. K.
      P:  Karl, M. S.
      SC:  Pete Brady
        1988  Killer's Inc.
        1990  Death Notice
        1991  Deerslayer
A:  Sibley, Celestine
      SC:  Kate Mulcay (see p. 190)
        1991  Ah, Sweet Mystery
```

    1992 Straight as an Arrow
    1993 Dire Happenings at Scratch Ankle
    1995 A Plague of Kinfolks

A: **Siegel, Doris**
  P: **Wells, Susan**
    SC: Anthony Ware
        1939 Murder Is Not Enough
        1940 Footsteps in the Air
        1942 Death Is My Name
        1947 The Witches' Pond

A: **Silberrad, Una L(ucy)**
    SC: John Bolsover
        SS   1911 The Affairs of John Bolsover

P: **Siller, Van**
    please see: **Van Siller, Hilda**

A: **Silva, Linda Kay**
    SC: Officer Delta "Storm" Stevens (see p. 65)
        1991 Taken by Storm
        1993 Storm Shelter
        1994 Weathering the Storm
        1995 Storm Front
        1996 Tropical Storm

A: **Silver, Victoria**
    SC: Lauren Adler & Michael Hunt
        1984 Death of a Harvard Freshman
        1986 Death of a Radcliffe Roommate

A: **Silverman, Marguerite R(uth)**
    SC: Chf. Insp. Christopher Adrian
        1945 The Vet It Was That Died
        1948 Who Should Have Died?
        1951 9 Had No Vet

P: **Simons, Roger**
    please see: **Punnett, Margaret w/ Ivor Punnett**

A: **Simonson, Sheila**
    SC: Lark Dailey Dodge
        1990 Larkspur
        1992 Skylark
        1993 Mudlark
        1996 Meadowlark
        1997 Malarkey

A: **Simpson, Doris**
  P: **Cohen, Anthea**
    SC: Nurse Agnes Carmichael (see p. 201)
        1982 Angel of Vengeance

1982   Angel Without Mercy
1983   Angel of Death
1984   Fallen Angel
1985   Guardian Angel
1986   Hell's Angel
1987   Ministering Angel
1988   Destroying Angel
1989   Angel Dust
1991   Recording Angel
1992   Angel in Action
1993   Angel in Love
1995   Angel in Autumn

A: **Simpson, Dorothy**
SC: Det. Insp. Luke Thanet (see p. 71)
1981   The Night She Died
1982   Six Feet Under
1983   Puppet for a Corpse
1984   Close Her Eyes
1985   Last Seen Alive
1986   Dead on Arrival
1987   Element of Doubt
1988   Suspicious Death
1989   Dead by Morning
1991   Doomed to Die
1992   Wake the Dead
1993   No Laughing Matter
1996   A Day for Dying

J: **Simpson, Helen (DeGuerry)**
please see: **Ashton, Winifred w/ Helen (DeGuerry) Simpson**

A: **Sims, L. V.**
SC: Sgt. Dixie T. Struthers
1987   Death Is a Family Affair
1987   Murder Is Only Skin Deep
1988   To Sleep, Perchance to Kill

A: **Sinclair, Fiona**
SC: Insp. Paul Grainger
1960   Scandalize My Name
1961   Dead of a Physician
        APA: But the Patient Died
1963   Meddle with the Mafia
1964   Three Slips to a Noose
1965   Most Unnatural Murder

A: **Singer, Shelley**
SC: Barrett Lake (see p. 233)
1993   Following Jane

A: **Smith, Barbara Burnett**
   SC: Jolie Wyatt
         1994 Writers of the Purple Sage
         1995 Dust Devils of the Purple Sage
         1996 Celebration in Purple Sage
         1997 Mistle Toe from Purple Sage
A: **Smith, Cynthia**
   SC: Emma Rhodes
         1996 Noblesse Oblige
         1997 Impolite Society
A: **Smith, Ellen Hart**
   P: **Revell, Louisa**
   SC: Julia Tyler
         1947 The Bus Station Murders
         1948 No Pockets in Shrouds
         1950 A Silver Spade
         1952 The Kindest Use a Knife
         1955 The Men with Three Eyes
         1957 See Rome and Die
         1960 A Party for the Shooting
A: **Smith, Evelyn E.**
   SC: Miss Susan Melville (see p. 204)
         1986 Miss Melville Regrets
         1987 Miss Melville Returns
         1989 Miss Melville's Revenge
         1991 Miss Melville Rides a Tiger
         1993 Miss Melville Runs for Cover
A: **Smith, J(ane) C. S.**
   SC: Quentin Jacoby
         1980 Jacoby's First Case
         1984 Nightcap
A: **Smith, Janet L.**
   SC: Annie MacPherson
         1990 Sea of Troubles
         1992 Practice to Deceive
         1994 A Vintage Murder
A: **Smith, Joan**
   SC: Loretta Lawson
         1987 A Masculine Ending
         1988 Why Aren't They Screaming?
         1990 Don't Leave Me This Way
         1993 What Men Say
         1995 Full Stop

A: **Smith, Joan G(erarda)**
    SC: Cassie Newton
        1989 Capriccio
        1990 A Brush with Death
A: **Smith, Julie**
    SC: Paul McDonald
        1985 True-Life Adventure
        1987 Huckleberry Fiend
    SC: Rebecca Schwartz (see p. 166)
        1982 Death Turns a Trick
        1984 The Sourdough Wars
        1986 Tourist Trap
        1991 Dead in the Water
        1993 Other People's Skeletons
    SC: Det. Skip Langdon (see p. 62)
        1990 New Orleans Mourning
        1991 The Axeman's Jazz
        1993 Jazz Funeral
        1994 New Orleans Beat
        1995 House of Blues
        1996 The Kindness of Strangers
        1997 Crescent City Kill
P: **Smith, Shelley**
    please see: **Bodington, Nancy Hermione Courlander**
A: **Spain, Nancy**
    SC: Johnny DuVivien
        1946 Death Before Wicket
        1946 Poison in Play
        1948 Murder, Bless It!
        1949 Death Goes on Skis
        1949 Poison for Teacher
    SC: Miriam Birdseye
        1949 Death Goes on Skis
        1949 Poison for Teacher
        1950 Cinderella Goes to the Morgue
            APA: Minutes to Murder
        1950 R in the Month
        1951 Not Wanted on Voyage
        1952 Out, Damned Tot!
J: **Spicer, Bart**
    please see: **Spicer, Betty Coe w/ Bart Spicer**
A: **Spicer, Betty Coe w/ Bart Spicer**
    P: **Barbette, Jay**
        SC: Harry Butten
            1950 Final Copy

1953 Dear Dead Days
       APA: Death's Long Shadow
1958 The Deadly Doll
1960 Look Behind You

A: **Spring, Michelle**
    SC: Laura Principal
           1993 Every Breath You Take
           1996 Running for Shelter

A: **Sprinkle, Patricia Houck**
    SC: Sheila Travis & Aunt Mary (see p. 267)
           1988 Murder at Markham
           1990 Murder in the Charleston Manner
           1991 Murder on Peachtree Street
           1992 Somebody's Dead in Snellville
           1993 Death of a Dunwoody Matron
           1994 A Mystery Bred in Buckhead
           1995 Deadly Secrets on the St. Johns

A: **Sproul, Kathleen**
    SC: Richard "Dick" Van Ryn Wilson
           1932 The Birthday Murder
           1933 Death and the Professors
                   APA: Death Among the Professors
           1934 Murder Off Key
           1935 The Mystery of the Closed Car

A: **Squire, Elizabeth Daniels**
    SC: Peaches Dann
           1994 Who Killed What's-Her-Name?
           1994 Remember the Alibi
           1995 Memory Can Be Murder
           1997 Whose Death Is It, Anyway?

P: **St. Clair, Elizabeth**
    please see: **Cohen, Susan Handler**

A: **St. Dennis, Madelon**
    SC: Sydney Treherne
           1932 The Death Kiss
           1932 The Perfumed Lure

A: **Stabenow, Dana**
    SC: Kate Shugak (see p. 81)
           1992 A Cold Day for Murder
           1993 A Fatal Thaw
           1993 Dead in the Water
           1994 A Cold-Blooded Business
           1995 Play with Fire

    1996 Blood Will Tell
    1997 Breakup
P: **Stacey, Susannah**
    please see: **Staynes, Jill w/ Margaret Storey**
A: **Stallwood, Veronica**
    SC: Kate Ivory
        1993 Death and the Oxford Box
        1995 Oxford Exit
        1996 Oxford Mourning
A: **Stand, Marguerite**
    SC: Bill Rice
        1964 Escape from Murder
        1965 Death Came with Darkness
        1966 Death Came in Lucerne
        1966 Death Came with Diamonds
        1966 Death Came with Flowers
        1968 Death Came to "Lighthouse Steps"
        1969 Death Came in the Studio
        1970 Death Came Too Soon
    SC: Pol. Const. Robins
        1964 Murder in the Camp
        1967 Diana Is Dead
P: **Stanton, Coralie**
    please see: **Hosken, Alice Cecil Seymour w/ Ernest Charles
        Heath Hosken**
A: **Stanton, Mary**
    P: **Bishop, Claudia**
        SC: Sarah & Meg Quilliam
            1994 A Taste for Murder
            1995 A Pinch of Poison
            1995 A Dash of Death
            1996 Murder Well-Done
            1997 Death Dines Out
A: **Staynes, Jill w/ Margaret Storey**
    P: **Eyre, Elizabeth**
        SC: Sigismondo (see p. 4)
            1992 Death of the Duchess
            1992 Curtains for the Cardinal
            1994 Poison for the Prince
            1995 Bravo for the Bride
            1996 An Axe for an Abbott
            1997 Dirge for a Doge
    P: **Stacey, Susannah**
        SC: Supt. Robert Bone (see p. 76)
            1987 Goodbye, Nanny Gray
            1988 A Knife at the Opera

1988 Body of Opinion
1990 Grave Responsibility
1992 The Late Lady
1995 Bone Idle
1995 Dead Serious

P: **Steele, V. M.**
    please see: **Firth, Violet Mary**
A: **Steinberg, Janice**
    SC: Margo Simon
               1995 Death of a Postmodernist
               1995 Death Crosses the Border
               1996 Death-Fires Dance
A: **Steiner, Susan**
    SC: Alex Winter
               1985 Murder on Her Mind
               1993 Library: No Murder Aloud
A: **Stenstreem, Ruth**
  P: **Babson, Marian**
    SC: A Pair of Related Novels
               1984 A Trail of Ashes
                      APA: Whiskers and Smoke
               1984 Death Swap
    SC: Douglas Perkins
               1971 Cover-Up Story
               1972 Murder on Show
                      APA: Murder at the Cat Show
               1989 Tourists Are for Trapping
               1990 In the Teeth of Adversity
    SC: Evangeline Sinclair & Trixie Dolan (see p. 101)
               1986 Reel Murder
               1989 Encore Murder
               1991 Shadows in Their Blood
               1993 Even Yuppies Die
               1995 Break a Leg, Darlings
J: **Stephenson, Anne**
    please see: **Brown, Susan w/ Anne Stephenson**
A: **Stevens, Frances M(oyer) R(oss)**
  P: **Hale, Christopher**
    SC: Lt. Bill French
               1935 Smoke Screen
               1937 Stormy Night
               1939 Murder on Display
               1940 Witch Wood
               1941 Dead of Winter

1942 Exit Screaming
1943 Hangman's Tie
1943 Murder in Tow
1945 Midsummer Nightmare
1945 Rumor Hath It
1948 Deadly Ditto
1949 He's Late This Morning
1950 Going, Going, Gone

J: **Stevens, Serita**
    please see: **Moore, Rayanne w/ Serita Stevens**

A: **Stevenson, Florence**
    SC: Kitty Telefair
1971 The Witching Hour
1971 Where Satan Dwells
1973 Altar of Evil
1973 Mistress of Devil's Manor
1974 The Sorcerer of the Castle
1975 The Silent Watcher

A: **Steward, Barbara w/ Dwight Steward**
    SC: Edgar Allan Poe
1978 Evermore
1979 The Lincoln Diddle

J: **Steward, Dwight**
    please see: **Steward, Barbara w/ Dwight Steward**

A: **Stewart, Flora**
    SC: Insp. Newsom
1966 Deadly Nightcap
1967 Blood Relations

J: **Stewart, Neil**
    please see: **Johnson, Pamela Hansford w/ Neil Stewart**

A: **Stockwell, Gail**
    SC: Kingsley Toplitt
1937 Death by Invitation
1938 The Embarrassed Murderer

A: **Stone, Elizabet M.**
    SC: Maggie Slone
1946 Poison, Poker and Pistols
1947 Murder at the Mardi Gras

P: **Storey, Alice**
    please see: **Shankman, Sarah**

J: **Storey, Margaret**
    please see: **Staynes, Jill w/ Margaret Storey**

A: **Storm, Joan**
    SC: Sarah Vanessa
1951 Dark Emerald

        1952 Bitter Rubies
        1953 Deadly Diamonds

A: **Strahan, Kay Cleaver**
    SC: Lynn MacDonald
        1928 The Desert Moon Mystery
        1929 Footprints
        1930 Death Traps
        1931 October House
        1932 The Meriweather Mystery
        1934 The Hobgoblin Murder
        1936 The Desert Lake Mystery

P: **Strange, John Stephen**
    please see: **Tillett, Dorothy Stockbridge**

A: **Struthers, Betsy**
    SC: Rosie Cairns
        1992 Found: A Body
        1994 Grave Deeds
        1995 A Studied Death

A: **Stuart (Ohlragge), Anne (Kristine)**
    SC: Ferris Byrd
        1985 Catspaw
        1988 Catspaw II
    SC: Maggie Bennett
        1987 At the Edge of the Sun
        1987 Darkness Before the Dawn
        1987 Escape out of Darkness

A: **Stubbs, Jean**
    SC: Insp. John Joseph Lintott
        1973 Dear Laura
        1974 The Painted Face
        1976 The Golden Crucible

A: **Stuyck, Karen Hanson**
    SC: Liz James
        1995 Cry for Help
        1996 Held Accountable
        1997 Lethal Lessons

A: **Sucher, Dorothy**
    SC: Sabina Swift & Vic Newman
        1988 Dead Men Don't Give Seminars
        1989 Dead Men Don't Marry

A: **Sullivan, Winona**
    SC: Sister Cecile
        1993 A Sudden Death at the Norfolk Cafe
        1995 Dead South

A: **Summerton, Margaret**
P: **Roffman, Jan**
    SC: Sgt. Ratlin
            1965 A Penny for the Guy
                  APA: Mask of Words
            1965 The Hanging Woman

A: **Sumner, Penny**
    SC: Victoria Cross
            1992 The End of April
            1995 Crosswords

A: **Swan (Burdett-Smith), Annie S.**
    SC: Anne Hyde
        SS 1908 Anne Hyde, Travelling Companion
    SC: Elizabeth Glen
        SS 1895 Elizabeth Glen, M. B.: The Experiences of a Lady
                Doctor
        SS 1897 Mrs. Keith Hamilton, M. B.

A: **Swan, Phyllis**
    SC: Anna J(agedinski)
            1979 Find Sherri!
            1979 Trigger Lady
            1979 You've Had It, Girl
            1980 The Death Inheritance

A: **Symons, Beryl (Mary E.)**
    SC: Insp. Henry Doight
            1928 The Devine Court Mystery
            1929 The Leering House
            1932 The Opal Murder Case
    SC: Jane Carberry
            1940 Jane Carberry Investigates
            1940 Jane Carberry: Detective
            1941 Jane Carberry and the Laughing Fountain
            1941 Magnet for Murder
            1947 Jane Carberry's Weekend

T

A: **Tait, Euphemia Margaret**
P: **Ironside, John**
    SC: Det. Insp. John Freeman
            1910 The Red Symbol
            1933 The Marten Mystery

P: **Tanner, Jake**
    please see: **Museo, Laura w/ Stephen Schermerhorn**
A: **Taylor, Bonnie w/ Matt Taylor**
    SC: Egan & Kingston
            1987 Neon Flamingo
            1991 Neon Dancers
A: **Taylor, Elizabeth Atwood**
    SC: Maggie Elliott
            1982 The Cable Car Murder
            1987 Murder at Vassar
            1992 The Northwest Murders
A: **Taylor, Jean**
    SC: Maggie Garrett
            1995 We Know Where You Live
            1996 The Last of Her Lies
A: **Taylor, Karen E.**
    SC: Det. Mitch Greer & Deidre Griffin
            1994 Blood Secrets
            1994 Bitter Blood
            1995 Blood Ties
A: **Taylor, Kathleen**
    SC: Tory Bauer
            1993 The Missionary Position
                 APA: Funeral Food
            1996 Sex and Salmonella
            1997 The Hotel South Dakota
A: **Taylor, L(aurie) A(ylma)**
    SC: J. J. Jamison (see p. 24)
            1983 Only Half a Hoax
            1984 Deadly Objectives
            1985 Shed Light on Death
            1989 A Murder Waiting to Happen
A: **Taylor, Mary Ann**
    SC: Pol. Chf. Emil Martin
            1980 Red Is for Shrouds
            1980 Return to Murder
J: **Taylor, Matt**
    please see: **Taylor, Bonnie w/ Matt Taylor**
A: **Taylor, Phoebe Atwood**
    SC: Asey Mayo (see p. 265)
            1931 The Cape Cod Mystery
            1932 Death Lights a Candle
            1933 The Mystery of the Cape Cod Players
            1934 Sandbar Sinister

1934 The Mystery of the Cape Cod Tavern
1935 Deathblow Hill
1935 The Tinkling Symbol
1936 Out of Order
1936 The Crimson Patch
1937 Figure Away
1937 Octagon House
1938 Banbury Bog
1938 The Annulet of Guilt
1939 Spring Harrowing
1940 The Criminal C.O.D.
1940 The Deadly Sunshade
1941 The Perennial Boarder
1942 The Six Iron Spiders
1942 Three Plots for Asey Mayo
1943 Going, Going, Gone
1945 Proof of the Pudding
1946 Punch with Care
1946 The Asey Mayo Trio
1951 Diplomatic Corpse

P: **Tilton, Alice**
  SC: Leonidas Witherall
    1937 Beginning with a Bash
    1938 The Cut Direct
    1939 Cold Steal
    1940 The Left Leg
    1941 The Hollow Chest
    1943 File for Record
    1944 Dead Ernest
    1947 The Iron Clew
      APA: The Iron Hand

J: **Tedeschi, Frank L.**
  please see: **Byfield, Barbara Ninde w/ Frank L. Tedeschi**
P: **Teilhet, Darwin L.**
  please see: **Teilhet, Hildegarde Tolman**
A: **Teilhet, Hildegarde Tolman**
  SC: Sam Hook
    1942 Hero by Proxy
    1945 The Double Agent
    1946 The Assassins

P: **Teilhet, Darwin L.**
  SC: Baron Von Kaz
    1936 The Crimson Hair Murders

1936 The Feather Cloak Murders
1940 The Broken Face Murders

P: **Tell, Dorothy**
please see: **Toopes, Dot**

A: **Temple, Lou Jane**
SC: Heaven Lee
1996 Death by Rhubarb
1997 Revenge of the Barbeque Queens

A: **Tepper, Sheri S.**
P: **Oliphant, B. J.**
SC: Shirley McClintock (see p. 274)
1990 Dead in the Scrub
1990 The Unexpected Corpse
1992 Death and the Delinquent
1992 Deservedly Dead
1994 Death Served Up Cold
1995 A Ceremonial Death

P: **Orde, A. J.**
SC: Jason Lynx (see p. 144)
1989 A Little Neighborhood Murder
1990 Death and the Dogwalker
1992 Death for Old Time's Sake
1993 Looking for the Aardvark
APA: Dead on Sunday
1995 A Long Time Dead
1997 Death of Innocents

P: **Tey, Josephine**
please see: **MacKintosh, Elizabeth**

A: **Thayer, (Emma Bedington) Lee**
SC: Peter Clancy (see p. 221)
1919 The Mystery of the Thirteenth Floor
1920 The Unlatched Door
1921 That Affair at "The Cedars"
1922 Q.E.D.
APA: The Puzzle
1923 The Sinister Mark
1924 The Key
1926 Poison
1927 Alias Dr. Ely
1928 The Darkest Spot
1929 Dead Men's Shoes
1930 They Tell No Tales
1931 Set a Thief
APA: To Catch a Thief

1931 The Last Shot
1932 The Glass Knife
1932 The Scrimshaw Millions
1933 Counterfeit
      APA: The Counterfeit Bill
1933 Hell-Gate Tides
1934 The Second Bullet
      APA: The Second Shot
1935 Dead Storage
      APA: The Death Weed
1935 Sudden Death
      APA: Red-Handed
1936 Dark of the Moon
      APA: Death in the Gorge
1936 Dead End Street
      APA: Murder in the Mirror
1937 A Man's Enemies
      APA: This Man's Doom
1937 Last Trump
1938 Ransom Racket
1938 That Strange Sylvester Affair
      APA: The Strange Sylvester Affair
1939 Lightning Strikes Twice
1939 Stark Murder
1940 Guilty!
1940 X Marks the Spot
1941 Hallowe'en Homicide
1941 Persons Unknown
1942 Murder Is Out
1942 Murder on Location
1943 Accessory After the Fact
1944 A Plain Case of Murder
1944 Five Bullets
1945 Accident, Manslaughter or Murder?
1945 Hanging's Too Good
1946 A Hair's Breadth
1946 The Jaws of Death
1947 Murder Stalks the Circle
1948 Out, Brief Candle!
1948 Pig in a Poke
      APA: A Clue for Clancy
1949 Evil Root
1950 Too Long Endured

1950 Within the Vault
    APA: Death Within the Vault
1951 Do Not Disturb
    APA: Clancy's Secret Mission
1951 Guilt Edged
    APA: Guilt-Edged Murder
1952 Blood on the Knight
1953 The Prisoner Pleads "Not Guilty"
1954 Dead Reckoning
    APA: Murder on the Pacific
1954 No Holiday for Death
1955 Who Benefits?
    APA: Fatal Alibi
1957 Guilt Is Where You Find It
1958 Still No Answer
    APA: Web of Hate
1959 Two Ways to Die
1960 Dead on Arrival
1961 And One Cried Murder
1966 Dusty Death
    APA: Death Walks in Shadow

A: **Thomas, Dicey**
  SC: Bertha Barstow
     1989 Statutory Murder
     1992 Just Plane Murder

A: **Thomson, June (Valerie)**
  SC: Insp. Finch (Rudd)
     1971 Not One of Us
     1973 Death Cap
     1974 The Long Revenge
     1977 A Question of Identity
     1977 Case Closed
     1979 Deadly Relations
         APA: The Habit of Loving
     1980 Alibi in Time
     1981 Shadow of a Doubt
     1982 To Make a Killing
         APA: Portrait of Lilith
     1984 Sound Evidence
     1985 A Dying Fall
     1986 The Dark Stream
     1987 No Flowers, by Request
     1988 Rosemary for Remembrance
     1989 The Spoils of Time

        1990 Past Reckoning
        1991 Foul Play
        1996 Burden of Innocence
    SC: Sherlock Holmes
        SS   1994 The Secret Files of Sherlock Holmes
        SS   1994 The Secret Chronicles of Sherlock Holmes

A: **Thurlo, Aimee w/ David Thurlo**
    SC: Ella Clah
        1995 Blackening Song
        1996 Death Walker

J: **Thurlo, David**
    please see: **Thurlo, Aimee w/ David Thurlo**

A: **Thynne, Molly**
    SC: Dr. Constantine
        1931 The Crime at the "Noah's Ark"
        1932 Murder in the Dentist's Chair
        1933 He Dies and Makes No Sign

A: **Tillett, Dorothy Stockbridge**
  P: **Strange, John Stephen**
    SC: Barney Gantt (see p. 181)
        1936 The Bell in the Fog
        1938 Rope Enough
              APA: The Ballot Box Murders
        1938 Silent Witnesses
              APA: The Corpse and the Lady
        1940 A Picture of the Victim
        1943 Look Your Last
        1948 Make My Bed Soon
        1952 Deadly Beloved
        1976 The House on 9th Street
    SC: Lt. George Honegger
        1941 Murder Gives a Lovely Light
        1948 All Men Are Liars
              APA: Come to Judgment
        1961 Eye Witness
    SC: Van Dusen Ormsberry
        1928 The Man Who Killed Fortescue
        1929 The Clue of the Second Murder
        1931 Murder on the Ten-Yard Line
              APA: Murder Game

P: **Tilton, Alice**
    please see: **Taylor, Phoebe Atwood**

A: **Tirbutt, Honoria**
  P: **Page, Emma**
    SC: Chf. Insp. Kelsey
      1981 Every Second Thursday
      1982 Last Walk Home
      1983 Cold Light of Day
      1985 Scent of Death
      1987 Final Moments
      1988 A Violent End
A: **Todd, Marilyn**
    SC: Claudia
      1995 I, Claudia
      1996 Virgin Territory
      1997 Man Eater
A: **Tone, Teona**
    SC: Kyra Keaton
      1983 Lady on the Line
      1985 Full Cry
A: **Toopes, Dot**
  P: **Tell, Dorothy**
    SC: Poppy Dillworth
      1990 Murder at Red Rook Ranch
      1990 Wilderness Trek
      1991 The Hallelujah Murders
      1992 The Goddess Murders
P: **Torrie, Malcolm**
    please see: **Mitchell, Gladys (Maude Winifred)**
A: **Travis, Elizabeth**
    SC: Ben & Carrie Porter
      1987 Deadlines
      1989 Under the Influence
      1990 Finders, Keepers
J: **Traynor, Anthony**
    please see: **Traynor, Page w/ Anthony Traynor**
A: **Traynor, Page w/ Anthony Traynor**
  P: **Anthony, Elizabeth**
    SC: Pauline Lyons
      1979 Ballet of Death
      1979 Ballet of Fear
A: **Trinchieri, Camilla**
  P: **Crespi, Camilla T.**
    SC: Simona Griffo (see p. 158)
      1994 The Trouble with Thin Ice

1995 The Trouble with Going Home
1996 The Trouble with a Bad Fit
1997 The Trouble with a Hot Summer

P: **Crespi, Trella**
SC: Simona Griffo (see p. 158)
1991 The Trouble with a Small Raise
1991 The Trouble with Moonlighting
1992 The Trouble with Too Much Sun

A: **Trocheck, Kathy Hogan**
SC: Callahan Garrity
1992 Every Crooked Nanny
1993 To Live and Die in Dixie
1994 Homemade Sin
1995 Happy Never After
1996 Heart Trouble
SC: Truman Kicklighter
1996 Lickety-Split
1997 Crash Course

J: **Trotman, Jack H.**
please see: **Harcourt, Palma w/ Jack H. Trotman**

A: **Truman, (Mary) Margaret**
SC: Mackensie Smith & Annabel Reed Smith (see p. 42)
1989 Murder at the Kennedy Center
1990 Murder at the National Cathedral
1992 Murder at the Pentagon
1994 Murder on the Potomac
1995 Murder at the National Gallery
SC: Washington, D.C.
1980 Murder in the White House
1981 Murder on Capitol Hill
1982 Murder in the Supreme Court
1983 Murder in the Smithsonian
1984 Murder on Embassy Row
1985 Murder at the FBI
1986 Murder in Georgetown
1987 Murder in the CIA
1996 Murder in the House

A: **Tucker, Kerry**
SC: Libby Kincaid (see p. 214)
1991 Still Waters
1992 Cold Feet
1993 Death Echo
1994 Drift Away

A: **Turnbull, Dora Amy Dillon**
P: **Wentworth, Patricia**

    SC: Benbow Smith & Frank Garratt
                  1931 Danger Calling
                  1933 Walk with Care

    SC: Insp. Ernest Lamb
                  1939 The Blind Side
                  1940 Who Pays the Piper?
                        APA: Account Rendered
                  1942 Pursuit of a Parcel

    SC: Miss Maud Silver (see p. 221)
                  1928 Grey Mask
                  1937 The Case Is Closed
                  1939 Lonesome Road
                  1941 In the Balance
                        APA: Danger Point
                  1943 Miss Silver Deals with Death
                        APA: Miss Silver Intervenes
                  1943 The Chinese Shawl
                  1944 The Clock Strikes Twelve
                  1944 The Key
                  1945 She Came Back
                        APA: The Traveler Returns
                  1946 Pilgrim's Rest
                        APA: Dark Threat
                  1947 Latter End
                  1947 Wicked Uncle
                        APA: Spotlight
                  1948 Eternity Ring
                  1948 The Case of William Smith
                  1949 Miss Silver Comes to Stay
                  1949 The Catherine Wheel
                  1950 The Brading Collection
                        APA: Mr. Brading's Collection
                  1950 Through the Wall
                  1951 Anna, Where Are You?
                        APA: Death at Deep End
                  1951 The Ivory Dagger
                  1951 The Watersplash
                  1952 Ladies' Bane
                  1953 Out of the Past
                  1953 Vanishing Point
                  1954 The Benevent Treasure
                  1954 The Silent Pool

1955 Poison in the Pen
1955 The Listening Eye
1956 The Fingerprint
1956 The Gazebo
    APA: The Summerhouse
1958 The Alington Inheritance
1961 The Girl in the Cellar

A: **Turnbull, Margaret**
  SC: Juliet Jackson
        1926 Madame Judas
        1928 Rogues' March
        1932 The Return of Jenny Weaver
        1934 The Coast Road Murder

A: **Tyre, Peg**
  SC: Kate Murray
        1994 Strangers in the Night
        1995 In the Midnight Hour

U

A: **Uhnak, Dorothy**
  SC: Det. Christie Opara (see p. 49)
        1968 The Bait
        1969 The Witness
        1970 The Ledger

V

A: **Vahey, John G. H.**
  P: **Clandon, Henrietta**
    SC: Penny & Vincent Mercer
          1935 Rope by Arrangement
          1936 This Delicate Murder
          1937 Power on the Scent
          1938 Fog off Weymouth
    SC: William Power
          1935 Rope by Arrangement
          1936 Good by Stealth
          1936 This Delicate Murder
          1937 Power on the Scent

A: **Valentine, Deborah**
    SC: Kevin Bryce
          1989 A Collector of Photographs
          1989 Unorthodox Methods
          1991 Fine Distinctions
J: **Van der Veer Lee, Marion**
    please see: **Saunders, Claire Castler w/ Marion Van der Veer Lee**
A: **Van der Veer Lee, Marion**
    P: **Lee, Babs**
    SC: Argus Steele
          1942 A Model Is Murdered
          1943 Passport to Oblivion
A: **Van Deventer, Emma M.**
    P: **Lynch, Lawrence**
    SC: Carl Masters
          1894 Against Odds
          1904 A Woman's Tragedy; or, the Detective's Task
          1908 Man and Master
    SC: Madeline Payne
          1884 Madeline Payne, the Detective's Daughter
               APA: *The Detective's Daughter; or Madeline Payne*
          1891 Moina; or, Against the Mighty
               APA: *Moina*
    SC: Neil Bathurst
          1879 Shadowed by Three
          1882 The Diamond Coterie
          1885 Out of the Labyrinth
    SC: Van Vernet
          1885 Dangerous Ground; or, the Rival Detectives
               APA: *The Rival Detectives; or, Dangerous Ground*
          1886 A Mountain Mystery; or, the Outlaws of the Rockies
A: **Van Gieson, Judith**
    SC: Neil Hamel (see p. 173)
          1988 North of the Border
          1990 Raptor
          1991 The Other Side of Death
          1992 The Wolf Path
          1993 The Lies That Bind
          1994 Parrot Blues
          1996 Hotshots
A: **Van Siller, Hilda**
    P: **Siller, Van**
    SC: Allan Stewart
          1965 A Complete Stranger

                    1966 The Mood of Murder
                    1967 The Biltmore Call
          SC: Pete Rector
                    1943 Good Night, Ladies
                    1946 Under a Cloud
          SC: Richard Massey
                    1943 Echo of a Bomb
                    1947 The Curtain Between
                              APA: Fatal Bride
A: **Van Urk, Virginia (Nellis)**
          SC: Tom Craig
                    1951 Speaking of Murder
                    1958 Grounds for Murder
A: **Van Vorst, Marie**
          SC: Jimmy Bulstrode
                    SS   1908 The Sentimental Adventures of Jimmy Bulstrode
                    SS   1918 After-Dinner Stories
P: **Venning, Michael**
          please see: **Craig, Georgiana Ann Randolph**
J: **Vetter, Louise**
          please see: **Lowry, Cheryl Meredith w/ Louise Vetter**
A: **Vincent, Lady Kitty (Edith Blanche)**
          SC: Gyp Kidnadze
                    1924 "No. 3"
                    1928 The Ruby Cup
                    1934 An Untold Tale
A: **Vivian, Margaret**
          SC: Dr. Jaz
                    SS   1933 Dr. Jaz

W

J: **Wahloo, Per**
          please see: **Sjowall, Maj w/ Per Wahloo**
P: **Wakefield, Hannah**
          please see: **Burton, Sarah w/ Judith Holland**
A: **Walker, Ir(m)a (Ruth) (Roden)**
          SC: Steve Rhoden
                    1963 Someone's Stolen Nellie Grey
                    1964 The Man in the Driver's Seat
                    1980 Murder in 25 Words or Less

A: **Walker, Mary Willis**
  SC: Molly Cates
      1994 The Red Scream
      1995 Under the Beetle's Cellar
P: **Wallace, C. H.**
  please see: **Burger, Rosaylmer**
A: **Wallace, Marilyn**
  SC: Sgt. Cruz & Sgt. Goldstein
      1986 A Case of Loyalties
      1988 Primary Target
      1992 A Single Stone
A: **Wallace, Mary**
  P: **Lynch, Miriam**
  SC: Nell Willard
      1979 Time to Kill
      1979 You'll Be the Death of Me
A: **Wallace (Estrada), Patricia**
  SC: Sydney Bryant
      1988 Small Favors
      1989 Deadly Grounds
      1991 Blood Lies
      1994 Deadly Devotion
A: **Wallingford, Lee**
  SC: Frank Carver & Ginny Trask
      1991 Cold Tracks
      1992 Clear-Cut Murder
A: **Wallis, Ruth (O.) Sawtell**
  SC: Eric Lund
      1944 No Bones About It
      1947 Cold Bed in the Clay
      1950 Forget My Fate
A: **Walsh, Jill Paton**
  SC: Imogen Quy
      1993 The Wyndham Case
      1995 A Piece of Justice
A: **Waltch, Lilla M.**
  SC: Lisa Davis
      1987 The Third Victim
      1988 Fearful Symmetry
P: **Walter, A. & H.**
  please see: **Walter, Alexia w/ Hubert Walter**
A: **Walter, Alexia w/ Hubert Walter**
  P: **Walter, A. & H.**
  SC: Sir Edgar Ewart
      1928 The Patriot
      1929 Betrayed

J: **Walter, Hubert**
   please see: **Walter, Alexia w/ Hubert Walter**
A: **Walz, Audrey Boyers**
   P: **Bonnamy, Francis**
      SC: Prof. Peter Uteley Shane
            1931 Death by Appointment
            1937 Death on a Dude Ranch
            1943 Dead Reckoning
            1944 A Rope of Sand
            1945 The King Is Dead on Queen Street
            1947 Portrait of the Artist as a Dead Man
                  APA: Murder as a Fine Art
                  APA: Self-Portrait of Murder
            1949 Blood and Thirsty
            1951 The Man in the Mist
A: **Ward-Thomas, Evelyn Bridget Patricia Stephens**
   P: **Anthony, Evelyn**
      SC: Davina Graham
            1980 The Defector
            1981 The Avenue of the Dead
            1982 Albatross
            1983 The Company of Saints
A: **Warmbold, Jean**
      SC: Sarah Calloway (see p. 183)
            1986 June Mail
                  APA: Dead Man Running
            1988 The White Hand
            1989 The Third Way
A: **Warner, Mignon**
      SC: Mrs. Edwina Charles (see pp. 23, 266)
            1976 A Nice Way to Die
                  APA: A Medium for Murder
            1978 The Tarot Murders
            1982 Death in Time
            1982 The Girl Who Was Clairvoyant
            1983 Devil's Knell
            1984 Illusion
            1985 Speak No Evil
A: **Warner, Penny**
      SC: Connor Westphal
            1997 Dead Body Language
            1998 Sign of Foul Play
            1999 Silence Is Golden

A: **Washburn (Reasoner), L(ivia) J.**
SC: Lucas Hallam (see p. 20)
1987 Wild Night
1989 Dead Stick
1990 Dog Heavies

J: **Watkins, Muriel**
please see: **Armitage, Audrey w/ Muriel Watkins**

A: **Watson, Clarissa**
SC: Persis Willum (see p. 208)
1977 The Fourth Stage of Gainsborough Brown
1980 The Bishop in the Back Seat
1985 Runaway
1988 Last Plane from Nice
1988 Somebody Killed the Messenger

P: **Webb, Martha G.**
please see: **Wingate, (Martha) Anne (Guice)**

A: **Weeks, Dolores**
SC: Dr. Scott Eason
1987 The Cape Murders
1988 The Friday Harbor Murders

A: **Wees, Frances Shelley**
SC: Michael Forrester
1931 The Maestro Murders
APA: Detectives, Ltd.
1931 The Mystery of the Creeping Man

A: **Weir, Charlene**
SC: Pol. Chf. Susan Wren
1992 The Winter Widow
1993 Consider the Crows
1995 Family Practice
1998 Murder: Take Two

A: **Welch, Pat**
SC: Helen Black
1990 Murder by the Book
1991 Still Waters
1993 A Proper Burial
1995 Open House
1996 Smoke and Mirrors

A: **Wells, Anna Mary**
SC: Dr. Hillis Owen & Miss Pomeroy (see p. 110)
1942 A Talent for Murder
1943 Murderer's Choice
1948 Sin of Angels

A: **Wells, Carolyn**
    SC: Alan Ford
        1916 The Bride of a Moment
        1917 Faulkner's Folly
    SC: Fleming Stone (see p. 221)
        1909 The Clue
        1911 The Gold Bag
        1912 A Chain of Evidence
        1913 The Maxwell Mystery
        1914 Anybody But Anne
        1915 The White Alley
        1916 The Curved Blades
        1917 The Mark of Cain
        1918 Vicky Van
            APA: The Elusive Vicky Van
        1919 The Diamond Pin
        1920 Raspberry Jam
        1921 The Mystery of the Sycamore
        1922 The Mystery Girl
        1923 Feathers Left Around
        1923 Spooky Hollow
        1924 Prillilgirl
        1924 The Furthest Fury
        1925 Anything But the Truth
        1925 The Daughter of the House
        1926 The Bronze Hand
        1926 The Red-Haired Girl
        1927 All at Sea
        1927 Where's Emily
        1928 The Crime in the Crypt
        1928 The Tannahill Tangle
        1929 The Tapestry Room Murder
        1929 Triple Murder
        1930 The Doomed Five
        1930 The Ghosts' High Noon
        1931 Horror House
        1931 The Umbrella Murder
        1932 Fuller's Earth
        1932 The Roll-Top Desk Mystery
        1933 The Broken O
        1933 The Clue of the Eyelash
        1933 The Master Murderer
        1934 Eyes in the Wall
        1934 The Visiting Villain

A: **Wendell, Sarah**
    SC: Dolly & The Old Buffer
            1973 The Old Buffer's Tale
            1979 Dolly and The Old Buffer Dig for Clews
            1984 Dolly and The Old Buffer in Oxford
            1990 Dolly and The Old Buffer Meet the Wolfman
            1990 Dolly and The Old Buffer on Kilimanjaro
            1991 Goodbye, Old Buffer
    SC: Dolly & The Wolfman
            1992 Dolly: Crystal Maker
            1993 Dolly, the Wolfman and the Fish Who Would Not Die
            1994 Jules Vern, Lady Dolly and the Blue Collar Cat
    SC: Henry & June
            1996 Henry and June, Tempted in the Tropics
            1997 Henry and June, Lured to the Latitudes

A: **Wender, Dorothea**
  P: **Wender, Theodora**
    SC: Prof. Glad Gold & Pol. Chf. Alden Chase
            1985 Knight Must Fall
            1986 Murder Gets a Degree

P: **Wender, Theodora**
  please see: **Wender, Dorothea**

P: **Wentworth, Patricia**
  please see: **Turnbull, Dora Amy Dillon**

A: **Wesley, Valerie Wilson**
    SC: Tamara Hayle (see p. 245)
            1994 When Death Comes Stealing
            1995 Devil's Gonna Get Him
            1996 Where Evil Sleeps
            1997 No Hiding Place

A: **Weston, Carolyn**
    SC: Al Krug & Casey Kellog
            1972 Poor, Poor Ophelia
            1975 Susannah Screaming
            1976 Rouse the Demon

A: **Wheat, Carolyn**
    SC: Cass Jameson (see p. 166)
            1983 Dead Man's Thoughts
            1986 Where Nobody Dies
            1995 Fresh Kills
            1996 Mean Streak
            1997 Troubled Waters

A: **Whelan, Hilary**
SC: Georges Albuisson & Jacques Andrieu
1995 Frightening Strikes
1995 A Shoulder to Die On
A: **Whitaker, Beryl (Salisbury)**
SC: John Abbot
1967 A Matter of Blood
1967 Of Mice and Murder
1967 The Chained Crocodile
1968 The Man Who Wasn't There
A: **White, Gloria**
SC: Ronnie Ventana (see p. 237)
1991 Murder on the Run
1993 Money to Burn
1995 Charged with Guilt
1997 Sunset and Santiago
A: **White, Teri**
SC: Blue Maguire & Spaceman Kowalski
1984 Bleeding Hearts
1986 Tightrope
A: **White, Valerie**
SC: John Case
1954 Case
1955 Case for Treachery
A: **Whitehead, Barbara**
SC: York Cycle of Mysteries
1988 Playing God
1990 The Girl with Red Suspenders
1991 The Dean It Was Who Died
1992 Sweet Death Come Softly
A: **Whitney, Polly**
SC: "Abby" Abagnarro & "Ike" Tygart
1994 Until Death
1995 Until the End of Time
1997 Until It Hurts
A: **Wilhelm (Knight), Kate (Gertrude)**
SC: Barbara Holloway (see p. 176)
1991 Death Qualified
1994 The Best Defense
1996 Malice Prepense
SC: Charlie Meiklejohn & Constance Leidl (see p. 111)
SS 1985 The Gorgon Field
1987 The Hamlet Trap
1988 The Dark Door

           1989 Smart House
           1990 Sweet, Sweet Poison
           1992 Seven Kinds of Death
      SS   1995 A Flush of Shadows
A: **Williams, Amanda Kyle**
     SC: Madison McGuire
           1990 Club Twelve
           1991 The Providence File
           1992 A Singular Spy
           1993 A Spy in Question
A: **Williams, Linda V.**
   P: **Grant, Linda**
     SC: Catherine Sayler (see p. 229)
           1988 Random Access Murder
           1990 Blind Trust
           1991 Love Nor Money
           1994 A Woman's Place
           1996 Lethal Genes
           1998 Vampire Bytes
A: **Williams, Margaret Wetherby**
   P: **Erskine, Margaret**
     SC: Insp. Septimus Finch
           1938 And Being Dead
                 APA: The Limping Man
                 APA: The Painted Mask
           1947 The Whispering House
                 APA: The Voice of the House
           1948 I Knew MacBean
                 APA: Caravan of Night
           1949 Give Up the Ghost
           1950 The Disappearing Bridegroom
                 APA: The Silver Ladies
           1952 Death of Our Dear One
                 APA: Don't Look Behind You
                 APA: Look Behind You, Lady
           1953 Dead by Now
           1955 Fatal Relations
                 APA: The Dead Don't Speak
                 APA: Old Mrs. Ommanney Is Dead
           1956 The Voice of Murder
           1958 Sleep No More
           1959 The House of the Enchantress
                 APA: A Graveyard Plot
           1961 The Woman at Belguardo

1963 The House in Belmont Square
   APA: No. 9 Belmont Square
1965 Take a Dark Journey
   APA: The Family at Tammerton
1967 Case with Three Husbands
1968 The Ewe Lamb
1970 The Case of Mary Fielding
1971 The Brood of Folly
1973 Besides the Wench Is Dead
1975 Harriet Farewell
1977 The House in Hook Street

A: **Williamson, Audrey (May)**
   SC: Supt. Richard York
      1979 Funeral March for Siegfried
      1980 Death of a Theatre Filly

A: **Wilson, Barbara (Ellen)**
   SC: Cassandra Reilly
      1990 Gaudi Afternoon
      1993 Trouble in Transylvania
   SC: Pam Nilsen
      1984 Murder in the Collective
      1986 Sisters of the Road
      1989 The Dog Collar Murders

A: **Wilson, G(ertrude) M(ary)**
   SC: Insp. Lovick
      1957 Bury That Poker
      1957 I Was Murdered
      1959 Shadows on the Landing
      1961 Witchwater
      1962 Roberta Died
      1963 Murder on Monday
      1964 Shot at Dawn
      1965 The Devil's Skull
      1967 Cake for Caroline
      1967 The Headless Man
      1968 Do Not Sleep
      1969 Death Is Buttercups
      1970 A Deal of Death Caps
      1971 The Bus Ran Late
      1972 She Kept On Dying

A: **Wilson, Karen Ann**
   SC: Samantha Holt
      1994 Eight Dogs Flying
      1995 Copy Cat Crimes

        1996 Beware Sleeping Dogs
        1997 Circle of Wolves

A: **Wiltz, Chris**
    SC: Neal Rafferty
        1981 The Killing Circle
        1987 A Diamond Before You Die
        1991 The Emerald Lizard

A: **Wingate, (Martha) Anne (Guice)**
    SC: Pol. Chf. Mark Shigata
        1988 Death by Deception
        1989 The Eye of Anna
        1991 The Buzzards Must Also Be Fed
        1992 Exception to Murder
        1993 Yakuza, Go Home!

P: **Martin, Lee**
    SC: Det. Deb Ralston (see p. 53)
        1984 Too Sane a Murder
        1986 A Conspiracy of Strangers
        1988 Death Warmed Over
        1988 Murder at the Blue Owl
        1989 Hal's Own Murder Case
        1990 Deficit Ending
        1990 The Mensa Murders
        1992 Hacker
        1993 The Day That Dusty Died
        1994 Inherited Murder
        1995 A Bird in a Cage
        1996 Genealogy of Murder

P: **Webb, Martha G.**
    SC: Tommy Inman
        1985 A White Male Running
        1986 Even Cops' Daughters

A: **Wings, Mary**
    SC: Emma Victor (see p. 286)
        1987 She Came Too Late
        1988 She Came in a Flash
        1996 She Came by the Book
        1997 She Came to the Castro

A: **Winke, Jennifer**
    SC: The Little Stranger
        1997 Surprise!
        1997 The Deed Is Done

A: **Winslow, Pauline Glen**
    SC: Supt. Merlin Capricorn (see p. 99)
        1975 Death of an Angel
        1976 The Brandenberg Hotel

1977 The Witch Hill Murder
1978 Coppergold
APA: *Copper Gold*
1980 The Counsellor Heart
APA: *Sister Death*
1982 The Rockefeller Gift

A: **Winsor, Diana**
SC: Tavy Martin
1972 Red on Wight
1974 The Death Convention

P: **Wolffe, Katherine**
please see: **Scott, Marian Gallagher**

A: **Wolzien, Valerie**
SC: Josie Pigeon
1995 Remodeled to Death
1996 Shore to Die
1997 Permit for Murder
1998 A House to Die For
SC: Susan Henshaw (see p. 288)
1988 Murder at the PTA Luncheon
1989 The Fortieth Birthday Body
1991 We Wish You a Merry Murder
1992 All Hallows' Evil
1992 An Old Faithful Murder
1993 A Star-Spangled Murder
1994 A Good Year for a Corpse
1994 'Tis the Season to Be Murdered
1995 Remodeled to Death
1996 Elected for Death

A: **Wood, Mrs. Henry (Ellen Price)**
SC: Johnny Ludlow
SS 1874 Johnny Ludlow
SS 1880 Johnny Ludlow, Second Series
SS 1885 Johnny Ludlow, Third Series
SS 1890 Johnny Ludlow, Fourth Series
SS 1890 Johnny Ludlow, Fifth Series
SS 1899 Johnny Ludlow, Sixth Series

P: **Woods, Sara**
please see: **Bowen-Judd, Sara Hutton**

A: **Woods, Sherryl**
SC: Amanda Roberts & Joe Donelli
1989 Body and Soul
1989 Reckless
1990 Stolen Moments
1991 Ties That Bind

1993 Bank on It
1993 Hide and Seek
1994 Wages of Sin
1995 Deadly Obsession
1995 White Lightning

SC: Molly DeWitt

1992 Hot Property
1992 Hot Secret
1993 Hot Money
1994 Hot Schemes
1995 Hot Ticket

A: **Worsley-Gough, Barbara**

SC: Aloysius Kelly

1954 Alibi Innings
1957 Lantern Hill

P: **Wray, I.**

please see: **Palliser, Iris**

P: **Wren, M. K.**

please see: **Renfroe, Martha Kay**

A: **Wright, Daphne**

P: **Cooper, Natasha**

SC: Willow King

1990 Festering Lilies
1991 Poison Flowers
1992 Bloody Roses
1993 Bitter Herbs
1995 Rotten Apples
1997 The Drowning Pool

A: **Wright, L(aurali) R.**

SC: Cassandra Mitchell & Sgt. Karl Alberg (see p. 75)

1985 The Suspect
1986 Sleep While I Sing
1990 A Chill Rain in January
1991 Fall from Grace
1993 Prized Possessions
1994 A Touch of Panic
1995 Mother Love
1996 Strangers Among Us

Y

A: **Yarbro, Chelsea Quinn**

SC: Charles Spotted Moon (see p. 23)

1976 Ogilvie, Tallant & Moon
APA: Bad Medicine

1979 Music When Sweet Voices Die
    APA: False Notes
1991 Poison Fruit
1992 Cat's Claw

A: **Yarbro, Chelsea Quinn w/ Bill Fawcett**
P: **Fawcett, Quinn**
    SC: Mme. Victoire Vernet (see p. 10)
        1993 Napoleon Must Die
        1993 Death Wears a Crown

A: **Yates, Margaret Tayler**
    SC: Anne "Davvie" Davenport McLean
        1937 The Hush-Hush Murders
        1939 Death Sends a Cable
        1941 Midway to Murder
        1942 Murder by the Yard

A: **Yeager, Dorian**
    SC: Elizabeth Will
        1994 Murder Will Out
        1995 Summer Will End
    SC: Victoria Bowering
        1992 Cancellation by Death
        1993 Eviction by Death
        1996 Ovation by Death

A: **York, Kieran**
    SC: Royce Madison
        1993 Timber City Masks
        1995 Crystal Mountain Veils

P: **York, Rebecca**
    please see: **Buckholtz, Eileen w/ Ruth Glick**
P: **Yorke, Margaret**
    please see: **Nicholson, Margaret Beda Larminie**

Z

A: **Zachary, Fay**
    SC: Dr. Liz Broward & Zack James
        1994 A Poison in the Blood
        1994 Blood Work

A: **Zaremba, Eve**
    SC: Helen Keremos (see p. 223)
        1978 A Reason to Kill
        1986 Work for a Million
        1987 Beyond Hope

1990 Uneasy Lies
1994 Butterfly Effect
1997 White Noise

A: **Zukowski, Sharon**
SC: Blaine Stewart
1991 The Hour of the Knife
1992 Dancing in the Dark
1994 Leap of Faith
1996 Prelude to Death
1997 Jungleland

APPENDIX I:
Series Character Chronology

This chronological listing is designed to assist readers in several ways. With this information, a series can be fixed in time. A favorite character can then be placed with her/his fictional counterparts. Often, writing style and vernacular reflect the era in which a book was written. Trends and character types also vary with different periods.

The first date of each entry marks the series character's first appearance in print. The second date shows when the last book in the series was published. The number of books in which each series character appears is next, followed by the series character's name in bold print. The Autonym appears under the series character's name.

1867–1868	2	**Valentine Hawkehurst** Braddon, M(ary) E(lizabeth)
1874–1899	6	**Johnny Ludlow** Wood, Mrs. Henry (Ellen Price)
1878–1917	13	**Ebenezer Gryce** Green, Anna Katharine
1879–1885	3	**Neil Bathurst** Van Deventer, Emma M.
1884–1891	2	**Madeline Payne** Van Deventer, Emma M.
1885–1886	2	**Van Vernet** Van Deventer, Emma M.
1894–1901	5	**Dr. Clifford Halifax** Meade (Smith), Elizabeth Thomasina
1894–1894	1	**Loveday Brooke, Lady Detective** Pirkis, C(atharine) L(ouisa)
1894–1908	3	**Carl Masters** Van Deventer, Emma M.
1895–1897	2	**Elizabeth Glen** Swan (Burdett-Smith), Annie S.

1897–1917	6	**Amelia Butterworth & Ebenezer Gryce** Green, Anna Katharine
1897–1897	1	**Lord Syfret** Kenealy, Arabella
1898–1899	2	**John Faunce** Braddon, M(ary) E(lizabeth)
1898–1898	1	**John Bell** Meade (Smith), Elizabeth Thomasina w/ Robert Eustace (Barton)
1899–1917	6	**Caleb Sweetwater** Green, Anna Katharine
1899–1899	1	**George Conway** Meade (Smith), Elizabeth Thomasina w/ Robert Eustace (Barton)
1899–1899	1	**Norman Head** Meade (Smith), Elizabeth Thomasina w/ Robert Eustace (Barton)
1899–1899	1	**Flaxman Low** Prichard, Katherine O'Brien w/ Vernon Hesketh Prichard
1900–1900	1	**Dr. Chetwynd & Dr. Paul Cato** Meade (Smith), Elizabeth Thomasina w/ Robert Eustace (Barton)
1900–1900	1	**Jim Burns** Penny, Mrs. Frank
1901–1901	1	**Gilchrist** Meade (Smith), Elizabeth Thomasina
1903–1903	1	**Madame Sara** Meade (Smith), Elizabeth Thomasina
1904–1904	1	**The Oracle of Maddox Street** Meade (Smith), Elizabeth Thomasina w/ Robert Eustace (Barton)
1904–1909	3	**Don Q** Prichard, Katherine O'Brien w/ Vernon Hesketh Prichard
1905–1925	8	**Bill Owen, The Old Man in the Corner** Orczy, Baroness (Emma Magdalena Rosalia Maria Josifa Barbara, Baroness Orczy)
1905–1940	14	**The Scarlet Pimpernel** Orczy, Baroness (Emma Magdalena Rosalia Maria Josifa Barbara, Baroness Orczy)

1906–1906	1	**Miriam Lemaire** Hosken, Alice Cecil Seymour w/ Ernest Charles Heath Hosken
1908–1908	1	**Anne Hyde** Swan (Burdett-Smith), Annie S.
1908–1918	2	**Jimmy Bulstrode** Van Vorst, Marie
1909–1925	4	**Millicent Newberry** Lee, Jennette (Barbour Perry)
1909–1942	61	**Fleming Stone** Wells, Carolyn
1910–1910	1	**Micah Faraday** Meade (Smith), Elizabeth Thomasina
1910–1910	1	**Lady Molly** Orczy, Baroness (Emma Magdalena Rosalia Maria Josifa Barbara, Baroness Orczy)
1910–1933	2	**John Freeman** Tait, Euphemia Margaret
1911–1911	1	**Lavie Jutt** Barclay, Marguerite w/ Armiger Barclay
1911–1922	3	**Joe Miller** Groner, Augusta
1911–1937	6	**Leticia "Tish" Carberry** Rinehart, Mary Roberts
1911–1911	1	**John Bolsover** Silberrad, Una L(ucy)
1912–1912	1	**Napoleon Prince** Edginton (Bailey), May (Helen Marion)
1912–1912	1	**Lady Weybridge** Evans, Marguerite Helen Jervis
1914–1915	2	**Mr. Gimblet** Bryce, Mrs. Charles
1914–1922	2	**Mercedes Quero** Locke, G(ladys) E(dson)
1915–1919	3	**Molly Morgenthau** Bonner, Geraldine
1915–1920	2	**Mr. Jones** Conyers, Dorothea (Smyth)
1915–1915	1	**Violet Strange** Green, Anna Katharine

1915–1918	2	**Hamilton Cleek** Hanshew, Hazel Phillips w/ Mary Hanshew
1916–1927	10	**Mitchell** Lincoln, Natalie S(umner)
1916–1917	2	**Alan Ford** Wells, Carolyn
1917–1917	1	**Cristina Raye** Grimshaw, Beatrice (Ethel)
1917–1923	5	**Timothy McCarty** Ostrander, Isabel (Egenton)
1918–1918	1	**M. Fernand** Orczy, Baroness (Emma Magdalena Rosalia Maria Josifa Barbara, Baroness Orczy)
1918–1923	8	**Pennington Wise** Wells, Carolyn
1919–1966	60	**Peter Clancy** Thayer, (Emma Bedington) Lee
1920–1984	47	**Hercule Poirot** Christie, Agatha
1920–1925	5	**Hamilton Cleek** Hanshew, Hazel Phillips
1920–1921	2	**Ferguson** Lincoln, Natalie S(umner)
1920–1921	2	**Barry O'Dell** Ostrander, Isabel (Egenton)
1920–1924	4	**The Shadowers, Inc.** Ostrander, Isabel (Egenton)
1921–1921	1	**M. Hector Ratichon** Orczy, Baroness (Emma Magdalena Rosalia Maria Josifa Barbara, Baroness Orczy)
1922–1931	2	**Briconi** Baskerville, Beatrice w/ Elliot Monk
1922–1973	5	**Tommy & Tuppence Beresford** Christie, Agatha
1922–1941	9	**Douglas Renfrew** Erskine, Laurie York
1922–1925	4	**Burton** Locke, G(ladys) E(dson)
1922–1927	5	**Jerry Boyne** MacGowan, Alice w/ Perry Newberry

1923–1942	24	**Henry Wilson** Cole, Margaret (Isabel Postgate) w/ G(eorge) D(ouglas) H(oward) Cole
1923–1927	3	**Furnival** Haynes, Annie
1923–1982	18	**Lord Peter Wimsey** Sayers, Dorothy L(eigh)
1923–1924	2	**Lorimer Lane** Wells, Carolyn
1924–1945	4	**Race** Christie, Agatha
1924–1944	23	**Pointer** Fielding, Dorothy
1924–1934	3	**Gyp Kidnadze** Vincent, Lady Kitty (Edith Blanche)
1925–1944	5	**Battle** Christie, Agatha
1925–1925	1	**Sandy** Conyers, Dorothea (Smyth)
1925–1925	1	**Guy Bannister** Crossley, Maude w/ Charles Thomas King
1925–1932	2	**Winston Barrows** Eades, M(aude) L.
1926–1927	2	**Septimus March** Bamburg, Lilian
1926–1941	5	**Everard Blatchington** Cole, Margaret (Isabel Postgate) w/ G(eorge) D(ouglas) H(oward) Cole
1926–1926	1	**Dr. Taverner** Firth, Violet Mary
1926–1934	4	**Juliet Jackson** Turnbull, Margaret
1927–1931	3	**Jack Strickland** Balfour, Eva w/ Beryl Hearnden
1927–1929	2	**Parrish Darby** Bamberger, Helen w/ Raymond Bamburger
1927–1935	10	**Scott Egerton** Malleson, Lucy Beatrice
1928–1932	3	**Sir John Saumarez** Ashton, Winifred w/ Helen (DeGuerry) Simpson

1928–1930	3	**Dexter Drake** Barker, Elsa
1928–1938	4	**Glyn Morgan** Lambert, Rosa w/ Dudley Lambert
1928–1928	1	**Patrick Mulligan** Orczy, Baroness (Emma Magdalena Rosalia Maria Josifa Barbara, Baroness Orczy)
1928–1936	7	**Lynn MacDonald** Strahan, Kay Cleaver
1928–1932	3	**Henry Doight** Symons, Beryl (Mary E.)
1928–1931	3	**Van Dusen Ormsberry** Tillett, Dorothy Stockbridge
1928–1961	32	**Miss Maud Silver** Turnbull, Dora Amy Dillon
1928–1929	2	**Sir Edgar Ewart** Walter, Alexia w/ Hubert Walter
1929–1989	27	**Albert Campion** Allingham (Carter), Margery (Louise)
1929–1931	2	**Gregory Lewis** Brown, Zenith Jones
1929–1932	5	**Sarah Keate & Lance O'Leary** Eberhart, Mignon (Good)
1929–1931	3	**Smith** Edington, Carmen Ballen w/ Arlo Channing Edington
1929–1930	3	**Stoddart** Haynes, Annie
1929–1931	2	**Tim Asher** Hultman, Helen Joan
1929–1930	2	**John Christmas** Jerrold, Ianthe (Bridgman)
1929–1940	3	**Bruce Perkins** Lilly, Jean
1929–1952	6	**Alan Grant** MacKintosh, Elizabeth
1929–1932	5	**Peter Piper** Mavity, Nancy Barr
1929–1984	68	**Dame Beatrice Adela Lestrange Bradley** Mitchell, Gladys (Maude Winifred)
1929–1931	3	**Kenneth Carlisle** Wells, Carolyn

1930–1941	7	**Philip "Spike" Tracy** Ashbrook, H(arriette) C(ora)
1930–1939	5	**James F. "Bonnie" Dundee** Austin, Anne
1930–1933	5	**Kane** Blair, Dorothy w/ Evelyn Page
1930–1950	14	**Evan Pinkerton** Brown, Zenith Jones
1930–1950	2	**Harley Quin** Christie, Agatha
1930–1985	20	**Miss Jane Marple** Christie, Agatha
1930–1931	3	**Miss Woolfe** Graham, (Matilda) Winifred (Muriel)
1930–1937	8	**Reynolds** Hamilton, Elaine
1930–1937	4	**Margetson** Keate, E(dith) M(urray)
1930–1943	7	**John Barrin** Lane, (Margaret) Gret
1930–1943	8	**Kate Marsh** Lane, (Margaret) Gret
1930–1934	2	**Peter Jerningham** Myers, Isabel Briggs
1930–1940	2	**Patrick Michael Doyle** Newell, Audrey
1930–1931	2	**Digby** Palliser, Iris
1930–1931	2	**Sebald Craft** Patterson, (Isabella) Innis
1930–1933	4	**John Smith** Plum, Mary
1930–1962	31	**Christopher McKee** Reilly, Helen
1930–1934	4	**Jimmy Lane** Ryerson, Florence w/ Colin Clements
1930–1932	2	**Colin Keats & Gwynn Leith** Shore, Viola Brothers
1931–1932	2	**Wade** Bristow, Gwen w/ Bruce Manning

534 • SILK STALKINGS

1931–1935	2	**Alice Penny** Burkhardt, Eve w/ Robert Ferdinand Burkhardt
1931–1932	2	**One Week Wimble** Burnham, Helen
1931–1948	4	**Tommy Rostetter** Campbell, Alice (Ormond)
1931–1940	6	**Li Moh** Cowdroy, Joan
1931–1931	1	**Guy Bannister** Crossley, Maude
1931–1934	2	**Everett Anderson** Daiger, K(atherine) S.
1931–1933	2	**Wylie King & Nels Lundberg** Davis, Clare w/ Burton Davis
1931–1933	3	**Benvenuto Brown** Gill, Elizabeth
1931–1932	2	**Hamilton Cleek** Hanshew, Hazel Phillips
1931–1933	4	**Wield** Peterson, Margaret Ann
1931–1959	47	**Robert Macdonald** Rivett, Edith Caroline
1931–1951	24	**Asey Mayo** Taylor, Phoebe Atwood
1931–1933	3	**Dr. Constantine** Thynne, Molly
1931–1933	2	**Benbow Smith & Frank Garratt** Turnbull, Dora Amy Dillon
1931–1951	8	**Peter Uteley Shane** Walz, Audrey Boyers
1931–1931	2	**Michael Forrester** Wees, Frances Shelley
1932–1933	2	**Joseph Kelly** Brown, Zenith Jones
1932–1950	4	**Nurse Hilda Adams (Miss Pinkerton)** Rinehart, Mary Roberts
1932–1935	2	**Angeline Tredennick** Sanborn, Ruth Burr
1932–1935	4	**Richard "Dick" Van Ryn Wilson** Sproul, Kathleen

1932–1932	2	**Sydney Treherne** St. Dennis, Madelon
1933–1934	2	**Peter Strangely** Black, E(lizabeth) Best
1933–1933	1	**Letitia Hawkins** Burgess, Ellen
1933–1934	2	**Jeremiah Irish** Child, Nellise
1933–1938	3	**Timothy Fowler** Colver, Anne
1933–1934	2	**Mr. Watson** Gardiner, Dorothy
1933–1934	2	**Woods** Muir, D(orothy) Erskine
1933–1939	2	**Montague Egg** Sayers, Dorothy L(eigh)
1933–1933	1	**Dr. Jaz** Vivian, Margaret
1934–1934	1	**John Primrose** Brown, Zenith Jones
1934–1934	1	**Parker Pyne** Christie, Agatha
1934–1935	2	**Clarice Claremont** Cranston, Claudia
1934–1934	1	**Susan Dare** Eberhart, Mignon (Good)
1934–1935	2	**Peggy Fairfield** Liddon, E(loise)
1934–1934	1	**Brother Felipe Bruno** Long, Gabrielle Margaret Vere Campbell
1934–1936	2	**M. Dupuy** Malleson, Lucy Beatrice
1934–1937	5	**Roderick Alleyn** Marsh, (Edith) Ngaio
1934–1936	3	**Colin Anstruther** Plain, Josephine
1935–1946	4	**Gramport** Barnett, Glyn
1935–1942	2	**Dennis Devore** Bennett, Dorothy

1935–1936	2	**Scott Stuart** Brawner, Helen w/ Francis Van Wyck Mason
1935–1936	2	**Dr. Benjamin Tancred** Cole, Margaret (Isabel Postgate) w/ G(eorge) D(ouglas) H(oward) Cole
1935–1937	2	**Frederick Hunt** Day (Lederer), Lillian w/ Norbert (Lewis) Lederer
1935–1935	1	**Pamela Wayne** Evans, Constance May
1935–1936	2	**Saunders** Firth, Violet Mary
1935–1953	8	**Hannasyde & Hemingway** Heyer, Georgette
1935–1946	5	**Patrick O'Brien** Irwin, Inez H(aynes)
1935–1959	16	**Elisha Macomber** Knight, Kathleen Moore
1935–1938	5	**James Greer** Marin, Muna Lee w/ Maurice C. Guiness
1935–1939	4	**Payran** Nisot, (Mavis) Elizabeth (Hocking)
1935–1939	6	**Rocky Allan** Rath, Virginia (Anne)
1935–1951	12	**Jane Amanda Edwards** Russell, Charlotte M(urray)
1935–1950	13	**Bill French** Stevens, Frances M(oyer) R(oss)
1935–1938	4	**Penny & Vincent Mercer** Vahey, John G. H.
1935–1937	4	**William Power** Vahey, John G. H.
1936–1946	7	**Simon Brade** Campbell, Harriette (Russell)
1936–1944	2	**Gorham** Cowdroy, Joan
1936–1954	19	**Anne & Jeffrey McNeill** DuBois, Theodora M.
1936–1936	2	**Dr. Joan Marvin** Eyles, (Margaret) Leonora (Pitcairn)
1936–1974	51	**Arthur G. Crook** Malleson, Lucy Beatrice

1936–1938	2	**Red Hanlon** Merrick, Mollie
1936–1940	2	**James Strange** Quinn, E(leanor) Baker
1936–1940	6	**Ryvet** Rivett, Edith Caroline
1936–1940	3	**Baron Von Kaz** Teilhet, Hildegarde Tolman
1936–1976	8	**Barney Gantt** Tillett, Dorothy Stockbridge
1937–1940	3	**Adam Quill** Abrahams, Doris Caroline w/ Simon Jasha Skidelsky
1937–1938	2	**Ballet Stroganoff** Abrahams, Doris Caroline w/ Simon Jasha Skidelsky
1937–1958	13	**Dr. David Wintringham** Ball, Doris Bell (Collier)
1937–1964	14	**Steven Mitchell** Ball, Doris Bell (Collier)
1937–1938	2	**Adelaide Adams** Blackmon, Anita
1937–1953	15	**Grace Latham & Col. John Primrose** Brown, Zenith Jones
1937–1948	5	**Headcorn** Campbell, Alice (Ormond)
1937–1939	2	**Dr. Nathaniel Bunce** Curtiss, E(lizabeth) M(angan)
1937–1937	2	**Carey Brent** Glidden, M(inna) W(esselhoft)
1937–1939	3	**Paul Vachell** Huxley, Elspeth (Jocelyn Grant)
1937–1939	3	**Daisy Jane Mott** Johnson, Enid w/ Margaret Lane
1937–1938	2	**Hook** Lane, (Margaret) Gret
1937–1939	2	**Simon Chard** Malim, Barbara
1937–1941	2	**Clive Granville** McKenna, Marthe
1937–1938	2	**Kingsley Toplitt** Stockwell, Gail

1937–1947	8	**Leonidas Witherall**
		Taylor, Phoebe Atwood
1937–1942	4	**Anne "Davvie" Davenport McLean**
		Yates, Margaret Tayler
1938–1941	4	**Dan Pardoe**
		Bowers, Dorothy (Violet)
1938–1941	2	**Eric Hazard**
		Budlong, Ware Torrey
1938–1941	2	**Mrs. Elizabeth Warrender**
		Cole, Margaret (Isabel Postgate) w/ G(eorge) D(ouglas) H(oward) Cole
1938–1939	3	**Mac McIntyre**
		Corne, M(olly)
1938–1940	2	**Glover**
		Eiker, Mathilde
1938–1959	18	**Mallett**
		Freeman, Kathleen
1938–1942	3	**Adam Drew & Katherine Cornish**
		Hanson, Virginia
1938–1946	7	**Stephen Mayhew**
		Hitchens, (Julia Clara Catherine) Dolores (Birk)
1938–1938	2	**Noah Bradshaw**
		Johnston, Madeleine
1938–1989	28	**Roderick Alleyn & Agatha Troy Alleyn**
		Marsh, (Edith) Ngaio
1938–1980	13	**Dr. Basil Willing**
		McCloy, Helen (Worrell Clarkson)
1938–1942	2	**Bill & Coco Hastings**
		Offord, Lenore Glen
1938–1942	5	**Mary Carner**
		Popkin, Zelda
1938–1947	8	**Michael Dundas**
		Rath, Virginia (Anne)
1938–1940	2	**Mr. Winkley**
		Rutland, Harriet
1938–1977	21	**Septimus Finch**
		Williams, Margaret Wetherby
1939–1940	2	**Mr. Hodson**
		Bidwell, Margaret
1939–1940	2	**Jack Thompson**
		Cameron, Evelyn

1939–1963	13	**Alister Woodhead** Clements, E(ileen) H(elen)
1939–1967	14	**John J. Malone & The Justuses** Craig, Georgiana Ann Randolph
1939–1943	5	**Peter & Janet Barron** Darby, Ruth
1939–1944	3	**Emma Marsh & Hank Fairbanks** Dean, Elizabeth
1939–1941	3	**Lyle Curtis & Susan Yates** Fetta, Emma Lou
1939–1942	3	**Chauncey O'Day** Gaines (Schultz), Audrey
1939–1953	17	**Desmond Shannon** Heberden, M(ary) V(iolet)
1939–1956	13	**Rachel & Jennifer Murdock** Hitchens, (Julia Clara Catherine) Dolores (Birk)
1939–1968	28	**William Austen** Hocking (Messer), (Mona Naomi) Anne
1939–1944	7	**Edward Trelawney** Long, Amelia Reynolds
1939–1946	4	**Hilea Bailey & Hilary D. Bailey III** Marting, Ruth Lenore
1939–1941	4	**Capt. Andy & Sue MacVeigh** Nearing, Elizabeth C.
1939–1964	7	**Matt Winters** Oellrichs, Inez H(ildegarde)
1939–1940	2	**Guy Northeast** Pullein-Thompson, Joanna M. C.
1939–1942	3	**Gregory Trent** Seifert, Adele
1939–1947	4	**Anthony Ware** Siegel, Doris
1939–1942	3	**Ernest Lamb** Turnbull, Dora Amy Dillon
1940–1949	7	**Christopher Storm** Barber, Willetta Ann w/ R(udolph) F(rederick) Schabelitz
1940–1946	3	**Hiram Odom** Boniface, Marjorie
1940–1942	5	**Toby Dyke** Brown, Morna Doris (MacTaggart)

1940–1941	2	**Lutie & Amanda Beagle** Chanslor, (Marjorie) Torrey (Hood)
1940–1951	16	**Henry Gamadge** Daly, Elizabeth (Theresa)
1940–1953	5	**Levy** Holding, Elisabeth Sanxay
1940–1942	3	**Tobin** Hughes, Dorothy B(elle)
1940–1941	2	**Agatha Welch** Johns, Veronica P(arker)
1940–1943	2	**Lord Winterstone** Johnson, Pamela Hansford w/ Neil Stewart
1940–1944	4	**Margot Blair** Knight, Kathleen Moore
1940–1963	26	**Pam & Jerry North** Lockridge, Frances (Louise Davis) w/ Richard (Orson) Lockridge
1940–1951	7	**Katherine "Peter" Piper** Long, Amelia Reynolds
1940–1963	26	**Tommy Hambledon** Manning, Adelaide Frances Oke w/ Cyril Henry Coles
1940–1941	2	**Christopher Gibson** Montgomery, Ione
1940–1966	9	**Haila & Jeff Troy** Roos, Audrey Kelley w/ William Roos
1940–1946	8	**Bill Grady** Shriber, Ione Sandburg
1940–1947	5	**Jane Carberry** Symons, Beryl (Mary E.)
1941–1979	4	**Charlesworth** Brand (Lewis), (Mary) Christianna (Milne)
1941–1983	9	**Cockrill** Brand (Lewis), (Mary) Christianna (Milne)
1941–1942	2	**Gypsy Rose Lee** Craig, Georgiana Ann Randolph
1941–1965	26	**Pat & Jean Abbott** Crane, Frances
1941–1944	3	**Ross Paterson** Field, Katherine
1941–1943	2	**Diego** Kelsey, Vera

1941–1943	2	**Sarah O'Brien** Marlett, Melba (Balmat)
1941–1943	2	**Andrea Reid Ramsay & David Ramsay** Matschat, Cecile Hulse
1941–1942	3	**Dr. Paul Prye** Millar, Margaret (Ellis Sturm)
1941–1942	2	**Eleanora Burke** Perdue, Virginia
1941–1943	3	**Powledge** Rea, M(argaret) P(aine)
1941–1961	3	**George Honegger** Tillett, Dorothy Stockbridge
1942–1945	3	**MacDougal Duff** Armstrong, Charlotte
1942–1946	4	**Christopher Saxe** Ashbrook, H(arriette) C(ora)
1942–1952	5	**Richard Tuck** Beynon, Jane
1942–1947	2	**Jacob Chaos** Bodington, Nancy Hermione Courlander
1942–1942	1	**John Charles Olson** Chute, M(ary) G(race)
1942–1958	3	**Bingo Riggs & Handsome Kusak** Craig, Georgiana Ann Randolph
1942–1944	3	**Melville Fairr** Craig, Georgiana Ann Randolph
1942–1954	2	**Sarah Keate** Eberhart, Mignon (Good)
1942–1962	13	**Gridley Nelson** Fenisong, Ruth
1942–1951	11	**Paul Kilgerrin** Heberden, M(ary) V(iolet)
1942–1944	2	**George White** Mannon, Martha w/ Mary Ellen Mannon
1942–1943	2	**D. A. Carey Galbreath** McCully, (Ethel) Walbridge
1942–1945	3	**Sands** Millar, Margaret (Ellis Sturm)
1942–1945	2	**Pettengill** Rowe, Anne (Von Meibom)

1942–1946	2	**Courtney Brade** Scott, Marian Gallagher
1942–1946	3	**Sam Hook** Teilhet, Hildegarde Tolman
1942–1943	2	**Argus Steele** Van der Veer Lee, Marion
1942–1948	3	**Dr. Hillis Owen & Miss Pomeroy** Wells, Anna Mary
1943–1945	3	**F. Millard Smyth** Boyd, Eunice Mays
1943–1944	2	**Andrew Torrent** Cores, Lucy (Michaela)
1943–1954	5	**Jim O'Neill** Disney, Doris Miles
1943–1966	19	**Grogan** Goyder, Margot w/ Anne N(eville) G(oyder) Joske
1943–1950	7	**Steve Carter** Long, Amelia Reynolds
1943–1945	2	**Bill Davies** Mason, Sara Elizabeth
1943–1948	2	**Miguel Urizar** McCloy, Helen (Worrell Clarkson)
1943–1945	2	**Christine Andersen** McCoy, Madeleine
1943–1944	2	**Mark Tudor** Nash, Anne
1943–1945	3	**Nell Winter & Doris "DoDo" Trent** Nash, Anne
1943–1956	4	**Lace White** Nolan, Jeannette Covert
1943–1959	4	**Todd McKinnon** Offord, Lenore Glen
1943–1946	2	**Pete Rector** Van Siller, Hilda
1943–1947	2	**Richard Massey** Van Siller, Hilda
1944–1949	5	**Kit Marsden Acton** Bramhall, Marion
1944–1949	4	**Lady Lupin Hastings, Clergyman's Wife** Coggin, Joan

1944–1987	4	**Dr. Sam: Johnson** de la Torre (Bueno) (McCue), Lillian
1944–1954	8	**Abbie Harris** Dean (Getz), Amber
1944–1950	5	**Alastair MacAlastair** Dick (Erikson), (Sibyl Cicely) Alexandra
1944–1945	2	**Lorna Donahue** Hill, Katharine
1944–1947	3	**Mark East** Lawrence, Hilda (Hildegarde Kronemiller)
1944–1946	2	**Mike James** Means, Mary w/ Theodore Saunders
1944–1972	35	**Dr. Manson** Radford, Mona Augusta Mangan w/ Edwin Isaac Radford
1944–1946	3	**Barry** Rowe, Anne (Von Meibom)
1944–1944	1	**Argus Steele** Saunders, Claire Castler w/ Marion Van der Veer Lee
1944–1950	3	**Eric Lund** Wallis, Ruth (O.) Sawtell
1945–1946	2	**John Davies** Bennett, Margot
1945–1947	2	**Nora Hughes & Larry Blaine** Davis, Lavinia R(iker)
1945–1948	5	**Randolph York** Durham, Mary
1945–1947	2	**Jenny Gilette & Hunter Lewis** Gresham, Elizabeth
1945–1952	6	**A. Pennyfeather** Hitchens, (Julia Clara Catherine) Dolores (Birk)
1945–1959	2	**Miles Pennoyer** Lawrence, Margery (H.)
1945–1947	3	**Peter Ponsonby** Leslie, Jean
1945–1957	6	**Patrick Laing** Long, Amelia Reynolds
1945–1945	1	**Cliveden Prince** Reubens, Aida
1945–1958	15	**Julian Rivers** Rivett, Edith Caroline

1945–1947	2	**Gregory Pavlov & O'Shaunnessey** Ryan, Jessica (Cadwalader)
1945–1948	2	**Lane Parry** Sarsfield, Maureen
1945–1948	2	**Ryan** Scherf, Margaret (Louise)
1945–1951	3	**Christopher Adrian** Silverman, Marguerite R(uth)
1946–1947	2	**Eve MacWilliams** Blizard, Marie
1946–1953	3	**Pat Campbell** Colter, Eli(zabeth)
1946–1971	8	**Jeff DiMarco** Disney, Doris Miles
1946–1948	2	**Dr. Anthony Post** Fahrenkopf, Anne w/ Ruth Fox (Hume)
1946–1952	2	**Jeff Strange** Gaines (Schultz), Audrey
1946–1951	3	**Rick Vanner** Heberden, M(ary) V(iolet)
1946–1947	2	**Tessie Venable** Holley, Helen
1946–1952	2	**Roderick "Drawers" Random** Kendall, Carol (Seeger)
1946–1949	2	**Elizabeth** Kilpatrick, Florence
1946–1963	17	**Merton Heimrich** Lockridge, Frances (Louise Davis) w/ Richard (Orson) Lockridge
1946–1956	2	**Douglas Grant** Millar, Florence N.
1946–1948	2	**Beau Smith & Pogy Rogers** Ross, Z(ola) H(elen Girdey)
1946–1949	5	**Johnny DuVivien** Spain, Nancy
1946–1947	2	**Maggie Slone** Stone, Elizabet M.
1947–1952	3	**Cam** Burbridge, Edith Joan
1947–1951	3	**Hortense Clinton** Hagen, Miriam-Ann

1947–1952	3	**Dennis Barrie** Long, Amelia Reynolds
1947–1959	2	**Peter Donnegan** Quick, Dorothy
1947–1952	4	**Homer Fitzgerald** Russell, Charlotte M(urray)
1947–1949	2	**Gale Gallagher** Scott, Margaret w/ Will(iam Charles) Oursler
1947–1960	7	**Julia Tyler** Smith, Ellen Hart
1948–1948	2	**Richard Hanard** Beynon-Harris, Vivian
1948–1963	5	**Emily & Henry Bryce** Scherf, Margaret (Louise)
1949–1959	3	**Mandrake** Coulson, Felicity Winifred Carter w/ John H. A. Coulson
1949–1951	3	**John Harland** Denniston, Elinore
1949–1955	3	**Marka de Lancey** Frost (Shively), Barbara
1949–1965	6	**Rev. Martin Buell** Scherf, Margaret (Louise)
1949–1953	4	**Lilly Wu & Janice Cameron** Sheridan, Juanita
1949–1952	6	**Miriam Birdseye** Spain, Nancy
1950–1977	2	**Chucky** Brand (Lewis), (Mary) Christianna (Milne)
1950–1951	2	**Flower** Field, Moira
1950–1973	5	**John Ripley** Gordon, Mildred w/ Gordon Gordon
1950–1963	2	**Hilda Trenton** Lyon, (Mabel) Dana
1950–1952	2	**Simon Ashton** Middleton, Elizabeth
1950–1962	5	**Ronald Price** Pullein-Thompson, Joanna M. C.
1950–1960	4	**Harry Butten** Spicer, Betty Coe w/ Bart Spicer

1951–1967	12	**George Marshall** Barling, Muriel Vere M.
1951–1954	2	**Clifford Flush** Branch, Pamela (Jean)
1951–1952	2	**Petunia Best & Max Frend** Chetwynd, Bridget
1951–1952	2	**Lord & Lady Tintagel** Davis, Julia
1951–1952	2	**Christopher Marsh** Durham, Mary
1951–1963	7	**Hugh Gordon & Liane Crawford** Gilruth, Susan
1951–1976	6	**Simon Drake** Nielsen, Helen
1951–1979	16	**George Felse & Family** Pargeter, Edith Mary
1951–1955	3	**Jim Little** Parker, Maude
1951–1953	3	**Sarah Vanessa** Storm, Joan
1951–1958	2	**Tom Craig** Van Urk, Virginia (Nellis)
1952–1961	3	**George Travers** Barling, Muriel Vere M.
1952–1956	2	**Benedict Breeze** Bayne, Isabella
1952–1957	3	**Richard Ringwood** Farrer, Katharine
1952–1957	3	**Ann McIntosh** McNamara, Lena Brooke
1953–1956	2	**Jolivet** Buchanan, Betty Joan
1953–1958	2	**Webster Flagg** Johns, Veronica P(arker)
1953–1954	4	**Norma "Nicky" Lee** Lee, Norma
1953–1956	2	**Father Keogh** Lindop, Audrey Erskine
1953–1954	2	**Charles Hillary** McGrew, Julia w/ Caroline K. Fenn

1953–1971	3	**Burnivel** Neville, Barbara Alison Boodson
1953–1958	4	**Al White** Pou, Genevieve Long
1954–1957	3	**Richard MacKay** Cushing, E(nid) Louise
1954–1961	5	**Gil Donan** Hood, Margaret Page
1954–1958	3	**Charles & James Latimer** Manning, Adelaide Frances Oke w/ Cyril Henry Coles
1954–1955	2	**Johnny Powers** McChesney, Mary F.
1954–1966	2	**Kelly** Roth, Holly
1954–1955	2	**John Case** White, Valerie
1954–1957	2	**Aloysius Kelly** Worsley-Gough, Barbara
1955–1966	9	**Baker** Brooks, Vivian Collin
1955–1970	11	**Hiram Potter** Denniston, Elinore
1955–1991	5	**Tom Ripley** Highsmith, (Mary) Patricia (Maugham)
1955–1960	2	**Jim Sader** Hitchens, (Julia Clara Catherine) Dolores (Birk)
1955–1959	2	**Collins & McKechnie** Hitchens, (Julia Clara Catherine) Dolores (Birk) w/ Hu(Bert) Hitchens
1956–1995	26	**John Coffin** Butler, Gwendoline
1956–1958	4	**William Winter** Butler, Gwendoline
1956–1961	3	**David Madden** Disney, Doris Miles
1956–1960	3	**Lathom Dynes** Edmiston, Helen Jean Mary
1956–1963	3	**Moss Magill** Gardiner, Dorothy
1956–1959	4	**Sally & Johnny Heldar** Hamilton, Henrietta

1959–1960	2	**Antoine Cirret** Hely (Younger), Elizabeth
1959–1993	19	**Henry Tibbett & Emily Tibbett** Moyes, Patricia
1959–1963	3	**James Flecker** Pullein-Thompson, Josephine (Mary Wedderburn)
1959–1974	16	**Fadiman Wace** Punnett, Margaret w/ Ivor Punnett
1960–1963	2	**Prentis** Backhouse, (Enid) Elizabeth
1960–1961	2	**Jerome Aylwin** Bowden, Jean
1960–1968	2	**Cardiff** Dennison, Dulcie Winifred Catherine Bailey
1960–1961	2	**Jim & Kate Harris** Feagles, Anita Macrae
1960–1966	6	**Herbert Broom** Hurt, Freda (Mary E.)
1960–1987	38	**Luis Mendoza** Linington, (Barbara) Elizabeth
1960–1964	2	**Forsythia Brown** Payes, Rachel
1960–1965	5	**Paul Grainger** Sinclair, Fiona
1961–1967	3	**Menendez** Blanc, Suzanne
1961–1963	3	**Bill Speed** Donovan, J(ean) B(ernadine)
1961–1963	2	**Horace Plummet** Healey, Evelyn
1961–1997	24	**John Putnam Thatcher** Henissart, Martha w/ Mary Jane Latsis
1961–1962	2	**Hedley Nicholson** Kelly, Mary
1961–1984	13	**Vic Varallo** Linington, (Barbara) Elizabeth
1961–1961	1	**Marcus Stubbs** Radford, Mona Augusta Mangan w/ Edwin Isaac Radford
1962–1965	3	**Remsen** Backus, Jean Louise

1962–1987 48 **Antony Maitland**
Bowen-Judd, Sara Hutton

1962–1996 18 **Charmian Daniels**
Butler, Gwendoline

1962–1965 2 **Nuri Iskirlak**
Fleming, Joan (Margaret)

1962–1965 4 **Hoani Mata**
Grayland, (Valerie) Merle (Spanner)

1962–1997 11 **Adam Dalgliesh**
James (White), P(hyllis) D(orothy) [Baroness James of
Holland Park]

1962–1985 13 **Jesse Falkenstein**
Linington, (Barbara) Elizabeth

1962–1964 2 **Bernard Simmons**
Lockridge, Frances (Louise Davis) w/ Richard (Orson)
Lockridge

1962–1964 2 **Paul Lane**
Lockridge, Frances (Louise Davis) w/ Richard (Orson)
Lockridge

1962–1964 3 **Steytler**
Milne, Shirley

1963–1968 15 **Hubert Bonisseur de la Bath**
Brochet, Jean Alexandre

1963–1968 5 **Marcus MacLurg**
Buchanan, Eileen-Marie Duell

1963–1974 3 **D. C. Randall (a cat)**
Gordon, Mildred w/ Gordon Gordon

1963–1980 3 **Steve Rhoden**
Walker, Ir(m)a (Ruth Roden)

1964–1966 2 **Dr. Henry Frost**
Ball, Doris Bell (Collier)

1964–1966 3 **Horton & Jordan**
Butler, Leslie

1964–1968 4 **Gibbon**
Cooper, (Evelyn) Barbara

1964–1972 5 **Salvador Borges**
Coulson, Felicity Winifred Carter w/ John H. A.
Coulson

1964–1970 3 **Basil**
Evans, Julie Rendel

1964–1997	12	**Kate Fansler** Heilbrun, Carolyn G(old)
1964–1968	2	**Christopher Jensen** Langley, Sarah
1964–1996	12	**Homer Kelly** Langton, Jane (Gillson)
1964–1986	13	**Ivor Maddox** Linington, (Barbara) Elizabeth
1964–1970	2	**Selena Mead** McGerr, Patricia
1964–1968	7	**Trevor Nicholls** Palmer, Madelyn
1964–1995	22	**Wilfred Dover** Porter, Joyce
1964–1997	17	**Reg Wexford** Rendell, Ruth
1964–1970	8	**Bill Rice** Stand, Marguerite
1964–1967	2	**Robins** Stand, Marguerite
1965–1969	4	**Patrick Shirley & Rupert "Rip" Irving** Brooks, Vivian Collin
1965–1967	4	**Steve Ramsay** Burger, Rosaylmer
1965–1965	2	**Ratlin** Summerton, Margaret
1965–1967	3	**Allan Stewart** Van Siller, Hilda
1966–1997	20	**Jim Qwilleran** Braun, Lilian Jackson
1966–1988	16	**Knute Severson** Forbes, DeLoris Florine Stanton
1966–1997	13	**Mrs. Emily Pollifax** Gilman (Butters), Dorothy
1966–1970	4	**Tami Shimoni** Hesky, Olga
1966–1967	3	**Christer Wick** Lange, Dagmar Maria
1966–1996	16	**C. D. Sloan** McIntosh, Kinn Hamilton

1966–1971	6	**Timothy Herring** Mitchell, Gladys (Maude Winifred)
1966–1971	4	**Edmund Brown** Porter, Joyce
1966–1972	5	**Phil Kramer** Sebenthal, Roberta Elizabeth
1966–1967	2	**Newsom** Stewart, Flora
1967–1971	3	**Julia Homberg** Ames, Sarah Rachel Stainer
1967–1969	2	**Dr. Nassim Pride** Buchanan, Eileen-Marie Duell
1967–1975	6	**Dr. Paul Holton** Hodges, Doris Marjorie
1967–1988	17	**Tom Pollard** Lemarchand, Elizabeth (Wharton)
1967–1971	5	**Matthew Furnival** Phillips, Stella
1967–1976	10	**Martin Beck** Sjowall, Maj w/ Per Wahloo
1967–1968	4	**John Abbot** Whitaker, Beryl (Salisbury)
1968–1968	2	**Henderson** Barling, Muriel Vere M.
1968–1969	3	**Tracy Larrimore & Mike Thompson** Burger, Rosaylmer w/ Julia Perceval
1968–1991	7	**Johnson Johnson** Dunnett, Dorothy (Halliday)
1968–1983	7	**Ben Safford** Henissart, Martha w/ Mary Jane Latsis
1968–1995	3	**Karen & Cheryl Nevitt** Mertz, Barbara L(ouise) G(ross)
1968–1971	2	**Ben Louis** Russell, E(nid)
1968–1978	4	**Dr. Grace Severance** Scherf, Margaret (Louise)
1968–1970	3	**Christie Opara** Uhnak, Dorothy
1969–1984	4	**Rapaso** Brown, Morna Doris (MacTaggart)

1969–1979	2	**Gail & Mitch Mitchell** Gordon, Mildred w/ Gordon Gordon
1969–1979	4	**Maurice Ygrec & Paul Michelin** Rippon, Marion (Edith)
1970–1973	2	**Bowman** Burrows, Julie
1970–1970	2	**Jefferson Shields** Carlon, Patricia (Bernadette)
1970–1976	5	**Patrick Grant** Nicholson, Margaret Beda Larminie
1970–1979	5	**The Honorable Constance Morrison-Burke** Porter, Joyce
1970–1990	25	**Tessa Crichton** Shaw, Felicity
1971–1976	4	**Ditteridge** Brown, Morna Doris (MacTaggart)
1971–1977	4	**Lucy Ramsdale** Dolson, Hildegarde
1971–1975	3	**Dr. William Ames** Freeman, Lucy
1971–1972	4	**Ira Yedder** Hershman, Morris
1971–1990	4	**Douglas Perkins** Stenstreem, Ruth
1971–1975	6	**Kitty Telefair** Stevenson, Florence
1971–1996	18	**Finch (Rudd)** Thomson, June (Valerie)
1972–1989	2	**Clovis Kelly** Babbin, Jacqueline
1972–1974	3	**Meredith** Brandes, Rhoda
1972–1973	4	**Jenny Gilette & Hunter Lewis** Gresham, Elizabeth
1972–1982	2	**Cordelia Gray** James (White), P(hyllis) D(orothy) [Baroness James of Holland Park]
1972–1974	3	**Laurie Grant & Stewart Noble** MacKintosh, May
1972–1989	4	**Jacqueline Kirby** Mertz, Barbara L(ouise) G(ross)

1972–1994	16	**Norah Mulcahaney** O'Donnell, Lillian (Udvardy)
1972–1976	3	**Al Krug & Casey Kellog** Weston, Carolyn
1972–1974	2	**Tavy Martin** Winsor, Diana
1973–1984	5	**Thea Crawford** Mann, Jessica
1973–1994	5	**Vicky Bliss** Mertz, Barbara L(ouise) G(ross)
1973–1994	16	**Melinda Pink** Moffat, Gwen
1973–1973	1	**Sara Hull** Piggin, Julia Remine
1973–1994	8	**Conan Flagg** Renfroe, Martha Kay
1973–1976	3	**John Joseph Lintott** Stubbs, Jean
1973–1991	6	**Dolly & The Old Buffer** Wendell, Sarah
1974–1976	2	**Kate Weatherley** Birmingham, Maisie
1974–1988	4	**Bosco of the Yard** Christopher, Laura Kim
1974–1975	4	**Barrington Hewes-Bradford** Granbeck, Marilyn w/ Arthur Moore
1974–1977	2	**Ann Hales** Ingate, Mary
1974–1976	3	**Guy Silvestri** Rennert, Maggie
1975–1988	4	**Henry Beaumont** Atkins, Meg (Margaret Elizabeth)
1975–1975	1	**Father Simon Bede & Helen Bullock** Byfield, Barbara Ninde w/ Frank L. Tedeschi
1975–1978	3	**Dr. Norah North** Duke, Madelaine (Elizabeth)
1975–1997	9	**Amelia Peabody Emerson & Radcliffe Emerson** Mertz, Barbara L(ouise) G(ross)
1975–1975	1	**Garson** Raskin, Ellen

1975–1982	6	**Merlin Capricorn** Winslow, Pauline Glen
1976–1979	3	**Father Simon Bede & Helen Bullock** Byfield, Barbara Ninde
1976–1987	4	**Julie Hayes** Davis, Dorothy Salisbury
1976–1977	2	**Will Woodfield** Foote-Smith, Elizabeth
1976–1978	2	**Jacques Brunel** Gavin, Catherine (Irvine)
1976–1978	2	**Rebeccah Rosenthal** Godfrey, Ellen
1976–1978	2	**David Haham** Haddad, C(arolyn) (A.)
1976–1977	2	**Lexey Jane Pelazoni** Head, (Joanne) Lee
1976–1997	9	**Anna Peters** Law (Trecker), Janice
1976–1977	2	**Jaime Sommers** Lottman, Eileen (Shurb)
1976–1993	2	**Natasha O'Brien & Max Ogden** Lyons, Nan w/ Ivan Lyons
1976–1981	2	**Hannah Land** MacKay (Smith), Amanda
1976–1982	3	**Tom Aragon** Millar, Margaret (Ellis Sturm)
1976–1985	7	**Mrs. Edwina Charles** Warner, Mignon
1976–1992	4	**Charles Spotted Moon** Yarbro, Chelsea Quinn
1977–1987	5	**Neil Carter** Dewhurst, Eileen (Mary)
1977–1994	11	**Jemima Shore** Fraser, Antonia (Pakenham)
1977–1982	3	**Dearborn V. Pinch** Green, Edith Pinero
1977–1997	18	**Sharon McCone** Muller, Marcia
1977–1980	3	**Mici Anhalt** O'Donnell, Lillian (Udvardy)

1977–1994	21	**Brother Cadfael** Pargeter, Edith Mary
1977–1988	5	**Persis Willum** Watson, Clarissa
1978–1980	8	**Tory Baxter** Baker, Marc(eil Genee Kolstad)
1978–1993	8	**Virginia Freer** Brown, Morna Doris (MacTaggart)
1978–1980	3	**Marilyn Ambers** Cohen, Susan Handler
1978–1980	6	**Terry Spring** Goulart, Ronald Joseph
1978–1979	7	**Maxine Reynolds** Grove, Martin
1978–1996	11	**Peter Shandy** MacLeod, Charlotte (Matilda Hughes)
1978–1984	5	**Steve Arrow** Mantell, Laurie
1978–1995	9	**Douglas Quantrill** Robinson, Sheila Mary
1978–1980	4	**Kay Barth** Schier, Norma
1978–1979	2	**Edgar Allan Poe** Steward, Barbara w/ Dwight Steward
1978–1997	6	**Helen Keremos** Zaremba, Eve
1979–1980	2	**Amy Tupper** Ball, Doris Bell (Collier)
1979–1980	2	**Megan Marshall** Collins, Michael
1979–1995	12	**Dr. Penelope Spring & Sir Tobias Glendower** Cook, Petronelle Marguerite Mary
1979–1980	2	**Adrienne Bishop** Ewing, Jan
1979–1979	2	**Charlotte Eliot** Filgate, C. Macartney
1979–1979	3	**Valerie Lambert** Grove, Martin
1979–1986	5	**C. B. Greenfield & Maggie Rome** Kallen, Lucille

1979–1990	3	**Janna Brill & Mahlon "Mama" Maxwell** Killough, (Karen) Lee
1979–1995	12	**Sarah Kelling Bittersohn & Max Bittersohn** MacLeod, Charlotte (Matilda Hughes)
1979–1980	2	**Kate Graham** Martin, Ian
1979–1979	3	**Carol Gates** McMahan, Ian
1979–1980	3	**Maggie Courtney** Pearson, Ann
1979–1997	17	**Thomas Pitt & Charlotte Ellison Pitt** Perry, Anne
1979–1984	2	**Richard Owen, Agent** Sharp, Marilyn (Augburn)
1979–1980	4	**Anna J(agedinski)** Swan, Phyllis
1979–1979	2	**Pauline Lyons** Traynor, Page w/ Anthony Traynor
1979–1979	2	**Nell Willard** Wallace, Mary
1979–1980	2	**Richard York** Williamson, Audrey (May)
1980–1981	3	**Richard Trenton** Bowen-Judd, Sara Hutton
1980–1981	4	**Jeremy Locke** Bowen-Judd, Sara Hutton
1980–1981	3	**Stephen Marryat** Bowen-Judd, Sara Hutton
1980–1994	8	**Anna Lee** Cody, Liza
1980–1981	2	**Dr. Gerritt DeGraaf** D'Amato, Barbara
1980–1987	2	**John Fenchurch & Bunce** Fiske, Dorsey
1980–1991	3	**Tom Maybridge** Gill (Trimble), B(arbara) M(argaret)
1980–1981	2	**Ronald Dobbs** Halpin, Mary D.
1980–1981	3	**Jean Darblay** Hardwick, Mollie

1980–1996	8	**Benjamin Jurnet** Haymon, S(ylvia) T(heresa)
1980–1981	3	**Dr. Peter Casey** Koehler, Margaret Hudson
1980–1982	2	**Robert Renwick** MacInnes, Helen (Clark)
1980–1992	5	**Madoc Rhys** MacLeod, Charlotte (Matilda Hughes)
1980–1994	5	**Delilah West** O'Callaghan, Maxine
1980–1983	3	**T. T. Baldwin** OCork, Shannon
1980–1984	2	**Quentin Jacoby** Smith, J(ane) C. S.
1980–1980	2	**Emil Martin** Taylor, Mary Ann
1980–1996	9	**Washington, D.C.** Truman, (Mary) Margaret
1980–1983	4	**Davina Graham** Ward-Thomas, Evelyn Bridget Patricia Stephens
1981–1989	3	**Hilary Tamar** Cockburn, Sarah
1981–1985	3	**Lettie Winterbottom** Cutter, Leela
1981–1996	7	**Robert Amiss** Edwards, Ruth Dudley
1981–1995	13	**Richard Jury** Grimes, Martha
1981–1993	5	**The Grub-and-Stakers** MacLeod, Charlotte (Matilda Hughes)
1981–1991	6	**Tamara Hoyland** Mann, Jessica
1981–1995	8	**Sigrid Harald** Maron, Margaret
1981–1997	9	**Sister Mary Teresa Dempsey** McInerny, Ralph
1981–1996	11	**Guarnaccia** Nabb, Magdalen
1981–1984	2	**Viera Kolarova** Powers, Elizabeth

1981–1996	13	**Luke Thanet** Simpson, Dorothy
1981–1981	1	**Barlow Dale** Siverns, Ruth
1981–1988	6	**Kelsey** Tirbutt, Honoria
1981–1991	3	**Neal Rafferty** Wiltz, Chris
1982–1986	4	**Michael Spraggue** Barnes, Linda (Appelblatt)
1982–1997	8	**Sarah Deane & Dr. Alex McKenzie** Borthwick (Creighton), J(ean) S(cott)
1982–1985	6	**Rev. Jabal Jarrett** Bream, Freda
1982–1985	2	**Helen Johnson** Dewhurst, Eileen (Mary)
1982–1996	13	**Kinsey Millhone** Grafton, Sue
1982–1986	2	**Rudolf Nilsen** Griffiths, Ella
1982–1985	3	**John Waltz** Labus, Marta Haake
1982–1988	3	**Nyla Wade** McConnell, Vicki
1982–1995	9	**V. I. Warshawski** Paretsky, Sara
1982–1992	4	**Mrs. Eugenia Potter** Rich, Virginia
1982–1995	13	**Nurse Agnes Carmichael** Simpson, Doris
1982–1993	5	**Rebecca Schwartz** Smith, Julie
1982–1992	3	**Maggie Elliott** Taylor, Elizabeth Atwood
1983–1995	8	**Andrew Basnett** Brown, Morna Doris (MacTaggart)
1983–1997	12	**Mike Yeadings & Angus Mott** Buchanan, Eileen-Marie Duell
1983–1995	6	**Jocelyn O'Roarke** Dentinger, Jane

1983–1987	6	**George Thorne** Harcourt, Palma w/ Jack H. Trotman
1983–1986	3	**Miss Harriet Unwin** Keating, H(enry) R(eymond) F(itzwalter)
1983–1990	3	**Roz Howard** Kenney, Susan (McIlvaine)
1983–1985	2	**The Widows** La Plante, Lynda
1983–1997	8	**Lloyd & Judy Hill** McGown, Jill
1983–1986	2	**Dr. Gordon Christy** Moore (Lee), Barbara
1983–1992	5	**Elizabeth Lamb Worthington** Morison, B(etty) J(ane)
1983–1985	2	**Elena Oliverez** Muller, Marcia
1983–1988	5	**Jake Samson & Rosie Vicente** Singer, Shelley
1983–1989	4	**J. J. Jamison** Taylor, L(aurie) A(ylma)
1983–1985	2	**Kyra Keaton** Tone, Teona
1983–1997	5	**Cass Jameson** Wheat, Carolyn
1984–1986	2	**Isamu "Sam Irish" Ohara** Ball, (Nanoni) Patricia (Maude Hamilton)
1984–1990	3	**Dr. Clio Rees Marsh & Harry Marsh** Bannister, Jo
1984–1987	3	**Dr. Tina May** Butterworth, Michael
1984–1995	6	**Ellie Simons Haskell** Cannell, Dorothy
1984–1986	2	**Clay & Linn Randolph** Carlton, Bea
1984–1993	5	**Andrea Perkins** Coker, Carolyn
1984–1997	10	**Jill Smith** Dunlap, Susan
1984–1986	3	**Vejay Haskell** Dunlap, Susan

1984–1997	6	**Kate Delafield** Forrest, Katherine V(irginia)
1984–1996	12	**David Webb & Ken Jackson** Fraser, Anthea
1984–1990	5	**Rev. Claire Aldington** Holland, Isabelle
1984–1993	3	**Gillian Adams & Edward Gisborne** Kelly, Nora
1984–1989	3	**Anthea & Justin Rutherford** Ley, Alice Chetwynd
1984–1987	4	**Birdie Linnett** Linscott, Gillian
1984–1989	3	**Iris Cooper & Jack Clancy** Marris, Kathrine
1984–1995	8	**Elizabeth MacPherson** McCrumb, Sharyn
1984–1996	9	**Lennox Kemp** Meek, M(argaret) R(eid) D(uncan)
1984–1995	5	**Charles Matthews** Meredith, D(oris) R.
1984–1991	7	**Penny Wanawake** Moody, Susan (Elizabeth)
1984–1984	1	**Sharon McCone** Muller, Marcia w/ Bill Pronzini
1984–1997	7	**Sister Mary Helen** O'Marie, Sister Carol Anne
1984–1990	5	**Patience C. McKenna** Papazoglou, Orania
1984–1987	3	**Enrico Caruso** Paul, Barbara
1984–1997	7	**Marian Larch** Paul, Barbara
1984–1995	10	**Jennifer Cain** Pickard, Nancy
1984–1993	10	**Robert Forsythe** Shannon, Doris
1984–1986	2	**Lauren Adler & Michael Hunt** Silver, Victoria
1984–1995	5	**Kate Baeier** Slovo, Gillian

1984–1987	2	**Judd Springfield** Smith, Alison
1984–1984	2	**A Pair of Related Novels** Stenstreem, Ruth
1984–1986	2	**Blue Maguire & Spaceman Kowalski** White, Teri
1984–1989	3	**Pam Nilsen** Wilson, Barbara (Ellen)
1984–1996	12	**Deb Ralston** Wingate, (Martha) Anne (Guice)
1985–1986	3	**Ellie Gordon** Bernell, Sue w/ Michaela Karni
1985–1997	3	**Flowers Detectives** Cannell, Dorothy
1985–1991	8	**Maggie Ryan** Carlson, P(atricia) M(cEvoy)
1985–1987	2	**Carole Loring** Carlton, Bea
1985–1997	13	**Hamish Macbeth** Chesney, Marion
1985–1996	9	**Paula Glenning** Clarke, Anna
1985–1988	2	**Kevin Blake** Douglas, Carole Nelson
1985–1997	7	**Stoner McTavish** Dreher, Sarah
1985–1987	4	**David Ballard & Michelle Merrill Ballard** Fell, Doris Elaine w/ Carole Gift Page
1985–1989	3	**Matthew Sinclair** Fennelly, Tony
1985–1996	5	**Jack Stryker** Gosling, Paula
1985–1989	2	**Jeanne Donovan** Granbeck, Marilyn
1985–1990	5	**Rain Morgan** Grant-Adamson, Leslie
1985–1986	2	**Largely Lee** Harris, Evelyn
1985–1995	13	**J. P. Beaumont** Jance, J(udith) A(nn)

1985–1987	2	**Louisa Evans** Johnston, Jane
1985–1992	6	**Liz Connors & Jack Lingemann** Kelly, Susan
1985–1993	8	**G. D. H. Pringle** Livingston, Nancy
1985–1993	8	**Fiddler & Fiora** Maxwell, Ann Elizabeth Lowell w/ Evan Maxwell
1985–1987	2	**Judith Hayes** Porter, Anna
1985–1987	2	**Paul McDonald** Smith, Julie
1985–1993	2	**Alex Winter** Steiner, Susan
1985–1988	2	**Ferris Byrd** Stuart (Ohlragge), Anne (Kristine)
1985–1986	2	**Glad Gold & Alden Chase** Wender, Dorothea
1985–1995	7	**Charlie Meiklejohn & Constance Leidl** Wilhelm (Knight), Kate (Gertrude)
1985–1986	2	**Tommy Inman** Wingate, (Martha) Anne (Guice)
1985–1996	8	**Cassandra Mitchell & Karl Alberg** Wright, L(aurali) R.
1986–1986	3	**Peregrine Connection** Buckholtz, Eileen w/ Ruth Glick
1986–1996	8	**George & Molly Palmer-Jones** Cleeves, Ann
1986–1995	4	**Tish McWhinny** Comfort, B(arbara)
1986–1990	4	**Rat Trapp** Corrington, Joyce H. w/ John William Corrington
1986–1997	3	**Joan Spencer** Frommer, Sara Hoskinson
1986–1992	3	**Nick Magaracz** Gallison (Dunn), Kate
1986–1991	2	**Luke Abbott** Gosling, Paula
1986–1993	2	**Theresa Fortunato** Green, Kate

1986–1989	3	**Sherlock Holmes**
		Greenwood, L(illian) B(ethel)
1986–1997	7	**Doran Fairweather Chelmarsh & Rev. Rodney Chelmarsh**
		Hardwick, Mollie
1986–1996	11	**Claire Malloy**
		Hess, Joan
1986–1988	2	**Theo Bloomer**
		Hess, Joan
1986–1996	9	**Peter Decker & Rina Lazarus Decker**
		Kellerman, Faye
1986–1994	4	**Calista Jacobs**
		Knight, Kathryn Lasky
1986–1986	4	**Guinevere Jones**
		Krentz, Jayne Ann
1986–1989	3	**Joanna Stark**
		Muller, Marcia
1986–1986	1	**Elena Oliverez**
		Muller, Marcia w/ Bill Pronzini
1986–1997	10	**August Didier**
		Myers, Amy
1986–1986	1	**Jane Bradshawe**
		Pardoe, Rosemary
1986–1987	2	**Fortune's Friends**
		Reynolds, Kay w/ Mike Reynolds
1986–1994	6	**Harriet Jeffries & John Sanders**
		Sale (Roe), (Caroline) Medora
1986–1987	2	**Rick & Rosie Ramsey**
		Santini, Rosemarie
1986–1993	5	**Miss Susan Melville**
		Smith, Evelyn E.
1986–1995	5	**Evangeline Sinclair & Trixie Dolan**
		Stenstreem, Ruth
1986–1992	3	**Cruz & Goldstein**
		Wallace, Marilyn
1986–1989	3	**Sarah Calloway**
		Warmbold, Jean
1987–1989	5	**Balthazar Marten**
		Adamson, M(ary) J(o)
1987–1997	7	**Carlotta Carlyle**
		Barnes, Linda (Appelblatt)

1987–1995	10	**Quin St. James & Mike McCleary** MacGregor, T(rish) J(aneshutz)
1987–1992	2	**The Body in the . . . Series** Marris, Kathrine
1987–1997	6	**Willa Jansson** Matera, Lia
1987–1992	2	**Jay Omega** McCrumb, Sharyn
1987–1993	4	**Lindsay Gordon** McDermid, Val
1987–1989	2	**Artie Weatherby** Miller, J(anice) M. T(ubbs)
1987–1990	2	**Finny Aletter** Montgomery (Ewegen), Yvonne
1987–1991	4	**Richard Baxter** Moore, Margaret
1987–1988	2	**Daisy Marlow** Morgan, D Miller
1987–1989	2	**Appollonia "Lonia" Guiu** Oliver, Maria-Antonia
1987–1991	6	**Jane Winfield & Andrew Quentin** Peterson, Audrey
1987–1992	5	**Peter Brichter & Kori Brichter** Pulver (Kuhfeld), Mary Monica
1987–1988	2	**Ed Jackson** Roberts, Nora
1987–1989	2	**Lloyd's of London** Shakespeare, L. M(arguerita)
1987–1988	3	**Dixie T. Struthers** Sims, L. V.
1987–1995	5	**Loretta Lawson** Smith, Joan
1987–1995	7	**Robert Bone** Staynes, Jill w/ Margaret Storey
1987–1987	3	**Maggie Bennett** Stuart (Ohlragge), Anne (Kristine)
1987–1991	2	**Egan & Kingston** Taylor, Bonnie w/ Matt Taylor
1987–1990	3	**Ben & Carrie Porter** Travis, Elizabeth

1987–1988	2	**Lisa Davis** Waltch, Lilla M.
1987–1990	3	**Lucas Hallam** Washburn (Reasoner), L(ivia) J.
1987–1988	2	**Dr. Scott Eason** Weeks, Dolores
1987–1997	4	**Emma Victor** Wings, Mary
1988–1991	2	**Meg Lacey** Bowers, Elisabeth
1988–1996	8	**Lady Margaret Priam** Christmas, Joyce
1988–1995	6	**Milton Kovak** Cooper, Susan Rogers
1988–1994	4	**Claudia Valentine** Day, Marele
1988–1996	9	**Gil Mayo** Eccles, Marjorie
1988–1990	3	**Linus Lintoul** Edmonds, Janet
1988–1989	2	**Georgia Lee Maxwell** Friedman, (Michaele) Mickey (Thompson)
1988–1989	6	**Nina McFall & Dino Rossi** Fulton, Eileen
1988–1997	6	**Helen West & Geoffrey Bailey** Fyfield (Hegarty), Frances
1988–1997	9	**Thomas Lynley** George, (Susan) Elizabeth
1988–1992	2	**Jane Tregar** Godfrey, Ellen
1988–1989	2	**Hana Shaner** Greth, (Le) Roma (Eshbach)
1988–1991	3	**Michael Ohayon** Gur, Batya
1988–1988	2	**Ann Tate** Haines, Carolyn
1988–1989	3	**Dawn Markey** Haines, Carolyn
1988–1995	2	**James Asher & Simon Ysidro** Hambly, Barbara

1988–1991	5	**Dick Tansey** Harcourt, Palma w/ Jack H. Trotman
1988–1988	2	**Jackson Fury** Jerina, Carol
1988–1990	2	**Emma Shaw** Jones, Hazel Wynn
1988–1989	2	**Galen Shaw & Julian Baugh** Long, Lydia
1988–1992	5	**Aline Scott** MacGregor, T(rish) J(aneshutz)
1988–1995	5	**Laura Di Palma** Matera, Lia
1988–1997	9	**Carole Ashton** McNab, Claire
1988–1993	5	**John Lloyd Branson & Lydia Fairchild** Meredith, D(oris) R.
1988–1997	5	**John McLeish & Francesca Wilson** Neel (Cohen), Janet
1988–1998	6	**Liz Sullivan, Bridget Montrose & Paul Drake** Roberts (Smith), Lora
1988–1990	2	**Hank Sullivan** Rooth, Anne Reed
1988–1998	9	**Benbow & Wingate** Sawyer, Corrine Holt
1988–1991	3	**Kate Maddox** Sawyer, Nancy Buckingham w/ John Sawyer
1988–1989	2	**Samantha Adams** Shankman, Sarah
1988–1997	6	**Richard Montgomery** Shepherd, Stella
1988–1991	3	**Pete Brady** Shuman, M. K.
1988–1995	7	**Sheila Travis & Aunt Mary** Sprinkle, Patricia Houck
1988–1989	2	**Sabina Swift & Vic Newman** Sucher, Dorothy
1988–1996	7	**Neil Hamel** Van Gieson, Judith
1988–1994	4	**Sydney Bryant** Wallace (Estrada), Patricia

1988–1992	4	**York Cycle of Mysteries** Whitehead, Barbara
1988–1998	6	**Catherine Sayler** Williams, Linda V.
1988–1993	5	**Mark Shigata** Wingate, (Martha) Anne (Guice)
1988–1996	10	**Susan Henshaw** Wolzien, Valerie
1989–1992	2	**T. D. Renfro** Azolakov, Antoinette
1989–1990	2	**Pat Goodenough** Bennett, Liza
1989–1996	7	**Jane Lawless & Cordelia Thorn** Boehnhardt, Patricia
1989–1996	5	**Clara Gamadge** Boylan, Eleanor
1989–1993	4	**Quint McCauley** Brod, D(eborah) C(obban)
1989–1996	8	**Jane Jeffry** Brooks, Janice Young
1989–1993	4	**Henry Bassett** Burden, Pat
1989–1993	2	**Wilson & Wilder** Bushell, Agnes
1989–1990	2	**Lady Indiana** Christopher, Laura Kim
1989–1991	2	**Abigail Doyle & Roz Benson** Collins, Anna Ashwood
1989–1993	4	**Bernard & Snooky** Dank, Gloria
1989–1994	3	**Georgina Powers** Danks, Denise
1989–1996	8	**Marcus Didius Falco & Helena Justina** Davis, Lindsey
1989–1994	3	**Kiernan O'Shaughnessey** Dunlap, Susan
1989–1995	2	**Lee Ofsted** Elkins, Charlotte w/ Aaron Elkins
1989–1991	2	**Martha "Moz" Brant** Femling, Jean

1989–1997	8	**Jessica Fletcher**
		Fletcher, Jessica & Donald Bain
1989–1995	4	**Kate Henry**
		Gordon, Alison
1989–1996	8	**Phryne Fisher**
		Greenwood, Kerry
1989–1996	4	**Mitchell "Mitch" Bushyhead**
		Hager, Jean
1989–1993	4	**Emma Chizzit**
		Hall, Mary Bowen
1989–1996	7	**Sheila Malory**
		Holt, Hazel
1989–1997	6	**Maggie MacGowen**
		Hornsby, Wendy (Nelson)
1989–1990	2	**Maggie Hill & Claire Conrad**
		Howe, Melodie Johnson
1989–1990	2	**Micky Douglas**
		Infante, Anne
1989–1997	8	**Kat Colorado**
		Kijewski, Karen
1989–1997	10	**Jeremy Faro**
		Knight, Alanna
1989–1991	3	**Diana Tregarde**
		Lackey, Mercedes
1989–1996	8	**Darina Lisle**
		Laurence, Janet
1989–1995	6	**Jefferson Birch**
		Lee, Wendi
1989–1997	7	**Xenia Smith & Leslie Wetzon**
		Meyers, Annette (Brafman)
1989–1997	6	**Nina Fischman**
		Piesman, Marissa
1989–1990	2	**James Roland**
		Quinton, Ann
1989–1993	2	**Annie FitzHugh**
		Roberts, Carey
1989–1993	2	**Miriam Winchester, Medicine Woman**
		Romberg, Nina
1989–1990	2	**Chris Martin**
		Roome, Annette

1989–1995	6	**Verity Birdwood** Rowe, Jennifer
1989–1995	2	**Beth Austin** Skom, Edith
1989–1990	2	**Cassie Newton** Smith, Joan G(erarda)
1989–1997	6	**Jason Lynx** Tepper, Sheri S.
1989–1992	2	**Bertha Barstow** Thomas, Dicey
1989–1995	5	**Mackensie Smith & Annabel Reed Smith** Truman, (Mary) Margaret
1989–1991	3	**Kevin Bryce** Valentine, Deborah
1989–1995	9	**Amanda Roberts & Joe Donelli** Woods, Sherryl
1990–1997	14	**Alice Nestleton** Adamson, Lydia
1990–1993	3	**Anna Southwood** Bedford, Jean
1990–1997	5	**Joanne Kilbourn** Bowen, Gail
1990–1996	5	**Mary Minor "Harry" Haristeen** Brown, Rita Mae w/ Sneaky Pie Brown
1990–1995	5	**Stephen Ramsay** Cleeves, Ann
1990–1997	10	**Holly Winter** Conant, Susan
1990–1997	8	**Dr. Kay Scarpetta** Cornwell, Patricia D(aniels)
1990–1997	7	**Cat Marsala** D'Amato, Barbara
1990–1997	7	**Goldy Bear** Davidson, Diane Mott
1990–1997	7	**Jeri Howard** Dawson, Janet
1990–1994	4	**Irene Adler** Douglas, Carole Nelson
1990–1992	6	**Jack Fleming & Charles Escott** Elrod, P(atricia) N(ead)

1990–1995	5	**James Fleming** Fallon, Ann C.
1990–1993	3	**Syd Fish** Geason, Susan
1990–1997	7	**Peter Bartholomew** Gunning, Sally
1990–1996	5	**Aurora Teagarden** Harris, Charlaine
1990–1994	2	**Nikki Trakos** Horansky, Ruby
1990–1994	4	**Jules Vern** Karl, Kimberly
1990–1995	3	**Claire Breslinsky** Kelly, Mary Anne
1990–1996	5	**Alison Hope & Nick Trevellyan** Kelly, Susan B.
1990–1995	6	**Edwina Crusoe, R.N.** Kittredge, Mary
1990–1991	2	**Sam Ryker** Krich, Rochelle Majer
1990–1993	5	**Winston Marlowe Sherman** Lorens, M(argaret) K(eilstrup)
1990–1997	8	**Charlotte Graham** Matteson, Stefanie
1990–1995	5	**Haskell Blevins** McCafferty, (Barbara) Taylor
1990–1996	4	**Spencer Arrowood** McCrumb, Sharyn
1990–1994	3	**Chicago Nordejoong** McKernan, Victoria
1990–1994	3	**Jazz Jasper & Omondi** McQuillan, Karin
1990–1994	3	**Hometown Heroes** McShea, Susanna H(ofmann)
1990–1996	5	**John Morrissey** Mitchell, Kay
1990–1996	7	**Dewey James** Morgan, Kate
1990–1992	4	**Jessica "Jesse" James** O'Brien, Meg

1990–1997	4	**Gwenn Ramadge** O'Donnell, Lillian (Udvardy)
1990–1997	8	**Faith Fairchild** Page, Katherine Hall
1990–1996	14	**Gregor Demarkian** Papazoglou, Orania
1990–1996	7	**William Monk** Perry, Anne
1990–1996	8	**Sister Joan** Peters, Maureen
1990–1995	3	**Michelle "Micky" Knight** Redmann, J. M.
1990–1994	5	**Abigail Patience Danforth** Rogers, Marian
1990–1996	6	**Melissa Craig** Rowlands, Betty
1990–1990	1	**Penelope Pettiweather** Salmonson, Jessica Amanda
1990–1993	3	**Sam Titus & Nicki Titus** Sandstrom, Eve K.
1990–1994	3	**Brigid Donovan** Saum, Karen
1990–1992	2	**Paris Chandler** Shah, Diane K.
1990–1997	5	**Samantha Adams** Shankman, Sarah
1990–1997	5	**Lark Dailey Dodge** Simonson, Sheila
1990–1994	3	**Annie MacPherson** Smith, Janet L.
1990–1997	7	**Skip Langdon** Smith, Julie
1990–1995	6	**Shirley McClintock** Tepper, Sheri S.
1990–1992	4	**Poppy Dillworth** Toopes, Dot
1990–1996	5	**Helen Black** Welch, Pat
1990–1993	4	**Madison McGuire** Williams, Amanda Kyle

1990–1993	2	**Cassandra Reilly** Wilson, Barbara (Ellen)
1990–1997	6	**Willow King** Wright, Daphne
1991–1997	6	**Sherlock Holmes** Andrews, Val
1991–1992	2	**Nick Hannibal & Molly Rafferty** Auspitz, Kate
1991–1996	3	**Jan Gallagher** Bailey, Jo
1991–1996	4	**Virginia Kelly** Baker, Nikki
1991–1992	2	**Andrew Taggart** Brandon, Ruth
1991–1993	2	**Mitch & Valerie Stevens** Brandt, Yanna w/ Nat Brandt
1991–1993	2	**Liz Wareham** Brennan, Carol
1991–1993	2	**Midge Cohen** Brill, Toni
1991–1997	4	**Julie Blake & Vic Paoli** Chapman, Sally
1991–1996	7	**Roger the Chapman** Clarke, Brenda Margaret Lilian Honeyman
1991–1997	11	**Judith McMonigle Flynn** Daheim, Mary
1991–1992	3	**Joss O'Bannion & Evan Glyndower** Duane, Diane w/ Peter Morwood
1991–1995	3	**Hannah Wolfe** Dunant, Sarah
1991–1993	2	**Dr. Bernadette Hebert** Ennis, Catherine
1991–1993	2	**Jess Koster** Fielding, Joy
1991–1995	4	**Wanda Mallory** Frankel, Valerie
1991–1993	3	**Amanda Knight** Fromer, Margot J.
1991–1994	2	**Sarah Fortune** Fyfield (Hegarty), Frances

1991–1997	8	**Kate Jasper** Girdner, Jaqueline
1991–1997	10	**Meredith Mitchell & Markby** Granger (Hulme), Ann
1991–1996	6	**Deaconess Theodora Braithwaite** Greenwood, D(iane) M.
1991–1996	5	**The Adept, Sir Adam Sinclair** Harris, Deborah Turner w/ Katherine Kurtz
1991–1997	6	**Bill Slider** Harrod-Eagles, Cynthia
1991–1997	4	**Alex Jensen** Henry, Sue
1991–1992	2	**Sophy Bancroft** Hocker, Karla
1991–1991	2	**Lane Montana** Hooper, Kay
1991–1997	5	**Vicki Nelson & Henry Fitzroy** Huff, Tanya
1991–1993	3	**Devon MacDonald** Jacobs, Nancy Baker
1991–1994	3	**Jane Tennison** La Plante, Lynda
1991–1996	6	**Nell Bray** Linscott, Gillian
1991–1997	6	**Robin Miller** Maiman, Jaye
1991–1997	13	**Miss Emily Seeton** Mason, Sarah J(ill)
1991–1995	3	**Dr. Maxene St. Clair** McGiffen, Janet
1991–1997	4	**Lucy Stone** Meier, Leslie
1991–1992	2	**Nathan Kendall** Mills, D(eanie) F(rancis)
1991–1993	2	**Jack Pharaoh** Moffat, Gwen
1991–1993	2	**Fanny Zindel** Moore, Rayanne w/ Serita Stevens
1991–1993	2	**Lucia Ramos** Morell, Mary

1991–1996	4	**Hubbert & Lil** Munger, Katy
1991–1996	2	**Whitney Logan** Munson, Douglas Anne
1991–1992	2	**B. F. Hopper** Museo, Laura w/ Stephen Schermerhorn
1991–1992	2	**CC Scott & Barbara Bettencourt** Plante, Pele
1991–1992	2	**Hollis Carpenter** Powell, Deborah
1991–1995	3	**Claire Sharples** Rothenberg, Rebecca
1991–1996	4	**Lauren Laurano** Scoppettone, Sandra
1991–1995	4	**Kate Mulcay** Sibley, Celestine
1991–1996	5	**Delta "Storm" Stevens** Silva, Linda Kay
1991–1992	3	**Simona Griffo** Trinchieri, Camilla
1991–1994	4	**Libby Kincaid** Tucker, Kerry
1991–1992	2	**Frank Carver & Ginny Trask** Wallingford, Lee
1991–1997	4	**Ronnie Ventana** White, Gloria
1991–1996	3	**Barbara Holloway** Wilhelm (Knight), Kate (Gertrude)
1991–1997	5	**Blaine Stewart** Zukowski, Sharon
1992–1997	6	**Jesus Creek, TN** Adams, Deborah
1992–1998	7	**China Bayles** Albert, Susan Wittig
1992–1995	2	**Blair Emerson** Amey, Linda
1992–1996	3	**Lee Squires** Andreae, Christine
1992–1996	3	**Lori Shepherd** Atherton, Nancy

1992–1996	3	**Smokey Brandon** Ayres, Noreen
1992–1997	7	**Sister Frevisse** Bacon, Gail w/ Mary Monica Pulver (Kuhfeld)
1992–1996	5	**Marti MacAlister** Bland, Eleanor Taylor
1992–1997	5	**Britt Montero** Buchanan, Edna
1992–1996	5	**David Middleton-Brown** Chase, Carol
1992–1996	5	**Agatha Raisin** Chesney, Marion
1992–1997	4	**Regan Reilly** Clark, Carol Higgins
1992–1997	9	**Jackie Walsh** Cleary, Melissa
1992–1997	3	**E. J. Pugh** Cooper, Susan Rogers
1992–1995	2	**Gloria Damasco** Corpi, Lucha
1992–1997	8	**Emma Lord** Daheim, Mary
1992–1997	4	**Mama (Candi) & Simone** DeLoach, Nora L.
1992–1994	2	**Ellie Bernstein** Dietz, Denise
1992–1994	3	**Alex Tanner** Donald, Anabel
1992–1997	8	**Midnight Louie** Douglas, Carole Nelson
1992–1994	2	**Annie McGrogan** Farrell, Gillian B.
1992–1992	2	**Laura Ireland** French, Linda
1992–1995	3	**Amanda Valentine** Fulton, Jennifer
1992–1997	7	**Freddie O'Neal** Garwood, Judith
1992–1996	3	**Matt Gabriel** Gosling, Paula

1992–1996	4	**Kate Kinsella** Green, Christine
1992–1994	2	**Catherine Edison** Haffner, Margaret
1992–1997	4	**Molly Bearpaw** Hager, Jean
1992–1997	9	**Christine Bennett** Harris, Lee
1992–1995	3	**Kate Millholland** Hartzmark, Gini
1992–1995	4	**David Silver** Hightower, Lynn S.
1992–1993	2	**Kristin Ashe** Jordan, Jennifer
1992–1994	3	**Dr. Samantha Turner** Landreth, Marsha
1992–1997	6	**Guido Brunetti** Leon, Donna
1992–1995	2	**Charlotte Sams** Lowry, Cheryl Meredith w/ Louise Vetter
1992–1997	5	**Deborah Knott** Maron, Margaret
1992–1995	2	**Elizabeth Blair** Marriott, Mary
1992–1995	4	**Jane da Silva** Marris, Kathrine
1992–1996	5	**Kate Brannigan** McDermid, Val
1992–1993	2	**William Hecklepeck** McKitterick, Molly
1992–1998	6	**The Tonneman Family of New York** Meyers, Annette (Brafman) w/ Martin Meyers
1992–1996	4	**"Charlie" Greene** Millhiser, Marlys
1992–1995	4	**Leah Hunter** Mitchell, Kay
1992–1997	5	**Glynis Tryon** Monfredo, Miriam Grace
1992–1994	2	**Blanche White** Neely, Barbara

1992–1993	3	**Beth Marie Cartwright** Owens, Virginia Stem
1992–1996	3	**Elizabeth Elliot** Peters, Elsa Kirsten
1992–1995	3	**Claire Camden** Peterson, Audrey
1992–1995	3	**Nell Fury** Pincus, Elizabeth
1992–1994	2	**Gabriel Dunn & Jake Myles** Press, Margaret
1992–1994	2	**Kit Powell** Robitaille, Julie
1992–1997	7	**Kate Shugak** Stabenow, Dana
1992–1997	6	**Sigismondo** Staynes, Jill w/ Margaret Storey
1992–1995	3	**Rosie Cairns** Struthers, Betsy
1992–1995	2	**Victoria Cross** Sumner, Penny
1992–1996	5	**Callahan Garrity** Trocheck, Kathy Hogan
1992–1998	4	**Susan Wren** Weir, Charlene
1992–1994	3	**Dolly & The Wolfman** Wendell, Sarah
1992–1995	5	**Molly DeWitt** Woods, Sherryl
1992–1996	3	**Victoria Bowering** Yeager, Dorian
1993–1996	3	**Alison Kaine** Allen, Kate
1993–1996	5	**Jeet & Robin Vaughan** Banks, Carolyn
1993–1996	4	**Liz Graham, Cal Donovan & Frank Shapiro** Bannister, Jo
1993–1997	5	**Anna Pigeon** Barr, Nevada
1993–1997	3	**Ian Roper** Bolitho, Janie

1993–1997	10	**Witherspoon & Mrs. Jeffries** Brightwell, Emily
1993–1994	2	**Morgana Dalton** Buckstaff, Kathryn
1993–1997	5	**Irene Kelly** Burke, Jan
1993–1997	3	**Maxey Burnell** Cail, Carol
1993–1994	2	**Brian Donodio** Callahan, Sheila MacGill
1993–1996	3	**Nan Robinson** Cannon, Taffy
1993–1995	2	**Marty Hopkins** Carlson, P(atricia) M(cEvoy)
1993–1997	6	**Cat Caliban** Carpenter, Lynnette
1993–1995	2	**Betty Trenka** Christmas, Joyce
1993–1997	3	**Eva "Bucket Nut" Wylie** Cody, Liza
1993–1994	2	**Kimmey Kruse** Cooper, Susan Rogers
1993–1997	5	**Duncan Kincaid & Gemma James** Crombie, Deborah
1993–1994	3	**Clively Close** Cummings, Barbara w/ Jo-Ann Power
1993–1995	3	**Ginevra Prettifield** Dawkins, Cecil
1993–1995	4	**Jack Prester & Maxx** Dengler, Sandy
1993–1995	5	**Joe Rodriguez** Dengler, Sandy
1993–1996	2	**Tyler Jones** Drury, Joan M.
1993–1996	3	**Claire Jennerette Claiborne** Dunbar, Sophie
1993–1995	2	**Dr. Jack Caleb & John Thinnes** Dymmoch, Michael Allen
1993–1994	2	**Rafferty & Llewellyn** Evans, Geraldine

1993–1998	6	**Amanda Hazard & Nick Thorn** Feddersen, Connie
1993–1996	3	**Alix Nicholson** Gilligan, Sharon
1993–1995	2	**Kate MacLean** Gilpatrick, Noreen
1993–1996	3	**April Woo & Jason Frank** Glass, Leslie
1993–1996	3	**Connor O'Neill & Fran Wilson** Green, Christine
1993–1994	2	**Ross** Grindle, Lucretia
1993–1997	6	**Anita Blake** Hamilton, Laurell K.
1993–1997	3	**Henrie O** Hart, Carolyn G(impel)
1993–1995	3	**Dr. Amy Prescott** Hendricksen, Louise
1993–1997	5	**Joanna Brady** Jance, J(udith) A(nn)
1993–1996	2	**Tristen Jade** Jon, Lori
1993–1998	5	**Laura Fleming** Kelner, Toni L. P.
1993–1996	3	**Kate Martinelli & Al Hawken** King, Laurie R.
1993–1996	3	**Lil Ritchie** Knight, Phyllis
1993–1994	2	**Jessie Drake** Krich, Rochelle Majer
1993–1996	2	**Terry Girard** Kunz, Kathleen
1993–1995	3	**Teal Stewart** Lamb, J. Dayne
1993–1995	3	**Maria Kallio** Lentolainen, Leena
1993–1997	3	**Sydney Sloane** Lordon, Randye
1993–1995	3	**Nancy Clue** Maney, Mabel

1993–1997	6	**Trewley & Stone** Mason, Sarah J(ill)
1993–1997	3	**Kathryn Mackay** McGuire, Christine
1993–1995	3	**Caley Burke** McKenna, Bridget
1993–1996	4	**Cassie Swann** Moody, Susan (Elizabeth)
1993–1996	4	**Catherine LeVendeur** Newman, Sharan
1993–1997	4	**Laura Ackroyd & Michael Thackeray** O'Connor, Maureen
1993–1995	3	**Joe Silva** Oleksiw, Susan (Prince)
1993–1997	5	**Barbara "Bo" Bradley** Padgett, Abigail
1993–1997	5	**Angelina Amalfi & Paavo Smith** Pence, Joanne
1993–1993	1	**Mrs. Eugenia Potter** Pickard, Nancy
1993–1997	5	**Roxanne Sydney** Poore, Dawn Aldridge
1993–1996	3	**Phoebe Siegel** Prowell, Sandra West
1993–1997	3	**Iris Thorne** Pugh, Dianne G.
1993–1997	4	**Lauren Maxwell** Quinn (Barnard), Elizabeth
1993–1997	5	**Owen Archer** Robb, Candace (M.)
1993–1997	9	**A Pennyfoot Hotel Mystery** Roberts, Doreen
1993–1997	4	**Julian Kestrel** Ross, Kate (Katherine J.)
1993–1994	3	**Laney Samms** Schmidt, Carol
1993–1996	5	**Barrett Lake** Singer, Shelley
1993–1996	2	**Laura Principal** Spring, Michelle

1993–1996	3	**Kate Ivory** Stallwood, Veronica
1993–1995	2	**Sister Cecile** Sullivan, Winona
1993–1997	3	**Tory Bauer** Taylor, Kathleen
1993–1995	2	**Imogen Quy** Walsh, Jill Paton
1993–1993	2	**Mme. Victoire Vernet** Yarbro, Chelsea Quinn w/ Bill Fawcett
1993–1995	2	**Royce Madison** York, Kieran
1994–1997	8	**Dr. Deirdre "Didi" Quinn Nightingale** Adamson, Lydia
1994–1998	4	**Kate Ardleigh & Sir Charles Sheridan** Albert, Susan Wittig w/ William J. Albert
1994–1997	3	**Emily "Em" Hansen** Andrews (Brown), Sarah
1994–1995	2	**Matilda Haycastle** Bailey, Michele
1994–1997	4	**Robin Light** Block, Barbara
1994–1997	3	**Sophie Greenway** Boehnhardt, Patricia
1994–1995	2	**Emily Silver** Brennan, Carol
1994–1996	2	**Thea Barlow** Caverly, Carol
1994–1997	3	**Dr. Gail McCarthy** Crum, Laura
1994–1996	2	**Toni Underwood** Davidson, Diane
1994–1996	4	**Miss Helma Zukas** Dereske, Jo
1994–1996	3	**Nicholas Segalla** Doherty, P(aul) C.
1994–1995	2	**Joanna McKenzie & James Carrick** Duffy, Margaret
1994–1996	2	**Saz Martin** Duffy, Stella

1994–1997	4	**Daisy Dalrymple & Alec Fletcher** Dunn, Carola
1994–1996	3	**Karen Hightower** Edghill, Rosemary
1994–1996	4	**Desiree Shapiro** Eichler, Selma
1994–1997	3	**Stephanie Plum** Evanovitch, Janet
1994–1996	2	**Margo Fortier** Fennelly, Tony
1994–1997	4	**Thea Kozak** Flora, Kate (Clark)
1994–1997	4	**Albenia "Benni" Harper** Fowler, Earlene
1994–1995	2	**Carmen Ramirez** Haddock, Lisa
1994–1997	4	**Tess Darcy** Hager, Jean
1994–1995	2	**Alex Danilov** Haley, Wendy
1994–1997	3	**Robin Hudson** Hayter, Sparkle
1994–1997	4	**Anneke Haagen & Karl Genesko** Holtzer, Susan
1994–1998	3	**Kate Austen** Jacobs, Jonnie
1994–1997	4	**Stella the Stargazer, a.k.a. Jane Austen Smith** Jorgensen, Christine T.
1994–1998	3	**Alex Plumtree** Kaewort, Julie
1994–1996	3	**Mary Russell & Sherlock Holmes** King, Laurie R.
1994–1996	3	**Brooke Cassidy & Matt Devlin** Kruger, Mary
1994–1995	2	**John Rawlings** Lampitt, Dinah
1994–1996	2	**Angela Matelli** Lee, Wendi
1994–1995	2	**Olivia Chapman** Logan, Margaret

1994–1997	2	**Tori Miracle** Malmont, Valerie S.
1994–1997	5	**Harriet Hubley** Manthorne, Jackie
1994–1995	3	**Jo Hughes** Mather, Linda
1994–1997	3	**Meredith Folger** Mathews, Francine
1994–1996	2	**Ashley Johnson & Elizabeth "Tenacity" Mendoza** McAllester, Melanie
1994–1997	4	**Schuyler Ridgway** McCafferty, (Barbara) Taylor
1994–1998	4	**Mackenzie Griffin** McCafferty, Jeanne
1994–1996	2	**Alix Thorssen** McClendon, Lise
1994–1995	2	**Gianna Maglione & Mimi Patterson** Mickelbury, Penny
1994–1997	4	**Magdalena Yoder** Myers, Tamar
1994–1997	3	**Jordan Myles** Navratilova, Martina w/ Liz Nickles
1994–1996	2	**Phoebe Fairfax** North, Suzanne
1994–1997	4	**Kathleen Mallory** O'Connell, Carol
1994–1997	4	**Queenie Davilov** Osborne, Denise
1994–1995	2	**Gail Connor** Parker, Barbara
1994–1996	2	**Max Bramble & Wylie Nolan** Reuben, Shelly
1994–1996	2	**Louise Eldridge** Ripley, Ann
1994–1997	4	**Lord Meren** Robinson, Lynda S(uzanne)
1994–1997	3	**Sano Ichiro** Rowland, Laura Joh
1994–1998	5	**Lydia Chin & Bill Smith** Rozan, S(hira) J(udith)

1994–1996	2	**Cat Wilde**
		Ruryk, Jean
1994–1995	2	**Ray & Kate Frederick**
		Schenkel, S(hirley) E.
1994–1995	2	**Angie DaVito**
		Shaffer, Louise
1994–1995	3	**Patricia Delaney**
		Short, Sharon Gwyn
1994–1997	4	**Jolie Wyatt**
		Smith, Barbara Burnett
1994–1997	4	**Peaches Dann**
		Squire, Elizabeth Daniels
1994–1997	5	**Sarah & Meg Quilliam**
		Stanton, Mary
1994–1995	3	**Mitch Greer & Deidre Griffin**
		Taylor, Karen E.
1994–1994	2	**Sherlock Holmes**
		Thomson, June (Valerie)
1994–1997	4	**Simona Griffo**
		Trinchieri, Camilla
1994–1995	2	**Kate Murray**
		Tyre, Peg
1994–1995	2	**Molly Cates**
		Walker, Mary Willis
1994–1997	4	**Tamara Hayle**
		Wesley, Valerie Wilson
1994–1997	3	**"Abby" Abagnarro & "Ike" Tygart**
		Whitney, Polly
1994–1997	4	**Samantha Holt**
		Wilson, Karen Ann
1994–1995	2	**Elizabeth Will**
		Yeager, Dorian
1994–1994	2	**Dr. Liz Broward & Zack James**
		Zachary, Fay
1995–1996	2	**Michael Croft**
		Adams, Jane
1995–1997	3	**Judith Thornton**
		Benke, Patricia D.
1995–1997	4	**Melanie Travis**
		Berenson, Laurien

1995–1996	2	**Ashley & Emily** Bruyer, Kris
1995–1997	3	**Father John O'Malley & Vicky Holden** Coel, Margaret
1995–1997	3	**Dorothy Martin** Dams, Jeanne M.
1995–1997	3	**Fremont Jones** Day, Dianne
1995–1998	2	**Nurse Molly Burke** Dreyer, Eileen
1995–1998	2	**Lisa King** Farrelly, Gail E.
1995–1997	3	**Sir Robert Carey** Finney, Pauline
1995–1996	3	**Frances "Fran" Tremaine Kirk** Furie, Ruthe
1995–1997	4	**Mother Lavinia Grey** Gallison (Dunn), Kate
1995–1997	3	**Grace de Rossa** Gibson, Maggie
1995–1997	2	**Sharon Hays** Gregory, Sarah
1995–1996	2	**Jules Clement** Harrison, Jamie
1995–1997	2	**Sam Jones** Henderson, Lauren
1995–1997	5	**Elena Jarvis** Herndon, Nancy
1995–1996	2	**Sonora Blair** Hightower, Lynn S.
1995–1996	2	**Gale Grayson & Katie Pru** Holbrook, Teri
1995–1996	2	**Lydia Miller** Hyde, Eleanor
1995–1997	2	**Kali O'Brien** Jacobs, Jonnie
1995–1996	2	**Natalie Gold** Jaffe, Jody
1995–1997	3	**Trevor Joseph** John, Katherine

1995–1996	2	**Maggie Garrett** Taylor, Jean
1995–1996	2	**Ella Clah** Thurlo, Aimee w/ David Thurlo
1995–1997	3	**Claudia** Todd, Marilyn
1995–1995	2	**Georges Albuisson & Jacques Andrieu** Whelan, Hilary
1995–1998	4	**Josie Pigeon** Wolzien, Valerie
1996–1997	2	**Lucy Wayles** Adamson, Lydia
1996–1998	3	**Biggie Weatherford** Bell, Nancy
1996–1997	2	**Cassidy James** Calloway, Kate
1996–1997	2	**Hollis Ball** Chappell, Helen
1996–1998	3	**Charlie Plato & Zack Hunter** Chittenden, Margaret
1996–1996	1	**Henry & Sunday Parker Britland IV** Clark, Mary Higgins
1996–1997	2	**Lindsay Chamberlain** Connor, Beverly
1996–1997	2	**Ruby Crane** Dereske, Jo
1996–1997	2	**Allison O'Neil** Douglas, Lauren Wright
1996–1997	2	**Barbara Simons** Epstein, Carole
1996–1997	2	**Alexandra Cooper** Fairstein, Linda
1996–1997	2	**Lupe Solano** Garcia-Aguilera, Carolina
1996–1997	4	**Patricia Anne & Mary Alice** George, Anne
1996–1997	3	**Matthew Bartholomew** Gregory, Susanna
1996–1997	2	**Theresa Galloway** Grimes, Terris McMahan

1996–1997	2	**Lily Bard** Harris, Charlaine
1996–1996	2	**Ellen North** Hoag, Tami
1996–1998	3	**Ruthie Kantor Morris** Horowitz, Renee
1996–1997	2	**Sister Agnes Bourdillon** Joseph, Alison
1996–1997	2	**Dr. Penelope Jessica "PJ" Gray** Kennett, Shirley
1996–1997	2	**Lorraine Page** La Plante, Lynda
1996–1997	2	**Hannah Trevor** Lorens, M(argaret) K(eilstrup)
1996–1997	2	**Texana Jones** Martin, Allana
1996–1996	2	**Jane Austen** Mathews, Francine
1996–1997	2	**Cassidy McCabe** Matthews, Alex
1996–1997	2	**Bert & Nan Tatum** McCafferty, Barbara Taylor w/ Beverly Taylor Herald
1996–1997	2	**Venus Diamond** Moody, Skye Kathleen
1996–1997	3	**Joe Grey, PI** Murphy, Shirley Rousseau
1996–1996	2	**Abigail Timberlake** Myers, Tamar
1996–1997	2	**Dr. Anne Menlo** O'Callaghan, Maxine
1996–1998	3	**Molly Masters** O'Kane, Leslie
1996–1997	2	**Andi Pauling** Roberts, Lillian M.
1996–1997	2	**Emma Rhodes** Smith, Cynthia
1996–1997	2	**Heaven Lee** Temple, Lou Jane
1996–1997	2	**Truman Kicklighter** Trocheck, Kathy Hogan

1996–1997	2	**Henry & June** Wendell, Sarah	
1997–1998	2	**Susanna, Lady Appleton** Emerson, Kathy Lynn	
1997–1997	2	**Fran Varady** Granger (Hulme), Ann	
1997–1998	2	**Mandy Dyer** Johnson, Dolores	
1997–1998	2	**Casey Jones** Munger, Katy	
1997–1997	2	**Cat Austen** Rubino, Jane	
1997–1997	2	**Helen Bradley** Rushford, Patricia H.	
1997–1998	2	**Maggie Dillitz** Sleem, Patty	
1997–1999	3	**Connor Westphal** Warner, Penny	
1997–1997	2	**The Little Stranger** Winke, Jennifer	

APPENDIX II:
Pseudonym to Autonym

There are any number of reasons for an author to use a nom de plume. A new name often gives an undeveloped aspect of an author's personality a chance to flourish. Several authors in our MASTER LIST have created a new pseudonym for each new series character. An author whose books are well known in one field may want to separate this work from her crime and mystery writing. Some team writers, in the true sense of collaboration, choose a single name under which their works appear.

A man may write under a female pseudonym thinking that readers may be more sympathetic toward a certain character developed by a woman rather than a man. In the not-so-distant past, many women chose to send their work to a publisher under a male pseudonym to improve chances of publication or publishers decreed that a woman adopt a male pseudonym or publish under her first initials. It was felt the market was more receptive to works by men.

Many earlier authors' real names were kept closely guarded secrets—sometime for decades. Today, some authors still desire anonymity for personal or professional reasons. Our policy is to reveal only those real names that have appeared in print elsewhere. We respect those who wish to remain pseudonymous.

This section makes it possible for readers familiar with only a pseudonym to discover the author's real name and any other pseudonyms she may have chosen to use. Readers may find that a favorite author's name is in fact a pseudonym. This list is compiled alphabetically by pseudonym (last name first). The autonym appears on the same line.

Pseudonym	Autonym
Aird, Catherine	*McIntosh, Kinn Hamilton*
Allan, Joan	*Grove, Martin*
Allen, Irene	*Peters, Elsa Kirsten*
Allen, Mary Ann	*Pardoe, Rosemary*
Anthony, Elizabeth	*Traynor, Page w/ Anthony Traynor*

Pseudonym	*Autonym*
Anthony, Evelyn	*Ward-Thomas, Evelyn Bridget Patricia Stephens*
Antill, Elizabeth	*Middleton, Elizabeth*
Aresbys, The	*Bamberger, Helen w/ Raymond Bamberger*
Arliss, Joen	*Martin, Ian*
Arnold, Margot	*Cook, Petronelle Marguerite Mary*
Ashe, Mary Ann	*Brand (Lewis), (Mary) Christianna (Milne)*
Babson, Marian	*Stenstreem, Ruth*
Bailey, Hilea	*Marting, Ruth Lenore*
Balfour, Hearnden	*Balfour, Eva w/ Beryl Hearnden*
Barbette, Jay	*Spicer, Betty Coe w/ Bart Spicer*
Barling, Charles	*Barling, Muriel Vere M.*
Barrington, Pamela	*Barling, Muriel Vere M.*
Barron, Stephanie	*Mathews, Francine*
Beaton, M. C.	*Chesney, Marion*
Beck, K. K.	*Marris, Kathrine*
Beecham, Rose	*Fulton, Jennifer*
Belfort, Sophie	*Auspitz, Kate*
Bell, Josephine	*Ball, Doris Bell (Collier)*
Berne, Karin	*Bernell, Sue w/ Michaela Karni*
Bishop, Claudia	*Stanton, Mary*
Black, Veronica	*Peters, Maureen*
Blackmur, L. L.	*Long, Lydia*
Blair, Marcia	*Baker, Marc(eil Genee Kolstad)*
Blake, Christina	*Halpin, Mary D.*
Bliss, Adam	*Burkhardt, Eve w/ Robert Ferdinand Burkhardt*
Bond, Evelyn	*Hershman, Morris*
Bonett, John & Emery	*Coulson, Felicity Winifred Carter w/ John H. A. Coulson*
Bonnamy, Francis	*Walz, Audrey Boyers*
Borton, D. B.	*Carpenter, Lynnette*
Bowen, Marjorie	*Long, Gabrielle Margaret Vere Campbell*
Brahms, Caryl & S. J. Simon	*Abrahams, Doris Caroline w/ Simon Jasha Skidelsky*
Bridge, Ann	*O'Malley, Lady Mary Dolling Saunders*
Browne, Lizbie	*Marriott, Mary*
Bruce, Jean	*Brochet, Jean Alexandre*

Pseudonym	Autonym
Burnes, Caroline	Haines, Carolyn
Burton, Anne	Bowen-Judd, Sara Hutton
Candy, Edward	Neville, Barbara Alison Boodson
Cannan, Joanna	Pullein-Thompson, Joanna M. C.
Carnac, Carol	Rivett, Edith Caroline
Castle, Jayne	Krentz, Jayne Ann
Caudwell, Sarah	Cockburn, Sarah
Challis, Mary	Bowen-Judd, Sara Hutton
Charles, Kate	Chase, Carol
Chipperfield, Robert O.	Ostrander, Isabel (Egenton)
Chisholm, P. F.	Finney, Pauline
Churchill, Jill	Brooks, Janice Young
Clandon, Henrietta	Vahey, John G. H.
Cockin, Joan	Burbridge, Edith Joan
Coffin, Geoffrey	Brawner, Helen w/ Francis Van Wyck Mason
Cohen, Anthea	Simpson, Doris
Colburn, Laura	McMahan, Ian
Coles, Manning	Manning, Adelaide Frances Oke w/ Cyril Henry Coles
Collins, Michelle	Collins, Michael
Cooper, Natasha	Wright, Daphne
Craig, Alisa	MacLeod, Charlotte (Matilda Hughes)
Crane, Hamilton	Mason, Sarah J(ill)
Crespi, Camilla T.	Trinchieri, Camilla
Crespi, Trella	Trinchieri, Camilla
Crosby, Lee	Budlong, Ware Torrey
Cross, Amanda	Heilbrun, Carolyn G(old)
Crowleigh, Ann	Cummings, Barbara w/ Jo-Ann Power
Curry, Avon	Bowden, Jean
Curzon, Clare	Buchanan, Eileen-Marie Duell
Dain, Catherine	Garwood, Judith
Dane, Clemence & Helen Simpson	Ashton, Winifred w/ Helen (DeGuerry) Simpson
Davey, Jocelyn	Raphael, Chaim
Dominic, R. B.	Henissart, Martha w/ Mary Jane Latsis
Draco, F.	Davis, Julia
Drake, Alison	MacGregor, T(rish) J(aneshutz)
Dukthas, Ann	Doherty, P(aul) C.

Pseudonym	Autonym
Edingtons, The	Edington, Carmen Ballen w/ Arlo Channing Edington
Egan, Lesley	Linington, (Barbara) Elizabeth
Ellery, Jan	Ewing, Jan
Erskine, Margaret	Williams, Margaret Wetherby
Evermay, March	Eiker, Mathilde
Eyre, Elizabeth	Staynes, Jill w/ Margaret Storey
Fawcett, Quinn	Yarbro, Chelsea Quinn w/ Bill Fawcett
Ferrars, E. X.	Brown, Morna Doris (MacTaggart)
Fickling, G. G.	Fickling, Gloria w/ Forrest Fickling
Fielding, A.	Fielding, Dorothy
Fitt, Mary	Freeman, Kathleen
Foley, Rae	Denniston, Elinore
Ford, Leslie	Brown, Zenith Jones
Fortune, Dion	Firth, Violet Mary
Fox, David	Ostrander, Isabel (Egenton)
Frazer, Margaret	Bacon, Gail w/ Mary Monica Pulver (Kuhfeld)
Frome, David	Brown, Zenith Jones
Gainham, Sarah	Ames, Sarah Rachel Stainer
Gaite, Francis	Manning, Adelaide Frances Oke w/ Cyril Henry Coles
Gallagher, Gale	Scott, Margaret w/ Will(iam Charles) Oursler
Gayle, Newton	Marin, Muna Lee w/ Maurice C. Guiness
Gilbert, Anthony	Malleson, Lucy Beatrice
Giroux, E. X.	Shannon, Doris
Glen, Alison	Lowry, Cheryl Meredith w/ Louise Vetter
Gordons, The	Gordon, Mildred w/ Gordon Gordon
Grant, Linda	Williams, Linda V.
Gray, Dulcie	Dennison, Dulcie Winifred Catherine Bailey
Gray, Gallagher	Munger, Katy
Green, Glint	Peterson, Margaret Ann
Grey, Robin	Gresham, Elizabeth
Grove, Marjorie	Grove, Martin
Haddam, Jane	Papazoglou, Orania
Hadley, Joan	Hess, Joan

Pseudonym	*Autonym*
Hale, Christopher	*Stevens, Frances M(oyer) R(oss)*
Hall, Patricia	*O'Connor, Maureen*
Hambledon, Phyllis	*MacVean, Phyllis*
Hamilton, Adam	*Granbeck, Marilyn w/ Arthur Moore*
Hamilton, Nan	*Ball, (Nanoni) Patricia (Maude Hamilton)*
Hanshew, Mary & Thomas Hanshew	*Hanshew, Hazel Phillips*
Hanshew, Thomas	*Hanshew, Hazel Phillips w/ Mary Hanshew*
Harris, Colver	*Colver, Anne*
Hart, Ellen	*Boehnhardt, Patricia*
Henderson, M. R.	*Granbeck, Marilyn*
Hervey, Evelyn	*Keating, H(enry) R(eymond) F(itzwalter)*
Hitchens, Bert & Dolores	*Hitchens, (Julia Clara Catherine) Dolores (Birk) w/ Hu(Bert) Hitchens*
Hobson, Polly	*Evans, Julie Rendel*
Holden, Genevieve	*Pou, Genevieve Long*
Hunt, Charlotte	*Hodges, Doris Marjorie*
Ironside, John	*Tait, Euphemia Margaret*
Irving, Alexander	*Fahrenkopf, Anne w/ Ruth Fox (Hume)*
Jackson, Marian J. A.	*Rogers, Marian*
Jones, Jennifer	*Johnson, Enid w/ Margaret Lane*
Kains, Josephine	*Goulart, Ronald Joseph*
Karl, M. S.	*Shuman, M. K.*
Kemp, Sarah	*Butterworth, Michael*
Kingsbury, Kate	*Roberts, Doreen*
Kruger, Paul	*Sebenthal, Roberta Elizabeth*
Lacey, Sarah	*Mitchell, Kay*
Laing, Patrick	*Long, Amelia Reynolds*
Lake, Deryn	*Lampitt, Dinah*
Lambert, Mercedes	*Munson, Douglas Anne*
Lang, Maria	*Lange, Dagmar Maria*
Langley, Lee	*Langley, Sarah*
Lathen, Emma	*Henissart, Martha w/ Mary Jane Latsis*
Lawrence, Margaret	*Lorens, M(argaret) K(eilstrup)*
Lee, Babs	*Van der Veer Lee, Marion*

Pseudonym	Autonym
Lee, Gypsy Rose	Craig, Georgiana Ann Randolph
Lee, W. W.	Lee, Wendi
Leek, Margaret	Bowen-Judd, Sara Hutton
Leonard, Charles L.	Heberden, M(ary) V(iolet)
Lewis, Lange	Beynon, Jane
Lombard, Nap	Johnson, Pamela Hansford w/ Neil Stewart
Lorac, E. C. R.	Rivett, Edith Caroline
Lynch, Lawrence	Van Deventer, Emma M.
Lynch, Miriam	Wallace, Mary
Mace, Merlda	McCoy, Madeleine
Mack, Evalina	McNamara, Lena Brooke
Macrae, Travis	Feagles, Anita Macrae
MacVeigh, Sue	Nearing, Elizabeth C.
Mannon, M. M.	Mannon, Martha w/ Mary Ellen Mannon
Mariz, Linda	French, Linda
Martin, Lee	Wingate, (Martha) Anne (Guice)
Maxwell, A. E.	Maxwell, Ann Elizabeth Lowell w/ Evan Maxwell
McCall, K. T.	Armitage, Audrey w/ Muriel Watkins
McClellan, Tierney	McCafferty, (Barbara) Taylor
McCormick, Claire	Labus, Marta Haake
McGrew, Fenn	McGrew, Julia w/ Caroline K. Fenn
Mead, Russell	Koehler, Margaret Hudson
Meade, L(illie) T(homas)	Meade (Smith), Elizabeth Thomasina
Meade, L. T.	Meade (Smith), Elizabeth Thomasina w/ Robert Eustace (Barton)
Melville, Jennie	Butler, Gwendoline
Meyers, Maan	Meyers, Annette (Brafman) w/ Martin Meyers
Michaels, Barbara	Mertz, Barbara L(ouise) G(ross)
Mills, Osmington	Brooks, Vivian Collin
Montross, David	Backus, Jean Louise
Morice, Anne	Shaw, Felicity
Neville, Margot	Goyder, Margot w/ Anne N(eville) G(oyder) Joske
O'Hara, Kenneth	Morris, Jean
O'Nair, Mairi	Evans, Constance May

Pseudonym	*Autonym*
Oliphant, B. J.	*Tepper, Sheri S.*
Olsen, D. B.	*Hitchens, (Julia Clara Catherine) Dolores (Birk)*
Orde, A. J.	*Tepper, Sheri S.*
Page, Emma	*Tirbutt, Honoria*
Paige, Robin	*Albert, Susan Wittig w/ William J. Albert*
Paull, Jessyca	*Burger, Rosaylmer w/ Julia Perceval*
Penn, John	*Harcourt, Palma w/ Jack H. Trotman*
Peters, Elizabeth	*Mertz, Barbara L(ouise) G(ross)*
Peters, Ellis	*Pargeter, Edith Mary*
Peters, Geoffrey	*Palmer, Madelyn*
Petrie, Rhona	*Buchanan, Eileen-Marie Duell*
Prichard, K. & Hesketh	*Prichard, Katherine O'Brien w/ Vernon Hesketh Prichard*
Quest, Erica	*Sawyer, Nancy Buckingham w/ John Sawyer*
Quill, Monica	*McInerny, Ralph*
Radford, E. & M. A.	*Radford, Mona Augusta Mangan w/ Edwin Isaac Radford*
Radley, Sheila	*Robinson, Sheila Mary*
Ramsay, Diana	*Brandes, Rhoda*
Rayter, Joe	*McChesney, Mary F.*
Revell, Louisa	*Smith, Ellen Hart*
Reynolds, Adrian	*Long, Amelia Reynolds*
Rice, Craig	*Craig, Georgiana Ann Randolph*
Robb, J. D.	*Roberts, Nora*
Roberts, Gillian	*Greber, Judith*
Robertson, Helen	*Edmiston, Helen Jean Mary*
Roffman, Jan	*Summerton, Margaret*
Roos, Kelley	*Roos, Audrey Kelley w/ William Roos*
Sandys, Oliver	*Evans, Marguerite Helen Jervis*
Saunders, Lawrence	*Davis, Clare w/ Burton Davis*
Scarlett, Roger	*Blair, Dorothy w/ Evelyn Page*
Scott, Denis	*Means, Mary w/ Theodore Saunders*
Sedley, Kate	*Clarke, Brenda Margaret Lilian Honeyman*
Shane, Susannah	*Ashbrook, H(arriette) C(ora)*
Shannon, Dell	*Linington, (Barbara) Elizabeth*
Shepherd, Joan	*Buchanan, Betty Joan*

Pseudonym	Autonym
Siller, Van	Van Siller, Hilda
Simons, Roger	Punnett, Margaret w/ Ivor Punnett
Smith, Shelley	Bodington, Nancy Hermione Courlander
St. Clair, Elizabeth	Cohen, Susan Handler
Stacey, Susannah	Staynes, Jill w/ Margaret Storey
Stanton, Coralie	Hosken, Alice Cecil Seymour w/ Ernest Charles Heath Hosken
Steele, V. M.	Firth, Violet Mary
Storey, Alice	Shankman, Sarah
Strange, John Stephen	Tillett, Dorothy Stockbridge
Tanner, Jake	Museo, Laura w/ Stephen Schermerhorn
Teilhet, Darwin L.	Teilhet, Hildegarde Tolman
Tell, Dorothy	Toopes, Dot
Tey, Josephine	MacKintosh, Elizabeth
Tilton, Alice	Taylor, Phoebe Atwood
Torrie, Malcolm	Mitchell, Gladys (Maude Winifred)
Venning, Michael	Craig, Georgiana Ann Randolph
Wakefield, Hannah	Burton, Sarah w/ Judith Holland
Wallace, C. H.	Burger, Rosaylmer
Walter, A. & H.	Walter, Alexia w/ Hubert Walter
Webb, Martha G.	Wingate, (Martha) Anne (Guice)
Wells, Susan	Siegel, Doris
Wells, Tobias	Forbes, DeLoris Florine Stanton
Wender, Theodora	Wender, Dorothea
Wentworth, Patricia	Turnbull, Dora Amy Dillon
Wolffe, Katherine	Scott, Marian Gallagher
Woods, Sara	Bowen-Judd, Sara Hutton
Wray, I.	Palliser, Iris
Wren, M. K.	Renfroe, Martha Kay
York, Rebecca	Buckholtz, Eileen w/ Ruth Glick
Yorke, Margaret	Nicholson, Margaret Beda Larminie

APPENDIX III:
Series Character to Writer

This appendix links the series character—arranged alphabetically by *first* name—to the writer. In this case, the term "writer" applies to both Pseudonym and Autonym—whichever name appears on the book jacket.

Because of the sheer number of law enforcement and military personnel represented, no rank or title is given to their name in this list. However, each individual's honorific is shown in the MASTER LIST. Physicians and members of the clergy are listed alphabetically by their honorific.

Readers may be familiar with a certain series character's name. By referring to this list, they can find the writer, then use the MASTER LIST to find all the titles of the books in which that character appears, as well as any other series characters created by the same author (Autonym).

Character	Writer
A Pair of Related Novels	Babson, Marian
A. Pennyfeather	Olsen, D. B.
A Pennyfoot Hotel Mystery	Kingsbury, Kate
Abbie Harris	Dean (Getz), Amber
"Abby" Abagnarro & "Ike" Tygart	Whitney, Polly
Abigail Doyle & Roz Benson	Collins, Anna Ashwood
Abigail Patience Danforth	Jackson, Marian J. A.
Abigail Timberlake	Myers, Tamar
Adam Dalgliesh	James (White), P(hyllis) D(orothy) [Baroness James of Holland Park]
Adam Drew & Katherine Cornish	Hanson, Virginia
Adam Quill	Brahms, Caryl & S. J. Simon
Adelaide Adams	Blackmon, Anita
Adrienne Bishop	Ellery, Jan
Agatha Raisin	Beaton, M. C.
Agatha Welch	Johns, Veronica P(arker)

Character	Writer
Al Krug & Casey Kellog	Weston, Carolyn
Al White	Holden, Genevieve
Alan Ford	Wells, Carolyn
Alan Grant	Tey, Josephine
Alastair MacAlastair	Dick (Erikson), (Sibyl Cicely) Alexandra
Albenia "Benni" Harper	Fowler, Earlene
Albert Campion	Allingham (Carter), Margery (Louise)
Alex Danilov	Haley, Wendy
Alex Jensen	Henry, Sue
Alex Plumtree	Kaewort, Julie
Alex Tanner	Donald, Anabel
Alex Winter	Steiner, Susan
Alexandra Cooper	Fairstein, Linda
Alice Nestleton	Adamson, Lydia
Alice Penny	Bliss, Adam
Aline Scott	Drake, Alison
Alison Hope & Nick Trevellyan	Kelly, Susan B.
Alison Kaine	Allen, Kate
Alister Woodhead	Clements, E(ileen) H(elen)
Alix Nicholson	Gilligan, Sharon
Alix Thorssen	McClendon, Lise
Allan Stewart	Siller, Van
Allison O'Neil	Douglas, Lauren Wright
Aloysius Kelly	Worsley-Gough, Barbara
Amanda Hazard & Nick Thorn	Feddersen, Connie
Amanda Knight	Fromer, Margot J.
Amanda Pepper	Roberts, Gillian
Amanda Roberts & Joe Donelli	Woods, Sherryl
Amanda Valentine	Beecham, Rose
Amber Mitchell & Liz Elliott	Brown, Susan w/ Anne Stephenson
Ambrose Usher	Davey, Jocelyn
Amelia Butterworth & Ebenezer Gryce	Green, Anna Katharine
Amelia Peabody Emerson & Radcliffe Emerson	Peters, Elizabeth
Amy Tupper	Bell, Josephine
Andi Pauling	Roberts, Lillian M.
Andrea Perkins	Coker, Carolyn
Andrea Reid Ramsay & David Ramsay	Matschat, Cecile Hulse

Character	Writer
Andrew Basnett	Ferrars, E. X.
Andrew Taggart	Brandon, Ruth
Andrew Torrent	Cores, Lucy (Michaela)
Andy & Sue MacVeigh	MacVeigh, Sue
Angela Matelli	Lee, Wendi
Angelina Amalfi & Paavo Smith	Pence, Joanne
Angeline Tredennick	Sanborn, Ruth Burr
Angie DaVito	Shaffer, Louise
Anita Blake	Hamilton, Laurell K.
Ann Hales	Ingate, Mary
Ann McIntosh	Mack, Evalina
Ann Tate	Burnes, Caroline
Anna J(agedinski)	Swan, Phyllis
Anna Lee	Cody, Liza
Anna Peters	Law (Trecker), Janice
Anna Pigeon	Barr, Nevada
Anna Southwood	Bedford, Jean
Anne & Jeffrey McNeill	DuBois, Theodora M.
Anne "Davvie" Davenport McLean	Yates, Margaret Tayler
Anne Hyde	Swan (Burdett-Smith), Annie S.
Anneke Haagen & Karl Genesko	Holtzer, Susan
Annie FitzHugh	Roberts, Carey
Annie Laurance Darling	Hart, Carolyn G(impel)
Annie MacPherson	Smith, Janet L.
Annie McGrogan	Farrell, Gillian B.
Anthea & Justin Rutherford	Ley, Alice Chetwynd
Anthony Ware	Wells, Susan
Antoine Cirret	Hely (Younger), Elizabeth
Antony Maitland	Woods, Sara
Appollonia "Lonia" Guiu	Oliver, Maria-Antonia
April Woo & Jason Frank	Glass, Leslie
Arabella Frant	Fearon, Diana
Argus Steele	Lee, Babs
Argus Steele	Saunders, Claire Castler w/ Marion Van der Veer Lee
Arly Hanks	Hess, Joan
Arthur G. Crook	Gilbert, Anthony
Artie Weatherby	Miller, J(anice) M. T(ubbs)
Asey Mayo	Taylor, Phoebe Atwood
Ashley & Emily	Bruyer, Kris
Ashley Johnson & Elizabeth "Tenacity" Mendoza	McAllester, Melanie

Character	Writer
August Didier	*Myers, Amy*
Aurora Teagarden	*Harris, Charlaine*
B. F. Hopper	*Tanner, Jake*
Baker	*Mills, Osmington*
Ballet Stroganoff	*Brahms, Caryl & S. J. Simon*
Balthazar Marten	*Adamson, M(ary) J(o)*
Barbara "Bo" Bradley	*Padgett, Abigail*
Barbara Holloway	*Wilhelm (Knight), Kate (Gertrude)*
Barbara Simons	*Epstein, Carole*
Barlow Dale	*Siverns, Ruth*
Barnaby	*Graham, Caroline*
Barney Gantt	*Strange, John Stephen*
Baron Von Kaz	*Teilhet, Darwin L.*
Barrett Lake	*Singer, Shelley*
Barrington Hewes-Bradford	*Hamilton, Adam*
Barry	*Rowe, Anne (Von Meibom)*
Barry & Dee Vaughan	*Jordan, Jennifer*
Barry O'Dell	*Chipperfield, Robert O.*
Basil	*Hobson, Polly*
Battle	*Christie, Agatha*
Beau Smith & Pogy Rogers	*Ross, Z(ola) H(elen Girdey)*
Ben & Carrie Porter	*Travis, Elizabeth*
Ben Louis	*Russell, E(nid)*
Ben Safford	*Dominic, R. B.*
Benbow & Wingate	*Sawyer, Corrine Holt*
Benbow Smith & Frank Garratt	*Wentworth, Patricia*
Benedict Breeze	*Bayne, Isabella*
Benjamin Jurnet	*Haymon, S(ylvia) T(heresa)*
Benvenuto Brown	*Gill, Elizabeth*
Bernard & Snooky	*Dank, Gloria*
Bernard Simmons	*Lockridge, Frances (Louise Davis) w/ Richard (Orson) Lockridge*
Bert & Nan Tatum	*McCafferty, Barbara Taylor w/ Beverly Taylor Herald*
Bertha Barstow	*Thomas, Dicey*
Beth Austin	*Skom, Edith*
Beth Marie Cartwright	*Owens, Virginia Stem*
Betty Trenka	*Christmas, Joyce*
Biggie Weatherford	*Bell, Nancy*
Bill & Coco Hastings	*Offord, Lenore Glen*
Bill Davies	*Mason, Sara Elizabeth*
Bill French	*Hale, Christopher*

Character	Writer
Bill Grady	Shriber, Ione Sandburg
Bill Owen, The Old Man in the Corner	Orczy, Baroness (Emma Magdalena Rosalia Maria Josifa Barbara, Baroness Orczy)
Bill Rice	Stand, Marguerite
Bill Slider	Harrod-Eagles, Cynthia
Bill Speed	Donovan, J(ean) B(ernadine)
Bingo Riggs & Handsome Kusak	Rice, Craig
Birdie Linnett	Linscott, Gillian
Blaine Stewart	Zukowski, Sharon
Blair Emerson	Amey, Linda
Blanche White	Neely, Barbara
Blue Maguire & Spaceman Kowalski	White, Teri
Bonnie Indermill	Berry, Carole (Summerlin)
Bosco of the Yard	Christopher, Laura Kim
Bowman	Burrows, Julie
Brett Nightingale	Kelly, Mary
Brian Donodio	Callahan, Sheila MacGill
Briconi	Baskerville, Beatrice w/ Elliot Monk
Brigid Donovan	Saum, Karen
Britt Montero	Buchanan, Edna
Brooke Cassidy & Matt Devlin	Kruger, Mary
Brother Cadfael	Peters, Ellis
Brother Felipe Bruno	Bowen, Marjorie
Bruce Perkins	Lilly, Jean
Burnivel	Candy, Edward
Burton	Locke, G(ladys) E(dson)
C. B. Greenfield & Maggie Rome	Kallen, Lucille
C. D. Sloan	Aird, Catherine
Caitlin Reece	Douglas, Lauren Wright
Caleb Sweetwater	Green, Anna Katharine
Caley Burke	McKenna, Bridget
Calista Jacobs	Knight, Kathryn Lasky
Callahan Garrity	Trocheck, Kathy Hogan
Cam	Cockin, Joan
Cardiff	Gray, Dulcie
Carey Brent	Glidden, M(inna) W(esselhoft)
Carl Masters	Lynch, Lawrence
Carl Pedersen	Hart (Shrager), Jeanne
Carlotta Carlyle	Barnes, Linda (Appelblatt)
Carmen Ramirez	Haddock, Lisa

Character	Writer
Carol Gates	Colburn, Laura
Carole Ashton	McNab, Claire
Carole Loring	Carlton, Bea
Casey Jones	Gray, Gallagher
Cass Jameson	Wheat, Carolyn
Cassandra Mitchell & Karl Alberg	Wright, L(aurali) R.
Cassandra Reilly	Wilson, Barbara (Ellen)
Cassidy James	Calloway, Kate
Cassidy McCabe	Matthews, Alex
Cassie Newton	Smith, Joan G(erarda)
Cassie Swann	Moody, Susan (Elizabeth)
Cat Austen	Rubino, Jane
Cat Caliban	Borton, D. B.
Cat Marsala	D'Amato, Barbara
Cat Wilde	Ruryk, Jean
Catherine Edison	Haffner, Margaret
Catherine LeVendeur	Newman, Sharan
Catherine Sayler	Grant, Linda
CC Scott & Barbara Bettencourt	Plante, Pele
Charles & James Latimer	Gaite, Francis
Charles Hillary	McGrew, Fenn
Charles Matthews	Meredith, D(oris) R.
Charles Spotted Moon	Yarbro, Chelsea Quinn
Charlesworth	Brand (Lewis), (Mary) Christianna (Milne)
"Charlie" Greene	Millhiser, Marlys
Charlie Meiklejohn & Constance Leidl	Wilhelm (Knight), Kate (Gertrude)
Charlie Parker	Shelton, Connie L.
Charlie Plato & Zack Hunter	Chittenden, Margaret
Charlotte Eliot	Filgate, C. Macartney
Charlotte Graham	Matteson, Stefanie
Charlotte Kent	Kittredge, Mary
Charlotte Sams	Glen, Alison
Charmian Daniels	Melville, Jennie
Chauncey O'Day	Gaines (Schultz), Audrey
Chicago Nordejoong	McKernan, Victoria
China Bayles	Albert, Susan Wittig
Chris Martin	Roome, Annette
Christer Wick	Lang, Maria
Christie Opara	Uhnak, Dorothy
Christine Andersen	Mace, Merlda

Character	Writer
Christine Bennett	Harris, Lee
Christopher Adrian	Silverman, Marguerite R(uth)
Christopher Gibson	Montgomery, Ione
Christopher Jensen	Langley, Lee
Christopher Marsden	Backhouse, (Enid) Elizabeth
Christopher Marsh	Durham, Mary
Christopher McKee	Reilly, Helen
Christopher Saxe	Shane, Susannah
Christopher Storm	Barber, Willetta Ann w/ R(udolph) F(rederick) Schabelitz
Chucky	Ashe, Mary Ann
Claire Breslinsky	Kelly, Mary Anne
Claire Camden	Peterson, Audrey
Claire Jennerette Claiborne	Dunbar, Sophie
Claire Malloy	Hess, Joan
Claire Sharples	Rothenberg, Rebecca
Clara Gamadge	Boylan, Eleanor
Clarice Claremont	Cranston, Claudia
Claude Warrington-Reeve	Bell, Josephine
Claudia	Todd, Marilyn
Claudia Valentine	Day, Marele
Clay & Linn Randolph	Carlton, Bea
Clifford Flush	Branch, Pamela (Jean)
Clive Granville	McKenna, Marthe
Cliveden Prince	Reubens, Aida
Clively Close	Crowleigh, Ann
Clovis Kelly	Babbin, Jacqueline
Cockrill	Brand (Lewis), (Mary) Christianna (Milne)
Colin Anstruther	Plain, Josephine
Colin Keats & Gwynn Leith	Shore, Viola Brothers
Collins & McKechnie	Hitchens, Bert & Dolores
Conan Flagg	Wren, M. K.
Connor O'Neill & Fran Wilson	Green, Christine
Connor Westphal	Warner, Penny
Cordelia Gray	James (White), P(hyllis) D(orothy) [Baroness James of Holland Park]
Courtney Brade	Wolffe, Katherine
Cristina Raye	Grimshaw, Beatrice (Ethel)
Cruz & Goldstein	Wallace, Marilyn
D. A. Carey Galbreath	McCully, (Ethel) Walbridge
D. C. Randall (a cat)	Gordons, The

Character	Writer
Daisy Dalrymple & Alec Fletcher	*Dunn, Carola*
Daisy Jane Mott	*Jones, Jennifer*
Daisy Marlow	*Morgan, D Miller*
Dame Beatrice Adela Lestrange Bradley	*Mitchell, Gladys (Maude Winifred)*
Dan Pardoe	*Bowers, Dorothy (Violet)*
Darina Lisle	*Laurence, Janet*
David Ballard & Michelle Merrill Ballard	*Fell, Doris Elaine w/ Carole Gift Page*
David Haham	*Haddad, C(arolyn) (A.)*
David Madden	*Disney, Doris Miles*
David Middleton-Brown	*Charles, Kate*
David Silver	*Hightower, Lynn S.*
David Webb & Ken Jackson	*Fraser, Anthea*
Davina Graham	*Anthony, Evelyn*
Dawn Markey	*Burnes, Caroline*
Deaconess Theodora Braithwaite	*Greenwood, D(iane) M.*
Dearborn V. Pinch	*Green, Edith Pinero*
Deb Ralston	*Martin, Lee*
Deborah Knott	*Maron, Margaret*
Dee Street	*Wakefield, Hannah*
Delilah West	*O'Callaghan, Maxine*
Delta "Storm" Stevens	*Silva, Linda Kay*
Dennis Barrie	*Reynolds, Adrian*
Dennis Devore	*Bennett, Dorothy*
Desiree Shapiro	*Eichler, Selma*
Desmond Shannon	*Heberden, M(ary) V(iolet)*
Devon MacDonald	*Jacobs, Nancy Baker*
Dewey James	*Morgan, Kate*
Dexter Drake	*Barker, Elsa*
Diana Tregarde	*Lackey, Mercedes*
Dick Tansey	*Penn, John*
Diego	*Kelsey, Vera*
Digby	*Wray, I.*
Ditteridge	*Ferrars, E. X.*
Dixie T. Struthers	*Sims, L. V.*
Dolly & The Old Buffer	*Wendell, Sarah*
Dolly & The Wolfman	*Wendell, Sarah*
Don Q	*Prichard, K. & Hesketh*
Doran Fairweather Chelmarsh & Rev. Rodney Chelmarsh	*Hardwick, Mollie*
Dorothy Martin	*Dams, Jeanne M.*

Character	Writer
Douglas Grant	*Millar, Florence N.*
Douglas Perkins	*Babson, Marian*
Douglas Quantrill	*Radley, Sheila*
Douglas Renfrew	*Erskine, Laurie York*
Dr. Alun Barry	*O'Hara, Kenneth*
Dr. Amy Prescott	*Hendricksen, Louise*
Dr. Anne Menlo	*O'Callaghan, Maxine*
Dr. Anthony Post	*Irving, Alexander*
Dr. Basil Willing	*McCloy, Helen (Worrell Clarkson)*
Dr. Benjamin Tancred	*Cole, Margaret (Isabel Postgate) w/ G(eorge) D(ouglas) H(oward) Cole*
Dr. Bernadette Hebert	*Ennis, Catherine*
Dr. Chetwynd & Dr. Paul Cato	*Meade, L. T.*
Dr. Clifford Halifax	*Meade, L(illie) T(homas)*
Dr. Clio Rees Marsh & Harry Marsh	*Bannister, Jo*
Dr. Constantine	*Thynne, Molly*
Dr. David Wintringham	*Bell, Josephine*
Dr. Deirdre "Didi" Quinn Nightingale	*Adamson, Lydia*
Dr. Elizabeth Chase	*Lawrence, Martha C.*
Dr. Gail McCarthy	*Crum, Laura*
Dr. Gerritt DeGraaf	*D'Amato, Barbara*
Dr. Gordon Christy	*Moore (Lee), Barbara*
Dr. Grace Severance	*Scherf, Margaret (Louise)*
Dr. Henry Frost	*Bell, Josephine*
Dr. Hillis Owen & Miss Pomeroy	*Wells, Anna Mary*
Dr. Jack Caleb & John Thinnes	*Dymmoch, Michael Allen*
Dr. Jaz	*Vivian, Margaret*
Dr. Joan Marvin	*Eyles, (Margaret) Leonora (Pitcairn)*
Dr. Kay Scarpetta	*Cornwell, Patricia D(aniels)*
Dr. Liz Broward & Zack James	*Zachary, Fay*
Dr. Manson	*Radford, E. & M. A.*
Dr. Maxene St. Clair	*McGiffen, Janet*
Dr. Nassim Pride	*Petrie, Rhona*
Dr. Nathaniel Bunce	*Curtiss, E(lizabeth) M(angan)*
Dr. Norah North	*Duke, Madelaine (Elizabeth)*
Dr. Paul Holton	*Hunt, Charlotte*
Dr. Paul Prye	*Millar, Margaret (Ellis Sturm)*
Dr. Penelope Jessica "PJ" Gray	*Kennett, Shirley*
Dr. Penelope Spring & Sir Tobias Glendower	*Arnold, Margot*

Character	Writer
Dr. Peter Casey	*Mead, Russell*
Dr. Sam: Johnson	*de la Torre (Bueno) (McCue), Lillian*
Dr. Samantha Turner	*Landreth, Marsha*
Dr. Scott Eason	*Weeks, Dolores*
Dr. Sylvia Strange	*Lovett, Sarah*
Dr. Taverner	*Fortune, Dion*
Dr. Tina May	*Kemp, Sarah*
Dr. William Ames	*Freeman, Lucy*
Duncan Kincaid & Gemma James	*Crombie, Deborah*
E. J. Pugh	*Cooper, Susan Rogers*
Ebenezer Gryce	*Green, Anna Katharine*
Ed Jackson	*Robb, J. D.*
Edgar Allan Poe	*Steward, Barbara w/ Dwight Steward*
Edmund Brown	*Porter, Joyce*
Edward Trelawney	*Long, Amelia Reynolds*
Edwina Crusoe, R.N.	*Kittredge, Mary*
Egan & Kingston	*Taylor, Bonnie w/ Matt Taylor*
Eleanora Burke	*Perdue, Virginia*
Elena Jarvis	*Herndon, Nancy*
Elena Oliverez	*Muller, Marcia*
Elena Oliverez	*Muller, Marcia w/ Bill Pronzini*
Elisha Macomber	*Knight, Kathleen Moore*
Elizabeth	*Kilpatrick, Florence*
Elizabeth Blair	*Browne, Lizbie*
Elizabeth Elliot	*Allen, Irene*
Elizabeth Glen	*Swan (Burdett-Smith), Annie S.*
Elizabeth Lamb Worthington	*Morison, B(etty) J(ane)*
Elizabeth MacPherson	*McCrumb, Sharyn*
Elizabeth Will	*Yeager, Dorian*
Ella Clah	*Thurlo, Aimee w/ David Thurlo*
Ellen North	*Hoag, Tami*
Ellie Bernstein	*Dietz, Denise*
Ellie Gordon	*Berne, Karin*
Ellie Simons Haskell	*Cannell, Dorothy*
Emil Martin	*Taylor, Mary Ann*
Emily & Henry Bryce	*Scherf, Margaret (Louise)*
Emily "Em" Hansen	*Andrews (Brown), Sarah*
Emily Silver	*Brennan, Carol*
Emma Chizzit	*Hall, Mary Bowen*
Emma Lord	*Daheim, Mary*
Emma Marsh & Hank Fairbanks	*Dean, Elizabeth*

Character	Writer
Emma Rhodes	Smith, Cynthia
Emma Shaw	Jones, Hazel Wynn
Emma Victor	Wings, Mary
Enrico Caruso	Paul, Barbara
Eric Hazard	Crosby, Lee
Eric Lund	Wallis, Ruth (O.) Sawtell
Erik March	Fickling, G. G.
Ernest Lamb	Wentworth, Patricia
Eva "Bucket Nut" Wylie	Cody, Liza
Evan Pinkerton	Frome, David
Evangeline Sinclair & Trixie Dolan	Babson, Marian
Eve Dallas	Robb, J. D.
Eve Elliott	Lee, Barbara
Eve MacWilliams	Blizard, Marie
Everard Blatchington	Cole, Margaret (Isabel Postgate) w/ G(eorge) D(ouglas) H(oward) Cole
Everett Anderson	Daiger, K(atherine) S.
F. Millard Smyth	Boyd, Eunice Mays
Fadiman Wace	Simons, Roger
Faith Fairchild	Page, Katherine Hall
Fanny Zindel	Moore, Rayanne w/ Serita Stevens
Father John O'Malley & Vicky Holden	Coel, Margaret
Father Keogh	Lindop, Audrey Erskine
Father Simon Bede & Helen Bullock	Byfield, Barbara Ninde
Father Simon Bede & Helen Bullock	Byfield, Barbara Ninde w/ Frank L. Tedeschi
Felix Guzman	Case, Peg w/ John Migliori
Ferguson	Lincoln, Natalie S(umner)
Ferris Byrd	Stuart (Ohlragge), Anne (Kristine)
Fiddler & Fiora	Maxwell, A. E.
Finch (Rudd)	Thomson, June (Valerie)
Finny Aletter	Montgomery (Ewegen), Yvonne
Flaxman Low	Prichard, K. & Hesketh
Fleming Stone	Wells, Carolyn
Flower	Field, Moira
Flowers Detectives	Cannell, Dorothy
Forsythia Brown	Payes, Rachel
Fortune's Friends	Reynolds, Kay w/ Mike Reynolds

Character	Writer
Fran Varady	Granger (Hulme), Ann
Frances "Fran" Tremaine Kirk	Furie, Ruthe
Frank Carver & Ginny Trask	Wallingford, Lee
Frankie Aguirre & Art Jefferson	Pearson, Ryne Douglas
Fred Vickery	Lewis (Brown), Sherry
Freddie O'Neal	Dain, Catherine
Frederick Hunt	Day (Lederer), Lillian w/ Norbert (Lewis) Lederer
Fremont Jones	Day, Dianne
Furnival	Haynes, Annie
G. D. H. Pringle	Livingston, Nancy
Gabriel Dunn & Jake Myles	Press, Margaret
Gail & Mitch Mitchell	Gordons, The
Gail Connor	Parker, Barbara
Gale Gallagher	Gallagher, Gale
Gale Grayson & Katie Pru	Holbrook, Teri
Galen Shaw & Julian Baugh	Blackmur, L. L.
Garret Mikaelian	Killough, (Karen) Lee
Garson	Raskin, Ellen
George & Molly Palmer-Jones	Cleeves, Ann
George Conway	Meade, L. T.
George Felse & Family	Peters, Ellis
George Honegger	Strange, John Stephen
George Marshall	Barrington, Pamela
George Thorne	Penn, John
George Travers	Barrington, Pamela
George White	Mannon, M. M.
Georges Albuisson & Jacques Andrieu	Whelan, Hilary
Georgia Lee Maxwell	Friedman, (Michaele) Mickey (Thompson)
Georgina Powers	Danks, Denise
Gianna Maglione & Mimi Patterson	Mickelbury, Penny
Gibbon	Cooper, (Evelyn) Barbara
Gil Donan	Hood, Margaret Page
Gil Mayo	Eccles, Marjorie
Gilchrist	Meade, L(illie) T(homas)
Gillian Adams & Edward Gisborne	Kelly, Nora
Ginevra Prettifield	Dawkins, Cecil
Ginger Barnes	Murray, Donna Huston

Character	Writer
Glad Gold & Alden Chase	Wender, Theodora
Gloria Damasco	Corpi, Lucha
Glover	Evermay, March
Glyn Morgan	Lambert, Rosa w/ Dudley Lambert
Glynis Tryon	Monfredo, Miriam Grace
Goldy Bear	Davidson, Diane Mott
Gorham	Cowdroy, Joan
Grace de Rossa	Gibson, Maggie
Grace Latham & John Primrose	Ford, Leslie
Gramport	Barnett, Glyn
Gregor Demarkian	Haddam, Jane
Gregory Lewis	Frome, David
Gregory Pavlov & O'Shaunnessey	Ryan, Jessica (Cadwalader)
Gregory Trent	Seifert, Adele
Gridley Nelson	Fenisong, Ruth
Grogan	Neville, Margot
Guarnaccia	Nabb, Magdalen
Guido Brunetti	Leon, Donna
Guinevere Jones	Castle, Jayne
Guy Bannister	Crossley, Maude
Guy Bannister	Crossley, Maude w/ Charles Thomas King
Guy Northeast	Cannan, Joanna
Guy Silvestri	Rennert, Maggie
Gwenn Ramadge	O'Donnell, Lillian (Udvardy)
Gyp Kidnadze	Vincent, Lady Kitty (Edith Blanche)
Gypsy Rose Lee	Lee, Gypsy Rose
Hagen	Hooper, Kay
Haila & Jeff Troy	Roos, Kelley
Hamilton Cleek	Hanshew, Hazel Phillips
Hamilton Cleek	Hanshew, Mary & Thomas Hanshew
Hamilton Cleek	Hanshew, Thomas
Hamish Macbeth	Beaton, M. C.
Hana Shaner	Greth, (Le) Roma (Eshbach)
Hank Sullivan	Rooth, Anne Reed
Hannah Barlow	Lachnit, Carroll
Hannah Land	MacKay (Smith), Amanda
Hannah Trevor	Lawrence, Margaret
Hannah Wolfe	Dunant, Sarah
Hannasyde & Hemingway	Heyer, Georgette
Harley Quin	Christie, Agatha

Character	Writer
Harriet Hubley	Manthorne, Jackie
Harriet Jeffries & John Sanders	Sale (Roe), (Caroline) Medora
Harry Butten	Barbette, Jay
Haskell Blevins	McCafferty, (Barbara) Taylor
Headcorn	Campbell, Alice (Ormond)
Heaven Lee	Temple, Lou Jane
Hedley Nicholson	Kelly, Mary
Helen Black	Welch, Pat
Helen Bradley	Rushford, Patricia H.
Helen Johnson	Dewhurst, Eileen (Mary)
Helen Keremos	Zaremba, Eve
Helen West & Geoffrey Bailey	Fyfield (Hegarty), Frances
Henderson	Barling, Charles
Henrie O	Hart, Carolyn G(impel)
Henry & June	Wendell, Sarah
Henry & Sunday Parker Britland IV	Clark, Mary Higgins
Henry Bassett	Burden, Pat
Henry Beaumont	Atkins, Meg (Margaret Elizabeth)
Henry Doight	Symons, Beryl (Mary E.)
Henry Gamadge	Daly, Elizabeth (Theresa)
Henry Tibbett & Emily Tibbett	Moyes, Patricia
Henry Wilson	Cole, Margaret (Isabel Postgate) w/ G(eorge) D(ouglas) H(oward) Cole
Herbert Broom	Hurt, Freda (Mary E.)
Hercule Poirot	Christie, Agatha
Hilary Tamar	Caudwell, Sarah
Hilda Trenton	Lyon, (Mabel) Dana
Hilea Bailey & Hilary D. Bailey III	Bailey, Hilea
Hiram Odom	Boniface, Marjorie
Hiram Potter	Foley, Rae
Hoani Mata	Grayland, (Valerie) Merle (Spanner)
Hollis Ball	Chappell, Helen
Hollis Carpenter	Powell, Deborah
Holly-Jean Ho	Lin-Chandler, Irene
Holly Winter	Conant, Susan
Homer Fitzgerald	Russell, Charlotte M(urray)
Homer Kelly	Langton, Jane (Gillson)
Hometown Heroes	McShea, Susanna H(ofmann)
Honey West	Fickling, G. G.
Hook	Lane, (Margaret) Gret

Character	Writer
Horace Plummet	Healey, Evelyn
Hortense Clinton	Hagen, Miriam-Ann
Horton & Jordan	Butler, Leslie
Hubbert & Lil	Gray, Gallagher
Hubert Bonisseur de la Bath	Bruce, Jean
Hugh Gordon & Liane Crawford	Gilruth, Susan
Ian Roper	Bolitho, Janie
Imogen Quy	Walsh, Jill Paton
Ira Yedder	Bond, Evelyn
Irene Adler	Douglas, Carole Nelson
Irene Kelly	Burke, Jan
Iris Cooper & Jack Clancy	Beck, K. K.
Iris Thorne	Pugh, Dianne G.
Isamu "Sam Irish" Ohara	Hamilton, Nan
Ivor Maddox	Linington, (Barbara) Elizabeth
J. J. Jamison	Taylor, L(aurie) A(ylma)
J. P. Beaumont	Jance, J(udith) A(nn)
Jack Fleming & Charles Escott	Elrod, P(atricia) N(ead)
Jack Pharaoh	Moffat, Gwen
Jack Prester & Maxx	Dengler, Sandy
Jack Strickland	Balfour, Hearnden
Jack Stryker	Gosling, Paula
Jack Thompson	Cameron, Evelyn
Jackie Walsh	Cleary, Melissa
Jackson Fury	Jerina, Carol
Jacob Chaos	Smith, Shelley
Jacqueline Kirby	Peters, Elizabeth
Jacques Brunel	Gavin, Catherine (Irvine)
Jaime Sommers	Lottman, Eileen (Shurb)
Jake Samson & Rosie Vicente	Singer, Shelley
James Asher & Simon Ysidro	Hambly, Barbara
James F. "Bonnie" Dundee	Austin, Anne
James Flecker	Pullein-Thompson, Josephine (Mary Wedderburn)
James Fleming	Fallon, Ann C.
James Greer	Gayle, Newton
James Roland	Quinton, Ann
James Strange	Quinn, E(leanor) Baker
Jan Gallagher	Bailey, Jo
Jane Amanda Edwards	Russell, Charlotte M(urray)
Jane Austen	Barron, Stephanie
Jane Bradshawe	Allen, Mary Ann

Character	Writer
Jane Carberry	Symons, Beryl (Mary E.)
Jane da Silva	Beck, K. K.
Jane Jeffry	Churchill, Jill
Jane Lawless & Cordelia Thorn	Hart, Ellen
Jane Tennison	La Plante, Lynda
Jane Tregar	Godfrey, Ellen
Jane Winfield & Andrew Quentin	Peterson, Audrey
Janna Brill & Mahlon "Mama" Maxwell	Killough, (Karen) Lee
Jason Lynx	Orde, A. J.
Jasper Tully	Davis, Dorothy Salisbury
Jay Omega	McCrumb, Sharyn
Jazz Jasper & Omondi	McQuillan, Karin
Jean Darblay	Hardwick, Mollie
Jeanne Donovan	Henderson, M. R.
Jeet & Robin Vaughan	Banks, Carolyn
Jeff DiMarco	Disney, Doris Miles
Jeff Strange	Gaines (Schultz), Audrey
Jefferson Birch	Lee, W. W.
Jefferson Shields	Carlon, Patricia (Bernadette)
Jemima Shore	Fraser, Antonia (Pakenham)
Jennifer Cain	Pickard, Nancy
Jenny Gilette & Hunter Lewis	Grey, Robin
Jenny Gilette & Hunter Lewis	Gresham, Elizabeth
Jeremiah Irish	Child, Nellise
Jeremy Faro	Knight, Alanna
Jeremy Locke	Challis, Mary
Jeri Howard	Dawson, Janet
Jerome Aylwin	Curry, Avon
Jerry Boyne	MacGowan, Alice w/ Perry Newberry
Jerry Zalman	Kraft, Gabrielle
Jess Koster	Fielding, Joy
Jesse Falkenstein	Egan, Lesley
Jessica "Jesse" James	O'Brien, Meg
Jessica Fletcher	Fletcher, Jessica & Donald Bain
Jessie Drake	Krich, Rochelle Majer
Jesus Creek, TN	Adams, Deborah
Jill Smith	Dunlap, Susan
Jim & Kate Harris	Macrae, Travis
Jim Burns	Penny, Mrs. Frank
Jim Little	Parker, Maude

Character	Writer
Jim O'Neill	Disney, Doris Miles
Jim Qwilleran	Braun, Lilian Jackson
Jim Sader	Hitchens, (Julia Clara Catherine) Dolores (Birk)
Jimmy Bulstrode	Van Vorst, Marie
Jimmy Lane	Ryerson, Florence w/ Colin Clements
Jo Beth Sidden	Lanier, Virginia
Jo Hughes	Mather, Linda
Joan Spencer	Frommer, Sara Hoskinson
Joanna Brady	Jance, J(udith) A(nn)
Joanna McKenzie & James Carrick	Duffy, Margaret
Joanna Stark	Muller, Marcia
Joanne Kilbourn	Bowen, Gail
Jocelyn O'Roarke	Dentinger, Jane
Joe Grey, PI	Murphy, Shirley Rousseau
Joe Miller	Groner, Augusta
Joe Rodriguez	Dengler, Sandy
Joe Silva	Oleksiw, Susan (Prince)
John Abbot	Whitaker, Beryl (Salisbury)
John Barrin	Lane, (Margaret) Gret
John Bell	Meade, L. T.
John Bolsover	Silberrad, Una L(ucy)
John Case	White, Valerie
John Charles Olson	Chute, M(ary) G(race)
John Christmas	Jerrold, Ianthe (Bridgman)
John Coffin	Butler, Gwendoline
John Davies	Bennett, Margot
John Farrel	Hitchens, Bert & Dolores
John Faunce	Braddon, M(ary) E(lizabeth)
John Fenchurch & Bunce	Fiske, Dorsey
John Freeman	Ironside, John
John Harland	Foley, Rae
John J. Malone & The Justuses	Rice, Craig
John Joseph Lintott	Stubbs, Jean
John Lloyd Branson & Lydia Fairchild	Meredith, D(oris) R.
John McLeish & Francesca Wilson	Neel (Cohen), Janet
John Morrissey	Mitchell, Kay
John Primrose	Ford, Leslie
John Putnam Thatcher	Lathen, Emma
John Rawlings	Lake, Deryn

Character	Writer
John Ripley	Gordons, The
John Smith	Plum, Mary
John Waltz	McCormick, Claire
Johnny Buchanan	McCall, K. T.
Johnny DuVivien	Spain, Nancy
Johnny Ludlow	Wood, Mrs. Henry (Ellen Price)
Johnny Powers	Rayter, Joe
Johnson Johnson	Dunnett, Dorothy (Halliday)
Jolie Wyatt	Smith, Barbara Burnett
Jolivet	Shepherd, Joan
Jordan Myles	Navratilova, Martina w/ Liz Nickles
Joseph Kelly	Ford, Leslie
Josie Pigeon	Wolzien, Valerie
Joss O'Bannion & Evan Glyndower	Duane, Diane w/ Peter Morwood
Judd Springfield	Smith, Alison
Judith Hayes	Porter, Anna
Judith McMonigle Flynn	Daheim, Mary
Judith Thornton	Benke, Patricia D.
Jules Clement	Harrison, Jamie
Jules Vern	Karl, Kimberly
Julia Homberg	Gainham, Sarah
Julia Probyn	Bridge, Ann
Julia Tyler	Revell, Louisa
Julian Kestrel	Ross, Kate (Katherine J.)
Julian Rivers	Carnac, Carol
Julie Blake & Vic Paoli	Chapman, Sally
Julie Hayes	Davis, Dorothy Salisbury
Juliet Jackson	Turnbull, Margaret
Kali O'Brien	Jacobs, Jonnie
Kane	Scarlett, Roger
Karen & Cheryl Nevitt	Michaels, Barbara
Karen Hightower	Edghill, Rosemary
Kat Colorado	Kijewski, Karen
Kate Ardleigh & Sir Charles Sheridan	Paige, Robin
Kate Austen	Jacobs, Jonnie
Kate Baeier	Slovo, Gillian
Kate Brannigan	McDermid, Val
Kate Delafield	Forrest, Katherine V(irginia)
Kate Fansler	Cross, Amanda

Character	Writer
Kate Graham	Arliss, Joen
Kate Henry	Gordon, Alison
Kate Ivory	Stallwood, Veronica
Kate Jasper	Girdner, Jaqueline
Kate Kinsella	Green, Christine
Kate MacLean	Gilpatrick, Noreen
Kate Maddox	Quest, Erica
Kate Marsh	Lane, (Margaret) Gret
Kate Martinelli & Al Hawken	King, Laurie R.
Kate Millholland	Hartzmark, Gini
Kate Mulcay	Sibley, Celestine
Kate Murray	Tyre, Peg
Kate Shugak	Stabenow, Dana
Kate Weatherley	Birmingham, Maisie
Katherine "Peter" Piper	Long, Amelia Reynolds
Kathleen Mallory	O'Connell, Carol
Kathryn Mackay	McGuire, Christine
Kay Barth	Schier, Norma
Kelly	Roth, Holly
Kelsey	Page, Emma
Kenneth Carlisle	Wells, Carolyn
Kevin Blake	Douglas, Carole Nelson
Kevin Bryce	Valentine, Deborah
Kiernan O'Shaughnessey	Dunlap, Susan
Kimmey Kruse	Cooper, Susan Rogers
Kingsley Toplitt	Stockwell, Gail
Kinsey Millhone	Grafton, Sue
Kit Marsden Acton	Bramhall, Marion
Kit Powell	Robitaille, Julie
Kitty Telefair	Stevenson, Florence
Knute Severson	Wells, Tobias
Kristin Ashe	Jordan, Jennifer
Kyra Keaton	Tone, Teona
Lace White	Nolan, Jeannette Covert
Lady Indiana	Christopher, Laura Kim
Lady Lupin Hastings, Clergyman's Wife	Coggin, Joan
Lady Margaret Priam	Christmas, Joyce
Lady Molly	Orczy, Baroness (Emma Magdalena Rosalia Maria Josifa Barbara, Baroness Orczy)
Lady Weybridge	Sandys, Oliver

Character	Writer
Lane Montana	Hooper, Kay
Lane Parry	Sarsfield, Maureen
Laney Samms	Schmidt, Carol
Largely Lee	Harris, Evelyn
Lark Dailey Dodge	Simonson, Sheila
Lathom Dynes	Robertson, Helen
Laura Ackroyd & Michael Thackeray	Hall, Patricia
Laura Di Palma	Matera, Lia
Laura Fleming	Kelner, Toni L. P.
Laura Ireland	Mariz, Linda
Laura Principal	Spring, Michelle
Lauren Adler & Michael Hunt	Silver, Victoria
Lauren Laurano	Scoppettone, Sandra
Lauren Maxwell	Quinn (Barnard), Elizabeth
Laurie Grant & Stewart Noble	MacKintosh, May
Lavie Jutt	Barclay, Marguerite w/ Armiger Barclay
Leah Gordon	Powers, Alexis
Leah Hunter	Lacey, Sarah
Lee Ofsted	Elkins, Charlotte w/ Aaron Elkins
Lee Squires	Andreae, Christine
Lennox Kemp	Meek, M(argaret) R(eid) D(uncan)
Leonidas Witherall	Tilton, Alice
Leticia "Tish" Carberry	Rinehart, Mary Roberts
Letitia Hawkins	Burgess, Ellen
Lettie Winterbottom	Cutter, Leela
Levy	Holding, Elisabeth Sanxay
Lexey Jane Pelazoni	Head, (Joanne) Lee
Li Moh	Cowdroy, Joan
Libby Kincaid	Tucker, Kerry
Lil Ritchie	Knight, Phyllis
Lilly Bennett	Kellogg, Marne Davis
Lilly Wu & Janice Cameron	Sheridan, Juanita
Lily Bard	Harris, Charlaine
Lindsay Chamberlain	Connor, Beverly
Lindsay Gordon	McDermid, Val
Linus Lintoul	Edmonds, Janet
Lisa Davis	Waltch, Lilla M.
Lisa King	Farrelly, Gail E.
Liz Connors & Jack Lingemann	Kelly, Susan
Liz Graham, Cal Donovan & Frank Shapiro	Bannister, Jo

Character	Writer
Liz James	Stuyck, Karen Hanson
Liz Sullivan, Bridget Montrose & Paul Drake	Roberts (Smith), Lora
Liz Wareham	Brennan, Carol
Lloyd & Judy Hill	McGown, Jill
Lloyd's of London	Shakespeare, L. M(arguerita)
Lord & Lady Tintagel	Draco, F.
Lord Meren	Robinson, Lynda S(uzanne)
Lord Peter Wimsey	Sayers, Dorothy L(eigh)
Lord Syfret	Kenealy, Arabella
Lord Winterstone	Lombard, Nap
Loretta Lawson	Smith, Joan
Lori Shepherd	Atherton, Nancy
Lorimer Lane	Wells, Carolyn
Lorna Donahue	Hill, Katharine
Lorraine Page	La Plante, Lynda
Louisa Evans	Johnston, Jane
Louise Eldridge	Ripley, Ann
Loveday Brooke, Lady Detective	Pirkis, C(atharine) L(ouisa)
Lovick	Wilson, G(ertrude) M(ary)
Lucas Hallam	Washburn (Reasoner), L(ivia) J.
Lucia Ramos	Morell, Mary
Lucy Ramsdale	Dolson, Hildegarde
Lucy Stone	Meier, Leslie
Lucy Wayles	Adamson, Lydia
Luis Mendoza	Shannon, Dell
Luke Abbott	Gosling, Paula
Luke Thanet	Simpson, Dorothy
Lupe Solano	Garcia-Aguilera, Carolina
Lutie & Amanda Beagle	Chanslor, (Marjorie) Torrey (Hood)
Lydia Chin & Bill Smith	Rozan, S(hira) J(udith)
Lydia Miller	Hyde, Eleanor
Lyle Curtis & Susan Yates	Fetta, Emma Lou
Lynn MacDonald	Strahan, Kay Cleaver
M. Dupuy	Gilbert, Anthony
M. Fernand	Orczy, Baroness (Emma Magdalena Rosalia Maria Josifa Barbara, Baroness Orczy)
M. Hector Ratichon	Orczy, Baroness (Emma Magdalena Rosalia Maria Josifa Barbara, Baroness Orczy)
Mac McIntyre	Corne, M(olly)

Character	Writer
MacDougal Duff	Armstrong, Charlotte
Mackensie Smith & Annabel Reed Smith	Truman, (Mary) Margaret
Mackenzie Griffin	McCafferty, Jeanne
Madame Sara	Meade, L(illie) T(homas)
Madeline Payne	Lynch, Lawrence
Madison McGuire	Williams, Amanda Kyle
Madoc Rhys	Craig, Alisa
Magdalena Yoder	Myers, Tamar
Maggie Bennett	Stuart (Ohlragge), Anne (Kristine)
Maggie Courtney	Pearson, Ann
Maggie Dillitz	Sleem, Patty
Maggie Elliott	Taylor, Elizabeth Atwood
Maggie Garrett	Taylor, Jean
Maggie Hill & Claire Conrad	Howe, Melodie Johnson
Maggie MacGowen	Hornsby, Wendy (Nelson)
Maggie Ryan	Carlson, P(atricia) M(cEvoy)
Maggie Slone	Stone, Elizabet M.
Mallett	Fitt, Mary
Mama (Candi) & Simone	DeLoach, Nora L.
Mandrake	Bonett, John & Emery
Mandy Dyer	Johnson, Dolores
Marcus Didius Falco & Helena Justina	Davis, Lindsey
Marcus MacLurg	Petrie, Rhona
Marcus Stubbs	Radford, E. & M. A.
Margetson	Keate, E(dith) M(urray)
Margo Fortier	Fennelly, Tony
Margo Simon	Steinberg, Janice
Margot Blair	Knight, Kathleen Moore
Marguerite Smith	Lee, Marie
Maria Kallio	Lentolainen, Leena
Marian Larch	Paul, Barbara
Marilyn Ambers	St. Clair, Elizabeth
Mark East	Lawrence, Hilda (Hildegarde Kronemiller)
Mark Shigata	Wingate, (Martha) Anne (Guice)
Mark Tudor	Nash, Anne
Marka de Lancey	Frost (Shively), Barbara
Martha "Moz" Brant	Femling, Jean
Marti MacAlister	Bland, Eleanor Taylor
Martin Beck	Sjowall, Maj w/ Per Wahloo

Character	Writer
Marty Hopkins	Carlson, P(atricia) M(cEvoy)
Mary Carner	Popkin, Zelda
Mary Minor "Harry" Haristeen	Brown, Rita Mae w/ Sneaky Pie Brown
Mary Russell & Sherlock Holmes	King, Laurie R.
Matilda Haycastle	Bailey, Michele
Matt Gabriel	Gosling, Paula
Matt Winters	Oellrichs, Inez H(ildegarde)
Matthew Bartholomew	Gregory, Susanna
Matthew Furnival	Phillips, Stella
Matthew Sinclair	Fennelly, Tony
Maurice Ygrec & Paul Michelin	Rippon, Marion (Edith)
Max Bramble & Wylie Nolan	Reuben, Shelly
Maxey Burnell	Cail, Carol
Maxine Reynolds	Grove, Marjorie
Medford	Roth, Holly
Meg Lacey	Bowers, Elisabeth
Megan Marshall	Collins, Michelle
Melanie Travis	Berenson, Laurien
Melinda Pink	Moffat, Gwen
Melissa Craig	Rowlands, Betty
Melville Fairr	Venning, Michael
Menendez	Blanc, Suzanne
Mercedes Quero	Locke, G(ladys) E(dson)
Meredith	Ramsay, Diana
Meredith Folger	Mathews, Francine
Meredith Mitchell & Markby	Granger (Hulme), Ann
Merlin Capricorn	Winslow, Pauline Glen
Merton Heimrich	Lockridge, Frances (Louise Davis) w/ Richard (Orson) Lockridge
Micah Faraday	Meade, L(illie) T(homas)
Michael Croft	Adams, Jane
Michael Dundas	Rath, Virginia (Anne)
Michael Forrester	Wees, Frances Shelley
Michael Hornsley	Salter, Elizabeth (Fulton)
Michael Ohayon	Gur, Batya
Michael Spraggue	Barnes, Linda (Appelblatt)
Michelle "Micky" Knight	Redmann, J. M.
Mici Anhalt	O'Donnell, Lillian (Udvardy)
Micky Douglas	Infante, Anne
Midge Cohen	Brill, Toni
Midnight Louie	Douglas, Carole Nelson

Character	Writer
Miguel Urizar	McCloy, Helen (Worrell Clarkson)
Mike James	Scott, Denis
Mike Yeadings & Angus Mott	Curzon, Clare
Miles Pennoyer	Lawrence, Margery (H.)
Millicent Newberry	Lee, Jennette (Barbour Perry)
Milton Kovak	Cooper, Susan Rogers
Miriam Birdseye	Spain, Nancy
Miriam Lemaire	Stanton, Coralie
Miriam Winchester, Medicine Woman	Romberg, Nina
Miss Emily Seeton	Crane, Hamilton
Miss Harriet Unwin	Hervey, Evelyn
Miss Helma Zukas	Dereske, Jo
Miss Jane Marple	Christie, Agatha
Miss Maud Silver	Wentworth, Patricia
Miss Susan Melville	Smith, Evelyn E.
Miss Woolfe	Graham, (Matilda) Winifred (Muriel)
Mitch & Valerie Stevens	Brandt, Yanna w/ Nat Brandt
Mitch Greer & Deidre Griffin	Taylor, Karen E.
Mitchell	Lincoln, Natalie S(umner)
Mitchell "Mitch" Bushyhead	Hager, Jean
Mme Victoire Vernet	Fawcett, Quinn
Molly Bearpaw	Hager, Jean
Molly Cates	Walker, Mary Willis
Molly DeWitt	Woods, Sherryl
Molly Masters	O'Kane, Leslie
Molly Morgenthau	Bonner, Geraldine
Montague Egg	Sayers, Dorothy L(eigh)
Morgana Dalton	Buckstaff, Kathryn
Moss Magill	Gardiner, Dorothy
Mother Lavinia Grey	Gallison (Dunn), Kate
Mr. Gimblet	Bryce, Mrs. Charles
Mr. Hodson	Bidwell, Margaret
Mr. Jones	Conyers, Dorothea (Smyth)
Mr. Watson	Gardiner, Dorothy
Mr. Winkley	Rutland, Harriet
Mrs. Edwina Charles	Warner, Mignon
Mrs. Elizabeth Warrender	Cole, Margaret (Isabel Postgate) w/ G(eorge) D(ouglas) H(oward) Cole
Mrs. Emily Pollifax	Gilman (Butters), Dorothy

Character	Writer
Mrs. Eugenia Potter	Pickard, Nancy
Mrs. Eugenia Potter	Rich, Virginia
Mrs. Norris	Davis, Dorothy Salisbury
Nan Robinson	Cannon, Taffy
Nancy Clue	Maney, Mabel
Napoleon Prince	Edginton (Bailey), May (Helen Marion)
Natalie Gold	Jaffe, Jody
Natasha O'Brien & Max Ogden	Lyons, Nan w/ Ivan Lyons
Nathan Kendall	Mills, D(eanie) F(rancis)
Nathan Shapiro	Lockridge, Frances (Louise Davis) w/ Richard (Orson) Lockridge
Neal Rafferty	Wiltz, Chris
Neil Bathurst	Lynch, Lawrence
Neil Carter	Dewhurst, Eileen (Mary)
Neil Hamel	Van Gieson, Judith
Nell Bray	Linscott, Gillian
Nell Fury	Pincus, Elizabeth
Nell Willard	Lynch, Miriam
Nell Winter & Doris "DoDo" Trent	Nash, Anne
Newsom	Stewart, Flora
Nicholas Segalla	Dukthas, Ann
Nick Hannibal & Molly Rafferty	Belfort, Sophie
Nick Magaracz	Gallison (Dunn), Kate
Nikki Holden & Roman Cantrell	Chase, Elaine Raco
Nikki Trakos	Horansky, Ruby
Nina Fischman	Piesman, Marissa
Nina McFall & Dino Rossi	Fulton, Eileen
Nina Reilly	O'Shaughnessy, Perri
Noah Bradshaw	Johnston, Madeleine
Nora Hughes & Larry Blaine	Davis, Lavinia R(iker)
Norah Mulcahaney	O'Donnell, Lillian (Udvardy)
Norma "Nicky" Lee	Lee, Norma
Norman Head	Meade, L. T.
Nuri Iskirlak	Fleming, Joan (Margaret)
Nurse Agnes Carmichael	Cohen, Anthea
Nurse Hilda Adams (Miss Pinkerton)	Rinehart, Mary Roberts
Nurse Molly Burke	Dreyer, Eileen
Nyla Wade	McConnell, Vicki
Olivia Chapman	Logan, Margaret

Character	Writer
One Week Wimble	Burnham, Helen
Owen Archer	Robb, Candace (M.)
Pam & Jerry North	Lockridge, Frances (Louise Davis) w/ Richard (Orson) Lockridge
Pam Nilsen	Wilson, Barbara (Ellen)
Pamela Wayne	O'Nair, Mairi
Paris Chandler	Shah, Diane K.
Parker Pyne	Christie, Agatha
Parrish Darby	Aresbys, The
Pat & Jean Abbott	Crane, Frances
Pat Campbell	Colter, Eli(zabeth)
Pat Goodenough	Bennett, Liza
Patience C. McKenna	Papazoglou, Orania
Patricia Anne & Mary Alice	George, Anne
Patricia Delaney	Short, Sharon Gwyn
Patrick & Ingrid Gillard	Duffy, Margaret
Patrick Grant	Yorke, Margaret
Patrick Laing	Laing, Patrick
Patrick Michael Doyle	Newell, Audrey
Patrick Mulligan	Orczy, Baroness (Emma Magdalena Rosalia Maria Josifa Barbara, Baroness Orczy)
Patrick O'Brien	Irwin, Inez H(aynes)
Patrick Shirley & Rupert "Rip" Irving	Mills, Osmington
Paul Grainger	Sinclair, Fiona
Paul Kilgerrin	Leonard, Charles L.
Paul Lane	Lockridge, Frances (Louise Davis) w/ Richard (Orson) Lockridge
Paul McDonald	Smith, Julie
Paul Vachell	Huxley, Elspeth (Jocelyn Grant)
Paula Glenning	Clarke, Anna
Pauline Lyons	Anthony, Elizabeth
Payran	Nisot, (Mavis) Elizabeth (Hocking)
Peaches Dann	Squire, Elizabeth Daniels
Peggy Fairfield	Liddon, E(loise)
Penelope Pettiweather	Salmonson, Jessica Amanda
Pennington Wise	Wells, Carolyn
Penny & Vincent Mercer	Clandon, Henrietta
Penny Wanawake	Moody, Susan (Elizabeth)
Peregrine Connection	York, Rebecca
Persis Willum	Watson, Clarissa

Character	Writer
Pete Brady	Karl, M. S.
Pete Rector	Siller, Van
Peter & Janet Barron	Darby, Ruth
Peter Bartholomew	Gunning, Sally
Peter Brichter & Kori Brichter	Pulver (Kuhfeld), Mary Monica
Peter Clancy	Thayer, (Emma Bedington) Lee
Peter Decker & Rina Lazarus Decker	Kellerman, Faye
Peter Donnegan	Quick, Dorothy
Peter Jerningham	Myers, Isabel Briggs
Peter Piper	Mavity, Nancy Barr
Peter Ponsonby	Leslie, Jean
Peter Shandy	MacLeod, Charlotte (Matilda Hughes)
Peter Strangely	Black, E(lizabeth) Best
Peter Uteley Shane	Bonnamy, Francis
Pettengill	Rowe, Anne (Von Meibom)
Petunia Best & Max Frend	Chetwynd, Bridget
Phil Kramer	Kruger, Paul
Philip "Spike" Tracy	Ashbrook, H(arriette) C(ora)
Phoebe Fairfax	North, Suzanne
Phoebe Siegel	Prowell, Sandra West
Phryne Fisher	Greenwood, Kerry
Pointer	Fielding, A.
Poppy Dillworth	Tell, Dorothy
Port Silva Mysteries	LaPierre, Janet
Powledge	Rea, M(argaret) P(aine)
Prentis	Backhouse, (Enid) Elizabeth
Queenie Davilov	Osborne, Denise
Quentin Jacoby	Smith, J(ane) C. S.
Quin St. James & Mike McCleary	MacGregor, T(rish) J(aneshutz)
Quint McCauley	Brod, D(eborah) C(obban)
Race	Christie, Agatha
Rachel & Jennifer Murdock	Olsen, D. B.
Rafferty & Llewellyn	Evans, Geraldine
Rain Morgan	Grant-Adamson, Leslie
Randolph York	Durham, Mary
Rapaso	Ferrars, E. X.
Rat Trapp	Corrington, Joyce H. w/ John William Corrington
Ratlin	Roffman, Jan
Ray & Kate Frederick	Schenkel, S(hirley) E.

Character	Writer
Rebecca Schwartz	Smith, Julie
Rebeccah Rosenthal	Godfrey, Ellen
Red Hanlon	Merrick, Mollie
Reg Wexford	Rendell, Ruth
Regan Reilly	Clark, Carol Higgins
Remsen	Montross, David
Rev. Claire Aldington	Holland, Isabelle
Rev. Jabal Jarrett	Bream, Freda
Rev. Martin Buell	Scherf, Margaret (Louise)
Reynolds	Hamilton, Elaine
Richard Baxter	Moore, Margaret
Richard "Dick" Van Ryn Wilson	Sproul, Kathleen
Richard Hanard	Beynon-Harris, Vivian
Richard Jury	Grimes, Martha
Richard MacKay	Cushing, E(nid) Louise
Richard Massey	Siller, Van
Richard Montgomery	Shepherd, Stella
Richard Owen, Agent	Sharp, Marilyn (Augburn)
Richard Ringwood	Farrer, Katharine
Richard Trenton	Burton, Anne
Richard Tuck	Lewis, Lange
Richard York	Williamson, Audrey (May)
Rick & Rosie Ramsey	Santini, Rosemarie
Rick Vanner	Heberden, M(ary) V(iolet)
Robert Amiss	Edwards, Ruth Dudley
Robert Bone	Stacey, Susannah
Robert Forsythe	Giroux, E. X.
Robert Macdonald	Lorac, E. C. R.
Robert Renwick	MacInnes, Helen (Clark)
Robin Hudson	Hayter, Sparkle
Robin Light	Block, Barbara
Robin Miller	Maiman, Jaye
Robins	Stand, Marguerite
Rocky Allan	Rath, Virginia (Anne)
Roderick Alleyn	Marsh, (Edith) Ngaio
Roderick Alleyn & Agatha Troy Alleyn	Marsh, (Edith) Ngaio
Roderick "Drawers" Random	Kendall, Carol (Seeger)
Roger Tejeda & Kate Byrd Teague	Hornsby, Wendy (Nelson)
Roger the Chapman	Sedley, Kate
Ronald Dobbs	Blake, Christina
Ronald Price	Cannan, Joanna

Character	Writer
Ronnie Ventana	*White, Gloria*
Rosie Cairns	*Struthers, Betsy*
Ross	*Grindle, Lucretia*
Ross Paterson	*Field, Katherine*
Roxanne Sydney	*Poore, Dawn Aldridge*
Roxy & Madisen	*Karl, Kimberly*
Royce Madison	*York, Kieran*
Roz Howard	*Kenney, Susan (McIlvaine)*
Ruby Crane	*Dereske, Jo*
Rudolf Nilsen	*Griffiths, Ella*
Ruthie Kantor Morris	*Horowitz, Renee*
Ryan	*Scherf, Margaret (Louise)*
Ryvet	*Carnac, Carol*
Sabina Swift & Vic Newman	*Sucher, Dorothy*
Sally & Johnny Heldar	*Hamilton, Henrietta*
Salvador Borges	*Bonett, John & Emery*
Sam Hook	*Teilhet, Hildegarde Tolman*
Sam Jones	*Henderson, Lauren*
Sam Ryker	*Krich, Rochelle Majer*
Sam Titus & Nicki Titus	*Sandstrom, Eve K.*
Samantha Adams	*Storey, Alice*
Samantha Adams	*Shankman, Sarah*
Samantha Holt	*Wilson, Karen Ann*
Sands	*Millar, Margaret (Ellis Sturm)*
Sandy	*Conyers, Dorothea (Smyth)*
Sano Ichiro	*Rowland, Laura Joh*
Sara Hull	*Piggin, Julia Remine*
Sarah & Meg Quilliam	*Bishop, Claudia*
Sarah Calloway	*Warmbold, Jean*
Sarah Deane & Dr. Alex McKenzie	*Borthwick (Creighton), J(ean) S(cott)*
Sarah Fortune	*Fyfield (Hegarty), Frances*
Sarah Keate	*Eberhart, Mignon (Good)*
Sarah Keate & Lance O'Leary	*Eberhart, Mignon (Good)*
Sarah Kelling Bittersohn & Max Bittersohn	*MacLeod, Charlotte (Matilda Hughes)*
Sarah O'Brien	*Marlett, Melba (Balmat)*
Sarah Spooner	*Kelman, Judith*
Sarah Vanessa	*Storm, Joan*
Saunders	*Steele, V. M.*
Savannah Reid	*McKevett, G. A.*
Saz Martin	*Duffy, Stella*

Character	Writer
Schuyler Ridgway	McClellan, Tierney
Scott Egerton	Gilbert, Anthony
Scott Stuart	Coffin, Geoffrey
Sebald Craft	Patterson, (Isabella) Innis
Selena Mead	McGerr, Patricia
Septimus Finch	Erskine, Margaret
Septimus March	Bamburg, Lilian
Sharon Hays	Gregory, Sarah
Sharon McCone	Muller, Marcia
Sharon McCone.	Muller, Marcia w/ Bill Pronzini
Sheila Malory	Holt, Hazel
Sheila Travis & Aunt Mary	Sprinkle, Patricia Houck
Sherlock Holmes	Andrews, Val
Sherlock Holmes	Greenwood, L(illian) B(ethel)
Sherlock Holmes	Thomson, June (Valerie)
Shirley McClintock	Oliphant, B. J.
Sigismondo	Eyre, Elizabeth
Sigrid Harald	Maron, Margaret
Simon Ashton	Antill, Elizabeth
Simon Brade	Campbell, Harriette (Russell)
Simon Chard	Malim, Barbara
Simon Drake	Nielsen, Helen
Simona Griffo	Crespi, Trella
Simona Griffo	Crespi, Camilla T.
Sir Edgar Ewart	Walter, A. & H.
Sir John Saumarez	Dane, Clemence & Helen Simpson
Sir Robert Carey	Chisholm, P. F.
Sister Agnes Bourdillon	Joseph, Alison
Sister Cecile	Sullivan, Winona
Sister Frevisse	Frazer, Margaret
Sister Joan	Black, Veronica
Sister Mary Helen	O'Marie, Sister Carol Anne
Sister Mary Teresa Dempsey	Quill, Monica
Skip Langdon	Smith, Julie
Smith	Edingtons, The
Smokey Brandon	Ayres, Noreen
Sonora Blair	Hightower, Lynn S.
Sophie Greenway	Hart, Ellen
Sophy Bancroft	Hocker, Karla
Spencer Arrowood	McCrumb, Sharyn
Stella the Stargazer, a.k.a. Jane Austen Smith	Jorgensen, Christine T.

Character	Writer
Stephanie Plum	Evanovitch, Janet
Stephen Marryat	Leek, Margaret
Stephen Mayhew	Olsen, D. B.
Stephen Ramsay	Cleeves, Ann
Steve Arrow	Mantell, Laurie
Steve Carter	Long, Amelia Reynolds
Steve Ramsay	Wallace, C. H.
Steve Rhoden	Walker, Ir(m)a (Ruth Roden)
Steven Mitchell	Bell, Josephine
Steytler	Milne, Shirley
Stoddart	Haynes, Annie
Stoner McTavish	Dreher, Sarah
Susan Dare	Eberhart, Mignon (Good)
Susan Henshaw	Wolzien, Valerie
Susan Wren	Weir, Charlene
Susanna, Lady Appleton	Emerson, Kathy Lynn
Swinton	Flower, Pat(ricia Mary Bryson)
Syd Fish	Geason, Susan
Sydney Bryant	Wallace (Estrada), Patricia
Sydney Sloane	Lordon, Randye
Sydney Treherne	St. Dennis, Madelon
T. D. Renfro	Azolakov, Antoinette
T. T. Baldwin	OCork, Shannon
Tamara Hayle	Wesley, Valerie Wilson
Tamara Hoyland	Mann, Jessica
Tami Shimoni	Hesky, Olga
Tavy Martin	Winsor, Diana
Teal Stewart	Lamb, J. Dayne
Terry Girard	Kunz, Kathleen
Terry Spring	Kains, Josephine
Tess Darcy	Hager, Jean
Tessa Crichton	Morice, Anne
Tessie Venable	Holley, Helen
Texana Jones	Martin, Allana
The Adept, Sir Adam Sinclair	Harris, Deborah Turner w/ Katherine Kurtz
The Body in the . . . Series	Beck, K. K.
The Grub-and-Stakers	Craig, Alisa
The Honorable Constance Morrison-Burke	Porter, Joyce
The Little Stranger	Winke, Jennifer
The Oracle of Maddox Street	Meade, L. T.

Character	Writer
The Scarlet Pimpernel	Orczy, Baroness (Emma Magdalena Rosalia Maria Josifa Barbara, Baroness Orczy)
The Shadowers, Inc.	Fox, David
The Tonneman Family of New York	Meyers, Maan
The Widows	La Plante, Lynda
Thea Barlow	Caverly, Carol
Thea Crawford	Mann, Jessica
Thea Kozak	Flora, Kate (Clark)
Theo Bloomer	Hadley, Joan
Theresa Fortunato	Green, Kate
Theresa Galloway	Grimes, Terris McMahan
Thomas Lynley	George, (Susan) Elizabeth
Thomas Pitt & Charlotte Ellison Pitt	Perry, Anne
Tim Asher	Hultman, Helen Joan
Timothy Fowler	Harris, Colver
Timothy Herring	Torrie, Malcolm
Timothy McCarty	Ostrander, Isabel (Egenton)
Tish McWhinny	Comfort, B(arbara)
Tobin	Hughes, Dorothy B(elle)
Toby Dyke	Ferrars, E. X.
Todd McKinnon	Offord, Lenore Glen
Tom Aragon	Millar, Margaret (Ellis Sturm)
Tom Craig	Van Urk, Virginia (Nellis)
Tom Maybridge	Gill (Trimble), B(arbara) M(argaret)
Tom Pollard	Lemarchand, Elizabeth (Wharton)
Tom Ripley	Highsmith, (Mary) Patricia (Maugham)
Tommy & Tuppence Beresford	Christie, Agatha
Tommy Hambledon	Coles, Manning
Tommy Inman	Webb, Martha G.
Tommy Rostetter	Campbell, Alice (Ormond)
Toni Underwood	Davidson, Diane
Tori Miracle	Malmont, Valerie S.
Tory Bauer	Taylor, Kathleen
Tory Baxter	Blair, Marcia
Tracy Larrimore & Mike Thompson	Paull, Jessyca
Trevor Joseph	John, Katherine

Character	Writer
Trevor Nicholls	Peters, Geoffrey
Trewley & Stone	Mason, Sarah J(ill)
Tristen Jade	Jon, Lori
Truman Kicklighter	Trocheck, Kathy Hogan
"Tubby" Hall	Hambledon, Phyllis
Tyler Jones	Drury, Joan M.
Ulysses Finnegan Donaghue	Shone, Anna
V. I. Warshawski	Paretsky, Sara
Valentine Hawkehurst	Braddon, M(ary) E(lizabeth)
Valerie Lambert	Allan, Joan
Van Dusen Ormsberry	Strange, John Stephen
Van Vernet	Lynch, Lawrence
Vejay Haskell	Dunlap, Susan
Venus Diamond	Moody, Skye Kathleen
Verity Birdwood	Rowe, Jennifer
Vic Varallo	Egan, Lesley
Vicki Nelson & Henry Fitzroy	Huff, Tanya
Vicky Bliss	Peters, Elizabeth
Victoria Bowering	Yeager, Dorian
Victoria Cross	Sumner, Penny
Viera Kolarova	Powers, Elizabeth
Violet Strange	Green, Anna Katharine
Virginia Freer	Ferrars, E. X.
Virginia Kelly	Baker, Nikki
Wade	Bristow, Gwen w/ Bruce Manning
Wanda Mallory	Frankel, Valerie
Washington, D.C.	Truman, (Mary) Margaret
Webster Flagg	Johns, Veronica P(arker)
Whitney Logan	Lambert, Mercedes
Wield	Green, Glint
Wilfred Dover	Porter, Joyce
Will Woodfield	Foote-Smith, Elizabeth
Willa Jansson	Matera, Lia
William Austen	Hocking (Messer), (Mona Naomi) Anne
William Hecklepeck	McKitterick, Molly
William Monk	Perry, Anne
William Power	Clandon, Henrietta
William Winter	Butler, Gwendoline
Willow King	Cooper, Natasha
Wilson & Wilder	Bushell, Agnes
Winston Barrows	Eades, M(aude) L.

Character	Writer
Winston Marlowe Sherman	*Lorens, M(argaret) K(eilstrup)*
Witherspoon & Mrs. Jeffries	*Brightwell, Emily*
Woods	*Muir, D(orothy) Erskine*
Wylie King & Nels Lundberg	*Saunders, Lawrence*
Xenia Smith & Leslie Wetzon	*Meyers, Annette (Brafman)*
York Cycle of Mysteries	*Whitehead, Barbara*

About the Authors

Victoria Nichols (right) and **Susan Thompson** (left), coauthors of the first edition of *Silk Stalkings,* have backgrounds in the fields of medical research and independent film production and distribution. For over fifteen years they have applied their considerable talents to the study of series mysteries by women authors. They are each members of Mystery Writers of America and Sisters in Crime. Photo courtesy of the authors.